Edited by Janis Sarra

Corporate Governance
in Global Capital Markets

UBCPre   Vancouver·Toronto

© UBC Press 2003

09 08 07 06 05 04 03   5 4 3 2 1

Printed in Canada on acid-free paper

National Library of Canada Cataloguing in Publication Data

Main entry under title:
  Corporate governance in global capital markets / edited by Janis Sarra.

  Includes bibliographical references and index.
  ISBN 0-7748-1004-1 (bound). – ISBN 0-7748-1005-X (pbk.)

  1. Corporate governance. 2. International economic integration. I. Sarra, Janis Pearl, 1954-

HD2741.C6735 2003   658.4'22   C2003-910778-7

Canadä

UBC Press gratefully acknowledges the financial support for our publishing program of the Government of Canada through the Book Publishing Industry Development Program (BPIDP), and of the Canada Council for the Arts, and the British Columbia Arts Council. This book has been published with the help of the K.D. Srivastava Fund.

UBC Press
The University of British Columbia
2029 West Mall
Vancouver, BC V6T 1Z2
604-822-5959 / Fax: 604-822-6083
www.ubcpress.ca

Contents

Foreword / vii
Purdy Crawford

Acknowledgments / xiii

Introduction / xv
Janis Sarra

**Part 1: Governance of the Corporation in the Context
of Global Markets**

1 Canadian Corporate Governance Reform: In Search of a Regulatory Role
for Corporate Law / 3
Stéphane Rousseau

2 Oversight, Hindsight, and Foresight: Canadian Corporate Governance
through the Lens of Global Capital Markets / 40
Janis Sarra

3 Governance, Mergers and Acquisitions, and Global Capital Markets / 85
Christopher C. Nicholls

**Part 2: Shareholder Activism and Control:
Accountability for Corporate Harms**

4 Canadian Institutional Shareholder Activism in an Era of Global
Deregulation / 111
Gil Yaron

5 Investor Control of Multinational Enterprises:
A Market for Corporate Governance Based on Justice and Fairness? / 131
Ronald B. Davis

6 The Interplay between Securities Regulation and Corporate Governance: Shareholder Activism, the Shareholder Proposal Rule, and Corporate Compliance with Law / 156
Cheryl L. Wade

7 Beyond Environmental Compliance, with a View to the Best Interests of the Company / 173
Robert Mansell and Brian Prill

Part 3: The Role of Directors in Governance Oversight: Domestic and International Lessons

8 Developments in US Boards of Directors and the Multiple Roles of Corporate Boards / 191
Lynne L. Dallas

9 The Governance of Commercial Crown Corporations: How Much Independence Can We Expect from Corporate Directors? / 225
Barry Slutsky and Philip Bryden

10 Synchronizing Individual Corporate Self-Interest Goals and Sector Development Responsibilities: The BC Seafood Processing Industry Experience / 248
Kathleen Porter and Joe Weiler

Part 4: Governance of the Financially Distressed Corporation

11 Under Pressure: Governance of the Financially Distressed Corporation / 275
Geoffrey B. Morawetz

12 Governance of the Financially Distressed Corporation in Global Capital Markets: Selected Aspects of the Financing and Governance of Canadian Enterprises in Cross-Border Workouts / 297
Edward A. Sellers, Natasha J. MacParland, and F. James Hoffner

13 The Role of Court-Appointed Officers in the Governance of Financially Distressed Corporations / 345
John Sandrelli

Contributors / 361

Index / 363

Foreword

Purdy Crawford

This book addresses the legal framework in which corporate governance operates, and offers strategies for directors, officers, and other stakeholders as corporations seek to compete in global capital markets. This foreword sets the context for this discussion by giving an overview of various pragmatic aspects of corporate governance, based on my varied experience as chief executive officer (CEO), board chair, and director. In Canada, the Dey guidelines issued by the Toronto Stock Exchange (now TSX) and reports such as *Beyond Compliance: Building a Governance Culture* are helpful in defining good governance practices.[1] While there continues to be debate about the extent to which corporate governance practices should be made mandatory, from a practical point of view, the guidelines do not necessarily fit all listed companies. Stock exchanges will experience pressure from companies in terms of their willingness to list if there are too many requirements, and the ease with which companies can move trading about makes these real concerns. In my view, two aspects should be mandatory. If companies are not conforming to a guideline, they should be required to specifically explain why they are not. Second, if a corporation does not have a non-executive chair of the board, it should be required to have an independent board leader or lead director. This would address potential conflicts of interest or the appearance of conflict that is created by having someone in the combined role of chair of the board and chief executive officer. The job content of the non-executive chair is extremely important; there should not be "two CEOs." Independent leadership and oversight are essential.

The corporate board is key to good governance. A corporate board should consist of a diversity of interests, including women, leaders of nonprofit organizations, some individuals lower down in the ranks of another organization who are on their way up, and people with different perspectives of the world and from different geographic regions. I am involved with a company engaging in considerable business activity in Japan, China, and Korea, and having a director from one or more of these nations would be helpful.

One difficulty is the distance they would be required to travel, which can make attendance by directors from distant regions difficult. Thus, how to achieve value on the board in this context is an ongoing challenge.

The board should meet from time to time in camera without any corporate officers present, including director/officers. These should be preset meetings, perhaps three times a year with the option of more frequent meetings, with sufficient time set aside for directors to have a frank discussion without the CEO present.

In seeking to attract independent directors, there has been an emphasis in Canada and the United States on having a board with a fair number of CEOs from other companies. My experience has been that while there are some outstanding CEOs on corporate boards, on the whole they do not have the time to fully perform the job of director. I became a much better director when I ceased to be a CEO.

Recruitment of directors is also important. The CEO should not recruit directors, as it sends the wrong message, namely, that the director is responsible to the CEO. The CEO has a role to play in order to ensure compatibility, but the recruiting should be done by the non-executive chair of the board or members of the nomination or corporate governance committee of the board.

In the debate about term limits for directors, an important factor to consider is whether a long-term director can remain independent. As boards seek younger directors, there is an issue of whether the same directors should be on a board for twenty to thirty years. It takes two or three years to really get a grip on a company, however, and a limit such as six years does not really permit a serious contribution unless the director has a unique background. There should be a mandatory retirement age for directors, perhaps seventy or seventy-two years. The nomination and corporate governance committee is essential to ensuring a well-functioning board, recruiting directors, measuring the performance of directors, and, increasingly, facilitating peer review for directors.

The directors' role is to monitor operations and provide leadership in adding value. It is difficult to draw a line delimiting directors' involvement in operations. Strategy development is very important to a company, and directors have a key role to play in this. The Dey guidelines on corporate governance could leave the impression that there is a piece of paper with the company's strategy written out and tied with a ribbon. The reality is far different: there are multiple strategies for multiple operations, strategies are continuously unfolding and changing, and directors have a key role to play in this ongoing strategic development process. Strategy is only as good as the people operating the business, whether they are implementing strategies or managing the day-to-day operations of the corporation. A key role for directors is ensuring the quality of the CEO and potential successors. An orientation program for directors is absolutely fundamental. Financial literacy is an important part of this. Even a director not on the audit committee needs to be financially literate, as everything ultimately comes down to numbers and the director must be able to ask questions and examine the assumptions behind the numbers. Directors should also be encouraged to acquire ongoing financial education, including taking courses at the company's expense in the areas where they do not have expertise.

An ideal board size is twelve to fifteen directors, but with the tendency towards appointing a new board committee for everything, a board that size might be insufficient. Moreover, if a director is not on a particular committee, he or she may not know enough about what is going on. One of the sponsors of the conference on global markets and corporate governance that was the genesis of this book, David McLean, the non-executive chair of Canadian National (CN), has developed a means of dealing with this that is extremely valuable. The board meets as a committee of the whole on several different issues, with different directors acting as chair of the committee. For example, the committee on strategy at CN is a committee of the whole board, but the chair is a person with considerable background in strategy. This enables maximum effectiveness, with the full involvement of all directors.

There are currently a number of issues with respect to director compensation. For example, the current practice of paying US directors in US dollars and Canadian directors in Canadian dollars creates a disparity in compensation of up to 40 percent. A fair compensation should be set and paid to all directors. Most directors serve on a board for the opportunity and the challenge, not the compensation. Some scholars in the United Kingdom and elsewhere have suggested that owning stock destroys a director's independence. I can appreciate the merits of this argument, but, on the other hand, owning a substantial number of shares in a company causes me as a director of that company to sit up and pay attention. Similarly, options are not problematic if they are properly valued as part of the total compensation package. There has been a tendency, particularly with high-tech companies, to award a huge number of options to the directors – in some cases, options that on a reasonable valuation basis were worth millions of dollars. There are different ways to value options; like valuing the warrants that a company issues to raise money, one usually uses some kind of variation of a Black Shoales method and the value can be anywhere from 15 percent to 45 percent of the value of underlying stock. Any options given to directors must be properly valued as part of the total package of director compensation.

An independent audit committee is fundamental to protecting the integrity of the company. Auditors should be told up front, and then reminded, that they are responsible to the audit committee and the board as a whole, not to management. It should be made clear that the audit committee wants to hear all the auditors' worries and concerns, and that if it does not, the auditors will be let go. Similarly, if the audit committee does not hear all the facts from management, those in such positions will also be let go. This is fundamental. There is a practice sometimes used in the United States that I find helpful: the auditors report to the audit committee not only the results under generally accepted accounting principles (GAAP) but also a reconciliation of what the results would be if the auditors applied what they might regard as preferable accounting, and what that reconciliation would mean. If it is insignificant, it probably does not much matter, but it is important information for audit committees.

I am more than a little concerned that some of the problems with auditors have been created by the companies they audit and the companies' boards of directors. The tendency to evaluate bids from audit firms based almost entirely upon the quoted fees for the audit work has helped to make audit work a commodity. It is more important to look at the quality of the people in the audit firm who are going to be responsible for the audit, and to have an understanding with them as to their responsibilities. Fees should be secondary. In Canada auditors are appointed by shareholders, whereas in the United States they are appointed by the board, but there is not much difference in substance. When consulting fees are added to audit fees, the more the audit firm is earning from the company, the greater the underlying pressure, conscious or otherwise, for the auditor to compromise. To be sure, there are auditors who receive all kinds of consulting fees who are very strong and independent and who would not compromise in any event, but the pressures are subtle and do exist. Another result of such consulting work is that the auditor ends up auditing what his or her consulting partners have helped to create. As a result of the collapse of the Enron Corporation in 2001 the major audit firms are starting to get out of the consulting business.

Frequently, the audit committee's mandate includes risk management, and the Canadian Institute of Chartered Accountants has provided guidance on risk management.[2] The CICA defines "risk" as anything that in a material way prevents the corporation from achieving its objectives. This is much broader than financial risk. For example, it can include the nonviability of a particular plant of the company that in turn drains the company of its resources. It includes both upside and downside risks to the corporation. Thus, risk should not be left solely to the financial department and the audit committee.

There is also an important role for the management resources and compensation committees of the corporate board, in facilitating development of leadership programs and reviewing the performance of senior officers. The compensation committee should, where needed, obtain its own independent compensation advice. New directors require training in compensation and in evaluating senior officers. A "360 review" consists of an evaluation by all the people around a particular manager of the manager's strengths and weaknesses, and a developmental program that responds to that assessment. Directors and officers are not just born with leadership qualities but can develop them if they are committed to doing so and have enough guidance and help. Incentive compensation provisions should have the potential for being substantial and the base salary should be kept relatively low, with tough performance criteria. Stock options can be "plain vanilla options" – that is, they vest over time regardless of performance – or performance conditions, such as achieving a certain return on investment, can be attached to options. The latter is preferable because of the noise of the market and the psychology of the market: one never quite knows where it is going, and a company has more control with underlying performance criteria. Good performance over a period will ultimately be reflected in the market.

One important aspect of leadership is the compensation committee's responsibility for reviewing the performance of the CEO, against both the corporate plan and personal objectives. The head of human resources is just as responsible to the chair of the compensation committee as to the CEO, and the former would want to hear comments from him or her about the performance of the CEO. The compensation committee should then make its own assessment and present it to a meeting of the board without the CEO present. The committee chair and/or a non-executive chair of the board, if there is one, would then meet with the CEO to review his or her performance. All of us have had trouble making the tough calls concerning termination of CEOs, and my own experience suggests that we are too cautious. Directors need to be concerned about a CEO who is defensive or evasive. It does not necessarily mean that he or she is not effective, but it is an early warning signal. A CEO who has self-confidence takes criticism well and uses it as a developmental tool.

While the corporate governance system has some defects, Enron was not a failure of the system but rather a failure of all the people in the system: management, the board, auditors, lawyers, investment bankers, advisors, rating agencies, and analysts. In this context, the Securities Industry Committee on Analyst Standards found that boards should be advised if the CEO starts "beating up" on analysts or other consultants if he or she does not like what they are saying.[3] This is a small part of what happened at Enron – a reporter taken to task for negative comments, a bond analyst sacked for being negative about Enron. Many people in the analytical world did not do their homework.

The issue of corporate social responsibility has sparked an interesting debate. The Canadian Democracy and Corporate Accountability Commission ("Broadbent Report") recommended social responsibility committees and social responsibility audits as part of the TSX guidelines. With the current

competition for listing, this could be hard to implement. I am for corporations being socially responsible and for the system to put pressure on companies to be so. Some companies, such as Suncor, are moving in this direction,
viewing this as a way to increase their value on the stock market. The
Broadbent Report also suggests that fiduciary obligation be changed to take
into account the interests of other stakeholders besides shareholders. There
are similar tests in some European countries and there are constituency
statutes in the United States, although the driving force in the US was the
market for corporate control. There is a problem, however, if the bottom
line for shareholders is seriously adversely impacted on a long-term basis,
namely, whether society will be able to create enough wealth to do all the
things we want to do to help people.

Good corporate governance is not an end in itself. The objective is to
create shareholder value on a long-term basis. "Long-term" means that interests of other stakeholders must be taken into account. If a company does
not provide a good place to work, how can it attract outstanding people? If
it does not contribute to communities, can it create superior value on a
long-term basis? A corporation's reputation for integrity is a most valuable
asset in creating value, and it would be difficult for a corporation to achieve
such a reputation if it did not concern itself with the interests of other
stakeholders. It follows that other models of operation can be effective in
creating value. My experience as a director of two American companies listed
on the New York Stock Exchange is that corporate governance in Canada is
at least as good as in the United States, but both nations have some distance
to go in enhancing governance. This book will expand the debate and discussion regarding optimal governance practice.

Source
Parts of this foreword were excerpted from the keynote address *Corporate Governance, the Be
All and End All?* delivered by Purdy Crawford to a University of British Columbia Faculty of
Law conference on global capital markets, emerging boards, and current issues in corporate governance in February 2002. Mr. Crawford is counsel, Osler, Hoskin and Harcourt,
chair of AT&T Canada, chair of the Five Year Review Committee of the *Securities Act* (Ontario), and former chair of the Securities Industry Committee on Analyst Standards.

Notes
1 Toronto Stock Exchange Committee on Corporate Governance in Canada, *Where Were the
  Directors? Guidelines for Improved Corporate Governance in Canada* (Toronto: Toronto Stock
  Exchange, 1994); Joint Committee on Corporate Governance, *Beyond Compliance: Building
  a Governance Culture,* Final Report (Toronto: TSX/CNDX/CICA, 2001).
2 P. Crawford, "Integrated Risk Management: A Director's View," comments to the Conference Board of Canada, February 2001 (on file with author).
3 Securities Industry Committee on Analyst Standards, *Setting Analyst Standards: Recommendations for the Supervision and Practice of the Canadian Securities Industry Analysts,* Final Report (Toronto: Ontario Securities Commission, October 2001).

Acknowledgments

The editor and authors would like to express our deep appreciation to the **David and Brenda McLean Endowment Fund** for providing funding support for this book.

The editor would also like to thank the University of British Columbia Faculty of Law for its continuing support, the editorial and production staff at UBC Press for their helpful assistance, and the contributing authors for their enthusiasm, diligence, and hard work in this collaborative project.

Research support to authors was also provided by Osler, Hoskin & Harcourt LLP, Torys LLP, Goodmans LLP and Fraser Milner Casgrain LLP and the Shareholder Association for Research and Education.

Introduction

Janis Sarra

This book draws together the work of legal scholars and practitioners from across North America to provide a comprehensive analysis of corporate governance issues in global capital markets. The collection of essays explores the theoretical underpinnings of corporate governance and provides concrete illustrations of different governance models and their outcomes. While the perspectives of the contributing authors differ, their common project is to explore different normative conceptions of the corporation in order to contribute to an analysis of global trends in corporate governance.

Although some scholars have claimed that the development of global capital markets will lead to the inevitable triumph of the market-centred system of corporate governance prevalent in Anglo-American law, the recent failures of large, publicly traded corporations in the United States cast doubt on claims of the ultimate superiority of that system. When this doubt is coupled with the existence of other forms of corporate governance throughout the world, the need for closer examination of potential alternatives or improvements in corporate governance becomes more evident. In examining the landscape surrounding governance of corporations in global markets, one needs analysis from differing points of view. Hence, this book has contributions from both legal scholars and senior practitioners.

These essays were first written and presented as papers at a conference on global capital markets and current trends in corporate governance, held at the Faculty of Law of the University of British Columbia in February 2002. The conference deliberations involved a lively and thoughtful exchange of views and commentary, which ultimately enhanced the contributions in this book. The chapters vary in length, depending on the complexity of the topic and as a result of being inclusive in terms of the diversity of views sought. Chapters 1 to 3, in particular, provide the comprehensive framework of norms theory, global governance trends, capital market differences, and developments in corporate board theory, which then ground the rest of the chapters that comment on more specific aspects of governance. The book measures diverse theoretical perspectives against the reality of corporate operations in current capital markets, exploring the norms that inform shifts in governance practice and the influence of regulatory regimes on governance change. Relationships both within and outside the firm are explored, including issues of accountability, ethics in decision making, and notions of efficiency in the generation of corporate wealth.

With changing capital and products markets, the landscape can be variable and uncertain, and this book explores a number a key questions from different vistas. The issues explored include the following: How can corporate boards enhance their structure or decision-making processes to meet the challenges of global markets? What are the theoretical underpinnings of current market-centred and bank-centred models of corporate governance? Are different governance norms entirely market-driven or are they a function of different historical and political choices? How do internal capital and management structures both create and respond to norms in decision making? Will divergent governance norms converge globally, given the movement of capital internationally and the cross-border nature of corporate activity? What is the role of debt in governance, and should it vary depending on the financial health of the corporation? Should directors and officers have any obligations to stakeholders other than shareholders? Given recent corporate failures such as Enron, how can securities regimes be constructed to protect the equity investments of diverse shareholders? What lessons do other governance structures in different domestic capital markets teach us? What should be the governance role of institutional and other equity investors? How can shareholders exercise their right to voice their preferences in terms of human rights or environmental sustainability? What is the appropriate role of public regulatory law in this area of "private" law? What are the particular challenges to governance of multinational corporations, and is there a market for investor control? What governance framework should assist directors and officers who are unable to see the horizon when the changing landscape places the corporation in financial distress? All these questions are touched on by the various contributors to this book. The analysis paints a vivid canvas of governance options, stakeholder interests, and the multilayered and complex texture of stewardship of the corporation.

This book builds on current corporate law scholarship. Legal scholarship in North America has to date reflected a particular normative view of the corporation in terms of the primacy of shareholder wealth maximization and liquidity of markets as the optimal measure of efficiency. This book offers a fuller analysis of governance challenges as domestic corporations and investors move outward into global capital markets. The governance structures most familiar to us arise from a conception of the corporation as a nexus of contractual relationships. Within this framework, agency cost theory is aimed at holding officers of widely held corporations accountable to equity investors, who are generally thought to be the only residual claimants to the firm's assets. The goal that flows from these notions is shareholder wealth maximization, aimed at an optimal return on investment of equity capital. Agency cost theory seeks to reduce inefficiency in the nexus of contractual relations' structure of the firm by advocating structural incentives to align the interests of corporate directors and officers with those of shareholders. Within this general approach, there are variations that ground governance in property rights, control of assets as the driving function, reduction of transaction costs, and, more recently, the role of norms as influencing contractual relationships by creating internalized sanctions on corporate conduct. Yet the vast majority of the world's corporations are closely held or blockheld, giving rise to a different set of governance challenges. This book explores the gap between the scholarship and the realities of governance within the shareholder wealth maximization paradigm. Moreover, it expands this legal scholarship by examining other interests implicated in the corporation, suggesting a variety of theoretical and practical approaches to account for these interests.

The first three chapters set out the macro-level governance issues in global capital markets, including the development of private norms theory, differences in capital and governance structures, and the effects of the increasingly global market for corporate control. The general theoretical and practical challenges having been set out, the next four chapters focus more particularly on the tensions between corporate directors and equity investors, specifically, whether there is a market for investor control that creates greater accountability for corporate social and economic harms. Following this discussion, three chapters examine directors and effective board oversight, both theoretically and practically. The final three chapters shift the focus to governance of the financially distressed corporation, a subject that has received little attention in corporate law scholarship, bringing the discussion full circle with respect to the growing complexity of governance in global capital markets.

In Chapter 1, Stéphane Rousseau examines whether or not there is a regulatory role for corporate law in the governance of corporations. He presents the theoretical justifications underlying the reliance of policy makers on private actors to identify and ensure adoption of positive corporate governance norms. Rousseau tracks the historical reasons for adoption of an enabling, as opposed to mandatory, corporate law regime. He then explores the relevance of the current social norms literature for corporate governance reform, giving the reader a clearer definition of corporate norms and a critique of the contributions and limits of such literature. Norms analysis is concerned with the boundary between legal and nonlegal enforceability of particular governance choices. Rousseau concludes that private enforcement mechanisms suffer from imperfections and need to be supplemented by public regulation that would give new meaning to shareholder voice in corporate governance. Rousseau's analysis sets the stage for Chapters 4 to 7 with respect to increasing shareholder activism. Boards of directors of publicly held corporations should be obliged to adopt their governance principles in a bylaw and submit the bylaw for shareholder approval annually. Rousseau further suggests that the mandatory examination of corporations' governance principles at the annual meeting would foster the participation of shareholders by reducing the costs of interventions.

Chapter 2 builds on Rousseau's analysis, juxtaposing the development of corporate law norms in Canada with those internationally. I suggest that current market pressure for convergence of governance norms and protection of equity interests comes primarily from Anglo-American corporations as capital moves outward, but this pressure is not purely market-driven. The private law aspects of such norms are situated in an extensive regulatory framework in Canada and the United States that protects a particular hierarchy of property. In this, the norms debate focuses largely on shareholder wealth maximization and reduction of associated agency costs, with share value considered the measure of optimal capital markets. This definition of "efficiency" includes a calculation of cost that frequently discounts or "externalizes" particular costs of corporate activity such as environmental or consumer harms. Yet there is countervailing pressure resisting such convergence, given the cultural, political, and economic structures of other capital market and corporate law regimes. Equity capital, rather than having primacy in terms of corporate goals, is ranked equally with recognition of the contributions of workers, creditors, and communities. In Chapter 2, I track some of these developments in continental Europe, Canada, the Pan-Pacific Region, and transition economies, suggesting that diverse systems give rise to different normative measures of "efficiency" and wealth generation. Canadian corporations seeking to participate in global markets need to develop an understanding of these different norms and governance structures, in order to appreciate and measure the signs of effective stewardship of the corporation.

In Chapter 3, Christopher Nicholls observes that the same forces of globalization that may lead to international convergence of governance practices in search of higher levels of operating efficiencies might also be expected to encourage greater uniformity in the rules relating to corporate control. Nicholls suggests that if US corporate governance norms are destined to become the world standard, then the market for corporate control, a key aspect of US governance, must also develop along American lines in other jurisdictions. The legal framework within which corporate control transactions occur will also need to converge, at least functionally. There have been recent indications that in traditional blockholder systems, there is growing acceptance of the value of fostering an active market for corporate control. Nicholls examines recent European initiatives in the takeover market, where takeover is viewed as having both wealth-maximizing and managerial discipline value. Cross-border acquisitions will inevitably have an impact on the sustainability of significant international legal and governance variations. Nicholls observes that whether or not this development represents a triumph in efficiency remains a matter of contention, and the shareholder primacy norm could lead to decisions that destroy firm value and thus decrease societal wealth. Shareholder wealth maximization as a socially valuable goal may be valid in some, but not all, contexts.

Having situated the governance debate within the larger capital and regulatory framework, the book turns its attention to the governance choices made by corporate actors. In Chapter 4, Gil Yaron suggests that recent amendments to Canadian corporations' law represent an acknowledgment of the role of shareholders in corporate governance. However, significant legal and institutional barriers remain, preventing efficient and effective engagement between shareholders and corporate officers. Yaron, as well as Ronald Davis and Cheryl Wade in the two chapters that follow, suggests that there is an enhanced role for the shareholder in facilitating responsible corporate governance. Institutional shareholders may be well situated in this respect because they are positioned to monitor the long-term performance of the corporation and the health of the economy. Yaron suggests that adoption of a concessionist view of the corporation, where the corporation is conceived of as an artificial entity whose separate legal personality is granted as a privilege by the state, would then acknowledge the responsibility of shareholders, their fiduciary agents, and the corporation to beneficiaries and the national economy. Yaron observes that such an approach requires that investors and firms take into consideration the implication of corporate decisions for both internal performance and externalities that impact on the corporation's ability to operate in the long-term interests of society. Under such a framework, institutional shareholder activism can be viewed as a mechanism to protect shareholders against investment risk and as a vehicle to direct governance towards creation of optimal long-term benefits while minimizing risks for beneficiaries, the corporation, and the economy as a whole in global capital markets.

In Chapter 5, Ronald Davis discusses investor control of multinational enterprises and the potential market for corporate governance based on justice and fairness. He observes that the emergence of multinational enterprises (MNEs) has made it increasingly difficult for incorporating states to govern MNE activities in other jurisdictions. MNEs are not currently held accountable for particular harms, such as environmental and human rights harms, in host nations. This is due to a combination of the international legal system's limited applicability to corporate conduct and the decreased accountability resulting from the draping of the corporate veil over international borders. Davis explores the possibility of investor control of the conduct of MNEs that violates international law norms. Pension funds, as increasingly large investors in global equity markets, do have the appropriate incentives to control such conduct. However, any development of such a market for good corporate governance is hindered by information asymmetries, costs of monitoring given the pension funds' diversified investment portfolios, lack of transparency measures, and the lack of a reliable method of determining the costs of harms to environmental, civil, and political rights. Davis reviews recent initiatives by the United Nations and European Union to increase the reliability of information about global corporate compliance with international norms and analyzes the weaknesses in the initiatives due to their voluntary nature. These difficulties in the regulation of the international conduct of MNEs are compounded by the domestic limits on shareholder participation in corporate governance. Davis concludes that while there is a potential for control of harmful corporate activities by global institutional investors, this should not be viewed as a complete solution. Public regulation is a necessary and complementary component of investor control.

In Chapter 6, Cheryl Wade contributes insights on the interplay between securities regulation and corporate governance, and, in particular, between the shareholder proposal rule and corporate compliance with antidiscrimination law. She suggests that while corporate governance problems created by the Enron bankruptcy and market outcomes post-September 11 will consume corporate directors and officers for some time, these events should not overshadow other serious issues of potential corporate wrongdoing. Wade analyzes the ongoing problem of workplace race and sex discrimination and the need for corporate boards to install systems that monitor discriminatory employment practices. The lack of clarity as to when unethical conduct becomes illegal conduct may identify a key problem that shareholders can assist corporate boards with in preventing the negative impact of discrimination. Wade looks at the costs to shareholder value, to employees, and to the public in cases where monitoring systems are not in place to ensure avoidance of discriminatory practices. She speculates that the persistence of workplace discrimination and the large costs of settlement of disputes arise because of the reluctance of corporate boards to accept the inevitability of wrongdoing on the part of some corporate managers and employees, especially in large publicly traded corporations. This can be remedied in part through shareholder proposals that call the board's attention to potential monitoring problems and that suggest that boards implement procedures regarding the monitoring of compliance with anti-discrimination laws in order to meet their duty of care obligations.

In Chapter 7, Robert Mansell and Brian Prill pick up the question of environmental harm and corporate responsibility, analyzing the challenges from the perspective of corporate officers. They suggest that the rise of environmental compliance concerns in Canadian corporate boardrooms was initially the result of director concerns about liability. However, the development of environmental management systems has created awareness that compliance is only a minimal requirement. The "best interests of the company" require that directors, in keeping with their legal obligations, address long-term environmental sustainability and proactive environmental strategies to ensure long-term corporate viability. Mansell and Prill observe that recent protests at world trade and finance summits are barometers of growing public concern with respect to how corporations manage the environmental impact of their activities. An environmentally proactive business strategy resulting in a sustainable production process is in the corporation's best interests, as well as providing benefits to the community. This requires a corporate paradigm shift from that of pollution control and regulatory compliance to one of resource productivity. This means implementing internal control and management information systems that reward employee ingenuity with respect to reducing the costs of production by converting wasted resources from pollution into additional revenue sources. Long-term sustainable business strategies require a corporate culture of innovation, and the ability to respond to change and to develop new technological processes that maximize resource efficiencies and reduce environmental impact.

The next three chapters examine the role of corporate boards, internationally and domestically. In Chapter 8, Lynne Dallas provides a comprehensive analysis of the multiple roles of corporate boards, with a particular focus on developments in US boards of directors. Dallas observes that as corporations have increased in their size and complexity, demands on their operations have required them to implement more complex organizational structures, a more diverse workforce, and a more formalized system of disclosure and auditing that assures shareholders of corporate well-being. She observes that the relational role of boards includes the use of board memberships to facilitate the sharing of information and perspectives between corporate stakeholders, in order to reduce uncertainty, gain access to resources, and ensure effective monitoring of the strategic direction of the corporation. She distinguishes between the business functions of boards, including strategic planning processes, which are often better performed by insiders, and the board's conflicts and monitoring role, best performed by outside directors. One solution may be the creation of a dual board structure that would benefit from the best of the governance skills of inside and outside directors, and the appointment of corporate ombudspersons to improve the flow of information to corporate boards. The current demands on corporate boards necessitate more careful consideration of the complex and sometimes conflicting functions that boards perform, and thus the multiple skills, expertise, and greater diversity of directors that are required.

At first glance, Chapter 9 appears to be an outlier in that it examines domestic Crown corporations. The link with other chapters becomes apparent, however, as Barry Slutsky and Philip Bryden examine the question of independence of corporate directors and the relationship between this independence and effective governance, whether the corporate entity is public or private. They consider the extent to which traditional public law and corporate law concepts provide directors of commercial Crown corporations with governance guidance. They conclude that traditional private corporate law rules contribute little towards finding the appropriate balance between independence and accountability of directors in this form of corporate governance, given the public interest aspects of activities carried out by such corporations. It is not obvious that either public law or private corporate law principles give such directors meaningful direction in how to resolve conflicts between efficiency goals and broader public policy objectives.

In Chapter 10, Kathleen Porter and Joe Weiler observe that the current focus on shareholders is too narrow a conception of the corporation. They suggest that governance should take account of the firm's full nexus of contractual relations with multiple collateral stakeholders. They provide a detailed case example of a seafood processing industry sector council that provides a private law model for synchronizing corporate self-interest with sectoral governance. Porter and Weiler argue that their model offers a governance approach that is superior to either market or statutory regulation by building collaborative relationships and decision making through broader involvement by internal company participants, something they describe as a "positive responsibility" approach to governance.

The final three chapters turn to governance of the corporation when it is financially distressed. Financial or economic distress may be the result of capital and product market fluctuations, currency changes, production inefficiencies, managerial shirking or excessive risk taking, or a variety of other factors. During the period in which decisions regarding the future of the corporation are being made, effective stewardship is essential to identifying the causes of the distress and the most positive outcomes. Geoffrey Morawetz commences this discussion in Chapter 11 by examining shifts in fiduciary obligation as corporations enter the "twilight period," the period after the directors and officers realize that there are serious financial or economic problems and before any formal proceedings are initiated. He explores remedies that may be available to creditors and other stakeholders if there is a failure in governance. The definition of successful workout has shifted in the past decade, including increased use of statutory restructuring tools to focus on viability as opposed to liquidation, the introduction of chief restructuring officers who take over stewardship of the corporation during the workout period, and the increased likelihood that creditors will convert some of their debt claims to equity in agreeing to a corporate restructuring. The implications of these changes for the stakeholder debate are not yet fully realized, but it is likely that there will be both up- and downstream influences in terms of governance norms. Morawetz discusses global initiatives in governance during insolvency, aimed at discerning optimal principles for governance of financially distressed corporations, including liability mechanisms and protection of creditors' interests through new levels of activism and oversight.

In Chapter 12, Edward Sellers, Natasha MacParland, and James Hoffner undertake a comprehensive analysis of refinancing of the financially distressed corporation. It is here that governance issues come full circle with the beginning of this book. With the entry of Canadian corporations into global capital markets, the governance issues have become increasingly complex. The discipline that these markets bring to bear on a corporation and its directors are heightened when dealing with financial distress. Sellers and co-authors focus on refinancing techniques in global capital markets and particular challenges to directors and officers in working out the financial problems of the corporation. In the managing of market relationships, stewardship of necessity shifts its focus from its equity relationships to debt relationships because it is unlikely that refinancing will come from further equity investment. Equally, however, maintaining market confidence and adhering to regulatory requirements is essential to the successful management of a corporation's distress. The value of both debt and equity during this period can be highly speculative, resulting in active secondary market activity, discounted debt trading, or over-the-counter trading. Thus, not only does governance attention shift from equity to debt investors but the creditors themselves are shifting, and frequently have diverse and conflicting interests in the outcome of the distress. This and the necessity of retaining employees, finding interim financing during the workout period, choosing the workout forum, deploying new oversight skills and resources, and garnering the support of creditors all pose new challenges and require creative new solutions.

Finally, in Chapter 13, John Sandrelli rounds out the discussion of governance of financially distressed firms by examining the role of court-appointed officers in the workout process. Governance issues are magnified during financial distress, made more complicated by the cross-border nature of most insolvencies. Currently, there are few Canadian corporations that do not participate in global debt and/or equity markets, even if their production facilities are located domestically. On financial distress, those investors and lenders engage Canada's domestic law in order to maximize the value of their claims. However, they may also import norms with respect to governance that shift stewardship of the corporation. Sandrelli observes that the financially distressed company requires at minimum an adjustment to its governance structure, and in some cases a complete overhaul. The use of a variety of court-appointed officers such as receivers, receiver-managers, monitors, and chief restructuring officers is in part aimed at easing the concerns of nervous lenders and suppliers. The governance and capital structure may be reorganized with a view to returning control to existing or new equity holders. Officers implicated in the process must engage in a balancing of interests during this uncertain period, as well as ensuring maximum value to claimants. Given that boards of directors may be ill equipped to deal with an insolvency workout, the business expertise and reputational capital of court-appointed officers assist in steering the corporate ship though the uncertain waters.

As this brief review of the contents of this volume illustrates, corporate governance is a topic that covers a broad range of issues involving the legal, economic, psychological, and social incentives informing the behaviour of corporate decision makers. The effects of the decisions they make permeate deeply the fabric of our society and, with the spread of global capital markets and multinational corporations, the fabric of other societies as well. The authors have made a valuable contribution to the ongoing discussion about whether the global corporation is subject to any control and, if so, by whom and through what mechanism.

Part 1
Governance of the Corporation in the Context of Global Markets

1
Canadian Corporate Governance Reform: In Search of a Regulatory Role for Corporate Law
Stéphane Rousseau

Corporate governance, which relates to the process and structure used to direct and manage the business of corporations, is seen as a critical determinant of corporations' growth, development, and success in this era of globalization and international competition.[1] Over the last two decades, it has attracted increasing attention from Canadian governments and regulators interested in providing a legal and institutional environment in which corporations can thrive.[2] Like their foreign counterparts, Canadian policy makers have established committees with the mandate to elaborate reform proposals to improve the governance of publicly held corporations.[3]

Although they have been numerous, the proposals put forward in Canada by corporate governance reform committees share two salient characteristics. First, they assume that reform of the corporate decision making of publicly held corporations is required in order to maximize social welfare. Second, they presuppose that the implementation of and compliance with the recommendations are private matters that should be left to the discretion of corporate actors. Corporate governance should be primarily regulated by private norms. The first characteristic has been extensively discussed. Scholars debate whether the goal of maximizing social welfare requires governance structures that maximize share value, or rather, that maximize "the wealth-creating potential of the corporation as a whole."[4] Others express doubts as to the existence of systemic problems affecting corporate decision making or the ability of governance structures to contribute to the maximization of social welfare.[5] In the course of this debate, however, the second characteristic of reform initiatives has received less attention, even though, as one commentator has noted, "perhaps the most serious issue underlying [corporate governance] developments and related proposals is the extent to which changes in ... oversight mechanisms should be driven by legislative or regulatory requirements, rather than developing over time in response to emerging commercial practice and community consensus."[6] This chapter makes a contribution towards bridging this gap in the current literature by discussing the role of public regulation in the implementation and enforcement of corporate governance reform proposals.

The remainder of this chapter is divided into two parts. The first part presents the theoretical justifications underlying the reliance of policy makers on corporate actors to ensure the implementation and compliance with the "good" corporate governance norms identified in their reform proposals. It then describes more specifically the approach taken by reform committees and gives some examples of the role of corporate actors as an alternative source of normativity. The second part analyzes the private implementation and enforcement mechanisms that are required for the governance norms to be implemented and enforced by corporate actors. It argues that there are indications that these mechanisms suffer from imperfections and need to be supplemented by public regulation. In this respect, it suggests that public regulation should seek to give a new meaning to shareholder voice in corporate governance.

Reform of the Corporate Governance Framework of Publicly Held Corporations: A Focus on Private Norms

Corporate governance is a major policy issue in Canada because it is a core feature of the country's competitiveness. It has attracted considerable attention from governments and regulators interested in providing a legal and institutional environment in which corporations can thrive. Despite this interest from policy makers, corporate governance remains primarily a private matter left to the discretion of corporate actors. In fact, reform committees have espoused an enabling approach by abstaining from imposing a definite set of governance norms on corporations. In this setting, value-maximizing governance norms are expected to be privately generated. They are to emerge from the interaction between members of the corporation, and are to be enforced by the same mechanism.

Theoretical Justifications for the Reliance on Private Corporate Governance Norms

Committees established to reform corporate governance have favoured dealing with this issue through an enabling approach. As discussed below, this enabling approach proceeds from the theory that the corporation is a nexus of contracts and that corporate law should generally defer to the wishes of the contracting parties. It is also consistent with the recent emerging norms literature that emphasizes the predominance of private norms in shaping the governance of corporations.

The Enabling Philosophy of Modern Corporate Law Statutes

In Canada the reform of corporate law undertaken by the Dickerson Committee at the beginning of the 1970s, of which the *Canada Business Corporations*

Act (CBCA) is the offspring, was founded on a contractual conception of the corporation.[7] For the members of the Committee, the role of corporate law was to facilitate the formation and organization of corporations tailored to the needs of their members. Thus, according to the Dickerson Committee, corporate law was to have fundamentally an enabling role: "The primary purpose of corporation laws is not regulatory. They are enabling acts, to authorize businessmen to organize and to operate their business, large or small, with the advantages of the corporate mechanism. They are drawn with a view to facilitate efficient management of business and adjustment to the needs of change."[8]

Concretely, the drafters of the *CBCA* implemented this enabling philosophy by putting forward a simple and flexible incorporation procedure as well as by dispensing company participants from unnecessary formalism. Since they remained wary of investor abuse by self-serving management, they proposed a web of legislative provisions designed to make directors responsible towards shareholders, and provided the latter with effective remedies to protect their rights and interests. The approach of the Dickerson Committee influenced the majority of provincial legislatures, which modelled their corporate statutes on the *CBCA*.

The underlying philosophy of modern Canadian corporate law statutes is consistent with the law and economics literature that emphasizes the centrality of "contractual" relations in corporations.[9] According to the dominant paradigm of this literature, corporations connect various contracts between shareholders, creditors, managers, employees, and suppliers, and can be seen as a nexus of contracting relationships.[10]

From a legal perspective, the conception of the corporation as a nexus of contracts implies that the role of corporate law should be to facilitate the formation of "contracts" among the members of the corporation.[11] In other words, corporate law should, in the ordinary course, have an enabling role. It should be left to members of the corporation to shape the rules governing their relationships.[12] It will generally avoid imposing mandatory rules on parties to the corporate contract: "Companies are heterogeneous and the preferences of company participants vary. Correspondingly, a legal standard is unlikely to suit all parties in all instances. If a law is mandatory, parties which are ill-served by it either simply have to endure the consequences or may incur substantial costs restructuring matters."[13]

In this context, the role of corporate law is to serve as a standard form contract that reduces the transaction costs of the negotiating parties while leaving them free to modify the default rules to suit their needs.[14]

The general consensus over the enabling role of corporate law has significant implications for corporate governance reform.[15] With respect to the agency problem associated with widely held corporations, it leads commentators to insist on the general effectiveness of market forces in controlling the conflicts of interest between managers and shareholders of widely held corporations.[16] According to commentators, market mechanisms such as the market for corporate control, executive compensation, the product market, and the managerial labour market, can readily reduce the divergence of interests between managers and shareholders and thus the agency costs that result from the separation of ownership and control.[17] Although these various market instruments do not entirely eliminate all concerns, their existence indicates that caution is warranted when discussing the opportunity of relying on mandatory corporate law rules to control the agency problem of widely held corporations.[18]

With respect to corporations characterized by the presence of controlling shareholders, Daniels and Iacobucci aptly underline that the concentration of ownership does not necessarily reduce the divergence of interests between managers and shareholders.[19] Indeed, it can create an agency problem between the controlling shareholder(s) and minority shareholders by facilitating entrenchment by management. Ownership concentration enables the controlling shareholder to realize self-serving transactions through the board of directors. At the same time, it reduces the disciplinary effect of market mechanisms such as the market for corporate control. In sum, where it enables the controlling shareholder to reap private benefits of opportunism that exceed the private costs of such behaviour, ownership concentration does not lead to an overall reduction of agency costs.

While acknowledging that market instruments may not play an effective role in deterring self-interested behaviour in such a setting, leading commentators tend to avoid proposing an expanded regulatory role for corporate law.[20] Thus, after noting that legal mechanisms such as the oppression remedy and securities legislation requirements protect minority shareholders to some extent, they tend to argue that further concerns about concentrated ownership problems need not lead to the enactment of new mandatory rules. Instead, government policy should seek to enhance the effectiveness of markets in the governance system, for instance, by fostering the disclosure of information, in order to lead them to exert better control of the agency problem associated with concentrated ownership.

The enabling philosophy is the dominant paradigm for conceptualizing corporate law in Anglo-American jurisdictions. Unsurprisingly, policy makers remain faithful to this philosophy in their efforts to improve corporate governance. As discussed below, they have therefore refrained from imposing mandatory rules on corporations, opting rather to leave it to corporate actors to implement and enforce the good governance practices that they promote.

The Role of Social Norms in Regulating the Behaviour of Corporate Actors

Interestingly, the adherence of reform committees to the enabling philosophy can also be explained by the emerging social norms literature, which emphasizes the predominance of private norms in shaping the governance of corporations. The interest in social norms has been gaining momentum since the publication of the foundational book by Robert Ellickson entitled *Order without Law* at the beginning of the 1990s.[21] This book convincingly underscored the importance of "informal systems of external social control," or "social norms," in regulating behaviour, and the necessity for law and economics to move away from legal centralism by taking into account the existence of these social norms.[22] Since that time, law and economics scholars have devoted considerable efforts to enriching the rational choice model in order to get a better understanding of the interconnection between the legal system and informal systems of social control.[23] Although they have been studied with respect to a multitude of legal issues, social norms have only recently begun to receive attention in the corporate law context.[24]

Before discussing the relevance of the social norms literature for corporate governance reform, it seems necessary to define the concept of norms. In this respect, it must be noted at the outset that numerous definitions are offered for this concept. Thus, Ellickson defines norms as "rules that emanate from social forces, distinguishing them from personal ethics (internalized rules), contracts (rules imposed by second party controllers), rules imposed by organizations, and laws (rules imposed by governments)."[25] For Marcel Kahan, norms are "rules, other than legal duties, that are regularly followed due to either an external punitive sanction administered by a third party or a related internalized sense of obligation."[26] Melvin Eisenberg considers norms as encompassing "all rules and regularities concerning human conduct, other than legal rules and organizational rules."[27] Richard Posner and Eric Rasmusen posit that a norm "is a social rule that does not depend on government for either promulgation or enforcement."[28]

As many have noted, this multiplicity of definitions unfortunately creates conceptual ambiguity.[29] While it is beyond the scope of this chapter to discuss thoroughly this terminology issue, it seems useful to agree on what "norm" signifies in order to conduct meaningful discussion and analysis. In this respect, Edward Rock and Michael Wachter have proposed a useful although somewhat inelegant designation for the concept of "norm" that synthesizes the various definitions offered by the literature: Norms are essentially nonlegally enforceable rules and standards (NLERS).[30] This conception of a norm "focuses attention on the boundary between legal and other third-party enforcement, just as the use of the implicit contracting language forces attention on the difference between self-enforcement and enforcement by third parties."[31] In other words, from a jurisdictional perspective, norm analysis is concerned with the boundary between legal and nonlegal enforceability. While they all share the characteristics of being nonlegally enforceable, NLERS come in different varieties:

> Some are truly self-enforcing in the sense that neither party has any incentive to breach. Some are self-enforced by feelings of guilt. Some are enforced directly by the parties themselves. Some are enforced by third parties through the application of peer pressure, shaming, or threats to one's reputation.[32]

Given the relative clarity of this definition, this chapter will use the concept of NLERS to discuss the significance of social norms for corporate governance.

The burgeoning literature on norms has led to an interest on the part of scholars in the role of NLERS in corporate law. As mentioned above, corporate law is essentially enabling, its role being to facilitate the conduct and organization of corporations. To some extent, it is nevertheless recognized that it has a regulatory role since it provides incentives and disincentives to corporate actors through the threat of liability. Still, as many have noted, corporate actors tend not to be primarily motivated by liability but rather by the prospect of financial gains.[33] In light of the work done on the operation of social norms in general, it is further argued that NLERS are also likely to exercise an influence on the behaviour of corporate actors.

Most notable among the research undertaken so far is the work of Rock and Wachter, who propose a theory of the relationship between legal and nonlegally enforceable rules and standards in the corporation and its implications in corporate law. Drawing on modern theories of the firm, Rock and Wachter argue that the principal feature of the firm is "to replace legal governance with nonlegally enforceable governance mechanisms."[34] The starting point of their analysis is the insight developed by Coase, where the concept of transaction costs is a central factor in delineating the boundaries of the firm.[35] Rock and Wachter remark that when transaction costs are low, parties can draft complete contracts that protect the integrity of their dealings. These complete contracts are then enforced through market discipline as well as judicial enforcement. However, when contracting is incomplete because of transaction costs, the market and the judiciary lose their effectiveness. Rock and Wachter contend that transactions are then brought inside the firm, where they are governed essentially by NLERS. Compliance with those governance arrangements is ensured by nonjudicial mechanisms, either self-enforcement or enforcement through nonlegal means.

In this model, the emergence and use of NLERS is enhanced by corporate law, which is seen "as a remarkably sophisticated mechanism for facilitating self-governance by NLERS."[36] Corporate law provides the foundation for the corporation to operate as a hierarchy by establishing the principle of centralized management, with shareholders electing the board of directors that is vested with the rights of residual control, that is, the authority to manage the corporation's business and affairs. More specifically, it provides management with the responsibility for determining the assets that will be owned by the corporation as well as the NLERS necessary to protect the integrity of transactions between the corporation and its shareholders and employees. At the same time, corporate statutes endow shareholders with ownership-type claims that enable them to exercise control over management.

On the one hand, the board, with its enormous discretion, has the ultimate responsibility and power to maximize the value of the corporation's assets and to craft the appropriate NLERS that protect the vulnerable specific investments of the various participants. But this needs to be done in a manner consistent with maximizing the shareholders' residual claim. If the directors fail to do so, shareholders can throw them out. That is why *only* shareholders get to vote for directors, a persistent feature of the corporate landscape. The fact that *only* shareholders get to vote is the critical feature of the standard corporation that fixes the goals of the board's exercise of discretion in drafting the NLERS of the firm.[37]

The governance of corporations through NLERS is further ensured by the business judgment rule, which maintains the primacy of NLERS and private enforcement by preventing parties from resorting successfully to third-party adjudicators.

The NLERS that emerge in the Rock and Wachter model can be firm-specific, such as the promotion of teamwork, boardroom composition, and fairness, with management selecting and enforcing them.[38] NLERS are not only firm-specific, however. They can spread from corporation to corporation to acquire a "transfirm" status.[39] While the process through which firm-specific norms obtain a transfirm status remains to some extent a puzzle, recent work by Melvin Eisenberg offers interesting insights into this process.

According to Eisenberg, the origin and adoption of social norms by corporate actors across firms result from changes in the corporate actor's belief systems brought about by new information or reasoned persuasion.[40] In other words, the diffusion of learning in the community helps firm-specific NLERS spread from firm to firm. Thus, for instance, it is a change in the belief system of the business community concerning the nature of the obligations of management that has led to an increased level of directorial care in the United States over the last ten years, rather than an increase in the threat of liability or the prospect of financial gains.[41] For Eisenberg, this change in the belief system was brought about by new information provided by an exogenous event, the rise of the takeover-bid institution, which highlighted the existence of a high level of managerial inefficiency.

Despite the apparent predominance of NLERS in the governance of corporations, there clearly remains a role for legal rules, as many have noted. The Rock and Wachter model indicates that the enabling function of corporate law serves to facilitate self-governance. In addition, corporate law fosters this type of governance through its expressive function that supports

NLERS and makes them "operational and meaningful through concreti-zation."[42] Besides, from a regulatory standpoint, corporate law can combat norms that decrease efficiency. For instance, detailed analysis of the causes underlying the recent wave of corporate scandals, which occurred in the wake of the Enron debacle, may reveal the role played by dubious norms, such as those governing auditor-firm relationships, and the need for regula-tory intervention.[43] Finally, as underlined by Posner and Rasmusen, legal rules have a role to play in the enforcement of norms.

In sum, norms scholars argue that the setting in which corporations op-erate provides fertile ground for norms to emerge and affect the behaviour of corporate actors. As Coffee summarizes, "corporate behaviour may be more shaped and determined by social norms than legal rules."[44] This theory provides an additional explanation for the reliance of reform committees on corporate actors to implement and enforce the good governance prac-tices they promote.

An Overview of the Reliance on Private Governance Norms

Over the last decades, corporate governance has been the subject of increas-ing attention from policy makers. Governments and regulators have estab-lished reform committees to review and suggest improvements to corporate decision making in Canada. Although set up at different periods in reaction to diverse events, the committees shared a fundamental characteristic: es-pousal of the enabling philosophy of corporate statutes. Thus, they have essentially left it to the discretion of corporate actors to shape their govern-ance framework. Corporate actors therefore have the ability to adopt the formal governance norms proposed by reform committees as well as to de-velop their own informal governance norms.

The Stock Exchanges' Guidelines on Corporate Governance

Concerns over corporate governance were raised not long after the enact-ment of the *Canada Business Corporations Act,* by the Royal Commission on Corporate Concentration (the "Bryce Commission") in 1978.[45] Although formed to review the nature and role of the concentration of corporate power in Canada and its consequences for public policy, the Commission devoted a part of its report to "Corporate Ownership, Control and Management."[46] As part of this inquiry, the Commission examined the role of the board of directors in large publicly held corporations, addressing issues that are strik-ingly familiar.

More specifically, the Commission remarked that "the contribution that might be made by boards and the significance to public corporations of the composition of boards"[47] were matters that had not been studied sufficiently in the past. Various factors were now causing a shift in attitude that required a revision of the board of directors' role. Thus, the Commission elected to participate in this revision by proposing its conception of this role.

According to the Commission, directors should play an expanded role in corporate decision making. By this, the Commission did not mean that the board should duplicate the responsibilities of the corporation's officers. Rather, it suggested that the board should assume the role of monitoring management: "The board should act as a check on the executive, be fully informed of the company's affairs, and be able to monitor the actions of management."[48] Hence, the Commission attempted to sketch out the various implications of this mandate of the board of directors, in terms of its structure and functions. In essence, the members of the Commission endorsed a fundamental principle that would be later restated by corporate governance committees, specifically, that the board of directors should be independent of management and therefore composed primarily of persons drawn from diverse backgrounds outside the corporation. Moreover, to achieve its monitoring role, the independent board should develop a more active audit committee as well as increase its direct contact with the corporation's independent auditors and outside counsel. Finally, directors should not sit on the boards of more than a few publicly held corporations, in order to be able to carry out their duties to the corporation.

Despite considering that these improvements to corporate decision making were necessary, the Bryce Commission abstained from recommending that these propositions be enacted in legislation:

> We think the results will be better if these views are adopted voluntarily rather than being imposed by law upon an antagonistic group, and then observed only with reluctance and formality. The final result might then be tokenism or cosmetic "window dressing." These are ideas that must work "not only in the courtroom but also in the boardroom." We hope that major Canadian companies will respond to these suggestions in a positive way, and will incorporate them into their formal operating activities.[49]

In the absence of support from legislators or regulators, however, the recommendations of the Commission went unheeded.

Although the issues raised by the Bryce Commission were considered again during the 1980s in the wake of serious failures in the financial services industry,[50] it is the work of the Toronto Stock Exchange Committee on Corporate Governance in Canada, chaired by Peter Dey (the "Dey Committee"), that brought this topic to the forefront of the regulatory agenda in the 1990s.[51] The work of the Dey Committee has received extensive commentary.[52] Briefly, the Committee was formed in 1993 to conduct a comprehensive study of corporate governance in Canada and to make recommendations to improve the manner in which Canadian corporations are governed.[53] It produced a report entitled *Where Were the Directors?* (the Dey Report) announcing a list of guidelines that aim to enhance the role of the board of directors in corporate decision making, an objective shared by the members of the Bryce Commission in their recommendations.

More specifically, the guidelines state that the board's responsibilities relate to the stewardship of the corporation and include the strategic planning process; the identification and monitoring of the principal risks of the business; the appointment, development, and succession of senior management; the implementation of an effective communications policy; and the adoption of relevant and reliable internal control systems. To ensure that the board can fulfill this stewardship role, the guidelines set forth recommendations with respect to its structure and functions. Thus, they recommend that boards be composed of a majority of unrelated directors, free from any interest or relationship that could influence their ability to exercise their judgment in the best interests of the corporation. In addition, they identify a number of governance-related functions that should be carried out by board committees, including the selection of unrelated directors, the assessment of management, and the responsibility for the corporation's overall governance system.

The guidelines announced in the Dey Report were well received by the Toronto Stock Exchange (TSX), which incorporated them in its *Company Manual*.[54] Although the guidelines are now part of the listing requirements of the TSX, this nevertheless imposes few constraints on listed corporations. In essence, the TSX *Company Manual* follows the recommendation of the Dey Report and abstains from making the guidelines mandatory. It encourages issuers to take into consideration the guidelines enacted, but leaves it to issuers to determine the extent of their compliance. Issuers need only disclose to shareholders their governance practices in their annual report or information circular, and discuss the extent to which they respect the guidelines and, to the extent that they do not, explain the reason for noncompliance. In sum, the *Company Manual* does not mandate substantive compliance with the guidelines; it requires only formal compliance, that is, disclosure of corporate governance practices made in light of the TSX guidelines.

Six years after the publication of the Dey Report, the members of the Dey Committee reconvened to examine the state of governance in Canada.[55] The findings of the Committee were mixed. While noting the considerable improvements made to corporate governance in Canada, the Committee expressed concerns that the commitment to good governance had lost momentum. Accordingly, it encouraged the TSX to launch a new review process of corporate decision making. In July 2000, the TSX followed this recommendation and formed a Joint Committee on Corporate Governance, chaired by Guylaine Saucier, in collaboration with the Canadian Institute of Chartered Accountants (CICA) and the Canadian Venture Exchange (CDNX) (the "Saucier Committee"). After more than a year of work, the Committee tabled its Final Report, *Beyond Compliance: Building a Governance Culture,* in November 2001.[56]

Following the approach taken by the Dey Committee, the Saucier Committee focused its inquiry on the board of directors. However, it arguably moved away from questions pertaining to board structures, dealt with by the Dey Report, to address more specifically "board functions."[57] Thus, in its Final Report, the committee proposed a series of fifteen recommendations that purportedly strengthen the board's stewardship role.

The thrust of the Saucier Committee's report is to enable the board to act independently in fulfilling its responsibilities. The report proposed to achieve this objective through two main groups of recommendations. The first group, which forms the pinnacle of the report, relates to the requirement for an "independent board leader" chosen from among the outside and unrelated directors. The independent board leader and unrelated directors would meet at every regularly scheduled meeting without management.[58] Specifically, the independent board leader would be empowered by the board to carry out functions that encompass providing leadership to enhance board effectiveness, managing the board, acting as a liaison between board and management, and representing the corporation to external groups. The independent board leader would also be charged with the responsibility to ensure regular assessments of the chief executive officer (CEO), the board and its committees, and the contribution of individual directors. In this respect, the Saucier Committee report recommends that boards of directors develop a formal mandate that sets out their responsibilities, and against which their assessment will be conducted.

The second group of recommendations aims to improve the effectiveness of audit committees.[59] Inspired by the US Blue Ribbon Committee report,[60] the Saucier Committee's report proposes guidelines with respect to the mandate and independence of audit committees, as well as to the financial literacy of committee members. Thus, it recommends that audit committees be composed solely of outside and unrelated directors who are financially literate. It states that at least one member of the committee should have accounting or related financial expertise. Audit committees should also adopt a formal mandate establishing the scope of their responsibilities, which should be disclosed to shareholders. Finally, it recommends that the audit committees exercise some oversight of the internal audit function and, where such a function does not exist, periodically request from management a review of the need for this function.

As mentioned earlier, the Saucier Committee's report retained the philosophy of the Dey Report with respect to enforcement:

> While there may be a place for regulating some aspects of corporate govern-
> ance, our view is that disclosure is a much better approach than attempting
> to regulate behaviour, if one is seeking to build a healthy governance cul-
> ture. Indeed, we believe that regulation aimed at changing board behaviour
> may turn out to be counterproductive.[61]

Thus, the Saucier Committee's report maintained the disclosure-based approach favoured by the Dey Report by recommending that the actual sections of the TSX *Company Manual* relating to corporate governance be amended to integrate its new proposals. Accordingly, upon the integration of the guidelines of the Saucier Committee's report in the *Manual*, corporations will have to provide a complete description of their system of corporate governance with specific references to each of the new guidelines.

Interestingly, although the Saucier Committee advocated the disclosure of meaningful information by the board,[62] it abstained from making recommendations that would lead issuers to attain this objective. In its Final Report, the Committee limited its recommendation to the statement that the "TSX should identify education, monitoring and enforcement measures that will ensure companies comply with the disclosure requirements."[63]

As the foregoing overview of the Dey and Saucier Committee reports indicates, Canadian corporate governance committees espoused an enabling approach by refraining from recommending that the guidelines they proposed become mandatory. This enabling approach, as seen above, is consistent with theoretical justifications that point to the ability of the corporation's members to regulate themselves and solve governance problems.[64] It is substantiated by more practical arguments that emphasize the need for flexible guidelines given the wide range of corporations subjected to them and the existence of various equally satisfying solutions to governance problems.[65] Given these arguments, governance committees have chosen not to mandate compliance with the guidelines enacted "but to secure sufficient disclosure so that investors and others can assess a listed company's corporate governance practices and respond in an informed way."[66]

Corporate Actors as an Alternative Source of Governance Norms: Some Examples

In parallel to the work of reform committees, various forces have coalesced to foster the emergence of NLERS pertaining to corporate governance. While a thorough inventory of those norms is beyond the scope of this chapter, it is appropriate to present a few salient examples of such informal governance norms as they underscore the ability of corporate actors to "regulate" themselves.[67]

At the management level, a significant change in the governance norms has been the transition from a managing board to a monitoring board over the last two decades.[68] Traditionally, according to the dominant concep-tion, the role of the board was to manage the business and affairs of the corporation. Rather inefficient for large publicly held corporations,[69] this role of the board of directors nevertheless remained the orthodoxy until the emergence of the monitoring model, which is now widely accepted by the business, investment, and legal communities. As Eisenberg notes, dif-ferent factors led to a change in belief systems in favour of the monitoring model:

> Partly the relevant communities were persuaded by a new idea. Not too long ago, the dominant idea was that the board had the function of manag-ing the business of the corporation, not of monitoring management. The business community, the investment community, the bar, and the courts became persuaded that the new monitoring idea was markedly better than the old managing idea.
>
> In addition, the information concerning managerial inefficiency that was transmitted by the spread between takeover-bid prices and market prices, which seems to have affected directors' belief-systems concerning the duty of care, also affected their belief-systems concerning the functions and struc-ture of the board.[70]

According to the monitoring model, the function of the board of a pub-licly held corporation is not to manage the business of the corporation. Rather, its function is "to select, regularly evaluate, fix the compensation of, and, where appropriate, replace the senior executives, and to monitor the conduct of the corporation's business to evaluate whether the business is being properly managed."[71] This model has now gained an obligatory character, given that public corporations and directors that do not respect it are criticized by the business and investment communities.[72]

At the ownership level, during the same period, institutional investors, the dominant shareholders of publicly held corporations, progressively aban-doned their passive approach to governance issues pursuant to which they traditionally respected the "Bay Street Rule" when dissatisfied with man-agement.[73] The "passivity norm" has been gradually replaced by an "activ-ism norm," following which institutional investors are getting more and more involved in corporate governance matters. As the works of MacIntosh and Montgomery have shown, institutions are increasingly exerting pressure on management, either directly through formal actions such as voting prox-ies or indirectly through behind-the-scenes diplomacy, to enhance the ac-countability of managers towards shareholders.[74] This shift from passivity to activism has been spurred by economic and legal developments that have been widely chronicled, such as the growth of the funds managed by insti-tutions, the concentration of institutional investments, limited investment opportunities, and regulatory changes.[75] While institutional investors' degree of adherence to the activism norm varies depending on the type of institution,[76] with public sector pension funds being among the most active investors, the emergence of the activism norm is nevertheless a significant development that enhances the monitoring of management. Institutional investor monitoring is now part of the governance system of publicly held corporations and contributes to the reduction of agency conflicts.

The emergence of these alternative governance norms is a testament to the ability of market participants to develop nonlegally enforceable rules and standards that affect the behaviour of corporate actors. However, the ability of market participants to produce such NLERS does not necessarily mean that there is no role for public regulation. The next part of this chapter examines the potential role that public regulation can play in the enforcement of such informal norms.

Implementation and Enforcement of Private Governance Norms: A Modest Role for Public Regulation

Pursuant to the approach taken by reform committees, corporate governance is expected to be improved by the interaction of corporate actors. More specifically, in publicly held corporations, negotiations cannot formally intervene between corporate actors. Improvements are to proceed from market pressures and social sanctions that should lead corporations to adopt the guidelines of the TSX and the NLERS that are value-maximizing. To the extent that these mechanisms work effectively, the elaboration of corporations' governance practices should be left to private actors. However, as discussed below, there are theoretical and empirical indications that private mechanisms suffer from imperfections and need to be supplemented by public regulation.

Shortcomings of Private Enforcement Mechanisms

The Market's Ability to Exert Pressure

The TSX guidelines on corporate governance are expected to be implemented and enforced by the market rather than by direct regulation. Specifically, it is assumed that mandatory disclosure of corporate governance practices by corporations will enable shareholders to compare them with the benchmark of the guidelines and form a judgment about the value of such practices.[77] In an efficient market, the shareholders' assessment would translate into share prices that adjust to reflect whether or not the practices are value-maximizing. In return, share price movements would exert pressure on directors to implement good corporate governance practices in order to maintain their corporation's access to the financial market as well as to prevent hostile takeovers. To summarize, the governance guidelines enacted by the TSX *Company Manual* are expected to be enforced by shareholder pressure, mediated by their evaluation of corporate shares.[78]

The effectiveness of this market regulation framework depends on two fundamental prerequisites.[79] First, shareholders must have access to an optimal level of information on the governance practices of corporations. Second, the information conveyed by corporations in this respect must be credible. It is possible, however, to question whether these prerequisites are met. As will be argued below, the current framework does not appear to be very conducive to effective disclosure. In parallel, the credibility of governance reporting by issuers remains wanting. In this respect, the succession of corporate scandals in the United States since the fall of Enron Corporation in 2001 provides serious anecdotal evidence in support of these critiques.

The Adequacy of Corporate Governance Disclosure

To enable the market to exert effective pressure on issuers, the TSX *Manual* requires listed companies to disclose their governance practices in their annual report or in their proxy circular. However, there are reasons to doubt that corporations meet the required level of disclosure in the current institutional setting.

It must be recognized from the outset that considerable discretion is left to issuers in reporting compliance with the governance guidelines enacted by the *Manual.* As one author notes:

> When the directors make the compliance statement ... they will have to assess whether they have complied with each of the Code's recommendations. They may find that they are asking themselves the question "how much is enough to establish compliance?" this could very well turn into "how much can we get away with?"[80]

This problem is compounded by the general character of some of the requirements contained in the guidelines. For instance, the TSX *Manual* guidelines establish that the "board of directors should review the adequacy and form of the compensation of directors and ensure that the compensation realistically reflects the responsibilities and risk involved in being an effective director."[81] Undoubtedly, this requirement leaves ample discretion to directors to decide what constitutes compliance. Such discretion now appears questionable in light of the recent analysis surrounding the Enron debacle, which challenges the ability of boards of directors to ensure the adequacy and integrity of disclosure.[82]

The directors' discretion is buttressed by the reluctance of the TSX to sanction inappropriate reporting of corporate governance practices. Theoretically, the Exchange can elect to suspend issuers from trading or delist them when they do not respect disclosure requirements. However, these sanctions are drastic measures that the Exchange is reluctant to use for disclosure violations, given that they also penalize the shareholders of the issuers at large, rather than just those responsible for the inadequate disclosure.[83] For this reason, where issuers do not comply with the disclosure policies, the Exchange would rather elect to send a warning letter advising the issuer of its failure to comply with its disclosure obligations. While such warnings are arguably effective "due simply to moral suasion and the generally responsible attitude with which companies approach their disclosure obligations,"[84] a cursory examination of corporate governance reporting in the proxy circular of TSX-listed corporations indicates that Exchange authorities have not enforced stringently the disclosure requirements. Indeed, anecdotal evidence indicates that considerable variations exist in the quality of reporting, which ranges from the terse to the very detailed.

In this context, it is the self-interest of firms that is the primary element determining the level of their compliance with the disclosure requirements of the TSX *Manual*.[85] The self-interest approach to disclosure is well known and states that issuers have significant incentives to voluntarily disclose information to investors.[86] Issuers' incentives to disclose information come more particularly from the impact of disclosure on firm value. Specifically, the argument posits that issuers will voluntarily disclose information to signal that their prospects are promising in order to differentiate themselves from low-quality firms. According to signalling theory, information that firms disclose or do not disclose is likely to be taken as a signal by investors.[87] Firms with "good news" or good investment projects have nothing to hide, since the disclosure of information will raise their value and allow them to distinguish themselves from firms with "bad news" or bad investment projects. Firms with no information also have incentives to disclose honest reports to avoid being confused with firms with bad news. Firms with bad news or bad investment projects must also disclose their unfavourable information, even if they would prefer not to do so, so that investors will not assume that they have even worse news. Therefore, firms that start disclosing information cannot stop their disclosure activities because investors will otherwise always assume the worst. Firms that do not disclose information "must suffer the cost of suspicion generated by nondisclosure or must convince investors that the numbers either would not be meaningful or that they would be too expensive to produce."[88]

In the context of corporate governance, this model implies that issuers should voluntarily disclose information on their practices until the marginal benefits of increments in information equal the marginal costs. This suggests in turn that the amount and quality of information provided should vary among issuers in order to reflect their different characteristics, which affect the costs and benefits of disclosure.[89] Stated differently, the characteristics of firms should affect their incentives to disclose their corporate governance practices. Firms that possess characteristics increasing the value of corporate governance reporting should therefore be associated with higher disclosure quality than others.

This proposition has recently been used in an empirical study examining "whether a firm's choice of disclosure quality on corporate governance practices was the result of a deliberate financial disclosure strategy explainable by certain internal and external determinants."[90] The study identified structural, performance, and governance variables that were likely to exercise an influence on the propensity of managers to select the quality of disclosure by corporations. More precisely, those variables were firm performance, size, level of financing activity, proportion of unrelated directors, and separation of the roles of chairman and chief executive officer. The study then analyzed the relationship between those variables and the Canadian Institute of Chartered Accountants' (CICA) evaluation of firms' corporate governance disclosure practices. The results, as summarized by the author, proved puzzling:

> We do not find any significant relationship between disclosure quality of governance practices and variables such as firm performance, size or level of financing activity which are often used to explain the quality level in the voluntary disclosure literature. Corporate governance variables such as the proportion of unrelated directors and the separation of the roles of chairman and chief executive are not significant either while, as predicted, the proportion of equity owned by management is only weakly positively related to disclosure quality.[91]

Given these results, it is difficult to assume that voluntary disclosure will lead corporations to report an adequate amount of corporate governance information.

In sum, the current framework does not appear to be very conducive to effective disclosure. The imperfections of the TSX *Manual* and of the voluntary disclosure model in this respect are further illustrated by a number of recent studies. For instance, a study of the corporate governance disclosure practice of 324 publicly held companies indicates that 51 percent of the companies reviewed did not report their practices against the guidelines of the TSX.[92] Likewise, recent CICA studies have highlighted the inadequacy of corporate governance reporting.[93]

These results concur with the general concerns that have regularly been voiced by regulators with respect to the degree of compliance by issuers with the current continuous disclosure requirements,[94] including, ironically, the Dey Committee: "We have the distinct sense that concerns exist about the ongoing disclosures of public companies. The concerns focus both on the timeliness of the release of information and upon the content of the releases."[95]

The preoccupations of the Committee were later restated by the Toronto Stock Exchange Committee on Corporate Disclosure set up to examine this particular issue. As part of its work, the Committee, chaired by Tom Allen, conducted a survey of market participants to assess the latter's perception of mandatory disclosure compliance. The Committee marshalled anecdotal evidence supporting the concerns expressed in the Dey Report by conducting a survey with analysts and retail investors.[96] While the analysts surveyed considered that issuers generally complied with the disclosure obligations, they stressed the existence of problems with respect to the sufficiency and timeliness of the information provided. The survey of retail investors supported this perception that information was not disclosed on a timely basis. In its assessment of the issuers' degree of compliance with disclosure requirements, the Committee identified junior issuers, particularly unlisted companies traded in the over-the-counter market, as an area of particular concern.[97] While the Saucier Committee recognized the inadequacies of corporate governance reporting in its Interim Report, it did not propose solutions to correct this problem in its Final Report.[98]

The Credibility of Disclosure

For corporate governance disclosure to be meaningful to shareholders, it must be credible; that is, shareholders must be able to differentiate between accurate reporting and window dressing. Indeed, notwithstanding its limitations, the voluntary model of disclosure aptly predicts that each issuer will have incentives to produce statements on its corporate governance practices that are "good news" for the market. Thus, as Belcher notes in her analysis of the Cadbury Report, "it follows that management have the incentive to produce a clean compliance statement which states that the company does comply with the Code."[99] Consequently, given the vagueness of the current disclosure requirements, issuers possess considerable latitude for reporting compliance creatively. In other words, managers have the incentives and the means to make disclosures that contain little useful information on their corporation's governance practices.

Enabling investors to differentiate between accurate and misleading disclosure of governance practices is critical to avoiding an adverse selection problem.[100] If they are unable to distinguish between good and bad corporate governance practices, investors will consider that individual firms have practices that reflect the average of the population of publicly traded firms. This will penalize firms that establish effective governance practices since they will receive the same valuation for their efforts as the average firms. Consequently, in such a setting, firms will not have incentives to develop good practices.

From this perspective, it is certainly puzzling that the TSX *Manual* does not mandate the auditing of corporate governance disclosure.[101] The verification of corporations' disclosure by auditors would provide an independent check on information accuracy that would enable investors to assess more accurately the credibility of the governance practices reported. Given the recent comments made by the Saucier Committee concerning the auditing of governance reporting, however, it is likely that the TSX *Manual* will not change its position on this in the course of the revision of its guidelines. In its Interim Report, the Committee remarked: "The thrust of our report is to encourage the development of a healthy governance culture. We believe that a requirement to audit disclosure statements would send the wrong signal. It would reinforce a compliance culture that we do not think is productive."[102] Although the Committee refrained from addressing this question in its Final Report, this omission can be taken to suggest that it considered the status quo adequate with respect to this question.

Proponents of the voluntary model of disclosure will argue that firms that develop good corporate governance practices have the incentives and the means to distinguish themselves from other firms, and thereby solve the adverse selection problem. More precisely, they can rely on reputable auditors, who can provide an independent check on information accuracy.[103] Accordingly, it may be argued that even though the TSX *Manual* does mandate the auditing of governance practices reporting, corporations with good practices will have their information audited on a voluntary basis, and that this will allow investors to distinguish quality in this respect.

While this proposition is true, it overlooks the fact that information costs will remain significant for investors in the presence of optional auditing. Indeed, it is important to emphasize that review by auditors fosters compliance with the standards by issuers. These standards benefit investors by increasing the uniformity of the presentation and the comparative value of the information disclosed.[104] In the absence of a general audit requirement with respect to corporate governance disclosure, investors will have to incur assessment and verification costs to compare audited reports with unaudited ones. Besides, a mandatory audit requirement would provide regulators with the opportunity to enact the necessary procedural safeguards to ensure the independence of the audit process and reduce the preoccupations spawned by the Enron scandal.

The Effectiveness of Private Sanctions

NLERS can constrain the behaviour of corporate actors in two broad ways.[105] First, they can compel actors to act in a certain way because the actors have internalized them. Internalization refers to the process in which the actors adhere to the norms "to the point where they obey them automatically, even when a failure to obey the norm would go unnoted by others."[106] Second, they can have an obligational effect on corporate actors because they are enforced by a third party who can impose sanctions or confer benefits, depending on whether the norms are breached or respected. In this respect, according to the norms literature, NLERS can be privately enforced by guilt, shunning, and shaming.[107]

Although NLERS pertaining to corporate governance may have been internalized to some extent by corporate actors, third-party enforcement appears to be crucial for such norms to have an obligational effect on members of the corporation.[108] Among the three main external enforcement mechanisms, shaming appears to be the most relevant to corporate governance. Shaming, as defined by Kahan and Posner, consists in "the process by which citizens publicly and self-consciously draw attention to the bad dispositions or actions of an offender, as a way of punishing him for having those dispositions or engaging in those actions."[109] It is directed at the offender's reputation and dignity, which it undermines through a publicly made condemnation. In doing so, shaming sanctions the offender but also influences potential offenders who can be deterred by the threat of such sanctions.

The role of shaming as an enforcement mechanism can be sketched against the background of two prominent general norms theories. First, according to Richard McAdams's theory of social esteem, individuals value and seek the esteem of others.[110] According to McAdams, this preference for esteem constitutes the driving force behind norm creation and enforcement. With respect to enforcement,[111] this theory suggests that individuals conform to social norms in order to maintain or gain the esteem of members of the community. Shaming from the community effectively sanctions norm violators by withholding from them the esteem they value. Second, in Eric Posner's model, norms have a signalling role that enables actors to reveal their true type.[112] By adhering to an obligational norm, an actor signals that he is a cooperator. Conversely, nonadherence signals that one is not a cooperative type. Thus, through his adherence or nonadherence to an obligational norm, an actor develops a reputation from which substantial benefits or penalties can be derived. In this model, shaming serves as a reputational sanction that affects the actor in his subsequent transactions.

From this perspective, shaming could arguably play a role in the enforcement of NLERS dealing with corporate governance, including those stated in the Toronto Stock Exchange's guidelines. Recent work by David Skeel emphasizes the role of shareholder activists in shaming corporations and directors that do not respect governance norms.[113] Skeel cites as an example of shaming the California Public Employees' Retirement System (CalPERS) focus list of underperforming firms, which identifies corporations that "are both poor economic performers and have corporate governance structures that do not ensure full accountability to company owners."[114] Skeel argues that such a list constitutes shaming in that it notifies the community that the corporations identified have transgressed a NLERS:

Although in times past the directors of large firms were not expected to do much at all, an increasingly powerful norm condemns directorial sloth and requires the board to exercise meaningful oversight. Directors who shirk these responsibilities, and firms that erect "accountability repellents," do so in violation of this norm. Private enforcers who call attention to these violations are therefore shaming the offenders in much the same way as a judge who orders a corporate polluter or price fixer to make a public confession of guilt.[115]

Shaming sanctions translate into concrete consequences for the corporations and directors targeted. They will lose esteem from the investment and business communities, to the extent that the norm infringed is shared by the latter. Moreover, investors may become reluctant to buy the corporations' securities and consumers may abstain from purchasing their products.

Thus, shaming could constitute an effective enforcement mechanism to ensure compliance with NLERS pertaining to corporate governance.[116] Indeed, the Canadian investment community is characterized by the presence of norms entrepreneurs, such as Fairvest, the Centre for Public and Corporate Governance, l'Association pour la protection des épargnants et investisseurs du Québec, and certain large public pension funds, that play a prominent role in the development and enforcement of governance norms.[117] Through public statements and interventions during shareholders meetings, these norms entrepreneurs can enforce NLERS by condemning the corporations and boards of directors that do not respect them. The enforcement activities of these norms entrepreneurs are complemented by the work of the financial press that communicates shaming sanctions or explicitly blames corporations and directors offending corporate governance norms. Shaming by norms entrepreneurs and the financial press can arguably sanction corporations and directors that stray away from governance norms, and deter potential offenders from following suit.[118]

The effectiveness of shaming should not be overstated. Undoubtedly, social esteem and reputation are valuable assets for corporations and their directors. It is unclear, however, whether shaming affects these assets in such a meaningful and significant way as to constitute a sanction and act as a deterrent. Indeed, some puzzling questions remain unanswered in this respect.

In the corporate governance context, shaming will most likely target corporate directors and managers, either directly or indirectly. Shaming sanctions will aim directly at managers and directors when they point towards the latter particularly. They will be intended for directors and managers indirectly when they are addressed at the corporation. In any case, given the intangible nature of the corporation, it appears that it is the directors' and managers' preference for esteem and reputation, as well as their vulnerability to shaming, that determines the effectiveness of the sanction.[119]

With respect to social esteem, it can be acknowledged that corporate managers and directors are likely to value power, prestige, and status, and to desire avoiding embarrassment.[120] Still, it is important to emphasize that the social status of corporate directors depends on various factors, such as the quality of the communications department and the directors' personality and appearance.[121] Moreover, social esteem can result from different types of actions that may not necessarily coincide with good governance practices and high-quality management: "A manager, for example, may increase her esteem by devoting her time to public causes, running a cool company, getting unusually high salary, introducing innovative products, or selling expensive watches."[122] Thus, while directors and managers undoubtedly value social esteem, the multiplicity of factors affecting this variable raises questions as to the impact of shaming sanctions for failing to respect corporate governance norms.

Likewise, it is possible to question the influence of shaming sanctions on the reputation of directors and managers. On the one hand, even assuming that adherence to the recognized governance norms conveys the signal of a cooperative management team, it must be acknowledged that the value of a reputation for cooperation is variable. It may be valuable for some corporate members while being less significant for others, depending on the assets that they own. This implies that shaming sanctions will have a variable effectiveness, as observed by Skeel:

> This suggests that managers who have less need to establish a reputation for co-operation will be more difficult to shame. If a manager's skills are so valuable that people transact with her regardless of her reputation, or if she actually benefits from a reputation as a "bad" type, shaming sanctions are less likely to prove effective.[123]

On the other hand, reputation is not a binary concept and nonconformity with governance norms may not destroy instantly all of the managers' and directors' reputational capital. Hence, shaming may work effectively only for the most blatant disrespect of corporate governance practices.

Finally, the effectiveness of shaming requires that both the enforcer and the enforcement community have access to adequate information.[124] As Margaret Blair and Lynn Stout have argued, it is possible to doubt that this requirement is met with respect to information about corporate governance:

> Even when other members of the business community can observe accusations and disagreements between and among shareholders, officers, and directors, they may find it hard to determine which side is at fault. Moreover,

in many cases they are unlikely to observe even the accusations and disagreements. The boardroom is a notoriously opaque environment. Even
in large firms, only the most public and bitter battles are reported in the
press. Smaller firms may go years without seeing their names – much less
their individual directors' or officers' names – mentioned in the *Wall Street
Journal*.[125]

In addition, as mentioned above, corporate governance reporting suffers
from significant imperfections that will impede the interventions of enforcers and the reaction of the enforcement community.

In the end, whether shaming sanctions affect in a meaningful and significant way social esteem and reputation is an empirical question. While David
Skeel has marshalled interesting evidence on shaming by shareholder activists, research remains very much in its nascent stage, and there is still a lack
of convincing evidence of the impact of shaming sanctions on the behaviour of corporate actors.

A Modest Role for Public Regulation: Giving a New Meaning
to Shareholder Voice in Corporate Governance

The corporate governance principles identified by reform committees are
expected to be implemented by shareholders by their evaluation of company securities and, to some extent, by informal sanctions such as shaming. As seen above, however, there is serious reason to believe that these
mechanisms suffer from shortcomings that reduce the pressure they create
on corporations. The mixed record of compliance of Canadian publicly held
corporations with the guidelines set forth in the Dey Report underlines the
deficiencies of the current enforcement mechanisms.[126] This indicates that
there may be a role for public regulation to enhance compliance with these
principles.

When discussing the role of public regulation in the enforcement of corporate governance principles, it is important not to lose sight of the theoretical justifications that support an enabling approach in this matter. As
discussed previously, they caution that regulation should not seek to enforce compliance with a definite set of governance principles and should as
much as possible leave it to corporate members to choose the applicable
principles. This approach receives support from empirical studies that demonstrate the ambiguous character of the relationship between received governance principles and firm value.[127] In such a context, it seems preferable
that the choice of governance structure remains a decision taken by the
corporation rather than by regulators.[128]

This preference for an enabling approach does not imply that public regulation cannot provide a meaningful contribution to enhance the quality of
corporate governance. Instead, it suggests that public policy should seek to

strengthen private enforcement mechanisms and avoid imposing specific governance principles on corporations. From this perspective, two sets of interventions seem apposite. First, regulators should take a more active stance to enhance the quality and credibility of governance reporting. While disclosure of governance practices is already mandatory for TSX-listed firms, evidence indicates that enforcement efforts by the Exchange could be buttressed in order to ensure compliance by corporations. In addition, a serious examination of the opportunity to have governance reporting submitted to an audit review, as was proposed in the United Kingdom by the Cadbury Report, should be undertaken by regulators.[129] In the absence of complete and credible disclosure of governance practices by corporations, private enforcement mechanisms will remain largely ineffective.[130]

Second, public policy should enhance shareholder participation in the setting of governance principles.[131] Indeed, one of the most puzzling aspects of the work undertaken by reform committees is the absence of any initiative aimed at ensuring the involvement of the shareholders meeting in the establishment of corporations' governance norms. Under the existing framework, shareholder intervention is expected to proceed primarily from the evaluation of corporate shares rather than from the exercise of their voting rights. The approach taken is especially striking given the critiques addressed by the Dey Committee to shareholders for their lack of involvement in corporate governance:

> Effective corporate governance depends heavily on the willingness of the owners to behave like owners and to exercise their rights of ownership, to express their views to boards of directors, and to organize and exercise their shareholder franchise if they do not receive a satisfactory response.[132]

> Shareholders get the governance they deserve and in our view shareholders have been too passive. Pressure from investors is necessary for boards to feel a sense of urgency – a healthy dynamic in the boardroom.[133]

> We are disappointed that the shareholders who have a responsibility to monitor the governance systems of corporations haven't identified weaknesses in governance systems sooner and thereby avoided these corporate failures. Institutional investors, such as pension funds, have special responsibilities to "regulate" the quality of governance.[134]

For its part, the Saucier Committee emphasized the importance of shareholder involvement in corporate governance, "particularly in Canadian capital markets where trading is especially thin and exit costs are high."[135] However, because of resource and time constraints, it refrained from examining how to foster shareholder participation in corporate governance.

At present, shareholder participation in the setting of governance princi-ples appears to be hindered by two significant barriers: the internal division of powers and shareholder apathy. The internal division of powers enacted by corporate statutes is well known to students of corporate law.[136] Accord-ing to corporate statutes, the board of directors is vested with the responsi-bility of managing or supervising the management of the business and affairs of the corporation.[137] Shareholders have the right to attend shareholders' meetings and vote on business matters brought before the meetings.[138] They are entitled to vote for the election and removal of directors, to authorize fundamental corporate operations and changes initiated by management, and to approve and initiate changes to bylaws.[139] However, unless they adopt a unanimous shareholders' agreement, shareholders do not have any direct power over the management of the corporation's business and affairs.[140] Moreover, they cannot compel the directors to make specific decisions even when they rely on the shareholder proposal mechanism.[141] To summarize, the powers of shareholders with respect to the business and affairs of the corporation are very limited.[142]

Given this division of power, the voting rights of shareholders do not cur-rently give them the power to compel the board of directors to comply with the governance guidelines of the TSX. The decision to conform to these guidelines is incumbent on the board of directors as part of its general man-date to manage or supervise the management of the business and affairs of the corporation. Thus, even if shareholders adopt a proposal to enjoin the directors to respect the guidelines, such a proposal will remain only advi-sory and will not impose any obligation on directors.[143] The only option currently open to shareholders is to express their dissatisfaction with how the governance guidelines are dealt with by voting against the directors standing for re-election. This may not prove to be very effective since share-holders may be reluctant to follow this course of action against individuals who are otherwise making a valuable contribution to the corporation.[144]

The "rational" apathy of shareholders is a second barrier that hinders their involvement in corporate governance issues.[145] Investors tend to hold a small fraction of the shares of individual publicly held corporations found in their portfolios. When dissatisfied with the management of the portfolio corporations, it appears more rational for them to sell their shares rather than initiate measures to address the problem. Indeed, an investor choos-ing to launch a campaign to contest the leadership of managers or propose governance changes will bear all of the costs of the intervention while re-ceiving only a fraction of the benefits that it can generate, based on the size of his or her investment. If every shareholder analyzes the issue in this per-spective, even value-enhancing interventions will not materialize. Co-operation between shareholders could alleviate this quandary by spreading the costs of intervention among those who benefit from it. However, a collective action problem "prevents them from structuring a co-operative arrangement which will increase the joint welfare of all concerned."[146] Shareholders will prefer to exit their investment by selling their shares on the market rather than attempt to improve matters.[147]

The rational apathy of shareholders is a pervasive phenomenon in widely held corporations. As many have noted since Berle and Means,[148] it magnifies the "agency cost problem" by giving managers the leeway to act opportunistically in their own interests rather than in the interests of shareholders.[149] Still, rational apathy is equally problematic in corporations characterized by the presence of a dominant shareholder. Apathy by minority shareholders enables the dominant shareholder to use the control of the corporation to realize self-serving operations detrimental to the corporation as a whole.[150]

Over the last decade, many have noted that shareholder apathy is likely to wane with the institutionalization of the securities market.[151] The staggering growth of the assets under management and the relatively small size of the Canadian market increasingly compel institutional investors to make substantial investments in individual corporations. At the same time, however, these factors reduce the ability of institutional investors to exit their investments, as they "are finding more often that they own too many shares in a corporation to liquidate their stake without the risk of disrupting the market and causing a drop in price."[152] Thus, rather than follow the Bay Street Rule when dissatisfied with management or confronted with majority shareholder abuses, institutions are expected to opt for the alternative strategy of taking an interventionist attitude to improve corporate governance.

Despite this enthusiasm, commentators emphasize the existence of countervailing forces that limit the extent of institutional investor involvement in corporate governance.[153] Some argue that institutional investors are subject to a web of legal constraints, such as takeover-bid regulation, proxy rules, and insider trading restrictions, which raise the cost of participation in corporate governance and induce passivity.[154] Others stress that institutional investors do not have the required incentives to engage in active monitoring even if regulatory barriers were reduced, because of market-driven and organizational constraints, such as conflicts of interest and remuneration schemes.[155] Finally, many underline the general reluctance of institutional investors towards public interventions and confrontation, which renders them more likely to adopt a collaborative approach rather than a conflictual one.[156]

Although they are diverse and numerous, these countervailing forces should not be overstated. As Professor Crête observes, "institutional investors have intervened regularly with regard to certain corporate governance issues, in addition to acting specifically in response to critical situations."[157]

However, their existence suggests that the involvement of institutional investors in corporate governance will take various intensities and translate into different types of interventions. Indeed, institutional investors tend to have a very pragmatic approach that is based on a cost-benefit analysis.[158] Therefore, to the extent that these constraints raise the cost of a particular intervention, they will likely have an impact on the decision of institutional investors as to whether to adopt an active or passive approach.

It must be acknowledged that so far institutional investors have not frequently resorted to direct action to foster compliance by corporations with the TSX corporate governance principles, even though the latter parallel those expressed in their own proxy guidelines.[159] While the compliance of corporations with the TSX principles may have been addressed by institutions through behind-the-scenes diplomacy, it can be argued that this issue would gain from being debated publicly.

Given these constraints, what role could public regulation play to enhance shareholder participation in the setting of corporate governance principles? It is suggested here that regulation should seek to foster shareholder voice on corporate governance issues.[160] Specifically, the boards of directors of publicly held corporations listed on the TSX or CDNX should be obliged to adopt their governance principles in a bylaw and submit it for the approval of shareholders at every annual meeting. The bylaw would be accompanied by an informative statement comparing the corporation's principles with the Exchange's governance guidelines that would inform shareholders about the level of compliance with the latter and the reasons for divergence. At the annual meeting, shareholders would then have the opportunity to review the governance principles of their corporation by being called upon to adopt, modify, or vote against them.

Mandating the approval of corporations' governance principles as a bylaw would yield a number of benefits. First, from a purely legal perspective, it would address the concern pertaining to the internal division of powers by indicating clearly that this issue falls within the competence of the general meeting and is not restricted to the board of directors. Shareholders would thereby be granted the power to intervene with respect to this matter not only through the price mechanism, but also periodically through the exercise of their voting rights, including their right to make a proposal. Furthermore, once adopted as a bylaw, the principles would create normative effects, as shareholders would have the power to enforce them by seeking a statutory remedy of compliance against the corporation and its directors and officers.[161]

Second, the mandatory examination of corporations' governance principles at the annual meeting would foster the participation of shareholders by reducing the cost of interventions. Indeed, the review of the governance principles would take place annually without shareholders having to raise the issue with the proposal mechanism. Unless they specifically elect to rely on this mechanism, shareholders would only have to determine whether they approve or reject the corporation's governance principles. Thus, shareholders would have the ability to pursue a "just vote no" strategy either by voting against the approval of the bylaw or by withholding proxy authority from management.[162] From the institutional investors' perspective, this opportunity would yield interesting advantages. Institutions would not have to bear the burden and the costs of having to publicly raise governance issues. They would have the ability to maintain their favoured ad hoc and reactive approach by simply voting on the corporation's governance principles in accordance with their proxy guidelines.[163] Alternatively, institutions would have the option of exercising quiet persuasion before the shareholders meeting on a board of directors undoubtedly more receptive, given the additional pressure created by the need to submit governance issues for the approval of shareholders.[164]

Finally, the power of shareholders to approve the governance principles would enhance the effectiveness of social sanctions. As Joseph Grundfest has noted, a "just vote no" campaign would undoubtedly tarnish the esteem and reputation of board members by underscoring the fact that the latter have undesirable traits or are uncooperative.[165] Thus, in order to maintain their social status and reputation, board members facing the prospect of such disapproval would be more inclined to cooperate with shareholders and enact governance principles that respect their expectations.

Critics will argue that this proposal will have little impact on the participation of shareholders and, therefore, on the enforcement of the TSX governance guidelines. On the one hand, they will stress that given that Canadian publicly held corporations are characterized by the presence of a dominant shareholder, submitting the governance principles to the general meeting will create little pressure for compliance.[166] On the other hand, they will express doubts as to whether shareholders will use this opportunity to adopt a more active stance towards corporate governance.

These critiques, while apposite, should not be overstated. Even though dominant shareholders "influence dramatically the outcome of votes at general meetings,"[167] the presentation and discussion of corporations' governance principles in light of the TSX principles may nevertheless have a significant effect on management's attitude towards the issues because of the publicity surrounding the event.[168] Moreover, this requirement would arguably have an expressive effect, that is, it would constitute a signal of the importance of the TSX principles for the community, as Eisenberg explains: "Adoption of a legal rule that is based on a social norm sends a message that the community regards the norm as especially important. This message increases both the likelihood that the norm will be internalized and the reputational penalties for violating the norm."[169] Thus, it could force directors, even backed by dominant shareholders, to analyze seriously their corporation's corporate governance principles and prepare a cogent argument justifying the differences with the TSX principles.[170] As one author notes: "Once a management is so distinguished the quality of its stewardship is at issue and debate can ensue over its performance and competence."[171] In turn, this would likely lead to better decision making with respect to corporate governance.

Besides, it must be recognized that the value flowing from increased participation does not "assume or require that all eligible shareholders will become intimately involved in the governance of public corporations."[172] As Grundfest remarks:

> Once shareholders have identified targets for "just vote no" campaigns, they can enter into negotiations with incumbent boards in an effort to obtain concessions that are responsive to shareholder concerns. If "just vote no" is perceived by management as a credible form of shareholder activism, then the mere threat of a well organized and responsibly targeted campaign may be sufficient to induce a meaningful management response. Under these circumstances, "just vote no" campaigns can achieve results without ever actually being implemented.[173]

Thus, while institutional investors would not exercise their voting rights at every annual meeting, the fact that they have the power to do so would help persuade corporations' management to assess their governance principles against the benchmark set by the TSX.[174]

Conclusion

In their proposals put forward to improve corporate governance, reform committees established by Canadian governments and regulators have favoured an enabling approach, according to which the choice of governance structure should remain a decision taken by members of the corporation rather than by regulators. Overall, they have refrained from advocating the enactment of rigid governance principles that would deprive corporations of the freedom to craft internal processes and structures tailored to their needs.

This approach rests on sound theoretical and empirical justifications. On the theoretical side, it is consistent with the contractarian doctrine derived from the nexus of contracts conception of the corporation as well as with the norms scholarship that argues that the setting in which corporations operate provides fertile ground for NLERS to emerge and affect the behaviour of corporate actors. On the empirical side, the emergence of alternative governance norms demonstrates the ability of market participants to develop NLERS.

The approach favoured by governments and regulators may, however, overstate the effectiveness of private mechanisms in ensuring the development of governance NLERS, and the implementation and enforcement of "good" governance practices. Indeed, these mechanisms suffer from shortcomings that raise doubts as to the ability of members of corporations to negotiate value-maximizing governance practices. As argued in this chapter, the preference for an enabling approach should not be taken as implying that public regulation cannot provide a meaningful contribution to enhance the quality of corporate governance. Rather, it provides a guide with respect to the form that public regulation should take. Thus, it is suggested here that public regulation should seek to strengthen private enforcement mechanisms while avoiding the imposition of specific governance principles on corporations.

Acknowledgments

This essay is part of a larger research project on corporate governance generously funded by the Social Science and Humanities Research Council of Canada and the Georg Stellari Foundation. Rea Hawi and Anne Talbot provided valuable research and editorial assistance.

Notes

1 R.J. Daniels and R. Morck, "Canadian Corporate Governance: The Challenge" in R.J. Daniels and R.K. Morck, eds., *Corporate Decision-Making in Canada* (Calgary: University of Calgary Press, 1996) 1 at 3.

2 See, for example, Daniels and Morck, *ibid.; Toronto Stock Exchange Committee on Corporate Governance in Canada, *Where Were the Directors? Guidelines for Improved Corporate Governance in Canada* (Toronto: Toronto Stock Exchange, 1994) [hereinafter *Dey Report*]; Joint Committee on Corporate Governance, *Beyond Compliance: Building a Governance Culture*, Final Report (Toronto: TSX/CNDX/CICA, 2001) [hereinafter *Beyond Compliance*]; Senate of Canada, Standing Senate Committee on Banking, Trade and Commerce, *Proceedings of the Task Force on Corporate Governance* (Ottawa: 1996); E.J. Waitzer, "What's Right about Corporate Governance" (1993) 15 O.S.C.B. 5575. Note also that there is a Corporate Governance Branch at Industry Canada that is namely responsible for the development and coordination of marketplace framework policies in the area of corporate law.

3 K.J. Hopt *et al.*, eds., *Comparative Corporate Governance: The State of the Art and Emerging Research* (Oxford: Clarendon Press, 1998). See also the *Corporate Governance Codes, Principles and Recommendations* compiled by the European Institute of Corporate Governance, <http://www.ecgi.org/codes/all_codes.htm>.

4 M.M. Blair, *Ownership and Control – Rethinking Corporate Governance for the Twenty-First Century* (Washington, DC: Brookings Institution, 1995) at 235; H. Hansmann and R.H. Kraakman, "The End of History for Corporate Law" (2001) 89 Georgetown L.J. 439.

5 J.G. MacIntosh, "If It Ain't Broke ... Why All the Cries for More Reform of Canada's Corporate Governance System? It's Never Worked Better" (1994) 7(4) Can. Inv. Rev. 37. Contrast S. Bhagat and B. Black, "The Uncertain Relationship between Board Composition and Firm Performance" (1999) 54 Bus. Law 921; I.M. Millstein and R.W. MacAvoy, "The Active Board of Directors and Performance of the Large Publicly Traded Corporation" (1998) 98 Colum. L. Rev. 1283.

6 J.C. Baillie, "Comments of a Business Lawyer on Rules Governing Boards of Canadian Public Corporations" (1996) 27 Can. Bus. L.J. 127 at 132-33.

7 J.S. Ziegel, "The *CBCA* – Twenty Years Later: Where Do We Go from Here?" [1994-95] *Meredith Lectures* 5.

8   R.W.V. Dickerson, J.L. Howard, and L. Getz, *Proposals for a New Business Corporations Law for Canada,* 1971, vol. 1, para. 8 (Ottawa: Information Canada), citing H.W. Ballantine, *Ballantine on Corporations* (Chicago: Callaghan and Company, 1946) at 41. See also *R. v. McClurg,* [1990] 3 S.C.R. 1020 at 1047, where Dickson C.J. states that the Saskatchewan Business Corporations Act "is facilitative – that is, it allows parties, with certain explicit restrictions to structure bodies corporate as they wish"; F. Iacobucci, J.R.S. Prichard, and M.L. Pilkington, *Canadian Business Corporations: An Analysis of Recent Legislative Developments* (Agincourt, ON: Canada Law Books, 1977) at 6.

9   In the law and economics literature, the concept of "contract" is broader than in the legal literature as it relates to the "network of relationships characterized by reciprocal expectations and behaviour." See B.R. Cheffins, *Company Law: Theory, Structure and Operation* (Oxford: Oxford University Press, 1997) at 36.

10 M.C. Jensen and W.H. Meckling, "Theory of the Firm: Managerial Behaviour, Agency Costs, and Ownership Structure" (1976) 3 J. Fin. Econ. 305.

11 See, in general, F.H. Easterbrook and D.R. Fischel, *The Economic Structure of Corporate Law* (Cambridge, MA: Harvard University Press, 1991).

12 Cheffins, *supra* note 9 at 250-53.

13 *Ibid.* at 262-63. See also L.E. Ribstein, "The Mandatory Nature of the ALI Code" (1993) 61 Geo. Wash. L. Rev. 984 at 991-98.

14 Cheffins, *ibid.*; H.N. Butler and L.E. Ribstein, "State Anti-Takeover Statutes and the Contract Clause" (1988) 57 U. Cin. L. Rev. 614 at 615; R.A. Epstein, *Simple Rules for a Complex World* (Cambridge, MA: Harvard University Press, 1995) at 248; Easterbrook and Fischel, *supra* note 11 at 34-35.

15 While there is a general consensus over the enabling role of corporate law, this does not imply that this conception is without flaw. For a good critique of this conception, see J.N. Gordon, "The Mandatory Structure of Corporate Law" (1989) 89 Colum. L. Rev. 1549.

16 For an overview of the argument, see J.S. Ziegel *et al., Cases and Materials on Partnerships and Canadian Business Corporations,* 2nd ed. (Toronto: Carswell, 1989) at 390-401.

17 See H.N. Butler, "The Contractual Theory of the Corporation" (1989) 11 Geo. Mason U. L. Rev. 99; H.N. Butler and L.E. Ribstein, "Opting Out of Fiduciary Duties: A Response to the Anti-Contractarians" (1990) 65 Wash. L. Rev. 1.

18 J.R. Macey, "Corporate Law and Corporate Governance: A Contractual Perspective" (1993) 18 J. Corp. L. 185 at 187.

19 R.J. Daniels and E.M. Iacobucci, "Some of the Causes and Consequences of Corporate Ownership Concentration in Canada" in R.K. Morck, ed., *Concentrated Corporate Ownership* (Chicago: University of Chicago Press, 2000) 81 at 83-84.

20 R.J. Daniels and P.N. Halpern, "Too Close for Comfort: The Role of the Closely Held Public Corporation in the Canadian Economy and the Implication for Public Policy" (1996) 26 Can. Bus. L.J. 11; P.N. Halpern, *Systemic Perspectives on Corporate Governance Systems* (Toronto: Rotman School of Management, 1999) at 34-36. See also J.G. MacIntosh and L. Schwartz, "Do Institutional and Controlling Shareholders Increase Corporate Value?" in Daniels and Morck, *supra* note 1, c. 8.

21 R.C. Ellickson, *Order without Law* (Cambridge, MA: Harvard University Press, 1991).

22 See, for example, R.D. Cooter, "Decentralized Law for a Complex Economy: The Structural Approach to Adjudicating the New Law Merchant" (1996) 144 U. Pa. L. Rev. 1643; R.C. Ellickson, "Law and Economics Discovers Social Norms" (1998) 27 J. Leg. Stud. 537; L. Lessig, "The New Chicago School" (1998) 27 J. Leg. Stud. 661; R.H. McAdams, Comment, "Accounting for Norms" [1997] Wis. L. Rev. 625.

23 See Symposium, "Law, Economics, and Norms" (1996) 144 U. Pa. L. Rev. 1643; Symposium, "Social Norms, Social Meaning, and the Economic Analysis of Law" (1998) 27 J. Leg. Stud. 537.

24 M.A. Eisenberg, "Corporate Law and Social Norms" (1999) 99 Colum. L. Rev. 1253 at 1254; Symposium, "Norms and Corporate Law" (2001) 149 U. Pa. L. Rev. 1607.

25 Ellickson, *supra* note 21 at 125-27.

26 M. Kahan, "The Limited Significance of Norms for Corporate Governance" (2001) 149 U. Pa. L. Rev. 1869 at 1872.

27 Eisenberg, *supra* note 24 at 1255.
28 R.A. Posner and E.B. Rasmusen, "Creating and Enforcing Norms, with Special Reference to Sanctions" (1999) 19 Int'l Rev. Law and Econ. 369.
29 See, for example, Kahan, *supra* note 26 at 1870-74.
30 E.B. Rock and M.L. Wachter, "Islands of Conscious Power: Law, Norms, and the Self-Governing Corporation" (2001) 149 U. Pa. L. Rev. 1619.
31 *Ibid.* at 1641.
32 *Ibid.*
33 See, for example, Kahan, *supra* note 26 at 1879-82.
34 Rock and Wachter, *supra* note 30 at 1621-22.
35 *Ibid.* at 1647-52.
36 *Ibid.* at 1623, 1654-61.
37 *Ibid.* at 1658-59.
38 See, for example, R. Cooter and M.A. Eisenberg, "Fairness, Character, and Efficiency in Firms" (2001) 149 U. Pa. L. Rev. 1717.
39 Rock and Wachter, *supra* note 30 at 1642-44.
40 Eisenberg, *supra* note 24 at 1262-63.
41 *Ibid.* at 1268-69.
42 *Ibid.* at 1276. See, more generally, C.R. Sunstein, "On the Expressive Function of Law" (1996) 144 U. Pa. L. Rev. 2021; D.M. Kahan, "Social Influence, Social Meaning, and Deterrence" (1997) 83 Va. L. Rev. 349; R. Cooter, "Expressive Law and Economics" (1998) 27 J. Leg. Stud. 585.
43 W.M. Bratton, *Enron and the Dark Side of Shareholder Value*, Public Law and Legal Theory Working Paper No. 35 (Washington, DC: George Washington University School of Law, 2002); J.N. Gordon, *What Enron Means for the Management and Control of the Modern Business Corporation: Some Initial Reflections*, Center for Law and Economic Studies, Working Paper No. 203 (New York: Columbia Law School, 2002); "Something Is Rotten" *The Economist* (25 July 2002) at 53. See also E.A. Posner, "Law, Economics, and Inefficient Norms" (1996) 144 U. Pa. L. Rev. 1697; P.G. Mahoney and C.W. Sanchirico, "Competing Norms and Social Evolution: Is the Fittest Norm Efficient?" (2001) 149 U. Pa. L. Rev. 2027.
44 J.C. Coffee, "Do Norms Matter? A Cross-Country Evaluation" (2001) 149 U. Pa. L. Rev. 2151.
45 Canada, *Report of the Royal Commission on Corporate Concentration* (Ottawa: Supply and Services Canada, 1978) [hereinafter *Bryce Commission*].
46 *Ibid.* at 283-337.
47 *Ibid.* at 293.
48 *Ibid.* at 294.
49 *Ibid.* at 297-98.
50 See, for example, Canada, *The Report of the Inquiry into the Collapse of the Canadian Commercial Bank and the Northland Bank* (Ottawa: Supply and Services Canada, 1986).
51 *Dey Report, supra* note 2.
52 See, for example, B.R. Cheffins, "Corporate Governance in the United Kingdom: Lessons for Canada" (1997) 28 Can. Bus. L.J. 69; C. Hansell, "Corporate Governance Disclosure in Canada: Background and Compliance" in L. Sarna, ed., *Corporate Structure, Finance and Operations* (Toronto: Carswell, 1998) 1 at 29; D.A. Thain, "The TSE Report: Disappointing" (1994) 59 Bus. Quart. 76.
53 The *Dey Report* was greatly influenced by the *Cadbury Report*. See A. Cadbury, *Report of the Committee on the Financial Aspects of Corporate Governance* (London: Burgess Science Press, 1992) [hereinafter *Cadbury Report*]; *Dey Report, supra* note 2 at 14.
54 Toronto Stock Exchange, *Company Manual*, ss. 472-75 [hereinafter *Company Manual*].
55 *The State of Corporate Governance in Canada* (Toronto: Toronto Stock Exchange and Institute of Corporate Directors, 2000).
56 *Beyond Compliance, supra* note 2.
57 *Ibid.* at 5-7. See also Joint Committee on Corporate Governance, *Beyond Compliance: Building a Governance Culture*, Interim Report (Toronto: TSX/CNDX/CICA, 2001) [hereinafter *Interim Report*] at 10-13. Leblanc, whose work has exercised an influence on the Saucier

Committee, refers to "board process" to designate "how a board of directors actually works and functions." See R. Leblanc, *Getting Inside the Black Box: Problems in Corporate Governance Research,* Background Paper for the Joint Committee on Corporate Governance (Toronto: N.p., 2001) at 14.

58 *Beyond Compliance, supra* note 2 at 16-18.

59 *Ibid.* at 27-32.

60 *Ibid.* at 46-50. See *Report and Recommendations of the Blue Ribbon Committee on Improving the Effectiveness of Corporate Audit Committees* (New York: New York Stock Exchange and National Association of Securities Dealers, 1999).

61 *Beyond Compliance, supra* note 2 at 10.

62 *Ibid.* at 10-11.

63 *Ibid.,* Recommendation No. 1, at 11. This recommendation replaces one of similar nature of the *Interim Report, supra* note 57 at 16-17, where it was suggested that the Institute of Corporate Directors and the Canadian Institute of Chartered Accountants work together "to promote full and fair disclosure of corporate governance practices."

64 *Supra* notes 2 and 57. On the disadvantages of legislative interventions, see also W.J. Braithwaite, "Who Is Best Suited to Introduce Corporate Governance Reform and Mutual Fund Governance Reform?" in Queen's Annual Business Law Symposium, *Securities Regulation: Issues and Perspectives* (Toronto: Carswell, 1995) 277 at 292-94; Hansell, *supra* note 52 at 38-40.

65 *Dey Report, supra* note 2 at 52.

66 B.R. Cheffins "Current Trends in Corporate Governance: Going from London to Milan via Toronto" (1999) 10 Duke J. Comp. and Int'l L. 5 at 26.

67 This section draws on the work of Eisenberg, *supra* note 24 at 1278-87. See also Rock and Wachter, *supra* note 30 at 1642-44.

68 See M.A. Eisenberg, "The Board of Directors and Internal Control" (1997) 19 Cardozo L. Rev. 237. For a more nuanced account, see J.E. Fisch, "Taking Boards Seriously" (1997) 19 Cardozo L. Rev. 265. Interestingly, this change is now reflected in s. 102 of the *Canada Business Corporations Act,* which recognizes that the role of directors is to manage or supervise the management of the business and affairs of the corporation: *Canada Business Corporations Act,* R.S.C. 1985, c. C-44 as am. by S.C. 2001, c. 14 [hereinafter *CBCA*].

69 H.M. Bybelezer, "The 'Corporate Governance' Debate and Modern Theory of the Firm: Some Lessons" in L. Sarna, ed., *Corporate Structure, Finance and Operations,* vol. 5 (Toronto: Carswell, 1988) at 59-65; R.A.G. Monks and N. Minow, *Corporate Governance* (Cambridge, UK: Blackwell, 1995) at 99-100.

70 Eisenberg, *supra* note 24 at 1280-81.

71 *Ibid.* at 1278.

72 Kathryn E. Montgomery and D.S.R. Leighton, "The Unseen Revolution is Here" (1993) 58(4) Bus. Quart. 39 at 42; W. Lilley, "And No Board to Break the Fall" *Report on Business Magazine* (July 1995) at 49; J. Wells, "Where Was the Board?" *Report on Business Magazine* (July 1993) at 43. For an example, see *In Re Standard Trustco Ltd.* (1992), 6 B.L.R. (2d) 241 (O.S.C.).

73 B.S. Black, "Agents Watching Agents: The Promise of Institutional Investor Voice" (1992) 39 UCLA L. Rev. 811; A.F. Conard, "Beyond Managerialism: Investor Capitalism?" (1988) 22 J. L. Reform 117; P.A. Koval, "Trends in Canadian Shareholder Activism" in The Canadian Institute, ed., *Duties and Liabilities of Officers and Directors* (Toronto: The Canadian Institute, 1992); J.G. MacIntosh, "The Role of Institutional and Retail Investors in Canadian Capital Markets" (1993) 31 Osgoode Hall L.J. 371; K.E. Montgomery, "Market Shift – The Role of Institutional Investors in Corporate Governance" (1996) 26 Can. Bus. L.J. 189.

74 MacIntosh, *ibid.;* Montgomery, *ibid.*

75 Eisenberg, *supra* note 24. See J.G. MacIntosh, "Institutional Shareholders and Corporate Governance in Canada" (1996) 26 Can. Bus. L.J. 145.

76 See R. Crête and S. Rousseau, "De la passivité à l'activisme des investisseurs institutionnels au sein des corporations: le reflet de la diversité des facteurs d'influence" (1997) 42 McGill L.J. 863.

77 *Beyond Compliance, supra* note 2 at 10-11; *Dey Report, supra* note 2 at 52; *Interim Report, supra* note 57 at 66-68. For a good summary of the argument, see A. Belcher, "Regulation by the

Market: The Case of the Cadbury Code and Compliance Statement" [1995] J.B.L. 321 at 323-25.
78 Braithwaite, *supra* note 64 at 294; *Cadbury Report, supra* note 53, para. 1.10; Hansell, *supra* note 52 at 50.
79 See Belcher, *supra* note 77 at 322; Hansell, *ibid.*
80 Belcher, *ibid.* at 321, discussing the adequacy of the disclosure of corporate governance practices with respect to the *Cadbury Report.*
81 *Company Manual, supra* note 54, s. 474.
82 Bratton, *supra* note 43; Gordon, *supra* note 43.
83 Cheffins, *supra* note 52, at 83. See also V. Finch, "Corporate Governance and Cadbury: Self-Regulation and Alternatives" [1994] J.B.L. 51 at 57.
84 Toronto Stock Exchange Committee on Corporate Disclosure, "Toward Improved Disclosure – Interim Report" (1996) 19 O.S.C.B. 8 at 57.
85 Belcher, *supra* note 77 at 339.
86 See, for example, G. Benston, "Required Disclosure and the Stock Market" (1973) 63 Am. Econ. Rev. 132; G. Benston, "The Effectiveness and Effects of the SEC's Accounting Disclosure Requirements" in H.G. Manne, ed., *Economic Policy and the Regulation of Corporate Securities* (Washington, DC: American Enterprise Institute for Policy Research, 1969) 23 at 24; F.H. Easterbrook and D.R. Fischel, "Mandatory Disclosure and the Protection of Investors" (1984) 70 Va. L. Rev. 669 at 673-77; G. Stigler, "Public Regulation of the Securities Markets" (1964) 37 J. Bus. 117 at 124.
87 H.E. Leland and D.H. Pyle, "Informational Asymmetries, Financial Structure, and Financial Intermediation" (1977) 32 J. Fin. 371.
88 G. Benston, "Required Periodic Disclosure under the Securities Acts and the Proposed Federal Securities Code" (1979) 33 U. Miami L. Rev. 1471 at 1476.
89 R. Labelle, *Corporate Disclosure of Governance Practices* (Montréal: École des HEC, 1999) at 7-8 (on file with author).
90 *Ibid.* at 4.
91 *Ibid.* at 20.
92 P. O'Callaghan and Associates with Korn/Ferry International, *Corporate Board Governance and Director Compensation in Canada, A Review of 2000*, cited in *Interim Report, supra* note 57 at 8.
93 Canadian Institute of Chartered Accountants, *Corporate Governance: A Review of Disclosure Practices in 1996*; Canadian Institute of Chartered Accountants, *Corporate Governance: A Review of Disclosure Practices in Canada*. Both available at <http://www.cica.com>.
94 See, for example, "Civil Liability for Continuous Disclosure Documents Filed under the Securities Act – Request for Comments" (1984) 7 O.S.C.B. 4910; E.J. Waitzer, "Making Continuous Disclosure Work Better" (1994) 17 O.S.C.B. 242.
95 *Dey Report, supra* note 2 at 49.
96 Toronto Stock Exchange Committee on Corporate Disclosure, *supra* note 84 at 25.
97 *Ibid.* at 26.
98 *Interim Report, supra* note 57 at 8.
99 Belcher, *supra* note 77 at 340
100 G.A. Akerlof, "The Market for Lemons: Quality and the Market Mechanism" (1970) 84 Q.J. Econ. 488; Leland and Pyle, *supra* note 87 at 371.
101 In the UK, corporate governance disclosure is submitted to an audit review. See Belcher, *supra* note 77 at 332-38.
102 *Interim Report, supra* note 57 at 67.
103 On the certification role of auditors, see generally R.J. Gilson and R.H. Kraakman, "The Mechanisms of Market Efficiency" (1984) 70 Va. L. Rev. 549 at 604; J.C. Coffee, *The Acquiescent Gatekeeper: Reputational Intermediaries, Auditor Independence and the Governance of Accounting*, Center for Law and Economic Studies, Working Paper No. 191 (New York: Columbia University Law School, 2001).
104 N. Campbell, "Compulsory Disclosure of Soft Information" (1993) 22 Can. Bus. L.J. 321 at 355; F.H. Easterbrook and D.R. Fischel, "Mandatory Disclosure and the Protection of Investors" (1984) 70 Va. L. Rev. 669 at 700-1.

105 Eisenberg, *supra* note 24 at 1257-61.
106 M.M. Blair and L.A. Stout, "Trust, Trustworthiness and the Behavioral Foundations Of Corporate Law" (2001) 149 U. Pa. L. Rev. 1735 at 1794. See also Cooter, *supra* note 22 at 1661-66.
107 Eisenberg, *supra* note 24 at 1260-61; D.A. Skeel, "Shaming in Corporate Law" (2001) 149 U. Pa. L. Rev. 1811 at 1821. For a more detailed taxonomy, see Posner and Rasmusen, *supra* note 28.
108 Norms of a moral character are more easily internalized than other norms. See generally K. Basu, "Social Norms and the Law" in P. Newman, ed., *The New Palgrave Encyclopedia of Economics and the Law* (New York: Macmillan, 1998) at 476-77; Eisenberg, *supra* note 24 at 1257-61; Cooter, *supra* note 22 at 1661-64; E.B. Rock, "Saints and Sinners: How Does Delaware Corporate Law Work?" (1997) 44 UCLA L. Rev. 1009 at 1013-14, 1104.
109 D.M. Kahan and E.A. Posner, "Shaming White-Collar Criminals: A Proposal for Reform of the Federal Sentencing Guidelines" (1999) 42 J. L. and Econ. 365 at 368.
110 R.H. McAdams, "The Origin, Development, and Regulation of Norms" (1995) 96 Mich. L. R. 338.
111 It is beyond the scope of this essay to discuss McAdams's theory in detail, especially the aspects dealing with norm creation.
112 E.A. Posner, "Law, Economics, and Inefficient Norms" (1996) 144 U. Pa. L. Rev. 1697.
113 Skeel, *supra* note 107.
114 CalPERS, *Focus List Selection Process*, <http://www.calpers-governance.org/alert/focus>.
115 Skeel, *supra* note 107 at 1825.
116 J.A. Grundfest, "Just Vote No: A Minimalist Strategy for Dealing with Barbarians inside the Gates" (1993) 45 Stanford L. Rev. 857 at 927.
117 For an overview of the interventions of norms entrepreneurs in corporate governance, see Crête and Rousseau, *supra* note 76; MacIntosh, *supra* note 73.
118 Grundfest, *supra* note 116 at 907-8; Skeel, *supra* note 107 at 1841-44.
119 See, however, Skeel, *ibid.* at 1829-35.
120 J.D. Cox and H.L. Munsinger, "Bias in the Boardroom: Psychological Foundations and Legal Implications of Corporate Cohesion" (1985) 48 Law and Contemp. Probs. 83 at 93-94; Grundfest, *supra* note 116 at 927.
121 Kahan, *supra* note 26 at 1896.
122 *Ibid.* at 1897.
123 Skeel, *supra* note 107 at 1834.
124 *Ibid.* at 1824-29; McAdams, *supra* note 110 at 362-64; S. Shavell, *Law Versus Morality as Regulator of Conduct*, Center for Law, Economics, and Business, Discussion Paper No. 340 (Cambridge, MA: Harvard Law School, 2001) at 14-16.
125 Blair and Stout, *supra* note 106 at 1795-96. See also J. Fanto, "Investor Education, Securities Disclosure, and the Creation and Enforcement of Corporate Governance and Firm Norms" (1998) 48 Cath. U. L. Rev. 15 at 23-26.
126 See Institute of Corporate Directors and Toronto Stock Exchange, *Five Years to the Dey* (Toronto, 1999), <http://tsers.com>; *Interim Report, supra* note 57 at 8; R. Blackwell, "Boardroom Reform Shows Little Progress, Study Says" *Globe and Mail* (3 January 2002) B3 (a review of board practices of the TSX 300 corporations made by Fairvest Corporation indicates that the corporations have made little progress in the improvement of their governance).
127 See, for example, Bhagat and Black, *supra* note 5; Millstein and MacAvoy, *supra* note 5.
128 For an alternative approach to corporate governance based on "reversible default rules," see L.A. Bebchuk and A. Hamdani, *Optimal Defaults for Corporate Law Evolution*, Center for Law, Economics, and Business, Discussion Paper No. 343 (Cambridge, MA: Harvard Law School, 2001), which argues that where public officials face a choice with respect to default rules, one more restrictive and one less restrictive with respect to management, they should favour the one that is more restrictive if they are unable to determine the one that is value-maximizing.
129 Finch, *supra* note 83 at 1994. See *Cadbury Report, supra* note 53; Committee on Corporate Governance, *Report of the Committee on Corporate Governance* (London, 1998) par. 6.6, Hampel Report, <http://www.ecgi.org/codes/country_documents/uk/hampel_index.htm>.

130   Fanto, *supra* note 125 at 23, 24; M.B. Fox, "Required Disclosure and Corporate Governance" in Hopt *et al., supra* note 3 at 701.

131   On the importance of shareholder participation in the implementation and enforcement of governance practices, see A. De Jong *et al., The Role of Self-Regulation in Corporate Governance: Evidence from the Netherlands,* Bradley Policy Research Center, Working Paper No. FR 00-20 (Rochester: University of Rochester, 2001).

132   *Dey Report, supra* note 2 at 47.

133   *The State of Corporate Governance, supra* note 55 at 2.

134   *Ibid.*

135   *Interim Report, supra* note 57 at 68.

136   See R.M. Buxbaum, "The Internal Division of Powers in Corporate Governance" (1985) 73 Calif. L. Rev. 1671; B. Welling, *Corporate Law in Canada – The Governing Principles* (Toronto: Butterworths, 1991) at 55-60.

137   See *CBCA, supra* note 68, s. 102. In *Canadian Jorex Ltd.* v. *477749 Alberta Ltd.* (1991), 85 Alta. L.R. (2d) 313 (C.A.), the Alberta Court of Appeal held that "the effect of this clause is that the directors' powers to manage a corporation's affairs are unlimited except to the extent these powers may have been circumscribed by the corporation's by-laws or U.S.A. [unanimous shareholder agreement]."

138   *CBCA, supra* note 68, ss. 132, 135, 140.

139   *Ibid.,* ss. 103, 106, 109, 173, 176, 183, 189.

140   Welling, *supra* note 136 at 468-80.

141   *Ibid.* See also *82009 Ontario Inc.* v. *Harold E. Ballard Ltd.* (1991), 3 B.L.R. (2d) 123 (Ont. Div. Ct.); *Ringuet* v. *Bergeron,* [1960] S.C.R. 672.

142   For a similar account in American corporate law, see P.V. Letsou, "Shareholder Voice and the Market for Corporate Control" (1992) 70 Wash. U. L.Q. 755 at 759-74.

143   B.R. Cheffins, "*Michaud* v. *National Bank of Canada* and Canadian Corporate Governance: A 'Victory' for Shareholder Rights?" (1998) 30 Can. Bus. L.J. 20 at 36-37; R. Crête, *The Proxy System in Canadian Corporations* (Montréal: Édition Wilson and Lafleur, 1986) at 210-15; Welling, *supra* note 136 at 475-80. See, however, *Michaud* v. *Banque nationale du Canada,* [1997] R.J.Q. 547 (C.S.), where Rayle J. suggested in an *obiter dictum* that shareholders may have the power to set the parameters of directors' remuneration in a proposal.

144   B.R. Cheffins and R.S. Thomas, *Should Shareholders Have a Greater Say Over Executive Pay? Learning from the US Experience,* Law and Economics Research Paper 01-6 (Nashville: Vanderbilt University Law School, 2001) at 15.

145   B.S. Black, "Shareholder Passivity Reexamined" (1990-91) 89 Mich. L. R. 520 at 576-91; E.F. Fama, "Agency Problems and the Theory of the Firm" (1980) 88 J. Pol. Econ. 288; Gordon, *supra* note 15 at 1575-771; E.B. Rock, "The Logic and (Uncertain) Significance of Institutional Shareholder Activism" (1991) 79 Geo. L.J. 445 at 453-64.

146   Cheffins, *supra* note 9 at 635-36. On collective action problems, see M. Olson Jr., *The Logic of Collective Action: Public Goods and the Theory of Groups,* 2nd ed. (Cambridge, MA: Harvard University Press, 1971).

147   D.R. Fischel, "The Corporate Governance Movement" (1982) 35 Va. L. Rev. 1259 at 1277-78.

148   A.A. Berle and G.C. Means, *The Modern Corporation and Private Property* (New York: Macmillan, 1932).

149   On agency problems, see Jensen and Meckling, *supra* note 10. For an overview of the agency problems, see A.G. Anderson, "Conflict of Interest: Efficiency, Fairness and Corporate Structure" (1978) 25 UCLA L. Rev. 738 at 774-77; Cheffins, *supra* note 143 at 25-33; Ziegel *et al., supra* note 16 at 390-95.

150   R.J. Daniels and J.G. MacIntosh, "Toward a Distinctive Corporate Law Regime" (1991) 29 Osgoode Hall L.J. 863.

151   See authorities cited at note 72.

152   Cheffins, *supra* note 52.

153   For a thorough overview of the arguments, see MacIntosh, *supra* note 75.

154   See, for example, Black, *supra* note 145.

155 See, for example, J.C. Coffee, Jr., "Liquidity versus Control: The Institutional Investor as Corporate Monitor" (1991) 91 Colum. L. Rev. 1277.

156 See, for example, Crête and Rousseau, *supra* note 76; Koval, *supra* note 73; Cheffins, *supra* note 143 at 60.

157 R. Crête, "Some Comments on the Impact of the Michaud Case" (1998) 30 Can. Bus. L.J. 73 at 77.

158 Crête and Rousseau., *supra* note 76 at 37.

159 See Cheffins, *supra* note 143 at 57-61. See, for example, OMERS, *Proxy Voting Guidelines*, <http://www.omers.com/investments/proxyvoting_guidelines/contents.htm>; Teachers, *Proxy Voting Guidelines*, <http://www.otpp.com/web/website.nsf/web/CGGuidelines>.

160 In the UK, the Department of Trade and Industry has proposed that shareholders be given the right to participate in the setting of executive compensation. For an analysis of the proposal, see Cheffins and Thomas, *supra* note 144.

161 *CBCA, supra* note 68, s. 247.

162 On the "just vote no" strategy, see in general Grundfest, *supra* note 116.

163 See K.E. Montgomery, "Survey of Institutional Shareholders" (1992) 4(4) Corp. Gov. Rev. 5 at 6-8; Crête and Rousseau, *supra* note 76 at 891-94.

164 Grundfest, *supra* note 116 at 907.

165 *Ibid.* at 927-31.

166 Cheffins, *supra* note 143 at 58-59.

167 *Ibid.*

168 Crête, *supra* note 157 at 83-85.

169 Eisenberg, *supra* note 24 at 1269-70.

170 Crête, *supra* note 157 at 83-85; Cheffins and Thomas, *supra* note 144 at 46.

171 Grundfest, *supra* note 116 at 924.

172 C. Goforth, "Proxy Reform as a Means of Increasing Shareholder Participation in Corporate Governance: Too Little, but Not Too Late" (1994) 43 Am. U. L. Rev. 379 at 434.

173 Grundfest, *supra* note 116 at 907.

174 See Crête, *supra* note 157 at 83-85.

2
Oversight, Hindsight, and Foresight: Canadian Corporate Governance through the Lens of Global Capital Markets
Janis Sarra

A benchmark of effective corporate governance is the quality of the corporate board's oversight of the activities of the corporation and its officers and agents. Oversight in this context means development and implementation of strategic planning, overseeing the decision making and risk assessment processes, and supervision of corporate officers to prevent shirking or self-dealing transactions. Ironically, the dictionary definition of "oversight" has another meaning – mistake, failure to notice, lapse, or omission.[1] In the wake of the collapse of Enron, WorldCom, and other large US publicly traded corporations, the issue is which is the operating meaning of oversight. These events raise questions of whether investors are adequately protected, how efficiency is measured, who participates in the risk/benefit decisions forming the basis of corporate transactions, and what other models are available internationally on which to draw. This chapter is but a snapshot in what is currently a highly dynamic regime. Governance has been on Canada's corporate law agenda for almost a decade, but recent events have created a new lens through which to explore these issues.

Those who are photographers will know that photographic paper is highly sensitive to light. A useful analogy can be drawn with capital markets and shareholder sensitivity to information. On the one hand, underexposure of corporate transactions and financial status can lead to a lack of transparency and poor decision making. When the proper information is ultimately exposed, the picture is quite different and investors who relied on the underdeveloped or undisclosed information suffer losses above those normally expected in the risk/return assessment of equity investments. This creates a lack of investor confidence, given the uncertainty in the quality of exposure of information. On the other hand, overexposure can make the markets unreadable and inaccessible. For example, Enron disclosed many of its corporate transactions, but disclosed them in such a complicated and opaque fashion that they were not discernible to most investors. When the full picture became clear, stock value plummeted, resulting in losses to Enron investors and a crisis in market confidence. While enhanced disclosure is important, its accessibility to retail investors is key. This chapter also suggests that notwithstanding a new lens focused on corporate governance, there are numerous critical issues that are being filtered out of the public debate. This is a function of the aperture setting, narrowly set at shareholder protection without advantage being taken of the opportunity to rethink some fundamental notions regarding corporate governance.

The rest of this chapter consists of three sections. The first examines board "oversight" as the indicium of effective corporate governance. It analyzes how the governance debate has been shaped in Canada and the lessons that can be drawn from international experience. Current market pressure for convergence of governance norms and protection of equity interests comes primarily from Anglo-American corporations as capital moves outward.[2] This pressure is not purely market-driven. The private law aspects of Anglo-American governance norms are situated in an extensive regulatory framework in Canada and the United States that protects a particular hierarchy of property. As a result, the norms debate focuses largely on shareholder wealth maximization and reduction of associated agency costs, with share value being considered the measure of optimal capital markets. "Efficiency" includes a calculation of cost that frequently externalizes particular costs of corporate activity such as environmental or consumer harms. In turn, the continuous disclosure regime encourages reporting to investors of "material change," with materiality defined narrowly to exclude costs borne by corporate investors other than shareholders. Concurrent with convergence pressure, however, there is countervailing pressure resisting such convergence, given the cultural, political, and economic structures of other corporate law regimes. Corporate law paradigms in continental Europe, the Pan-Pacific Region, and transition economies are examined for both their normative approach and the challenges that they pose for effective governance. In many of these models, equity capital, rather than having primacy in terms of corporate goals, is ranked equally with recognition of the contributions of workers, creditors, and communities. Canadian corporations seeking to participate in global markets need to develop an understanding of these different norms and governance structures, in order to appreciate and measure the signs of effective stewardship of the corporation.

The second section examines "hindsight," the lessons learned (or not) from recent failures of Anglo-American corporate governance. There has been considerable attention post-Enron to whether or not current regulatory controls are adequate to protect investors, and much activity by securities regulators to enhance the continuous disclosure regime. While attention has focused on equity investors, the reforms may still not afford the level of protection that hindsight suggests will truly enhance our "investor consumer" protection regime. Moreover, it is obvious that protection of other corporate stakeholders is not captured by these initiatives.

The last section then focuses on "foresight," providing suggestions as to how corporate governance can be further enhanced. It focuses on both domestic and international governance issues, including the results of a qualitative survey of Canadian directors undertaken in 2002. This section highlights the need for an ongoing project of governance reform if Canadian corporations are to fully participate in global markets.

Oversight: Effective Governance of the Corporation

Governance of the corporation includes the structure by which corporate decisions are made so that capital can be raised cost-effectively, assets are utilized in the efficient generation of wealth, and corporate officers are accountable to those investing in the firm in a manner that controls agency costs.[3] Within the normative framework of Canadian corporate law, these activities are undertaken with the objective of shareholder wealth maximization. This objective in turn drives corporate conduct and the accountability mechanisms that govern.

Governance Norms: The Narrow Aperture of Voluntary Guidelines

Corporate norms have been described as nonlegally enforceable standards or systems of cooperation driven by a common understanding rather than externally imposed laws.[4] Law and economics scholars have used norms analysis to explain particular corporate conduct that does not easily fit into the pure market-driven conception of the corporation, suggesting that corporate officers engage in stewardship of the corporation influenced by norms that bridge the gap between efficiency-enhancing activity and duties of care and loyalty.[5] Norms influence the conduct of corporate officers in their complex interactions internally with managers and employees, and externally with creditors, shareholders, and the public.[6] Stéphane Rousseau has undertaken a thoughtful analysis of the current norms debate in Chapter 1. In this chapter, the term "corporate governance norms" is used to describe the confluence of articulated and unarticulated rules that govern decision making in the corporation. However, these rules or standards of corporate stewardship evolve in the context of the larger public policy and regulatory framework of corporate law, securities law, and a highly developed scheme of credit enforcement and bankruptcy law, which provide the normative "muscle" to encourage particular kinds of governance behaviour. The force of these laws is frequently assumed, in that the debate focuses on the contribution that privately generated corporate norms make to enhance shareholder wealth maximization without full consideration of the regulating effects of such laws.

In Canada, as with most developed market economies, a public regulatory framework supports and respects property ownership, shareholder rights, and other public policy standards that create and delimit the role of the corporate legal personality and its decision makers. Limited liability specifies a division of value between shareholders and other claim holders, such as tort claimants, consumers, suppliers, and other creditors, which in turn can induce insiders to make suboptimal investment choices in terms of the welfare of all claim holders.[7] Governance is also affected by the existence or absence of numerous constraints on corporate activity, such as "investor consumer" protection through standards for disclosure, regulated forums for securities transactions, prohibitions on insider trading, and other measures designed to facilitate access to capital while affording basic protections to minority shareholders.[8] Corporate governance is shaped by public laws that recognize, to varying degrees, the interests of shareholders, creditors, workers, and others in terms of director and officer liability for employment standards, gender and race discrimination laws, environmental protection, and particular transactions that place the solvency of the corporation at risk. Public regulation to protect property rights is increasing, while there is simultaneously a move towards fewer standards regulating corporate conduct with respect to workers and other stakeholders. Within this highly codified regulatory protection of private property, there are no mandatory standards of corporate governance other than statutory and common law codification of fiduciary obligation that create a benchmark against which the activities of corporate managers are measured. The benchmark of "in the best interests of the corporation" is broadly worded but normatively narrowly defined as shareholder wealth maximization.

Canadian corporate governance norms have been shaped by the Toronto Stock Exchange (TSX), which accounts for 90 percent of equity trading in Canada.[9] A series of studies and consultation processes – generating reports such as *Where Were the Directors* (the Dey Report) in 1994; *Five Years to the Dey*, which reported survey results of 600 corporate officers five years later; and *Beyond Compliance: Building a Governance Culture* in 2001 – considered whether one could codify principles for good governance and whether such norms should be imposed by public law or encouraged as best governance practice.[10] Stéphane Rousseau has canvassed these studies in Chapter 1. The TSX has issued nonmandatory guidelines for governance, but sets no minimum governance requirements for listing other than disclosure of governance practices. One-half of publicly traded Canadian corporations do not have formalized governance rules. Rather, norms have developed in the context of business decision making, tempered by statutes imposing liability for particular kinds of conduct. Post-Enron, the TSX has announced new amended voluntary guidelines for governance, discussed in the section "Foresight" below. The guidelines continue to be voluntary because of the TSX's conclusion that its mandate is disclosure of governance systems rather than the setting of minimum standards.[11] This despite the fact that the TSX's own study, *Beyond Compliance,* concluded that there are continuing deficiencies in governance, in terms of risk assessment processes, board independence, director training, and strategic planning processes for boards.[12] Fifty-one percent of listed corporations do not report their governance practices measured against the TSX guidelines.[13]

The Camera Itself: Normative Underpinnings of Corporate Law

Elsewhere, I have discussed at length the different theoretical approaches to corporate law, their normative underpinnings, and the need to expand our understanding of the full range of investments in the corporation.[14] Canadian corporate governance is modelled largely on the contractarian approach, which suggests that implicit and explicit contracts are the mechanism by which stakeholders protect their interests in their dealings with the corporation and its managers.[15] Shareholders are considered the only residual claimants (after payment of all debts) to the firm's assets, and thus have the greatest incentive to monitor corporate directors' and officers' conduct.[16] The goal that flows from these notions is shareholder wealth maximization, aimed at an optimal return on investment of equity capital.[17] Yet shareholders suffer from information asymmetries, free-rider problems, lack of incentives to invest in the acquisition of expertise, and the costs of monitoring. Agency cost theory seeks to reduce inefficiency in the nexus of contractual relations' structure of the firm by advocating structural incentives to align the interests of corporate directors and officers with those of shareholders.[18]

The Canadian contractarian view of corporate governance reinforces share value as the optimal indicator of efficiency in corporate activity. This view of corporate governance has been buttressed by statutory and judicial support for the notion that the objective of the corporation is shareholder wealth maximization, with judicial deference to business judgments that accomplish that end.[19] Efficiency generally means the allocation of financial and other corporate resources to put assets to their highest use while controlling transaction costs. Hence, legal and governance rules should be constructed to ensure that resources are allocated to their optimal use, measured as shareholder wealth maximization. In turn, this will generate value that will ultimately benefit society as a whole.[20] Any rights of creditors or employees ought to be strictly limited to contractual and statutory rights.[21] Although there are a number of pricing mechanisms, efficiency is frequently measured by present share value as the measure of shareholder confidence in managers and the market's overall assessment of the governance of the corporation.[22] Failures in the market's ability to price accurately are generally attributed to information asymmetries, with the solution being to create greater transparency in governance and corporate transactions in order for investors to monitor and respond, primarily through exit, if dissatisfied with board oversight or managerial decisions. Yet exit by investors can send untimely and inaccurate signals to managers through imperfect markets.[23]

Norms as nonlegally enforceable standards influence board composition and corporate culture, set standards for corporate charitable acts (or not), create the pressure to operate effectively where there are sufficiently competitive markets, and generally govern relationships within a firm.[24] While the norms literature makes important observations about the norms that are part of the corporate culture, it can fail to acknowledge that these very norms are grounded in pre-existing hierarchies within the firm. Contractarianism does not acknowledge that current market models are based on a particular historical distribution of property, and that the governance systems they generate have redistributional effects that continue to shift value to property owners. It fails to acknowledge that the initial distribution of property, economic, and political rights then determines the scope of possible economic outcomes when looking at market allocations of resources, goods, and services.[25] A shareholder wealth maximization paradigm thus has distributional consequences that are made invisible using a purely contractarian analysis. The contractarian view allows for ease of accountability, given that corporate officers are accountable only to shareholders and given its single equity capital-maximizing objective. It does, however, have weaknesses in terms of discerning shareholder wealth maximization given the diversity of investors and different risk capabilities and investment timelines. Moreover, the narrow focus results in the creation of "externalities" and an artificial distinction between costs of firm activity that are accounted for within the corporation and those that are not. Thus, corporations are free to externalize numerous costs by having others bear the costs of decisions that create production or market efficiencies for the corporation but that may harm employees or communities, or have serious economic and social consequences from their effects on the environment. Yet the logic of a contractarian approach should be to recognize, value, and account for all implicit and express contracts and thus for all costs associated with particular governance decisions. If there is to be accurate accounting of such externalities, the question is why those bearing the risk of loss and actual losses do not have their interests routinely accounted for in corporate decision making.[26]

More recently, socio-economics scholars, and to some extent communitarian scholars, have suggested that in generating wealth, governance should ensure that the corporation is accountable to communities in which it operates, in advancing public policies of investor protection, environmental protection, and employment standards.[27] In Chapter 8, Lynne Dallas points to empirical data that suggest that a corporate board representing diverse interests is an effective means of acquiring resources, reducing environmental uncertainty, making optimal use of the skills of diverse participants, and ensuring that decision making takes account of the context in which the corporation operates.[28] A challenge for the socio-economic model, however, is to develop an acceptable method to determine what are socially optimal goals and to respond to the question of why corporate officers are better situated than public policy makers to determine those goals.

Widening the Lens to Assess Other Governance Models

The international movement of capital is unprecedented in volume and value, requiring Canadian corporations to assess their governance regime and the ability to effectively compete for capital internationally. With the emergence of global capital markets, the governance debate continues to situate itself as a purely property-based regime, focusing on the need to protect those property rights under vastly differing legal and political systems. However, the globalization of capital markets should not lead one to assume that free markets will function effectively absent an adequate regulatory and governance framework. The financial market failures in Russia and Asia in the late 1990s are examples of this. Global capital flows give rise to the potential for opportunism by insider controlling shareholders or foreign investors. Key to the attraction of "patient capital" is the ability to offer corporate governance systems that are clearly articulated and adhered to, within regulatory and legal frameworks that support contractual and ownership rights.[29] Thus, capital market controls are aimed at allocating risks and distributing the costs of shifts in capital markets domestically or outside the state.[30]

Liquidity of markets is frequently viewed as key to healthy governance. Yet Ross Buckley has suggested that it can be illusory because capital markets that are deep and efficient in good times can rapidly become thin, volatile, and illiquid during periods of economic downturn.[31] Tracking the early protectionist development of US markets, Buckley suggests that developing or transition economies may similarly be better served by barriers to the free movement of capital. For example, many Asian nations already have the domestic capital to finance their economic development. Buckley suggests that if this capital were to remain invested domestically, as an economy's own capital markets deepen and the regulatory systems mature, the state could then liberalize capital movement. He argues that the real moral hazard of international capital markets is not the risk of self-dealing but rather the devastating impact on the poor who bear the burden in the debtor countries that experience the financial crisis. This has not been accounted for in the discussion on global capital markets.

The shift to global capital markets squarely raises the issue of whether there will be a convergence in corporate governance norms. Factors such as the legal and regulatory regime influence the ability of capital markets to act as an effective tool for channelling investments efficiently. Capital markets simultaneously contain the language of free market while advocating state regulatory control to protect private property. The link manifests itself in a variety of ways. For example, emerging and transition economies are frequently plagued by underdeveloped securities markets, inadequate regulatory frameworks to protect investments, inadequate exit mechanisms, in some cases corruption, and a judicial system unable to provide timely and effective remedies for these issues.[32] Even in developed market economies, however, there have been some notable failures in the ability of shareholders, the market, or securities regulators to detect and/or control managerial misconduct.[33] The Enron fiasco in the United States is the most recent and notorious example of this. Depending on the capital structures of these economies, controlling shareholders, corporate boards, auditors, banks, and other institutional lenders were thought to be carefully monitoring corporate decision makers.

As capital has moved outward, it has encountered different corporate governance paradigms. For example, in some continental European countries, with different historical development and civil law traditions, the bank-centred capital structure and governance model moved corporations away from a pure shareholder wealth maximization norm. In contrast to the US, which used public laws to severely restrict the activities of banks, banks in Germany and other continental European economies were allowed to obtain ownership stakes and to offer securities trading services to customers. Public regulation thus facilitated the ability of banks to act as direct equity owners, creditors, and blockholders with a strong governance role.[34] These regulatory choices resulted in the underdevelopment of securities markets, because capitalization did not require liquid securities markets, and thus underdevelopment of minority shareholder protections.[35] The monitoring role of banks and other blockholders also resulted in a model of corporate governance with greater focus on the value of human capital contributions in addition to share wealth maximization. Public regulatory choices have also been made in European Union (EU) countries in terms of recognition of a role for employees in corporate governance, and laws reallocating the costs of corporate activity that negatively impacts on employees and other stakeholders. For example, the EU Acquired Rights Directive, adopted as legislation in several EU member states, limits the ability of an acquiring bidder to lay off excess employees in the immediate aftermath of a takeover.[36] This protects employees and tempers the takeover market in these economies.

The link between capital markets and corporate governance has been described as being either path-dependent or a function of markets. Governance models are path-dependent in that corporations reflect the historical, legal, and political frameworks in which they operate. Bebchuk and Roe observe, for example, that Anglo-American corporate governance is a function of path-dependence rather than a natural evolution towards efficiency, with norms developed in response to widely dispersed capital and existing political and social institutions, reflecting enormous power inequities.[37] An alternative view is that global capital markets will create convergence notwithstanding political and historical influences. The mobility of capital, mergers, cross-listing on international stock exchanges, the move to international accounting standards, and the global transfer of both debt and equity will result in convergence of corporate governance norms. Coffee argues that there is functional convergence, that securities markets are growing rapidly in countries where they were previously underdeveloped, and that private law and exchanges will create protection for investors in the absence of state intervention as a response to the competition for capital.[38] Yet Visentini observes that capital markets may overrule domestic legislation in allocation of economic resources, and there is a danger that global companies will not be adequately regulated in any jurisdiction.[39] Ronald Davis echoes this in Chapter 5, in his discussion of investor control of multinational corporations. Elsewhere, I have suggested that path-dependence and market convergence theory are not mutually exclusive.[40] Historical economic and political structures set strong normative and regulatory frameworks in which corporate governance practice is determined. The majority of the world's corporations continue to be closely, domestically held, including family-owned and state-owned enterprises, or held as part of an intricate set of cross-holdings.[41] Governance of corporations is shaped by their internal capital, share, and management structures. While convergence pressure is likely to result in some alteration of these regulatory frameworks, it is unlikely to result in complete convergence as the result of the move to global capital markets.

For example, capitalization of US corporations was accomplished by equity investments of numerous widely dispersed shareholders and through investment of retained earnings, resulting in a predominance of corporate structures where strong managers controlled the corporation and dispersed shareholders lacked the information, resources, and incentive to effectively monitor these managers – hence, a "separation of ownership and control."[42] This vested power in those with little equity stake and little direct accountability. Thus, corporate governance mechanisms have been aimed at controlling opportunistic behaviour by powerful managers in order to protect dispersed shareholders, while reducing the agency costs of such monitoring and aligning of interests. The regulatory system responded to the governance problems that were a consequence of widely dispersed ownership through securities regulation, consumer protection laws, and corporations' laws apportioning responsibility and liability among the corporate legal personality and directors and officers in their fiduciary capacity. Within this regulatory system, corporations are left with a variety of options for public and private financing.

The ownership structure of Anglo-American corporations has been changing, however, and while the majority of shares continue to be widely held, there is increasing concentration of ownership by institutional investors. Pension funds now hold more than 25 percent of equity in US corporations.[43] These developments have created new tensions in accountability and governance. For example, jurisprudence according high deference to business judgments has worked in some instances to diminish accountability. Current initiatives to reform US securities regulation, through rigid interpretation of the ordinary business exception and heavy restriction of shareholder participation regarding social policies, have extended a trend towards diminishing shareholder participation and thus the ability of shareholders to hold managers accountable for any corporate actions not directly related to share value maximization.[44] There has been a simultaneous increase in institutional shareholder activism, aimed at enhancing corporate accountability and increasing the independence of corporate boards and audit committees. This activism has taken the form of "voice" in the sense of informal influences on corporate officers and more direct intervention in the form of proposing new directors, increased use of proxy voting, shareholder proposals, and relationship investing. Mechanisms to influence the market for corporate control, such as poison pills and breakup fees, that have a tendency to entrench managers, are being systematically attacked by institutional shareholders.[45] Institutional investors have the resources and information to monitor managers. Moreover, while the prospect of exit affords these investors bargaining power, other regulatory restrictions hinder exit, thus leaving voice as the de facto option.

In contrast to the Anglo-American model, the governance challenge in closely held, cross-held, or blockheld corporate structures such as those in Germany, Italy, Japan, and other parts of Asia has been to protect the interests of minority shareholders from powerful controlling shareholders or blockholders.[46] The continental European model of corporate governance is a function of closely held or blockheld domestic capital structures, and public policy choices about the role of multiple stakeholders such as creditors and workers. Generally, the influence of banks as large blockholders varies depending on whether the power is over debt or equity markets.[47] For example, in Belgium, France, and Sweden, banks are an integral part of links between different business groups, and thus their monitoring is manifested through that means.[48] For closely held corporations or those with complex cross-holdings, blockholding, or pyramid structures, governance problems are created by alignment of the interests of managers with controlling shareholders or blockholders. This is frequently to the detriment of minority shareholders and foreign shareholders because their interests are disregarded or economic benefits are extracted through self-dealing transactions.

German corporations are highly leveraged, and debt, as well as the equity that banks vote on behalf of investors' deposits, plays a strong governance role. This capital structure historically resulted in little need for developed securities markets. This was further influenced by public policy that recognizes the importance of lending institutions and employees within the governance structure of the corporation. The result is a governance structure with less pressure to maximize short-term shareholder value and more attention to other stakeholders. While capital is less liquid, corporations are also less subject to the volatility that accompanies rapid changes in investor confidence. For example, rapid capital market changes do not result in immediate labour shedding and thus the negative impact on employees is generally less extreme. As Germany has sought to attract international capital to remain competitive globally, allowing corporations to diversify their capital structures, there are more active securities markets, although these are still ancillary to the banks as the primary source of capital.[49] Only recently have there been changes to governance structures to enhance minority shareholder accountability, such as new insider trading rules, in part a result of greater competition for capital.

Corporate governance objectives in Germany have also been mandated by the statutory framework. National wage adjustment programs, legislated co-determination structures, national retraining programs, and public policy that obliges the corporation to consider workers' interests have shifted the governance focus and resulted in a more comprehensive means of addressing structural changes to corporations. With the high risk of expropriation of their human capital investments removed, workers in turn acquired higher firm loyalty and interacted with managers to develop more cooperative production models and work practices. Governance has been aimed at encouraging the board to manage for the good of the enterprise, including both equity investors and the public welfare. This is reflected in the co-determination model, a two-tier corporate board structure in which workers and shareholders participate on a supervisory board and daily decision making is undertaken by a separate managerial board. In the workplace, co-determination has translated into works councils, essentially collaborative processes to enhance production, health and safety, and workers' voice in strategic planning. Corporate officers, through a series of collaborative strategies, pursue both shareholder wealth maximization and the economic and social health of the enterprise and its workers. However, the two-tier board structure, while designed to reflect different stakeholder interests, has created a different kind of accountability concern. While the supervisory boards of the largest corporations consist of equal numbers of employees and shareholders, "employee" membership on the board includes supervisors, professionals, and unionized workers, whose interests frequently diverge. Board oversight is undermined by infrequent board meetings, unduly large and unwieldy board size, and untimely and inadequate disclosure to board members. There is also a problem of managers bypassing the supervisory board, thereby exacerbating accountability problems.[50] The banks participate both as equity holders on the supervisory board and as blockholders intervening directly with managers. The latter raises concern regarding any control premiums that they may be extracting. Moreover, German law allows for a broader scope of shareholder participation at general meetings, a role employed by banks.[51] Thus, concerns about shareholder rights are those faced by minority shareholders in light of "strong blockholders and weak owners."[52]

Within corporations with a high concentration of shareholding, there is considerable difference in controlling shareholder voting, with the UK dominated by institutional investors such as life insurance companies and financial institutions, whereas Austrian, Italian, and French ownership is dominated by family, individual, and nonfinancial companies.[53] Many corporations in these jurisdictions are a complex arrangement of pyramid and/ or cross-holdings, where a few shareholders or blockholders exert considerable influence over corporate decision making.[54] Lack of transparency regarding ownership, voting control, and transactions that may benefit particular blocks of shareholdings also creates potential for abuse and hinders outside investors' ability to assess the stewardship of the corporation. Thus, the governance issues differ from those presented by dispersed ownership.

Japanese corporations present yet another governance model, which will likely undergo some transition with recent changes to corporate and securities law. Characterized in the post-occupation era by a system of cross-holdings, *Keiretsus* were structured vertically, with suppliers having a direct governance role in terms of their relations with the corporation, and horizontally, where there is a lead bank and a number of member firms.[55] Banks as debt holders were also frequently the largest equity holders, and corporate governance structures emerged to utilize this pattern of ownership, debt, and control.[56] This resulted in little dependence on capital markets, low liquidity because of the size and complexity of cross-holdings, and underdevelopment of securities regulation. Japan's corporate governance was also influenced by powerful social and cultural relationships through suppliers clubs and presidents clubs. Corporate governance has emphasized protection of employee and creditor interests, which are considered at least as important as shareholder interests.[57] This stakeholder model arises out of a complex postwar economic and political history, in which long-term employment evolved in response to massive labour unrest and production takeover strikes.[58] The illiquidity of Japanese labour and capital markets created a higher incentive to invest in workers over the long term, in turn creating corporate structures and cultures that were stable and that resulted in highly productive collaboration.[59] This stakeholder model has been buttressed by judicial decisions that have protected workers' human capital investments.[60]

Thus, Japanese capital and governance structures worked to create a wealth maximization model not aimed purely at shareholder wealth maximization. It includes a normative conception of longtime employment, with advancement in the corporation frequently measured by contributions to the team process, as opposed to individual contributions, and these powerful cultural norms shape how efficiency and wealth are measured. It has been only in the past five years that the first real wave of labour shedding has hit Japan. This is integrally linked to more active securities markets, which tend to reward labour shedding in terms of market price.[61] The current capital structure of Japanese corporations is changing, with a slow reduction in cross-shareholdings and a declining role for the banks in both provision of capital and governance. This trend is a function of new regulatory change that re-established pure holding companies, deregulated stock investments by pension funds, and implemented substantial change to corporate accounting practices.[62] Shareholder activism is at a nascent stage. Derivative litigation was rarely used because of the high costs of filing and limited recovery possibilities. Recent lowering of these costs has resulted in a boom in derivative suits, although expensive bonding requirements still act to deter shareholders, and remedies are frequently available only where there has been illegal conduct.[63]

Japanese corporate law is undergoing further transition, with new *Commercial Code* amendments effective 2003 that will allow corporations to opt for an Anglo-American model of governance or retain the dual monitoring auditor system (*Kansayaku*).[64] Combined with shifts in securities regulation, shareholder activism, and the notion of Japanese lifetime employment, there is an important issue of whether these shifts represent a move towards an optimal governance paradigm. The evolution is tempered by particular norms that drive Japanese corporate law. Notwithstanding normative pressure internationally to discount the value of human capital contributions, Japanese directors are still hesitant to move to a pure shareholder wealth maximization model. More than 2,400 corporations list on Japanese exchanges, compared with 60 Japanese corporations on US and UK exchanges.[65] Most domestically held corporations still continue to value the lifetime employment norm. It may be that the governance model that evolves will adopt the best elements of increased transparency, corporate accountability, enhanced shareholder protection, employee long-term employment protections, and production synergies, which would allow Japanese corporations to compete internationally but retain those elements of corporate community that have long been considered a primary objective of the social and economic life of Japan.

In Asia, the majority of corporations are still closely held, by individuals or families or by a series of cross-holdings or pyramid holdings.[66] When Asia experienced its financial crisis in 1998-99, the lack of good governance controls and, in particular, the lack of minority shareholder protection, led to market crashes and some expropriation of wealth by controlling shareholders.[67] Such regimes also suffer from a lack of transparency that can diminish investor confidence and encourage such rent seeking by controlling shareholders. However, characterizing such capital and governance structures as "crony capitalism" masks more complex normative underpinnings of corporate governance in these nations. While there is a risk of extraction of control premiums and in some cases corruption, corporations have been successful in generating wealth and economic activity. There is also a powerful culture of cooperation in business relations, recognition of team as opposed to individual contribution, and corporate activity as part of society. Chinese, Asian, and Pan-Pacific corporations are frequently governed based on notions of social cohesion, nonconfrontational commercial relationships, and the firm's contributions and place in the social ordering.[68] This can result in governance that protects more diverse investments in the firm. As a result, there is resistance to wholesale adoption of Anglo-American norms. Berglof and von Thadden suggest that, notwithstanding these differences in governance norms, there is evidence that shareholders are relatively well protected in these systems, and that other governance mechanisms such as channelling of resources between firms within a group plays a role in directing capital to its most productive use. The governance challenge is thus one of "strong managers, related investors," requiring the strengthening of human capital, the accumulation of domestic capital, and governmental accountability.[69] Moreover, Branson has argued that the effect of globalization on Asian economies has been less self-sustaining economic activity, increased poverty, and greater vulnerability by developing nations dependent on international capital that engages in regulatory arbitrage.[70]

With the global competition for capital, initiatives in various jurisdictions indicate that there is a continuing tension between Anglo-American approaches to investor protection and private law initiatives to enhance corporate governance under bank-centred, family- or state-controlled models. Individual states have been influenced by domestic corporations in trying to discern principles for best governance practice, such as the Viénot Report in France in 1999, the Olivencia Report in Spain in 1998, the Code for Corporate Governance issued by the Italian Stock Exchange in 1999, and a host of other initiatives that have ensured that the governance debate remain high on the agenda of capital markets regulators and participants. The market pressure for convergence of corporate governance norms is most acute where there is risk of expropriation of investors' capital within economic systems with poor regulatory protection. Numerous Asian corporations have also moved towards independent board members and international auditing standards, as a means of regaining investor confidence.[71] Those with resources to promote governance reform have created international fora, such as the Organization for Economic Cooperation and Development (OECD) and the World Bank joint Global Governance Forum to promote acceptance of corporate governance principles, based largely on the Anglo-American model of governance.[72]

Other governance initiatives do not closely align with the Anglo-American model. In France, corporate governance continues to be driven by a stakeholder model, in which shareholder interest is but one of the interests considered in decision making. In the European Union, efforts at harmonization of corporate governance and corporate law have been slowed because of fundamental normative disagreements about stakeholder conceptions of the corporation, especially between Germany and the UK.[73] Korea's Code of Best Practice for Corporate Governance, developed in 1999, emphasizes enhanced shareholder rights and remedies and independent corporate boards, yet it also emphasizes protection of stakeholder rights, creditors, employees, consumer and environmental protection, and stakeholder participation in management monitoring.[74] India's Draft Report on Corporate Governance addresses market pressures for transparency, board reform to include independent directors and audit committees, and enhanced shareholder protections, while still emphasizing as a first principle that "the fundamental objective of corporate governance is the enhancement of long-term shareholder value while at the same time protecting the interests of other stakeholders such as employees creditors, customers and society at large."[75]

Changes in the capital and governance structures of transition economies represents yet another wave of capital market influence on firms. Katharina Pistor has examined changes in twenty-four transition economies from 1990 to 1998, where the governance challenge has been to facilitate the financing and restructuring of the pre-existing state-owned enterprise sector.[76] The mass privatization schemes that were aimed at dispersed share ownership and accompanying structures resulted instead in rapid concentrations of capital, and thus blockholder control. While there have been recent moves to create legal protection of minority shareholder rights, Pistor suggests that it is less than clear that this will change the trend towards equity concentration, particularly given the lack of small-investor confidence and the underdevelopment of securities market protection. Those nations that adopted a direct sales method of privatization acquired capital structures that were blockholdings by strategic investors.[77] Pistor suggests that this trend towards concentrated holdings is path-dependent in terms of the prewar corporate codes that reflected not only socialist principles but also key provisions on shareholder and creditor rights. She observes that it also reflects early transition to market economic activity even prior to the collapse of socialism, and cites Hungary as an example. This history and more recent reform created constraints on policy choices in governance for transition economies. The level of shareholder and creditor protection was low at the outset of economic transition, except creditor rights in the CEE/Baltic nations.[78] Yet Pistor concludes that the increase in legal rules protecting shareholder and creditor rights are the result of foreign technical assistance in system design and of efforts to harmonize rules for nations seeking EU membership, as opposed to responses to market pressure.

Pistor tracks developments across cumulative indices, such as voice, exit, protection of minority shareholder rights, agency problems, and stock market integrity indices. She concludes that shareholder voice is the most strongly developed and market integrity the weakest, and that formal legal change in transition economies is converging despite differences in pre-socialist legal heritage.[79] The corporate governance model that is emerging in many of these nations is neither market-centred nor bank-centred, but rather a control model that includes relatively concentrated ownership but a strong role for banks on a short-term debt basis only. It illustrates that hybrid models may be possible in global capital markets, notwithstanding considerable pressure to import pre-existing Anglo-American norms. Other scholars have raised similar tentative conclusions for transition economies, arguing that the shareholder protection paradigm is far too narrow and that governance mechanisms in these nations reflects a much broader conception of stakeholder.[80] Berglof and von Thadden suggest that transition economies are in the early part of their firm life cycle, and thus liquid markets are not as important as effective restructuring post-privatization, including the need for regulatory protection and enforcement. They suggest that the problem is managers' theft, exploitation of suppliers and customers, and failure to pay employees and the government, calling this a governance challenge of "omnipotent managers, little resistance."[81]

Thus, challenges in corporate governance internationally are complex. In trying to discern optimal governance strategies for Canadian corporations in global markets, we need to be cognizant of our pre-existing normative assumptions in order to be conscious of how they affect our understanding of different corporate regimes and the governance challenges generated. Effective oversight needs to encompass this broader understanding of governance across different normative conceptions of the corporation.

Hindsight: The Filters through Which Investors Assess the Governance of the Corporation

Having canvassed issues raised by different models globally, we can gain new insight on the need for effective oversight from recent failures in Anglo-American governance. The hindsight acquired post-Enron is one that has focused on transparency guarantees and prevention of self-dealing transactions, both of which are very important to well-functioning capital markets. However, there continue to be filters in the way in which these and other issues are being addressed. This section commences with a very brief discussion of the lessons from Enron, although the reader is advised to consult the extensive documentation and analysis of Enron's collapse. While the response has consisted of heightened disclosure requirements and some prohibitions on self-dealing, it may not afford sufficient protection to equity investors. Moreover, the failure to place the interests of other corporate investors in the picture is significant, particularly because of the multiple harms to unsecured creditors, employees, and others as a result of Enron's collapse.

Enron and the Systemic Failures of Governance

In December 2001, Enron Corporation was listed as the seventh largest company in the US, with over $100 billion in annual gross revenues.[82] With its collapse, shareholders lost more than $60 billion in market value, 20,000 employees lost their jobs, and creditors lost billions in trade and other credit. Enron's primary activity, trading in energy contracts as essentially marketable commodities, had been considered highly innovative. The strategy required heavy financing, which Enron accomplished through a series of complicated transactions in which it inappropriately hedged its own risks and failed to disclose both the risks inherent in this strategy and its off-balance sheet liabilities. This created the conditions ripe for officer self-dealing transactions, to the detriment of the corporation and its investors.

The US Senate committee that investigated Enron reported in July 2002 that for the most part, Enron's corporate board knew of and sanctioned these transactions. The board ignored indicators that reporting of the corporation's transactions pushed the limits of generally accepted accounting principles (GAAP). Board members approved the movement of multiple entities off the corporation's books, while guaranteeing massive debts. The board waived conflict-of-interest prohibitions and inappropriately allowed officers to set up businesses, resulting in officers extracting millions of dollars in personal profits at the expense of the corporation. The board approved the "Raptor" transactions, which inappropriately used special purpose entities (SPEs) that appeared to hedge millions of dollars in volatile investments, when essentially Enron was inappropriately hedging its own risk, unknown to its investors and creditors.[83] The result was that losses of almost $1 billion were concealed from the market by creating an appearance that the investments were hedged by a third party, i.e., that the third party was obligated to pay Enron the amount of those losses, when in reality an independent third party did not exist.[84] These transactions were sanctioned by Enron's external auditor, which was also heavily dependent on Enron for lucrative consulting fees that made up half of its $50 million in annual fees from the corporation.[85]

The Enron directors were in a position to prevent many of the failures in governance that occurred, but failed in their oversight role because of a board culture that created unquestioning loyalty. The Senate Committee Report concluded that the Enron directors failed in their fiduciary obligations to safeguard Enron shareholders, including allowing the corporation to engage in inappropriate conflict-of-interest transactions, extensive off-the-books activities, and excessive executive compensation. The Senate committee found that the Enron board of directors knowingly allowed Enron to conduct billions of dollars in off-the-books activity to make its financial condition appear better than it was, and the directors failed to ensure adequate public disclosure of these liabilities, thus contributing to Enron's collapse. Independence of board members was compromised by financial ties between the company and certain board members, including lucrative consulting fees in addition to their director's compensation, and major financial donations to organizations in which board members were directly involved and from which they received income.[86] Finally, the Senate committee found that the Enron board failed to ensure the independence of the company's auditor, allowing Arthur Andersen to provide internal audit and consulting services as well as serve as Enron's outside auditor.[87] Enron highlights the economic and social harm caused by lack of effective board oversight. Its collapse revealed deficiencies in the disclosure regime, securities protections, accounting standards, and professional codes of conduct.

Lessons for Canadian Corporate Governance
The first reaction of Canadian securities regulators and stock exchanges was that "an Enron" could not happen in Canada. Seriously reduced investor confidence and mass exit from securities markets indicate that investors are not as confident. In Canada, the hallmarks of good governance have been effective and independent oversight of the corporate board, transparency of corporate transactions, director accountability to shareholders, and auditors and similar professionals as gatekeepers or protectors of the integrity of the disclosure process. All of these elements are present in the US regime as well. Alone or in combination, however, they did not provide a check on corporate misconduct. Thus, at least to some degree, a similar governance failure could occur in Canada. Effective oversight requires corporate directors able to think separately and independently from corporate officers. It is not sufficient merely to appoint corporate directors who do not meet the statutory definition of related directors. Rather, the board requires an ability to represent and present diverse views on corporate activity, and healthy discussion and debate on the efficacy, goals, and risks of any particular transactions that affect the financial and economic health of the corporation.

Scholars Lynne Dallas and Marleen O'Connor have written about the dynamics of corporate boards and the problems associated with a lack of diversity of views and backgrounds, including the inability to question particular transactions, the need for conformity, the failure to bring diverse views to consideration of strategic decisions, fewer skill sets and experience to contribute to risk assessment, and a sense of morality that precludes questioning or challenge of group decisions.[88]

Shareholders have attempted to reduce agency problems and align managers' interests with those of equity investors by compensation practices that give managers equity or options. However, this can also create non-alignment of interests, because lack of diversification of managers' holdings may discourage appropriate risk taking, unlike the interest of diversified equity holders, or they may give rise to accounting practices with respect to options that mask actual return to shareholders. This appears to have occurred in Enron. Notwithstanding this, current suggestions that corporations report stock options on their financial statements are strongly resisted by Canadian publicly traded corporations.

To the extent that the Senate committee viewed Enron as a failure in fiduciary obligation, it was a failure not only to shareholders but also to others implicated in the corporation's economic activity. In part, this is the result of normative pressure to report sustained short-term earnings in order to impress shareholders. The Senate committee found that Enron directors failed to meet their fiduciary obligation to engage in careful oversight, with disastrous results for equity investors and others. In this respect, casting fiduciary obligation narrowly was detrimental to the long-term interests of equity investors. Enron's misconduct was particularly egregious because of the large number of smaller investors who sustained losses, including workers who had tied much of their surplus income in Enron as a retirement strategy. There is a distinction between equity investors who have tied their life savings in the markets in hopes of securing their share in the supposed "culture of generous equity return," and larger investors, whose actual capital investment is a much more substantial amount in dollar terms but represents a smaller portion of their equity investments at risk. Institutional investors are compelled by their fiduciary and trust obligations to diversify risk, and thus the impact of one corporate failure on overall capital is minimized. Moreover, many larger investors are managers of other people's capital, and their personal equity capital is therefore not at risk. Thus, shareholders have radically different risk capabilities, investment timelines, diversification capabilities, and information and resources to monitor corporate activity. Not only does this influence the short-term versus long-term investment and return timelines but it also has direct implications for the type of risks in which shareholders wish corporations to engage. While optimal investment practice assumes diversification of portfolios and ease of exit if equity investors are dissatisfied with corporate performance, these make huge assumptions about the sophistication of investors. It also requires a deeper appreciation of the power relationships, even within the existing shareholder wealth maximization paradigm. It is not enough merely to disclose corporate activity; it is also necessary to create a regulatory framework that recognizes these differences.

Voluntary Corporate Governance Standards

In 2002 the TSX issued new proposed disclosure requirements and amended voluntary guidelines on corporate governance.[89] The guidelines include enhanced disclosure of the number of unrelated directors on the corporate board, a suggestion that audit committees should be composed only of unrelated directors, and suggestion of a charter that sets out the audit committee's roles and responsibilities.[90] The guidelines recommend that all members on the audit committee should be financially literate, with at least one member having accounting or related financial expertise. The Practice Note attached to the guidelines states, however, that an acceptable definition of financial literacy is the "ability to read and understand a balance sheet, an income statement and a cash flow statement." An acceptable definition of accounting or related financial expertise is the ability to analyze and interpret a full set of financial statements, including notes, in accordance with GAAP.[91] Even for voluntary guidelines, these suggest a very low threshold for financial literacy, and thus do not respond to the governance failures highlighted by Enron.

The TSX guidelines also emphasize the role of the board in stewardship of the corporation, including strategic planning processes; adoption of ongoing succession planning, risk assessment processes, and evaluation of senior officers, including the CEO; and establishment of structures and procedures to ensure that the board can function independently and to ensure the integrity of the corporation's internal control and management information systems. The TSX survey found that less than 30 percent of boards are engaged in strategic planning and fewer than 40 percent have a formal process for oversight of risk management.[92] The guidelines emphasize the need for board independence, which can be accomplished through the use of lead directors or other means to ensure that the board discharges its responsibilities. The TSX has decided that it will not require a lead director or non-executive board chair as a condition of listing companies, even though its own Joint Corporate Governance Project recommended this in 2001 as an important feature of effective governance.[93] Only one-third of listed corporations have a non-executive chair or lead director.[94] The guidelines suggest that the board of directors should be constituted with a majority of unrelated directors. They stop short, however, of requiring the corporation to disclose the nature of the relationship of related directors with the corporation, although this is critical to shareholder assessment of the ability of the directors to effectively oversee the activities of corporate officers. The TSX fails to recommend that corporations disclose the results of shareholder votes. It does not create any guidelines for director remuneration, nor does it require compensation committees to be composed exclusively of unrelated directors. The proposed guidelines also do not suggest that auditor's fees be reported broken down on the basis of services performed. Many of these governance changes are suggestions that have been highlighted in the public discourse post-Enron, and yet they have not been implemented.

The only actual requirement is that corporations report their governance practices, something that most have neglected to do in the past despite its being a requirement.[95] The TSX views its role as providing the framework for issuers to disclose their corporate governance practices "in order for the market to reward or sanction them."[96] Moreover, the corporate governance guidelines continue to be exclusively shareholder-focused. They are silent on the need for or benefits of board diversity, based on gender, race, or stakeholder interest.

The TSX guidelines promote governance from the perspective of maximizing shareholder value; thus, they are firmly situated in the Anglo-American corporate governance paradigm. While maximizing shareholder value is a key objective, it does not provide a complete analysis of factors involved in governance. The survey on which the guidelines were based indicated that one deficiency may be the level of preparedness for participation of Canadian publicly traded corporations in international capital markets.[97] Yet there are no recommendations that appear to address this, such as board diversity, including cross-cultural and cross-national representation, or director training that is aimed at acquiring an understanding of diverse capital market and governance structures internationally. The TSX has acknowledged the changing nature of the investment community; one-half of all Canadians own shares, primarily through mutual funds, and while roughly one-half are inactive investors, there is a growing number of small investors taking "concerned" interest in investing through access to the Internet.[98] The TSX assumes a governance structure that does not allow for small-investor activism. Rather, disclosure is encouraged so that such investors can "exit" if dissatisfied with corporate performance. The liquidity of the market becomes the primary measure of corporate success, rather than a more textured view of the relationship between corporate officers and multiple interested investors. Unlike in other jurisdictions, the "stakeholder" debate has been largely ignored in the series of regulatory or policy initiatives of the TSX and its brother organizations. The Dey Report was the exception, in recognizing the importance of stakeholder relationships. Although the mandate of the TSX is arguably narrower and focuses on shareholder protection through good governance, the guidelines are proffered as a relatively complete assessment of the requirements for governance reform, expressly aimed at aligning Canadian capital markets with those of the United States. Notions of good governance, if anything, have thus narrowed since the Dey Report.

Moreover, there is a fundamental tension between the scope of governance activity that should be regulated and that which should be encouraged as efficiency-enhancing, with a view towards shareholder wealth maximization. These initiatives do not explore three underlying issues, specifically, that the "enabling" debate takes place in the context of an already highly regulated system that creates an "investor protection" culture; that the scope and nature of shareholder participation or activism is underdeveloped in Canadian corporate governance; and that the more fundamental question of whether there are other stakeholders in the corporation who contribute inputs and who may be entitled to upside benefits of wealth generation is not addressed.

Securities Disclosure
Canadian capital markets are governed by a disclosure-based regulatory regime, designed to protect investors. While the Canadian regime is one of "continuous disclosure," the information that investors receive is primarily filtered through corporations, their agents, and other actors. As the Enron debacle revealed, there is considerable malleability in the reporting of financial information and even generally accepted accounting principles can mask the consequences of particular transactions, such as how special purpose entities are reported or the nonconsolidation of stock options on the corporate balance sheet. Thus, there are deficiencies in the disclosure regime that require correction. Moreover, although Canadian listed companies are required to disclose material changes by filing a material change report with securities regulators and issuing a public release, the definition of "material" is narrow in terms of both what *is* material to shareholders and what, although arguably not part of the bottom line of the financial statements, investors might be interested in.[99]

There is no doubt that regulatory change post-Enron is aimed at restoring investor confidence in the markets. Corporate restatements of financial positions are a response to market volatility and fear of liability. Such restatements have been buttressed by legislative initiatives such as the *Sarbanes-Oxley Act of 2002,* aimed at protecting investors by improving the accuracy and reliability of corporate disclosure pursuant to US securities laws.[100] In both Canada and the United States, public company accounting oversight boards have been created to protect the interests of the investing public. In July 2002, Canadian securities regulators issued a new policy of best practices in disclosure, including that companies must have written disclosure policies, that a senior officer or committee must police this policy, and that there are specified financial, operational, and structural data that companies must release in a fair and careful manner.[101] "Material" information is now defined to include data on changes to accounting policies, changes in rating agency decisions, and any exceptions to corporate ethics or conduct practices that are put in place for key employees. These best practices will increase transparency, but it is evident that their implementation is being resisted.[102] Securities regulators have also become increasingly vigilant in investigating and enforcing the current continuous disclosure regime, with added resources and public sanctions.[103]

As a direct outcome of Enron's collapse, the Canadian Accounting Standards Board (ASB) has issued new guidelines on consolidation of special purpose entities and disclosure of guarantees, aimed at enhancing transparency.[104] These developments are important, although they also highlight a more systemic underlying issue, the malleability of accounting standards in general. The Canadian ASB is also involved in discussions with the International Accounting Standards Board, which was recently established to promote harmonization of accounting standards that will provide reliable financial reporting to enhance investor confidence in global capital markets. It may also facilitate the exchange of lessons with respect to the rigour of accounting standards, and perhaps ultimately reduce those aspects of the malleability that work to the detriment of diverse investors who rely on the financial reporting in their investment decisions.

Industry Analysts

Analysts have a highly influential role in capital markets. "Sell-side" analysts support trading revenue by interpreting publicly disclosed company information and making recommendations on good securities investments for their firm's clients.[105] They are one of the filters through which corporate activity is reported, in their advice to the investing public.[106] Unlike other areas of securities law, there is minimal regulation of analysts and thus inadequate enforceable standards.[107] Retail investors frequently assume that investment advice is more objective than that disclosed by the corporation, and are often unaware that conflicts of interest may exist because the analyst is undertaking paid research for the company or has holdings with the corporation. Institutional investors are less likely to face this problem, as they tend to have their own in-house analysts.

If this filter obscures the financial status of the corporation, there is serious detriment to stakeholders. The Securities Industry Committee on Analyst Standards, chaired by Purdy Crawford, issued its Final Report in late 2001, making extensive recommendations for the supervision and practice of Canadian securities industry analysts.[108] The Committee recommended mandatory disclosure of conflicts to ensure that investors have enough information to understand the basis for the analyst's research recommendations and to be informed of conflicts of interest of the analyst resulting from securities holdings by the analyst or the analyst's firm, or remuneration paid for research.[109] Particular conflicts would be prohibited completely; for example, an analyst serving as an officer, director, employee, or adviser of a company would be prohibited from issuing research on that company. The report also recommends a number of best practices involving how research and recommendations are reported and disclosure of their underlying assumptions, and suggests that public companies should not pressure analysts, directly or indirectly, in order to influence the outcome of research. It also recommends that analyst meetings and conference calls be open to the media and investors.[110] Given the potential for self-dealing in the absence of adequate standards, corporate boards need to exercise oversight in terms of the relationship between the corporation, its management, and investment analysts and dealers.[111] These recommendations will enhance investor protection by regulating one of the important filters through which capital markets operate.

Creditors

Under Anglo-American governance models, creditors are assumed to have bargained a risk premium in the cost of credit. However, this ignores the complexity and diversity of creditors. The more senior the creditor, the more likely it is to have bargained a risk premium and secured its interest against corporate assets or other forms of protection. Pension fund beneficiaries have some protection bargained for them through standards imposed by pension legislation. Thus, while secured creditors will not benefit from upside gains of a shareholder-driven concept of efficiency, their losses have been controlled. However, thousands of creditors are unsecured and unable to either diversify risk or bargain a risk premium. They include small trade suppliers, repair persons, employees, local governments to which payment for taxes and utilities is owed, and claimants harmed by environmental or consumer torts. These creditors are considered fixed or contingent claimants, and corporate decision making is not required to take account of their interests in maximizing value. Thus, efficiency, as currently normatively defined, allows for corporate decisions that shift assets away from creditors, often transferring value that could be used to satisfy these claims, unless the shift is excessive enough to render the corporation insolvent and creditors have access to oppression or bankruptcy remedies. At the point of bankruptcy, however, unsecured creditors receive no value or only a severely discounted value for their claims, given the hierarchy of credit realization in bankruptcy. The decision making that shifted assets out of unsecured creditors' reach has occurred at a point very much prior to actual insolvency, and their interests, which may be severely prejudiced by particular corporate transactions, need not be accounted for in determinations of efficiency.

Resources should be utilized optimally in corporate activity, and how optimal use is measured is key. Accuracy of costing may require tempering traditional efficiency measures to encompass maximizing value by considering diverse investments in the firm.[112] This definition of optimal use includes recognition of diverse inputs into productive activity. The starting point of measuring efficiency could be to consider what interests and investments are at stake in the corporation, and to acknowledge that there are competing efficient decisions. Such decision making could make Pareto improvements *if* costs are fully accounted for, including complex costs such as harm to long-term sustainability and the social and economic costs of adjustments in employment markets.

Foresight

Foresight is defined as the exercise of insight, prudence, prescience, and care for the future.[113] In corporate law, risk management, strategic planning processes, and succession planning are to provide the foresight in governance of the corporation. These are all important considerations in governance. However, foresight also requires some thought as to how governance should further develop. This section discusses current regulatory and other changes and raises questions about whether they are adequate to address effective corporate governance in global capital markets.

There is no doubt that there needs to be enhanced investor protection, and new securities regulations, industry analyst standards, and amendments to corporate laws to enhance shareholder protection are important steps. However, these are aimed at allowing Canadian corporations to participate domestically. It is less clear that they assist in the move to, and continued participation in, global markets. In Chapter 5, Ronald Davis writes about the difficulties with monitoring the conduct of global corporations. This affects the domestic governance regime as well. This section provides some initial thoughts on the foresight that needs to be exercised, viewed from the respective lenses of investors, directors, and other stakeholders.

Domestic Governance

Not requiring disclosure of corporate harms as part of the securities regime creates *ex ante* incentives on the part of corporate officers to externalize the costs of some activities, because they need not be reported or they can be reported as benefits to the corporation. The social and economic effects of labour shedding are a good illustration of this. While the financial statement records a savings in massive downsizing, the costs to the individuals from loss of deferred income and pension benefits, costs of relocating, social costs to family, and ripple economic effects on the community are not part of the disclosure, as they are not "material" to the bottom line of corporate profit. As egregious as Enron-type failures in disclosures to investors are, the attention that has been given to correcting the financial disclosure regime is in part a function of property interests that were harmed. Yet securities regulation does not operate in a vacuum. It is situated in complex public and private law norms regarding harms and protections for multiple interested parties. The securities system should better recognize that equity investors may well have an interest in greater disclosure of the nature of corporate transactions that impact on these multiple concerns. In the same vein, investor education has been aimed at discerning fraud, a focus reinforced post-Enron. Almost no attention is paid to education to promote diversification and reduction of risk, a key factor in the harms caused to Enron employees as shareholders. Moreover, little education or skills building is given to shareholders to facilitate their ability to make investment choices that reflect personal social and economic beliefs. These issues are symptomatic of much larger systemic change that is required.

In Canada, shareholder rights and remedies are codified in both corporate and securities laws, and are governed by a mixed federal and provincial legislative scheme. Shareholder activism in Canada has been confined largely to "exit" as opposed to "voice," partly the result of corporate laws that until recently limited the scope of shareholder activism. Amendments to the *Canada Business Corporations Act (CBCA)* in 2001 included a number of provisions relating to corporate governance and enhancing shareholder involvement in corporate decision making.[114] The principal changes are directed towards enhanced access to disclosure, removal of former prohibitions on shareholder communications, and use of new technologies in communication. The reforms are also aimed at enhanced participation, including the ability of corporations to hold electronic meetings, and revised proxy rules aimed at facilitating shareholder communication. There are also new shareholder remedies, such as liberalized proposal rules, the ability to commence a civil action for insider trading, limited new protection for minority shareholders on a squeeze-out, and provisions governing unanimous shareholder agreements.

Shareholder proposal provisions are generally aimed at enhancing the accountability of corporate officers and providing shareholders an increased opportunity to participate in governance decisions. The new shareholder provisions in the *CBCA* have elements that may both enhance and detract from this objective. A shareholder must alone or in combination hold 1 percent of the total number of outstanding voting shares or shares with a fair market value of $2,000 for at least six months before being entitled to submit a shareholder proposal.[115] While shareholders can combine their shares to accomplish this, it is unclear why the threshold was necessary when there was no evidence of abuse of the proposal provisions when there was no threshold. The threshold appears to unnecessarily exclude small investors. The reforms do increase the potential scope and content of shareholder proposals. Prior to the amendments, corporate officers could refuse to circulate a shareholder proposal on the ground that "it clearly appears that the proposal is submitted ... primarily for the purpose of promoting general economic, political, racial, religious, social or similar causes."[116] This provision had the effect of halting efforts by shareholders to use the proposal process to inject corporate accountability and responsibility factors into decision making.[117] The new language allows corporate officers to refuse to circulate a proposal where it "clearly appears that the proposal does not relate in a significant way to the business or affairs of the corporation."[118] This language is on its face more expansive and could eliminate a key barrier to shareholder proposals. However, it is based on the language of US statutes, and in the US there has been an uneven history of deference on the part of the Securities and Exchange Commission (SEC) and the courts to exclusion of shareholder proposals.[119]

The recent changes to the *CBCA* also increase the ability of shareholders to communicate with one another, although the statute imposes an arbitrary limit of fifteen shareholders allowed to communicate before dissident proxy circular requirements are activated.[120] Shareholders can now publicly communicate their intention to vote a particular way in public speeches, press releases, websites, and other broadcast media without activating the solicitation prohibitions.[121] Given the recent enactment of these measures, it is too early to gauge the potential for shareholder activism. Unlike the United States, Canada has not had a strong history of shareholder proxy or proposal activism.[122] This is likely to change. Organizations such as the Shareholder Association for Research and Education (SHARE) are working with institutional shareholders to submit shareholder proposals that afford a wider expression of investor preferences, a means of enhancing social responsibility, and ultimately greater accountability of managers.[123] The Ontario Teachers' Pension Plan (OTPP) has focused on relationship investing, aimed at maximization of long-term shareholder value through best governance practices. It advocates requiring corporations to publicly disclose the details of all votes taken at annual or special meetings of shareholders.[124] The OTPP also promotes pension law change to emphasize the duty of investment managers to vote their proxies and to disclose to beneficiaries how they voted; currently only 60 percent of these shares are regularly voted.[125]

Recently, institutional shareholders representing $500 billion in assets ($350 billion invested in Canadian publicly traded corporations) formed the Canadian Coalition for Good Governance.[126] The group includes pension funds, mutual funds, and money managers, and its express goal is to align the interests of corporate managers with those of shareholders through informal influence and use of proxy voting, a move likely to enhance governance.

However, the alignment of shareholder and managerial interests does not always mean that the interests of other stakeholders will be protected. It is premature to speculate on the effect of the Coalition's future activities. A key question will be how these investors approach the interests of stakeholders and the question of balancing those interests with those of their own beneficiaries. In many cases, these interests are aligned. The timeline that these shareholders focus on is also important, because short-term return, as opposed to long-term investment, tends to push corporate managers into making decisions that harm workers and create short-term earnings in order to keep investors satisfied. In this respect, there may be a qualitative difference between pension funds, which are trustees for pensioners and workers, and other institutional investors whose objective is short-term return. Scholars such as Susan Stabile and Ronald Davis have suggested that pension funds may offer a means of greater corporate democracy because of the economic power they wield, depending on how they view their fiduciary and trust obligations.[127]

The View from Directors Now

In 2002 the University of British Columbia Faculty of Law conducted a qualitative survey (UBC Governance Survey) of thirty-one corporate directors, holding forty-six directorships on boards of Canadian publicly traded corporations.[128] While the full results have yet to be reported, the initial data offer some important insights into directors' current views of governance. Ninety percent of those surveyed suggested that a non-executive board chair or lead director is fundamental to effective governance. The rationale given was that it affords the board a greater measure of independence in its oversight activities and enhances the corporation's ability to avoid conflicts of interest. According to the TSX, however, only 30 percent of its listed corporations have separated the role of board chair and CEO. Given that it enhances investor confidence and protection of the corporate law regime, it is unclear why the TSX resists making it a mandatory practice, other than the conclusion that managers of Canadian publicly traded corporations are resistant to an independent check on corporate conduct. Absent listing requirements, this percentage is not likely to shift in the short term.

Closely following in terms of the top priorities of the directors surveyed in the UBC Governance Survey was overwhelming support for establishing effective and independent corporate governance committees that promote enhanced disclosure and formalized strategic planning processes. Considerable value was also accorded to in-camera meetings, where directors can assess officer decisions and performance without those officers present. While the UBC Governance Survey revealed that directors intuitively found strong links between good governance practice and corporate performance, they indicated that measuring this link quantitatively is extremely difficult. Most were confident that effective oversight prevents surprises in terms of corporate or officer misconduct. About one-third mentioned the need for enhanced vigilance with respect to audit committees and auditor independence, and in some cases, reconsideration of the amount of consulting work external auditors receive from the firm.

Five Years to the Dey in 1999 indicated that 85 percent of corporate officers believe that director liability is not a deterrent to recruiting directors. Rather, it is the limited pool of experienced directors and the problem of directors holding too many directorships that create a scarcity of directors.[129] These survey results debunk the myth that the liability regime is a deterrent to recruitment of qualified directors who can exercise effective oversight. Canadian case law clearly sets out the expectations of directors under both statutory regimes and the common law, and generally creates a high threshold before directors and officers will be held personally liable.[130] Enhanced insurance and indemnification in corporate statutes has created further protection for corporate directors.

In the UBC Governance Survey, 80 percent of the directors surveyed identified the need for more gender diversity on corporate boards and acknowledged that diversity of views can enhance governance, as long as there is a shared goal of effective governance and a willingness to work together. An effective corporate governance committee responsible for director recruitment and evaluation processes was considered essential. However, almost all attributed the current lack of diversity to the fact that there is not a pool of CEOs who are women, since CEO experience is still viewed as an essential prerequisite to board membership. In the foreword to this book, Purdy Crawford, one of Canada's pre-eminent CEOs and directors, has debunked this myth, suggesting that a variety of skills and experience is essential to an effective corporate board. Several acknowledged that there may be increased opportunities for women with financial expertise, given the normative push for financial literacy post-Enron. Directors on resource-related corporate boards noted the importance of specialized skills of corporate directors, and international experience and geographic representation corresponding to the corporation's business activities. Only two directors discussed the merits of having diverse stakeholders represent the interests of workers, consumers, or community members. About one-half indicated that there had been little or no discussion about racial minority representation, suggesting that the focus is "on skills as opposed to representation by particular groups." One board has a First Nations director to give a First Nations perspective with respect to the corporation's activities within a particular region. Several directors mentioned the need to attract directors from international regions in which the corporation operates, but reported obstacles to moving in this direction. Travel presents a significant barrier to effective participation, and the experience has generally been that telephone participation in board meetings is not an effective substitute for in-person exchange. There was quite pronounced resistance to any regulatory measures that would require more diverse representation on corporate boards.

Interestingly, few directors surveyed reported that their corporations have formal director training programs. All had orientation sessions, and new directors had the opportunity to meet with corporate officers. However, the survey clearly indicated that many directors believe that anyone who does not have sufficient CEO or director experience so that training is not required should not be appointed to the board. This, of course, is a self-fulfilling cycle. If the directors are not diverse, they are unlikely to hire senior officers that reflect the gender and racial makeup of either the corporation or its larger community. Without that senior officer experience, these groups will not be appointed to corporate boards. Without this diversity, corporate conduct that is not considered material to the balance sheet is unlikely to be seriously addressed. One director who was chair of his board was "pleasantly surprised" to find that 60 percent of the corporation's rank and file workers owned stock in the corporation, but had been unaware of this commitment by employees to the corporation's future prospects prior to responding to that question in the survey. Similar responses indicate that directors continue to view workers as fixed capital claimants rather than as long-term investors through their shareholdings and human capital contributions. There was, however, some evidence of concern that employees not under-diversify their risk in terms of equity investments in the corporation, given the harm caused to Enron employees by concentrated shareholdings as their retirement strategy.

The majority of directors surveyed in the UBC Governance Survey indicated that long-term shareholder value is consistent with directors giving consideration to social responsibility issues, including environmental and safety issues. One-half of the directors surveyed suggested that risk assessment now include environmental risks and risks associated with catastrophic events, in addition to financial and intellectual property risks. About 75 percent of those surveyed linked performance and social responsibility. Several directors discussed the conduct of their corporation internationally and the commitment to social responsibility in diverse economies. Two observed that their corporation had experienced fewer adjustment harms with political unrest in other jurisdictions, because their firm had already been engaged in community consultations in terms of their operations there. Thirty percent of directors indicated that this new attention to corporate social responsibility has been driven by institutional and other shareholders, which have focused the board's attention on these issues if the corporation is to retain that investment. This is interesting, in light of the discussions by Gil

Yaron, Ronald Davis, and Cheryl Wade in the chapters that follow, in terms of the potential for shareholder activism to create corporate social and economic accountability.

Refocusing Fiduciary Obligation on All Investments in the Corporation

One of the most disappointing aspects of the governance debate post-Enron is that fiduciary obligation is not being more fully conceptualized. Clearly, its current manifestation has limits even for shareholder protection. Yet there is a more fulsome analysis of the corporation that recognizes wealth maximization as the product of multiple inputs, equity capital investors, debt lenders, trade creditors, employee labour, loyalty, and innovative contributions, and community infrastructure that supports the corporation's activities. These are all investments in the firm. Elsewhere, I have suggested that the interests of creditors, workers, and other stakeholders run along a continuum of fixed and residual interest. The shareholder wealth maximization paradigm should be recast to recognize this continuum of investments and interests in the corporation.[131] Yet the shareholder primacy norm continues to be deeply embedded in Canadian and US corporate law. While the language of corporate law specifies decision making in the "best interests of the corporation," that language has been consistently interpreted by the courts as the best interests of the shareholders. This creates normative pressure to maximize short-term shareholder return, which in turn creates *ex ante* incentives to move liabilities off the balance sheet and externalize harms to workers, consumers, and other creditors. However, shareholders are not the only investors in the firm.

The 1994 Dey Report suggested that boards need to take account of other stakeholder interests in pursuit of wealth-maximizing goals and long-term viability of the corporation. Almost a decade later, however, the debate in Canada about stakeholder interest and reconception of the corporation is at a nascent stage. A January 2002 report by the Canadian Democracy and Corporate Accountability Commission has advanced this debate by conducting national hearings and making a set of recommendations aimed at enhancing corporate governance.[132] A survey conducted for the Commission found that 72 percent of Canadians accept the right of corporations to make profits but also want corporations to accept a broader sense of accountability that extends beyond profit maximization. Eighty percent of Canadians want corporate social responsibility standards established, and a requirement that companies report their compliance with such standards so that shareholders and consumers can make informed decisions. Thirty-six percent of those surveyed were equity capital investors, and the survey results revealed consistency in these views about corporate social responsibility across both shareholding and nonshareholding survey participants.

The survey indicates that the public concerns differ from those that are the focus of current dialogue among securities regulators, stock exchanges, and corporate officers, which persist in pursuing governance reform in the narrow context of the shareholder primacy normative model.

The Commission's recommendations for reform of corporate governance include urging corporations to develop governance structures that facilitate a corporate culture supportive of corporate social responsibility, defined as the corporation responding to interests in addition to the interests of shareholders, including those of employees, suppliers, customers, and communities. It recommends requiring corporations to establish a corporate social responsibility board committee and appoint a senior executive as ombudsperson responsible for corporate social responsibility. The Commission also recommends that corporations should be required to disclose any corporate social responsibility policies and practices in their annual reports or information circulars as a condition of listing on Canadian stock exchanges – setting out their approach and assessing the extent to which their practices conform to corporate social responsibility guidelines set out in stock market listing rules. These corporate social responsibility guidelines should be developed by government with reference to established international indices of corporate social responsibility. The Commission recommended amending the statutory fiduciary obligation of directors to allow directors to take into account other stakeholder interests in acting in the best interests of the corporation. The recommendations call for large companies to provide "social audit" information on the implementation of corporate social responsibility policies and practices, and suggest that there should be a new law protecting employees against adverse employment consequences for "whistle blowing" on corporate noncompliance with laws.

The Commission also urges Canadian governments to work diligently to ensure proper enforcement of existing corporate, securities, consumer, health and safety, criminal, environmental, food, water, and other standards. It recommends that Canadian pension plan managers be expressly allowed to take corporate social responsibility matters into account and should disclose this in their statement of investment policies; that the Canadian government should promote multilateral inclusion of a "social clause" in trade agreements and promote a convention to outlaw violations of basic human rights, workers' rights, and environmental standards as a prerequisite to membership in trade organizations.

The recommendations are aimed at providing enhanced information to investors and the public, but also requiring corporate structures that would have to make individual choices about corporate social responsibility and disclose these choices. The recommendations on fiduciary obligation, while important, need to be accompanied by enforceable remedies by stakeholders with a direct interest in the corporation, or such change would only mirror US constituency statutes, which in some instances have reduced rather than increased accountability to stakeholders. The Commission also makes an important link between the public and private law aspects of corporate activity and electoral democracy. Elsewhere, I have noted that the current shareholder wealth maximization paradigm is a function of long-standing property relations, and the wealthiest equity investors are not going to divest their holdings in favour of a fundamental reconceptualization of the corporation.[133] However, this does not preclude multiple shorter-term strategies and new legislative standards that require corporations to fully disclose and account for their conduct. Statutory provisions enacting the Commission's recommendations could also facilitate a potential alignment of the interests of shareholders, workers, and other stakeholders in having the corporation successfully generate wealth, sustain employment, and reduce human rights, environmental, and other harms.

Wide-Angle View of Governance in Global Markets

Capital Structure: A Normative or Market-Driven Choice?
Governance choices are driven largely by access to capital. The capital structure of the corporation both shapes the internal mechanisms that ensure effective oversight and planning and responds to the regulatory regime that sets the climate for capital investment.[134] However, differing capital structures also generate different tensions among corporate constituencies over the potential for utilizing corporate assets for self-interested behaviour at a cost to other constituents. Diversification of ownership creates accountability problems between managers and dispersed shareholders, whereas concentration of ownership reduces potential for liquidity but allows for lower-cost monitoring. Concentrated voting power creates higher incentives to monitor, but also a risk of blockholder/managerial collusion to the detriment of small shareholders.[135]

The move towards more liquid capital markets presents these investors with the benefits of easier exit but also the problem of reduced ability to monitor managers. Thus ownership and governance structures influence and reflect one another. If the corporation takes a higher portion of debt, the risk is shifted to creditors, and equity holders will tolerate higher risk because they do not have to share any upside benefits. This may explain why firms with block holding tend to be more highly leveraged, as well as why many mergers and acquisitions are highly leveraged. The counter balance is that the high cost of "risky" debt can divert a considerable portion of any upside value to creditors. Thus, the broadly accepted link between concentrated ownership and level of monitoring needs to be qualified to account for leveraging. Although there are higher agency costs of debt, an ownership structure that shifts risk to creditors can mitigate these costs in order to achieve higher monitoring. Following Enron, the claims that the Anglo-American model of corporate governance generated optimal shareholder protection and would inevitably triumph in global capital markets are certainly less compelling. A recognition that all forms of corporate governance involve tensions among those who invest in the corporation is a first step towards recognizing that normative choices are implicated in the capital structure chosen and that the structure's normative impact is also affected by the regulatory context in which it operates.

The normative aspects may become clearer as a result of the growth of multinational corporations. The accompanying increase in mergers and acquisitions has also brought about the need to merge corporate governance structures that function in different economic systems. The assumption has been that more active capital markets will lead to unquestioning adoption of Anglo-American models of corporate governance that are characteristic of liquid capital markets. It is equally plausible, however, that new hybrid models of governance will emerge to reflect more complex capital structures, cross-border ownership, and cross-corporate culture. A corporation owned and registered in one country will be required to comply with domestic law, and also with foreign public laws in terms of governance, consumer protection, anti-discrimination laws, officer liability, and credit systems, thus creating governance models that cross boundaries and systems.[136] While it may seem convenient to global capital investors, the discussion above indicates that it may be impracticable to expect that North American norms of governance will be imported wholesale into corporations operating in diverse systems. Equally, however, investors will be hesitant to invest their capital in jurisdictions where there is legitimate concern over property rights, shareholder remedies, and accountability by corporate decision makers for their governance decisions. As countries seek international capital, much of it grounded in Anglo-American securities regimes, they will be required to move towards a system of enhanced protection of shareholder interests, to the possible detriment of other corporate investors and community members.

The concern about liquid capital markets internationally is key, but it masks an equally important issue that Anglo-American investors face. Capital investors have difficulty not only with weaknesses in minority shareholder rights but also with the more communitarian norms reflective of corporate governance in other countries. Co-determination potentially allows for alliances between workers and minority shareholders in terms of maximizing wealth of the enterprise. Arguably, both could benefit from enhanced monitoring of managers on the shop floor and at the board level. A co-determination model that situated information, decisions, and accountability within the supervisory board could address many of the shareholder concerns raised. One would then be left with the one issue where there is truly normative disagreement, specifically that under German and similar governance models, corporations are managed in the interests of broader numbers of stakeholders. It is this disagreement that needs to be made transparent in the governance debate, because it challenges the Anglo-American shareholder wealth maximization paradigm. Comparative corporate governance scholars frequently assume that efficiency, broadly defined as shareholder wealth maximization and externalization of numerous costs, is the single goal of corporate governance. Only rarely is this narrow concept of efficiency challenged in Anglo-American economies, and governance thus does not take account of other normative policy goals that create optimal wealth maximization, with the costs measured differently.

The Anglo-American paradigm has been that employees do not have investments in the corporation greater than the wage/effort bargain, and thus corporate decision makers should not be accountable to them. Only more recently is there some recognition that the nature of human capital investment may be specialized or beyond fixed capital claims such that their interests need to be accounted for in governance of the corporation.[137] In countries with co-determination models of corporate governance, there are stated objectives of working collectively for the good of both the enterprise and the employees.[138] Co-determination as a conceptual model thus requires further study, in order to draw on those elements of collaboration that may assist in protecting the interests of stakeholders in the governance of the corporation, and that may be amenable to adapting to change in rapidly evolving markets.

Convergence: Real or an Optical Illusion?

The governance debate has resulted in some convergence towards a conceptual understanding of effective corporate governance as necessary to enhancing corporate performance, effectively monitoring activities of managers, and protecting shareholder rights. This debate and the resulting framework, however, have been largely situated within a structure of widely dispersed share ownership that continues to characterize US corporations but that does not reflect the ownership structure of the majority of the world's corporations. The governance debate has also been situated in the context of clear regulatory rules under securities and corporations legislation, comprehensive mechanisms for enforcement, an independent judiciary to enforce shareholder remedies, and a strong common-law tradition of fiduciary obligation. Thus, much of Anglo-American scholarship focuses on the private law aspects of corporate governance because the developed regulatory framework and strong independent judicial system is an operating assumption. Anglo-American scholars take for granted a well-defined system of ownership registration and property protection. Although there have been some notable failures in the North American governance regime, for the most part corporations operate within a regulatory regime that minimizes the risk of such failures, and the regime has in place an infrastructure that will generally respond to the discovery of regulatory failures.[139] Investor protection will normally be given more weight because of the importance of private property in this regime and because investor protection failures tend to have high profiles. In such cases, the state will intervene and collaborate with the private sector to respond to the particular regulatory deficiency.

There is political and social resistance to wholesale importation of Anglo-American private law norms, and this resistance may or may not counter market pressure for convergence.[140] Moreover, importing these norms and practices may not be effective in dealing with the problems of corporate governance that differ from those to which the Anglo-American model responds. Nevertheless, there may be pressure to adopt these norms from investors who will be reluctant to invest in corporations whose governance norms are unfamiliar. Although there is unlikely to be full convergence of governance norms given the different political, economic, and ownership structures internationally, any convergence to date as corporations seek access to global capital is taking the form of movement towards market-based models. This is not, however, a purely market-based trend. While there are public regulatory changes to facilitate the development of securities markets in bank-centred economies, there have not been concurrent regulatory changes to facilitate the movement of foreign banks into the United States or other market economies. Thus, the current arena for competition for capital will be Europe and other economies where banks have played a significant role in governance.[141] The current shifts in securities markets outside of North America should not be taken as a pure market decision in terms of efficient and fully competing capital structures; capital markets continue to be shaped by political choices.

Keeping the Public Interest in Focus

While there is growing recognition that certain regulatory systems must be in place to facilitate movement of capital and provide exit mechanisms in case of firm failure, there are concurrent normative pressures to dismantle other regulatory frameworks in terms of environmental standards and social safety nets.[142] This is a deeply contested debate among scholars and policy makers. There is also debate as to how market convergence will affect protection for stakeholders such as employees. Thus, Anglo-American governance theory is preoccupied with potential rent seeking by employees and with the distributional effects of any governance structures that recognize and value workers as human capital investors. In part, this is because human capital investments are not properly accounted for in valuing inputs to corporate economic activity. Moreover, there is a normative assumption that competitive markets can externalize third-party harms and do not need to take account of this in costing and making efficiency determinations. These assumptions have become key to the Anglo-American shareholder wealth maximization paradigm. Given increasing pressure to compete for global capital, much of it coming from Anglo-American investors, there is pressure on countries such as Germany, France, Italy, and Japan to move towards the Anglo-American model and thus to rethink their recognition and protection of employees and other stakeholders. It is no surprise, given the self-interest of capital investors, that market pressure for convergence of corporate governance norms has not been accompanied by concurrent market pressure to protect employees, small creditors, or other stakeholders in these jurisdictions.

Corporations are dependent on the availability of cost-effective capital. In North America, much of that capital depends on securities markets and secondary trading to establish the corporation's creditworthiness. This dependence gives large investors enormous power to influence corporate activity in their own interests. Absent externally imposed standards on how capital is used and how costs are accounted for, corporations will necessarily conduct their activities with a careful eye on market reaction. While facilitating the expression of investor preferences should strengthen corporate accountability, investors represent only a fraction of society, the fraction that has surplus property to invest. Capital markets cannot and should not replace public law standards and enforcement. What is required is a conception of the corporation that integrates public policy across a range of issues, instead of isolating the securities regime as "private law."

Different governance models internationally accord different priority and treatment to multiple investors, recognizing the diverse inputs into the firm's productivity and generation of wealth. This requires both private law recognition of the value of these inputs and public law protections, given the information asymmetries and inequitable bargaining power such stakeholders face. Best practices of corporate governance should include a strong commitment to compliance with public law and the spirit of laws that are aimed at redressing systemic discrimination, providing protection against tort harms, and preventing violations of labour and environmental standards. Costs need to be measured to account for harms that are currently considered externalities and thus not recorded as costs on the corporate balance sheet. There needs to be a cross-cultural theory of corporate governance that recognizes different normative conceptions of the corporation, and different normative goals for corporate activity.

Conclusion

The norms for effective governance, while important for Canadian corporations domestically, are likely underdeveloped as corporations move into global capital markets in search of either capital or investment opportunities. Governance in the context of global markets requires a deeper understanding of cross-national and cross-cultural economic activity, including an appreciation of how corporate boards exercise oversight and in whose interests. The embracing of norms of transparency and international accounting standards is a shift in governance internationally, in large measure due to market pressure for convergence. Disclosure is a key feature of liquid capital markets, enabling corporations to attract and retain capital, and enabling investors to monitor the use of their equity capital and to influence corporate behaviour by exit. Disclosure of corporate objectives could include policies relating to business ethics and environmental and other public policy commitments, which would enable investors to evaluate the relationship of the corporation and the communities in which they operate.[143]

A key issue for global capital is how to assess risk and potential return when the corporation is operating in another country with different regulatory and cultural norms. The disclosure problem squarely raises the issue of the extent to which managers and controlling shareholders should be accountable to minority and foreign investors. Transparency was historically less of a concern in closely held corporations, because controlling shareholders monitored managers. With the growing diversity of capital structures, however, there are new risks in terms of accountability for rent seeking by controlling shareholders aligned with managers.

Consideration of governance models has also underplayed the powerful role of financial institutions in shaping corporate governance policy in a globally integrated economy. This is particularly the case with respect to the role of international monetary funds and centralized financial institutions in emerging or transition economies.[144] These institutions have had a powerful influence on the debate regarding when and where state regulatory intervention is necessary or beneficial and where it "interferes" with the free flow of capital. It has shaped the debate regarding protection of equity capital as a fundamental principle, to the exclusion of consideration of other kinds of investments, with distributional consequences for economic wealth.[145]

Regulatory reforms are sought to facilitate the global movement of capital by ensuring protection of equity interests, particularly foreign capital and minority investors, in terms of recognition and enforcement of property rights. The importation of international accounting and auditing standards is also sought, to enhance protection of financial institutions and other investors. Yet deregulation is sought to free up labour markets, to encourage free trade and generally discourage regulation that inhibits investment. Thus, regulation is sought to facilitate the global movement of equity capital while the same considerations are not part of the debate for human capital investors. Pressure for these reforms completely bypasses the debate regarding why property in this context is a higher-valued commodity than human capital or other investments. Only costs internal to the corporation are measured in determining efficiency, primarily through the measure of return to shareholders. These inherent tensions stem from the underlying assumptions and deeply embedded norms that the optimal approach to a globally integrated economy is to maximize efficiency by facilitating the ability of corporations, investors, and lenders to compete in global capital markets. While there is no doubt that such competition is a prerequisite for continued economic growth, it may cast the paradigm too narrowly. Arguably, strong political, economic, and social norms will act as a barrier to any fundamental changes in corporate governance absent legislative intervention in the "market." These barriers will be erected because the transaction costs of accomplishing this fundamental change may be viewed as too high, and benefits of a redistributive nature pose too great a challenge to existing property norms to be acceptable to many shareholders.

Acknowledgments

I would like to express my appreciation to the David and Brenda McLean Endowment Fund for providing funding support for this project. My sincerest thanks to Purdy Crawford and Ronald B. Davis for their insightful comments on an earlier draft. Thanks also to the UBC Faculty of Law students who conducted the survey of Canadian corporate directors: Paule Stewart, Michelle Isaak, Marianne Smith, Jamala McRae, Joel Whysall, and Toireasa Jespersen Nelson. Parts of this chapter were drawn from a previously published article: J. Sarra, "Corporate Governance in Global Capital Markets, Canadian and International Developments" (2002) 76 Tulane L. Rev. 1691.

Notes

1 Microsoft Word for Windows 1998 Thesaurus, accessed 1 September 2002; see also *The Oxford Concise Dictionary* (Oxford: Oxford University Press, 1999).
2 John Coffee, "The Rise of Dispersed Ownership: The Roles of Law and the State in the Separation of Ownership and Control" (2001) Yale L.J. 70; Ira Millstein, "Remarks to the Global Conference on Corporate Governance" (July 2000), at 4, <http://www.oecd.org>.
3 Gustavo Visentini, "Comparability and Competition between European and American Corporate Governance: Which Model of Capitalism?" (1998) 33 Brook. J. Int. Law 833 at 835; F. Barca, "Alternative Models of Control: Efficiency, Accessibility and Market Failures," in John E. Roemer, ed., *Property Relations, Incentives and Welfare, International Economics Association* (London: Macmillan, 1997) at 195. In this chapter, "investment" is broadly defined to include equity, debt, human capital, and other contributions to the firm's wealth-generating activities.
4 Eric Posner, "Law, Economics and Inefficient Norms" (1996) 144 U. Pa. L. Rev. 1697 at 1699; Edward Rock and Michael Wachter, "Islands of Conscious Power, Law, Norms and the Self-Governing Corporation" (2001) 149 U. Pa. L. Rev. 1619; Mel Eisenberg, "Corporate Law and Social Norms" (1999) 99 Colum. L. Rev. 1253 at 1256; Marcel Kahan, "The Limited Significance of Norms for Corporate Governance" (2001) 149 U. Pa. L. Rev. 1869; P. Mahoney and C. Sanchirico, "Competing Norms and Social Evolution: Is the Fittest Norm Efficient?" (2001) 149 U. Pa. L. Rev. 2027.

5 See, for example, Margaret Blair and Lynn Stout, "Trust, Trustworthiness and the Behavioural Foundations of Corporate Law" (2001) 149 U. Pa. L. Rev. 1735.

6 J. Sarra, "Corporate Governance in Global Capital Markets, Canadian and International Developments" (2002) 76 Tulane L. Rev. 1691-1748; E. Posner and E.B. Rasmusen, "Creating and Enforcing Norms, with Special Reference to Sanctions" (1999) 19 Int'l Rev. Law and Econ. 369 at 369.

7 Kose John and Lemma Senbet, "Corporate Governance and Board Effectiveness" (1998) 22 J. Bank. and Fin. 371 at 398.

8 Marco Becht, *Strong Blockholders, Weak Owners and the Need for European Mandatory Disclosure. The European Corporate Governance Network Executive Report* (Bruxelles: ECGN, 1997) at 35-36.

9 Toronto Stock Exchange, <http://tsx.com>.

10 Toronto Stock Exchange Committee on Corporate Governance in Canada, *Where Were the Directors? Guidelines for Improved Corporate Governance in Canada* (Toronto: Toronto Stock Exchange, 1994) [hereinafter *Dey Report*]; Institute of Corporate Directors and Toronto Stock Exchange, *Five Years to the Dey* (Toronto, 1999) [hereinafter *Five Years to the Dey*], <http://TSX.com>; TSX News Release, 17 June 1999, <http://TSX.com/news>; Joint Committee on Corporate Governance, *Beyond Compliance: Building a Governance Culture*, Final Report (Toronto: TSX/CNDX/CICA, 2001) [hereinafter *Beyond Compliance*].

11 TSX News Release, *ibid.*

12 Thirty-nine percent of corporations did not have any formal process for risk assessment: *Five Years to the Dey, supra* note 10.

13 *Ibid.*

14 J. Sarra, "Corporate Governance Reform: Recognition of Workers' Equitable Investments in the Firm" (1999) 32 Can. Bus. L.J. 384.

15 M.C. Jensen and W.H. Meckling, "Theory of the Firm: Managerial Behaviour, Agency Costs and Ownership Structure" (1976) 3 J. Fin. Econ. 305 at 305-15.

16 John Braithwaite and Peter Drahos, *Global Business Regulation* (Cambridge, UK: Cambridge University Press, 2000).

17 F.H. Easterbrook and D.R. Fischel, *The Economic Structure of Corporate Law* (Cambridge, MA: Harvard University Press, 1991) at 36-38; E. Fama and M. Jensen, "Separation of Ownership and Control" (1983) 26 J. L. and Econ. 301 at 315; O. Hart, "An Economist's View of Fiduciary Duty" (1993) 43 U.T.L.J. 299 at 303.

18 Jensen and Meckling, *supra* note 15; S. Grossman and O. Hart, "The Costs and Benefits of Ownership: A Theory of Vertical and Lateral Integration" (1986) 94 J. Pol. Econ. 691; R. Rajan and L. Zingales, "Power in a Theory of the Firm" (1998) 113 Q. J. Econ. 387; J. Sarra, "Convergence versus Divergence, Global Corporate Governance at the Crossroads: Governance Norms, Capital Markets and OECD Principles for Corporate Governance" (2001) 33 Ottawa L. Rev. 177-223.

19 R. Daniels, "Must Boards Go Overboard? An Economic Analysis of the Effects of Burgeoning Statutory Liability on the Role of Directors in Corporate Governance" (1994-95) 24 Can. Bus. L.J. 229 at 231.

20 L. Kaplow and S. Shavell, "Should Legal Rules Favour the Poor? Clarifying the Role of Legal Rules and Income Tax in Redistributing Income" (2000) 29 J. Leg. Stud. 821.

21 J. Macey and G. Miller, "Corporate Stakeholders: A Contractual Perspective" (1993) 43 U.T.L.J. 400 at 427.

22 Eugene Fama, "Market Efficiency, Long-Term Returns and Behavioural Finance" (1998) 49 J. Fin. Econ. 283.

23 Lynne Dallas, "The Relational Board: Three Theories of Corporate Boards of Directors" (1996) 22 J. Corp. L.1 at 42.

24 Rock and Wachter, *supra* note 4 at 1643-45.

25 Barbara Ann White, "Essay: Feminist Foundations for the Law of Business: One Law and Economics Scholar's Survey and Review" (1999) 10 UCLA Women's L.J. 39 at 42, 51, 74.

26 Sarra, *supra* note 14.

27 Marleen O'Connor, "The Human Capital Era, Reconceptualizing Corporate Law to Facilitate Labour-Management Co-operation" (1993) 78 Cornell L. Rev. 899 at 958; L.E. Mitchell, "Co-operation and Constraint in the Modern Corporation: An Inquiry into the Causes of

Corporate Morality" (1995) 73 Texas L. Rev. 477 at 501-2; M. O'Connor, "Restructuring the Corporation's Nexus of Contracts: Recognizing a Fiduciary Duty to Protect Displaced Workers" (1991) 69 N.C. L. Rev. 1189 at 1195; David Millan, "Communitarianism in Corporate Law: Foundations and Law Reform Strategies," in L.E. Mitchell, ed., *Progressive Corporate Law* (Boulder, CO: Westview Press, 1995).

28 See Lynne Dallas's discussion in Chapter 8 of this book. See also Lynne L. Dallas, "Two Models of Corporate Governance: Beyond Berle and Means" (1988) 22 U. Mich. L.J. 85.

29 Millstein, *supra* note 2; OECD, *Principles for Corporate Governance* (OECD, 1999), <http://www.oecd.org>; Rafael La Porta *et al.*, "Corporate Ownership around the World" (1998), <http://nberws.nber.org/papers>.

30 Ross Buckley, "Managing Global Capital Flows, Options for Debtor Countries" (Melbourne: Monash University, 2000); S. Edwards, "How Effective Are Capital Controls?" (1999) at 3, <http://www.nber.org/papers/w7413>.

31 Buckley, *ibid.* at 4, 11, 20-21.

32 Ira Millstein, "A Private Sector Perspective on Corporate Governance," Latin American Corporate Governance Roundtable sponsored by the OECD and World Bank (26 April 2000), <http://www.oecd.org>.

33 The RT Capital and Bre-X scandals in Canada are good examples of this. *Re RT Management Capital Inc. et al.* (20 July 2000) Order of the Ontario Securities Commission, <http://www.osc>; J. MacIntosh, "Lessons of Bre-X (?) Some Comments" (1999) 32 Can. Bus. L.J. 223; Jeffrey Gordon, "Pathways to Corporate Convergence? Two Steps on the Road to Shareholder Capitalism in Germany" (1999) 5 Colum. J. European Law 219 at 221.

34 Visentini, *supra* note 3 at 849.

35 Raphael La Porta *et al.*, "Legal Determinants of External Finance" (1997) 52 J. Fin. 1131; J. Gordon, "The Mandatory Structure of Corporate Law" (1989) 89 Colum. L. Rev. 1549 at 1555.

36 European Union Acquired Rights Directive, Eur. Rep. (9 January 1999) (Lexis, Nexis Library, Curnws File).

37 L. Bebchuk and M. Roe, "A Theory of Path Dependence in Corporate Ownership and Governance" (1998) Stanford L. Rev. See also Curtis Milhaupt, "Property Rights in Firms" (1998) 84 Va. L. Rev. 1145; John Coffee, "The Future as History: Prospects for Global Corporate Governance" (1999) 93 Northwestern U. L. Rev. 641; Raphael La Porta *et al.*, "Corporate Ownership around the World" (1999) 54 J. Fin. 471; T. Nenova, "The Value of Corporate Votes and Control Benefits: A Cross-Country Analysis, <http://papers.ssrn.com/paper.taf?abstract_id=237809>.

38 Coffee, *supra* note 2 at 7.

39 Visentini, *supra* note 3.

40 Sarra, *supra* note 6.

41 F. Barca and M. Becht, eds., *Ownership and Control: A European Perspective* (Brussels: Free University of Brussels, 1999).

42 A. A. Berle and G.C. Means, *The Modern Corporation and Private Property* (New York: Commerce Clearing House, 1932) at 355, 356.

43 S. Nesbitt, "Long-term Rewards from Shareholder Activism: A Study of the CalPERS Effect" (1994) J. Applied Corp. Fin. (winter) at 75.

44 C. Ayotte, "Re-evaluating the Shareholder Proposal Rule in the Wake of *Cracker Barrel* and the Era of Institutional Investors" (1999) 48 Cath. U. L. Rev. 511 at 539.

45 C. Mayer , Peter Moores Professor of Management Studies Lecture, Oxford University (Brussels: ECGN, 2000) at 8.

46 Mark Roe, *Strong Managers, Weak Owners: The Political Roots of American Corporate Finance* (Princeton, NJ: Princeton University Press, 1994); Becht, *supra* note 8.

47 Roberta Romano, "Comment on LaPorta, Lopez-de-Silanes and Shleifer, Corporate Ownership around the World" (1999) European Corporate Governance Network, <mbecht@ulb.ac.be> (copyright with owners).

48 Becht, *supra* note 8 at 37; Visentini, *supra* note 3 at 838.

49 Visentini, *supra* note 3 at 840-41.

50 Viet Dinh, "Co-determination and Corporate Governance in a Multinational Business Enterprise" (1999) J. Corp. L. 975 at 979-83.

51 Visentini, *supra* note 3 at 844.
52 Becht, *supra* note 8 at 4.
53 Colin Mayer, "Firm Control," Lecture, Oxford University (18 February 1999), citing C. Mayer and J. Franks, "Ownership and Control" in C. Mayer and J. Franks, ed., *Trends in Business Organization* (Tubingen: JCB Mohr, 1995) at 6-7.
54 *Ibid.* at 11; L. Zingales, "The Value of the Voting Right: A Study of the Milan Stock Exchange Experience" (1997) 7 Rev. Fin. Studies 125.
55 The term *Keiretsus* in this respect is used by North American scholars on a broader basis than in Japan. See Masafumi Nakahigashi and Janis Sarra, "Balancing Social and Corporate Culture in the Global Economy: The Evolution of Japanese Corporate Structure and Norms" (2003) 24 Law and Policy 299-350.
56 S. Prowse, "The Structure of Corporate Ownership in Japan" (1992) 47 J. Fin. 1121 at 1126.
57 Roe, *supra* note 46 at 101; Masahiko Aoki, "Toward an Economic Model of the Japanese Firm" (1990) 28 J. Econ. Lit. 1.
58 Ronald J. Gilson and Mark J. Roe, "Lifetime Employment: Labour Peace and the Evolution of Japanese Corporate Governance" (1999) 99 Colum. L. Rev. 508 at 531.
59 *Ibid.*
60 *Ibid.* at 526.
61 For a discussion of these developments, see Nakahigashi and Sarra, at 55.
62 Nakahigashi and Sarra, *ibid.;* Curtis Milhaupt and Mark West, "Institutional Change and M&A in Japan, Diversity through Deals" (2002), <http://204.60.194.172/milhauptwest.htm>.
63 Mark West, "Why Shareholders Sue: The Evidence from Japan" (2001) 30 J. Leg. Stud. 351.
64 Nakahigashi and Sarra, *supra* note 55.
65 *Ibid.*
66 Coffee, *supra* note 2 at 70.
67 *Ibid.*
68 D. Branson, "The Very Uncertain Prospect of Global Convergence in Corporate Governance" (2001) 34 Cornell Int'l L.J. 321 at 338.
69 Erik Berglof and Ernst-Ludwig von Thadden, *The Changing Corporate Governance Paradigm: Implications for Transition and Developing Countries* (Stanford, CA: Center for Advanced Study in Behavioral Sciences, 1999) at 18-23.
70 Branson, *supra* note 68 at 353, 358.
71 Asian Corporate Governance Association, *Building Stronger Boards and Companies in Asia: A Concise Report on Corporate Governance Policies and Practices* [ACGN, 2000, on file with the author].
72 Global Corporate Governance Forum; see also European Association of Securities Dealers, "Corporate Governance Principles and Recommendations" (2000), <http://www.easd.com>, which propose "Pan-European Principles for Corporate Governance" that are remarkably Anglo-American shareholder-centric.
73 Coffee, *supra* note 2 at 14; Branson, *supra* note 68 at 337.
74 Committee on Corporate Governance, *Code of Best Practice for Corporate Governance* (Korea: Committee on Corporate Governance, 1999).
75 Draft report of the Kumar Mangalam Committee on Corporate Governance at 6.
76 Katharina Pistor, *Patterns of Legal Change: Shareholder and Creditor Rights in Transition Economies*, Working Paper No. 49 (European Bank for Reconstruction and Development, 2000), <http://www.ebrd.com/pubs/index.htm>.
77 *Ibid.* at 3 and the studies cited therein.
78 Pistor notes a distinction in the pretransition legal frameworks of countries with German legal heritage, such as Croatia, the Czech Republic, Estonia, Hungary, Poland, and Slovenia (what she calls the CEE/Baltics); those initially receiving French law, including Bosnia, Herzegovina, Albania, Macedonia, Bulgaria, and Romania; and those comprising the former republics of the Soviet Union, except the Baltic states: *ibid.* at 6.
79 Using a different set of indices to measure creditor rights, she suggests that legal reform such as strong *ex post* control rights are responsive to problems in protection of rights, as opposed to proactive or pre-existing norms; these are remedies that allow creditors to invalidate pre-bankruptcy transactions, and that allow creditors to hold shareholders,

particularly parent companies, liable for debt incurred by corporations just prior to bankruptcy: *ibid.* at 20.

80 Berglof and von Thadden, *supra* note 69.

81 *Ibid.* at 19, 20, 26.

82 Report of the Permanent Subcommittee on Investigations of the US Senate Committee on Governmental Affairs, *The Role of the Board of Directors in Enron's Collapse,* 8 July 2002, Report 107-70, 107th Congress, 2d session at 6 [hereinafter *Senate Committee Report*]; Faith Kahn, "Remember the Titans, Enron and the Fallen Towers of Trade" (2002) 76 Tulane L. Rev.

83 *Senate Committee Report, ibid.* at 46-48. See also the *Report on Investigations by the Special Investigative Committee of the Board of Directors of Enron Corporation* (1 February 2002) [hereinafter *Powers Report*] at 97.

84 *Senate Committee Report, supra* note 82 at 44; *Powers Report, ibid.* at 25 at 4, 25, 99, 133.

85 *Senate Committee Report, ibid.* at 44.

86 *Ibid.* at 55-56.

87 *Ibid.* at 55.

88 Dallas, *supra* note 28.

89 Toronto Stock Exchange, Request for Comments, Corporate Governance Policy – Proposed New Disclosure Requirements and Amended Guidelines (26 April 2002), <http://www.tsx.com>.

90 "Unrelated director" is defined as a director who is independent of management and is free from any interest and any business or other relationship that could, or could reasonably be perceived to, materially interfere with the director's ability to act with a view to the best interests of the company, other than interests and relationships arising from shareholding: Toronto Stock Exchange, *Company Manual,* s. 472, Corporate Governance Guidelines [hereinafter *Company Manual*].

91 *Ibid.,* s. 473(12), Guidelines.

92 *Beyond Compliance, supra* note 10 at 22.

93 *Ibid.*

94 *Five Years to the Dey, supra* note 10 at 5-6.

95 *Company Manual, supra* note 90, s. 472.

96 *Ibid.* at 2.

97 *Five Years to the Dey, supra* note 10 at 6.

98 Barbara Stymiest, President and CEO, Toronto Stock Exchange, "Capital Market Trends" (May 2000), <http://TSX.com/news>.

99 For a discussion of this, see J. Sarra, "Rose-Coloured Glasses, Opaque Financial Reporting and Investor Blues: Enron as Con and the Vulnerability of Canadian Corporate Law" (2002) 73 St. John's L. Rev., New York 101.

100 H.R. 3763, 107 Congress 2002, July 2002.

101 Canadian Securities Administrators (CSA) Disclosure Policy, <http://www.osc.gov.on.ca/>.

102 The TSX urging its listed companies to write the CSA, <http://www.tse.com/en/medianews/newsreleases/>.

103 Ontario Securities Commission, Communiqué, "OSC Increases Continuous Disclosure Reviews – More Staff, Higher Targets, Deficient Companies to Be Named" (15 August 2002), <http://www.osc.gov.on.ca>.

104 Since 2000, the ASB has been engaged in a program to harmonize Canadian accounting standards with those in the United States: <http://www.osc.gov.on.ca>.

105 The term "analyst" applies to several functions: "sell-side" analysts work at full-service investment dealers; those typically employed by institutional investors are on the "buy-side"; and other analysts, frequently classified as independent, sell their research on a subscription basis: *ibid.*

106 *Ibid.*

107 There is a voluntary Code of Ethics and Standards in use internationally, issued by the Association for Investment Management: *ibid.*

108 Securities Industry Committee on Analyst Standards, *Setting Analysts Standards: Recommendations for the Supervision and Practice of Canadian Securities Industry Analysts,* Final Report (Toronto: TSX, Investment Dealers Association, 2001), <http://www.TXE.com>.

109 *Ibid.* at 46-47. Disclosure of conflicts would be required in each research report and recommendation, including: where the Pro-Group (a defined term) holds any class of a company's securities (long or short) that in the aggregate exceed 5 percent of outstanding securities of that class; where the analyst or his or her associates hold or are short in any of the company's securities, directly or through derivatives; and where remuneration has been received from the company for services or if the firm has acted as underwriter or advisor within 24 months preceding the report or recommendation. For a discussion of Pro-Group and IDA By-Law 29.15, see *ibid.* at 11. There are also recommendations regarding transparency and readability of the disclosure.

110 *Ibid.* at 71.

111 Purdy Crawford, Response to the Draft Recommendations of the *Beyond Compliance* Report, on file with author, cited with permission.

112 Sarra, *supra* note 14.

113 Word Thesaurus, *supra* note 1.

114 *Canada Business Corporations Act,* R.S.C. 1985, c. C-44, as am. by S.C. 2001, c. 14 [hereinafter *CBCA*], in force 24 November 2001; *Canada Business Corporations Regulations,* SOR/01-2139, <http://canada.gc.ca/gazette/hompar2-2_e.html>; Industry Canada's "Regulatory Impact Analysis Statement," 2001 <http://strategis.ic.gc.ca/SSG/cs01381e.html>.

115 *CBCA, supra* note 114, s. 137(1.1).

116 S. 137(5) of the *CBCA,* prior to the most recent amendments.

117 Re *Varity Corp. and Jesuit Fathers of Upper Canada* (1987), 60 O.R. (2d) 640 (C.A.).

118 *CBCA, supra* note 114, s. 137(5)(b.1).

119 See Chapter 6 of this book.

120 *CBCA, supra* note 114, s. 150.

121 *Ibid.,* ss. 68, 147.

122 Janis Sarra, "Shareholders as Winners and Losers under the Amended *CBCA*," (forthcoming, 2003, Can. Bus. L.J.).

123 SHARE, <http://www.share.ca/>.

124 OTPP, Submission to the Standing Senate Committee on Banking Trade and Commerce (26 May 2002) at 4, <http://www.otpp.com/web/website>.

125 *Ibid.* at 3.

126 OTPP, "Institutional Investors Form Coalition to Fight for Improved Corporate Governance" (27 June 2002), <http://www.otpp.com/web/website.nsf/web/coalitionforcorpgov>.

127 Susan Stabile, US Senate Committee Presentation (2001); Ronald B. Davis, "Enron and Two Aspects of the Pension Puzzle" (September 2002) (on file with author).

128 The survey was conducted between 5 January and 1 May 2002, through in-depth telephone and in-person interviews conducted by six UBC Faculty of Law students. Each interview lasted from thirty minutes to two hours, and participants were given the questions in advance. The results are currently being tabulated and will be publicly reported, although the directors asked for strict confidentially in terms of attributing particular statements.

129 *Five Years to the Dey, supra* note 10 at 18.

130 For a discussion of this issue, see J. Sarra and R.B. Davis, *Director and Officer Liability in Corporate Insolvency* (Toronto: Butterworths, 2001) c. 2 and the cases cited therein.

131 Sarra, *supra* note 6.

132 Canadian Democracy and Corporate Accountability Commission, *The New Balance Sheet, Corporate Profits and Responsibility in the 21st Century* (January 2002) [hereinafter *The New Balance Sheet*].

133 Sarra, *supra* note 14.

134 M. Jensen, "The Modern Industrial Revolution, Exit and the Failure of Internal Control Systems" (1993) 48 J. Fin. 862 at 863-65; H. Manne, "Mergers and the Market for Corporate Control" (1965) 73 J. Pol. Econ. 110; William Carney, "The Legacy of the 'Market for Corporate Control' and the Origins of the Theory of the Firm" (1999) 50 Case Western Reserve L. Rev. 215; Becht, *supra* note 8 at 23.

135 Becht, *supra* note 8 at 23; R. Heinrich, "Complementarities in Corporate Governance: Ownership Concentration, Capital Structure, Monitoring and Pecuniary Incentives." Working Paper (Kiel Institute of World Economics, Duesternbrooker, Germany, 2000) at 10.

136 D. Logue and J. Seward, "Anatomy of a Governance Transformation: The Case of Daimler-Benz" (1999) 62 Law and Contemporary Problems 87.

137 Sarra, *supra* note 14 at 418-29; M.M. Blair, *Ownership and Control: Rethinking Corporate Governance for the Twenty-First Century* (Washington, DC: Brookings Institution, 1995).

138 *Mitbestimmungsgesetz* (1996) 5 Commercial Laws of Europe 483-91; *Betriebsverfassungsgesetz (Works Constitution Act, 1992)* (Germany), as amended February 2001, 87ff, 94-96ff, 111ff.

139 For example, in response to the Bre-X scandal in Canada, a joint Toronto Stock Exchange/Ontario Securities Commission Task Force addressed standards for listing mining sector corporations: "Setting New Standards: Recommendations for Public Mineral Exploration and Mining Companies" (Toronto: TSX/OSC, 1999).

140 Jamie Allen, "Code Convergence in Asia: Smoke or Fire?" (2000) Corporate Governance Int'l at 1. Allen is Secretary General, Asian Corporate Governance Association (ACGA), <http://www.acga>.

141 Visentini, *supra* note 3 at 845.

142 Sarra, *supra* note 14 at 385.

143 Sarra, *supra* note 18.

144 J. Wolfensohn, "A Proposal for a Comprehensive Development Framework," <http://www.worldbank.org>; World Bank, *The State in a Changing World* (World Bank, 1997); J. Stiglitz, "More Instruments and Broader Goals: Moving toward the Post-Washington Consensus," <http://www.wider.unu.edu/stiglitz>.

145 OECD, *Principles for Corporate Governance* (OECD, 1999), <http://www.oecd.org>; United Nations Development Programme, *Human Development Report* (United Nations, 1999).

3
Governance, Mergers and Acquisitions, and Global Capital Markets
Christopher C. Nicholls

Mergers and acquisitions have recently been described as "undoubtedly among the most significant macroeconomic phenomena of the industrialized West during the last twenty years."[1] The recent volume of M & A activity had been especially large, at least prior to the dampening effects of the 2001 market slowdown, the shock of the 11 September terrorist attacks, and recent uncertainty plaguing global capital markets. The value of deals announced worldwide in 2000, for example, has been estimated at more than US$3.3 trillion.[2] While the vast majority of such transactions are negotiated, rather than unsolicited or hostile bids, the number of hostile bids is still significant. For a variety of reasons, including, among others, increasing international pressures to achieve economies of scale and the abolition of pooling of interests accounting (which necessarily limited the range of suitable acquisition partners and led to negotiated mergers), it is not improbable that the number of hostile bids may increase in future.

The United States is often thought to be the centre of most hostile takeover activity. Various explanations for this apparent feature of American markets have been offered, including the widespread phenomenon of dispersed share ownership of American public corporations, the high degree of US competition, and the acceptance of the economic benefits of an active market for corporate control. One commentator has even ambitiously suggested the possibility that "hostile takeovers are more likely in countries that score high on Masculinity and Individualism, or respectively, on Mastery and Autonomy."[3] The empirical data support the view that hostile bids were more prevalent in the United States during the 1980s; although more recently (i.e., over the past five years), based upon available empirical data, the position seems somewhat more ambiguous. For example, Weston and Weaver report that in 1997, 0.5 percent of all merger and acquisition transactions in the United States were hostile, compared with 1.2 percent in the rest of the world.[4] In 1998, 0.2 percent of US transactions were hostile, compared with 1.1 percent in the rest of the world.[5] In 1999, 7 percent of US transactions were hostile, compared with 22.2 percent in the rest of the world.[6]

The study of merger and acquisition activity, particularly hostile takeover bids, is linked to the issue of corporate governance because of the external discipline said to be provided by contestability of corporate management or, as it is usually called, the market for corporate control.[7] Indeed, as Macey and Miller have written, "the market for corporate control lies at the heart of the American system of corporate governance."[8]

What is less clear is whether the market for corporate control has emerged as an essential element in American corporate governance because of distinctive features of the US regime, including laxity in mandatory US corporate law protections for shareholders and the absence of effective monitoring by controlling shareholders, or whether, instead, stronger corporate law protections and concentrated share ownership have not developed in the United States because an active market for corporate control has made these developments unnecessary.

The uncertain explanation for the prominence of the market for corporate control as a feature of American governance clutters the otherwise tidy theory that international corporate governance practices ought to be expected to converge as increasing globalization puts pressure upon firms to achieve ever higher levels of operating efficiencies.[9] American "market system" corporate law and governance practices have long differed from structures arising in countries with so-called blockholder systems, such as Germany. But many commentators have questioned whether it is the relentless pursuit of efficiency or merely path-dependency that accounts, in whole or in part, for the development of the features of either system.[10]

The same forces of globalization that are thought to lead to international convergence of internal corporate governance practices might also be expected to encourage greater uniformity in the rules relating to corporate control. In particular, if, as some commentators argue, US corporate governance norms are destined to become the world standard,[11] then surely the market for corporate control – which plays such a key role in American governance – must also develop along American lines in other jurisdictions. Yet, if there is to be convergence in the operation of the market for corporate control, then the legal framework within which corporate control transactions occur will also need to converge, at least functionally.[12] Thus, similar questions arise as to the inevitabilty or desirability of international convergence of takeover rules, among other things.

Unquestionably, the market/blockholder dichotomy that has been identified as a barrier to the development of universal corporate law and corporate governance standards is also highly relevant to the prospect of the international convergence of rules governing mergers and acquisitions, especially those applicable to hostile takeover bids. There have been recent indications, however, notwithstanding the narrow failure in July 2001 of a new European takeover directive, that even in traditional blockholder systems, there is growing acceptance of the value of fostering an active market for corporate control. Whether this development represents the inevitable triumph of efficiency or a bold leap of economic faith remains a matter of contention. It is worthwhile to consider how the prospects for convergence in corporate control regimes fits within the broader issue of converging governance standards.

Legal Systems and the Impetus for Convergence

As Douglass North has observed, in a world of incomplete information, institutions play an essential role, and formal rule changes that depart from informal institutional mechanisms can threaten to destabilize a political system.[13] Accordingly, any comparative study of corporate law and corporate governance must be wary of too hastily concluding that apparent evidence of inherent "superiority" of any single national system necessarily means that other, "laggard" systems are inevitably destined to either evolve into "higher" forms or face inevitable decline and eventual economic extinction. Nonetheless, a growing body of scholarship does suggest that, in a world where capital can move easily across borders in pursuit of the highest returns, companies will enjoy a competitive advantage in the form of lower cost of capital when they operate subject to legal systems and pursuant to corporate governance standards that enhance shareholder value and provide adequate protection for investors, particularly those investors holding minority equity interests. For this reason, where jurisdictional differences in legal rules or governance norms impair firm value, one should expect to see pressure within such jurisdictions to reform.

Seeking thus to link financing and investment patterns to jurisdictional variations in corporate laws and governance, commentators have reported correlations between certain features of domestic legal systems and observed patterns of corporate financing,[14] suggesting that "strong" legal systems facilitate the advantageous use of external finance by corporations operating thereunder, while "weak" legal systems impose inefficient financing constraints upon corporations.[15]

In the mergers and acquisitions context, these systemic differences are important because of their relationship to the emergence of concentrated share ownership, a key factor in the development of an active market for corporate control. Specifically, poor legal protection for minority investors is said to be correlated with enhanced private benefits of control for insiders and holders of control blocks of equity. Thus, as Coffee,[16] La Porta *et al.*,[17] and others have concluded, an explicit connection may be drawn between the strength of legal protections for minority shareholders and the development of blockholder systems, the existence of which, in turn, affects the corporate control dynamic. Put simply, it is argued that in systems that do not afford adequate minority shareholder protection, minority equity interests are largely illiquid; accordingly, investors have an incentive to take large positions and, thereupon, to actively monitor management. Systems in which controlling share interests are the norm will also afford the holders of such blocks the opportunity to receive benefits in excess of their proportionate "share" of the corporation's cash flows. And as discussed further below, the presence (or absence) of a controlling shareholder has a profound and often determinative impact on the efficacy of the market for corporate control as a managerial discipline.

Market systems, such as those of the United States and the UK, are thought, according to this theory, to afford minority shareholders sufficient protections to ensure that their interests remain marketable. Such shareholders feel considerably less vulnerable and so have reduced incentive to protect themselves by acquiring large equity stakes. A corollary effect of greater minority shareholder protection, however, is that share ownership in American firms tends to be more dispersed, and problems with undertaking collective action consequently militate against effective monitoring. Although American institutional shareholders may often assume an active role in firm governance, their effectiveness in this area, according to financial economists, remains uncertain.[18] The key implication of this story, however, is that there is less impetus for investors to acquire control blocks, and consequently more scope for the operation of the market for corporate control.

In highly competitive international markets, it has been argued, international governance differences are not indefinitely sustainable. The very survival of firms may depend upon the proliferation of investor-friendly rules and norms. According to this story, then, we should expect to see convergence of legal and governance systems, absent other barriers, although precisely what form that convergence will or ought to take remains a matter of contention.[19]

Of course, this convergence theory is open to criticism. One might reasonably question, after all, whether or not differences between countries that supposedly share similar systems are not at least as great as between systems themselves. Further, some commentators have posited that this explanation of inevitable convergence overlooks important cultural factors that could, indeed, lead to a very different outcome from that predicted by the convergence model.[20] Moreover, as Bebchuk and Roe have argued, there is reason to believe that the development of corporate governance systems is path-dependent, and that significant international differences could indeed persist, "notwithstanding the forces of globalization and efficiency."[21] In addition, one notes that according to one explanatory model, there is a link between distinctive American share ownership patterns and weak shareholder protections in American corporate law, whereas according to another explanatory model, it is the relative weakness of shareholder protections in civil law jurisdictions that account for observed differences in ownership patterns. The difficulty is that both convergence and nonconvergence stories can plausibly explain observed international developments to date, leaving those of us who are not content to substitute dogma for analysis in the uncomfortable position of not knowing in which direction public policy and law ought properly to be nudged.

If the question of convergence of governance norms is complex and uncertain, the prospects for convergence of the framework within which corporate control transactions may be effected are doubly so. Corporate control transactions necessarily engage not only internal corporate governance practices but also external regulation. As Hansmann and Kraakman have observed, corporate governance practices are likely to converge internationally more rapidly than corporate legislation;[22] and in the corporate control context, corporate governance norms and practices are often intimately linked to the structure of a jurisdiction's corporate and securities legislation. Moreover, the market for corporate control may operate through multiple channels, including proxy contests, sales of control blocks, and even ostensibly friendly merger transactions, as well as hostile takeover bids. Each of these mechanisms is subject to its own complicated overlay of legal and procedural considerations. The balance of this chapter, however, focuses primarily on hostile bids because they, necessarily, involve attempts to shift control on both sides of the principal/agent divide by not only unequivocally bypassing managers but also displacing economic rather than merely managerial control.

Agency Problems and the Market for Corporate Control

The Firm

Theories of the firm, capital structure, financial intermediation, and corporate governance are necessarily interconnected. Firms provide the means by which resources are pooled for indivisible enterprise,[23] and securities evidence the financial claims through which the resources of dispersed investors are aggregated and deployed in the real economy. Once the providers of capital and the users of capital are distinct, governance issues are unavoidable.[24] While pooling of capital permits firms to reach levels of size sufficient to benefit from optimal economies of scale,[25] the larger the public firm, it has been suggested, the greater becomes the risk of corporate governance problems.[26]

The Agency Problem and the Putative Shareholder Primacy Norm

The importance of the market for corporate control derives from the inevitable agency problems encountered in modern firms where ownership (or perhaps, more technically, residual economic benefit)[27] and control are separate.

The identification of a governance "problem" implies a departure from some idealized norm, however. Accordingly, the framing of an idealized corporate regime usefully begins with an articulation of the descriptive and normative significance of the shareholder primacy norm – a notion, chiefly articulated in US academic writing, that the primary (or perhaps exclusive) duty of corporate directors is to act in the interests of the shareholders. A conventional rationalization of shareholder primacy notes that while other corporate constituents' interests are protected by explicit contract or external regulation, the shareholder's residual economic interest enjoys no such protection. It is thus appropriate that the directors' fiduciary duty be owed to the shareholders alone. Indeed, it is argued that such a duty is efficient, since the shareholders have the best incentive to monitor directors' performance,[28] leading to better-managed corporations and healthier national economies. The celebrated American judicial decision that remains the strongest twentieth-century statement of this proposition and that has become a mainstay of law school corporate law courses is the 1919 American case of *Dodge* v. *Ford Motor Co,*[29] and a widely-cited English decision pointing in a similar direction is *Parke* v. *Daily News Ltd.*[30]

The shareholder primacy norm is much beloved by law and economics scholars,[31] financial economists,[32] and dogmatic conservatives generally.[33] Some critics have challenged the shareholder primacy norm, however, at least at the descriptive if not the normative level, arguing that strong evidence exists to show that corporations are not, in fact, run solely with shareholders' interests in mind.[34] To be sure, this criticism alone is not fatal to the recognition of a fiduciary duty to shareholders (rather than to the corporation as an entity) because, as Macey has argued, the fiduciary duty may itself best be understood as a residual claim of the shareholders; accordingly, shareholders remain free to bargain away some portion of the duty (to accommodate, for example, the securing of adequate credit, the hiring of good employees, etc.). Whatever is not bargained away, however, remains the shareholders' alone.[35] More trenchant criticisms of the putative norm have been raised, though, and, whatever the normative power of the shareholder primacy model, it does not seem unfair to suggest that the legal pedigree of shareholder primacy is at least questionable in the United States,[36] and arguably rests on even less substantial foundations in Canada.

In the United States, to begin with, it has been suggested that the shareholder primacy norm was originally developed, more than a century before the Dodge/Ford decision, in the context of resolving disputes between majority and minority shareholders, not between shareholders and other corporate stakeholders. Simply put, when courts first asserted that corporations must be operated for the benefit of all the stockholders, the emphasis was intended to be placed upon the word "all" not upon the word "stockholders."[37] This interpretation is consistent with the conclusion reached by Joseph

H. Sommer following a historical review of US banking legislation.[38] Sommer concludes that the very development of the business corporation as the dominant form of business organization in America can be understood in terms of an attempt to address fears of exploitation by majority business owners:

> The eighteenth-century business community preferred corporate govern-ance in business affairs for the same reason it preferred Constitutional gov-ernance in political affairs: members needed to limit their creature's own power. The late eighteenth-century corporate charter provided unique pro-tection against expropriation by majority stockholders, protection that other forms of organization could not supply.[39]

Nor, for example, did the famous American study of the emergence of the modern corporation by Berle and Means,[40] as Cynthia Williams has recently noted,[41] embrace a shareholder primacy norm, but rather concluded that the corporation "should not be operated solely for the benefit of sharehold-ers"[42] owing to the "concentration of [corporate] power in the economic field."[43]

In the Canadian legal context, there are more complications still. It is simple enough to state what the duty of directors of a Canadian corpora-tion is: "to act honestly and in good faith with a view to the best interests of the corporation." That is the language found in the *CBCA*[44] and in many other Canadian provincial corporate statutes.[45] Occasionally, Canadian prac-titioners choose to paraphrase (or, more precisely, to rephrase) the direc-tors' mandate as a duty "to act in the best interests of the corporation and the shareholders."[46] This alternative formulation, it may be thought, is only intended to state in practical terms what must be implicit in language that would otherwise place directors in the curious position of owing their fe-alty to an inanimate legal fiction.[47] It is important to reiterate, however, that the typical Canadian corporate statute does not, in fact, refer to a spe-cific directorial duty to shareholders, and omission of the word "sharehold-ers" was evidently deliberate and not merely drafting oversight.[48] Some early common law decisions spoke of directors' duties in relation to sharehold-ers,[49] but it is not clear to what extent these early statements have been, or ought to be, qualified by more refined concepts of the corporation as legal entity and express statutory formulations of directors' duties.[50] At least one reading of the leading *Percival* v. *Wright*[51] decision casts doubt on the exist-ence of such a fiduciary duty to shareholders – at least in all circumstances. *Martin* v. *Gibson*[52] has on occasion been cited for the proposition that the shareholders comprise the company and so are the only rightful beneficiar-ies of directors' duties;[53] but a close reading of *Martin* suggests that the court was there expounding a view, as Sommer discusses in the context of older

American authorities,[54] relating to the relationship of majority to minority shareholders, not the relationship of shareholders to other potential corporate stakeholders. The influential Dey Report expressed support for the shareholder primacy norm,[55] but the more recent report of the Saucier Committee was more ambivalent in its discussion of the subject,[56] notwithstanding that a research report prepared for the Committee advanced a shareholder primacy view.[57] Perhaps most importantly, however, Canadian courts continue, from time to time, to question the bald assertion that a corporation is synonymous with its shareholders.[58]

Of course, for lawyers, although perhaps not for financial economists, there are also troublesome technical difficulties with which to grapple in attempting to define a duty to shareholders as a legal matter. Is the duty of the directors, for example, to maximize dividends? One can hardly imagine any Canadian lawyer or judge seriously entertaining such an outlandish proposition. Dividend policy is, in any event, according to modern financial economic theory, largely irrelevant to firm (and common share) value, except perhaps as a signalling mechanism,[59] and the very fact that the declaration of dividends remains entirely within the directors' discretion makes any suggestion of a duty to maximize dividends wholly untenable. In the simplest sense, it has long been recognized that, ultimately, the value of any financial claim must bear some relation to the generation of cash flows.[60] Still, it is clear that there is certainly no duty to maximize dividend payments. Should the shareholder primacy norm be regarded, then, as a duty to maximize corporate profits? Or something else? Financial economists have an elegant answer to the question: the most sensible goal for corporate directors to pursue is to ensure the maximization of shareholder wealth[61] through the maximization of the firm's share price, or, perhaps equivalently, to maximize some agreed measure of *economic* (rather than accounting) profit,[62] such as EVA.[63]

But even putting aside questions of the legal pedigree and practical interpretation of the shareholder primacy norm, a more fundamental problem with the concept remains. The welfare effects of the shareholder primacy norm have not infrequently been challenged. Perplexing questions remain as to whether the unabashed pursuit of shareholder interest – Milton Friedman's famous article aside[64] – does indeed ultimately serve the public good. Commentators have noted that, assertions to the contrary notwithstanding,[65] the shareholder primacy norm could, in fact, lead to decisions that destroy firm value,[66] and so decrease societal wealth. There are at least two dimensions to this issue. First, is the general argument in support of shareholder wealth maximization as a socially valuable goal valid in any case? Second, even if the argument is sound within certain legal contexts, is it necessarily valid in all contexts?[67]

Shareholder Primacy and the Market for Corporate Control

A comprehensive review of the implications of the shareholder primacy norm is well beyond the scope of this chapter. It need only be noted here that it is sometimes said that the shareholder primacy norm has assumed special significance in the context of the market for corporate control.

To understand the role of shareholder primacy in the context of corporate control, it is useful to recall the central economic argument said to support the value of fostering an active market for corporate control. The basic insight of Manne, that the threat of takeovers can enhance shareholder value by serving as an effective check on potentially opportunistic managers, has been extended in the agency cost literature, by Jensen and others.[68] The empirical literature generally supports the proposition that takeovers increase the value of target companies,[69] and that jurisdictions that inhibit the launching of hostile bids adversely affect the value of corporations incorporated there.[70] This view is further buttressed by findings that adoption of takeover defences by a firm leads to a decrease in the value of that firm, although, to be fair, the shareholder wealth effects of takeover defences remains a matter of some debate.[71] Nor is the long delay between the "discovery" of the potential benefits of contesting management and the widespread appearance of hostile takeovers in the United States necessarily inconsistent with the notion that the value of takeovers is genuine and easily recognized. Rather, the apparently sudden proliferation of hostile bids may, it has been suggested, be linked to certain macroeconomic factors. Specifically, commentators have suggested that what may have prompted the apparently sudden interest in the 1980s in seeking to unlock value through hostile takeovers may have been the sustained period of high real interest rates in the 1980s that raised investors' opportunity cost of capital, and so accelerated demands on corporate managers to deliver superior returns on equity.[72]

Needless to say, however, the view that hostile bids have beneficial effects upon the value of target companies specifically and for society more generally has occasionally been challenged. For example, Stein has argued that the observed increase in target company share prices accompanying the launching of a bid may simply be the result of the bid's signalling effect upon the price of shares that were previously being (improperly) underpriced by the market.[73] How such underpricing (or discounting) may have arisen has itself fuelled academic inquiry.[74] Moreover, the effect of bids on the value of *acquiring*, as opposed to *acquired*, corporations is somewhat more equivocal.[75] Further, there are skeptics who argue that – despite the apparent empirical evidence to the contrary – takeover bids may not, in fact, be wealth enhancing,[76] may encourage managers of firms vulnerable to takeover to inefficiently pursue short-term opportunities at the expense of increasing long-term value,[77] and may not be an effective discipline on managers because of minority shareholder free-riding problems[78] or because of the significant scope left for managerial opportunism given standard bid premia;[79] and that they may be pursued for a variety of reasons – such as managerial hubris[80] or the pursuit of personal prestige[81] – that have little to do with a rational calculation aimed at unlocking value.

More specifically, however, if hostile bids do, in fact, increase value, then it is important to understand the source of this value creation. It is in relation to this issue that the analysis of the market for corporate control is fundamentally affected by the shareholder primacy issue. As Mitnick has noted: "If the firm operates to the benefit of its shareholders then expropriation of excess contract value would be both rational and justified. However, if the firm should be managed for the benefit of stakeholders – labor, contracting parties, and creditors – then [hostile takeovers could actually result in welfare losses]."[82]

Moreover, if an effective market for corporate control is value enhancing, and if laws and governance norms tend to move towards ever-more efficient forms, then at least two phenomena are puzzling. First, in the United States, where the market for corporate control is said to be most vigorous, the sudden wave of takeovers in the 1980s prompted many US states to seek to protect local firms from hostile raiders through the enactment of anti-takeover "constituency statutes."[83] Although the first generation of these statutes encountered constitutional obstacles,[84] later versions survived constitutional challenge[85] and continue in place today. This proliferation of state anti-takeover constituency statutes, according to Roe, resulted not from any concerns about the adverse social effects of takeovers but rather from a power struggle. He argues that the explosion of corporate merger activity in the 1980s disrupted the relative managerial autonomy enjoyed within such corporations earlier in the century, and that subsequent anti-takeover legal reforms are best viewed as the product of successful power jockeying by those same corporate managers.[86]

However, even if one dismisses these developments as the actions of corporate "rogue" states, may one still reasonably assume that global pressures will indeed lead corporate laws and governance practices throughout the world to reflect the shareholder/director relationship implicit in the law of the state that is so often identified as the leading US (public) corporate law jurisdiction, namely, Delaware? Is the Delaware standard, in other words, to be viewed as the most economically efficient, the polestar that should now guide the development of takeover law in all other jurisdictions?

At first glance, such a proposition may seem to embody an apparent contradiction. The presumed economic benefits of an active market for corporate control would seem to suggest that jurisdictions that favoured a less prominent role for directors of companies subject to hostile bids would be rewarded by the marketplace. In many key respects, however, Delaware is not such a jurisdiction. Indeed, a leading Delaware jurist has described the Delaware law of corporate control as based upon a director-centred model rather than upon a model that would give "primacy to the stockholders' right to react to tender offers without substantial target board involvement."[87] Indeed, the fact that Delaware law is so widely favoured by large US corporations despite its apparent weaknesses (especially in the takeover context) has been identified by Black and Kraakman as proof of path-dependency in the US corporate charter competition.[88] Of course, it ought not to be forgotten that while Delaware law has come to *permit* defensive measures, it does not mandate them. It is for this reason that Easterbrook and Fischel have argued that takeover defence measures are simply another basis for healthy firm competition:

> Promoting or deterring tender offers is just one of the dimensions in which firms compete. Left alone, corporations could offer investors as many different regimes of tender offer bidding and defense as they now offer different investment instruments and governance structures. The more beneficial a structure for investors, the more likely it is to survive.[89]

Moreover, although Delaware law is broadly tolerant of directors' defensive measures, subject to consistently affirmed principles of perception of threat and reasonableness of managerial response,[90] the Delaware courts are guided by a certain shareholder primacy principle in the sale of control context. The Delaware courts have recognized that where directors of a company being sold do not act to maximize current value for their existing shareholders, such shareholders will, among other things, forever lose the opportunity to obtain a premium for the purchase of their shares.[91] It is this special case of shareholder primacy that is said, in particular, to explain the so-called *Revlon* duty[92] under Delaware law, including the famous "qualification" to the duty that arises in the case of share exchange offers by publicly traded offerors with no controlling shareholder.[93]

While the implications of the *Revlon* duty appear to have become reasonably well settled in Delaware and the circumstances in which such a duty will be triggered have also, over time, become passably transparent,[94] three points warrant mention here. First, the development of the *Revlon* duty was, arguably, necessary in Delaware in order to counterbalance the otherwise "director-centered model"[95] of takeover law chosen by the Delaware courts in the 1980s. Second, the shareholder primacy aspect of the *Revlon* duty has been specifically rejected by legislation in many other US states.[96] In other words, there has not been convergence even within the United States with respect to this issue. Finally, it is not clear that the governance implications of Delaware takeover law have, in fact, been adopted outside the United States, either in Canada[97] or elsewhere. The principles of corporate governance of the Organization for Economic Cooperation and Development (OECD), for example, expressly depart from the Delaware standard, a fact that was recently noted by the Chief Justice of the Delaware Supreme Court.[98] But if the absence of convergence is merely evidence of the fact that the Delaware regime is not optimal for public companies, what, then, is to be made of the fact that Delaware is so favoured by large US corporations?[99] If convergence is the inevitable result of relentless pressure to increase shareholder value, why have these pressures not appeared to have such an impact in the United States? If the answer is that factors other than a drive for optimal efficiency, such as path-dependency,[100] explain US corporate law and governance evolution, then could such other factors not also be expected to shape the development of the legal regimes under which corporate control transactions are carried out internationally? Moreover, one questions whether certain US-style legal reforms have been proposed internationally, premised, perhaps, on the assumption that US models must be market-oriented because they have emerged in a market system.

While it would be foolish indeed to draw hasty conclusions about the prospect for convergence based on this very superficial canvass, one only notes that there may be more to the governance convergence question than the conventional observation of differences in patterns of shareholdings and shareholder protection measures in the US and UK market systems on the one hand and the European (especially German) blockholder system on the other. In fact, the most recent European initiative suggests that Europe may be moving towards a system that – formally at least – is far more conducive to a shareholder-centred market for corporate control than any US state. This initiative is briefly discussed in the next section.

Recent European Initiatives

It is sometimes asserted that European views on takeovers can be neatly bifurcated. The UK market model is, like the US model, conducive to takeovers, an attitude embodied in the City Code on Takeovers and Mergers, which, one commentator suggests, referring to Rule 21 of the Code, "embodies the philosophy that shareholders own the company and the board manages it."[101] This observation, however, may reflect an American attempt to re-create the British in their own image. The Code's General Principles do not unequivocally advance a theory of the shareholders as "owners" of the corporation, saying, rather: "It is the shareholders' interest taken as a whole, *together with those of employees and creditors,* which should be considered when the directors are giving advice to shareholders."[102]

Rule 21 itself does impose restrictions on defensive measures involving the issuance of shares and major asset sales, and the payment of breakup fees (or "inducement fees," as the rule calls them). But such provisions are surely aimed at curbing management opportunism rather than recognizing shareholders as the "owners" of the corporation.

As for the rest of Europe's approach to corporate takeovers, the saga of the so-called Thirteenth Directive in Europe is by now well known. Beginning its life over thirteen years ago, quietly abating in 1994 then resurfacing in renewed form in 1996, the Thirteenth Directive was passed by the European Council in 2000, but ultimately defeated in the European Parliament in July 2001 (in a remarkable tie vote), owing largely, it is generally agreed, to opposition against the measure rallied by Germany.[103] Indeed, the apparent intransigent opposition of Germany, in particular, to any legal reforms that might enhance the European market for corporate control has often been cited as evidence of the continental divide on the matter.

In response to the failure of the Thirteenth Directive, the European Commission established a "High Level Group of Company Law Experts" under the chairmanship of Jaap Winter to provide advice on the creation of new pan-European takeover rules. The High Level Group released its report on 10 January 2002[104] and, to the surprise of some observers, Germany appears prepared to support the initiative.[105] Accordingly, the report represents a significant development, and merits at least brief discussion here.

The report specifically recognizes the wealth-creating and managerial discipline value of takeovers:

> Takeovers are a means for bidders to create wealth by exploiting synergies between their existing business and the target company. Many European companies will need to grow to an optimal scale to make effective use of the integrating internal market ... Actual and potential takeover bids are an important means to discipline the management of listed companies with dispersed ownership, who after all are the agents of shareholders ... Such discipline of management and reallocation of resources is in the long term in the best interests of all shareholders and society at large.[106]

The report further advocates a takeover regime guided by two principles: the primacy of the shareholder's right to decide whether or not to tender to a bid, and proportionality between risk-bearing capital and control. From these principles, the report derives a view of takeover defences that would allow considerably less scope than Delaware law for directors to institute defensive measures in response to hostile bids, a distinction that the report itself expressly acknowledges.[107]

Where a company's corporate charter contains takeover-impeding measures (whether these were passed before or after the bid was launched), the report recommends that a successful bidder ought to be able to "break through" such measures, provided the bid has been accepted by a specified super-majority of the target company's shareholders.[108] The effect of such breakthrough rights would be to ensure that a bidder who acquires a specified super-majority of a target company's shares enjoys all the normal incidents of control, subject to mandatory co-determination rules in countries where such rules exist.[109] The breakthrough rule would not, however, attempt to address barriers that arise as a result of pyramidal holding structures,[110] which are, evidently, common in Europe and indeed are thought to represent one of the important ways in which shareholdings in many jurisdictions differ from shareholding patterns in US and UK companies.

Conclusion

Formal and informal pressures for international convergence of corporate governance practices will undoubtedly increase in the coming decade. Cross-border acquisitions, in particular, must inevitably have an impact on the sustainability of significant international legal and governance variations. But while it is certainly plausible to assert that we should expect to see convergence of governance norms in response to the development of an international market for corporate control that is unfettered by inefficient, protectionist rules, the story is a complex one and public policy makers should be careful not to mistake the plausible for the incontrovertible.

Notes

1 Yedidia Z. Stern, "A General Model for Corporate Acquisition Law" (2001) J. Corp. L. 675 at 676.

2 Patricia A. Vlhakis, "Takeover Law and Practice 2001" in Practising Law Institute, *33rd Annual Institute on Securities Regulation* (New York: PLI, 2001) at 291.

3 Amir N. Licht, "The Mother of All Path Dependencies: Toward a Cross-Cultural Theory of Corporate Governance Systems" (2001) 26 Delaware J. Corp. L. 147 at 199.

4 J. Fred Weston and Samuel C. Weaver, *Mergers and Acquisitions* (New York: McGraw Hill, 2000) at 115.

5 *Ibid.*

6 *Ibid.*

7 The significance of the market for corporate control as an effective managerial discipline was first identified by Henry Manne in his seminal paper "Mergers and the Market for Corporate Control" (1965) 3 J. Pol. Econ. 110.

8 Jonathan R. Macey and Geoffrey P. Miller, "Corporate Governance and Commercial Banking: A Comparative Examination of Germany, Japan, and the United States"(1995) 48 Stanford L. Rev. 73.

9 The "market" system/"blockholder" system dichotomy is frequently referred to in comparative corporate governance literature. See, for example, William W. Bratton and Joseph A. McCahery, "Comparative Corporate Governance and the Theory of the Firm: The Case" (1999) 38 Colum. J. Transnat'l L. 213. See also Rafael La Porta *et al.*, "Corporate Ownership around the World" (1999) 54 J. Fin. 471.

10 Canada would appear to more closely resemble a "blockholder" than a market system. For example, as Morck has found, based on Canadian and American studies from the 1980s, only 16 percent of the largest Canadian corporations were widely held, compared with 50 percent of the largest US firms: Randall Morck, "On the Economics of Concentrated Ownership" (1996) 26 Can. Bus. L.J. 63 at 69. Of course, it is possible that ownership concentration is diminishing, and at least one theoretical model would predict that, as Canadian companies become larger, they will also become more widely held. However, Daniels and

Halpern's research suggests that precisely the opposite pattern has been observed in Canada, namely, that "the evidence suggests that ownership concentration increased over a period in which there was sustained economic growth and decreased when growth was reduced": Ronald J. Daniels and Paul Halpern, "Too Close for Comfort: The Role of the Closely Held Public Corporation in the Canadian Economy and the Implications for Public Policy" (1996) 26 Can. Bus. L.J. 11 at 32. Daniels and Halpern suggest, preliminarily, that the development of concentrated corporate ownership in Canada might be explained by reference to "the delayed effects of industrial development, the distortionary effects of government trade and investment protection policy, and, to a lesser degree, on the role of the Canadian banks in efficient debt monitoring": *ibid.* at 45.

11 See, for example, Hansmann and Kraakman, *infra* note 22.

12 See the discussion in Chapter 2 of this book.

13 Douglass C. North, *Institutions, Institutional Change and Economic Performance* (Cambridge, UK: Cambridge University Press, 1990).

14 See, for example, Rafael La Porta *et al.,* "Investor Protection and Corporate Governance" (2000) 58 J. Fin. Econ. 3; Rafael La Porta *et al.,* "Legal Determinants of External Finance" (1997) 52 J. Fin. 1131.

15 Among the most important of these commentaries are the works of La Porta *et al.* See, for example, Rafael La Porta *et al.,* "Law and Finance" (1998) 106 J. Fin. 52; "The Quality of Government" (1999) 15 J. L. Econ. and Org. 222; "Investor Protection and Corporate Governance" (2000) 58 J. Fin. Econ. 3. They conclude, among other things, that, "as a general rule ... civil law countries, particularly French civil law countries, are more interventionist than common law countries. The inferior protection of the rights of outside investors in civil law countries may be one manifestation of this general phenomenon." To similar effect are the conclusions of Bernard Black, who posits that the development of strong securities markets is dependent upon the existence of institutional norms that ensure adequate disclosure of corporate information to minority equityholders along with assurances that managerial opportunism will be contained or eliminated. See Bernard S. Black, "The Core Institutions that Support Strong Securities Markets" (2000) 55 Business Lawyer 1565; and "The Legal and Institutional Preconditions for Strong Securities Markets" (2001) 48 UCLA L. Rev. 781. The argument for convergence does assume that capital can, and will, flow readily across international borders in the absence of barriers. However, financial economists have observed that, in fact, investors tend to have a (perhaps irrational) home country investment bias. See, for example, Ian Cooper and Evi Kaplanis, "Home Bias in Equity Portfolios and the Cost of Capital for Multinational Firms" (1995) 8 J. Applied Corp. Fin. 95.

16 John C. Coffee, Jr., "The Future as History: The Prospects for Global Convergence in Corporate Governance and Its Implications" (1999) 93 Northwestern U. L. Rev. 641 at 647.

17 La Porta *et al., supra* note 9 at 496, conclude that a "comparison of countries with good and poor shareholder protection shows that widely-held firms are more common in countries with good protection."

18 Burkhart, Gromb, and Panunzi argue that, even where shareholder monitoring is *ex post* efficient, it can have an *ex ante* disincentive effect on managerial incentive. See Mike Burkhart, Denis Gromb, and Fausto Panunzi, "Large Shareholders, Monitoring, and the Value of the Firm" (1997) Q. J. Econ. 693. For a broader review of the financial economic literature on institutional investor activism, see Roberta Romano, "Less Is More: Making Institutional Investor Activism a Valuable Mechanism of Corporate Governance" (2001) 18 Yale J. on Reg. 174. For a discussion of the issue in the Canadian context, see Robert Yalden, "Concentrated Control, Institutional Investors and Shareholder Responsibilities" (1996) 26 Can. Bus. L.J. 86; and Jeffrey G. MacIntosh, "Institutional Shareholders and Corporate Governance in Canada" (1996) 26 Can. Bus. L.J. 145.

19 The Hampel Committee, for example, suggested that "there are signs that market development may lead to convergence, with greater emphasis than before in continental Europe on 'shareholder value'": see *Committee on Corporate Governance Final Report* (London: The Committee on Corporate Governance and Gee Publishing, 1997) para. 1.4. There are competing views, for example, as to whether fundamental "indivisible" features of so-called

"blockholder" systems (such as those of Germany) on the one hand and market systems (such as those of the US and the UK) on the other affect or constrain such convergence. See, for example, Bratton and McCahery, *supra* note 9, in which the authors survey the literature in which the arguments are advanced with respect to the prospects for "hybrid" convergence on the one hand and hegemonic convergence (reflecting the ultimate triumph of the market system) on the other. The authors conclude that a hybrid theory of international convergence lacks merit.

20 Bratton and McCahery, *supra* note 9. See also Thomas J. Courchene, "Corporate Governance as Ideology" (1996) 26 Can. Bus. L.J. 202, esp. at 203: "national approaches to corporate governance are inextricably linked to the underlying societal values, with the feedbacks going in both directions. Indeed, it probably could not be otherwise." The impact for Canada, Courchene notes, is a curious one: "We espouse a German-style social contract but we have latched on to American-style corporate governance" (at 207).

21 Lucian A. Bebchuk and Mark J. Roe, "A Theory of Path Dependence in Corporate Governance and Ownership" (1999) 52 Stanford L. Rev. 127.

22 See Henry Hansmann and Reinier Kraakman, "The End of History for Corporate Law" (2001) 89 Geo. L.J. 439 at 455.

23 Sirri and Tufano, for example, argue that the development of the corporate form was a crucial step in facilitating pooling, which was advantageous both for firms (which could access the capital necessary to grow to optimal size) and individual investors (for whom pooling offered advantages of diversification, liquidity, and cost-effective monitoring of their investments). They even argue that pooling provided for more equitable distribution of wealth. Without pooling, only the wealthy could finance large firms and, to the extent that such large firms enjoyed economies of scale, they could outperform smaller firms, ensuring that the wealthiest investors became wealthier still. See Erik R. Sirri and Peter Tufano, "The Economics of Pooling" in Dwight B. Crane *et al.*, eds., *The Global Financial System: A Functional Perspective* (Boston: Harvard Business School Press, 1995) at 81.

24 This is the problem of the separation of ownership and control most often associated with the seminal work of Adolf Berle and Gardiner Means, *The Modern Corporation and Private Property* (New York: Macmillan, 1932).

25 The question of what economic factors will determine the optimal size of firms has been canvassed at length. One of the earliest theoretical examinations of the issue was Ronald H. Coase's paper, "The Nature of the Firm" (1937) 4 Economica 386. More recent theories include Oliver Hart's incomplete contracting or property rights model. See Oliver Hart, *Firms, Contracts, and Financial Structure* (Oxford: Clarendon Press, 1995).

26 See, for example, Michael C. Jensen, "The Modern Industrial Revolution, Exit, and the Failure of Internal Control Systems" (1993) 48 J. Fin. 831.

27 Margaret Blair has said that "the notion that a corporation's assets are the property of shareholders is intellectually dishonest, and any thoughtful legal scholar or economist knows it." Quoted in *Transcripts of Proceedings – Corporate Charity: Societal Boon or Shareholder Bust?* (1998) 28 Stetson L. Rev. 52 at 67.

28 See, for example, Frank H. Easterbrook and Daniel R. Fischel, *The Economic Structure of Corporate Law* (Cambridge, MA: Harvard University Press, 1991).

29 N.W.668.

30 [1962] 1 Ch. 927.

31 See, for example, Easterbrook and Fischel, *supra* note 28.

32 The suggestion that corporations ought to be operated with the goal of maximizing shareholder wealth is a standard feature of corporate finance texts. See, for example, Zvi Bodie and Robert C. Merton, *Finance* (Upper Saddle River, NJ: Prentice Hall, 2000) at 11. (Bodie and Merton are, however, careful to qualify this rule to make clear that it is subject to legal and ethical constraints, and further include an express assumption "that the goal of maximizing shareholder wealth does not necessarily conflict with other desirable social goals." *Ibid.* at note 3). Steven Kaplan has argued that a departure from the shareholder wealth maximization goal destroys value, and that, indeed, just such value destruction occurred in the United States prior to the 1980s, when "top executives were as loyal to employees and other stakeholders as they were to shareholders. This loyalty led to under-utilized

resources." The takeover activity of the 1980s, he argues, helped correct this unfortunate situation. See Steven Kaplan, "Riding on the Benefits of the LBO Wave" in Financial Times, *Mastering Finance* (London: Pitman Publishing, 1998) 405 at 407.

33 Perhaps the most famous articulation of the shareholder primacy norm came from Milton Friedman in his celebrated *New York Times Magazine* article "The Social Responsibility of Business Is to Increase Its Profits" *N.Y. Times Magazine* (13 September 1970). As has been noted by many subsequent commentators, the dominant view among finance academics is that corporations ought to maximize shareholder wealth, not corporate profits.

34 Margaret M. Blair and Lynn A. Stout, "A Team Production of Corporate Law" (1999) 85 Va. L. Rev. 247.

35 Jonathan R. Macey, "Fiduciary Duties as Residual Claims: Obligations to Nonshareholder Constituencies from a Theory of the Firm Perspective" (1999) 84 Cornell L. Rev. 1266.

36 See, for example, Margaret M. Blair and Lynn A. Stout, "Director Accountability and the Mediating Role of the Corporate Board" (2001) 79 Wash. U.L.Q. 403 at 406, in which the writers suggest that, despite the recent apparent dominance of the shareholder primacy norm in the academic and business commentary, "the 'shareholder primacy' claim seems at odds with a variety of important characteristics of US corporate law. Despite the emphasis legal theorists have given shareholder primacy in recent years, corporate law itself does not obligate directors to do what the shareholders tell them to do. Nor does corporate law compel the board to maximize share value. To the contrary, directors of public corporations enjoy a remarkable degree of freedom from shareholder command and control. Similarly, the law grants directors wide discretion to consider the interests of other corporate participants in their decision making – even when this adversely affects the value of the stockholders' shares." Of course, most students of corporate governance are familiar with the celebrated law review exchange between Adolf Berle and Merrick Dodd in the 1930s. Berle argued in favour of the shareholder primacy norm; Dodd favoured what today might be dubbed the stakeholder constituency view. See A.A. Berle, Jr., "Corporate Powers as Powers in Trust" (1931) 44 Harv. L. Rev. 1049; E. Merrick Dodd, Jr., "For Whom Are Corporate Managers Trustees?" (1932) 45 Harv. L. Rev. 1145; A.A. Berle, Jr., "For Whom Corporate Managers *Are* Trustees: A Note" (1932) Harv. L. Rev. 1365.

37 D. Gordon Smith, "The Shareholder Primacy Norm" (1998) J. Corp. L. 277.

38 Joseph H. Sommer, "The Birth of the American Business Corporation: Of Banks, Corporate Governance, and Social Responsibility" (2001) 49 Buffalo L. Rev. 1011.

39 *Ibid.* at 1013.

40 Adolf A. Berle, Jr., and Gardiner C. Means, *The Modern Corporation and Private Property* (New York: Macmillan, 1932).

41 Cynthia A. Williams, "The Securities and Exchange Commission and Corporate Social Transparency"(1999) 112 Harv. L. Rev. 1199 at 1215-21.

42 *Ibid.* at 1219.

43 *Ibid.*, quoting Berle and Means, *supra* note 40.

44 *Canada Business Corporations Act,* R.S.C. 1985, c. C-44, s. 122(1)(a) [hereinafter *CBCA*].

45 See *Business Corporations Act* (Alberta), R.S.A. 1981, c. B-15, s. 117; *Corporations Act* (Manitoba), R.S.M. 1987, c. C.225, s. 117; *Business Corporations Act* (New Brunswick), R.S.N.B. 1981, c. B-9.1, s. 79; *Corporations Act* (Newfoundland), R.S.N. 1990 c. C-36, s. 203; *Business Corporations Act* (Ontario), R.S.O. 1990, c. B16, s. 134(1)(a); *Business Corporations Act* (Saskatchewan), R.S.S. 1978, c. B-10, s. 117.

46 See James E.A. Turner, "A Guide For Directors: How Directors Can Navigate the Potential Problems of M and A's" *Ivey Business Journal* (July/August 2000) 74: "directors are so-called fiduciaries. That means that they have a duty to act honestly and in good faith for the benefit of the corporation *and its shareholders* ... The requirement that directors act in the best interests of the corporation means that they must act in the best interests of the shareholders as a whole, *in the sense that the shareholders are the ultimate owners of the corporation"* (emphasis added).

47 L.C.B. Gower commented on this untenable position in this way: "Despite the separate personality of the company it is clear that directors are not expected to act on the basis of what is for the economic advantage of the corporate entity disregarding the interests of its

members. They are, for example, clearly entitled to recommend the payment of dividends to the members and are not expected to deny them a return on their money by ploughing back all the profits so as to increase the size and wealth of the company": *Gower's Principles of Modern Company Law*, 5th ed. (London: Sweet and Maxwell, 1992) at 554.

48 The Dickerson Committee specifically declined "to give precision to the notion of 'the best interests of the corporation.'" See R.V. Dickerson *et al., Proposals for a New Business Corporations Law for Canada (Vol. I)*, para. 241. The Committee did, however, appear to reject the shareholder primacy view, referring to a passage in Gower's *Modern Company Law*, 3rd ed., in which Gower had described the shareholder primacy view as "anachronistic." The Dickerson Committee indicated that Gower's characterization was "charitabl[e]." See also *Parke* v. *Daily News Ltd., supra* note 30.

49 See, for example, *Re Iron Clay Brick Mfg. Co.* (1889), 19 O.R. 113, in which Robertson J. states that a director must give "his whole ability, business knowledge, exertion and attention to the best interests of the shareholders who had placed him in that position," at 123.

50 See, for example, Bruce Welling *et al., Canadian Corporate Law* (Toronto: Butterworths, 1996). The authors, after describing as a summary of the nineteenth-century articulation of the directors' duty the case of *Re Iron Clay Brick Mfg. Co., ibid.*, suggest that the language in this case may be subject to qualification owing to "the impact of certain subsequent judicial rulings – corporations being recognized as legal persons separate from the shareholder collective in 1897" (at 227).

51 [1902] 2 Ch. 421.

52 (1907), 15 O.L.R. 623. See, in particular, p. 632, where Boyd C. states: "Now, the persons to be considered and to be benefited are the whole body of shareholders – not the majority, who may for ordinary purposes control affairs – but the majority plus the minority – all in fact who, being shareholders, constitute the very substance (so to speak) of the incorporated body."

53 See *Teck Corp. Ltd.* v. *Millar* (1973), 33 D.L.R. (3d) 288 [hereinafter *Teck*].

54 See Sommer, *supra* note 38.

55 See Toronto Stock Exchange Committee on Corporate Governance in Canada, *Where Were the Directors? Guidelines for Improved Corporate Governance in Canada* (Toronto: Toronto Stock Exchange, 1994) [hereinafter *Dey Report*] para. 2.2(2): "We define the principal objective of directing and managing the business and affairs of the corporation as enhancing shareholder value." To be sure, however, the Report does go on to introduce some politically important qualifications to this statement: para. 2.2(4).

56 Joint Committee on Corporate Governance, *Beyond Compliance: Building a Governance Culture*, Final Report (Toronto: TSX/CNDX/CICA, 2001) at 7: "The object of good governance is to promote strong, viable and competitive corporations. Boards of directors are stewards of the corporation's assets, and their behaviour should be focused on adding value to those assets by working with management to build a successful corporation and enhance shareholder value." By way of comparison, in the UK, the Hampel Committee, in its report on corporate governance, appears to adopt a much clearer version of the shareholder primacy norm, stating that "the single overriding objective shared by all listed companies ... is the preservation and the greatest practicable enhancement over time of their shareholders' investment": para. 1.16. This duty, they explain, "is to shareholders both present and future": para. 1.18.

57 Richard Leblanc, *Getting Inside the Black Box: Problems in Corporate Governance Research*, <http://www.cica.ca/multimedia/Download_Library/Research_Guidance/Risk_Management_Governance/GettingInside_Leblanc.pdf>. "Although the beneficiary of the fiduciary duty is 'the corporation,' a legal fiction, in practice and in jurisprudence, the ultimate duty is becoming fairly well-established, and that is to act in the interests of all shareholders."

58 See, for example, *Rogers Communications Inc.* v. *Maclean Hunter Ltd.*, [1994] O.J. No. 408 per Farley J.: "The influence of the American experience seems to pervade – shareholder concerns appear uppermost, possibly without appreciating that the Supreme Court of Canada in *Ringuet* v. *Bergeron* ... discussed the concept of the corporation as being more than just an aggregate of shareholder interests. Our business and legal culture may be affected by the US

experiences, however, we do have a separate culture even in these areas." One of the most well-known Canadian judicial comments on the shareholder/stakeholder issue is found in the judgment of Berger J. in *Teck*, *supra* note 53: "If today the directors of a company were to consider the interests of its employees no one would argue that in doing so they were not acting *bona fide* in the interests of the company itself. Similarly, if the directors were to consider the consequences to the community of any policy that the company intended to pursue, and were deflected in their commitment to that policy as a result, it could not be said that they had not considered *bona fide* the interests of the shareholders." This "stakeholder constituency" statement, however, formed no essential part of the judgment since, in fact, counsel for the party seeking to impugn the actions of the defendant directors in the case appeared to accept that those directors, in resisting the overtures of the plaintiff, Teck, were acting with a view to maximizing the firm's share value. "They [the directors] ... believed that the value of Afton's shares ... would decline under Teck's management." Accordingly, the actions of the defendant directors in *Teck* would, it seems, have been upheld even applying a strict rule of shareholder primacy.

59   The economic irrelevance of a firm's dividend policy is associated with the work of Franco Modigliani and Merton Miller. See especially Franco Modigliani and Merton Miller, "Dividend Policy, Growth and the Valuation of Shares" (1961) 34 J. Bus. 411. For a discussion of the theory that a change in dividend policy may be used as a signalling device where information asymmetries exist between firm managers and shareholders, see William F. Sharpe *et al.*, *Investments*, 3rd Canadian ed. (Toronto: Prentice Hall Canada, 2000) at 549. For a more formal discussion of financial signalling, see Stephen A. Ross, "The Determination of Financial Structure: The Incentive Signalling Approach" (1977) 8 Bell J. Econ. 23.

60   It was John Burr Williams, writing in 1938, who emphasized the importance, in valuing common shares, of considering the dividends paid to the shareholders' shares, noting that earnings "are only a means to an end, and the means should not be mistaken for the end. Therefore we must say that a stock derives its value from its dividends, not its earnings": John Burr Williams, *The Theory of Investment Value* (Cambridge, MA: Harvard University Press, 1938) at 57. Williams, of course, was writing before the revolutionary papers on capital structure and dividend irrelevance published by Modigliani and Miller in the late 1950s and early 1960s. But even in the post Modigliani-Miller world, the significance of cash distributions to share valuation has been recognized. Warren Buffett, for example, has defined the intrinsic vale of a corporation's share in terms of "the discounted value of the cash that can be taken out of a business during its remaining life": Warren E. Buffett, *Berkshire Hathaway Inc. An Owner's Manual*, cited in Christopher C. Nicholls, *Corporate Finance and Canadian Law* (Toronto: Carswell, 2000) 87 (note 31).

61   See Bodie and Merton, *supra* note 32 at 11. Bodie and Merton are careful to emphasize that they do not advocate a shareholder wealth maximization rule that ignores legal and ethical considerations: "This rule ... assumes that managers do not make decisions that are illegal or unethical." As indicated below, the *Dey Report* on corporate governance concluded that the objective of a corporation was to enhance shareholder value. See *Dey Report*, *supra* note 55. The impact of modern financial theory on the interpretation of directors' legal duties has been adverted to by Hu, who declared in 1990 that "the law pertaining to the pecuniary objectives of the corporation has been rendered obsolete by modern financial theory": Henry T.C. Hu, "Risk, Time, and Fiduciary Principles in Corporate Investment" (1990) 38 UCLA L. Rev. 277 at 295.

62   The OECD's Business Sector Advisory Group on Corporate Governance asserted that "most industrialized societies recognize that generating long-term economic profit (a measure based on net revenues that takes into account the cost of capital) is the corporation's primary objective" (*Corporate Governance: Improving Competitiveness and Access to Capital in Global Markets, A Report to the OECD by the Business Sector Advisory Group on Corporate Governance* [OECD, 1998] at 2). Although certainly the use of economic profit has become common among many corporations, it is not clear that such widespread use has gained any legal recognition that would justify the claim that "societies" recognize the pursuit of such a measure as a corporation's primary objective. The OECD Principles of Corporate Governance adopted in 1999, although purporting to "build upon" (among other things)

the Advisory Group's work (OECD, *OECD Principles of Corporate Governance* [OECD, 1999] at 3) was far more equivocal on the question of shareholder primacy, and included express language dealing with the importance of nonshareholder constituents (part 3, at 7).

63 EVA is an acronym for "Economic Value Added," a trademark of Stern Stuart and Co. For a discussion of EVA, see Christopher C. Nicholls, *Corporate Finance and Canadian Law* (Toronto: Carswell, 2000) at 132-33.

64 Friedman, *supra* note 33.

65 It was Charles Erwin Wilson, a former president of General Motors, who, as a nominee for US Secretary of Defense in 1953, articulated the supposed relationship between corporate prosperity and national prosperity when he uttered the famous statement, "For years I thought what was good for our country was good for General Motors, and vice versa."

66 See, for example, Margaret M. Blair and Lynn A. Stout, "Director Accountability and the Mediating Role of the Corporate Board" (2001) 79 Wash. U.L.Q. 403.

67 See, for example, Mark J. Roe, "The Shareholder Wealth Maximization Norm and Industrial Organization" (2001) 149 U. Pa. L. Rev. 2063. Roe argues that the shareholder wealth maximization norm will increase societal wealth where there is significant industry competition. In markets characterized by monopolies, however, the pursuit of such a norm may actually lead to lower GNP.

68 Michael Jensen, "Agency Costs of Free Cash Flow, Corporate Finance and Takeovers" (1986) 76 Am. Econ. Rev. 323.

69 See, for example, Weston and Weaver, *supra* note 4 at 116: "Event studies of merger announcements show that returns to targets are always positive; the positive returns are even higher with multiple bidders. Returns to bidders tend to be around zero and negative with multiple bidders. Event studies have been shown to be relatively good predictors of subsequent performance. Industry-adjusted postmerger performance of merging firms show that they perform better than nonmerging firms in the same industries."

70 See, for example, Robert Daines, "Does Delaware Law Improve Firm Value" (2001) 62 J. Fin. Econ. 525 at 527: "I find that firms domiciled in states that raise significant barriers to hostile bids are worth significantly less and may receive fewer bids." See also Jonathan M. Karpoff and Paul H. Malatesta, "The Wealth Effects of Second-Generation Takeover Legislation" (1989) 25 J. Fin. Econ. 291, in which the authors report that the initial public announcement of the passage by a state of anti-takeover legislation was followed, on average, by a small decline in the value of firms incorporated there. See also Roberta Romano, "A Guide to Takeovers: Theory, Evidence, and Regulation" (1992) 9 Yale J. on Reg. 119 at 177, in which the author concludes: "Because the overwhelming balance of research views takeovers favorably, the more restrictive of takeovers, the more ill-conceived the regulation."

71 For a recent canvass of the competing academic and practitioners' views on the effect of the adoption of takeover defences – especially shareholder rights plans (or poison pills) – see John C. Coates IV, "Empirical Evidence on Structural Takeover Defences: Where Do We Stand?"(2000) 54 U. Miami L. Rev. 783.

72 See, for example, Margaret M. Blair, "Financial Restructuring and the Debate about Corporate Governance" in Margaret M. Blair, ed., *The Deal Decade: What Takeovers and Leveraged Buyouts Mean for Corporate Governance* (Washington, DC: Brookings Institution, 1993) at 3.

73 Jeremy C. Stein, "Takeover Threats and Managerial Myopia" (1998) 96 J. Pol. Econ. 61.

74 See, for example, Reinier Kraakman, "Taking Discounts Seriously: The Implications of 'Discounted' Share Prices as an Acquisition Motive" (1988) 88 Colum. L. Rev. 891. Kraakman considers, in particular, two possible explanations for observed discounted stock prices: the "misinvestment hypothesis" and the "market hypothesis."

75 See Weston and Weaver, *supra* note 4. See also Sudip Datta, Mai Iskandar-Datta, and Kartik Raman, "Executive Compensation and Corporate Acquisition Decisions" (2001) 56 J. Fin. 2299, in which the authors "document a strong positive relation between equity-based compensation (EBC) received by acquiring managers and stock price response around and following corporate acquisitions."

76 See, for example, Martin Lipton, Comment on Mark Roe's paper, in Blair, ed., *supra* note 72.

77 Stein, *supra* note 73.

78 See Sanford J. Grossman and Oliver D. Hart, "Takeover Bids, the Free-Rider Problem, and the Theory of the Corporation" (1980) 11 Bell J. Econ. 42. Grossman and Hart argue that

minority shareholders who believe a bid will succeed and that the bidder will add value to the target firm, will refuse to tender to a bid. Their proposed solution is for corporations to include in their corporate charters provisions that would allow a successful bidder to exclude nontendering minority shareholders from any subsequent gains in firm value.

79 See, for example, Richard A. Posner, "Law and Theory of Finance: Some Intersections" (1986) 54 Geo. Wash. L. Rev. 159 at 167: "The fact remains that tender offers are made at very high premiums over the current market price of the target firm's stock ... This suggests a large margin within which managers can divert wealth from shareholders to themselves without worrying about inviting a takeover that may cost them their jobs."

80 Richard Roll, "The Hubris Hypothesis of Corporate Takeovers" (1986) 59 J. Bus. 197.

81 Christopher Avery, Judith A. Chevalier, and Scott Schaefer, "Why Do Managers Undertake Acquisitions? An Analysis of Internal and External Rewards for Acquisitiveness" (1998) 14 J. L. Econ. and Org. 24.

82 Scott Mitnick, "Cross Border Mergers and Acquisitions in Europe: Reforming Barriers to Takeovers" (2001) 2001 Colum. Bus. L. Rev. 683 at 698. Mitnick quotes a passage from Tim Jenkinson and Colin Mayer, Hostile Takeovers 16 (1994) in support of this proposition, paraphrased here.

83 Roberta Romano studied several of the state anti-takeover statutes, concluding that they were passed chiefly at the behest of potential takeover targets in vulnerable states. See Roberta Romano, "The Political Economy of Takeover Statutes" (1987) 73 Va. L. Rev. 111. Bebchuk and Ferrell have argued that US states have incentives to pass legislation that is overly protective of managers, and have done so to the detriment of shareholder interests. See Lucian Arye Bebchuk and Allen Ferrell, "Federalism and Corporate Law: The Race to Protect Managers from Takeovers" (1999) 99 Colum. L. Rev. 1168.

84 See *Edgar* v. *MITE Corp.*, 457 U.S. 624 (1982).

85 See *CTS Corp.* v. *Dynamics Corp.*, 481 U.S. 69 (1987). For a recent consideration of the possibility that such statutes could run afoul of the so-called "takings clause," see Lynda J. Oswald, "Shareholders v. Stakeholders: Evaluating Corporate Constituency Statutes under the Takings Clause" (1998) J. Corp. L. 1.

86 Mark J. Roe, "Takeover Politics" in Margaret M. Blair, ed., *The Deal Decade: What Takeovers and Leveraged Buyouts Mean for Corporate Governance* (Washington, DC: Brookings Institution, 1993) at 321.

87 Vice Chancellor Leo E. Strine, Jr., "Categorical Confusion: Deal Protection Measures in Stock-for-Stock Merger Agreements" (2001) 56 Bus. Law 919 at 925.

88 Bernard Black and Reinier Kraakman, "Path-Dependent Competition for Corporate Charters: Manager Choice, Shareholder Veto" (Paper delivered at American Law and Economics Association Annual Meeting, Yale University, May 1999).

89 Easterbrook and Fischel, *supra* note 28 at 167.

90 See, for example, *Unocal* v. *Mesa Petroleum*, 493 A.2d 946 (Del. Super. Ct. 1985); *Unitrin, Inc.* v. *American General Corp.*, A.2d 1361 (Del. Supr. Ct. 1995). For a brief overview of the Delaware jurisprudence in the takeover context, see Nicholls, *supra* note 63 at 341-45. For a more detailed treatment of the topic, see Dennis J. Block and Michael B. Arouh, "Public Company M and A: Recent Developments in Corporate Control, Defensive Mechanisms and Other Deal Protection Techniques" in Practising Law Institute, *supra* note 2 at 467.

91 See, for example, William T. Allen, Jack B. Jacobs, and Leo E. Strine, Jr., "Function over Form: A Reassessment of Standards of Review in Delaware Corporation Law" (2001) 56 Bus. Law. 1287.

92 The *Revlon* duty refers to the duty of the board of directors of a corporation triggered when a sale of control or breakup of the company becomes inevitable. The duty was first articulated by the Delaware Supreme Court in *Revlon, Inc.* v. *MacAndrews and Forbes Holdings Inc.*, 506 A.2d 173 (1986), in these words: "The duty of the board thus changed from the preservation of [the target] as a corporate entity to the maximization of the company's value at a sale for the stockholders' benefit" (at 182).

93 This exception was implicit in the court's decision in *Paramount Communications, Inc.* v. *Time, Inc.*, 571 A.2d 1140 (Del. Supr. Ct.1989), and was more fully refined in *Paramount Communications, Inc.* v. *QVC Network Inc.*, 637 A.2d 34 (Del. Supr. Ct. 1994). The exception has since become a well-understood and accepted part of Delaware takeover law. See, for

example, Leo E. Strine, Jr., "Categorical Confusion: Deal Protection Measures in Stock-for-Stock Merger Agreements" (2001) 56 Bus. Law 919 at 921. See also Allen *et al., supra,* note 91 at 1291, and note 11. Curiously, this gloss on the *Revlon* duty does not appear to have received significant attention in Canada.

94   Needless to say, ambiguities remain, for example, in the context of bids consisting of both cash and stock components. See, for example, *In Re Lukens Inc. Shareholders Litigation,* 757 A.2d 720 (Del. Ch. 1999). It should also be noted that Black and Kraakman (*supra* note 88) have argued that Delaware is by no means transparent on these issues.

95   Strine, *supra* note 93 at 925. Stephen M. Bainbridge, it should be noted, has recently argued that one may reconcile a "director primary" model of corporate law (which he argues is normatively superior to a "shareholder primary" model) with the proposition that the goal of business corporations is to maximize shareholder wealth. The key to this reconciliation for Bainbridge is that while the board of directors controls the corporation (and is not merely exercising power delegated by the shareholders), the "corporate contract ... required directors to maximize shareholder wealth." See, e.g., Stephen M. Bainbridge, "Director Primacy in Corporate Takeovers: Preliminary Reflections" (2002) 55 Stanford L. Rev. 791 at 811-12.

96   Because the Delaware takeover jurisprudence arises from particular norms of Delaware corporate law that are, arguably, not found in Canadian corporate law, it is somewhat curious that Canadian courts have not been more often invited to consider precedents from other US states for guidance in the takeover context.

97   The Ontario Court of Appeal has expressly declared that "Revlon is not the law in Ontario": *Maple Leaf Foods Inc.* v. *Schneider Corp.* (1998) 32 O.R. (3d) 177. The aspect of the Revlon duty rejected by the Court was the suggestion, as originally formulated in the original Delaware decision in *Revlon, Inc.* v. *MacAndrews and Forbes Holdings Inc.,* 506 A.2d 173 (Del. Supr. Ct. 1986), that directors operating in the "Revlon zone" must conduct an auction. However, use of the term "Revlon duty" appears to have evolved in Delaware since 1986, and, as used today by American attorneys, reflects a more flexible duty that would seem quite consistent with the Ontario Court of Appeal's views on the proper role of a target company's board. The suggestion that directors of a target company undergoing a change of control transaction are under a duty to maximize shareholder value – but not necessarily to do so by way of an auction – has also been confirmed by other Canadian courts. See, for example, *Re Pacifica Papers Inc.,* [2001] B.C.J. 1484.

98   E. Norman Veasey, "Should Corporation Law Inform Aspirations for Good Corporate Governance Practices – or Vice Versa?" (2001) 149 U. Pa. L. Rev. 2179 at 2184.

99   There is, of course, an extensive academic literature that seeks to explain why more than half of the largest US corporations have chosen to incorporate (or reincorporate) in Delaware. Originally, commentators divided on the question of whether Delaware's success in attracting corporate charters represented the culmination of a "race to the bottom" (in which state governments competed to provide manager-friendly legislation that compromised shareholder protection) or conversely – since shareholders generally had to approve reincorporations – whether Delaware's success in fact heralded its victory in a "race to the top" (in which statutes providing increased managerial flexibility in fact enhanced shareholder value). The landmark paper espousing the "race to the bottom" thesis was William L. Cary, "Federalism and Corporate Law: Reflections upon Delaware" (1974) 83 Yale L.J. The landmark "race to the top" paper was Ralph K. Winter, Jr., "State Law, Shareholder Protection, and the Theory of the Corporation" (1977) 6 J. Leg. Stud. 251. Much subsequent work has appeared on the topic. One interesting insight on this topic has been offered by William Bratton. He contends that the turning point for Delaware's charter-competition success came in 1938, with the US Supreme Court's decision in *Erie Railroad Co.* v. *Tompkins,* 304 U.S. 64 (1938). In *Tompkins,* the Supreme Court held that "except in matters governed by the Federal Constitution or by acts of Congress, the law to be applied in any case is the law of the state" (at 78). The significance of this holding in the corporate charter context, according to Bratton, was this: prior to *Tompkins,* the Delaware judiciary was effectively constrained from straying excessively from federal common law principles because plaintiffs in many instances could choose to litigate corporate law matters in the

federal rather than the state courts. Thereafter, the Delaware state courts became, effectively, the sole arbiter of disputes involving Delaware corporate law, and so had greater latitude to develop a unique Delaware corporate law jurisprudence. See William W. Bratton, "Berle and Means Reconsidered at the Century's Turn" (2001) J. Corp. L. 737 at 768.

100 See Black and Kraakman, *supra* note 88.

101 Mitnick, *supra* note 82 at 703.

102 City Code on Takeovers and Mergers, General Principles, para. 9, <http://www. thetakeoverpanel.org.uk> (accessed 23 January 2002).

103 For a journalistic view on the failure of the directive, see "Pull up the Drawbridge" *Economist* (7 July 2001). For a more detailed treatment of the "rise and fall of the Thirteenth Directive," see Mitnick, *supra* note 82 at 690-92.

104 *Report of the High Level Group of Company Law Experts on Issues Related to Takeover Bids* (Brussels, 10 January 2002).

105 See Paul Hofheinz, "Legal Panel Recommends Expansion of Shareholder Rights in Takeovers" *Wall Street Journal* (11 January 2002).

106 *Supra* note 104 at 19.

107 *Ibid.* at 39-41.

108 *Ibid.* at 29-35. The Report suggests that an appropriate "breakthrough" threshold should be at least 75 percent. There is a parallel to such a break-through threshold in Delaware. Under the *Delaware General Corporation Law,* a corporation is not permitted to engage in a business combination with an interested stockholder for three years following the date on which the shareholder became interested, unless the transaction is approved by a two-thirds vote of the minority shareholders. (An interested stockholder essentially means a shareholder holding at least 15 percent of the corporation's outstanding stock.) However, where the interested stockholder owns at least 85 percent of the shares, there is no such restriction. (See *Delaware General Corporation Law,* s. 203.)

109 *Ibid.* at 33.

110 *Ibid.* at 38-39.

Part 2
Shareholder Activism and Control: Accountability for Corporate Harms

4
Canadian Institutional Shareholder Activism in an Era of Global Deregulation
Gil Yaron

We regard informed, measured, and responsible institutional
shareholder activism to be one of the linchpins of a modern system
of corporate governance. We are also of the opinion that, given the
right legal framework, Canadian institutional investors can play a
constructive and responsible role in corporate governance.

– Ronald J. Daniels and Randall Morck[1]

One of the most profound transformations in modern North American society has been the shift of institutional power from the nation-state to corporate enterprise. This changing dynamic in governance is attributable to
the diminished role of the state in neoliberal societies through deregulation, and the emergence of the multinational corporation. The coming into
favour of free market, neoliberal ideology has facilitated a virtually global
deregulation agenda. Nation-states around the world continue to support a
"market friendly system of regulation, in which governments often delegate numerous responsibilities to the private sector."[2] International agreements, such as the World Trade Organization and the Free Trade Agreement
of the Americas, seek to establish an international rules-based system for
facilitating trade and eliminating existing trade barriers, thereby reducing
the ability of state governments to take unilateral actions to protect local
economies.[3] For the most part, Canada has adopted this neoliberal ideology
at both federal and provincial levels.[4]

Moreover, as Ronald Davis details in Chapter 5 of this book, the emergence of the multinational enterprise (MNE) has made it increasingly difficult for incorporating states to govern MNE activities in other jurisdictions.[5]
The United Nations' *World Investment Report 2000* estimates "that there are
approximately 63,000 parent firms with around 690,000 foreign affiliates
and a plethora of inter-firm arrangements ... rendering it [the multinational

corporation] a formidable force in today's world economy."[6] Of the 100 largest economies in the world, fifty-one are corporations.[7] These larger enterprises carry on increasingly more complex activities and transactions, often in remote locations without independent oversight by host states.

As a result of this institutional shift, increasing attention is being placed on the development and implementation, both by the state and by industry, of national and international corporate governance standards.[8] To date, developments in this area have focused on the creation of standards to support the fiduciary duties of directors to act in the best interest of the corporation, and to protect shareholder value. The establishment of corporate governance standards has been accompanied by the formulation of corporate responsibility benchmarks (i.e., corporate codes of conduct, reporting standards, and process-based standards).[9] While it remains to be seen how effective these various initiatives will be in engendering a more responsible corporate sector, their voluntary nature (with the exception of binding trade-related agreements) and process-based perspective raise doubts about their sufficiency as an adequate accountability framework for free enterprise that addresses the potential impacts of corporate activity on all stakeholders, including employees, communities, and the environment.

In their books *The Rise of Fiduciary Capitalism* and *The New Global Investors,* James P. Hawley and Andrew T. Williams and Robert A.G. Monks identify the institutional investor as a new voice for promoting prudent corporate governance.[10] Hawley and Williams characterize the American institutional investor as a "universal owner," one that "holds in its portfolio a broad cross section of the economy, holds its shares for the long term, and on the whole does not trade except to maintain its index."[11] Universal owners are concerned with minimizing investor risk by maintaining adequate diversification and minimizing externalities through the application of a portfolio-based approach to investment management.[12] As fiduciaries, long-term investors, and majority owners, they are not concerned with short-term returns on investment but rather long-term performance to meet the needs of present and future beneficiaries. Accordingly, corporations in which they invest must operate in a financially, socially, and environmentally responsible manner that supports a healthy and sustainable economy. Consequently, "a universal owner's cumulative long-term return is determined not merely by the performance of each individual firm it owns, but by the performance of the economy as a whole."[13]

This chapter considers the validity of the universal owner hypothesis in the context of the Canadian economy, and the theoretical and policy justifications for enhanced institutional shareholder activism in Canadian corporate governance.[14] It begins by considering whether the Canadian institutional investor reflects the nature of its American counterpart. It then posits a theoretical framework for institutional shareholder activism and assesses the degree to which the current legal and market conditions, particularly recent amendments to the *Canada Business Corporations Act (CBCA)*, support or impede it.[15] It is the observation of this author that while shareholder activism may play a legitimate role in monitoring the activities of the firm, the legal and procedural framework remains fraught with legal and structural barriers.

The approach advocated here is an enhanced role for the shareholder in facilitating responsible corporate governance for several reasons. The particular orientation of the institutional investor towards mitigating long-term risk places it in the position of monitoring the long-term performance of the corporation and the health of the economy, society, and natural environment. Institutional shareholders, indeed all shareholders, also possess the ability to engage corporations with respect to international operations outside the purview of state government.

It is important to emphasize that none who advocate for increased shareholder rights view it as a surrogate for government regulation.[16] As Ron Davis points out in Chapter 5, "investor control is complementary to public regulation, rather than a substitute for the absence of such regulation." The arguments made in this chapter fully recognize the limitations of institutional shareholders acting as proxy for the interests of other stakeholders in society.[17] However, as Stéphane Rousseau alludes to in Chapter 1 of this book, institutional shareholders provide a mechanism for a voice in the debate over corporate governance that goes beyond traditional private norms. Accordingly, while this chapter is not to be interpreted as advocating against state involvement in the national economy, it recognizes the diminishing presence of the state and attempts to outline one market mechanism to assist in mediating among stakeholder interests.

The Canadian Institutional Investor as Universal Owner

The nature of corporate ownership in Canada has changed significantly over the past decade with the replacement of the retail investor by the institutional investor as the major player in Canadian equity markets.[18] It is the unique characteristics of the institutional investor that suggest possibilities in enhancing responsible corporate governance. Unlike individual shareholders, institutional investors are intermediaries investing assets on behalf of beneficiaries. In a trust context, institutional investors must comply with fiduciary duties of prudence and loyalty, which require that investment decisions be made in the best interests of the beneficiaries.[19] Alternatively, institutional investors act as agent on behalf of the collective interest of the *real* owners of capital, which include a majority of individuals in society, particularly through pension plans and retail mutual funds. The result is that the agency model and differentiation of interests between management and owners becomes more complex as owners are supplanted by agents representing their collective interest in the market.[20]

These unique characteristics of the institutional investor as fiduciary and investor in a broad cross section of the Canadian economy give it a unique role. It is argued that its responsibility should be to invest with a long-term view to satisfying the financial requirements of beneficiaries *and* ensuring a sustainable social and economic framework necessary to provide adequate returns for future beneficiaries.[21] For each institutional investor, its stock performance "depends crucially on the macroeconomic performance of the economies in which it is invested."[22] As articulated by Robert Monks, a leading authority on corporate governance, the universal owner (or "global investor") "is likely to make good decisions for the long-term benefit of society, because it can afford in most cases to take a long-term view, and a diversified view. An ordinary domestic investor may need to reap profits in the short term."[23]

If one accepts this role for the institutional investor, the question is to what extent Canadian institutional investors have the potential to influence Canadian enterprise, as Hawley, Williams, and Monks postulate with respect to their American counterparts? Hawley and Williams identify universal owners by three fundamental common characteristics: size, portfolio composition, and investment strategies.[24] While data for Canada are not as robust as those available for American institutional investors, limited information suggests that Canadian institutional investors, particularly trusteed pension funds, are emerging as universal owners within the Canadian equity market.[25]

With respect to size, both the assets and equity ownership of institutional shareholders have increased significantly over the past several decades, although not to the extent of their American counterparts.[26] In 2000, Canadian institutional investors had amassed $2.86 trillion dollars in assets, 12.49 percent invested directly in equity.[27] Institutional shareholders owned 30.9 percent of all Canadian-based corporations on the Toronto Stock Exchange, down from 37.2 percent in 1990.[28] Organization for Economic Cooperation and Development (OECD) figures indicate that the financial assets of institutional investors in Canada have risen from 68.6 percent of the nation's GDP in 1992 to 111.3 percent in 2000.[29]

By far, the majority of institutional equity is held by trusteed pension plans. At the end of the second quarter of 2001, trusteed pension plans in Canada managed assets valued at $568.6 billion, 40 percent invested in stocks, up from 20 percent in 1990.[30] Over one-third of institutional shares, representing 10.4 percent of the value of all Canadian-based corporations on the Toronto Stock Exchange (12.9 percent of the TSE 300), were held by trusteed pension plans, down from 17.89 percent (21.50 percent of the TSE

Table 1

Total dollar value of assets and shares for Canadian institutional investors

Year	2000	1990	1980	1970	1961
Total assets ($ million)	2,862,398	1,292,933	484,768	111,486	42,007
Total shares ($ million)	357,408	104,301	32,698	10,339	3,268
Shares as % of total assets	12.49	8.07	6.75	9.27	7.78

Source: Statistics Canada, *National balance sheet accounts – 1806* (Table 378-0004). CANSIM II Database.

Table 2

Total dollar value of assets and shares for trusteed pension plans

Year	2000	1990	1980	1970	1961
Total assets ($ million)	480,235	197,896	51,159	11,109	4,082
Total shares ($ million)	120,335	50,211	9,086	2,416	415
Shares as % of total assets	25.06	25.37	17.76	21.75	10.17

Source: Statistics Canada, *National balance sheet accounts – 1806* (Table 378-0004). CANSIM II Database.

300) in 1990 (see Table 1).[31] These represent significant increases over total historical asset and equity levels in years dating back to 1961 (see Table 2).[32] Similarly, plan portfolios usually reflect a broad cross section of the Canadian equity market through indexation and diversification.

It is also of interest to observe that preliminary empirical surveys suggest a change in the perceptions of beneficiaries regarding the desired objectives of institutional investors and their role as fiduciary agents. A recent national poll conducted after the economic decline in 2001 and the tragic attacks on the World Trade Center of 11 September indicates that the interests of a majority of individual shareholders and beneficiaries of pension plans want institutional investments to be made in companies with good social responsibility records, reinforcing findings of an earlier 1997 UK national opinion poll.[33]

These preliminary data, while not as robust as those for American institutional investors, indicate a significant role for Canadian institutional investors in the Canadian equity market and an ability to claim a role as universal owners, if not individually, then collectively.

Theoretical Framework for a Broad-Based Mandate for Institutional Shareholder Activism

Starting with the ground-breaking work of Berle and Means identifying the differentiation between ownership and management, there has been extensive consideration of the place of the shareholder in the theory of the firm.[34] The emergence of the institutional shareholder necessitates a revisitation of the theoretical context framing the role of the shareholder in the governance of private enterprise.

The prevailing contractual theory of the firm, canvassed by Janis Sarra in Chapter 2 of this book, asserts the right of the shareholder as owner to oversee the governance of the corporation by management through the exercise of votes attached to shares in the corporation.[35] It is this rationale that has resulted in the creation of shareholder rights in corporate law, particularly rights pertaining to the submission of shareholder proposals, voting of proxies, and communications between shareholders with respect to the solicitation of proxies.[36] However, this paradigm is limited to considering the rights and responsibilities of shareholders and the individual corporate legal entities through their contractual relationships established through statute and private agreement. It fails to incorporate the relationship of these parties to other stakeholders outside of any contractual relationships established by the corporation.

In contrast, the fiduciary responsibilities of the universal shareholder to society, as represented by its beneficiaries, are more fully realized in the context of a concessionist theory of the firm. Concessionism conceives of the corporation "as an artificial entity whose separate legal personality is granted as a privilege by the state."[37] Reflected in the corporate practice of chartering until the middle of the nineteenth century, concessionist theory includes two key ideas. The first is the notion that the corporation as an artificial or fictional entity exists "only in the contemplation of law."[38] The second is that the corporation is "an emanation of the state, created by revocable grant."[39] The latter element gives to the corporation a public character. Accordingly, the owners of the firm are not only responsible for achieving the purposes of the corporation itself but are also accountable to the state for ensuring that the corporation does not violate terms of its charter or cause harm in the course of carrying out its activities. Concessionist theory in this manner goes beyond the alternative contractualist theoretical paradigm, which views the firm as a nexus of contracts, where parties define their rights and responsibilities solely with respect to each other through contract, to considering the relationship of the firm to society as a whole.

A concessionist view acknowledges responsibility of shareholders, their fiduciary agents, and the firm to beneficiaries and the national economy. Within this model, investors and firms take into consideration the implications of company decisions on internal performance *and* externalities as they impact the corporation's ability to operate in the long-term interest of society. It is in this framework that institutional shareholder activism becomes viewed not only as a mechanism to protect shareholders against investment risk but also as a vehicle for directing firm governance in a way that optimizes long-term benefits and minimizes risk for beneficiaries, the firm, and the economy as a whole.

Institutional Shareholder Activism

Aside from the empirical and theoretical justification for the institutional investor as universal owner, the concerns of institutional investors as fiduciaries require consideration of whether institutional shareholder activism in areas of corporate governance and corporate social and environmental performance enhance corporate financial performance.

The active engagement of the investor in corporate governance in Canada has matured quite rapidly in the last several years. Survey data from the Shareholder Association for Research and Education (SHARE) indicate that the number of shareholder proposals considered by shareholders increased from less than 3 in each year from 1982 to 1996 to 63 and 39 in 2000 and 2001, respectively.[40] In addition, numerous institutional investors have implemented investment policies and proxy voting guidelines that direct trustees and money managers on corporate/shareholder dialogue and the voting of proxies.[41] Academics,[42] religious institutional investors,[43] and shareholders from across Canada[44] have been advocating for a more equitable regime to address concerns regarding the business and affairs of corporations in Canada. Increasing interest has been expressed in shareholder activism, particularly by institutional investors as a means of managing risk and enhancing investment performance. As Jeffrey MacIntosh asserts: "The concentration of economic power, expertise, and incentives in the hands of institutional investors is a means of overcoming collective action problems and ensuring that both corporate managers and controlling shareholders are well monitored."[45] The evidence reviewed in this section suggests that improvements to the framework for institutional shareholder activism in Canada could have positive implications for investors and companies and positive macro implications for the well-being of national and global economies.[46]

The issue is to what extent can institutional shareholder activism improve corporate performance through enhancement of governance and social and environmental practices.[47] While it is premature to draw conclusions from or causal relationships between institutional shareholder activism and corporate performance, studies conducted to date indicate a positive correlation with respect to shareholder engagement on traditional corporate governance matters.[48] One study by Stephen L. Nesbitt concluded that the value of California Public Employees' Retirement System (CalPERS) investments improved relative to the S&P index in the years following activist intervention.[49] A second study, by Tim Opler and Jonathan Sokobin, arrived at the same conclusion for a group of public and private pension funds, which collectively own over $800 billion in financial assets.[50] Hawley and Williams observe that "active ownership matters even if specific governance features do not," suggesting that the performance of all firms may be improved by the targeting of a few firms with shareholder proposals.[51] It is possible that shareholder activism has simply put pressure on corporations to increase short-term returns at the expense of long-term considerations that may have adverse impacts on the economy, society, and/or environment. However, the studies to date do reinforce the neutral proposition that shareholder activism does in principle have the capacity to influence corporate decision making and performance.

Studies also support the conclusion of pension regulators that proxies are valuable pension plan assets.[52] Recent American studies have demonstrated that proxy activities by institutional investors targeted at underperforming firms can lead to desired changes in corporate behaviour, although findings to date have found little or no general effect from proxy activity.[53] Hawley and Williams suggest that this may be due to the unrelatedness of the measures to performance or the obfuscation of the relationship by other factors.[54] Clearly, more study in all of these areas is warranted.

Legal Framework

Having put forward a possible theoretical framework for institutional shareholder activism and presented some initial empirical support to suggest its relevance in improving corporate performance, we can now consider whether the legislative and market framework in Canada, specifically recent amendments to the *CBCA*, achieve the intended effect of "improv[ing] the legal framework for federal corporations by enhancing shareholder decision input in decision making."[55] Here we consider the extent to which the new legal framework provides an effective and efficient mechanism for facilitating corporate/shareholder dialogue, mitigating investor risk, and promoting a sustainable economy.

Shareholder activism has its roots in the earliest governance frameworks of the modern corporation. In common law days, the corporation was largely a communal venture. The shareholder meeting was vitally important to the operation of the business corporation. It provided the forum for stockholders to avail themselves of the judgment and acumen of all those participating in the company meeting. Common law placed no obligation on corporate management to reference views of nonmanagement in any corporate documents on matters to be discussed at shareholder meetings.[56] Corporate management also did not have to provide notice of dissident proposals in a Notice of Meeting.[57] The only recourse for shareholders was to requisition a special meeting. Assigning proxies was frowned upon in the belief that voting by proxy would likely encourage absences from meetings and nonparticipation in corporate affairs.[58]

Statutory rules governing shareholder proposals and shareholder communications were introduced into federal law with the enactment of the

CBCA in 1975.[59] With the growth of the corporate form and the separation of ownership from management, shareholders had the need for their rights in the governance of the corporation to be spelt out.[60] The accepted view was that the statutory rights of shareholders, including the ability to circulate shareholder proposals and communicate among shareholders, was necessary to balance the interests of owners with those of management.[61] More generally, the *CBCA* established a new model reducing government oversight of corporate management through regulation and advancing various mechanisms under which shareholders and other actors could directly enforce their rights and engage more actively in the governance of the firm.

The paucity of shareholder actions in the last twenty-five years is undoubtedly the consequence of numerous factors. Commentators have provided various explanations for this, including the difficulty in coordinating and communicating among shareholders, agency costs, free-rider problems, and concentration of ownership among publicly traded Canadian corporations.[62] However, academics and investors agree that the primary impediment, aside from institutional capacity,[63] has been the hostile legislative framework in federal and provincial corporate statutes.[64]

The old federal rules allowed registered shareholders only to file proposals of up to 200 words in length with corporations provided that they were filed on time and were not submitted for the purpose of redressing a personal grievance or "promoting general economic, political, racial, religious, social or similar causes."[65] Communication between shareholders was permitted but severely restricted by virtue of the definition of "solicitation" in relation to the soliciting of proxies under the *CBCA*.[66] Restrictive interpretations of the rules by the courts narrowed their scope even further.[67]

The recent amendments to the *CBCA*, brought into force on 24 November 2001 after nine years of lobbying by shareholders led by faith-based institutional investors through the Taskforce on the Churches and Corporate Responsibility, represent a significant and positive change to the framework governing federally incorporated corporations in Canada.[68] Both their scope and content are insufficient, however. With respect to scope, the *CBCA* applies to more than 155,000 corporations in Canada, but to only 800 publicly traded corporations and 144 of the TSE 300 index. This leaves a majority of large-cap corporations incorporated under provincial corporate statutes, yet only six provinces provide rules for shareholder proposal and communications.[69] Requirements in each jurisdiction differ, in some cases significantly.[70] Lack of uniformity could potentially have a distorting effect on the market to the extent that corporations use the difference as a factor in deciding to move their place of incorporation to avoid such rules. Amendments to British Columbia's corporate legislation proclaimed but not in force give no indication of any intention to harmonize with the federal regime.

Nevertheless, the amendments to the *CBCA* go some way to addressing the concerns identified. Of significance are five changes to the rules governing shareholder proposals and communications:

- Beneficial shareholders may now file shareholder proposals.[71]
- The word count for proposals is increased to 500.[72]
- Shareholders now have to meet eligibility requirements. Shareholders must have held a minimum of $2,000 worth of shares or 1 percent of total outstanding shares for a period of no less than six months prior to submitting a proposal.[73]
- Proposals must be submitted at least ninety days prior to the anniversary date of the Notice of Meeting of the corporation.[74]
- The definition of "solicitation" has been clarified, allowing shareholders to communicate freely with each other without issuing a dissident proxy circular provided that the shareholder is not seeking to obtain the ability to vote another shareholder's proxy on his or her behalf.[75]

The most important change, however, is the elimination of the exclusion regarding the subject matter of proposals. Under the new rules, proposals must "relate in a significant way to the business or affairs of the corporation," and are no longer excludable merely because they address matters of a general economic, political, racial, religious, or social nature.[76] This ground for exclusion severely constrained shareholders (as evidenced by the number of proposals challenged and rejected by corporations) and set an unreasonable threshold for shareholders to meet. Based largely on SEC Rule 14-8, American jurisprudence suggests how this American-based threshold is to be interpreted and applied. However, this provision awaits consideration by Canadian courts.

Unfortunately, the piecemeal application of the American framework[77] and unique approaches taken by the federal government to address certain concerns of shareholders and industry leave various problems unlikely to be addressed until the five-year review of the *CBCA* in 2007.[78]

Dispute Resolution Forum

In the United States, when a dispute arises between shareholders and management regarding the circulation of a proposal, the matter is referred to the Securities and Exchange Commission (SEC) to provide a nonbinding ruling on the acceptability of the proposal's content. In most instances, the parties accept this ruling, thereby avoiding costly and time-consuming recourse to the courts. No such administrative process exists in Canada. Shareholders of both federally and provincially incorporated companies must apply to the courts in instances where a company refuses to circulate a proposal or challenges the rights of shareholders in this area. The cost and time requirements associated with legal challenges entrenches the problem of free ridership and fiduciary apathy since only the largest institutional investors could possibly find it economically justifiable when balancing the costs of pursuing the issue against the potential benefits to their beneficiaries.[79]

Filing Reference Date

The new *CBCA* rules introduce a new deadline for submitting shareholder proposals that has caused considerable confusion for shareholders. Under the new rules, the corporation must receive proposals ninety days prior to the anniversary date of the Notice of Meeting.[80] Those advancing this new reference date argue that corporations require more time to process proposals before circulating them. While the new reference date addresses this concern, it is problematic for a number of reasons. First, shareholders do not receive the Notice of Meeting at the time it is issued. The Notice is circulated to shareholders but only with other management proxy circular materials distributed several months after the Notice of Meeting is issued.[81] Second, the reference date is unique among North American corporate legislation. The new *CBCA* regulations do require that companies publish the submission deadline in their annual proxy circular, but it remains to be seen how many corporations will adhere to this requirement.[82] If companies do legitimately require more time to review proposals submitted by shareholders, this need for more time should be accommodated using the more transparent reference date of the company's annual general meeting rather than the obscure date of the Notice of Meeting, and simply increasing the prescribed number of days the proposal must be filed in advance.

Identifying and Communicating with Beneficial Owners

As noted, the new *CBCA* rules permit beneficial shareholders to file proposals, but shareholders continue to be thwarted in their efforts to communicate with beneficial shareholders because they are not identified on the company's register of shareholders. Furthermore, registered shareholders are not required to provide lists of their beneficial shareholders. Without being able to identify beneficial shareholders, it is exceedingly difficult to communicate information about issues pertaining to the corporation.

Another emerging wrinkle is the problem of identifying the beneficial shareholder for the purpose of submitting proposals. Under the *CBCA*, the registered shareholder must provide proof of beneficial ownership on behalf of the beneficial shareholder upon the corporation's request.[83] In many instances, pension funds and mutual funds in Canada are established pursuant to a trust agreement. In this context, the beneficiaries of the fund are the plan beneficiaries and unitholders, respectively, not the board of trustees or the investment manager. One would therefore presume that the unitholders *collectively*, or more typically the manager on their behalf by virtue of assignment of the unitholders' rights to the manager in the trust agreement, have the right to submit a shareholder proposal. However, uncertainty regarding who actually maintains beneficial ownership in the property of the shares has resulted in certain custodians, as registered shareholders, refusing to provide a statement of proof of beneficial ownership. This problem has been remedied in the United States, where beneficial owners have had the right to file proposals for years, by the inclusion of a more expansive definition of beneficial owner.[84]

Furthermore, recent experience with the new rules also reveals problems with the requirement that the registered shareholder provide proof of beneficial ownership. In Canada, the registered shareholder on behalf of most institutional investors is the Canadian Depository System (CDS). The CDS is not able to provide statements of proof as required by the *CBCA* and custodians have been unwilling to act on behalf of the CDS in issuing a statement of proof. Consequently, beneficial owners are unable to satisfy this requirement if requested to do so by the corporation.

Institutional and Market Factors

In addition to concerns pertaining to the law, significant market barriers identified nearly a decade ago persist to a greater or lesser extent, impeding the effectiveness and efficiency of institutional shareholder activism.[85]

Disclosure of Information

As Ronald Davis identifies in Chapter 5, one of the principal problems facing investors is the lack of access to adequate information in a timely and continuous manner. At present, securities regulation requires disclosure of "material changes" in the corporation in a timely and continuous manner, but does not apply this standard of disclosure to "material facts."[86] As evidenced by the impacts of workplace discrimination lawsuits and environmental liabilities,[87] policies and activities in these areas can have significant impacts on shareholder value, and shareholders should be informed about them in a full, continuous, and timely manner.

Dual-Class Share Structures

A significant number of public Canadian companies continue to maintain dual-class share structures, allowing a relatively small number of shareholders to wield control even though they own only a small percentage of the firm. In 2000, 126 out of 795 companies listed on the TSE maintained dual-class share structures, compounded by the fact that 90 (72 percent) of these companies also had a controlling shareholder with more than 50 percent of outstanding voting shares.[88] This arrangement persists despite empirical evidence demonstrating that dual-class recapitalizations tend to lead to entrenchment of management and depressed firm value.[89] Canadian corporate law requires special shareholder votes when dual-class structures are created, thereby enabling shareholders to object to opportunistic dual-class recapitalizations. Still, dual-class structures persist within corporate Canada, in part due to vested interests and management control of proxies.

Control of Proxy Voting Mechanism

The apparatus for managing proxies continues to be retained in the hands of management rather than an independent third party.[90] Consequently, management is able to communicate with beneficial shareholders directly, lobby shareholders in advance of votes, and monitor advance voting leading up to an annual general meeting. Furthermore, in many instances, public companies in Canada do not allow for confidential voting, which adds indirect pressure on various institutional investors to vote in line with management's recommendations.

Concentration of Ownership

While ownership concentration of public companies in Canada has lessened in recent years,[91] a significant number are still owned by a small group of controlling shareholders.[92] Studies in both Canada and the United States suggest that this phenomenon is detrimental to corporate performance for various reasons, including the entrenchment of management, the extraction of private benefits from firms by majority shareholders, and the tendency of controlling shareholders, particularly second-generation controllers, to perform poorly as managers.[93]

Investor Apathy

Institutional investors have traditionally taken a passive role in the investment process, despite statements by Canadian and American regulators affirming that proxy votes are valuable plan assets and that voting or delegating the voting of plan assets is part of the duties of plan fiduciaries.[94] Many attribute this to the "free-rider" phenomenon, where efficiencies dictate that smaller shareholders rely on the efforts of larger institutional investors to assert their rights and interests. Less discussed is the institutionalized subjugation of beneficial shareholders through their inability to submit shareholder proposals in all provincial jurisdictions and the delegation of voting rights to investment managers. According to one British author, "there is no history or expectation that pension fund trustees will exercise any active ownership role in relation to the shares held. That has never been seen as their role and it would be frowned upon by their corporate managements."[95] This perception is supported by results of a 1992 American survey that found that a "perceived or explicit mandate as passive owner" was the fourth top reason given by institutional investors for not engaging in shareholder activism.[96]

Conflict of Interest

A much-neglected and tabooed issue is conflict of interest at both the institutional and individual fiduciary level. Professor MacIntosh refers to "institutional co-option," where "the administrators of the pension fund of corporation A will not become activists in respect of the fund's holdings of corporation B in the expectation that the administrators of the pension fund of corporation B will show similar restraint in respect of its holdings in corporation A."[97] Similarly, MacIntosh notes that insurance companies may see their corporate clients withdraw their business if the fund managers do not vote with management.[98] While virtually impossible to verify, these assertions are particularly serious with respect to management trustees of pension plans that allow the interests of a given corporation to override those of plan members.

Resources

Institutional investors have traditionally cited limited time and resources as the two major reasons for not engaging in shareholder activism.[99] While these reasons continue to be of issue, the relaxing of rules governing shareholder activism in Canada, changing interpretations of the duties of fiduciaries, increasing trustee education, greater coordination of engagement efforts, and evidence demonstrating superior performance by actively trusteed investments all point towards growing acceptance of shareholder activism among institutional investors.

Other Issues

Commentators have identified a number of additional concerns about the role of institutional investors in corporate governance, including agency-related problems (i.e., agency accountability, moral hazards associated with failures to monitor investment managers, adverse selection of investment management, historical underperformance of investment managers, political pressure in the case of public pensions, and management compensation structures),[100] institutional concerns beyond ownership concentration (i.e., free ridership and cross-ownership),[101] and other market-related factors (i.e., lack of liquidity and corresponding increased exit costs).[102] These issues are beyond the scope of this chapter but merit renewed consideration in the context of new investor realities.

Conclusion

This chapter has considered the case for a larger role for institutional investors in the governance of publicly traded Canadian corporations in the context of global deregulation. It is suggested that acceptance of a concessionist paradigm of the firm in contrast to the classical contractualist framework, the fiduciary relationship of institutional investor to beneficiary, and empirical support linking shareholder activism with enhanced corporate performance collectively demonstrate the potential role of the institutional investor in supporting healthy corporate governance in a deregulated and global economy.

The recent amendments to federal corporate legislation in Canada represent part of a trend towards acknowledging the role of shareholders in corporate governance. These advances are coupled with increased interest by institutional investors, increasing institutional capacity to coordinate shareholder activism, and the development of proxy guidelines by pension and mutual funds. While existing studies provide some evidence in this regard, additional study is necessary to better understand this dynamic.

These initiatives are driven by a belief that institutional shareholder democracy is supportive of both improved specific investment performance and the possibility of long-term benefits for beneficiaries by mobilizing investment capital in a manner that promotes a sustainable economy.

Significant legal and institutional barriers remain that prevent efficient and effective engagement between shareholders and management. In the context where the corporation has become the primary institution in society, the challenge for Canadian corporate law is not only to provide a proper framework for shareholder democracy but also to embrace a broader notion of corporate democracy that acknowledges the involvement of all stakeholders in the governance of the firm.

Notes

1 Ronald J. Daniels and Randall Morck, *Canadian Corporate Governance Policy Options, Discussion Paper Number 3* (Ottawa: Industry Canada, 1996) at 101.

2 Virginia Haufler, *A Public Role for the Private Sector: Industry Self-Regulation in a Global Economy* (Washington, DC: Carnegie Endowment for International Peace, 2001) at 1, citing Alfred Aman, "Administrative Law for a New Century" in Aseem Prakash and Jeffrey A. Hart, eds., *Globalization and Governance* (London: Routledge, 1999).

3 See, for example, Robert Boyer and Daniel Drache, *States against Markets: The Limits of Globalization* (New York: Routledge, 1996); Saskia Sassen, *Globalization and Its Discontents* (New York: New Press, 1998).

4 Department of Foreign Affairs and International Trade, *Opening Doors to the World: Canada's International Market Access Priorities 2000* (Ottawa: DFAIT, 2001). The British Columbia Securities Commission has commenced a parallel "Deregulation Project" to produce a new *Securities Act and Rules* by the end of 2003: see British Columbia Securities Commission, *BC Notices*, Doc. No. 2001/78 (20 November 2001).

5 But see Paul N. Doremus *et al.*, *The Myth of the Global Corporation* (Princeton, NJ: Princeton University Press, 1998).

6 United Nations Conference on Trade and Development, *World Investment Report 2000: Cross-border Mergers and Acquisitions and Development* (New York: United Nations, 2000) at 1.

7 Sarah Anderson and John Cavanagh, *Top 200: The Rise of Corporate Global Power* (Washington, DC: Institute for Policy Studies, 2000), <www.ips-dc.org/reports/top200text.htm>.

8 Toronto Stock Exchange Committee on Corporate Governance in Canada, *Where Were the Directors? Guidelines for Improved Corporate Governance in Canada* (Toronto: Toronto Stock Exchange, 1994); Joint Committee on Corporate Governance, *Beyond Compliance: Building a Governance Culture*, Final Report (Toronto: TSX/CNDX/CICA, 2001); OECD, *OECD*

Guidelines for Multinational Enterprises, <http://www1.oecd.org/daf/investment/guidelines/mnetext.htm>; *Global Reporting Initiative,* <http://www.globalreporting.org>.

9   Rhys Jenkins, *Corporate Codes of Conduct: Self-Regulation in a Global Economy* (Geneva: United Nations Research Institute for Social Development, 2001); TCCR Benchmark project.

10   James P. Hawley and Andrew T. Williams, *The Rise of Fiduciary Capitalism* (Philadelphia: University of Pennsylvania Press, 2000); Robert A.G. Monks, *The New Global Investors: How Shareowners Can Unlock Sustainable Prosperity Worldwide* (Oxford: Capstone Publishing, 2001).

11   Hawley and Williams, *ibid.* at xv.

12   *Ibid.* at 5.

13   *Ibid.* at xv.

14   Shareholder activism includes a myriad of activities, including corporate-shareholder dialogue, letter writing to corporations, submission of shareholder proposals, proxy voting, and litigation. Shareholder activism has focused predominantly on the private norms associated with corporate governance; however, institutional investors, such as CalPERS, have explicitly defined corporate governance more broadly beyond board process to include the financial, social, and environmental practices of corporations.

15   *Canada Business Corporations Act,* R.S.C. 1985, c. C-44, as am. by S.C. 2001, c. 14.

16   Hawley and Williams, *supra* note 10 at 3, citing Robert A.G. Monks and Nell Minow, *Corporate Governance* (Cambridge, MA: Basil Blackwell, 1995) at 268-70: "This is an agenda that can be addressed only by government in conjunction with a 'universal shareholder.'"

17   Michel Patry and Michel Poitevin, "Why Institutional Investors Are Not Better Shareholders" in R.J. Daniels and R.K. Morck, eds., *Corporate Decision-Making in Canada* (Calgary: University of Calgary Press, 1995) 341 at 341; Alan Shipman, *The Market Revolution and Its Limits: A Price for Everything* (London: Routledge, 1999) at 288-89.

18   J.G. MacIntosh, "The Role of Institutional and Retail Shareholders in Canadian Capital Markets" (1993) 32 Osgoode Hall L.J. 371 at 411 [hereinafter *MacIntosh (1993)*].

19   These fiduciary duties have evolved, albeit slowly, over time and continue to respond to changes in investment practices. See Gil Yaron, "The Responsible Pension Trustee: Re-Interpreting the Principles of Prudence and Loyalty in the Context of Socially Responsible Institutional Investing" (2001) 20(4) Estates, Trusts and Pensions J. 305.

20   Hawley and Williams, *supra* note 10 at 2.

21   This mandate conflicts with the interests of corporate directors, who are charged with acting in the interest of the corporation and money managers under pressure to obtain short-term gains to enhance their placement in the market. See Allan Sykes, *Capitalism for Tomorrow: Reuniting Ownership and Control* (Oxford: Capstone Publishing, 2000) at 105.

22   Hawley and Williams, *supra* note 10 at 13.

23   Monks, *supra* note 10 at 105.

24   Hawley and Williams, *supra* note 10 at 5, 14. The authors also note that as a group, they also invest in the same large, liquidity-traded companies.

25   Institutional investors include banks, trusteed pension plans, life insurance companies, trust and mortgage loan companies, local credit unions, caisses populaires, insurance companies, and investment funds. For the purpose of this paper, reference to institutional investors is focused primarily on trusteed pension funds because of their larger presence in the Canadian equity market and their historic leadership in institutional shareholder activism.

26   Hawley and Williams, *supra* note 10 at 5. (Institutional shareholders owned 59.9 percent of the largest 1,000 US firms in 1997.)

27   See Statistics Canada, *National Balance Sheet Accounts – 1806* (Table 378-0004), CANSIM II Database. These figures do not include equity ownership by foreign institutional investors. High levels of ownership concentration in Canadian firms have traditionally undermined these figures. However, recent studies suggest this has become less of a consideration with increased dilution in ownership over recent years. See *infra* note 100.

28   TSE Review, December 2001; Statistics Canada, *ibid.* The TSE is represented here as a proxy for the Canadian equity market.

29   OECD, "Recent Trends: Institutional Investor Statistics" (2001) 80 Financial Market Trends 46.

30 Statistics Canada, *Quarterly Estimates of Trusteed Pension Plans (Second Quarter 2001)* (Ottawa: Statistics Canada, 2001); OECD, *ibid.* at 47.

31 TSE Review, *supra* note 28.

32 These figures do not include investment through various pooled and indexed funds, which are significant given that many plans use indexation as a strategy. See *MacIntosh (1993)*, *supra* note 18 at 443.

33 Vector Research, public opinion poll (Toronto: Canadian Democracy and Corporate Accountability Commission, 2001). The survey of 2,006 adults conducted between 28 September and 8 October 2001 found that 54 percent of shareholders want pension funds that invest in firms with a good record of social responsibility even if it resulted in somewhat lower benefits to the shareholder. Fifty-nine percent of wealthy shareholders (i.e., incomes greater than $100,000) endorsed this view. See also Russell Sparkes, "SRI Comes of Age" (2000) Pension Investor citing a national opinion poll conducted in Britain during September 1997 for the Ethical Investment Research Service (EIRIS).

34 Adolph A. Berle and Gardiner C. Means, *The Modern Corporation and Private Property* (New York: Macmillan, 1932).

35 B.R. Cheffins, *Company Law: Theory, Structure, and Operation* (Oxford, UK: Oxford University Press, 1997).

36 See, for example, Robert W.V. Dickerson *et al.*, *Proposals for a New Business Corporations Law for Canada*, vol. 1 (Ottawa: Information Canada, 1971) at 95.

37 Mary Stokes, "Company Law and Legal Theory" in W. Twining, ed., *Legal Theory and Common Law* (Oxford, UK: B. Blackwell, 1986) at 162. Concessionism is distinguished from the theoretical concept of communitarianism discussed by Janis Sarra in Chapter 2 of this book. While the intended relation is the same, concessionism mandates a subservient relationship of the corporation to the state and society, whereas communitarianism relies on corporate voluntarism to support the public good.

38 Chris Tollefson, *Theorizing Corporate Constitutional Rights: Revisiting "Santa Clara" Revisited* (LL.M. Thesis, York University, 1992) at 13 citing *Dartmouth College* v. *Woodward*, 17 U.S. 518 at 636 (1819) (per Marshall Ch. J.).

39 *Ibid.*

40 Shareholder Association for Research and Education, "Shareholders Back Calls for Disclosure on Board Independence" (2001) 1(2) Prospectus 2; Moira Hutchinson, *The Promotion of Active Shareholdership for Corporate Social Responsibility in Canada* (Toronto: Michael Jantzi Research Associates, 1996) appendices. These figures do not include management proposals successfully opposed by shareholders, shareholder proposals that were withdrawn prior to a vote, or shareholder proposals not circulated by the corporation on grounds that the subject matter of the proposal was excludable. Nor does it capture shareholder involvement through corporate-shareholder dialogue, which is the preferred mode of institutional engagement.

41 See, for example, Ontario Teachers' Pension Plan, which publicly discloses its proxy voting guidelines and proxy voting records, <http://www.otpp.com>; Canadian Press, "OMERS Airs Ethical Guidelines" *Globe and Mail* (28 January 2002) B3. For additional examples, see Shareholder Association for Research and Education, *Incorporating Active Trustee Practices into Pension Plan Investment Policies* (Vancouver: SHARE, 2002), <http://www.share.ca>.

42 See, for example, *MacIntosh (1993)*, *supra* note 18 at 411; Jeffrey G. MacIntosh, "Institutional Shareholders and Corporate Governance in Canada" (1995-96) 26 Can. Bus. L.J. 145 at 167 [hereinafter *MacIntosh (1995-96)*].

43 For the history of the churches in Canadian shareholder activism, see Hutchinson, *supra* note 40. See also P.A. Koval, "Trends in Canadian Shareholder Activism" in The Canadian Institute, *Duties and Liabilities of Officers and Directors* (19 November 1992).

44 See Canada, Senate Standing Committee on Banking, Trade and Commerce, "Proceedings of the Senate Standing Committee on Banking, Trade and Commerce, First Session, Thirty-seventh Parliament" (14 March and 4 April 2001).

45 *MacIntosh (1993)*, *supra* note 18 at 376, 438. Patry and Poitevin, *supra* note 17 at 364, also point out additional efficiencies with respect to institutional shareholder activism, including the presence of professional management, scale, and the ability to share information

with other institutional investors. MacIntosh addresses various concerns about increased institutional investor presence in the market, including concerns regarding the diminished pool of savings available for investment (at 434), impairment of the allocative efficiency of primary markets (at 434), impact on the efficiency of the price discovery mechanism (at 434), and the impairment of secondary market liquidity (at 440).

46 See Bernard S. Black, "Shareholder Passivity Reexamined" (1990) 89 Mich. L. R. 520; Jeffrey G. MacIntosh, "Institutional Investors and Corporate Governance in Canada" (Conference paper prepared for Canadian Corporate Governance: An Interdisciplinary Perspective, C.D. Howe Institute, 10-11 February 1994); Mark J. Roe, "A Political Theory of American Corporate Finance" (1991) 91 Colum. L. Rev. 10; Jeffrey G. MacIntosh and Lawrence P. Schwartz, "Do Institutional and Controlling Shareholders Increase Corporate Value?" in R.J. Daniels and R.K. Morck, eds., *Corporate Decision-Making in Canada* (Calgary: University of Calgary Press, 1995) 303 at 332.

47 The issue of whether good corporate governance improves corporate performance is beyond the scope of this chapter and is debated elsewhere in the literature. The following studies only contemplate the relationship between conventional corporate governance issues and corporate performance. For a review of American data, see Hawley and Williams, *supra* note 11, c. 6. See also MacIntosh and Schwartz, *supra* note 46 at 303; McConnell and Servaes, *infra* note 48; Paul A. Gompers, Joy L. Ishii, and Andrew Metrick, *Corporate Governance and Equity Prices* (Cambridge, MA: National Bureau of Economic Research, 2001), <http://papers.nber.org/papers/W8449>; R. La Porta *et al.*, *Investor Protection and Corporate Value* (NBER Working Paper 7403); Ronald F. Felton *et al.*, "Putting a Value on Board Governance" (1996) 4 McKinsey Quarterly. There is also an extensive literature on the impacts of externalities on investment performance. See, e.g., Glen Dowell, Stuart Hart, and Bernard Yeung, *Do Corporate Global Environmental Standards Create or Destroy Market Value?* (Washington, DC: Social Investment Forum, 2001).

48 See B.S. Black, "The Value of Institutional Investor Monitoring: The Empirical Evidence" (1992) 39 UCLA L. Rev. 895; J.J. McConnell and H. Servaes, "Additional Evidence on Equity Ownership and Corporate Value" (1990) 27 J. Fin. Econ. 595.

49 Wilshire Associates, *The CalPERS Effect* (19 July 1995) [unpublished]. The study examined the performance of sixty-two companies targeted by CalPERS over a five-year period. Results indicated that while the stock of these companies trailed the S&P 500 Index by 89 percent in the five-year period before CalPERS acted, the same stocks outperformed the index by 23 percent in the following five years, adding approximately $150 million annually in additional returns. This survey has been regularly updated since 1995, with results showing the same positive impact of active critical minority shareholding on the share relative valuation on the market.

50 Tim C. Opler and Jonathan Sokobin, *Does Coordinated Institutional Activism Work? An Analysis of the Activities of the Council of Institutional Investors* (October 1995), <http://fisher.osu.edu/fin/journal/dice/papers/1995/95-5.pdf>. The study documents the performance of ninety-six firms that appeared on the Council's focus lists in 1991, 1992, and 1993 relative to several control groups. Firms on Council focus lists experienced poor share price performance in the year before being included on a focus list. In the year after being listed, these firms experienced an average share price increase of 11.6 percent above the S&P 500. Given that the mean equity market value of Council-listed firms was $3.42 billion, the total abnormal dollar gain of these firms was estimated at $39.7 billion.

51 Hawley and Williams, *supra* note 10 at 123.

52 Office of the Superintendent of Financial Institutions Canada, *Guideline for the Development of Investment Policies and Procedures for Federally Regulated Pension Plans* (Ottawa: OSFI, 2000).

53 Hawley and Williams, *supra* note 10 at 122-23.

54 *Ibid.*

55 *CBCA* Regulatory Impact Analysis Statement at 1.

56 *Campbell* v. *Australian Mutual Provident Society* (1908) 24 T.L.R. 623.

57 L.C.B. Gower, *Modern Company Law*, 3rd ed. (London: Stevens, 1969) at 479.

58 Frank D. Emerson and Franklin C. Latchman, *Shareholder Democracy: A Broader Outlook for Corporations* (Cleveland: The Press of Western Reserve University, 1954) at 6. Interestingly,

Britain's *Myners Report on Institutional Investment* and South Africa's *King Report on Corporate Governance for South Africa – 2002* both suggest a return to this view by recommending the imposition of sanctions on directors, management, and shareholders who fail to attend shareholder meetings of companies in which they are invested. Similar censure is recommended for directors and managers of financial institutions who do not personally attend or send representatives to shareholder meetings of companies in which they have a certain prescribed level of investment.

59 *Canada Business Corporations Act*, S.C. 1974-75, c. 33.

60 Cheffins, *supra* note 35.

61 See clause-by-clause analysis of the proposed changes to the *CBCA*, part 12 (4 June 2001), <http://strategis.ic.gc.ca/SSG/cl00178e.html>.

62 Koval, *supra* note 43; *MacIntosh (1995-96), supra* note 42.

63 Shareholder proposals increased significantly in the last five years with the stronger coordination of the churches through the Taskforce on the Churches and Corporate Responsibility, the creation of l'Association de protection des épargnants et investisseurs du Québec, the Shareholder Association for Research and Education, and various institutional investors with activist mandates. See SHARE survey findings, *supra* note 40.

64 *MacIntosh (1993), supra* note 18 at 382; Koval, *supra* note 43 at 34-43; Senate Standing Committee on Banking, Trade and Commerce, *supra* note 44.

65 *CBCA, supra* note 15, s. 137.

66 *Ibid.*, s. 150(1)(b).

67 See, for example, *Verdun* v. *Toronto-Dominion Bank*, (1996) 139 D.L.R. (4th) 415 (S.C.C.), beneficial owner not entitled to submit proposals; *Re Varity Corp. and Jesuit Fathers of Upper Canada et al.* (1987), 41 D.L.R. (4th) 384 (Ont. C.A.), aff'g 38 D.L.R. (4th) 157 (Ont. H.C.J.), proposal excluded as being politically motivated.

68 For a detailed history of shareholder activism in Canada, see Hutchinson, *supra* note 40. See also Koval, *supra* note 43.

69 Aside from federal legislation, the jurisdictions with shareholder proposal provisions include Ontario, Manitoba, Alberta, Newfoundland, New Brunswick, and the Northwest Territories.

70 For example, Ontario's filing deadline for shareholder proposals is 60 days prior to the anniversary date of the company's annual general meeting. Other provinces set the deadline at 90 days. The *CBCA*'s recent amendments make the deadline 90 days prior to the anniversary date of the company's Notice of Meeting. See *CBCA, supra* note 15, s. 137(5)(a) and *Canada Business Corporations Regulations 2001*, SOR/DORS/2001-512 (22 November 2001), s. 50 (Canada Gazette Part II, vol. 135(25) at 2683) [hereinafter *CBCA Regulations*].

71 *CBCA, ibid.*, s. 137(1).

72 *Ibid.*, s. 137(3); *CBCA Regulations, supra* note 70, s. 49.

73 *CBCA, ibid.*, s. 137(1.1); *CBCA Regulations, ibid.*, s. 47.

74 *CBCA, ibid.*, s. 137(5)(a); *CBCA Regulations, ibid.*, s. 50.

75 *CBCA, ibid.*, s. 147.

76 *Ibid.*, s. 137(5)(c).

77 *Proposals of Security Holders*, (2001) 17 C.F.R. 240, Rule 14-8.

78 *CBCA, supra* note 15.

79 Industry Canada is presently inquiring into the creation of a dispute resolution mechanism, but it is not expected to be considered for inclusion in the federal regime until the five-year review of the *CBCA* in 2007.

80 *Supra* note 70. Under the old rules, proposals had to be received ninety days prior to the anniversary date of the company's annual general meeting.

81 Notices of Meeting are generally posted earlier on the SEDAR website.

82 *CBCA Regulations, supra* note 70, s. 58 (z.8).

83 *CBCA, supra* note 15, s. 137(X).

84 *Definition of Beneficial Ownership*, (2001) 17 C.F.R. 240, Rule 13b-3.

85 *MacIntosh (1995-96), supra* note 42 at 158.

86 For a discussion of possible information contained under the definition of material fact, see Memorandum from Director of Division of Corporation Finance to Acting Chairman

Laura Unger on the subject "Response to letter dated 2 April 2001 from Congressman Wolf" (SEC, 8 May 2001) at 2.

87   See Chapters 5 and 6 of this book.

88   William M. MacKenzie, "Out of Control" (2000) 12(6) Corp. Gov. Rev. 1 at 2; *MacIntosh (1995-96), supra* note 42 at 162 citing K.E. Montgomery and D.S.R. Leighton, "The Unseen Revolution Is Here" (1993) 58(1) U.W.O. Bus. Quar. 38. In the early 1990s, approximately 200 companies listed on the TSE had dual-class share structures, while 18 percent of the TSE Composite Index had restricted or nonvoting shares.

89   G. Jarrell and A. Poulson, "Dual Class Recapitalizations as Antitakeover Mechanisms: The Recent Evidence" (1988) 20(1/2) J. Fin. Econ. 129-52.

90   Emerson and Latchman, *supra* note 58 at 4; Michael J. Whincop, *An Economic and Jurisprudential Genealogy of Corporate Law* (Ashgate, Aldershot, UK: Dartmouth Publishing, 2001) at 124.

91   R. Daniels and J. MacIntosh, "Toward a Distinctive Canadian Corporate Law Regime" (1991) 29 Osgoode Hall L.J. 863; R. Daniels and P. Halpern, "The Role of the Closely Held Public Corporation in the Canadian Economy and the Implications for Public Policy" (1995) Can. Bus. L.J.; *MacIntosh (1993), supra* note 18; Patry and Poitevin, *supra* note 17 at 352-53.

92   MacKenzie, *supra* note 88. A review of 795 corporations listed on the TSE 300 in 2000 found that 25 percent of companies had no shareholder with more than 10 percent of all outstanding voting shares in the company; 52 percent of companies had no shareholder with more than 20 percent of outstanding voting shares; and 77 percent had no shareholder with more than 50 percent of voting shares. This, however, does not account for the cooperation of shareholders in practice. The current data contrast starkly with early studies that found that in more than three-fourths of Canadian corporations reviewed, one large blockholder controlled 20 percent or more of the voting shares, and in over half of the firms, a single blockholder controlled more than 50 percent of the voting shares. See also P. Someshwar Rao and Clifton R. Lee-Sing, "Governance Structure, Corporate Decision-Making and Firm Performance in North America," and R.J. Daniels and R. Morck, "Canadian Corporate Governance: The Challenge" in R.J. Daniels and R.K. Morck, eds., *Corporate Decision-Making in Canada* (Calgary: University of Calgary Press, 1996) 3.

93   R. Morck and D. Stangeland, "Large Shareholders and Corporate Performance in Canada" (1994) [unpublished]. See also B. Johnson *et al.*, "An Analysis of the Stock Price Reaction to Sudden Executive Deaths: Implications for the Managerial Labour Market" (1985) 7 J. Acct. and Econ. 151; M. Barclay and C. Holderness, "The Law and Large Block Trades" (1992) 35 J. L. and Econ. 265-94; M. Barclay, C. Holderness, and J. Pontiff, "Private Benefits from Block Ownership and Discounts on Closed End Funds" (1993) 33 J. Fin. 263-91.

94   Office of the Superintendent of Financial Institutions Canada, *supra* note 52; Letter from Department of Labour re Employees' Retirement Program (23 February 1994) ("Avon letter"), <http://www.lens-library.com/info/dolavon.html>.

95   Sykes, *supra* note 21 at 51.

96   K.E. Montgomery, "Survey of Institutional Shareholders" (1992) 4(4) Corp. Gov. Rev. 5 at 10.

97   *MacIntosh (1995-96), supra* note 42 at 160 citing R. Romano, "Public Pension Fund Activism in Corporate Governance Reconsidered" (1993) 93 Colum. L. Rev. 795.

98   *MacIntosh (1995-96), ibid.*

99   Montgomery, *supra* note 96 at 10.

100 Patry and Poitevin, *supra* note 17 at 354-63; *MacIntosh (1993), supra* note 18 at 443; Romano, *supra* note 97. But see Keith Ambachtsheer, "Public Pension Power in Canada: For Good ... or for Evil?" (Summer 2000) Canadian Investment Review.

101 Patry and Poitevin, *ibid.* at 355, 365; *MacIntosh (1993), ibid.*

102 Patry and Poitevin, *ibid.*

5
Investor Control of Multinational Enterprises: A Market for Corporate Governance Based on Justice and Fairness?
Ronald B. Davis

> Today, the paramount challenge that we as lawyers – academics and practitioners alike – face is to acknowledge fully the simple truth that the free market is not an end in itself, but rather a means to an end. Maximization of efficiency is always subject to corrective considerations of justice and fairness.
>
> – Gunther Handl[1]

Is control of the harmful activities of multinational enterprises (MNEs) with respect to the environment and to human, political, and social rights by their investors a credible and likely prospect? This chapter commences a discussion regarding both the potential for, and the barriers to, investor control over MNEs' international activities. The first section following this introduction briefly highlights the problem of MNE control, given the international character of MNE organizations, the national jurisdiction of the legal systems of home and host states, and the absence of international fora to regulate and arbitrate on such conduct. The problem arises from the interaction of two factors. First, the present system of international law is primarily a system governing interactions among nation-states, not the actions of private parties, including MNEs. The second factor is the limited liability attached to the corporate legal form – "the corporate veil." The corporate veil ordinarily limits the liability for harms caused by corporate operations to the assets of the corporation. The corporate veil shields both the individuals at the corporation who made the decisions causing the harm and/or the investors in the corporation from personal liability for those harms. When the corporate veil is draped across international boundaries, unique issues of accountability and control arise, issues that do not arise when corporate activity is confined to a single state.

Having identified the absence of effective public law mechanisms to hold MNEs accountable for harmful conduct, the chapter then examines proposals outlined by Robert Monks in his book *The New Global Investors*. Monks's proposals focus on the control potential of pension funds as investors in MNEs.[2] The proposals are an important contribution to the discussion regarding institutional shareholder activism. However, it is unlikely that their full potential to control MNE activity will be realized until enforceable international standards, and a system for credible, consistent reporting on the compliance of MNEs with those standards, are also brought into existence.

The following section then analyzes both the potential for, and barriers to, investor control of MNEs' harmful international activity. These factors are illustrated using the events surrounding a large release of mine tailings and wastewater at the mine operated by Marcopper Mining Corporation in the Philippines. The events demonstrate the difficulties that arise when a complex web of private international contractual relations and the "corporate veil" interact with a host country's regulatory initiatives concerning corporate activity within its jurisdiction.

The next section reviews the necessity for reliable and comparable information concerning the effects of MNEs' activities on the environment and the social, civil, and political rights of the host countries' citizens in order to have a market for socially responsible corporate governance. Recent initiatives by the United Nations Environment Project and the European Union are attempts to improve the quality and comparability of such information about MNE activity. However, neither initiative will create a mandatory, enforceable disclosure regime for MNE effects on a host country's environment or its citizens' social, civil, and political rights.

The potential for control of these harmful activities by corporate investors is examined in the following section. It concludes that this potential should not be exaggerated or offered as a substitute for public regulation. The division of power between investors and managers in corporate law constitutes an important limiting factor. While the involvement of investors in the control of MNEs is important, it will reach its optimal level only in circumstances where a vital role for public regulation is recognized as an important component of the legal and social framework for corporate accountability. Investor control is complementary to public regulation, rather than a substitute for the absence of such regulation.

Problems with National Control of MNE International Activity

MNEs are organizations that, while created in one state, operate in several states through subsidiary corporate entities created in each country of operation, through contractual links in supply and delivery chains, and/or through licensing and franchise agreements.[3] As private entities, MNEs are subject to the national law of the states in which they operate, and may also have been granted certain rights under treaties between states, rights that can be enforced in the courts of the applicable state. Certain treaties also provide for protection of investor rights against state action through binding international arbitration. Arbitration provides a dispute resolution mechanism for claims against the state by investors claiming that the state regulatory or legislative actions harmed their investments. Thus, a forum exists for private actors to hold public state actors accountable for decisions that harm equity investments. In contrast, however, there is no international forum in which these enterprises can be held accountable for their actions in breach of fundamental international law and conventions concerning human rights, the environment, and social/political rights. International law assigns this function to the courts of the various states, exercising their national jurisdiction over activities of the corporations that originate in or affect their territory.[4]

Problems arise because of a number of factors. There is the reluctance of home and/or host governments to take action against MNEs due to their importance to the country's economy or the government's complicity as investors in or beneficiaries of the company's activities.[5] There is an inability of the host country to impose the full sanctions of its law on the responsible parties because the corporate structure insulates the controlling corporation (domiciled in the home country) from adverse consequences of regulatory action in the host country. The home country may be unable to impose the full sanctions of its laws on the corporation controlling the MNE for harms arising in the host country because the MNE's corporate structure creates a separate corporation in the host country. That corporation is not ordinarily subject to the jurisdiction of the home country's courts for its actions in the host country. In some instances, there is the likelihood that the home country court, even where it finds it has jurisdiction to hear a case against the MNE for the actions of its subsidiaries in another country, will exercise its discretion not to hear the case on the grounds of one or more of the prudential doctrines, such as *forum non conveniens,* state action, comity, or public policy. Finally, there is the difficulty of the lack of a forum capable of exercising jurisdiction over the MNEs on the basis of universality jurisdiction, other than under the *Alien Tort Claims Act*[6] in the United States federal courts.

Given these difficulties with the control of international MNE activity by nation states, the issue is whether there is a potential for such control to be exercised by the MNE's equity investors, who by doing so would create accountability mechanisms absent from current international law. In this respect, Robert Monks has begun to examine this potential for a particular class of equity investors, pension funds with investments in global equity markets.

Monks's Theory of Investor Activism as a Normative Control on Corporate Action

In *The New Global Investors*, Robert Monks expresses his concern that the large MNEs have a "license ... to do what they will," and that this licence can then be used to create either beneficial investments or social problems symptomatic of the "problem of unlimited license."[7] He proposes that corporations be controlled through active participation in corporate governance by their shareholders. He points to evidence that pension funds own a large proportion of global equity, estimating that they may own up to 77 percent of the equity in the largest 1,000 companies in the world.[8] His economic rationale for the intervention of this group of investors to protect the human, social, environmental, and political rights of people around the world is that this group of investors cannot "externalize" these costs in the same manner as domestic investors because they are investors in every market:

> The Global Investor is likely to make good decisions for the long-term of society, because it can afford in most case to take a long-term view, and a diversified view. An ordinary domestic investor may choose to invest in a corporation that externalizes the brunt of the harm that it is doing. But importantly, nothing is external to a global shareowner. Institutions having investments in all countries have virtually no incentive to permit environmental and hiring practices in the poorest countries that can only have the impact of competing with their own investments elsewhere.[9]

In his view, the only shareholder group that is capable of both being active investors and being held accountable for their exercise of power in a legitimate fashion are pension fund fiduciaries. Monks suggests that the pension funds are more legitimate wielders of corporate power than the unfettered management of large corporations because "they have more of a stake in the good of society and the world."[10] Thus, as investors with a stake in the health and well-being of the global economy, the pension funds serve as a proxy for the economic interests of the citizens of the world.

Monks believes that the development of "global values" by the Organization for Economic Cooperation and Development (OECD), the World Bank, and globalization protesters will converge over time through the need and desire for investment capital. He envisions a cost/benefit "arbitrage" by different societies that will result in the attraction of the optimum external investment. He concludes his analysis by urging governments to "remove the obstacles they have created to the working of a free market in corporate governance."[11] However, this is not a call for the withdrawal of government involvement in this area. Rather, he calls for a clear governmental requirement that fiduciaries must actively vote their shares. He also suggests that governments permit the pension plan participants to enforce this duty in the courts and/or that governments enforce it themselves.[12]

By way of background, it is important to situate Monks's proposals in the context of the legal regime governing investment of pension funds. Pension funds are monies contributed to fund pensions for employees. The employer, and in some cases both the employer and the employee, contribute to the funds. Contributions are made in return for services rendered to the employer's business by the employees. However, the pensions are payable to employees only when they reach retirement age, many years after the contributions have begun to be made to the pension fund. The level of contributions is designed to provide sufficient money to fund future pension payments, provided they are invested and generate earnings for a number of years until payments commence.

Thus, although the pension plan's funds are designed for the ultimate benefit of the employees in the plan, the funds are not directly under their control; rather, they are held in the name of the pension plan's trustees or plan administrators. The common law and pension statutes have dealt with the problems that might arise as a result of the lack of direct control of the funds assets by imposing fiduciary duties towards the employee-beneficiaries of the pension fund on the trustees or plan administrators. The duties imposed on pension fund fiduciaries include loyalty to the beneficiaries and prudence with respect to investments.[13]

Pension fund fiduciaries do not typically invest in equities directly. Rather, they retain professional investment managers to either provide advice or carry out the fund's investment program under the supervision of the fund fiduciaries. Often the shares are held in the name of the investment manager or in the name of the trust company used to hold the fund's assets.

One of the aspects of the duty of prudent investment is a requirement to maintain adequate diversification of investments. It is possible to reduce the risk to the fund from its investments to a level where the risk to the fund is reflected in the expected returns and the investments consist of a wide-ranging portfolio of stocks that will reflect those available in the equity market.[14] Many pension statutes require pension fund fiduciaries to adopt formal, written investment policies and goals that constitute binding guidelines for the pension fund's investment managers. These written policies are also provided to the pension fund's beneficiaries and to pension-regulating agencies. Thus, there is a mechanism by which the fiduciaries and their investment managers may be accountable to the fund's beneficiaries if their investment policies and goals are breaches of their fiduciary duty and/or if they invest in a manner that is not permitted by the policy.

Once the pension fund has invested in a corporation's equities, the pension fund fiduciaries have access to certain levers of control over the corporation through their power to vote their shares in shareholder meetings and in elections of the corporation's board of directors. The pension fund's beneficiaries, as employees, residents of certain communities, and persons who suffer any adverse changes to the local environment, have an interest in the attempts to externalize certain costs of corporate activity. They have an interest in potential costs that may be imposed on the corporation in order to compensate those who are harmed. In addition, because they are diversified investors in all or most of the equity market, any externalization of these costs is an illusory benefit to them. Since they will also be investors in those competitors disadvantaged by the successful externalization, they will not receive any overall financial benefits from the externalization since the gain to the externalizing corporation will be counterbalanced by the losses sustained by the non-externalizing corporations. Thus, for pension funds with diversified investments, there is no "benefit" to be reaped in the traditional "cost/benefit analysis" by which such externalizing activity is usually justified as generating increased shareholder wealth.[15] They also have an interest in potential harms to their future employment, to their civic and political rights, and to their environment if corporations engage in unrestrained externalization of these harms. This interest is reflected in certain survey results that indicate that pension fund beneficiaries do not want their pension fund's investments to be used to support corporations that impose these harms on their society, economy, or environment.[16]

The Potential for, and Barriers to, Investor Control of International Activity

Monks's proposals are a useful starting point for a discussion of the potential for control of the international activities of MNEs by their investors. The question remains, however, of how, if the course of action urged by Monks is adopted, pension fund trustees as MNE investors in the developed world can realistically control an MNE to prevent violations of the human, economic, social, or political rights of the citizens of another country?

There are two means for control by pension fund investors. First, control can be delivered through the imposition of significant costs on an MNE for such violations. Second, there is a control potential through a market for socially responsible corporations, similar to the consumer market for sustainable harvesting and fair-trade labelling on consumer products. Control would be exercised in the first instance through a legal system imposing liability for compensatory damages on the MNE for violations of these rights. These costs, or rather the potential for incurring these costs, would cause corporate management and/or its shareholders to either ensure that their operations do not violate these rights, or withdraw investment, or refuse to invest where the risks of being implicated in such violations is too high. The second source of control would depend on pension fund trustees acting on information about the international activities of MNEs' subsidiaries by refusing to invest in corporations that violate human, economic, social, or political rights or by exercising control over the corporations they have invested in to prevent such violations.

However, as the international legal system is presently constructed, the first method does not present a realistic alternative for control because legal persons, including MNEs, can ordinarily be subjected to such costs only through legal actions in the host state where the violations have occurred. Although it is possible that some legal action may be taken against the MNE in its home state, the likelihood of success is subject to a number of doctrinal constraints that substantially diminish the ability of such "home state liability" to act as a reliable control on an MNE's operations.[17]

Marcopper: An Illustrative Example of the Problems of International Regulation

A recent situation in the Philippines provides a useful illustration of the difficulties that arise for environmental enforcement activities as a result of draping the corporate veil over international borders. The *Globe and Mail* reported on unsuccessful attempts by the Philippine government to force a Canadian mining company, Placer Dome Inc., to take steps to prevent the catastrophic failure of a dam retaining millions of tonnes of waste water and tailings at the Marcopper mine site.[18] The mine was owned and operated by the Marcopper Mining Corporation, a Philippine corporation. It had been in operation since 1969.[19] In its 1996 annual report, Placer Dome reported that there had been a large accidental release of 4 million tonnes of tailings at the "39.9 percent owned Marcopper Mine" in March of that year.[20] Placer Dome indirectly owned 39.9 percent of the stock of Marcopper.[21] It had three of the eight directors on Marcopper's board.[22]

The release of tailings into a nearby river system occurred around a concrete plug in a tunnel at the base of a Marcopper holding pit.[23] Since the discharge, Placer Dome has conducted extensive environmental studies and has undertaken to restore the river to the condition it was in prior to the 1996 spill.[24] Placer Dome undertook this work voluntarily, as its position is that it is under no legal obligation, as a minority shareholder, to conduct a cleanup.[25] In addition to indirectly owning 39.9 percent of the shares, Placer Dome had provided guarantees of certain indebtedness for loans granted to the Marcopper Mining Corporation.[26] At the time of the tailings pit incident in 1996, $20 million of the guaranteed debt remained outstanding. Following the release and the shutdown of Marcopper's operations, Placer Dome offered to acquire the balance of the outstanding principal of the debt by assignment.[27] Placer Dome also recorded a $43 million provision against earnings, which represented the outstanding balance of the loan it had guaranteed and its estimate of the costs of repairing the concrete plug, remediating the tailings released, and setting up a compensation fund. The provision also took into account the expected proceeds of insurance policies.[28]

In March 1997, Placer Dome reached an agreement with Marcopper's controlling Philippine owner to transfer Placer Dome's interest in Marcopper to Marcopper. Placer Dome repaid the outstanding debt it had guaranteed and had its subsidiary, a Cayman Islands company called MR Holdings, acquire the debt and collateral security from the lender. Placer Dome's shares in MR Holdings were then transferred to "a group of Philippine financial investors." The foregoing details concerning the fate of its shares in Marcopper were revealed by Placer Dome in a press release following "erroneous news reports" based on court documents filed in a Philippine court action by MR Holdings.[29] MR Holdings described itself as a wholly owned subsidiary of Placer Dome when it filed a third-party claim seeking to prevent the sheriff from auctioning Marcopper's assets to satisfy a court judgment in favour of an unsecured creditor.[30] Placer Dome was never a party to the court proceedings. The Philippine Supreme Court recently held that based on the record before it, Marcopper and Placer Dome should not be considered as one and the same entity.[31] Thus, in the Philippine courts, the corporate veil has not been pierced, and Marcopper and Placer Dome are legally distinct entities.

Two issues arising out of the tailings release remain outstanding, however. The first is an acceptable method for the disposal of the tailings removed from the river. The second is the structural integrity of the Marcopper tailings pit and dams on the Marcopper property. Soon after the release of the tailings, Placer Dome formed a separate entity, Placer Dome Technical Services Philippines (PDTS), to complete the cleanup.[32] Marcopper and PDTS sought the approval of various Philippine government agencies for a plan to remove the tailings from the river and dispose of them in a deepwater ocean site off the Philippine coast. Marcopper submitted an application in 1997 and PDTS submitted an environmental impact study in 1999; no permit for the disposal was issued until August 2001. That permit, dated January 2001, had already expired when it was issued.[33] The expired permit was withdrawn by Philippine authorities one week later. The issuance of the permit was even more puzzling because in April 2001, a regional official of the Philippine Department of Environment and Natural Resources (DENR) had indicated that the DENR favoured returning the tailings to the pit from which they had escaped.[34] The final decision on a tailings disposal method was to be taken following a study by the United States Geological Survey (USGS), which was retained by the province of Marinduque to act as the consultant with respect to "all possible cleanup options available for the rehabilitation and restoration of the tailings spills in affected areas."[35]

The second issue concerns the stability of the tailings pit and dams on the Marcopper mine site. An engineering report funded by PDTS was prepared pursuant to an Engineering Study Agreement between the Philippine Mines and Geosciences Bureau of the Department of Environment and Natural Resources, Marcopper, and PDTS.[36] The findings of this study were brought before the Philippine House of Representatives on 5 September 2001 in a speech by the Representative from the Marcopper mine site district, and were referred to the Committee on Ecology.[37] According to newspaper reports, the study advised that there was imminent danger of failure of one of the dams. It went on to advise that such a failure would result in property damage and potential loss of life.[38] The report also pointed out that a second drainage tunnel in the tailings pit could also fail due to the pressure of rising waters in the pit, and more than 100,000 people living in the vicinity would be affected.[39] The Ecology Committee began to investigate the operations of Marcopper Mining and issued an invitation to Placer Dome to testify. Placer Dome refused the invitation, saying that it had no current information to contribute that was not already in the engineering consultant's report or known to Marcopper, the mine's owner. Following the publicity about the findings of the report, the DENR Secretary issued an order in a letter dated 11 October 2001 to Placer Dome, PDTS, and Marcopper, requiring them to secure the dam and tailings pit.[40] Placer Dome responded by requesting that the order be withdrawn because it had no legal responsibility for the Marcopper mine's structures.[41]

Placer Dome then announced that it had concluded that its presence was causing politically-based rather than merit-based decision making, and decided that Marcopper's principal shareholder, as a local company, would be more effective.[42] In November 2001, therefore, Placer Dome reached an agreement with Marcopper and its controlling shareholders to have Marcopper complete the river cleanup by removing the tailings and replacing them in Marcopper's tailings pit.[43] This cleanup will be funded by PDTS using funds in an escrow account earmarked for the cleanup payments to Marcopper. An initial payment was made by Placer Dome to the controlling shareholder. It is Placer Dome's position that it has no further role to play "in addressing the issues on the Marcopper mining site," which it says are the responsibility of the owner and operator, Marcopper.[44] Nevertheless, according to Placer Dome, as of February 2002, it had spent approximately US$70 million to replace the plug in the Marcopper tailings pit, clean the river to the extent possible without a final decision on where the tailings would be deposited, and repay the $21 million loan to Marcopper from the Asia Development Bank that Placer Dome had guaranteed.[45] In December 2001, PDTS closed its office and exited the Philippines.[46]

Thus, Placer Dome still intends to fund the remediation of the 1996 tailings release, although it has contracted with Marcopper to have it obtain the necessary permits and actually perform the work. Payment for work performed will not be made until an engineering firm retained by Placer Dome certifies that the work has been satisfactorily completed. It is not clear where Marcopper is going to obtain the funds to pay for the cleanup, since it will have to expend some funds in order to perform the work necessary to obtain certification and payment from the escrow account, although its principal shareholder has received the initial payment from Placer Dome. Even more problematic, however, is whether Marcopper has funding to carry out the repairs required to the tailings pit and dams at the Marcopper site. Placer Dome's position is that these are the responsibility of Marcopper. The funding it has agreed to provide is for the removal of the tailings from the river. In a recent interview, Mr. Bernardino, a director of Marcopper and owner of F Holdings, Inc. (which has been identified in a newspaper report and during Ecology Committee hearings as Marcopper's principal shareholder)[47] indicated that he did not see any need to repair the tailings pit or dams and that he wanted to start returning the tailings to the pit without waiting for the USGS study results.[48]

Placer Dome expends considerable resources in its worldwide operations on long-term sustainability, including some resources directed at remediation. However, what is at issue is how decisions are made with respect to environmental protection and remediation, the quantum of resources directed to these activities, and the accountability mechanisms in place for an MNE operating in numerous countries and employing thousands of employees in those countries. When assessing the reports concerning the Marcopper situation, one has to keep in mind that unlike privately held MNEs, Placer Dome is subject to mandatory public disclosure. In addition, its public commitment to sustainable operations make it subject to a level of scrutiny to which privately held corporations without this commitment are not subjected. As well, Placer Dome, as a minority shareholder, was under no obvious legal obligation to pay for remediation of the tailings spill and arguably could have restricted its losses to the payment of its loan guarantees. Placer Dome has certainly taken that position regarding any legal liability for the condition of the Marcopper dams and tailings pit, which it says are the responsibility of the mine's owner and operator, Marcopper.

Not everyone agrees with Placer Dome's position regarding Marcopper, however. More recently, the *Globe and Mail* reported that a Philippine congressman from the region in which the Marcopper mine is located claimed that Placer Dome was running away from both the weakened dams and the 1996 spill into the river. A Placer Dome spokesperson denied the charge and said it had set aside enough money in a trust fund to clean up the site.[49] In a letter to employees, Placer Dome's president and chief executive officer referred to these newspaper reports as false and misleading, reiterating the company's position that it had no legal obligation to take any steps concerning either the Marcopper spill or the condition of the structures.[50] Placer Dome was created in 1987 by the amalgamation of three Canadian mining corporations, Placer Development Limited, Dome Mines Limited, and Campbell Red Lake Mines Limited.[51] In its preliminary survey, the USGS reviewed the historical literature concerning the Marcopper mine in which it was reported that the mine was under "design and management control" of Placer Development Limited.[52] Marcopper Mining Corporation was formed to mine the copper discovered by Placer Development on Marinduque Island. Placer Development guaranteed the original loan taken out to finance the mine's development.[53] According to newspaper reports, Philippine ruler Ferdinand Marcos owned 50 percent of Marcopper's shares through a company called Performance Investments Corporation, until they were seized by the Philippine government in 1986, following his overthrow; they were sold to an investor in 1994.[54] In addition, according to Catherine Coumans, a longtime critic of Marcopper's operations in the Philippines, Placer Development, and then Placer Dome, provided the individuals who served as presidents and resident managers of Marcopper until 1997, pursuant to terms in the loan guarantees that the companies provided to the lenders in return for the loans to Marcopper.[55] For some of these individuals, employment at Marcopper was preceded and followed by further employment at Placer Development or one of the Placer Dome companies.[56]

The foregoing recitation of events is not an assertion that Placer Dome is legally liable for either the tailings spill or the upkeep of the Marcopper mine structures. Rather, it is offered as an example of the kinds of informational barriers that inhabitants of both host countries and home countries will face in trying to determine such an issue. As matters stand, some of the terms of the agreement between Placer Dome and Marcopper and its principal shareholder for the cleanup of the tailings remain confidential.[57] The complex web of private contractual relations between the banks, Placer Dome, and Marcopper, including the hiring of Placer employees by Marcopper to serve as president and resident manager, also have their details and significance veiled by private contracts. The intervention of private contractual arrangements, even where publicly traded companies are involved, certainly presents a daunting task for host country inhabitants who might wish to try and follow the decision-making responsibilities. Finally, there is the corporate veil, a legal protection that is expressly designed to shield shareholders, such as Placer Dome, from liability beyond the value of their investment in the corporation. Placer Dome wrote off its entire investment in Marcopper, plus the estimated costs of the cleanup. It then transferred its equity in Marcopper to Marcopper's other shareholder. Thus, it has incurred the costs of the tailings release to the full extent required by the limited liability provided by the corporate veil. Nevertheless, the

Philippines' DENR Secretary was willing to order Placer Dome to assume responsibility for repairing the tailings pit and dam. Whether or not the Secretary had the legal right to issue such an order to Placer Dome, subsequent events show that even a host country willing to enforce its standards against an MNE may be frustrated by the MNE's corporate veil, where the MNE withdraws from the host state.

These differing views regarding responsibility highlight the problem of informational asymmetries. The lack of an international forum to deal with such claims results in the information being disseminated primarily through media accounts. Yet pension funds need transparency in order to assess and potentially act in cases of alleged corporate misconduct. It is also evident that there is an inadequate judicial forum to resolve these conflicts between officials of the host state and the MNE. The chances of being able to pursue Placer Dome in a Canadian court for either a mandatory order requiring it to repair the dam and other structures in the Philippines or for the environmental damage and loss of life if the dam does ultimately fail are very remote, regardless of the existence of any actual legal merit to such a claim against Placer Dome.

Canadian courts' jurisdiction over Placer Dome as a Canadian corporation would not be an issue. However, there are the practical problems of commencing a lawsuit in a land thousands of miles from home. Moreover, the plaintiffs would have to establish subject-matter jurisdiction, based on some theory of either "vicarious liability" for the acts of the Philippine corporation, or on the theory of direct liability for a failure to supervise a foreign corporation as a significant shareholder.[58] In order to establish the second theory, the plaintiffs would have to establish actual control, since as a minority shareholder, where there is also a single majority shareholder, Placer Dome's relationship with Marcopper will not fit comfortably into the parent-subsidiary model of liability. Any application by injured citizens of the host nation would also have to meet the defendant's arguments that a Canadian court was a *forum non conveniens*.[59]

Although the plaintiffs might also consider a claim under the *Alien Tort Claims Act (ATCA)*[60] in the federal courts of the United States, they would once again face the problems of subject-matter jurisdiction and *forum non conveniens*, with the additional problem of establishing personal jurisdiction over Placer Dome.[61] Subject matter jurisdiction has been taken under *ATCA* with respect to the actions of corporations "only for the most egregious violations of civil and political rights and for violations of international humanitarian law."[62] Subject-matter jurisdiction has specifically been denied in cases of environmental abuses.[63] Given US federal courts' requirement for state action to establish subject-matter jurisdiction under the *ATCA*, the current efforts of the Philippine government to force Placer Dome to repair the dam might lead to a finding of lack of subject-matter jurisdiction in any suit against Placer Dome under *ATCA*.[64]

In Order to Have a Market, You Have to Be Able to Measure

Thus, the cost/benefit arbitrage by different nations resulting in the optimum level of external investment depends for its efficacy on the costs imposed by restraints on MNEs' activities through the legal system. However, such arbitrage under the existing legal system will fail to provide the expected optimization of investments because the MNE will be able to "externalize" the costs of harmful operations onto the people, economy, and government of the host state and thus invest in non-optimal operations. Monks appears to expect that pension fund trustees as the "owners" of the MNE would require investment optimization through the exercise of some form of restraints on managerial discretion.

However, in order for the trustees to impose limits on a corporation's management, they first need to know what its management is doing with respect to the environment and human, social, and political rights in host countries. Second, they need to be able to provide MNEs with clear guidelines for permissible and impermissible activity in these areas. For pension fund trustees, a cost/benefit "arbitrage" would not be possible without some reliable method of determining the costs, including the harm to the environment and social, civil, and political rights, of particular investments in the absence of clearly enforceable laws as a benchmark for assessing these costs. Investors need both appropriate standards and a reliable source of information if the "arbitrage" is going to lead to anything but further harmful exploitation in the name of profitable returns for the MNE.

This same lack of standards and reliable information about compliance with those standards also undermines the second source of control of the MNE envisioned by Monks – a free market in corporate governance.[65] Monks assumes that pension fund trustees or their investment managers will have access to the kind of information about the international activities of subsidiary corporations of the parent MNE that will allow them to make judgments about these activities' effects on the environment and the social, civil, and political rights of the host country's citizens. He also assumes that there is agreement on the appropriate standards of compliance to be applied, as well as on the effects of MNEs' activities on these rights. Pension fund trustees would invest in those MNEs that respected these rights and divest their holdings from MNEs that did not, and/or seek changes in corporate policy through the exercise of their power as shareholders.

However, as has been pointed out with respect to the attempts to control MNEs through the consumer market, meaningful standards of behaviour and reliable information about the compliance of the MNE with those standards in all aspects of its operations are extremely scarce.[66] Without such information, pension funds will not be able to either effectively control management of the MNE and/or determine which corporations are engaged in activities that harm their interests as global investors. It is highly unlikely that the funds will be able to justify the costs of doing the on-site research necessary in the absence of verifiable audits of corporate activities overseas, in view of the diversified investment portfolios each fund is legally required to maintain. Diversification limits the amount of resources a pension fund can justify expending to with respect to a single investment.[67] In such circumstances, pension funds will have to rely on information produced by third parties. Thus, merely having the pension fund trustees committed to trying to control the management of an MNE will not necessarily generate either clear guidelines or reliable information about the compliance of the MNE and its subsidiary corporations with such guidelines.

In addition, some of the lessons from the financial markets would indicate the need for international standards and credible, consistent reporting on compliance in order for a corporate governance market to work. As Stéphane Rousseau points out in Chapter 1 of this book, a regime of voluntary disclosure of corporate governance information makes it difficult to distinguish between accurate reporting and window dressing, and this may lead to an adverse selection problem. That is, if the information that the investors have about the quality of corporate governance does not enable them to distinguish the corporations with good corporate governance from those with problematic governance, this difference will not be reflected in their prices.[68] Corporate law tries to mitigate the problems for financial markets caused by asymmetric information by mandating regular disclosure of relevant financial information and regulating insider trading. However, in the area of corporate governance, and especially with respect to compliance with international norms of human rights and environmental, political, and social rights, there is no highly developed regulatory scheme of disclosure and verification to mitigate the inability of investors to judge corporate quality.

Recent Initiatives by the United Nations Environment Project and the European Union

There are some recent initiatives that may improve the quality and comparability of information available about an MNE's operations. The Coalition of Environmentally Responsible Economies (CERES) and the United Nations Environment Project (UNEP) have jointly convened an ambitious project, funded by UNEP, called the "Global Reporting Initiative" (GRI). The GRI has developed "Sustainability Reporting Guidelines" to be used by MNEs to provide information with respect to their economic, environmental, and social performance globally. The purpose of the guidelines is summarized as follows:

The GRI seeks to make sustainability reporting as routine and credible as financial reporting in terms of comparability, rigour, and verifiability ...

A generally accepted framework for sustainability reporting will enable corporations, governments, NGOs, investors, labour, and other stakeholders to gauge the progress of organisations in their implementation of voluntary initiatives and toward other practises supportive of sustainable development. At the same time, a common framework will provide the basis for benchmarking and identifying best practises to support internal management decisions.[69]

The GRI is creating a permanent organization to promote and develop the guidelines. The members of the permanent organization include the reporting corporations themselves, UNEP, nongovernmental organizations, and some national government agencies. Although the current guidelines provide for self-reporting, the GRI is attempting to obtain consensus on an appropriate set of rules addressing independent "verification" or "assurance" concerning any reports generated using the GRI guidelines.

However, reporting under these guidelines, as with many other such initiatives, is entirely voluntary. In addition, the reports themselves do not provide any standards against which to judge the types and levels of activities reported. They provide information about the trends in the various activities reported, and leave it to the individual investor to determine whether sufficient progress is being made and whether the level of activity reported is acceptable or not. For example, engineering reports concerning the state of environmental controls could be reported as an investment in environmental engineering by the parent corporation. There does not appear to be any mechanism that would require the corporation to link the commissioning of the report to its willingness to follow the report's recommendations.

Similarly, a European Parliament proposal that a committee of the European Parliament could serve as a temporary European Monitoring Platform is based on voluntary participation. All interested parties could both praise companies that are acting in accordance with international standards and criticize companies that fail to comply, and this praise and criticism would also provide increased information to activist investors.[70] The proposed participation and reporting by companies would be voluntary and motivated by a desire to "show their stakeholders that they are conforming with best practice."[71] The European Parliament saw this platform as merely a temporary measure while the European Commission and Council developed the legal basis for a binding code and monitoring system in the European Union (EU) in accordance with its resolution.[72]

In 2001 the Commission of the European Union issued two communications dealing with globalization. The first is a communication setting out the EU's approach to the issue of social governance and promotion of core labour standards in its trading relations with other states (Core Labour Standards Communication).[73] In the communication, the Commission rejects sanctions as the appropriate method for promoting such standards. Instead, the Commission preferred strengthening the role of the International Labour Organization (ILO) and its complaint mechanisms by providing technical assistance to the ILO.[74] The communication also approves of denying preferential access to EU markets to products from countries that permit violations of the ILO's core conventions.[75]

The Commission also published a Green Paper on corporate social responsibility (CSR).[76] The Green Paper envisions the role of the European Union as that of "promoting" CSR through provision of a "framework" that provides transparency, coherence, and best practices, and by assisting in development of the appropriate evaluation and verification tools. The Green Paper does not discuss the European Parliament's 1998 resolution concerning a model code of conduct for MNEs and the creation of a Monitoring Platform. The potential for the creation of such a model code is present in the proposed framework, and it could arguably result from the consultation process following the issuance of the Green Paper.[77] However, the Commission was expressly refraining from making any concrete proposals in the Green Paper because the discussions concerning the role of the EU in corporate social responsibility were only at the preliminary stage.[78]

In July 2001, following the consultation, the Commission issued a Communication to European Institutions and Member States setting out a proposed strategy on CSR for the Commission (hereinafter EU Communication).[79] The EU Communication presented a definition of corporate social responsibility that emphasized its voluntary nature, its intimate links with sustainable development, and its dimension of exceeding minimum legal standards.[80] It also recognized the global dimensions of CSR by referring to the need to develop an effective system of "global governance," including social and environmental dimensions. The EU Communication then went on to refer to globalization bringing "increased exposure to transboundary economic criminality, requiring an international response."[81] However, the international response envisioned by the Commission is to follow the strategies of encouraging compliance with international standards, and using trade preferences to encourage compliance as outlined in the Core Labour Standards Communication discussed above, and extending those strategies to all areas of corporate social responsibility.[82] The Commission also identified problems with transparency and comparability of standards for measuring CSR and, in response to this and other problems, created an EU Multi-stakeholder Forum on CSR, which is to report in the summer of 2004 on a number of topics, including:

- effectiveness and credibility of codes of conducts, to be based on internationally agreed principles, in particular the OECD guidelines for multinational enterprises
- development of commonly agreed guidelines and criteria for CSR measurement, reporting, and assurance
- definition of commonly agreed guidelines for labelling schemes, supporting the ILO core conventions and environmental standards
- disclosure on pension and retail funds Socially Responsible Investing (SRI) policies.[83]

Thus, although the Commission appears to recognize that there is a problem of "transboundary economic criminality" requiring a response, it does not propose that the EU take the initiative in developing the needed international response. However, given the status of CSR as an activity over and above that of compliance with the law, one would think that defining that compliance and the means to ensure it would be an important step in promoting CSR.

The Role of the Investor in the Control of Corporate Activity: The Myth of Ownership

Scholars writing on the problems of corporate governance generally have stated the problem as one arising from the separation of "ownership" and "control" and characterized the management of the corporation and/or its board of directors as the "agents" of the shareholders.[84] It is a uniquely indirect form of agency, however.[85] Although corporate law provides shareholders with the right to make proposals to the annual general meeting of shareholders, these proposals, even if they receive majority support, may only be advisory and the board of directors need not comply with their direction.[86] Thus, there are substantial legal obstacles to the use of shareholder proposals as the means by which the directors of MNEs will be compelled to refrain from international conduct that violates human, environmental, social, and political rights.[87] In an earlier paper, Monks himself recognized that under the current legal regime, the governance role of shareholders was "advisory."[88]

Institutional investors in the United States have recently begun submitting shareholder proposals containing amendments to the corporation's bylaws.[89] This power is also found in Canadian corporate statutes.[90] The debate over the use of the bylaw amendment power by shareholders in the United States has centred on two issues: (1) the appropriateness of its use in a corporate law regime that gives management control over the corporation's operations; and (2) whether the board of directors may either amend or revoke shareholder-imposed bylaws following their enactment.[91] While this debate is likely to continue for some time where corporations are widely held, the opportunities for such a debate in the Canadian context are restricted by the pervasive presence of controlling shareholders in those corporations.[92] Where these controlling shareholders are themselves foreign corporations that are widely held, it may be possible for Canadian global investors to pursue the enactment of bylaws with respect to the parent corporation's operations, and thus seek to implement good corporate governance of the Canadian subsidiary indirectly.

To the extent that some of the managerial excesses that Monks wishes the global investors to restrain are capable of being described as unlawful activity, there may also be potential for the use of the doctrine of *ultra vires* in order to restrain particular activity. At least one US scholar has carefully reviewed the arguments for the availability of shareholder remedies for *ultra vires* acts under state corporate law with respect to unlawful activity by corporate managers.[93] He concludes that although the concept is no longer applicable to most corporate activities, it remains applicable to unlawful activity by a corporation.[94] Shareholders can obtain injunctive relief and damages for *ultra vires* acts without having to pass the procedural hurdles and overcome the judicial deference to management decision making in the "business judgment rule" applied in US state courts in shareholder derivative suits.[95] The remedies would also be available to shareholders to restrain the harmful activities of MNEs where those activities contravene the laws of the host state and/or international law where that law is applicable to the corporation.[96]

These obstacles are not insurmountable, but they do represent serious impediments to the ability of global investors to commence the project urged on them by Monks. Despite the impediments to their participation in corporate governance activities, institutional investors continue to pursue changes and develop novel strategies to overcome them.[97] In addition to shareholder proposals, some pension funds have developed strategies such as communication with the directors about concerns, withholding votes from directors, and even initiating a proxy battle for control.[98] Thus, the difficulty experienced by global investors in exerting a degree of control over management to date has not led them to desist.

However, one factor will greatly inhibit any efforts they may make to ensure that corporations abide by international legal norms that protect human rights, political and social rights, and the environment. Global investors need an assessment of the impact of corporate activities on these rights based on enforceable standards and verifiable evaluations of corporate compliance. This information must also be readily available and produced in a cost-efficient manner, otherwise the market for corporate governance will become a market for "lemons" and collapse under the weight of investor disbelief. All of the tools available to shareholders for attempting to exert control over management are dependent on the shareholder being able to access reliable information about corporate activities and their impact. Without this information, the relationship between the global investors and management may deteriorate to the level of complicity in corporate exploitation described in the following disturbing portrait of multinational corporate activity:

> In the multinational sphere, however, the evils imagined result from managers over performing, relentlessly pursuing profit through economic imperialism, excessive regulatory arbitration, degradation of the environment and plantation production. The United States style corporate governance model, which convergence advocates say should or already does dominate on global fronts, contemplates an underperforming or self dealing manager, not an over performing one. Put another way, in the international sphere, the senior managers and dispersed owners share an interest in financial returns that is less hampered, or not hampered at all, by an agency cost problem. Their interests are in alignment rather than out of alignment, as traditional corporate governance theory hypothesizes. Why this is so is a matter for conjecture. Perhaps it is because of the larger stakes and the absence of significant obstacles, the "easy pickings" as it were in the multinational sphere.[99]

Branson has also pointed out that so-called "soft-law," including voluntary corporate codes of conduct, will melt before a sustained assault by corporate "scoff-laws" and the resulting defection of other corporate managers in the face of their apparent success. Only enforceable standards can resist such an assault.[100]

Conclusion: A Cost/Benefit Analysis as a Source of Justice and Fairness?

The Global Reporting Initiative and the European Union initiatives are in a nascent stage and do not yet provide generally accepted standards or a mechanism by which compliance with standards by MNEs can be measured. Thus, we are left with a condition in which the pension fund trustees will lack the basic tools with which to either conduct an "arbitrage" of the costs and benefits of MNE activities or to subject the MNE to the "market" for good corporate governance. The efficacy of the proposal that pension fund trustees exercise control over the worst excesses of the MNEs in which they invest depends on the existence of concrete international standards for behaviour and a reliable means of measuring and reporting on compliance with those standards. Absent such international standards, it is difficult to envision a cost/benefit analysis as a source of justice and fairness. Lack of universally accepted standards also raises questions as to what constitutes "justice" and "fairness," and who should make the normative determinations of the content of these concepts.

Although standards and verification measures exist or are being developed as voluntary efforts, governments appear reluctant to insist that MNEs comply with the standards and submit to verification. At this point, home state governments appear satisfied to promote, rather than require, good corporate citizenship from the MNEs created in their jurisdiction, at least insofar as their activities in host countries are concerned. Without decisive government action, however, the ability of pension fund trustees to exert control will depend on their ability, as investors in MNEs, to justify the costs they incur to exercise control over those activities that cause harm to internationally recognized rights. Where those costs become excessive, important human, social, and environmental rights will be at risk from the uncontrolled activity of MNEs. It seems counter to considerations of justice and fairness that the reach of international law and the protection it affords those Filipinos living below the retaining dam of the Marcopper mine site (assuming it is even applicable to their circumstances) would be entirely dependent on the cost/benefit analysis of a pension fund trustee in the developed world.

Acknowledgments
This chapter is part of a larger project for which I received financial support from a Social Sciences and Humanities Graduate Fellowship and a Capital Markets Research Fellowship from the Faculty of Law, University of Toronto. I would like to thank Janis Sarra and the participants at the conference "Global Capital Markets, Merging and Emerging Boards: Current Issues in Corporate Governance," held at the Faculty of Law, University of British Columbia, on 8 and 9 February 2002, for their comments on an earlier draft of this chapter. I would also like to thank the anonymous reviewers for their kind assistance and helpful comments. Any errors are, of course, my own.

Notes
1 Gunther Handl, "The Present State of International Environmental Law – Some Cautionary Observations" (1999) 29 Environmental Policy and Law 28 at 30.
2 Robert A.G. Monks, *The New Global Investors: How Shareowners Can Unlock Sustainable Prosperity Worldwide* (Oxford: Capstone Publishing, 2001).
3 Sol Picciotto, "What Rules for the World Economy" in Ruth Mayne and Sol Picciotto, eds., *Regulating International Business* (New York: St. Martin's Press, in association with Oxfam, 1999) 6 at 6-7
4 U. Baxi, "Mass Torts, Multinational Enterprise Liability, and Private International Law" (1999) 276 Receueil des Cours 297 at 339-40.
5 Douglas M. Branson, "The Very Uncertain Prospect of 'Global' Convergence in Corporate Governance" (2001) 34 Cornell Int'l L.J. 321 at 356, noting that Unilever-Best's production and sales exceeds the GDP of all but about fifty nations.
6 U.S.C.S. s. 1350 (2002) (Alien's action for tort).
7 Monks, *supra* note 2 at 176.
8 *Ibid.* at 92.
9 *Ibid.* at 105.
10 *Ibid.* at 180-81.

11 *Ibid.* at 188.
12 *Ibid.* at 133-34.
13 Gil Yaron, "The Responsible Pension Trustee: Reinterpreting the Principles of Prudence and Loyalty in the Context of Socially Responsible Institutional Investing" (2001) 20 Estates, Trusts and Pensions J. 305.
14 John H. Langbein and Richard A. Posner, "Market Funds and Trust-Investment Law" [1976] 1 American Bar Foundation Research Journal 1 examines the proposition that a market portfolio will, over the long term, outperform mutual funds whose managers attempt to pick stocks whose stock prices are undervalued with respect to the expected return on investment. They based their support for this proposition on the efficient capital markets hypothesis, in which the price of the stock accurately reflects all publicly available information about the corporation. They speculated that in the future it might be contrary to the fiduciaries' duty of prudence to fail to invest in a market fund portfolio given the lower management costs and maximum diversification provided. They amplified and clarified their support for these propositions a year later in John H. Langbein and Richard A. Posner, "Market Funds and Trust-Investment Law: II" [1997] 1 American Bar Foundation Research Journal 1.
15 Monks, *supra* note 2 at 105 makes this point with respect to global investors and externalization, but it may also be true for pension funds whose assets are invested in a "market fund" consisting of a portfolio of all the stocks in a national or regional equity market.
16 A telephone poll of 2,006 Canadians, Marc Zwelling, "Analysis of the Public Opinion Poll Conducted for the Canadian Democracy and Corporate Accountability Commission 2001 Vector Research" (2001), <http://www.corporate-accountability.ca> (accessed 18 January 2002), found that 54 percent wanted their pension funds invested in socially responsible corporations and that 51 percent were willing to accept slightly lower returns on those investments to make socially responsible investments; Yaron, *supra* note 13, reports that a national opinion poll of 700 adults in Great Britain in September 1977 conducted by Ethical Investment Research Service found that 73 percent wanted ethically screened pension funds, if there was no reduction in investment returns, while another 29 percent would have accepted reduced returns from ethically screened investments; see also May 1999 Millennium Survey highlighting importance of corporate social responsibility to citizens of twenty European and North American countries, summarized at <http://www.environics.net/eil/millennium/>.
17 "Host countries are often unwilling or unable to impose criminal sanctions or provide civil remedies, and home countries generally do not exercise jurisdiction over the extraterritorial acts of multinational corporations": The Editors, "Developments in the Law – International Criminal Law: Part V, Corporate Liability for Violations of International Human Rights Law" (2001) 14 Harv. L. Rev. 2025 at 2025 citing S. Joseph, "Taming the Leviathans: Multi-National Enterprises and Human Rights" (1999) 46 Neth. J. Int'l Law 171 at 175-79.
18 Simon Cooper, "Placer Dome Gets Flood Warning" *Globe and Mail* (23 October 2001) A10.
19 Geoffrey S. Plumlee *et al.*, "An Overview of Mining-Related Environmental and Human Health Issues, Marinduque Island, Philippines: Observations from a Joint US Geological Survey – Armed Forces Institute of Pathology Reconnaissance Field Evaluation, May 12-19, 2000," United States Geological Survey Open-File Report 00-397 (2000), <http://pubs.usgs.gov/of/2000/ofr-00-0397/> (accessed 15 August 2002).
20 Placer Dome Inc., Edgar Filing, Securities and Exchange Commission, *Annual Report 1996* at 20 and at 64, note 14 f. to consolidated financial statements (ARS1997).
21 Letter of Jay K. Taylor, CEO Placer Dome Inc., to Employees of Placer Dome Inc. (8 February 2002) at 1.
22 Allan Robinson, "Placer Dome Cleanup Threatened" *Globe and Mail* (6 November 2001) Business. The information concerning the directors was provided in an interview of Placer Dome president Jay Taylor.
23 Securities and Exchange Commission, ARS, *supra* note 20 at 20.
24 Placer Dome Inc., Corporate News Release, "Marcopper Spill Update #8." <http://www.placerdome.com/newsroom/content/current/marcopper8.html> (accessed 2 February 2002).
25 Taylor, *supra* note 21 at 3.

26 Securities and Exchange Commission, *supra* note 20 at 64.
27 *Ibid.*
28 *Ibid.*
29 Placer Dome Inc., Press Release, "Placer Dome Has No Stake in Marcopper" (8 April 1999) in Public Company Filings – SEDAR <http://www.sedar.com/search/search_form_pc_en.htm> (accessed 15 August 2002).
30 *MR Holdings, Ltd.* v. *Sheriff Carlos P. Bajar, Sheriff Ferdinand M. Jandusay, Solidbank Corporation and Marcopper Mining Corporation,* No. G.R. No. 138104, <http://www.supremecourt.gov.ph/2002/toc/2002apr.htm> (Unreported, Supreme Court of the Philippines [Third Division], Sandoval-Gutierrez, Melo, Vitug, Panganiban, and Carpio, 11 April 2002).
31 *Ibid.*
32 Taylor, *supra* note 21 at 1.
33 *Ibid.*
34 World Reporter (TM) – Asia Intelligence Wire, "Final Marcopper Tailing Cleanup Set" (2001) *BusinessWorld (Philippines).* Available on Westlaw, a commercial database (accessed 6 September 2002) (identifier: Westlaw 2001 WL 17162622).
35 *Ibid.*
36 Taylor, *supra* note 21 at 2.
37 Republic of the Philippines, House of Representatives, *Journal,* No. 21 (5 September 2001) (Reyes, E.).
38 Robinson, *supra* note 22.
39 *Ibid.;* Vinia M. Datinguinoo, "Another Mining Disaster Looms in Marinduque" *Philippine Headline News Online* (15 April 2002), <http://www.newsflash.org/2002/04/ht/ht002427.htm> (accessed 15 August 2002); Delfin T. Mallari Jr., "Same Stories Remain 5 Years After Marinduque Mine Spill" *Philippine Daily Inquirer* (11 November 2001), available on Westlaw, a commercial database (accessed 6 September 2002) (identifier: Westlaw 2001 WL 29110547).
40 Cooper, *supra* note 18; Mallari, *supra* note 39.
41 Datinguinoo, *supra* note 39.
42 Taylor, *supra* note 21 at 1-2.
43 *Ibid.* at 2.
44 *Ibid.* at 2-3.
45 These amounts do not include the amounts Placer Dome has committed to pay Marcopper's controlling shareholder to complete the tailings remediation: Taylor, *supra* note 21 at 3. According to testimony provided in 2002 by Marcopper officers before a committee of the Philippine Congress, Placer Dome has received about $11 million in insurance payments: Congress of the Philippines Committee Affairs Department, "GMA Acts on M'dque Mining Disaster" (27 February 2002) 10(67) Committee News Ecology Committee, <http://www.congress.gov.ph/committees/commnews_det.php?newsid=191> (accessed 6 September 2002).
46 Taylor, *supra* note 21 at 3.
47 Datinguinoo, *supra* note 39; Congress of the Philippines Committee Affairs Department, *supra* note 45.
48 Vinia M. Datinguinoo, "Another Mining Disaster Looms in Marinduque, Part 2" *Philippine Headline News Online* (15 April 2002), <http://www.newsflash.org/2002/04/ht/ht002430.htm> (accessed 15 August 2002).
49 Jeff Sallot, "Philippines Accuses Mining Giant of Turning Its Back on Cleanup Job" *Globe and Mail* (29 January 2002) A8.
50 Taylor, *supra* note 21.
51 Placer Dome Inc., "Corporate Profile" <http://www.placerdome.com/company/profile.html> (accessed 7 September 2002).
52 Plumlee *et al., supra* note 19 at 6 citing D.W. Zandee, "Tailing Disposal at Marcopper Mining Corporation" in Institution of Mining and Metallurgy, ed., *Asian Mining '85* 35 (1985).
53 Shawn McCarthy, "Marcos Connection Haunts Placer Dome Mining Record" *Toronto Star* (21 February 1989), <http://www.library.newscan.com/Biblio/Frames/FrameMain.asp> (accessed 23 August 2002).

54 *Ibid.* Just before the Marcopper tailings spill, Imelda Marcos filed a suit in the Philippines alleging ownership of the Marcopper shares on behalf of the Marcos estate: Prudencio R. Europa, "PCGG Asks Marcoses to Prove Ownership of Assets" (14 March 1996) 24(11) *Filipino Reporter.* Available on Westlaw, a commercial database (accessed 6 September 2002) (identifier: Westlaw 1996 WL 15670742).

55 Catherine Coumans, "Backgrounder on Placer Dome in Marinduque, Philippines" *Mining Watch Canada Publications* (2002), <http://www.miningwatch.ca/publications/Marinduque_backgnd.html> (accessed 6 September 2002); and see McCarthy, *supra* note 53, which reports that "Marcopper presidents have come from the ranks of the Canadian partner."

56 Alexander (Sandy) Laird is reported to have joined Placer Development Group in 1960 and worked for them in British Columbia until 1968, when he became resident manager at the Marcopper Mining Corporation. In 1971 he returned to work for Placer Development as senior mining engineer, operations. He eventually became a senior vice president at Placer Dome Inc.: see biographical note at Metallurgy and Petroleum Canadian Institute of Mining, "President 1997-1998, Alexander (Sandy) Laird" (2002), <http://www.cim.org/about/presidentsALaird.cfm> (accessed 5 September 2002). John E. Loney, who was Marcopper Mining Corporation president at the time of the tailings release, was subsequently the president of Placer Asia Pacific; for a letter reporting on the divestment of Marcopper investments, see John E. Loney, "Cleaning Up the Spill," *Asiaweek.com* Letters and Comment (1997), <http://www.pathfinder.com/asiaweek/97/0502/letters.html> (accessed 5 September 2002).

57 Congress of the Philippines Committee Affairs Department, *supra* note 45.

58 *Lubbe* v. *Cape PLC,* [2000] 4 All England Reports 268 (H.L.) ("Lubbe v. Cape") at 271.

59 These arguments by a defendant were accepted with some enthusiasm by a Quebec court in a case involving a similar kind of harm from an operating mine in Guyana: *Recherces Internationales Quebec* v. *Cambior Inc.,* [1998] No. 2554, Q.J. Quicklaw (Que. S.C.); special costs of $50,000 were awarded against the plaintiffs in a later proceeding: *Recherces Internationales Quebec* v. *Cambior Inc.,* [1999] No. 1581, JQ Quicklaw (Que. S.C.).

60 U.S.C.S. s. 1350, *supra* note 6.

61 If this Canadian corporation has no contacts in the United States, or those contacts are conducted through subsidiaries, there may not be sufficient presence to establish jurisdiction – *Doe* v. *Unocal Corp.,* 27 F. Supp. 2d 1174 (C.D. Cal. 1998) ("Unocal") – although in another case, establishing an investor relations office in New York was sufficient to establish general personal jurisdiction – *Wiwa* v. *Royal Dutch Petroleum Co.,* 226 F.3d 88 (2d Cir. 2000) ("Wiwa"), *cert.* denied, 69 U.S.L.W. 3628 (U.S. Mar. 26, 2001) (No. 00-1168).

62 The Editors, *supra* note 17 at 2037.

63 *Ibid.* citing *Beanal* v. *Freeport McMoran Inc.,* 969 F. Supp. 362 at 370 (E.D. La. 1997) ("Beanal").

64 In addition, a plaintiff would have to establish that the corporation and the host state were acting jointly with respect to the alleged violation, unless it involved acts of piracy, slave trading, genocide, and war crimes for which the corporation alone could be held liable under international law: *ibid.* at 2037 citing *Kadic* v. *Karadic,* 70 F.3d 232 at 239-44 (2d Cir. 1995) ("Kadic").

65 Monks, *supra* note 2 at 188.

66 Naomi Roht-Arriaza, "Private Voluntary Standard-Setting, the International Organization of Standardization and International Environmental Lawmaking" (1995) 6 Yearbook of International Environmental Law 10 at 152-53, points out that the ISO 14000 standard requires neither public information on performance nor adherence to any particular standard, merely the implementation of certain management systems. See also M. Shaughnessy, "The United Nations Global Compact and the Continuing Debate about the Effectiveness of Corporate Voluntary Codes of Conduct" (2001) Columbia Journal of Environmental Law and Policy: 2000 Yearbook 159, reporting the problem of voluntary codes' lack of a legal mechanism to enforce compliance.

67 Other limits that may also apply are similar to those that apply in cases of dispersed share ownership among individuals – they will be able to reap only a part of the total increase in the value of the corporation that is proportionate to the percentage of shares they own,

and the rest of the benefit will go to other shareholders who did not expend the resources to generate the benefits. See the discussion of "rational apathy" in J.G. MacIntosh, "Institutional Shareholders and Corporate Governance in Canada" (1996) 26 Can. Bus. L.J. 145 at 152-54.

68 George A. Akerlof, "The Market for 'Lemons': Quality Uncertainty and the Market Mechanism" (1970) 84 Q. J. Econ. 488 at 490-91.

69 "Global Reporting Initiative Overview" <http://www.Globalreporting.Org/AboutGRI/Overview.Htm> (accessed 2 November 2001).

70 Rapporteur Richard Howitt, European Parliament, *Report on EU Standards for European Enterprises Operating in Developing Countries: Towards a European Code of Conduct,* Committee on Development and Cooperation, No. PE 228.198/fin. (17 December 1998).

71 *Ibid.*

72 *Ibid.* at 7, para. 9.

73 Commission of the European Communities, *Promoting Core Labour Standards and Improving Social Governance in the Context of Globalization,* Communication to the Council, the European Parliament and the Economic and Social Committee, Communique COM (2001) 416 final (18 July 2001).

74 *Ibid.* at 14.

75 *Ibid.* at 16-17.

76 Commission of the European Communities, *Promoting a European Framework for Corporate Social Responsibility,* Green Paper COM (2001) 366 final (18 July 2001).

77 *Ibid.* at 22.

78 *Ibid.* at 23.

79 Commission of the European Communities, *Communication from the Commission Concerning Corporate Social Responsibility: A Business Contribution to Sustainable Development,* Communication to European Institutions, Member States, Social Partners and Other Concerned Parties COM (2002) 347 final (2 July 2002).

80 *Ibid.* at 5.

81 *Ibid.* at 6.

82 See text accompanying notes 73-75, *supra;* Commission of the European Communities, *supra* note 79 at 22-25.

83 Commission of the European Communities, *ibid.* at 17-18.

84 Larry D. Soderquist and Robert P. Vecchio, "Reconciling Shareholders' Rights and Corporate Responsibility: New Guidelines for Management" (1978) 27 Duke L.J. 819, writing more than twenty years ago, identified problems with the ownership model and reported on surveys indicating that shareholders thought of themselves more as investors rather than owners.

85 MacIntosh, *supra* note 67 at 152-53, characterizes the control powers of shareholders as "episodic."

86 Brian R. Cheffins, "*Michaud* v. *National Bank of Canada* and Canadian Corporate Governance: A 'Victory for Shareholder Rights'?" (1998) 30 Can. Bus. L.J. 20 at 36-37, pointed out that corporate law vests the management of the corporation in the board of directors and, with few exceptions, the directors are not bound by shareholder resolutions concerning the management of the corporation, even if they receive majority support. However, R. Crete, *The Proxy System in Canadian Corporations: A Critical Analysis* (Montreal: Wilson and Lafleur Martel, 1986) at 197-98, notes that the absence of the express statutory exclusion of shareholder proposals dealing with ordinary business (found in US legislation) does provide several interpretive problems concerning the division of power between shareholders and directors.

87 J.N. Gordon, "Shareholder Initiative: A Social Choice and Game Theoretic Approach to Corporate Law" (1991) 60 U. Cincinnati L. Rev. 347 at 351-52, points out that management has absolute control over decision making and over the agenda, since there is no binding shareholder initiative power. In Chapter 4 of this book, Gil Yaron notes that in Canada shareholder proposals are governed by provincial legislation; only six provinces have rules for shareholder proposals, and the requirements differ considerably.

88 Robert A.G. Monks, "Relationship Investing" (Presented at the Conference on Relational Investing of the Institutional Investor Project, Center for Law and Economic Studies, Columbia University School of Law, 6-7 May 1993) [unpublished]. Monks proposed two structural reforms: bylaw amendments to provide "long-term shareholders" with the power to nominate candidates for election by all shareholders to a committee (whose members would be paid by the corporation with a budget to engage professionals) that would monitor the directors; and the use of corporate governance "turnaround" companies to negotiate corporate governance improvements on behalf of index fund investors in return for compensation if the governance improvement is successful.

89 Lawrence A. Hamermesh, "Corporate Democracy and Stockholder-Adopted By-laws: Taking Back the Street?" (1998) 73 Tulane L. Rev. 409.

90 MacIntosh, *supra* note 67 at 153.

91 Hamermesh, *supra* note 89 at 428-67, 468-79; John C. Coffee Jr., "The Bylaw Battlefield: Can Institutions Change the Outcome of Corporate Control Contests?" (1997) 51 U. Miami L. Rev. 605; J.N. Gordon, "'Just Say Never'? Poison Pills, Deadhand Pills and Shareholder Adopted Bylaws: An Essay for Warren Buffet" (1997) 19 Cardozo L. Rev. 511; Jonathan R. Macey, "The Legality and Utility of the Shareholder Rights Bylaw" (1998) 26 Hofstra L. Rev. 835.

92 R.J. Daniels and P. Halpern, "Too Close for Comfort: The Role of the Closely Held Public Corporation in the Canadian Economy and the Implications for Public Policy" (1995-96) 26 Can. Bus. L.J. 11 at 12, notes that the vast majority of companies listed on the Toronto Stock Exchange 300 were controlled by a single shareholder; MacIntosh, *supra* note 67 at 155-56; however, Yaron, in Chapter 4 of this book, cites evidence that the level of concentration in publicly traded companies has diminished in recent years.

93 Kent Greenfield, "Ultra Vires Lives! A Stakeholder Analysis of Corporate Illegality (with Notes on How Corporate Law Could Be Used to Reinforce International Law Norms)" (2002) 87 Va. L. Rev. 1279.

94 *Ibid.* at 1314.

95 *Ibid.* at 1351-56. However, Greenfield recognizes that the shareholder will first have to become aware of the unlawful corporate activity in time to make injunctive proceedings meaningful.

96 *Ibid.* at 1369-78. Although the notion that the corporation (or any other nonstate actor) is directly subject to international law is contested (see *Kadic* v. *Karadic, supra* note 64), some scholars have argued they are subject to human rights and similar international law; see Jordan J. Paust, "Other Side of Right: Private Duties Under Human Rights Law" (1992) 5 Harvard Human Rights Journal 51.

97 J.E. Zanglein, "From Wall Street Walk to Wall Street Talk: The Changing Face of Corporate Governance" (1998) 11 DePaul Bus. L.J. 43 at 79-80, reports on the use of binding bylaw shareholder proposals submitted by various institutional investors leading to their adoption in one case and their withdrawal after the management complied in two others; see also Hamermesh, *supra* note 89.

98 *Ibid.* at 81-85, reporting on the activities of large public pension plans and TIAA-CREF; Yaron, in Chapter 4 of this book, analyzes the potential impact of recent changes to Canada's federal corporate statute that remove some prior restrictions on the participation of institutional shareholders in the shareholder proposal process as well as broaden the scope of proposals to include social, political, economic, and racial matters that would include those activities that violate international norms.

99 Branson, *supra* note 5 at 361.

100 Douglas M. Branson, "Teaching Comparative Corporate Governance: The Significance of 'Soft Law' and International Institutions" (2000) 34 Ga. L. Rev. 669 at 696-97.

6

The Interplay between Securities Regulation and Corporate Governance: Shareholder Activism, the Shareholder Proposal Rule, and Corporate Compliance with Law
Cheryl L. Wade

The Corporate Scandals of 2001 and 2002 and the Need for Greater Vigilance in All Areas of Corporate Law Compliance

In the months preceding the conference that resulted in this book, a dismal story of alleged corporate misconduct that led to the bankruptcy of the energy giant Enron Corporation began to unfold. In the months after the conference, charges of unprincipled and perhaps illegal conduct at companies other than Enron erupted. Alleged accounting fraud by the managers of WorldCom Inc. sparked the filing of a Securities and Exchange Commission (SEC) civil suit and a criminal investigation of the company's former chief financial officer and its former controller.[1] At the time of the conference, Enron was the largest bankruptcy in US history. Incredibly, now that WorldCom has filed for bankruptcy, it has replaced Enron in size and magnitude, but not notoriety.

In 2002 several other companies became embroiled in controversies relating to alleged managerial and directorial misconduct. Adelphia Communications Inc. filed for bankruptcy, and the SEC and federal prosecutors investigated claims that the company had guaranteed billions of dollars in loans to the company's former chief executive officer and his sons.[2] At Qwest Communications International, the SEC and the Justice Department investigated stock sales by senior officers who may have enriched themselves by engaging in accounting practices that overstated revenue and understated costs.[3] ImClone Systems Incorporated's chief executive officer was accused of violating federal securities laws in an insider trading scandal that involved lifestyle and entertainment personality Martha Stewart.[4] The SEC investigated the accounting practices of Tyco International Ltd., and in an unrelated matter, the Manhattan District Attorney in New York City indicted Tyco's former chief executive officer for evading over $1 million in New York state's sales tax.[5] The SEC examined accounting practices at Aon, a large insurance broker.[6]

The conference that ultimately led to this book was organized to consider current corporate governance issues "as Canada moves into global capital markets."[7] The 11 September terrorist attacks[8] and the claims of executive and directorial misconduct at Enron and other companies present two of the most pressing corporate governance problems in the United States at this point in time. Business leaders struggle to find the best paradigm for good corporate citizenship and social responsibility as the United States wages its war on terrorism. Corporate leaders also grapple with efforts to make good corporate governance decisions in the aftermath of seemingly ubiquitous claims of corporate misconduct. Corporate boards and managers could not have anticipated the Enron bankruptcy and other corporate scandals. Boards and managers could not have anticipated the effect these events would have on all companies, even honest ones, as investors lost confidence and questioned whether securities regulation is able to ensure the kind of financial transparency that enables them to make informed investment decisions.[9]

The impact of the corporate scandals of 2001 and 2002 was sweeping because more Americans owned stock than in earlier decades.[10] Financial losses to investors and employees were unprecedented. Public outrage and investor dissatisfaction were acute,[11] even though observers debated whether the public's new concern about and intolerance for corporate fraud would endure.[12] The discourse among lawmakers concerning the scandals was extensive.[13] Unfortunately, however, the discussion was plagued with political grandstanding when Democrats argued that President Bush and Vice President Cheney, when they served as corporate director of Harken Energy and chief executive officer of Halliburton Company, respectively, engaged in the same kind of corporate misconduct that they condemned in their speeches.[14] This political wrangling risked replacing real corporate governance reform with empty political rhetoric. Fortunately, this did not happen, and modest but concrete changes in corporate governance occurred. For example, Coca-Cola decided to change its accounting practices to include stock options as expenses without being required to do so by law.[15] Also, many chief financial officers reported that they increased financial disclosure in the months after the Enron scandal became public.[16] Rules of corporate governance have also changed. On 10 July 2002, the SEC adopted new rules for research analysts.[17] The SEC has requested that NASDAQ and the New York Stock Exchange adopt new rules relating to corporate board independence and shareholder involvement in corporate governance matters.

The most significant legislative response to the corporate scandals of 2001 and 2002 was the enactment of the *Sarbanes-Oxley Act of 2002* (hereinafter the *2002 Act*). President Bush described the *2002 Act* as "the most far-reaching reforms of American business practices since the time of Franklin

Delano Roosevelt."[18] Among other things, the *2002 Act* enhances criminal penalties for corporate fraud, creates a "Public Company Accounting Oversight Board to oversee the audit of public companies that are subject to the securities laws," and requires enhanced financial disclosure.

While charges of managerial misconduct and directorial slothfulness were made against several companies in 2001 and 2002, the Enron story endures as the archetypical narrative of corporate misconduct and irresponsibility. For this reason, in this chapter I analyze the social significance of the recent allegations of corporate wrongdoing by reference to the Enron episode. The corporate governance problems created by the Enron bankruptcy will consume directors and managers for quite some time. These issues, however, should not completely overshadow other types of corporate wrongdoing and the need for boards to investigate and monitor corporate compliance with law in a way that mitigates resulting corporate injury. The public discourse has focused on financial disclosure and the type of misconduct that affects a company's fiscal circumstances. The Enron debacle should inspire enhanced directorial oversight in other areas of potential employee and executive misconduct. After considering the allegations of the blatantly unethical and perhaps illegal conduct of Enron's senior executives, corporate boards should become more vigilant about ensuring corporate compliance with *all* applicable law. Boards should guard against the shortsightedness that is often characteristic of today's directors. The Enron debacle teaches that boards can expect executives to comply with the law only when board oversight creates a corporate culture of honesty and accountability.

Discrimination: A Corporate Governance Matter

The conduct of corporate officers at Enron seems to have been so egregious, and the Enron board's oversight so lacking, that most observers are shocked by the failure in corporate governance that contributed to Enron's bankruptcy. This chapter, however, explores corporate wrongdoing beyond the financial crises that plagued Enron, WorldCom, Adelphia, Qwest, and other companies. These debacles offer important lessons that are applicable in *all* areas of corporate compliance with law. They offer potential insights into human nature that should lead boards to question the trust they typically place in corporate managers and employees. The scandals offer an invaluable lesson for the boards of large publicly held companies. They teach that boards should not be surprised when their employees or officers fail to comply with the law.

This chapter explores the ongoing problem of workplace racial and sex discrimination and the reasons why boards should install systems that adequately monitor discriminatory employment practices. Workplace discrimination is a persistent problem that has plagued several publicly held companies in the past decade. In the 1990s, several large publicly held companies, most notably Texaco and Coca-Cola, paid millions of dollars to settle class action suits alleging racial discrimination.[19] While the causes and existence of discrimination deserve serious consideration, the accounting scandals of 2002 have extinguished scrutiny of workplace sexism and racism. The accounting scandals, however, offer illuminating lessons for corporate managers who will inevitably face allegations of workplace discrimination in the future. Future allegations are inevitable because discrimination persists, and because women and employees of colour are willing to litigate race and gender inequities in the workplace. The Enron debacle and the other stories of alleged corporate wrongdoing offer potential guidance for corporate boards and managers about the causes of other types of corporate wrongdoing such as discrimination. The corporate scandals of 2001 and 2002 also demonstrate the costs to investors and the general public of financial wrongdoing. Other types of unethical corporate behaviour, such as discrimination, also have the potential to negatively affect a company's financial circumstances.

The Enron saga and the recently settled racial discrimination suits provide illuminating comparisons for corporate governance scholars. The Enron bankruptcy was caused, in part, by a failure in corporate governance.[20] Enron's directors breached fiduciary duties when they failed to monitor their managers' compliance with accounting and financial standards. The widespread racial discrimination at Texaco and Coca-Cola that led to the filing of class actions alleging bias in hiring and promotion, and blatant racial harassment, are also the result of corporate governance failures. Board members and senior executives failed to monitor their employees' compliance with anti-discrimination laws. The problems at Enron, Texaco, and Coca-Cola are costly. Employees at the three companies suffered personal and pecuniary losses. Enron's shareholders lost value. The losses to Texaco and Coca-Cola shareholders were temporary, but the potential for significant harm to shareholder value is clear. There are also costs to society in general when corporate employees discriminate (Texaco and Coca-Cola) and mislead the investing public (Enron).

Another comparison between Enron on the one hand and Texaco and Coca-Cola on the other lies in the fact that in both contexts it is rarely clear when unethical conduct becomes illegal conduct. At Texaco and Coca-Cola, for example, and in response to most allegations of discrimination, there is a debate about whether hiring and promotion decisions are discriminatory or merely the result of a meritocracy. In the Enron context, "reasonable people can disagree within bounds over accounting."[21] Commenting on the investigation of alleged accounting fraud at Qwest Communications International, a former chief of enforcement at an SEC regional office acknowledged the difficulty of distinguishing mere error from fraud in this context.[22]

This chapter explores the ways in which shareholders can help boards understand the realities of racial and gender inequities in the workplace. I examine the potential for shareholders to communicate with corporate boards about the negative impact of discrimination on shareholder profits. The lesson that Enron offers in this context is that corporate boards should not be surprised when employees allege pervasive discrimination within large publicly held companies. Canadian investors and issuers should understand the potential power of shareholder, employee, and community activism in the United States and the conceivable effect of such activism on corporate boards.[23] Managers should consider the continuing problem of workplace discrimination, the increased willingness of employees and shareholder activists to litigate discrimination issues, and the meteoric rise in amounts paid to settle discrimination claims. Companies that are forced to pay large amounts to settle discrimination suits suffer pecuniary losses from the actual settlements,[24] and from the attendant negative publicity.[25] Ultimately, of course, these are shareholder losses.

The rise in the number of discrimination complaints, and in the amounts paid by companies to settle discrimination suits, is a corporate governance issue. "'Corporate governance' refers to how decisions are made and, more importantly, how disputes are settled within publicly traded corporations."[26] "'Corporate governance' is a term that in the United States generally refers to the relationships among the professional managers of a publicly held corporation, its board of directors, and its shareholders."[27] Workplace discrimination is a corporate governance issue because shareholders rely on boards to monitor managers in a way that encourages compliance with the laws that prohibit discrimination. Corporate boards that inadequately monitor compliance with anti-discrimination laws reduce, rather than maximize, shareholder wealth.

The inadequate monitoring of corporate compliance with the law is a breach of the directorial and managerial duty of care owed shareholders, and is contrary to the shareholder primacy paradigm, in which shareholder profits are to be maximized, that is the fundamental tenet of US state corporation law.[28] Elsewhere, I apply the language of the Delaware Chancery Court in *In re Caremark International Inc. Derivative Litigation*[29] to the conduct of corporate managers at Texaco and Coca-Cola, two companies that paid large amounts to settle racial discrimination litigation in the 1990s.[30] In *Caremark,* the Chancery Court described the type of directorial and managerial conduct that would breach the fiduciary duty of care owed to shareholders. The Court advised that a board's "sustained or systematic failure" to monitor compliance with the law would amount to a duty of care breach.[31] A board's egregious failure to monitor employees' compliance with the law that resulted in losses due to fines and penalties imposed upon the company may make it possible for shareholders to recover those losses in a derivative action.

In *Caremark*, the court approved the settlement of a derivative suit. The suit was brought by shareholders who alleged that the company's failure to comply with federal and state law applicable to health care providers was the result of the failure of the board and officers to adequately monitor corporate employees. The Chancellor in *Caremark* described the kind of board inaction that would violate the duty of care. The conduct described in *Caremark* as violative of the duty of care is the kind of conduct that led to losses suffered by the shareholders of Texaco and Coca-Cola when the companies paid large amounts to settle.[32] There was a sustained and systematic failure of the directors and managers of Texaco and Coca-Cola to investigate and monitor alleged racial discrimination. *Caremark*, however, is merely a settlement opinion, so it has no precedential value.

There has been no indication that the deference courts give to directorial and managerial decision making under the business judgment rule is waning. The business judgment rule grants a broad immunity to the decisions of corporate management. The rule embodies a policy of judicial deference to directorial and managerial decision making and "exists to protect and promote the full and free exercise of the managerial power granted to ... directors."[33]

After the debacle at Enron, however, corporate governance commentators should explore the wisdom of the almost invariably automatic presumption under the business judgment rule that the decisions of corporate boards and officers are the exercise of valid business judgment. This exploration should proceed with great care in order to avoid the negative impact on corporate decision making that judicial deference under the rule prevents.[34]

The business judgment rule is a practice of judicial deference to the decisions of corporate officers and directors. Courts defer under the rule only when officers and directors satisfy the fiduciary duties of loyalty and care that they owe shareholders. Officers and directors owe a duty of loyalty to shareholders that includes avoidance of conflicts of interest. They also owe shareholders a duty of care that includes monitoring and investigating corporate compliance with the law. It is this fiduciary obligation that seems to be breached by the managers of companies who ignore racial discrimination allegations without adequately investigating them. Courts should more carefully consider allegations made by plaintiff shareholders that directors and officers breached the fiduciary duty of care.

My observation about the business judgment rule is best illustrated by considering directorial and managerial conduct at Texaco and Enron before problems at these companies became public. Consider the response of Texaco's vice president of human resources to suggestions from African American employees about adopting practices undertaken by other businesses to achieve workplace diversity and to avoid discrimination. The vice president "slammed his hand on the table ... and bellowed: 'You people must have lost your minds! I think you're a bunch of militants! I've been here for thirty-three years and I can tell you right now that Texaco will not even consider any of these crazy proposals! ... The next thing you know we'll have Black Panthers running down the halls or ... in front of the building!'"[35] The "crazy" proposals rejected by Texaco's vice president included suggestions such as "basing managers' bonuses in part on how well they implemented diversity, or starting a black employees association, or beefing up recruiting from black colleges."[36]

Texaco shareholders filed a derivative suit against the company, its board, and some of its officers, claiming duty of care breaches. Incredibly, in approving a settlement of the claim and reducing the plaintiffs' attorneys' fees, the court observed that the shareholders were not likely to have prevailed in their duty of care argument if the case had been tried. Perhaps the court came to this conclusion because Texaco's vice president of human resources was not named as a defendant. Plaintiffs' attorneys should have named the vice president as one who clearly breached his fiduciary duty of care by not taking steps that may have avoided the negative publicity associated with the filing and settling of racial discrimination litigation. This negative publicity risked shareholder losses and is obviously antithetical to shareholder wealth maximization goals. The vice president failed to satisfy his duty of care by not investigating the discrimination allegations. Moreover, the court that heard the Texaco shareholders' duty of care case should have been less pessimistic about the outcome of the case for plaintiffs. If the case had not been settled, an excellent argument could have been made establishing that senior executives failed to monitor compliance with antidiscrimination laws under the principles articulated in *Caremark*.

Analysis of directorial and managerial conduct at Enron in the months preceding its bankruptcy reveals that board members and executives not involved in the alleged wrongdoing breached their duty of care. The Enron board's inattention to the details that brought Enron down, and the willingness of Enron executives not involved in allegedly fraudulent behaviour to keep quiet about suspected misconduct on the part of the company's chief financial officer and other wrongdoers, are duty of care violations. Consider, for example, the statements of some observers that Enron's former chief executive officer, Kenneth Lay, was not aware of the allegedly fraudulent conduct of Andrew Fastow, Enron's former chief financial officer.[37] The assertion that Lay's hands-off approach to corporate governance left him unaware of egregious wrongdoing is tenable only if he had no notice of the potential misconduct. In *Graham* v. *Allis-Chalmers Mfg. Co.*,[38] the Delaware Supreme Court made clear that board members violate the duty of care to ensure compliance with law when they have notice of noncompliance. As chairman of Enron's board, Lay's duty to investigate noncompliance on the part of his executives was triggered once he received the infamous memorandum from Sherron Watkins stating that she was "incredibly nervous that [Enron] will implode in a wave of accounting scandals."[39] Because Lay violated the fiduciary duty of care, his decisions and conduct should not enjoy the protection of the business judgment rule. The trouble at companies such as Enron, WorldCom, ImClone, Adelphia, and Tyco may indicate that duty of care violations are more common than courts have suspected. This means that courts, in light of the scandals of 2001 and 2002, should be careful to avoid deferring to business conduct and decision making that may breach the duty of care.

The Continuing Problem of Discrimination, Shareholder Activism, and Improving Corporate Cultures

Workplace discrimination in the United States endures, despite prohibitions against employment inequities based on race, gender, religion, and national origin under Title VII of the *Civil Rights Act* of 1964.[40] In recent years, discrimination complaints filed with the Equal Employment Opportunity Commission have increased.[41] Many large US companies have paid huge amounts to settle discrimination claims. In 1996, Texaco settled a racial discrimination suit for $176 million.[42] Racial discrimination suits were settled by Shoney's in 1992 for $134.5 million,[43] and Coca-Cola in 2000 for $192.5 million.[44] In 1997 Publix Supermarkets paid $81.5 million and Home Depot paid at least $104 million, and in 1998 Mitsubishi paid $34 million to settle sexual harassment or sex discrimination claims.[45] The *Civil Rights Act* of 1991 enhanced employers' potential liability for workplace discrimination, and since its passage, the number of employment discrimination claims has increased significantly. "The 1991 *Civil Rights Act* broadened the range of remedies available ... to include future pecuniary losses, pain and suffering, inconvenience, mental anguish, loss of enjoyment of life, other pecuniary losses and punitive damages."[46]

The number of racial discrimination claims filed with the Equal Employment Opportunity Commission has exceeded the number of complaints alleging other types of workplace discrimination.[47] "As minorities gain entry to the companies that once spurned them, charges of racial harassment on the job have almost doubled, to 6,249 [in 1999] from 3,272 in 1990 ... The acts cited ranged from slurs to nooses hung in doorways."[48] "The number of victims receiving payouts from employers has tripled, to 1,750 [in 2000] from 513 in 1998."[49]

Why does workplace discrimination persist? I conclude that one explanation is the reluctance of boards to accept the inevitability of wrongdoing on the part of at least some corporate employees and executives – especially in large publicly held companies. The accounting practices and other alleged wrongdoing that led to the Enron collapse is illustrative. Enron's board should not have deferred to the financial decisions made by the managers they were supposed to monitor. *BusinessWeek* reported that Enron's former chief executive officer "created and embodied the in-your-face Enron culture, where risk-taking, deal-making, and 'thinking outside the box' were richly rewarded, while controls appeared loose at best."[50] The Enron implosion offers lessons for the way the relationship between boards and managers should change. Boards cannot assume that their executives and employees are complying with the law. They should have monitoring systems in place that provide a basis for believing in the honesty of corporate managers.

This observation is especially relevant in the context of racial discrimination, where companies such as Texaco and Coca-Cola were plagued with racially toxic corporate cultures.[51] Critical race theorists have argued convincingly that racism is a permanent component of American society,[52] and that more often than not, today's discriminatory practices result from unconscious racism.[53] In a large publicly held company with hundreds, perhaps thousands, of employees, racial or gender bias can be expected. Most agree that racism and sexism persist in US society. The workplace is a mere microcosm of society and will be affected by the same biases that continue to plague our communities.

Some discriminatory practices in the workplace are *not* unconscious. Texaco and Coca-Cola employees described corporate cultures that allowed blatantly racist jokes and pranks.[54] The Enron debacle demonstrates that too often, board members bury their heads in the sand, refusing to accept the inevitability of human wrongdoing within their companies. This kind of constructive ignorance led to the huge settlements recently paid by large companies to racial discrimination victims.

What we learned from the Enron incident and the Texaco and Coca-Cola racial discrimination settlements is that this failure in directorial oversight is extremely costly. When boards fail to do their jobs, employees and communities are harmed. Shareholders are harmed when stock value falls as a result of negative publicity and large judgments or settlements are paid to disgruntled workers. When boards fail to monitor adequately, plaintiffs' lawyers often hold the board accountable by litigating.[55] Any issuer or investor should understand the magnitude of these potential losses.

Before litigation is filed, shareholders should attempt to inspire boards to adequately perform their functions as monitors. One way to do so is to submit shareholder proposals that call the board's attention to potential monitoring problems. This is what the shareholders of Walt Disney Company did to avoid Enron-type problems within their firm.[56] Disney shareholders asked Disney managers to include a proposal requesting that "Disney bar its outside auditor from also doing consulting work" for the company. The Disney proposal, submitted by an institutional investor, was resisted by management, but the SEC required Disney's managers to include it in proxy materials so that shareholders may vote because the proposal raises "significant policy issues." In the racial discrimination context, activists have purchased corporate stock as a way to gain access to corporate managers and influence their employment practices.

Professor Lawrence E. Mitchell's inquiry into the causes of corporate immorality led him to observe that "the narrow role assigned to stockholders limits their ability, at least practically, to participate in formulating and realizing the corporation's goals as moral actors."[57] The shareholder proposal process may provide the kind of shareholder participation that inspires corporate morality and compliance with the law.

The Shareholder Proposal Process

Because discrimination persists, shareholder activists may, and should, attempt to communicate with managers and other shareholders about discriminatory corporate cultures. They may do so under United States federal securities law, specifically Section 14 of the *Securities Exchange Act* of 1934 (hereinafter the *Exchange Act*). Rule 14a, promulgated by the SEC pursuant to the authority granted to it by Congress under the *Exchange Act,* governs management's solicitation of shareholder proxies. Section 14 of the *Exchange Act* provides a process for shareholders to communicate with management and other shareholders on issues relating to corporate governance. Rule 14a-8, the shareholder proposal rule, requires corporate managers to include in the proxy materials sent to shareholders any shareholder proposal that satisfies the procedural and substantive prerequisites enumerated by the SEC under the rule.[58] If a shareholder proposal satisfies the requirements under the rule, management must include it in the proxy statement. This means that the company pays for the distribution of the proposal along with other proxy materials. This gives the rest of the shareholders a chance to vote on the proposal. If the proposal does not satisfy the SEC's prerequisites for inclusion, management can exclude it. If it is excluded, shareholders will not be able to communicate with other shareholders at the company's expense.[59]

Shareholders may draft proposals that suggest changes in corporate policy on which other shareholders may vote.[60] Shareholders have asked their fellow shareholders to vote on a variety of issues, such as the appropriateness of a corporate policy to do business in South Africa before the dismantling of apartheid, or a corporate decision to sell napalm during the war in Vietnam.[61] More germane to the thesis in this chapter, shareholders have submitted proposals that relate to alleged discriminatory conduct within the companies they own.[62]

The process of submitting a shareholder proposal, and the traditionally instinctive reaction of managers to use one or more of the thirteen bases for excluding such proposals, has been unnecessarily adversarial. Consider one of the substantive bases relied on by management to exclude a shareholder proposal – the "ordinary business operations" exclusion under Rule 14a-8(i)(7). Under 14a-8(i)(7), managers may exclude any shareholder proposal that relates to the company's ordinary business operations because such a pro- posal intrudes upon the province of corporate officers to manage the corpo- ration's day-to-day affairs.[63]

The SEC staff's interpretation of which proposals relate to ordinary busi- ness operations has been confused. Employment-related proposals, for ex- ample, that concern a company's hiring and promotion of minority or women employees, cover ordinary business operations – employment deci- sion making. These proposals also relate to the significant social policy of ameliorating the effects of discrimination. After a difficult period of con- flicting interpretations, the SEC concluded that it was not able to distin- guish proposals that involved significant policy from those that merely relate to ordinary business operations. In 1998 the SEC reversed itself and it now, once again, determines whether the shareholder proposal relates to a sig- nificant social issue. If it does, it must be included, even if it also relates to ordinary business matters.

The SEC's vacillation on whether to apply the social policy test to employment-related proposals to determine whether they should be in- cluded in a company's proxy materials was caused by the difficulties in determining whether the shareholder proposal process was an appropriate forum for social and political discourse. One commentator, in reviewing the appraisals of a process that allows for social and political discourse in proxy materials under Rule 14a-8, observed that critics feared access to the proxy process by "grandstanding social/political activists."[64] Critics were afraid that the rule would become "an open-ended tool for social/political activists."[65] This perspective also explains corporate management's typical resistance to the inclusion of shareholder proposals that raise social policy issues.

While commentators have criticized access to the proxy process for share- holder activism related to social and political issues, shareholder proposals that deal with traditional corporate governance issues are clearly not within a company's ordinary business operations. Traditionally, Rule 14a-8 has been "a potent tool for corporate governance reform" facilitated by shareholders proposing "limits on golden parachutes and executive pay, repeal of stag- gered boards, redemption of poison pills, reduction of supermajority voting requirements, opting out of anti-takeover statutes, establishment of confi- dential voting, and greater roles for outside directors."[66]

Institutional investors concerned about the losses that result when corpo- rate discrimination is alleged, employees who are victims of discrimination and who hold shares of the company for which they work, and activist groups that purchase corporate securities as a means of influencing management policies regarding discrimination may submit shareholder proposals addressing the problem of workplace discrimination. Shareholder activists should draft proposals that embody fiduciary duty ideals. The proposals should suggest that boards implement or re-examine corporate policies and procedures regarding the monitoring of compliance with anti-discrimination laws. The proposals should focus corporate boards on the duty of care owed shareholders to adequately monitor corporate compliance with anti-discrimination laws in a way that will help to avoid the pecuniary losses that accompany discrimination allegations. Such proposals are a matter of social policy, but they are also a matter of corporate governance. These proposals concern social *and* corporate policy. Proposals that concern a board's duty of care should not be excluded as ordinary business operations, and the shareholder proposal process is an appropriate forum for such proposals, assuming they survive the rule's other bases for exclusion.

Since, as I conclude, proposals that discuss discriminatory employment practices as breaches of fiduciary duty are corporate governance matters that do not fall within the exclusion for ordinary business operations under Rule 14a-8(i)(7), corporate managers should be less resistant to the inclusion of such proposals. Even if managers conclude that it would be best to exclude such proposals under one or more of the rule's other exclusions, they should be responsive to suggestions from shareholders that enhanced monitoring of compliance with discrimination law may be required. In fact, some recent shareholder proposals "have led managers to negotiate settlements ... the rule has served as a springboard for direct shareholder access to directors and management."[67] Corporate boards and managers, recognizing that shareholder input about fiduciary breaches and the failure to uncover workplace discrimination are appropriate because such proposals are not ordinary business matters, may more adequately respond to shareholder concerns, thereby avoiding pecuniary losses to their companies and shareholders. They may also help to avoid the less tangible losses suffered by society in general, and individuals in particular, as a result of persistent discrimination.

Conclusion

Section 14 of the *Securities Exchange Act* of 1934 provides a process for shareholders to communicate with management and other shareholders on issues relating to the governance of the corporation. Employees who own shares in the company may use the shareholder proposal process to convey concerns about workplace discrimination. Institutional shareholders and socially responsible shareholders may also submit shareholder proposals.

The corporate scandals of 2001 and 2002 can serve to inform the thinking of corporate governance jurists concerning the frequency of managerial and directorial duty of care breaches. Consideration of the social significance of the scandals reveals another lesson. There will be a proliferation of litigation in the aftermath of the scandals.[68] Shareholders who communicate with management on corporate governance issues, and management's willingness to listen, may prevent the litigation that ensues when corporate governance problems are not remedied.

Institutional investors are more likely than individual investors to recognize the need for corporate governance changes at their companies. For example, institutional investors recognized problems at WorldCom and sold off their holdings while individual investors held their stock on the recommendation of analysts that predicted the company's bright future.[69] Labour union pension funds have joined in the public and political demand for corporate governance reform.[70] The shareholder proposal process is one way for pension funds to express their desire for reform. Institutional investors concerned about the losses that result from the negative publicity that accompanies discrimination allegations may do the same.

One question to explore is whether there is any real value in the shareholder proposal process. Proposals are precatory. Shareholders may only suggest, never demand, changes in corporate governance. This is the only feasible way to do business in large publicly held companies, where it would be impossible for boards and managers to accommodate hundreds of shareholders. Because shareholders fail to vote in favour of most proposals, the real value of the process may be in the opportunity it provides for shareholders to communicate about a company's policy regarding the investigation and monitoring of compliance with anti-discrimination laws. With the help of corporate attorneys, shareholder proponents may be able to draft proposals that inspire corporate diligence in monitoring discrimination, and that do not run afoul of the SEC's prerequisites for including the proposal in materials sent to the rest of the shareholders. In other words, the discussion of corporate policy in a proposal may encourage more effective oversight of corporate compliance with anti-discrimination laws. Moreover, shareholders who regularly make proposals are sometimes given the opportunity to have quiet conversations with management during which they can discourage the breaches of the duty of care that occur when managers ignore discrimination allegations.

Richard Delgado and Jean Stefancic have questioned whether speech changes racial reality. They observed that as a society, we do not recognize that conduct is discriminatory until decades later.[71] I conclude, however, that if there is no discussion of racial unfairness, or other types of discrimination, at the time it takes place, there will be no recognition of the issues – even decades later.

Notes

1 See generally Kurt Eichenwald, "For WorldCom, Acquisitions Were Behind Its Rise and Fall" *New York Times* (8 August 2002) A1; Charles Haddad and Steve Rosenbush, "Frantically Paddling to Keep WorldCom Afloat" *BusinessWeek* (22 July 2002) 38; Carl Hulse, "Lawmakers Say Files Show Flagrant WorldCom Fraud" *New York Times* (16 July 2002) C7; Jared Sandberg, Deborah Solomon, and Rebecca Blumenstein, "Inside WorldCom's Unearthing of a Vast Accounting Scandal" *Wall Street Journal* (27 June 2002) A1; Kelly Greene and Rick Brooks, "WorldCom Staff Now Are Saying 'Just Like Enron'" *Wall Street Journal* (27 June 2002) A9; Michael Schroeder, "SEC Files Civil Suit against WorldCom" *Wall Street Journal* (27 June 2002) A3.

2 See generally "Those Very Public Arrests of Executives" *New York Times* (28 July 2002) 4; Geraldine Farbrikant, "Adelphia Fails to Make Note Payment" *New York Times* (12 May 2002) C1; Jonathan D. Glater, "Mad as Hell: Hard Time for White-Collar Crime" *New York Times* (28 July 2002) WK5.

3 See generally David Leonhardt, "Qwest Officials Made Millions in Stock Sales" *New York Times* (30 July 2002) C1; Simon Romeo, "Echoes of Other Scandals Haunt a Chastened Qwest" *New York Times* (30 July 2002) C4; "Qwest: Another under a Cloud" *BusinessWeek* (22 July 2002) 44.

4 See Marc Peyser, "The Insiders" *BusinessWeek* (1 July 2002) 38.

5 Mark Maremont and Laurie P. Cohen, "Former Tyco CEO Is Charged with Two New Felony Counts" *Wall Street Journal* (27 June 2002) A3.

6 Joseph B. Treaster, "Aon Reports US Investigation of Its Accounting" *New York Times* (8 August 2002) C1.

7 This language is taken from the description of the conference on "Global Capital Markets, Merging and Emerging Boards: Current Issues in Corporate Governance," held at the Faculty of Law, University of British Columbia in February 2002.

8 Several important corporate governance questions arise with respect to the attacks of 11 September 2001. In the aftermath of the tragic events and the recession that followed, how can corporate boards and managers maximize shareholder profits while at the same time attending to the security and safety of its nonshareholder constituents such as employees and the communities in which they do business?

9 See generally Nanette Byrnes, "Paying for the Sins of Enron" *BusinessWeek* (11 February 2002) 35 (describing "Enronitis" as a decline in stock values as investors sold holdings fearing that the accounting practices of other companies were similar to Enron's practices).

10 See Daniel Akst, "Shocked by Scandals? These Are Nothing" *New York Times* (7 July 2002) 4.

11 See for example, Adam Liptak, "Not Answering Can Raise Lots of Questions" *New York Times* (10 July 2002) 7; "Bush Speech Leaves Investors Wanting Action" *Wall Street Journal* (10 July 2002) C1.

12 Glater, *supra* note 2.

13 See, for example, Jeanne Cummings, Jacob M. Schlesinger, and Michael Schroeder, "Bush Crackdown on Business Fraud Signals New Era" *Wall Street Journal* (10 July 2002) A1; David E. Sanger, "Bush, on Wall St., Offers Tough Stance" *New York Times* (10 July 2002) A1; Richard A. Oppel Jr., "Bush and Democrats Still Deeply Split on What Needs to Be Done" *New York Times* (10 July 2002) C5.

14 See Paula Dwyer, "The Ghosts That Won't Go Away" *BusinessWeek* (22 July 2002) 34 (describing Bush's tenure on the board of Harken Energy Corp., when he profited from stock sales a few days before the company was forced to restate accounting errors). See also Mike McNamee and Stephanie Anderson Forest, "The Cheney Question" *BusinessWeek* (22 July 2002) 35 (describing accounting irregularities investigated by the Securities and Exchange Commission at Halliburton Co., where Dick Cheney served as chief executive before becoming vice president).

15 David E. Sanger and Rochard A. Oppel, Jr., "Senate Approves a Broad Overhaul of Business Laws" *New York Times* (16 July 2002) A1.

16 See "True Confessions from CFOs" *BusinessWeek* (12 August 2002) 40.

17 Lee Walczak, "Let the Reforms Begin" *BusinessWeek* (22 July 2002) 26.

18 Elisabeth Bumiller, "Bush Signs Bill Aimed at Fraud in Corporations" *New York Times* (31 July 2002) A1.
19 See, for example, Bari-Ellen Roberts and Jack White, *Roberts vs. Texaco: A True Story of Race and Corporate America* (New York: Avon Book, 1998) at 274-75; Jack E. White, "Texaco's High-Octane Racism Problems: Piles of Cash and Substantial Reforms Fail to Reverse the Call for Boycott" *TIME* (25 November 1996) 34; Greg Winter, "Coca-Cola Settles Racial Bias Case" *New York Times* (17 November 2000) A1; "Class Action Alleges Race Discrimination at Coca-Cola Inc." *Legal Intelligencer* (26 April 1999).
20 See "The Lessons from Enron" *Economist* (9-15 February 2002) 9.
21 "Reforms Fail if They Paralyze CEOs" *BusinessWeek* (12 August 2002) 116.
22 David Leonhardt, "Qwest Officials Made Millions in Stock Sales" *New York Times* (30 July 2002) C1.
23 For example, the Rainbow/PUSH Coalition created the Wall Street Project to monitor the impact of corporate activity on poor communities and people of colour. See Joseph Kahn, "Jackson Challenges Capital of Capital" *New York Times* (16 January 1999) 3. The Project has purchased the shares of US corporations in order to play a role in influencing the decisions of corporate managers and directors. See Jesse L. Jackson Sr., "Making the Wall Street Bulls Run Righteously" *Essence* (October 1998) 186.
24 For example, significant earnings decreases were suffered by Shoney's and Home Depot as a result of the amounts paid to settle discrimination claims. See Michelle McCann, "Shareholder Proposal Rule: Cracker Barrel in Light of Texaco" (1998) 39 UBC L. Rev. 965; "Home Depot Shareholders React to Company's Diversity Problems" *Business Wire* (14 April 1998).
25 See, for example, Dorothy J. Gaiter, "Eating Crow: How Shoney's, Belted by a Lawsuit, Found the Path to Diversity" *Wall Street Journal* (16 April 1996) B4 (reporting that when word of a racial discrimination suit reached the public, Shoney's stock price fell significantly); Rochelle Sharp, "Mitsubishi Picketing Concerning Lawsuits Is Readied by Groups" *Wall Street Journal* (8 May 1996) B3 (reporting that consumer groups responded to a sexual discrimination suit by boycotting the company, causing significant financial and public relations setbacks).
26 David Sciulli, *Corporate Power in Civil Society* (New York: New York University Press, 2001) at 10.
27 Robert Hamilton, "Corporate Governance in America 1950-2000: Major Changes but Uncertain Benefits" (2000) 25 Iowa J. Corp. L. 349.
28 *Cf. Dodge* v. *Ford Motor Co.,* 170 N.W.668 (Mich. 1919).
29 A.2d 959 (Del. Ch. 1996).
30 Cheryl L. Wade, "Racial Discrimination and the Relationship between the Duty of Care and Corporate Disclosure" (2002) 63 U. Pitt. L. Rev. 389
31 *In re Caremark International Inc. Derivative Litigation,* 698 A.2d 959 at 971 (Del. Ch. 1996).
32 Corporate officers at Texaco, for example, ignored Texaco employees who complained of racially discriminatory employment practices. This executive inaction, and directorial failure to exercise appropriate oversight, allowed the problem to fester. Eventually, the company paid over $175 million to settle a class action racial discrimination suit. See Roberts and White, *supra* note 19 at 274-75.
33 *Zapata Corp.* v. *Maldonado,* 430 A.2d 779 at 782 (Del. 1981).
34 Judicial deference to directorial and managerial decision making is justified because this approach shields boards and officers from an inordinate level of liability to which they would be subjected under ordinary negligence rules. Also, this judicial deference seeks to deter "overly cautious corporate decisions" that may preclude profit maximization. *Joy* v. *North,* 692 F.2d 880 at 886 (2d Cir. 1982).
35 Roberts and White, *supra* note 19 at 147-48.
36 *Ibid.* at 146.
37 See, for example, William J. Holstein, "Harvesting the First Crop of Enron Tales" *New York Times* (28 July 2002) BU6.
38 A.2d 125 (Del. Supr. Ct. 1963).
39 Peter C. Fusaro and Ross M. Miller, *What Went Wrong at Enron* (Hoboken, NJ: John Wiley and Sons, 2002) at 185. See also Emily Thornton and Wendy Zellner, "The Real Story of the Watkins Memo," *BusinessWeek* (12 August 2002) 8.

40 U.S.C. 2000e-2(a)(1) (1964). Title VII provides: "It shall be an unlawful employment practice for an employer ... to fail or refuse to hire or to discharge any individual, or otherwise to discriminate against any individual with respect to his compensation, terms, conditions, or privileges of employment, because of such individual's race, color, religion, sex, or national origin."

41 "Not since the height of the civil rights movement in the 1960s have there been so many race, sex and age discrimination lawsuits ... [T]he number of companies with employees in litigation against them rose to 63 percent in 1995, a 10 percent increase over 1993": Connie Aitcheson, "Corporate America's Black Eye" *Black Enterprise* (April 1997) 109 at 110. "The EEOC has thousands of pending investigations and lawsuits regarding civil rights violations in the workplace": Eric L. Smith, "Playing the Corporate Race Card" *Black Enterprise* (January 1997) 19.

42 See Roberts and White, *supra* note 19 at 274-75; White, *supra* note 19 at 34.

43 See McCann, *supra* note 24 at 967.

44 See Winter, *supra* note 19; "Class Action Alleges Race Discrimination at Coca-Cola Inc.," *supra* note 19.

45 See Steven M. H. Wallman, "Equality Is More than 'Ordinary Business'" *New York Times* (30 March 1997) 12; Robert S. Whitman, "Employment Liability: From the Courtroom to the Proxy Ballot" (1998) 19 Corp. Board 11.

46 Alan L. Rupe and Jane Holt, "Who Is Disabled in Kansas" (1996) 35 Washburn L.J. 272.

47 *Ibid.* at 274-75.

48 Winter, *supra* note 19.

49 Amy Martinez, "Fighting Discrimination with What Business Fears: Big-Dollar Lawsuits" *Palm Beach Post* (4 March 2001) 1A.

50 Wendy Zellner, "Jeff Skilling: Enron's Missing Man" *BusinessWeek* (11 February 2001) 38 at 39 and 40.

51 See Roberts and White, *supra* note 19 at 274-75; "Portrait of a Company Behaving Badly" *TIME* (16 March 1998) 46 at 46-51; Winter, *supra* note 19; "Class Action Alleges Race Discrimination at Coca-Cola Inc.," *supra* note 19.

52 See, for example, Derrick Bell, *Faces at the Bottom of the Well: The Permanence of Racism* (New York: Basic Books, 1992).

53 "Americans share a common historical and cultural heritage in which racism has played and still plays a dominant role. Because of this shared experience, we also inevitably share many ideas, attitudes, and beliefs that attach significance to an individual's race and induce negative feelings and opinions about nonwhites. To the extent that this cultural belief system has influenced all of us, we are all racists. At the same time, most of us are unaware of our racism": Charles Lawrence, "The Id, the Ego, and Equal Protection: Reckoning with Unconscious Racism" (1987) 39 Stanford L. Rev. 317 at 322.

54 See, for example, Anne Fisher, "Texaco: A Series of Racial Horror Stories" *Fortune* (May 1998) 186.

55 See, for example, Michael Drummond, "Class-Action Warrior" *Salon.com, Inc.* (28 January 2002). Several attorneys now specialize in race discrimination litigation. See Martinez, *supra* note 49; Carrie Johnson, "Tech Firms Face Bias Suits; As Boom Times Wane, Litigation Spreads" *Washington Post* (23 February 2001) E01.

56 See Miles Weiss, "'Disney Can't Bar Vote on Auditor Conflicts,' SEC Says," *Bloomberg News* (20 December 2001).

57 Lawrence E. Mitchell, "Cooperation and Constraint in the Modern Corporation: An Inquiry into the Causes of Corporate Immorality" (1995) 73 Texas L. Rev. 477 at 497.

58 The preamble to Rule 14a-8 provides: "This rule addresses when a company must include a shareholder's proposal in its proxy statement and identify the proposal in its form of proxy when the company holds an annual or special meeting of shareholders. In summary, in order to have your shareholder proposal included on a company's proxy card, and included along with any supporting statement in its proxy statement, you must be eligible and follow certain procedures. Under a few specific circumstances, the company is permitted to exclude your proposal, but only after submitting its reasons to the Commission."

59 "If a shareholder proposal satisfies the [SEC's] conditions, management must include it in the company-funded proxy statement and give the body of shareholders a chance to vote

on it. If the proposal does not, management can effectively block shareholder access to the proxy machinery for initiating corporate reforms": Alan R. Palmiter, "The Shareholder Proposal Rule: A Failed Experiment in Merit Regulation" (1994) 45 Ala. L. Rev. 879.

60   See George W. Dent Jr., "SEC Rule 14a-8: A Study in Regulatory Failure" (1985) 30 N.Y. Law School L. Rev. 1.

61   See *Medical Committee for Human Rights* v. *SEC*, 432 F.2d 659 (D.C. Cir. 1970).

62   See, for example, Cracker Barrel Old Country Store, Inc., SEC No-Action Letter, [1992-1993 Transfer Binder] Fed. Sec. L. Rep. (CCH) P76,418 (17 February 1993); *Amalgamated Clothing and Textile Workers Union* v. *Wal-Mart Stores, Inc.*, 821 F. Supp. 877 (S.D.N.Y. 1993).

63   See Amendments to Rules on Shareholder Proposals, Exchange Act Release No. 34-40018, 17 C.F.R. 240. 14a-8. Rule 14a-8(i)(7) allows management to exclude a proposal if it "deals with a matter relating to the company's ordinary business operations."

64   Palmiter, *supra* note 59 at 901, questioning the appropriateness of exclusions based on content and proposing numerical limitations.

65   *Ibid.* at 903.

66   *Ibid.* at 883-84.

67   *Ibid.* at 884.

68   See, for example, Robert Frank, "Deloitte, Adelphia Are Squaring Off in a Blame Game" *Wall Street Journal* (10 July 2002) C1.

69   Eichenwald, *supra* note 1.

70   See Steven Greenhouse, "Labor to Press for Changes in Corporate Governance" *New York Times* (30 July 2002) C7.

71   See Richard Delgado and Jean Stefancic, "Images of the Outsider in American Law and Culture: Can Free Expression Remedy Systemic Social Ills?" (1992) 77 Cornell L. Rev. 1258 at 1279.

7
Beyond Environmental Compliance, with a View to the Best Interests of the Company
Robert Mansell and Brian Prill

The 1990s saw issues of environmental compliance move front and centre in the boardrooms of Canada, pushed there as a result of directors' and officers' concerns about liability. Regulators recognized that imposing personal responsibility on officers and directors was an effective tool for increasing the compliance of corporations. The result has been the development of systems of environmental management to ensure compliance and reduce the risk of liability. These same systems have made directors aware that environmental compliance is only a minimal requirement and that acting in the best interests of the company may require addressing long-term environmental sustainability in considering corporate strategy. There has been much legal analysis of directors' obligations to ensure compliance. An area still to be explored involves the responsibilities and limitations of a director, assuming that the director wishes to exercise the powers of the board in a proactive fashion to reduce the environmental risks to the corporation. Whereas Ronald Davis and Cheryl Wade explored related questions from the perspective of investors in Chapters 5 and 6, this chapter examines issues of environmental sustainability from the perspective of directors. It explores the legal obligations of directors to act in the best interests of the company, and demonstrates that implementing proactive environmental strategies to ensure the long-term financial viability of the corporation is in keeping with those legal obligations.

Best Interests of the Company
Section 122 of the *Canada Business Corporations Act (CBCA)* states:[1]

> 122. (1) Every director and officer of a corporation in exercising their powers and discharging their duties shall
>> (a) act honestly and in good faith with a view to the best interests of the corporation; and

(b) exercise the care, diligence and skill that a reasonably prudent person would exercise in comparable circumstances.[2]

This broad statement, echoed in most provincial corporate legislation, is supposed to set out a director's duty for overseeing the management of the company, including its policies on sustainability. Mr. Justice Berger considered this duty to "act honestly and in good faith with a view to the best interests of the corporation" in *Teck Corporation Ltd.* v. *Miller et al.*, stating that "directors must act in good faith [and] there must be reasonable grounds for their belief."[3] In other words, when a director or board of directors makes a decision to implement a proactive environmental business strategy, this decision must be undertaken in "good faith" and there must be "reasonable grounds" to support the belief that this is in the best interests of the company.[4] Reasonable grounds, therefore, implies more than an affinity for environmental issues. It implies some method of information review and analysis of the information presented.

This decision in *Teck* has most recently been adopted in *Rio Tinto Canadian Investments Ltd.* v. *Labrador Iron Ore Royalty Income Fund (Trustee of)*,[5] where Mr. Justice Farley quoted from *Pente Investment Management Ltd. (Maple Leaf)* v. *Schneider* (1999).[6] In *Maple Leaf*, Ms. Justice Weiler, for the Ontario Court of Appeal, stated:

> The mandate of the directors is to manage the company according to their best judgment; that judgment must be informed judgment; it must have a reasonable basis. If there are no reasonable grounds to support an assertion by the directors that they have acted in the best interests of the company, a court will be justified in finding that the directors acted for an improper purpose.
>
> ...
>
> One way of determining whether the directors acted in the best interests of the company, according to Farley J., is to ask what was uppermost in the directors' minds after a "reasonable analysis of the situation.
>
> ...
>
> It must be recognized that the directors are not the agents of the shareholders. The directors have absolute power to manage the affairs of the company even if their decisions contravene the express wishes of the majority shareholder ... There may be a conflict between the interests of individual groups of shareholders and the best interests of the company.[7]

What is clear from this statement is that the director's duty to act is "to act in the best interests of the corporation" and not in the best interests of any specific shareholder. However, when a director is acting in the best interests of the corporation, it would be difficult to argue that the shareholders do not benefit, even if it is possible that other stakeholders of the corporation may also benefit. In Mr. Justice Berger's analysis of directors' responsibilities in *Teck*, he refers to the United States Supreme Court decision of Judge Jackson in *State Tax Commission v. Aldrich et al.*,[8] where Jackson states that the "classical theory [of a director's duty] ... must yield to the facts of modern life. If today the directors of a company were to consider the interests of its employees [or] ... the consequences to the community ... it could not be said that they had not considered the bona fide interests of the shareholders."[9] The 1994 Dey Report[10] on corporate governance, analyzed at some length by Stéphane Rousseau in Chapter 1, echoes the proposition that corporations no longer operate in isolation and that shareholders are not the only group of stakeholders directors should consider in providing sustainable, long-term strategic guidance to the corporation.

The Dey Report: Balancing Shareholder and Stakeholder Interests
The Dey Report put forth the proposition that while the primary purpose of the directors of a corporation is to enhance shareholder value, "the interests of shareholders will not be well served if the interests of other stakeholders are not considered."[11] In the current business climate, it is obvious that certain elements of the public are clamouring for increased consideration in corporate decision making. The recent protests at world trade and finance summits are merely a reflection of that concern. While these protests provide significant material for debate over the tactics used, they have also raised public awareness and increased concern with respect to how corporations manage the environmental and social impacts of their activities. Corporations who ignore these barometers of social action do so at their own peril. The outcome of this heightened awareness is most clearly seen in increased legislation and regulation designed to intervene in corporate activity. Additionally, corporations and consumers are seeing increased costs related to environmental and social impacts, and increased restrictions on access to resources.[12]

Directors' responsibility for stakeholders' interests is not a new issue. A variety of legislation already exists that mandates directors to consider the interests of other stakeholders when making decisions. For example, the *Income Tax Act*[13] mandates the withholding and filing of income tax on behalf of another person. When directors are evaluating strategic business plans and the available resources, they already understand that monies reserved for income tax payments on behalf of their employees are not a part of the available resource base. These assets are held in trust for the benefit of the stakeholders, and they may not be used for other corporate purposes.

In *Soper* v. *Canada (C.A.),*[14] the court talks of the "positive duty to act where a director obtains information, or becomes aware of facts, which might lead one to conclude that there is, or reasonably could be, a problem with remittances." While the decision is with regard to nonpayment of income tax withholdings, this same duty would apply to issues of fiscal stewardship, environmental liabilities, or any other area of corporate governance. Applying the principle in *Soper* to environmental issues, this means that when a director becomes aware of an environmental problem, the director has a duty to act on the problem.

This type of obligation to be proactive regarding certain corporate obligations found full expression in environmental legislation in the late 1980s and early 1990s. For example, the Ontario *Environmental Protection Act* includes the following express obligation for officers and directors:

> 194. (1) Every director or officer of a corporation that engages in an activity that may result in the discharge of a contaminant into the natural environment contrary to this Act or the regulations has a duty to take all reasonable care to prevent the corporation from causing or permitting such unlawful discharge.

> 194. (3) A director or officer of a corporation is liable to conviction under this section whether or not the corporation has been prosecuted or convicted.[15]

The first, and most significant, prosecution under this section was that of *R.* v. *Bata Industries Ltd.*[16] In the now infamous *Bata* decision, the court set out some details of what was expected of officers and directors in discharging this obligation. The requirements, reduced to their essence, were that the board be kept appropriately informed of environmental issues; review them, with the assistance of appropriate outside expertise where needed; and provide direction on environmental management to ensure compliance.

In *R.* v. *Bata Industries Ltd., Bata, Marchant and Weston,* the Ontario Ministry of Environment (MOE) charged the company with a number of offences relating to the discharge of waste from leaking drums onto the ground and into the groundwater.[17] In addition, the MOE charged Thomas Bata (chairman of Bata Industries Ltd.), Douglas Marchant (president of Bata Industries Ltd.), and Keith Weston (general manager and vice president on site) with failing to take all reasonable care to prevent a discharge, contrary to Section 194 of the *Environmental Protection Act*. The facts were relatively straightforward, and not unusual in the late 1980s, when the offences occurred. Bata Industries Ltd. was storing drums of waste chemicals, solvents, and similar materials behind the plant. Plant personnel had sought quotes for waste disposal for these drums, but the original quote had been too expensive and the company had sought a cheaper alternative. The drums remained in place over a long period of time, from 1986 through 1989, when they were finally removed. During this time, leaks had occurred from the drums, which resulted in the charges of causing or permitting a discharge into the natural environment.

The three directors and officers were charged with failing to take all reasonable care to prevent such a discharge. Ultimately, the company was found guilty of causing and permitting a discharge, and both the president and the on-site general manager and vice president were convicted under Section 194. The chairman, Thomas Bata, was acquitted based on bulletins issued from his office requiring appropriate measures to be taken with respect to waste management. In his reasons, the trial judge made clear that this was a first case, and that both the level of fine and the evaluation of the standard for taking reasonable care to prevent the corporation from causing or preventing a discharge were very much influenced by that. It is likely that the level of due diligence that was sufficient to result in an acquittal for Mr. Bata would not be sufficient today.

In sentencing the directors, the trial judge provided a great deal of guidance on what due diligence consisted of with respect to this type of charge. First, he looked at whether the board of directors had established a pollution prevention "system," including supervision, inspection, mandated improvement in business methods, and the exhortation of people under the director's or officer's control or influence. Such a system would have to be sufficient, within the terms and practices of the industry, to ensure compliance with environmental laws, ensure that officers report back periodically to the board on the operation of the system, and ensure that officers are instructed to report any substantial noncompliance to the board in a timely manner.

The judge stated that the directors are responsible for reviewing environmental compliance reports provided by the officers of the company, but are justified in placing reasonable reliance on the reports provided by officers, consultants, counsel, or other informed parties. They need to be assured that officers are promptly addressing environmental concerns and that they are being made aware of the standards of their industry and other industries that deal with similar environmental effects, and they are to personally react when they realize that the system has failed.

This general structure resulted in boards and management of major companies throughout Canada setting up environmental management systems to ensure that they could specifically address all of the requirements outlined by the court in the *Bata* decision. The systems resulted in regular reviews of environmental performance and compliance throughout a number of industries, with regular reports to boards of directors detailing corporate performance measured against both compliance with environmental law and industry standards.

What directors quickly learned in receiving the information generated under these systems was that compliance was no simple matter. They also quickly learned that environmental management was as much about reducing and managing impacts as it was about achieving compliance. A board's expertise in identifying environmental risks, and the potential for advantage from environmental management, grew rapidly as a result of these legal requirements. As the management systems and structures evolved, so did the ability of directors to formulate corporate strategy in the context of environmental management. A growing number of corporations have recognized that they must maintain a sophisticated level of understanding of the environmental aspects of the business, effectively manage those risks, and ensure that a strategic vision for that management is implemented throughout the company. This growing recognition, in our view, fits closely with the general obligations of directors, as those obligations have come to be understood during the past few years.

The directors of a corporation have a duty to act in the best interests of the company, whether to avoid risk or to capitalize on opportunity. This duty to act must be supported by knowledge and information, and, where a director lacks either, the duty extends to utilizing the skills of experts in the field to inform the director of the potential risks or opportunities. Section 124 of the *CBCA* absolves directors from liability when they rely in good faith on the reports of industry experts when they evaluate strategic business options. This is in response to the obligation for directors to be "reasonably prudent" when exercising their "care, diligence and skill." Interestingly, Section 122 does not call for reasonably skilled directors; it calls for "reasonably prudent" ones. This is to ensure that skill is not the measure of a director's ability; prudence and wisdom are. Knowledge can be obtained from a variety of sources; prudence and the wisdom as to how to apply it are another matter, however. Effectively, what these sections imply is that the *Act* provides protection for directors who seek to pursue shareholder value in an informed and responsible fashion.

As stated above in *Maple Leaf*, the director's duty is to the corporation and not to a specific shareholder or group of shareholders.[18] This duty to the best interests of the corporation even supersedes the wishes of any shareholder the director may specifically represent on the board. Where a director who is a nominee of a specific group of shareholders is placed in a position where the interests of the shareholder, short-term or long-term, are in conflict with the "best interests of the corporation" and that director fails to act in the "best interests of the corporation," that director may be held in conflict of interest.[19]

One of the objectives of corporate governance that the Dey Report identified was that "corporate strategies should be developed by taking a longer term view of the direction of the corporation."[20] The case law cited above makes it clear that for directors to fulfill their obligations under Section 122 of the *CBCA*, they must make informed and reasonable decisions based on the best interests of the company and not those of an individual shareholder. Combine Section 122 of the *CBCA* with the Dey Report recommendation that directors be responsible for the pursuit of "sound long-term strategies" and "ensuring financial viability," and it becomes readily apparent that one of the mandates of the directors is to provide guidance and direction for the implementation of sustainable business strategies.[21] A sustainable business strategy is one that evaluates the financial, environmental, and social risks of a business plan and considers what resources the corporation has available to mitigate these risks. The Dey Report refers to the need to balance stakeholder interests with shareholder interests, and to the implementation of an effective, sustainable strategic plan that has thoroughly evaluated these risks as the best way to accomplish this balancing act.[22]

Stewardship
The Dey Report identified five major responsibilities of directors, which the Toronto Stock Exchange subsequently included in their corporate governance guidelines. The five responsibilities of effective corporate governance that directors should assume are:

1 the adoption of a strategic planning process
2 the identification and monitoring of principal risks to the business and ensuring the implementation of appropriate systems to manage these risks
3 succession planning, including the appointment, training, and monitoring of senior management
4 a communications policy for the corporation
5 the integrity of the corporation's internal control and management information systems.[23]

The identification and monitoring of environmental risks through the implementation of appropriate management systems can be as important a feature of a strategic planning process as financial management. Depending on the information that went in to the formulation of a business strategy, environmental risk management can be a cost of business or an increased source of revenue, or both. Whether or not an environmental management strategy becomes a cost of business or a revenue stream may depend on how well the board understands the principal risks of the business and how much research has gone into the development of a long-term sustainable strategic plan for the business.

Michael Porter and Class van der Linde point out that pollution activities are the result of inefficient production processes.[24] Whenever any inputs of production are disposed of as a waste product, there is inefficiency. This inefficiency is a waste of valuable resources and increases the cost of production, which is in turn passed on to the consumer as an increased cost of consumption. This increased cost of consumption then diverts scarce consumption resources away from other products that may be equally desirable to the consumer. Increasing efficiency, by reducing waste in the form of pollution, works to correct that.

One example of an industry that improved its environmental performance and reduced its costs is the Dutch tulip industry. This industry was constantly being faced with increased regulations with respect to the use of pesticides and fertilizers, which was having an effect on its business and production. In search of a solution, innovative producers within the industry devoted a portion of their resources to developing a closed-loop system of tulip production. By removing their bulbs from the earth and placing them in a rock wool bed nourished by a circulating water bath, these producers lowered their risk of disease and pest infestation and reduced their costs for pesticides and fertilizers.[25] Admittedly, there was an initial outlay of capital with respect to research and development in choosing to implement such a strategy, and directors and shareholders who are primarily motivated by short-term gains may be reluctant to implement such a strategy. These directors and shareholders, however, were set on developing sustainable corporate strategies and, as a result, have seen their long-term investment result in lower operational costs and higher profits.

Comparing this example with the director's duty to act in the best interests of the company, it becomes apparent that this environmentally proactive business strategy resulted in a sustainable production process that was in the corporation's best interests and that provided additional stakeholder benefits to the community. An accomplishment such as this requires a corporate paradigm shift from that of pollution control and regulatory compliance to one of resource productivity, however. This means implementing internal control and management information systems that reward innovation and employee ingenuity with respect to reducing the costs of production and regulatory compliance by converting wasted resources in the form of pollution into additional revenue sources. Dow Chemical California is a company that made this switch when increased regulation forced it to redesign its wastewater processes. By doing this in such a way that waste output from one production process could be used as an input to production in a different area of the plant, Dow effectively converted a $250,000 process redesign cost into a research and development project that increased production efficiencies and resulted in annual savings of $2.4 million.[26]

Max Clarkson calls this paradigm shift a move from the shareholder model of capitalism to the stakeholder model of capitalism, and maintains that "successful corporations are in fact managed in order to satisfy, and retain the participation of their primary stakeholder groups."[27] Mr. Justice Berger in *Teck* also recognized that where directors consider the need of employees or that of the community, it does not mean that they have not considered the bona fide interests of the shareholder. Mr. Justice Farley summarized this most succinctly in *Ballard,* where he stated:

> It seems to me that while it would be appropriate for a director to consider the individual desires of one or more various shareholders (particularly his "appointing" shareholder) in order to come up with a plan for the operation of a corporation, it would be inappropriate for that director (or directors) to only consider the interests of certain shareholders and to either ignore the others or worse still to act in a way detrimental to their interests. The safe way to avoid this problem is to have the directors act in the best interests of the corporation (and have the shareholders derive their benefit from a "better" corporation).[28]

What becomes apparent from the general discourse on directors' duties is that as long as the directors are implementing strategies that they reasonably believe are in the interests of the corporation, the courts will not intervene. This also means that where directors implement a long-term sustainable development strategy and believe that this strategy is in the best interests of the corporation, then even if it is in opposition to the wishes of any specific group of shareholders, the directors should follow the course of action with the most sustainable strategic plan containing a long-term view to the best interests of the corporation. The prevailing judicial opinions indicate that the directors' first loyalty is to the corporation, and that considering a shareholder's wish over the well-being of the corporation places the director in a conflict of interest.[29]

Sustainable Strategic Planning

The Saucier Committee report entitled *Beyond Compliance: Building a Corporate Governance Culture* noted that "strategic planning is much more than developing a business plan" and that "directors are not there to manage the business, but are responsible for overseeing management and holding it to account."[30] The report refers to a 1999 survey indicating that "almost 30 percent of boards had no input or involvement in strategic planning, other than formal approval of the plan, and almost 40 percent of boards had no formal process for oversight of risk management."[31] (Stéphane Rousseau discussed these findings in Chapter 1.) Given that directors can be held personally liable under most environmental legislation for failure to properly manage environmental risks, this points to a significant gap in the current culture of corporate governance.[32]

The adoption of the Dey Report by the Toronto Stock Exchange is one example of using corporate governance guidelines to motivate change. Under Section 473, every listed company must disclose, on an annual basis, its approach to corporate governance in the company's annual report or information circular. Where the company's system is different from the guidelines listed in Section 474, the company must explain the differences or explain why the guidelines are inapplicable. The Saucier Committee recommended that these guidelines need to be "amended to *make it clear* that the board's responsibility *goes beyond* the 'adoption of a strategic planning process'"[33] (emphasis added). It recommended that the "board should be responsible for contributing to the development of the strategic plan."[34]

This requires change in the corporate governance model that many corporations use today. Royston Greenwood and C.R. Hinings hypothesize that change is a reaction to external and internal pressures as they act within an organization.[35] Two external pressures act on organizations to create change: market pressure and institutional pressure. Institutional pressure is pressure from regulatory agencies, professional institutions, social expectations, and the actions of other leading organizations. Section 122(1)(b) of the *CBCA* is an example of a legal institutional pressure that asks directors to "exercise the care, diligence and skill that a reasonably prudent person would exercise in comparable circumstances." Various statutes that impose director liability for noncompliance are also examples of institutional pressure as applied to corporate governance. The work done by Dianne Saxe suggests that Greenwood's hypothesis that institutional pressure from environmental regulation increases compliance is correct.[36] It is also clear from the recommendations in the Dey Report and from the Saucier Committee that directors need to take a more active role in risk analysis and strategic planning. The Dey and Saucier Committees' recommendations that disclosure requirements with respect to corporate governance practices be strengthened is one way of increasing institutional pressure on directors to take a more active role in long-term sustainable strategic business planning. This type of planning requires that directors become involved and exercise sound business judgment based on information and knowledge provided by experts in the field in determining which strategic plan is in the best interests of the corporation. It is part of the directors' responsibility to exercise sound business judgment and provide guidance to management in choosing sustainable business strategies that provide for long-term corporate viability.

In *Schafer* v. *International Capital Corp.*, Mr. Justice Baynton states that the fundamental principle in the "Canadian version" of the sound business judgment rule is a "presumption that ... the directors of a corporation make an informed decision."[37] The directors' duty is to weigh the advantages against the disadvantages and make the decision that is in the best interests of the corporation. With respect to developing a sustainable strategic plan, this would imply that directors have a duty to look at the alternatives and make an informed decision based on long-term financial viability. Assessing environmental expenses accurately is as important a part of the production equation as assessing labour and resource expenses. When left out of the production cost equation, directors leave themselves open to being blindsided by personal as well as corporate liability. One of the criticisms the court had for the actions of one of the corporate officers in *Bata*[38] was that he did not exercise an informed business judgment when he chose to reject a waste disposal proposal as a result of price. In the *Bata* decision, it will be recalled, the site manager had rejected a proposal for the disposal of the drums that ultimately leaked and caused the problem, simply because the price was too high. He subsequently obtained a proposal that was lower, and was prepared to accept it without any further investigation as to the differences. The court felt that there was a duty to investigate further, to understand the reasons for the difference in price and the different services outlined in the two quotes he had received.

This has a bearing for directors today when deciding on which business strategies to implement. Business strategies are based on a choice of options. When confronted with implementing a long-term sustainable business strategy, there may be some immediate capital costs, as mentioned earlier in the Dow Chemical example, but the long-term advantages may outweigh the short-term disadvantages. In resource-based industries, this may mean harvesting later rather than earlier. In manufacturing industries, it may imply developing new technologies to use resources more efficiently.

The work done by Sanjay Sharma and Harrie Vredenburg indicates that when effectively used, sustainable business strategies actually stimulate innovation and increase competitive advantages.[39] Sharma and Vredenburg conducted a study of seven companies in the oil and gas industry to investigate the hypothesis that proactive environmental business practices stimulate innovation and increase revenue streams. The companies ranged from juniors to majors and were all surveyed and ranked according to their environmental responsiveness. Of the seven companies, two were ranked as being environmentally proactive and five were ranked as being environmentally reactive. Sharma and Vredenburg then measured the levels of innovation within these companies based on how many innovations and patents they attributed to their position on environmental responsiveness.

The results were significant. Over a fifteen-year period from 1980-1995, the two environmentally proactive firms could account for 132 innovations (of which 93 were patented), whereas the five environmentally reactive firms could account for only 38 (16 of which were patented).[40] The environmentally proactive corporations achieved more than three times the number of innovations or patents than the environmentally reactive ones. These innovations or patents helped the proactive corporations develop additional revenue streams or technologies that gave them a competitive advantage over the reactive corporations. Using comparative case studies, Sharma and Vredenburg discovered that the companies that implemented proactive environmental strategies also exhibited:

- a capability for higher-order learning
- a capability for continuous innovation
- a capability for stakeholder integration.[41]

The development of these capabilities is among the factors to which this study attributed the proactive companies' ability to maintain their competitive advantage in the oil and gas industry.

In considering what is in a corporation's best interests, directors should also take into account the corporation's reputation. "Intangible organizational assets, such as reputation, are seen as important sources of sustainable competitive advantage."[42] While some directors may hold that the costs of sustainable environmental management strategies are high, spills and other types of environmental disasters can not only have an effect on a company's reputation but also affect its stock price.

A study by Robert Klassen and Curtis P. McLaughlin indicates that good environmental management reduces costs or increases revenues.[43] This study also revealed that environmental awards and environmental disasters had a significant impact on shareholder value. Based on a seven-year study, an environmental award increased a company's share price by an average of $0.37 per share, whereas a negative environmental incident decreased the average share price by $0.70 per share. Effectively, a negative environmental incident affected shareholder value three times worse than a positive environmental award. The conclusion reached in this study was that environmental awards increased investor confidence in a company's ability to perform. Therefore, even if a director were to take a position that his or her responsibility was only to the shareholder, this study indicates that by not developing environmentally sustainable business practices and effectively taking into account other stakeholders a director is liable to reduce shareholder value, expose himself or herself or the corporation to liability, and tarnish the corporation's reputation. Good corporate governance in today's marketplace requires that directors exercise the "care, diligence and skill [of a] reasonably prudent person" when assessing all areas of a corporation's performance, including environmental policies, strategic direction, production processes, and financial results.

Managing Change

The three major studies on corporate governance – the Dey Report, *Five Years to the Dey,* and *Beyond Compliance* – all suggest that the model of corporate governance in Canada is under pressure to change.[44] The disclosure requirements in the Toronto Stock Exchange (TSE) *Company Manual* are also a call for change in accountability in corporate governance. Along with a call for change, however, there is also resistance to change. The Dey Report introduced the issue of "liability chill" into its discussion of developing an adequate human resource base from which to select competent directors to ensure good corporate governance.[45] It expressed disappointment at a report of a Federal Government Interdepartmental Working Group that stated that director liability was "limited to a handful of companies that were in severe financial difficulty."[46] The TSE report *Five Years to the Dey* examined this issue and determined that if there was a problem in recruiting directors, it resulted from a lack of qualified candidates, not "liability chill." This phenomenon appears to conform to the management change theories of Danny Miller[47] and Royston Greenwood.[48]

Miller's study concludes that as companies mature and develop, they simplify their processes. However, this simplification of processes eventually leads to lower organizational performance because past success patterns become the familiar norms. This in turn leads to less tolerance for ideas that deviate from past success factors. Corporations then lose their ability to deal with randomness and become stagnant. This becomes especially harmful in competitive environments and, given that many firms are using environmental or social responsibility strategies to gain competitive advantage, creates a resistance to governance strategies that incorporate other stakeholders.

Greenwood's work on radical change identified the same resistance to change that Miller identified, and it examined how the pressure from the external business environment affected the firm's internal resistance to change.[49] According to Greenwood, the ability of a firm to change its model of strategic planning is tied to the manner in which a firm responds to external pressures and how these external pressures cause a firm to restructure its internal power dynamics. For a firm to effectively succeed at changing its strategic planning model, the power to implement change needs to be allocated to those who are willing to align the firm's strategic planning model with the new business environment. This allocation of power can be done through retraining or through succession planning. Greenwood's theory is in harmony with the TSE guidelines' call for corporate governance to accept responsibility for "succession planning, including appointing, training, and monitoring senior management." Where management is either unwilling or unable to adequately address the forces of environmental competitiveness it is the board's responsibility to insist on retraining of the senior management, so that the corporation can remain competitive; or consider developing succession strategies, so that the appropriately trained personnel can occupy the senior management positions.

Undertaking a strategy of environmental competitiveness requires commitment from the top down. This includes the directors on the board and the senior management team doing more than paying lip service to a long-term sustainable business strategy. A sustainable business strategy requires the accumulation of human capital that is a mix of interpersonal relationships, firm culture, and reputation among buyers and suppliers.[50] Once achieved, this asset becomes difficult to copy because it creates a nebulous quality within a company that drives its motivation and innovation. This in turn provides a company with a sustainable competitive advantage because of its competitors' inability to copy it.

An asset accumulation strategy of this type develops over years. Where a director elects to recommend that a corporation develop a sustainable strategic business plan, of necessity this means working towards the best interests of the company over an extended period. A director whose priorities are in conflict between a shareholder with a short-term reward horizon as opposed to long-term corporate viability will be faced with the task of gathering the required information to adequately explain to investors why the long-term strategy is in the corporation's best interests. While this may be challenging at times, this task is merely one of the group of responsibilities that directors take on when they accept a position as a member of a corporation's governing body. The case law referred to above always holds that directors are responsible for making informed decisions that are in the best interests of the corporation, whether they agree or disagree with any particular shareholder's position on the issue.

Conclusion

A review of the case law regarding directors' responsibilities shows that directorship is much more than a figurehead position. It is a position that requires informed involvement and prudent decision making. Where knowledge is lacking, it requires investigation, analysis of the reports obtained, and the turning of one's mind to adopting a business strategy that one believes will help ensure the corporation's long-term financial viability. This means considering all the risks that the business may face, including environmental, fiscal, and social risks, including risks to reputation, and then implementing a strategy that is in the corporation's best interests.

By so doing, directors should also achieve the best results for the shareholders. Best results should not be confused with quick results, as the implementation of long-term sustainable business strategies requires the accumulation of human capital capable of sustaining a corporate culture of innovation, and the ability to respond to change. Even a significant increase in the level of compliance cannot be accomplished overnight. Given the complexity of social, environmental, and regulatory issues that corporations face today, only by developing a culture of innovation will they attain the critical mass required to develop new technological processes that maximize resource efficiencies and reduce environmental impact.

Therein lies the director's vulnerability and strength. The director's role is not one of providing hands-on management. It is to provide objective reflection on where the corporation has been and where it should be going; to provide strategic advice that will ensure that the corporation is a long-term financially viable entity. There will undoubtedly be many corporations whose operations have minimal environmental risks and where strategic management does not require extensive consideration of sustainability. For most companies, however, the identification of risks and opportunities related to sustainability are crucial to corporate success, particularly over the long term. The obligation of today's director is to provide leadership that takes into consideration all of the stakeholders that contribute to a corporation's prosperity and all risks that can damage it. This requires recognition that the sustainable development of a corporation as an environmental concept is not so far from the sustainable growth of a corporation as a concept of financial viability.

Notes

1 *Canada Business Corporations Act,* R.S.C. 1985, c. C-44, as am. by S.C. 2001, c. 14, s. 135 (Sched., s.43) [hereinafter *CBCA*].
2 *Ibid.,* s. 122(1).
3 *Teck Corporation Ltd.* v. *Miller et al.* (1972), 33 D.L.R. (3d) 288 at 315 (B.C.S.C.) [hereinafter *Teck*].
4 *Ibid.*
5 *Rio Tinto Canadian Investments Ltd.* v. *Labrador Iron Ore Royalty Income Fund (Trustee of),* [2001] O.J. No. 2440 (Ont. Sup. Ct. Comm. List), para. 16 [hereinafter *Rio Tinto*].
6 *Pente Investment Management Ltd. (Maple Leaf)* v. *Schneider* (1999), 42 O.R. (3d) 177 (Ont. C.A.) [hereinafter *Maple Leaf*].
7 *Ibid.,* para. 33 as quoted in *Rio Tinto, supra* note 5, para. 16. See also *Ontario Inc.* v. *Harold E. Ballard Ltd.* (1991), 3 B.L.R. (2d) 113 at 123 (Ont. Ct. (Gen. Div.)) [hereinafter *Ballard*]; *Maple Leaf, supra* note 6, para. 33 as quoted in *Rio Tinto, supra* note 5, para. 16
8 *State Tax Commission* v. *Aldrich et al.,* 316 U.S. 174 at 192 (U.S. Sup. Ct. 1942).
9 *Teck, supra* note 3 at 314.
10 Toronto Stock Exchange Committee on Corporate Governance in Canada, *Where Were the Directors? Guidelines for Improved Corporate Governance in Canada* (Toronto: Toronto Stock Exchange, 1994) [hereinafter *Dey Report*].
11 *Ibid.* at 8.
12 An example of the concern for sustainable development practices is the *Canadian Environmental Assessment Act* (1992), c. 37; brought into force 22 December 1994.
13 *Income Tax Act,* R.S.C. 1952, c. 148, s. 227.
14 *Soper* v. *Canada (C.A.),* [1998] 1 F.C. 124 (F.C.A.), para. 53 [hereinafter *Soper*].

15 *Environmental Protection Act* R.S.O. 1990, Ch. E. 19.
16 *R.* v. *Bata Industries Ltd.,* 25 O.R. (3d) 321 (Ont. C.A.) [hereinafter *Bata*].
17 *Regina* v. *Bata Industries Ltd., Bata, Marchant and Weston,* 9 O.R. (3d) 329 (Ont. Ct. [Prov. Div.]).
18 *Maple Leaf, supra* note 6, para. 34.
19 *PWA Corp.* v. *Gemini Group Automated Distribution Systems Inc.,* (1993) 101 D.L.R. (4th) 15 (Ont. Ct. (Gen. Div.)) [hereinafter *PWA*].
20 *Dey Report, supra* note 10 at 7.
21 *Ibid.*
22 *Ibid.* at 21.
23 Toronto Stock Exchange, *Company Manual,* s. 474, at 421 [hereinafter *Company Manual*].
24 Michael E. Porter and Class van der Linde, "Green and Competitive: Ending the Stalemate" (1995) September/October Harv. Bus. Rev. 120 at 122.
25 *Ibid.* at 121.
26 *Ibid.* at 126.
27 *Dey Report, supra* note 10 at 21.
28 *Ballard, supra* note 7 at 171-72.
29 *PWA, supra* note 19.
30 Joint Committee on Corporate Governance, *Beyond Compliance: Building a Governance Culture,* Final Report (Toronto: TSX/CNDX/CICA, 2001), <http://www.cica.ca/multimedia/ Download_Library/Research_Guidance/Risk_Management_Governance/Governance_Eng_ Nov26.pdf> [hereinafter *Beyond Compliance*].
31 *Ibid.*
32 *Canadian Environmental Protection Act,* 1999, s.c. 1999, c. 33, s. 280.
33 *Beyond Compliance, supra* note 30 at 23.
34 *Ibid.*
35 For a complete analysis on organizational change, see Royston Greenwood and C.R. Hinings,"Understanding Radical Organizational Change: Bringing Together the Old and New Institutionalism" (October 1996) 21(4) Acad. Mgmt. J. 1022 at 1025.
36 Dianne Saxe, *Environmental Offences: Corporate Responsibility and Executive Liability* (Aurora: Canada Law Book, 1990) at 28, confirms that director prosecution significantly increases efforts at environmental compliance.
37 *Schafer* v. *International Capital Corp.,* [1996] S.J. No. 770 (Sask. Q.B) para. 25 [hereinafter *Schafer*].
38 *R.* v. *Bata Industries Ltd.,* (1992) 9 O.R. (3d) 329.
39 Sanjay Sharma and Harrie Vredenburg, "Proactive Environmental Strategy and Development of Comparatively Valuable Organizational Capabilities" (1998) 19 Strategic Mgmt. J. 729.
40 *Ibid.* at 742.
41 *Ibid.* at 749.
42 Urs Daellenbach, Sanjay Sharma, and Harrie Vredenburg, *A Dynamic Theory of Corporate Reputation Formation and Stability.* Working Paper, University of Calgary.
43 Robert D. Klassen and Charles P. McLaughlin, "The Impact of Environmental Management on Firm Performance" (August 1996) 42(8) Mgmt. Science 1199.
44 Institute of Corporate Directors and Toronto Stock Exchange, *Five Years to the Dey* (Toronto, 1999).
45 *Dey Report, supra* note 10 at 36.
46 *Ibid.*
47 Danny Miller, "The Architecture of Simplicity" (1993) 18(1) Acad. Mgmt. Rev. 116.
48 Greenwood and Hinings, *supra* note 35.
49 The business environment includes all of the forces working within society: legal, regulatory, social, political, as well as pressures within the firm's specific industry.
50 Jay Barney, "Firm Resources and Sustained Competitive Advantage" (1991) 17(1) J. Mgmt. 99.

Part 3
The Role of Directors in Governance Oversight: Domestic and International Lessons

8
Developments in US Boards of Directors and the Multiple Roles of Corporate Boards
Lynne L. Dallas

As corporations have increased in size and complexity, so have the demands on their operations, requiring more complex organizational structures, such as departments and divisions, a more diverse workforce possessing various levels and areas of expertise, and a more formalized system that assures shareholders of corporate well-being through formal disclosure reports and the hiring of independent auditors. The demands on corporate boards of directors have also changed. These demands require boards to perform a multitude of functions that call for attention to the structure of boards and to their composition and practices. Insufficient changes have been made, however, to accommodate these multiple roles of corporate boards.

This chapter is about the multiple roles of corporate boards, which include the manager-monitoring, relational, and strategic management roles of boards. The main focus for legal reform of corporate boards has been on their manager-monitoring (or supervisory) role. To better perform this function, corporations have made a number of changes in the composition and structure of boards. For instance, they have changed their boards' structure by creating board committees to specialize in various subject areas. They have also given attention to the composition of their boards to ensure the necessary expertise for these committees and the independence of board members from management. In addition, boards are increasingly adopting the practice of having outside directors meet separately from the chief executive officer (CEO).

The second role of boards, the relational role, is less well understood. It refers to the use of board memberships to facilitate the sharing of information and perspectives among corporations and their various stakeholders, such as shareholders, consumers, and the legal and financial community, and to ensure the corporation the continued support of these stakeholders. Traditionally, approximately 26 percent of board members have been selected to perform relational functions.[1] In recent years, the interest of the business community in forming more diverse boards points to the continued importance of the relational role of boards. Diversity in terms of the presence of women, minority, and foreign directors on boards is intended to enable corporations to better relate to their domestic and foreign consumers and employees. The third role of boards, the strategic role, is generally subsumed within the manager-monitoring and relational roles of boards. A separate strategic role of boards is indicated, however, to the extent that boards engage in strategic management, which refers to the development and implementation of corporate strategy at the board level. This chapter explains how these roles more accurately describe board functions than the description of board functions as control, service, and strategy.

The multiple roles of boards often come into conflict with each other. The relational role can conflict with the manager-monitoring role when board members selected to perform relational functions have business relationships with the corporation and are therefore not independent of management, as is desirable for manager monitoring. Similarly, the emergence of a strategic management role for boards (to the extent that it is occurring) is not necessarily a positive development because the performance of this role by boards may detract from the time spent on manager monitoring by boards. Also, if insiders are best at this strategic management function, it may dictate a more insider (executive officer)-dominated board at the expense of independent directors, who are advisable for effective manager monitoring.

A recent meta-analysis has found that both insider-dominated and outsider-dominated boards are associated with more successful corporations in terms of return on assets.[2] In this chapter, I explore a number of alternative explanations for these findings. I propose an interpretation that is based on the perception that boards perform multiple roles. Insider-dominated boards perform some roles more effectively than outsider-dominated boards, particularly strategic management. Outsider-dominated boards perform other functions better than insider-dominated boards, particularly manager-monitoring functions, to the extent that the outside directors are truly independent of management, unlike the board of Enron Corporation prior to its collapse.[3] Both boards perform relational and some monitoring functions. This analysis suggests a number of reforms for corporate boards that will enable them to perform their multiple functions more effectively.

The findings of the meta-analysis suggest the potential for enhancing board performance by the use of a dual board structure. This structure would consist of an insider-dominated board, composed of insiders and outside (relational) board members who would not necessarily be independent of management (a "business review" board), and an outsider-dominated board, composed solely of independent directors (a "conflicts" board).[4] First, the conflicts board is designed to decrease the pressures on independent directors from inside directors to conform to management wishes in areas where management has conflicts of interest. The organization of this conflicts board is a logical step in the process of board reform that began with increasing the number of outside directors on corporate boards and their committees, and that has extended more recently to having outside directors meet separately from the full board. The formation of this conflicts board takes the social dynamics of groups seriously and insists on the independence of outside directors. A related proposal, although one also applicable to single board systems, is that independent directors appoint a corporate ombudsperson who would have access to all corporate meetings and information concerning the corporation.[5] The corporate ombudsperson would serve the independent directors full-time for a three-year period, and would report to independent directors and also to shareholders in the corporation's annual report. Improving the flow of information is important for a board with outside directors and can be accomplished by having a board ombudsperson and also by establishing a strategic planning committee that provides a forum for outside directors to meet with management. Would the Enron debacle have occurred had Enron utilized a separate conflicts board composed of truly independent directors and sought to improve the flow of information to these independent directors as suggested by this proposal?

Second, the business review board would, as previously noted, consist of inside directors and outside directors (who may or may not be independent of management). I suggest that the performance of the insider-dominated board reported in the meta-analysis may indicate the advantage of group decision making by peers (fellow executives), which may decrease corporate politics and the chances of a dominant CEO becoming convinced of his invincibility, as appeared to have been the case with Enron CEO Jeffrey Skilling.[6] In addition, the quality of decisions is enhanced in ambiguous and uncertain situations when diverse perspectives are shared, and this sharing is encouraged when persons are in similar social positions (for example, all directors of the corporation). The business review board would make business decisions not within the jurisdiction of the conflicts board and would have various advantages in performing relational, strategic management, and some monitoring functions.

To avoid confusion, it is important to point out that the dual board structure proposed here is not the same as the two-tiered board structure found in Germany. The division of functions in the two-tiered German board system is of supervision and management. Both boards in the dual board structure perform supervision: the conflicts board mainly performs manager monitoring and the business review board mainly performs relational monitoring.[7] In addition, neither board in the German system is composed solely of independent outside directors, unlike the recommendation for the conflicts board in the dual board system. In Germany supervisory boards consist of employees and many directors having business relationships with the corporation. In addition, the dual monitoring boards are not restricted in the way German supervisory boards are in conducting the business and affairs of the corporation. One feature of the German system that US corporations may wish to consider is having employee representatives on their boards (or, in the dual board system, on business review boards). Employee directors would not only likely protect the employees' stake in the corporation, which, for example, was substantially impacted by Enron's governance, but would also bring diverse perspectives to corporate boards.[8]

In this chapter, I first discuss recent developments in board structure, composition, and practices that accommodate the manager-monitoring and relational roles of US boards of directors. I then explore the multiple roles of corporate boards, theoretically and empirically, and address issues relating to the strategic role of boards. I then turn to interpretations of recent empirical literature on corporate boards and proposals for reforming US boards of directors.

Developments in Manager Monitoring by US Boards of Directors

More effective supervision of managers by boards is the objective of various reforms in recent years in the structure, composition, and practices of boards of directors of US public corporations. These reforms are encouraged by developments in fiduciary duty law whereby courts apply a more deferential standard of review when reviewing corporate decisions made by independent directors.[9] Thus, reforms to change the composition of boards to include more independent directors are supported by these decisions. In addition, the experience of shareholders in the 1980s with board approvals of defensive tactics that had the effect of defeating takeovers that shareholders favoured highlighted managerial dominance of corporate boards. This experience has also had the effect of spurring board reform, particularly because institutional ownership has increased.[10] These institutional investors have become increasingly active in corporate governance as exit has become a less viable option and as norms have changed that permit them to take actions to facilitate board reform, including the establishment of institutional investor associations.[11]

Trends towards Outside Directors on US Corporate Boards

Probably the most significant trend in board governance in the US in the last twenty years is the increase in the number and proportion of outside directors on corporate boards of directors.[12] This increase has coincided naturally with a decrease in the number and proportion of corporate insiders on boards. Proxy statement data for 1998 show that corporate boards of public corporations in the US average eleven directors, with two inside directors.[13] This represents a decrease in the number of inside directors from

1993, when boards averaged three inside directors, and from 1973, when boards averaged five inside directors.[14] In a study comparing the composition of US boards of directors in 1970 and 1980, the decrease in inside directors was offset by independent directors on boards. Independent directors included public and professional directors, private investors, and directors employed by nonrelated business organizations.[15] The proportion of relational outside directors consisting of financiers, consultants, legal counsel, and directors employed by related businesses did not change significantly during this period.[16]

This trend towards fewer inside directors was fuelled by the objective of making boards more independent from management. As early as 1975, Melvin Eisenberg made a persuasive case for having boards composed of a majority of outside directors who are independent of management in his foundational book *The Structure of the Corporation.*[17] Psychological studies confirm the considerable pressures on directors to conform to the wishes of corporate insiders, and thus the importance of true independence.[18] Today, numerous codes of best practices proposed and adopted in the US and abroad by national stock exchanges, professional organizations, and blue ribbon committees of academicians, legal practitioners, and business leaders recommend independent-outside directors on corporate boards of directors for more effective manager monitoring.[19]

Developments in US Board Committees

Attempts to improve manager monitoring have also been made in recent years by changing board structure through the use of committees. Management literature supports the use of committees for effective board functioning.[20] Committees enhance the effectiveness of boards by permitting directors to use and develop expertise in specialized areas and to focus their energies on a subset of issues confronting the corporation. The number of public corporations who now have audit committees composed of outside directors (although not necessarily independent directors) is a dramatic example of the increasing focus on manager monitoring by US boards. Audit committees of boards are intended to implement and support the boards' manager-monitoring functions by periodically reviewing the corporations' processes for compiling financial data, its internal controls, and the independence of the corporation's external auditors.[21] According to 1998 proxy statements, all public corporations have audit committees with an average of zero insiders on these committees.[22] Such committees have had widespread support from a variety of sources, including national stock exchanges, professional organizations, and blue ribbon committees formed in the US and abroad.[23]

Another board committee considered important to effective manager monitoring by boards is the compensation committee, which is responsible for setting and reviewing executive compensation. There is a consensus in the US that good board practice requires a compensation committee composed of independent directors.[24] According to a 1999 survey, 96 percent of the corporations surveyed have compensation committees composed solely of outside directors (although these directors are not necessarily independent directors).[25] This study chastised boards that have insiders on their compensation committees, explaining that outside directors are necessary for boards "to properly oversee their fiduciary responsibilities and operate independently of management."[26]

The third most popular manager-monitoring committee of boards is the nominating committee, which is responsible for recommending board members to shareholders. Having a nominating committee consisting of independent directors is considered good board practice.[27] According to 1998 proxy statements, 74 percent of public corporations have nominating committees composed, on average, entirely of outside directors.[28]

Of course, having these committees does not guarantee effective manager monitoring. Concern that the quality of financial reporting by US corporations is on the decline has recently received substantial national attention. Arthur Levitt, the former chairperson of the Securities and Exchange Commission, in 1998, cautioned corporations against the manipulation of numbers (referred to as "earnings management") that may assist corporations in attaining short-term competitive advantage but that in the long run will undermine confidence in US capital markets.[29] The actual functioning of audit committees has varied among corporations from being thorough to perfunctory and from having expert, professional committee members to having members who do not understand the basic principles of financial reporting.[30] Proposals to address this situation were made by a Blue Ribbon Committee sponsored by the New York Stock Exchange and the National Association of Securities Dealers, whose report, issued in 1999, focused on the important role of the board audit committee in providing active and independent oversight.[31] In 2000, the Securities and Exchange Commission adopted new rules and amendments based in large measure on the recommendations of this Blue Ribbon Committee.[32] Further reforms are receiving considerable national attention as a result of accounting irregularities at Enron and other corporations.[33] The *Sarbanes-Oxley Act of 2002*, passed in the wake of Enron, required public corporations to have audit committees that are composed solely of independent directors and to disclose whether at least one member is a "financial expert."[34] The New York Stock Exchange (NYSE) in its proposed rules to the Securities and Exchange Commission has also promulgated rules dealing with the independence, authority, and responsibility of audit committees.[35] As for compensation committees, they may have difficulty in monitoring executive compensation. This difficulty is arguably reflected in the dramatic recent rise in US executive compensation,[36] the increasing use of stock options that may create inappropriate managerial incentives,[37] and in the growing differences in the levels of compensation of US executives compared with the compensation of the lowest paid corporate employees and corporate executives in other nations.[38] As for board nominating committees, they often do not consider shareholder nominees, which is a serious failing.[39] The NYSE, in its proposed rules, requires listed companies to have compensation and nominating board committees, which are to consist solely of independent directors and also specifies their duties and responsibilities.[40]

Other Recent Developments in Board Practices
Increasing sophistication in monitoring is exhibited in recent board developments. A number of public corporations are establishing standing board committees to review corporate governance processes.[41] One survey found that 56 percent of responding companies have corporate governance committees.[42] One study notes that "increasingly, the corporate governance committee or the full board is appointing committee chairmen and members of the committees of the board with the concurrence of the chairman/CEO, instead of having these appointments made by the CEO alone."[43] A number of boards are also evaluating their own performance and, to a lesser extent, the performance of individual board members.[44] One survey found that 20 percent of the corporations surveyed evaluate individual directors formally and, as evidence of this emerging norm, that 73 percent believe that this is a good corporate practice.[45] Independent directors are also meeting separately from the board to consider matters.[46] The NYSE, in its proposed rules, requires outside directors to meet "at regularly scheduled executive sessions without management."[47] This practice goes some way to counter the social dynamics of boards that can stymie independent decision making.[48]

US corporations have not taken steps to adopt certain proposals for improving manager monitoring. They have not appointed independent directors as chairpersons of boards or as "lead directors." The leadership of boards by independent directors could have a positive effect on the social dynamics of boards.[49] A 1999 survey of public corporations, however, found that only 9 percent of responding corporations had independent director chairpersons, 30 percent had lead directors, and the remaining corporations had no plans to implement either of these reforms.[50]

Another proposal is to limit the number of directorships that a single director may hold. This proposal is designed to ensure that directors have sufficient time to attend to the affairs of the corporation.[51] Few corporations have adopted this proposal,[52] although corporations are increasingly limiting the number of directorships that their executive officers may hold.[53] This proposal is problematic to some, however, because it does not guarantee that a director will spend any length of time on corporate affairs and does not take into account that some individuals may prefer to spend their time on board affairs rather than on other pursuits.

A primary responsibility of the board of directors is to appoint the successor to the current CEO. Directors of US corporations believe that improvements are needed in this area. A survey of public directors reveals that "many are critical of the management succession process."[54] Based on 1998 proxy statements, however, only 32 percent of public corporations have management succession committees.[55]

In conclusion, a number of changes have occurred in corporate structures, composition, and practices that are designed to improve the manager-monitoring functions of boards. These reforms include increasing the percentage of outside directors on corporate boards, creating committees composed predominantly of outside directors that specialize in important subjects that require objective assessments, having outside directors meet separately from the whole board, decreasing the CEO's control over the appointment of board and committee members, and encouraging the review of board and board members' performance. More attention, however, needs be given to the subject of whether outside directors are truly "independent." For example, as the facts are coming to light about Enron, it appears that many outside directors were not independent but were benefiting from various kinds of financial relationships with Enron.[56] In addition, attention needs to be given to the leadership of boards through independent chairpersons or independent lead directors and to the methods by which independent directors are kept informed of important issues concerning the corporation. Enron directors claim, for example, that they were unaware of Enron's accounting problems,[57] which would be much harder to maintain had independent directors appointed a corporate ombudsperson to keep them informed.

Developments in the Relational Monitoring by US Boards
United States boards of directors are not limited to performing manager monitoring; they also perform relational monitoring. Relational monitoring addresses the corporation's substantial environmental uncertainties. The corporation obtains access to information, advice, support and/or legitimacy by furthering relationships with stakeholders through board memberships.

Shareholders
A relationship that is important to the corporation is its relationship with shareholders. A 1999 study reports a "cultural change" in the last few years in the US with respect to the relationship between shareholders and boards of directors of public corporations that "correspond[s] to a growing awareness by board members of their duty to properly represent the shareholders

who elected them as directors."[58] Given that the prevailing legal theory provides that directors should operate corporations to benefit shareholders, this "change" in culture may seem mysterious. Managerialism has predominated, however, as the mode of governance of US public corporations. Although substantial attention has been given in the past to ensuring the professionalism of managers, the operative goals of the corporation have been largely undefined. The increasing power of institutional shareholders has changed the culture in which corporations operate today.[59] Confronted with the formal legal doctrine of shareholder primacy, directors are currently pressured by institutional shareholders to specify how their decisions serve the interests of shareholders.

In this vein, attempts are made to align the interests of directors with those of shareholders. A recent trend is to compensate outside directors in whole or in part with stock and/or stock options in order to align their financial interests with those of shareholders.[60] One study shows that 88 percent of companies offered stock compensation in 1998, compared with only 33 percent in 1990.[61] Unfortunately, it is becoming increasingly apparent that stock options do not align the interests of directors and shareholders. Because accounting rules do not require stock options to be recognized as expenses, corporate profits reported to shareholders are inflated.[62] This accounting rule also encourages the issuance of large amounts of options. Eventually corporate resources are diverted from real investments to share repurchases to satisfy the options once they are exercised.[63] In addition, compensation with stock options encourages "earnings management" or the manipulation of reported financial results to affect stock prices. Enron is an example of the damage that earnings management can cause.[64]

Diversity on Corporate Boards

The role of the board in providing an avenue for shareholders to influence the corporation is consistent with the formal views of the corporation as intended to further shareholder interests.[65] Competing views of the corporation are found in US case law and commentary, however. For example, Adolph Berle and E. Merrick Dodd, in their famous debate in the 1930s, considered the significance of the separation of control from ownership resulting from the ownership of shares by dispersed, public shareholders.[66] Berle and Dodd ultimately agreed that the corporation was not only a profit-making entity but also an institution with social responsibilities.[67] Dodd claimed that "business is permitted and encouraged by the law primarily because it is of service to the community rather than because it is a source of profits to its owners."[68] Case law is found that supports the existence of a fiduciary duty of directors to the corporate entity as distinct from its shareholders.[69] Under this conception of fiduciary duty, directors are trustees for the corporation and arguably for the stakeholders who comprise it. In more recent years, this view has been codified in a number of constituency statutes, enacted in over one-half of the states in the US, that permit directors to take into account in decision making the interests of stakeholders, at least in a tender offer situation.[70] Moreover, in the important corporate law state of Delaware, which does not have a constituency statute, the Delaware Supreme Court has stated that directors may take into account the interests of employees, consumers, and other stakeholders in making decisions as long as these decisions have a mere rational relationship to furthering a shareholder interest.[71]

In addition, there is increasing interest by US public corporations in representing the interests of a diverse society on corporate boards.[72] This development arguably represents a recognition of the value of stakeholder capitalism, although the discussion among directors and other businesspersons proceeds emphatically in the traditionally acceptable context of enhancing shareholder value. One study of board best practices, which is based on the opinions of working groups of corporate executives, investors, and directors throughout the US, found that "diversity is [considered] a key part of good governance."[73] Diversity was defined to include diversity in terms of gender, race, and culture as companies become international. The study reports considerable consensus among the working groups that there are substantial economic arguments in favour of diversity on corporate boards as "companies broaden the scope of what they consider relevant to creating shareholder value to include things like workplace practices and customer satisfaction."[74]

A substantial number of directors, particularly of the largest corporations, consider it important to have minority representation on the board. The reason is "to better reflect the changing marketplace and the growth in minority market segments."[75] Service industries such as motels, restaurants, telephones, and airlines that have substantial minority employees are found to have more minority representation on boards, which indicates a labour stakeholder orientation.[76] In addition, there is substantial support for having women on corporate boards to perform relational functions.[77] James Preston, retired CEO of Avon Products, states that because "60 percent of all purchases in this country are made by women, having women on the board just makes good business sense."[78] Women on boards permit the corporation to send important signals to current female managers and potential recruits.[79]

It should not be lost sight of the fact that minorities and women on boards contribute to the performance of all board roles. For example, the consideration of women and minorities permits the corporation to take advantage of the full range of intellectual capital available to the corporation.[80] As one CEO of a Fortune 1000 company said of women, "when you open positions to both sexes, you double the number of people in the top 10, or in the top 1 percent of ability in the marketplace."[81] Moreover, a study finds that women are not "token" directors but are on the board due to their business expertise and access to information and resources that the corporation requires. The percentage of female outside directors with corporate backgrounds rose from 13.3 percent in 1987 to 37.6 percent in 1996, ten years later.[82] Moreover, the percentage of women serving as outside directors who represent organizations that provide services to the corporation rose from 13.3 percent in 1987 to 32.6 percent in 1996.[83]

Some studies have examined whether there are sex-based biases in the appointment of women directors to board committees. A recent study based on 1983 data found sex-based biases in committee assignments, even after controlling for experience-based characteristics.[84] This study observed that female directors were as qualified as, if not better qualified than, their male counterparts on most characteristics examined. Women were favoured for public affairs committee memberships over men, and men were favoured for the more powerful compensation and executive committees.[85] These data are dated, however, and the small number of female directors make reliance on this study, as well as on studies attempting to link the presence of female or minority directors to corporate performance, problematic.

A survey of corporate directors found that 20 percent of directors expressed the desire to add a foreign director to their boards "to enhance their global perspective."[86] Although time and distance barriers exist to having non-US directors on corporate boards, these barriers are being overcome by fewer (but possibly longer) board meetings and video teleconferencing.[87] A study of global corporations found that these corporations added foreign directors to their boards to acquire an in-depth understanding of new markets, comprehend a new customer base, deal with demands of international investors, and gain credibility in certain capital markets or political environments.[88]

The discussion concerning board diversity in the US takes place in the context of improving corporate returns for shareholders. Shareholders, including institutional investors, have been active in using the corporate proxy machinery to further diversity within the company, including on boards. Shareholder board diversity proposals at Cypress Semiconductor and American Power Conversion have received supporting votes as high as 43.8 percent and 30.1 percent, respectively.[89] Although business leaders indicate little support for constituency or special interest directors on boards,[90] the issues focused on for improving returns to shareholders include stakeholder concerns: workplace practices and/or customer satisfaction.[91] Corporations with diverse boards are expected to have greater sensitivity to these stakeholder issues;[92] thus, diverse boards enable these corporations to more effectively relate to their socio-economic environment. Boards also perform other relational roles that facilitate the corporation's interactions with its environment. Corporations benefit from understanding their legal and financial environment and supplier markets. Between 1970 and 1980, 26 percent of board members were financiers, consultants, legal counsel, and directors employed by related businesses.[93]

In summary, boards perform various relational roles by having persons on their boards who assist the corporation in dealing with environmental uncertainties. These persons lend legitimacy to the corporation and help the corporation in its operations by, among other things, assisting it in effectively relating to shareholders and various other stakeholders of the corporation.

Roles of Corporate Boards: Theories and Empirical Studies

The board of directors is expected to perform a number of functions. This has confounded the empirical literature on corporate boards and has made it difficult to find definitive answers concerning principles of board composition, structure, and process. This section explores board theories and empirical findings on corporate board functioning.

Manager Monitoring and the Shareholder Relational Role of Corporate Boards

Agency cost theory, originating in research in finance and economics, explains that corporate boards are used to reduce agency costs, which are "costs imposed on the principal [shareholders] when an agent with discretionary authority [management] takes actions to help himself, rather than the principal."[94] Boards of directors are intended to ensure that managers act in the interests of shareholders rather than in their own personal interest.[95] This theory embraces the manager-monitoring role of boards and the shareholder relational role of boards. Manager monitoring is intended to curtail managerial self-dealing, negligence, and the lack of professionalism on the part of management in attending to the affairs of the corporation. Boards mediate the relationship between the shareholders of the corporation and management by providing the appropriate oversight and incentives to management to protect the interests of shareholders.

Three agency cost theories are offered that are relevant to board composition. The first theory focuses on the importance of outside directors to effective manager monitoring. According to this theory, the board performs manager monitoring primarily by providing a forum for competition among top managers for the top management position.[96] The outside directors on the board "act as arbiters in disagreements among internal managers,"[97] rank internal managers,[98] and provide appropriate incentives to managers to act in the interests of shareholders.[99] This agency cost theory that relies on outside directors to evaluate competing executives suggests that a mix of both inside and outside directors on boards enhances board performance.

The second, more recent, agency cost theory focuses on the role of inside directors in monitoring the CEO directly, without the outside directors playing a role.[100] This agency cost theory, which I refer to as the "managerial-incentive theory," claims that inside directors are superior to outside directors in evaluating the CEO. According to this theory, because of their superior access to information concerning strategic decision making by the CEO, inside directors are better at evaluating the CEO and providing the CEO with appropriate incentives to engage in strategic risk taking.[101] This theory recommends an insider-dominated board for more effective manager monitoring.

The third agency cost theory is called the "substitute" hypothesis. This theory claims that manager monitoring by corporate boards may in certain situations be less cost-effective than other forms of corporate monitoring, in which case these other forms of monitoring shall "substitute" for manager monitoring by corporate boards.[102] For example, it is argued that in certain industries, stock ownership by managers,[103] increased corporate leverage,[104] and increased dividend payouts[105] will provide managers with appropriate incentives, thus negating the need for manager monitoring by corporate boards of directors. Thus, according to the substitute hypothesis, no general recommendation applicable to all corporations is appropriate concerning the composition of corporate boards.

The first agency cost theory, which predicts a reduction of agency costs by the presence of outside directors on corporate boards, has been tested in studies examining situations where managers have conflicts of interest with shareholders. These studies try to test the ability of outside directors to engage in effective manager monitoring, although they do not determine whether this monitoring occurs through the outside directors' observation of competition among inside directors. Empirical studies test the relationship between the proportion of outside directors on corporate boards and the adoption of anti-takeover devices, which are presumed to be harmful to shareholders but beneficial to managers. These studies report mixed results.[106] These results are not surprising, however, because whether these anti-takeover devices operate to benefit or harm shareholders depends on the context in which they are used. In addition, studies on the relationship of the proportion of outside directors on corporate boards and the level of executive compensation report inconsistent findings.[107] Levels of executive compensation, however, are arguably more a reflection of industrial norms and market constraints than the manager-monitoring capability of individual boards.[108] Studies on executive turnover may be more reflective of the benefits of outside directors on corporate boards. These studies have more consistently found a positive relationship between the proportion of outside directors on corporate boards and executive turnover.[109] A problem with most of theses studies, however, is that they fail to differentiate between independent and non-independent outside directors. The outside directors studied often include directors with business relationships with the corporation and directors who may have significant social relationships with the CEO.

In addition, the independence of outside directors is diminished by their serving on boards with inside directors. Psychological studies on group behaviour indicate that members of groups operate under social pressures that encourage conformity to the group, or lack of objectivity.[110] Studies also show "a correlation between the capacity to exert influence and one's position in a hierarchical social structure."[111] CEOs often assume the leadership position on boards. Particularly as board chairpersons, CEOs exert considerable influence over outside board members. Thus, the structure of corporate boards does not support independence on the part of outside directors. It is therefore not surprising that studies often do not find differences in boards when some additional outside directors are added. Some outside directors do exercise more independence than others, and the dominance of these directors on important committees of the board may have positive effects, but the socialization process of board group memberships often robs these directors of much-needed independence. It is also important to point out that the empirical literature is further confounded by those situations where non-independent outside directors have interests that are negatively affected by managerial self-dealing or negligence. In those situations, non-independent directors have incentives to effectively monitor management.

The second agency cost theory, the managerial-incentive theory, is discussed later in this chapter.[112] The third theory, the substitute hypothesis, which predicts that agency cost reduction methods may "substitute" for having outside directors on corporate boards, has received at most moderate empirical support.[113] There is mixed support for the proposition that increased leverage, high dividend payouts, and stock ownership substitute for outside directors on corporate boards.[114]

The Broad Relational Roles of Corporate Boards

This section introduces the resource dependence theory, which explains the relational role of corporate boards. The resource dependence theory, grounded in sociology and organizational behaviour theory, explains that corporations seek to decrease uncertainty by gaining access to needed resources (tangible and intangible) through board memberships.[115] Outside board members permit the corporation to: (1) coordinate with its external environment; (2) obtain advice and access to information from directors with differing backgrounds, skills, and networks; (3) enhance the support, status, and legitimacy of the corporation in the eyes of relevant audiences; and (4) effectuate monitoring of the strategic direction of the corporation.[116] Inside directors perform similar functions for the corporation by reflecting the views and diverse interests of various departments and functional units within the corporation itself. Thus, the board, according to resource dependence theory, is used as a "bridging strategy"[117] or "boundary spanning"[118] device that enables the corporation to mediate its relationships with various stakeholders and others comprising its external and internal environment. According to the resource dependence perspective, women, minority, and foreign directors provide advice, support, and enhanced status and legitimacy to the corporation's operations. These functions may also be provided by bankers, environmentalists, major suppliers, and customers on corporate boards. Thus, "because of their prestige in their professions and communities, directors are able to extract resources for successful company operations ... these activities are believed to enhance the firm's legitimacy in society and to help it achieve goals of efficiency and improved performance."[119]

Resource dependence theory also explains the two-way relationship represented by board memberships.[120] The corporation benefits from having relational board members. Internal and external interests, however, also benefit from the ability of relational directors to influence the corporation. For example, a woman on the board may influence the corporation to consider human resource issues of particular concern to women. A banker or lawyer may influence the amount of corporate attention directed to financial or regulatory concerns. An inside director employed by a foreign division or a sales division of the corporation may gain attention for the needs of his or her division. An important factor determining the ability of these board members to influence corporations is the perceived dependence of the corporations on the resources provided by these members, which perception in turn is influenced by the board members themselves.[121]

Related to the resource dependence theory is the strategic contingency perspective, which explains that a corporation's environment, strategy, and past performance are strategic contingencies facing the corporation. Board composition reflects these strategic contingencies, which are important to the corporation's effectiveness and survival.[122] Studies have shown that corporations that utilize board memberships to acquire resources for the corporation enhance their performance.[123] For example, in the nonprofit sector, positive associations were found between board composition and the ability of nonprofit agencies to raise funds.[124] In a study of 80 corporations, deviations from a ratio of inside to outside directors deemed responsive to external concerns was related to poor performance.[125] Moreover, in a survey of the CEOs of 119 Fortune 500 corporations, environmental uncertainty was found to be related to the proportion of outside directors on corporate boards.[126] Uncertainties regarding the corporations' customers, competitors, suppliers, technology, and economic and political circumstances were considered. The authors concluded that having higher proportions of outside directors on corporate boards was a viable way of "co-opting the environment and reducing uncertainty surrounding strategy development and execution."[127]

Strategic Roles of Corporate Boards

A board of directors' monitoring and relational functions concerning corporate strategy include the following: (1) involvement in setting the corporation's overall goals or missions; (2) overseeing and setting guidelines for the development and implementation of corporate strategy; (3) pointing out strategic opportunities and issuing warnings about environmental threats; and (4) evaluating senior executives with regard to their choice of strategic initiatives and implementation of strategic choices.[128] These monitoring and relational functions concerning corporate strategy are more specifically referred to as "strategic monitoring." More controversial, however, is whether the board should also engage in "strategic management," that is, in the actual development and implementation of corporate strategy.[129] Although particular situations may warrant a board's involvement in strategic management, such involvement at the very least duplicates corporate management's responsibilities, with all the attendant problems that duplication entails. There are advantages in having management perform strategic management functions because of the time they have to devote to such efforts and because of their expertise. Moreover, separating strategic management and monitoring functions creates a structure designed to enhance accountability.

According to the resource dependence theory, directors are boundary-scanning agents who have access to important information that enables them to assist corporations in setting goals, embracing opportunities, and avoiding threats. Moreover, as agency cost theory points out, the monitoring of managerial performance requires attention to corporate strategy, including overseeing and evaluating the development and implementation of corporate strategy by executive officers. Thus, the manager-monitoring and relational monitoring functions of the board involve corporate strategy. Boards perform a third role, however, when they perform strategic management functions.

While this chapter describes board roles as monitoring, relational, and possibly strategic management, some organizational literature refers to board roles as service, strategy, and control. The latter categorization of board roles is problematic, however. For example, the service role of boards is defined as "enhancing company reputation, establishing contacts with the external environment, and giving advice and counsel to executives."[130] These functions are explained by the resource dependence perspective on corporate boards, but the "service" depiction of these functions neglects the two-way nature of the resource dependence perspective. That is, board members not only provide services but also obtain opportunities to influence the corporation through board memberships. These service and influence functions are more appropriately referred to as the relational role rather than the service role of boards.

In addition, the "control" role is subsumed within monitoring and relational functions, and is a misleading description of board functions. Although the board has the legal power to control the corporation, at most it monitors the corporation and influences corporate policy; control is primarily in the hands of management. This reality is reflected in provisions of US state statutes on board responsibilities, and in the more recent recommendations of the American Law Institute's Principles of Corporate Governance that specify separately the control functions of management and the monitoring functions of boards.[131] Finally, the "strategy" role of boards is potentially quite broad and may encompass strategic monitoring and strategic management. While the manager-monitoring and relational roles cover the former function, they do not necessarily cover the latter. Thus, if boards perform or ought to perform strategic management functions, there is a third role of boards that is more accurately called the strategic management role of boards. Categorizing the board roles as monitoring, relational, and possibly strategic management is, therefore, more accurate and helpful than describing board roles as service, control, and strategy.

In terms of strategy, a recent survey of over 1,000 directors of large US corporations indicates that corporate boards are becoming increasingly active in strategic monitoring and possibly strategic management:

> Over 40 percent of our respondents say their boards spend considerable time on strategy and over 60 percent contend that they are deeply involved in the strategy-setting process. Surprisingly, 54 percent say they participate in an annual retreat or special planning session. And a very strong 80 percent believe that their boards have sufficient and relevant expertise to evaluate strategic options. Again, we recognize that there are many companies that leave the strategic planning function almost exclusively to the CEO as part of the management process, but our respondents strongly suggested that it is the board's responsibility to become involved in both the setting and the review of strategic goals.[132]

The answer to a specific question by these respondents indicates that boards mainly perform strategic monitoring functions. In this question, the respondents were asked to choose the statement that best describes their board's role concerning corporate strategy: (1) reviews strategy after it is developed, (2) helps develop the strategy, or (3) plays no role. Over 60 percent of respondents chose answer (1), indicating that their boards review strategy after it is developed, that is, their boards perform strategic monitoring rather than strategic management functions.[133]

Research on Outside Directors and the Multiple Roles of Corporate Boards

The empirical literature has been mixed on whether there is a positive, negative, or no relationship between inside/outside board member composition and corporate performance.[134] However, a recent meta-analysis of such studies found a curvilinear relationship between inside/outside board member composition and return on assets (ROA), although not return on equity.[135] That is, boards more dominated by either outside or inside directors were found to have a positive effect on return on assets. The following subsections explore alternative explanations of these findings.

Different Strategies

Assuming that the findings of this study are replicated in future studies, the authors of the meta-analysis suggest that a board composed of predominantly outside or inside directors may support alternative business strategies, with each set of strategies providing avenues for improved corporate performance. The choice of strategies may follow from the inside directors' greater firm-specific knowledge and the outside directors' access to information and connections external to the corporation. The researchers speculate as follows:

> Note that insiders' greater knowledge of company affairs and internal operations is compatible with a focus on asset allocation strategies and attainment of related efficiencies, therefore, with movement to stronger ROA through control of working assets. In contrast, outsiders' greater knowledge about and experience with external affairs seems more consistent with the formulation of environmental strategies, leading to strengthened ROA though the enhancement of income sources and streams.[136]

Similarly, another researcher suggests that differences in information may cause outside directors to focus on new market entry through venturing and acquisition activities and inside directors to focus on internal business and product development.[137]

Thus, boards composed predominantly of inside directors or outside directors may pursue different strategies that positively affect corporate performance. Note that the "different strategies" interpretation of the findings of the meta-analysis suggests a strategic management role for boards. It does not ascribe less risk taking to outsider-dominated boards, though, as does the agency cost managerial-incentive theory.[138]

Different Managerial Incentives

The agency cost managerial-incentive theory has been offered to explain the advantages of an insider-dominated board,[139] although it does not explain the advantages of an outsider-dominated board that were also found by the meta-analysis. Like the "different strategies" explanation for the perform-ance implications of board composition, this explanation focuses on the different informational sources of inside/outside directors. However, rather than informational differences affecting a board member's preferences for strategies, these differences are claimed to affect a board's method of evalu-ating managers, which in turn supposedly impacts the corporation by af-fecting the managers' choices of more or less risky strategies. The argument is that outside directors are at a disadvantage relative to insiders in evaluat-ing the CEO, that is, in discriminating between corporate financial "out-comes" that are the result of bad decision making by the CEO and outcomes that are due to factors beyond the CEO's control. This explanation main-tains that inside directors with firm-specific knowledge are better at evalu-ating the CEO and, therefore, that they can enhance the CEO's commitment and willingness to pursue risky strategies through investments and research and development (R&D).

In the terminology of this managerial-incentive theory, outside directors are said to rely on "outcome" or "financial" controls, whereas inside direc-tors are said to rely on "behavioural" or "strategic" controls through ob-serving the actual behaviour of the CEO. The managerial-incentive theory predicts that the choice of controls impacts strategic decision making by the CEO by affecting his or her incentives. Outcome controls are claimed to shift the risk of poor results from shareholders to the CEO and cause the CEO to adopt more risk-averse strategies. Thus, in corporations with more outside directors, who are expected to utilize outcome controls, corpora-tions are predicted to pursue more risk-averse strategies, such as unrelated diversification and less expenditure on capital investments and R&D, than boards composed of more inside directors.

Recently, some studies have suggested that insider boards are more suc-cessful than outsider boards at supporting risk-taking activities by corpora-tions. A recent study of entrepreneurship activity found that corporations with more inside directors engaged in more entrepreneurial activities.[140] Another study found a positive relationship between the percentage of in-side directors on boards of Fortune 500 corporations and R&D spending.[141] R&D spending, however, may not reflect risk-taking activities but rather may reflect internal inefficiencies when corporations decide to keep funds rather than distribute them to shareholders.[142] Moreover, without relating the entrepreneurial activities in the former study to corporate performance, it is difficult to judge whether these activities are advantageous to corpora-tions. A recent study of small and large airlines found that both small and large airlines performed better "to the degree that their competitive behaviors resembled those of the average or typical, small and large airline."[143] This study suggests benefits to competitive conformity. It may be that "small (or large) firms that are doing badly are inclined to engage in extreme, deviant behavior but that those performing well tend to engage in risk-averse conformist behavior." This explanation is consistent with prospect theory, which suggests that persons become more risk-seeking when faced with returns below target.[144] More extreme strategic behaviours are observed by corporations in a downward spiral towards bankruptcy.[145]

In a study of California general hospitals, the relationship between a board dominated by outside directors and the use of either outcome or behavioural controls was tested directly by surveying board members on their actual criteria for evaluating CEOs.[146] This study found that boards consisting of higher percentages of outside directors were not associated with an emphasis on outcome controls. It also found mixed support for the relationship between outcome controls and risk-averse strategies. A negative relationship was found between the use of outcome controls and capital expenditures, but no relationship was found between outcome controls and unrelated diversification.

This study also found a negative relationship between the use of outcome controls for evaluating CEOs and both the frequency of board meetings and the existence of board-level strategic planning committees. Thus, interactions between CEOs and boards diminish the use of outcome controls. The authors of this study explain:

> The results of this study suggest that board composition may not be the sole factor influencing the board's access to information about the CEO's performance-related behavior. In fact, we showed that outsiders may have better access to information about the quality of the top manager's decision making than suggested by the [managerial-incentive] literature. Besides tighter board-CEO linkages through more frequent board meetings and the presence of a strategic planning committee, outsiders may successfully develop informal communication with "inside" management officials whose opinion they trust and respect.[147]

This study suggests that especially in corporations with outside directors, considerable attention should be given to the flow of information within the corporation and to the establishment of a board-level strategic planning committee.[148] Note that a corporate ombudsperson would also improve the flow of information to outside directors.

Homogeneous/Heterogeneous Groups
Although the heterogeneity/homogeneity group research has focused mainly on management teams rather than boards, it is suggested that the reason corporations with either insider- or outsider-dominated boards have higher ROAs is because these boards are more homogeneous than boards

consisting of more equal numbers of inside and outside directors. In fact, however, insider- and outsider-dominated boards are not more homogeneous, and are even unlikely to have the same degree of heterogeneity. Moreover, homogeneous groups are not necessarily superior.[149] As group theory has shown, heterogeneous groups tend to make higher-quality decisions in matters involving creative and judgmental decision making.[150] Heterogeneous groups also have an advantage in solving problems having verifiably correct answers when heterogeneity "increases the probability of the group containing members who are capable of determining the correct answer to the problems being solved"[151] or when diversity increases "the amount of attention and discussion paid to each group member's individual solution."[152] In terms of manager monitoring, diversity "may promote the airing of different perspectives and reduce the probability of complacency and narrow-mindedness in the board's evaluation of executive proposals."[153] Such a board can produce a wider range of solutions for problems and decision criteria for evaluating corporate options. Heterogeneity also mitigates various cognitive biases in decision making.[154] Thus, even if insider- and outsider-dominated boards were more homogeneous, this homogeneity would not necessarily explain better performance.

Conflicting Multiple Roles of Corporate Boards

I propose another interpretation of the findings of the meta-analysis. This interpretation recognizes that boards are expected to perform multiple roles, with the effective performance of these roles requiring different kinds of directors. Some boards perform some roles better than others, depending on their composition. An outsider-dominated board that consists of mainly independent directors may achieve a group dynamic necessary for effective manager monitoring. Another kind of outsider-dominated board that is composed of both independent and non-independent outside directors may more successfully assist the corporation in relating to its external environment. An insider-dominated board may arguably enable more insiders to communicate effectively with outside directors on the board who provide advice and counsel. The insider-dominated board may also reap the advantages of peer-group decision making when inside directors confer among themselves on strategic management issues.

As previously noted, the manager-monitoring role of boards conflicts with the relational role of boards to the extent that the presence of inside and non-independent outside directors on corporate boards prevent independent outside directors from objectively monitoring management. Although a structure that has important monitoring committees consisting of predominantly independent directors (such as the auditing, compensation, and nominating committees discussed in this chapter) may mitigate conformity pressures, a board dominated by independent directors is expected to be more successful at resisting these pressures.[155] In addition, the manager-monitoring role of boards conflicts with the strategic management role to the extent that the latter role requires more inside directors to serve on boards.

If conflicts exist between board roles and the advantages of different kinds of boards are better understood, it may be possible to modify the board's structure to enhance the performance of multiple board roles. For example, if insider boards engage in more strategic management and are more successful at these functions than outsider boards, it may be due to the benefits of group decision making on issues involving some complexity and ambiguity. That is, the main benefit of an insider board may be that it levels the hierarchy among executive officers by creating a more peerlike structure.[156] For example, consider the German two-tiered board structure with a supervisory and management board: the two-tiered board structure permits collegial monitoring of management by the management board. The management board of a German corporation usually consists of the corporation's "top seven or so operating executives."[157] This flattening of the executive hierarchy means that the chairman of the management board in Germany is "the first among equals rather than the first among lessers usually associated with US chief executive officers."[158] Of course, corporations vary with some having very strong chairmen. Nevertheless, this structure has a number of advantages. The leveling of the hierarchy can result in greater accountability. There is less of a chance of a dominant individual becoming convinced of his invincibility. As one observer notes "[t]he trouble with dominant figures is their increased propensity as time goes on to listen less, believe their own hyperbole, and as a consequence to make bad mistakes."[159] There are fewer instances of this occurring in German corporations than in United States corporations.[160]

The danger of placing too much power in the hands of CEOs is confirmed by an Enron officer's description of Enron CEO Jeffrey Skilling: "Over the years, Jeff changed. He became more of a creature of his own creation. His hubris came to outweigh some of the more attractive parts of his personality. He became more intolerant, more opinionated, more bombastic. Jeff was always right, and that got worse. He had a little bit of a God syndrome."[161]

One knowledgeable observer of corporate practice notes that "a committee is actually a more efficient way of running a large and complex modern corporation than relying on a powerful and charismatic leader."[162] This is not only due to the cult of personality. There is support for this view in psychological studies that indicate that decision making in ambiguous or uncertain situations is best done by groups rather than by individuals.[163] Moreover, persons in more proximate social positions are more likely than those in disparate positions to bring disagreements and opposing perspectives into the open for discussion.[164] Less political behavior can also be expected for a top management team in which members are peers. A study of top management teams in the microcomputer industry found less evidence of politics in teams when power was not centralized in the CEO.[165] Politics is characterized by behind the scenes coalition formation, office lobbying, cooptative attempts, withholding information and the controlling of agendas.[166] Thus, the advantages of insider-dominated boards found by the meta-analysis may reflect the advantages of group decision making on strategic management issues by executive officers serving in proximate social positions on these boards.

A restructuring proposal that is consistent with my interpretation of the meta-analysis on the multiple roles of corporate boards and that takes advantage of group decision making among top corporate officers is the *dual board structure*. This structure consists of a manager-monitoring board composed of only independent directors (the "conflicts board") and a relational board composed of a mix of different kinds of directors (the "business review board").[167] The business review board would perform various relational and strategic management functions (and some monitoring functions) and would be composed of a mix of inside directors and relational outside directors. This board would have the advantages of group decision making among top executives but would also perform important relational functions and some monitoring functions through the presence of relational outside directors. The conflicts board would have group dynamics more consistent with objective manager monitoring by being composed solely of independent outside directors. Attention should also be given to the flow of information to these independent directors. The appointment by independent directors of a corporate ombudsperson who would have access to all meetings and information concerning the corporation and would report to these directors would enhance their ability to engage in effective manager monitoring.[168] The formation of board-level strategic planning committees would also facilitate important communication between outside directors and management.

The dual board structure would have the effect of allowing boards to perform potentially conflicting functions by persons best able to perform each function. As the corporation has created divisions and departments to specialize in the many tasks required of the corporation as its operations have become more complex, so must the board of directors give attention to the many roles it is expected to perform and to the characteristics of persons best suited to perform those functions. The dual board structure also draws on the benefits of group decision making. In ambiguous and uncertain situations, group decision making can prove beneficial. This insight also provides support for restructuring the US system to provide for employee directors who would further enhance the manager-monitoring and relational functions of corporate boards by, among other things, bringing diverse perspectives and information to the attention of boards.[169]

Conclusion

In this chapter, I have explored developments in board structure, composition, and practices that are designed to improve the manager-monitoring capability of corporate boards of directors. These developments have included an increase in the percentage of outside directors on corporate boards and board committees. In addition, board committees have been formed to specialize in areas where managerial oversight is particularly important. Attention has also been given to decreasing the role of the CEO in the appointment of board chairpersons and committee members. These functions are increasingly being performed by the full board or a corporate governance committee. Board practices have also developed to enhance the objectivity and effectiveness of boards. Outside directors often meet separately from the full board, and boards have put in place methods for reviewing the performance of the full board and/or individual board members. Few corporations have adopted certain proposals, however, for improving the performance of their boards, such as appointing a lead director or chairperson who is an independent director, limiting the number of directorships that board members may simultaneously fill, and forming management succession committees, despite substantial criticism of the management succession process by many directors. Perhaps more important, too little attention has been given to whether the outside directors are truly independent of management, as the Enron debacle has demonstrated.

In addition to the manager-monitoring role of boards, I have also discussed the relational role of boards. Corporations relate to their shareholders through the presence of shareholder representatives on their boards. In addition, a portion of board memberships are held by various persons who assist corporations in relating to their nonshareholder stakeholders. More recently, the diversity movement on corporate boards has exemplified the importance of the relational functions of corporate boards. Diverse directors are intended to relate corporations to their consumers and employees, both domestic and foreign. Diversity also has an additional benefit in uncertain and ambiguous environments in which diverse perspectives have the potential to improve the quality of decision making. These reasons also support the giving of additional attention to providing employee representation on corporate boards.

Finally, boards also perform functions relating to corporate strategy. I have delineated the various strategy-related functions that boards may perform. Although most of these functions are subsumed within the manager-monitoring and relational roles of corporate boards, a third role may be emerging, which I refer to as strategic management. Strategic management functions are usually performed by management, and there are good reasons for this allocation of functions. However, there are advantages to peer-group decision making on strategic management subjects, which suggests advantages to the restructuring of boards to provide for a business review board in a dual board system.

Considerable theoretical and empirical literature supports the importance of outside directors to the board's performance of relational and manager-monitoring functions. A recent meta-analysis of board studies finds that both insider- and outsider-dominated boards are associated with corporations with higher ROAs. These findings may indicate that both insider- and outsider-dominated boards have advantages that offset their disadvantages. The potential for improving board effectiveness lies in maximizing the advantages of both kinds of boards through a dual board structure. As previously explained, the structure I propose is not the German two-tiered board structure but a structure that is specially suited to the performance of the multiple roles of corporate boards. The dual board consists of a "conflicts board," which is composed solely of independent directors, and a "business review board," which consists of a mix of different kinds of directors who need not be independent.

Without attention to board structure, the multiple roles of boards will conflict because the persons ideally suited to perform some board functions are not ideally suited to perform other board functions. In addition to the dual board structure, I recommend the appointment of corporate ombudspersons by independent directors and the formation of strategic management committees to improve the flow of information to outside directors. I also recommend employee directors who have an incentive to protect their stake in the corporation and who can provide diverse perspectives and information to improve the quality of board decision making. As corporate organizations change to accommodate the needs of a more complex, changing environment, so must the structure, composition, and practices of corporate boards.

Acknowledgments

I appreciate the financial support for this research from the University of San Diego School of Law, and the helpful editorial comments of Janis Sarra. Copyright for this chapter belongs to Lynne L. Dallas, 2001. All rights reserved, except permission granted to UBC Press to publish this chapter.

Notes

1 Barry D. Baysinger and Henry N. Butler, "Corporate Governance and the Board of Directors: Performance Effects of Changes in Board Composition" (1985) 1(1) J. L. Econ. and Org. 101 at 113.
2 John A. Wagner III, J.L. Stimpert, and Edward I. Fubana, "Board Composition and Organizational Performance: Two Studies of Insider/Outsider Effects" (1998) 35(5) J. Mgmt. Studies 655.
3 Prior to Enron's collapse, it was listed as the seventh largest publicly traded company in the US with over $100 billion in gross revenues. It was widely admired for its transformation of an old line energy company into a high-tech global company. It filed for bankruptcy on 2 December 2001. As a result of its aggressive accounting and off-book activities, its assets

had to be written down by as much as $24 billion. Its stock plummeted from $90 per share in August of 2000 to forty cents per share in December 2001. Many Enron employees lost their jobs and significant retirement savings that were heavily invested in Enron stock. See Senate Report No. 107-70, *The Role of the Board of Directors in Enron's Collapse,* prepared by the Permanent Subcommittee on Investigations of the Committee on Governmental Affairs, 1, 6 (8 July 2002).

4   For a detailed exploration of this proposal, see Lynne L. Dallas, "Proposals for Reform of Corporate Boards of Directors: The Dual Board and Board Ombudsperson" (1997) 54(1) Wash. and Lee L. Rev. 91 [hereinafter *Dual Board*].

5   *Ibid.* at 130-36.

6   See *infra* text accompanying notes 156-66.

7   As explained later in this chapter (see text accompanying note 119), the relational role of boards involves a two-way relationship. The relational director serves the corporation and enhances its ability to perform. At the same time, the relational director is in a position to monitor the corporation to ensure its consideration of the interests of the relational director, whether those interests are to comply with legal regulations or to consider the advancement of its female employees.

8   Lynne L. Dallas, "The New Managerialism and Diversity on Corporate Boards of Directors," (2002) 76 Tulane L. Rev. 1363 [hereinafter "New Managerialism"]; Howard Fineman and Michael Isikoff, "Lights Out: Enron's Failed Power Play" *Newsweek* (21 January 2002) 15.

9   State courts in the US apply deferential standards to corporate decision that are approved by independent directors. See *Smith* v. *Van Gorkum,* 488 A.2d 858 (Del. 1985), applying deferential business judgment rule; *Aronson* v. *Lewis,* 473 A.2d 805 (Del. 1984), excusing demand requirement; *Auerbach* v. *Bennett,* 393 N.E.2d 994 (N.Y. 1979), deferring to independent litigation committee in dismissing shareholder derivative action.

10 Institutional ownership in the US increased from 15.8 percent in 1970 to 38 percent in 1981, 44.8 percent in 1986, and 53.3 percent in 1990: James P. Hawley, "Political Voice, Fiduciary Activism, and the Institutional Ownership of US Corporations: The Role of Public and Noncorporate Pension Funds" (1995) 38 Sociological Perspectives 415 at 417. Large institutional investors doubled their share of the common stock market from 1980 to 1996, and by 1996 controlled over one-half of that market: Paul A. Gompers and Andrew Metrick, "Institutional Investors and Equity Prices" (2001) 116(1) Q. J. Econ. 229.

11 Bernard S. Black, "Shareholder Passivity Reexamined" (1990) 89 Mich. L. R. 520 at 570-75; Alfred F. Conard, "Beyond Managerialism: Investor Capitalism?" (1988) 22 U. Mich. J.L. Ref. 117 at 143-44; Patrick J. Ryan, "Rule 14a-8, Institutional Shareholder Proposals, and Corporate Democracy" (1988) 23 Ga. L. Rev. 97 at 157-63. See, for example, CalPERS, "Corporate Governance Core Principles and Guidelines: US," <http://www.calpers.governance.org/principles/domestic/us/page04.asp>.

12 Korn/Ferry International, *26th Annual Board of Directors Study* (1999) at 11 [hereinafter *26th Annual Board Study*].

13 *Ibid.*

14 *Ibid.*

15 Baysinger and Butler, *supra* note 1 at 111-14.

16 *Ibid.* at 113-14.

17 Melvin Aron Eisenberg, *The Structure of the Corporation* (Boston: Little, Brown, and Company, 1976) at 139-85. See *26th Annual Board Study, supra* note 12 at 5, which found that it was generally accepted among US public corporations that "boards are composed primarily of independent directors who have no significant ties or conflicts of interest with the company."

18 See, for example, James D. Cox and Harry C. Munsinger, "Bias in the Boardroom: Psychological Foundations and Legal Implications of Corporate Cohesion" (1985) Law and Contemp. Probs. 83; *Dual Board, supra* note 4 at 104-11.

19 For example, American Law Institute, *Principles of Corporate Governance: Analysis and Recommendations,* Part 3A.01 (St. Paul, MN: American Law Institute Publishers, 1994) at 110;

NYSE, *Corporate Accountability and Listing Standards Committee, Recommendations Submitted for SEC Approval*, Recommendation No. 1 (2002); John C. Shaw, "The Cadbury Report, Two Years Later" in Klaus J. Hopt and Eddy Wymeersch, eds., *Comparative Corporate Governance* (New York: Walter de Gruyter, 1997) at 22-25, 33-35; F.F. DuPlessis, "Corporate Governance: Some Reflections on the South African Law and the German Two-Tiered Board System" in Fiona Patfield, ed., *Perspectives in Company Law*, vol. 2 (Boston: Kluwer Law International, 1997) at 131. Numerous definitions are offered for independent directors. Basically, a director will be considered independent if he or she: (1) has never been an employee of the corporation or any of its subsidiaries; (2) is not a relative of an employee of the company; (3) provides no services to the company; (4) is not employed by any firm providing major services to the company; and (5) receives no compensation from the company, other than director fees; National Association of Corporate Directors, *Report of the NACD Blue Ribbon Commission on Performance of Chief Executive Officers, Boards, and Directors* (Washington, DC: NACD, 1994) at 13-35. Definitions of independence are found in the *Investment Company Act* of 1940, the *Securities and Exchange Act* of 1934, and the *Internal Revenue Code*, and have been developed by the Federal Deposit Insurance Corporation (FDIC), American Law Institute, Business Roundtable, National Association of Securities Dealers, New York Stock Exchange, and Council of Institutional Investors. See CalPERS, "Corporate Governance Principles," <http://www.calpers-governance.org/principles/domestic/us/page14.asp>.

20 Diana Bilimoria and Sandy Kristin Piderit, "Board Committee Membership: Effects of Sex Based Bias" (1994) 37(6) Acad. Mgmt. J. 1453.

21 American Law Institute, *supra* note 19, Part 3A.03 at 115-16.

22 *26th Annual Board Study, supra* note 12 at 14.

23 *Report and Recommendations of the Blue Ribbon Committee on Improving the Effectiveness of Corporate Audit Committees* (New York: New York Stock Exchange and National Association of Securities Dealers, 1999), <http://www.nasd.com> and <http://www.nyse.com> [hereinafter *Blue Ribbon Committee Report*]; A. Cadbury, *Report of the Committee on the Financial Aspects of Corporate Governance* (London: Burgess Science Press, 1992), s. 4.35(b) [hereinafter *Cadbury Report*], <http://www.independentdirector.co.uk/cadbury.htm>; "The NASDAQ Stock Market Listing Requirements" (12 October 2000), <http://www.nasdaq.com>; "The Draft Report of the Committee Appointed by the SEBI on Corporate Governance under the Chairmanship of Shri Kumar Mangalam Birla" (September 1999), <http://www.sebi.gov.in>.

24 The Conference Board, *Board Diversity in US Corporations: Best Practices for Broadening the Profile of Corporate Boards*, Research Report No. 1230-99-RR (New York: Conference Board, 1999) at 22.

25 Spencer Stuart Board Index 9. According to 1998 proxy statements, 99 percent of US public corporations had compensation committees composed, on average, of only outside directors: *26th Annual Board Study, supra* note 12 at 13.

26 Spencer Stuart Board Index 9.

27 The Conference Board, *supra* note 24 at 22.

28 *26th Annual Board Study, supra* note 12 at 13.

29 Chairman Arthur Levitt, Securities and Exchange Commission, "The 'Numbers Game'" (Remarks for New York University Center for Law and Business, 28 September 1998), <http://www.sec.gov/gov/news/speeches/spech220.txt>. For a discussion of earnings management, see Dallas, "New Managerialism," *supra* note 8.

30 Levitt, *supra* note 29.

31 *Blue Ribbon Committee Report, supra* note 23.

32 SEC Release No. 34-42266 (12 October 2000), <http://www.sec.gov/rules/final/34-42266.htm>.

33 Fineman and Isikoff, *supra* note 8 at 24.

34 Sarbanes-Oxley Act of 2002, Pub. L. No. 107-204, sec. 301, 407, 116 stat. 74 (to be codified at 15 U.S.C. sec. 7264). The Sarbanes-Oxley Act further places responsibility on corporate officers for financial reports and internal controls for financial reporting. *Ibid.* at 302 and 404.

35 NYSE, *supra* note 19, Recommendation Nos. 5-7 (2002).

36 The salaries and bonuses of CEOs rose by 93 percent between 1980 and 1994, and stock options by 683 percent: Brian J. Hall and Jeffrey B. Liebman, "Are CEOs Really Paid Like Bureaucrats?" (1998) 63 Q. J. Econ. 653 at 661-62; see also 1999 Spencer Stuart Board Index 7: "Twenty-six percent [of US directors surveyed] feel that CEO compensation is too high, but 50 percent think it is just right and 23 percent think it is generally in line with economic conditions."

37 Dallas, "New Managerialism," *supra* note 8; see *infra* text accompanying notes 60-64 on stock options.

38 Lawrence Mishel, Jared Bernstein, and John Schmitt, *The State of Working America, 2000-2001* (Ithaca, NY: ILR Press, 2001) at 211.

39 The Conference Board, *supra* note 24 at 23.

40 NYSE, *supra* note 19, Recommendations Nos. 4-5.

41 *26th Annual Board Study, supra* note 12 at 6.

42 *Ibid.* at 6: the corporate governance committee usually assumes the functions of the nominating committee. See The Conference Board, *supra* note 24 at 21.

43 *26th Annual Board Study, supra* note 12 at 6.

44 *Ibid.* A 1998 survey of US corporate directors shows that "139 companies (23 percent of sample) had a formal board evaluation process. However, only 58 companies (9 percent) had an evaluation process for individual board members." The Conference Board, *supra* note 24 at 28.

45 *26th Annual Board Study, supra* note 12 at 8.

46 *Ibid.* at 24-25, concerning US corporations: "69 percent of respondents report that their outside directors meet in executive session other than for compensation matters, without the CEO present. However, this does vary according to type and size of company. While only 56 percent of insurance companies meet in executive session, 75 percent of the largest companies ($20 billion and over) do. Respondents report that such meetings take place three times a year on average."

47 NYSE, *supra* note 19, Recommendation No. 3.

48 *Dual Board, supra* note 4 at 104-11.

49 See, for example, Robert S. Baron, Norbert L. Kerr, and Norman Miller, *Group Process, Group Decision, Group Action* (Pacific Grove, CA: Brooks/Cole Publishing, 1992) at 73; Susan E. Jackson, "Consequences of Group Composition for the Interpersonal Dynamics of Strategic Issue Processing" (1992) 8 Advances in Strategic Mgmt. 345 at 370-71.

50 *26th Annual Board Study, supra* note 12 at 8: independent director chairmen were defined as non-executive chairmen who are also not former employees of the corporation.

51 National Association of Corporate Directors, *Report of the NACD Blue Ribbon Commission on Performance of Chief Executive Officers, Boards, and Directors* (Washington, DC: NACD, 1994) at 12 [hereinafter *NACD Report*].

52 *26th Annual Board Study, supra* note 12 at 8 (proposal considered a "lost cause"); The Conference Board, *supra* note 24 at 12.

53 Spencer Stuart Board Index 2.

54 *26th Annual Board Study, supra* note 12 at 7: "Twenty-three percent [of directors surveyed] say most companies do a poor job, twenty-seven percent say the CEO dominates the process and thirty percent say the board gets involved too late."

55 *Ibid.* at 13.

56 Christopher H. Schmitt, Julian E. Barnes, and Megan Barnett, "As Enron Fell, Even Its Outside Board Members Had Become Insiders" *US News and World Report* (11 February 2002) 28.

57 Mark Babineck, "Enron Debacle Exposes Board Conflicts" *Californian AC Times* (17 February 2002), <http://www.nctimes.net/news/2002/20020217/60100.html>.

58 *Ibid.* at 5.

59 "New Managerialism," *supra* note 8.

60 *26th Annual Board Study, supra* note 12 at 5.

61 The Conference Board, *supra* note 24 at 32. Based on 1998 proxy statement data, 84 percent of US public corporations compensated directors with some form of stock, compared with 78 percent in 1997 and 62 percent in 1995. *26th Annual Board Study, supra* note 12 at 18.

62 Matthias Benz, Marcel Kucher, and Alois Stutzer, "Stock Options: The Managers' Blessing: Institutional Restrictions and Executive Compensation," U. of Zurich IEER Working Paper No. 61 (13 October 2000) at 5-6, <http://Papers.ssrn.com/so13/papers.cfm?abstract_id =251009>; Dallas, "New Managerialism," *supra* note 8; Daniel Murray, "Employee Stock Options: The Fed Joins in" Report No. 142 (London: Smithers and Co., 2000) at 1, 13.

63 Daniel A. Bens, Venky Nagar, and M.H. Franco Wong, "Real Investment Implications of Employee Stock Option Exercises" Social Science Research Network (29 December 2000) at 27, <http://papers.ssrn.com/sol3/papers.cfm?abstract_id=254708>; "New Managerialism," *supra* note 8.

64 Levitt, *supra* note 29; Dallas, "New Managerialism," *supra* note 8.

65 Lynne L. Dallas, "Two Models of Corporate Governance: Beyond Berle and Means" (1988) 22(1) U. Mich. J.L. Ref. 19 at 95-96, describing the relationship between the corporation and shareholders as one of informal or formal cooptation.

66 Compare Adolph Berle, "For Whom Corporate Managers Are Trustees: A Note" (1932) 45 Harv. L. Rev. 1365, with E. Merrick Dodd, "For Whom Are Corporate Managers Trustees?" (1932) 45 Harv. L. Rev. 1145, and E. Merrick Dodd, "Is Effective Enforcement of the Fiduciary Duties of Corporate Managers Practicable?" (1934) 2 U. Chicago L. Rev. 194.

67 See Adolf Berle, *The 20th Century Capitalist Revolution* (New York: Harcourt Brace, 1954) at 169; Adolf Augustus, "Corporate Decision-Making and Social Control" (1968) 24 Bus. Law 149 at 150.

68 Dodd, *supra* note 66 at 1149.

69 *McQuade* v. *Stoneham*, 263 N.Y.323 at 334; 189 N.E.234 at 238 (1934)(Lehman, J., concurring); *Jackson* v. *Hopper*, 76 N.J.Eq. 592, 75 A. 568, 571 (Ct. Err. and App. 1910), stating that "the corporation itself is an entity, wholly separate and distinct from the individuals who compose and control it." See also Margaret M. Blair and Lynn A. Stout, "A Team Production Theory of Corporate Law" (1999) 85 Va. L. Rev. 247 at 287-315; Thomas A. Smith, *The Efficient Norm for Corporate Law: A Neotraditional Interpretation of Fiduciary Duty* (1999) Mich. L. R. 214, 243 n. 70.

70 See James J. Hanks Jr., "Playing with Fire: Nonshareholder Constituency Statutes in the 1990's" (1991) 21 Stetson L. Rev. 97.

71 *Revlon, Inc.* v. *MacAndrews and Forbes Holdings, Inc.*, 506 A.2d 173 at 182 (Del. 1986); *Unocal* v. *Mesa Petroleum*, 493 A.2d 946 at 955 (Del. Super. Ct. 1985).

72 For an extended discussion of the significance of this development, see "New Managerialism," *supra* note 8.

73 The Conference Board, *supra* note 24 at 6. The report states that the diversity focus does not change the board's obligations as fiduciaries to represent all shareholders, but "rather helps a board fulfill its duties and mission."

74 *Ibid.* at 7. The report states that "shareholder value is strengthened when intangibles such as diversity, workplace practices, and customer satisfaction permeate a company."

75 *26th Annual Board Study, supra* note 12 at 13. According to 1998 proxy statements, 60 percent of public corporations have ethnic minorities on their boards, with 39 percent of the companies having African-Americans on their boards, 12 percent Latino directors, and 9 percent Asian directors. *26th Annual Board Study, supra* note 12 at 11. See also 1999 Spencer Stuart Board Index 6. Ethnic minorities account, however, for only 6 percent of Fortune 500 company directors. *26th Annual Board Study, supra* note 12 at 11. Based on a survey of directors, 29 percent of US companies plan to increase the numbers of African-American directors, 14 percent to increase the number of Latino directors, and 10 percent to increase the number of Asian directors: *ibid.,* at 12-13. Minorities are also under-represented in the executive suite: Dan R. Dalton and Catharine M. Daily, "The Other Ceiling" (1998) 35 Across the Board 19. Moreover, minority women of colour are under-represented in the managerial labour force compared with their participation in the total labour force: Margaret Blackburn White and Joseph Potts, "Just the Facts: Women of Color in US Corporations" (1999) 7(3) Diversity Factor 8.

76 Gerald E. Fryxell and Linda D. Lerner, "Contrasting Corporate Profiles: Women and Minority Representation in Top Management Positions" (1989) 8 J. Bus. Ethics 341.

77 Unlike the glass ceiling women have reached in seeking to enter the executive suite (The Conference Board, *supra* note 24 at 26), women have made slow but steady progress in the boardroom. Fortune 500 companies with one or more women on their boards increased from 69 percent in 1993 to 88 percent in 1998: *ibid.* at 16-17. This represents an increase in the percentage of total board seats held by women from 8.3 percent in 1993 to 11.1 percent in 1998: *ibid.* at 17 (percentages vary by industry). See also *26th Annual Board Study, supra* note 12 at 11; 1999 Spencer Stuart Board Index 6. Larger companies tend to have more women on their boards: The Conference Board, *supra* note 24 at 18 (corporations located in the US Northeast also tend to have more women on their boards). The percentage of Fortune 500 companies with more than one female director increased from 29.2 percent in 1993 to 37.6 percent in 1998, with 6.8 percent of such companies in 1998 having three or more women directors: *ibid.* at 17. Bilimoria says that "although 85 percent of CEOs considered it important to have female directors, 48 percent found female candidates 'difficult to identify' and cited this as a reason for current low levels of female directorships": Diana Bilimoria, "Women Directors: The Quiet Discrimination" (17 July 1995) 19 The Corporate Board, at 10 n. 93. There is currently no consensus on whether qualified women are available to increase the number of women on corporate boards: Donna Dillon Manning, "Women Directors: A CEO Priority" (1995) 19 Directors and Boards 21.

78 Catherine M. Daily, S. Trevis Certo, and Dan R. Dalton, "A Decade of Corporate Women: Some Progress in the Boardroom, None in the Executive Suite" (1999) 20 Strategic Mgmt. J. 93 at 94.

79 *Ibid.* at 94, 98.

80 *Ibid.* at 96-97.

81 Manning, *supra* note 77 at 20.

82 Daily, Certo, and Dalton, *supra* note 78.

83 *Ibid.*

84 Bilimoria and Piderit, *supra* note 20. But see I.F. Kesner, "Directors' Characteristics and Committee Membership: An Investigation of Type, Occupation, Tenure and Gender" (1988) 31 Acad. Mgmt. J. 66.

85 Bilimoria, *supra* note 77. Women directors of U.S. companies are most likely to be on audit and social/corporate responsibility committees (14 and 15 percent, respectively) and least likely to be on executive committees (6 percent). They are most likely to chair social/corporate responsibility committees (21 percent): The Conference Board, *supra* note 24 at 30.

86 Spencer Stuart Board Index 5.

87 *Ibid.* at 7.

88 The Conference Board, *Globalizing the Board of Directors: Trends and Strategies* (pamphlet) (New York: Conference Board, 1999) at 15.

89 Susan Williams, "2001 Background Report E, Board Diversity" (2001) 4 IRRC Social Issue Service 2-3.

90 *Ibid.* at 9-10; *NACD Report, supra* note 51 at 11-12.

91 The Conference Board, *supra* note 24 at 9. See also Manning, *supra* note 77 at 19. In a survey of over one-third of the CEOs of Fortune 1000 companies, the following percentages of CEOs sought to have women directors to: (1) exemplify commitment to diversity to shareholders (60 percent); (2) exemplify commitment to advancing women (59 percent); (3) enhance the ability to recruit and retain women (46 percent); (4) initiate discussions about issues that affect female employees (29 percent); (5) reflect female consumers' perspectives (26 percent); and (6) contribute a perspective different from those of male directors (49 percent).

92 For example, one report observes that issues like family life and flexible work arrangements are given greater prominence in companies that attract both female executives and female board members: The Conference Board, *supra* note 24 at 8, 27. The Executive Leadership Council proposes that companies conduct a self-audit that would include making "key stakeholder evaluations."

93 Baysinger and Butler, *supra* note 1 at 113.

94 Larry Ribstein and Peter V. Letson, *Business Associations,* 3rd ed. (New York: Matthew Bender, 1996) at 4.

95 Rita D. Kosnik, "Greenmail: A Study of Board Performance in Corporate Governance" (1987) 32 Admin. Sci. Q. 163 at 167-68; Shaker A. Zahra and John A. Pearce II, "Boards of Directors and Corporate Financial Performance: A Review and Integrative Model" (1998) 15 J. Mgmt. 291 at 301.

96 Eugene F. Fama, "Agency Problems and the Theory of the Firm" (1980) 88 J. Pol. Econ. 288 at 293. See generally Eugene F. Fama and Michael C. Jensen, "Separation of Ownership and Control (1983) 26 J. L. and Econ. 301 at 314-15: board as "top level court of appeal of the internal agent [labour] market."

97 Fama and Jensen, *ibid.* at 315.

98 *Ibid.* at 314.

99 *Ibid.* See also Fama, *supra* note 96 at 293.

100 Barry Baysinger and Robert E. Hoskisson, "The Composition of Boards of Directors and Strategic Control: Effect on Corporate Strategy" (1990) 15 Acad. Mgmt. Rev. 72.

101 See *infra* text accompanying note 139.

102 Chenchuramaiah Bathala and Ramesh P. Rao, "The Determinants of Board Composition: An Agency Theory Perspective" (1995) 16 Managerial and Decision Econ. 59; James A. Brickley and Christopher M. James, "The Takeover Market, Corporate Board Composition and Ownership Structure: The Case of Banking" (1987) 30 J. L. and Econ. 161.

103 Bathala and Rao, *ibid.* at 62. But see Benjamin E. Hermalin and Michael S. Weisbach, "The Determinants of Board Composition" (1988) 19 Rand J. Econ. 589 at 594, whose findings contradict the predictions of substitute hypothesis when family directors are considered.

104 Bathala and Rao, *ibid.* But see John A. Pearce and Shaker A. Zahra, "Board Composition from a Strategic Contingency Perspective" (1992) 29 J. Mgmt. Studies 411 [hereinafter *Board Composition*], finding a positive relationship between increased proportions of outside directors on corporate boards and increased leverage; Jeffrey Pfeffer, "Size and Composition of Corporate Boards of Directors: The Organization and Its Environment" (1972) 17 Admin. Sci. Q. 218 at 224, finding an inverse relationship between higher debt/equity ratios and the proportion of inside directors on corporate boards.

105 Bathala and Rao, *ibid.* But see Michael H. Schellenger *et al.,* "Board of Director Composition, Shareholder Wealth, and Dividend Policy" (1989) 15 J. Mgmt. 457 at 465, finding that support for substitution hypothesis is not confirmed regarding relationship between the proportion of outside directors on the board and dividend payouts.

106 Kosnik, *supra* note 95 at 163; Laura Linn, "The Effectiveness of Outside Directors as a Corporate Governance Mechanism: Theories and Evidence" (1996) 90 NWU L. Rev. 898; Paul Mallette and Karen L. Fowler, "The Effects of Board Composition and Stock Ownership on the Adoption of Poison Pills" (1992) 35 Acad. Mgmt. J. 1010; Paula L. Rechner *et al.,* "Corporate Governance Predictors of Adoption of Anti-Takeover Amendments: An Empirical Analysis" (1993) 12 J. Bus. Ethics 371.

107 Brickley and James, *supra* note 102; Hamid Mehran, "Executive Compensation Structure, Ownership, and Firm Performance" (1995) 38 J. Fin. Econ. 163.

108 John M. Bizjak, Michael L. Lemmon, and Lalitha Naveen, "Has the Use of Peer Groups Contributed to Higher Levels of Executive Compensation?" (11 December 2000), <http://papers.ssrn.com/sol3/papers.cfm?abstract_id=252544>.

109 For example, Michael S. Weisbach, "Outside Directors and CEO Turnover" (1988) 20 J. Fin. Econ. 421; Linn, *supra* note 106.

110 Cox and Munsinger, *supra* note 18; *Dual Board, supra* note 4 at 107-10.

111 John C. Turner, *Social Influences* (Pacific Grove, CA: Brooks/Cole Publishing, 1991) at 136-41.

112 See *infra* text accompanying notes 139-48.

113 See *supra* notes 102-5.

114 *Ibid.*

115 Catherine M. Daily and Charles Schwenk, "Chief Executive Officers, Top Management Teams, and Boards of Directors: Congruent or Countervailing Forces?" (1996) 22(2) J. Mgmt.

185; *Board Composition, supra* note 104 at 417-18; Dallas, *supra* note 65 at 91-94; Zahra and Pearce, *supra* note 95 at 297-99.

116   Daily and Schwenk, *ibid.* at 190-91, 194, 196; Lynne L. Dallas, "The Relational Board: Three Theories of Corporate Boards of Directors" (1996) 22(1) J. Corp. L. 1 at 12-13; *Dual Board, supra* note 4 at 102; Zahra and Pearce, *supra* note 95 at 297-99.

117   Dallas, *supra* note 64 at 91-94; Zahra and Pearce, *supra* note 95.

118   Daily, Certo, and Dalton, *supra* note 78 at 95.

119   Zahra and Pearce, *supra* note 95 at 297. The singular focus on the managerial monitoring function of corporate boards in the US legal academy has tended to downplay the important relational roles that boards perform. Professor Eisenberg has argued that the corporations may gain access to resources, such as advice, information, and legitimacy, by means other than board memberships: Eisenberg, *supra* note 17 at 157-58. However, board members provide the corporation with relevant advice and information on a continuing basis due to their membership on the board, thus providing the corporation with assistance as its circumstances change. Moreover, the information is provided in a setting where joint deliberation is possible and where all members possess fiduciary duties to act in the best interest of the corporation. Many outside board members are CEOs of other corporations who would not provide resources to the corporation if they were not board members. CEOs' acceptance of board memberships as opposed to independent consulting contracts is a socially acceptable way for CEOs to interact with corporations other than their own. Also, the lure of board memberships to CEOs lies not in the opportunity to provide independent advice but more in the experience of interacting with other knowledgeable individuals on business problems, and the prestige associated with board memberships. *26th Annual Board Study, supra* note 12 at 31; Jay W. Lorsch and Elizabeth MacIver, *Pawns or Potentates: The Reality of America's Corporate Boards* (Boston, MA: Harvard Business School Press, 1989) at 23-30; Cox and Munsinger, *supra* note 18 at 96-97.

120   Dallas, *supra* note 65 at 92-97.

121   Jeffrey Pfeffer and Gerald Salancik, *The External Control of Organizations: A Resource Dependence Perspective* (New York: Harper and Row, 1978) at 43, 53; J. Thompson, *Organizations in Action* (New York: McGraw-Hill, 1967) at 31; David J. Hickson *et al.*, "Organizations as Power" (1981) 3 Res. Organ. Behav. 151 at 159-60; R.M. Emerson, "Power-Dependence Relations" (1962) 27 Am. Soc. Rev. 31 at 32.

122   *Board Composition, supra* note 104 at 415.

123   Zahra and Pearce, *supra* note 95 at 297-99.

124   Keith G. Provan, "Board Power and Organizational Effectiveness among Human Service Agencies" (1980) 23 Acad. Mgmt. J. 221 at 226-27; Mayer N. Zald, "Urban Differentiation Characteristics of Boards of Directors and Organizational Effectiveness" (1967) 73 Am. J. Soc. 261 at 268.

125   Pfeffer, *supra* note 104 at 226.

126   *Board Composition, supra* note 104.

127   *Ibid.* at 432.

128   Zahra and Pearce, *supra* note 95 at 302.

129   Kenneth R. Andrews, "Directors' Responsibility for Corporate Strategy" (1980) Harv. Bus. Rev. 30.

130   Zahra and Pearce, *supra* note 95 at 292. These functions have also been referred to as "institutional" functions whereby "boards help to link the organization to its external environment and secure critical resources, including prestige and legitimacy": Jerry Goodstein, Kanak Gautam, and Warren Boeker, "The Effect of Board Size and Diversity on Strategic Change" (1994) 15 Strategic Mgmt. J. 241.

131   For example, Del. Code Ann. tit. 8, Sec. 141(a) (1991); American Law Institute, *supra* note 19, Part III, ss. 3.01 and 3.02.

132   *26th Annual Board Study, supra* note 12 at 6-7.

133   *Ibid.* at 41.

134   Baysinger and Butler, *supra* note 1 at 104; Rajeswararao S. Chaganti *et al.*, "Corporate Board Size, Composition and Corporate Failures in Retailing Industry" (1985) 22 J. Mgmt. Studies 400; William Q. Judge, "Correlates of Organizational Effectiveness: A Multilevel Analysis

of a Multidimensional Outcome" (1994) 13 J. Bus. Ethics 1 at 7; Hamid Mehran, "Executive Compensation Structure, Ownership, and Firm Performance" (1995) 38 J. Fin. Econ. 163 at 180; *Board Composition, supra* note 104 at 433; Stuart Rosenstein and Jeffrey G. Wyatt, "Outside Directors, Board Independence, Shareholder Wealth" (1990) 76 J. Fin. Econ. 175 at 190; Schellenger *et al., supra* note 105; Zahra and Pearce, *supra* note 95 at 309. A recent meta-analysis found little evidence of a linear relationship between board composition measured by the proportion of outside/inside board members and corporate performance: Dan R. Dalton *et al.*, "Meta-Analytic Reviews of Board Composition, Leadership Structure, and Financial Performance" (1998) 19 Strategic Mgmt. J. 269.

135 Wagner, Stimpert, and Fubana, *supra* note 2.

136 *Ibid.*

137 Shaker A. Zahra, "Governance, Ownership and Corporate Entrepreneurship: The Moderating Impact of Industry Technological Opportunities" (1996) 39(6) Acad. Mgmt. J. 1713 [hereinafter *Governance*], discussing outside directors who own large blocks of stock. See also *Board Composition, supra* note 104, finding that boards with larger proportions of outside directors tend to pursue strategies of external growth and diversification. The outsider/insider director board classification scheme has been criticized for failing to capture the external/internal orientation of board members. Using an attitudinal survey of directors of nine publicly held banks, the outsider/insider director classification did not reflect the external/internal orientation of board members. See John A. Pearce II, "The Relationship of Internal Versus External Orientations to Financial Measures of Strategic Performance" (1983) 4 Strategic Mgmt. J. 297 In addition, the study found a positive association between bank profitability and a high internal/low external orientation. The definitions of internal and external orientation used in this study, however, are problematic. The definitions, for example, bear no relationship to the manager-monitoring/relational roles of the board described in this chapter and fail to capture the wide variety of functions that board members may perform.

138 See text accompanying notes 101-2 and 139.

139 Baysinger and Hoskisson, *supra* note 100; see text accompanying notes 100-1.

140 *Governance, supra* note 137, including such activities as innovation, entering new businesses by expanding operations, and strategic renewal in revitalizing the corporation's operations by changing the scope of its business or competitive approach.

141 Barry D. Baysinger, Rita D. Kosnik, and Thomas A. Turk, "Effects of Board and Ownership Structure on Corporate R and D Strategy" (1991) 34(1) Acad. Mgmt. J. 205.

142 *Governance, supra* note 137. R&D expenses may also serve a relational role by signalling to shareholders the corporation's commitment to innovation.

143 Ming-Jer Chen and Donald C. Hambrick, "Speed, Stealth, and Selective Attack: How Small Firms Differ from Large Firms in Competitive Behavior" (1995) 38(2) Acad. Mgmt. J. 453.

144 Amos Tversky and Daniel Kahneman, "The Framing of Decisions and the Psychology of Choice" (1981) 30 Science 18.

145 Donald C. Hambrick and Richard A. D'Aveni, "Large Corporate Failures as Downward Spirals" (1988) 33 Admin. Sci. Q. 1.

146 Rafik I. Beekun, Yvonne Stedham, and Gary J. Young, "Board Characteristics, Managerial Controls and Corporate Strategy: A Study of US Hospitals" (1998) 24(1) J. Mgmt. 3.

147 *Ibid.* at 9.

148 Daily and Schwenk, *supra* note 115 at 191: outside directors can easily acquire the information needed by "requesting this information" from top management team members, "regardless of their service on the board."

149 For a discussion of the advantages and disadvantages of homogeneous versus heterogeneous groups, see "New Managerialism," *supra* note 8.

150 *Ibid.*

151 See generally Jackson, *supra* note 49 at 359.

152 John P. Wanous and Margaret A. Youtz, "Solution Diversity and the Quality of Group Decisions" (1986) 29 Acad. Mgmt. J. 149 at 157.

153 "New Managerialism," *supra* note 8; Goodstein, Gautam, and Boeker, *supra* note 130 at 245.

154 *Ibid.*

155 *Ibid.*

156 Lynn L. Dallas, "Evolutionary Institutional Approach to Corporate Law" [manuscript on file with author].

157 Steven N. Kaplan, "Top Executives, Turnover, and Firm Performance," (1994) 10 J.L. Econ. and Org. 142, 143; Spencer Stuart European Index: Current Board Trends and Practices at Major European Corporations 12 (Amsterdam: Spencer Stuart, 1999).

158 Kaplan, *supra* note 157, at 147.

159 Jonathan P. Charkham, *Keeping Good Company: A Study of Corporate Governance in Five Countries* (New York: Oxford University Press, 1994) at 361.

160 *Ibid.*

161 Evan Thomas *et al.*, "Every Man for Himself" *Newsweek* (US ed.) (18 February 2002) 22.

162 Charkam, *supra* note 159, at 361.

163 Don Hellriegel, John W. Slocom, and Richard W. Woodman, *Organizational Behavior* (St. Paul, MN: West Publishing Company, 1983); Robert J. Haft, "Business Decisions by the New Board: Behavioral Science and Corporate Law," (1981) 81 Mich. L. R. 1 at 9-12.

164 Kathleen M. Eisenhardt and L.G. Bourgeois III, "Politics of Strategic Decision Making in High-Velocity Environments: Toward a Mid-Range Theory," (1988) 31 Acad. Mgmt. J. 737.

165 *Ibid.*

166 *Ibid.*

167 *Dual Board, supra* note 4.

168 *Ibid* at 130-36.

169 Dallas, *supra* note 8.

9

The Governance of Commercial Crown Corporations: How Much Independence Can We Expect from Corporate Directors?
Barry Slutsky and Philip Bryden

In June 1994, the British Columbia government announced a decision to build, at a total cost of $210 million, three fast car ferries as part of the ten-year capital plan for the British Columbia Ferry Corporation (BC Ferries), a wholly owned provincial Crown corporation. The delivery of the fast ferries was delayed by more than two years from what was originally scheduled, and the project was more than $200 million over budget.[1] When the ferries eventually came into service, it was discovered that they were not well suited for use on the Ferry Corporation's routes in British Columbia's coastal waters, and they were ultimately withdrawn from service and put up for sale. At the time this chapter was written, a buyer had not yet been found for the fast ferries.

In a report entitled *A Review of the Fast Ferry Project: Governance and Risk Management*, British Columbia Auditor General George Morfitt stated:

> For governance to be effective, all those assigned responsibility must have clearly defined roles and the opportunity to carry out those roles. In our opinion, lack of these key features was the main cause of the problems arising in the fast ferry project (detailed in our report, following). We commented in our November 1996 "Study of Crown Corporations Governance" that improvements in governance are needed in British Columbia's Crown corporations. The fast ferry project illustrates how much still needs to be done in this area.[2]

The report then went on to discuss whether it was still appropriate for ferry services to be delivered to British Columbians through a Crown corporation:

> The idea of using Crown corporations to deliver publicly-provided services of a commercial nature is sound. Properly applied, such an administrative mechanism can be more cost-effective than direct service by government

because it gives more room for the application of business practices. However, BC Ferries has not been allowed to apply these practices in an organized and consistent way.

The Act setting up BC Ferries provides for cabinet, not the corporation's board, to make most key decisions, including approving route additions or deletions, approving fares, tolls and other charges, and approving corporate borrowings. Also, since capital plans need cabinet approval and capital budgets need Treasury Board approval, construction of ferries or terminals is also ultimately a government decision. In short, the corporation does not have control over most significant decisions that affect its financial and operating performance.

Most key business decisions are made outside BC Ferries (and, at times, contrary to BC Ferries' advice), by elected officials who also have responsibility for many other important areas of government. As a result, decisions about BC Ferries' business are often ad hoc and lack consistency. For example, decisions about fares have not always been integrated with decisions about subsidies, routes, capital expenditures, or service levels.

This means that the government is unlikely to get the benefits of a Crown corporation approach – a serious disadvantage, given that BC Ferries operates an essential part of the province's transportation system, and is vital to the social and financial well-being of many Vancouver Island and other coastal communities.

In 1981, the Select Standing Committee on Crown Corporations of the Legislative Assembly carried out a review of BC Ferries. Its report noted: "The future effectiveness of the ferry system would seem to require that the directors have somewhat greater control over these important aspects of their business ... [The] present division of responsibilities between the Lieutenant-Governor in Council and the board creates a situation in which the clarity of the board's mandate to plan, develop, and operate the ferry system is clouded." In our opinion, the committee's comments are still valid today.[3]

Three propositions underlying the Auditor General's advice concerning the failure of the fast ferry project deserve consideration. The first is that that there are conceptually sound reasons for governments to use Crown corporations to provide services of a commercial nature. In other words, even in situations where goods or services might otherwise be available from private providers, there can be sound justifications for a governmental decision to use a government-owned corporate vehicle to provide those goods or services as an instrument to pursue public policy goals.[4] The second is that the choice of using a commercial Crown corporation as a means of pursuing public policy goals carries with it an implication that some degree of corporate autonomy from governmental control is needed for the corporation to achieve these goals. The third is that more, rather than less, corporate autonomy from government is desirable, or at a minimum that directors of Crown corporations ought to have a better understanding of their responsibility to act independently from government direction and the capacity to do so effectively.

The goal of this chapter is to explore the third proposition, and more particularly to consider the extent to which traditional Canadian public law and corporate law concepts do, or do not, provide directors of commercial Crown corporations with meaningful guidance on how to play this independent role. It is one thing to say that in principle the directors of commercial Crown corporations ought to exercise more autonomy within a framework of ultimate accountability to government for the performance of the enterprise, and quite another to give operational effect to that commitment in a meaningful fashion. For the reasons set out below, we are of the view that the traditional legal rules we employ in exercising judicial control over administrative action and imposing duties on the directors of private corporations are unlikely to contribute much, if anything, to our ability to provide a clearer definition of the appropriate balance between the independence and accountability of directors in this form of corporate governance, or support to the directors in the performance of this independent role. This chapter treats the public law and corporate law dimensions of this issue separately, but we acknowledge that there is some overlap in the reasons for which similar conclusions are reached with respect to each branch of the law.

Background: Autonomy and Accountability of Crown Corporations

Before exploring the chapter's central theme, however, it is useful to pause and reflect for a moment on the first two propositions that underlie the Auditor General's advice, because they form the backdrop to the chapter's consideration of the third. If we return to the first proposition, that there is a legitimate public policy role to be played by commercial Crown corporations, it is obvious that this assumption, or at least its application in the case of particular enterprises, is highly debatable. Not only has there been a lively academic discussion of the virtues and vices of privatization of functions formerly performed by Crown corporations,[5] but there are also many examples of the phenomenon in this country and elsewhere from which commentators can draw lessons. The privatization debate clearly carries significant implications for the governance of Crown corporations, but we hope to be able to sidestep it by making three observations.

The first is that, as far as we can tell, the case for public as distinct from private enterprise is not made on the basis that public ownership represents a superior form of organization from the exclusive standpoint of economic efficiency. As a number of commentators have pointed out, there are several reasons to believe that state-owned corporations will have difficulty matching the performance of private companies from the standpoint of wealth maximization. These include the absence of a market for shares that can be used as a signal of shareholder assessment of managerial performance; a correspondingly weak threat of takeover of control, which tends to weaken managerial performance incentives; a tendency to undervalue the full opportunity cost of the capital tied up by public enterprises; and a tendency towards weak monitoring by private sector debt holders because of implicit government guarantees of at least some of the enterprise's debts.[6] It is unnecessary for the purposes of this chapter to evaluate the soundness of these arguments in general or in any particular situation. It is enough to observe that where a government comes to the conclusion that the pursuit of economic efficiency or wealth maximization is its sole public policy goal in relation to a particular enterprise, industry, or sector, it is increasingly unlikely that the government will choose the creation of a commercial Crown corporation as a vehicle for pursuing that goal. Correspondingly, the abandonment of other public policy goals in favour of an exclusive focus on an enterprise's capacity for wealth maximization would appear to lead governments in the direction of divestiture of ownership of existing enterprises rather than of restructuring their governance systems.[7] For the purposes of this chapter, this means that it is reasonably safe to conclude that where Canadian governments make use of commercial Crown corporations, there must be some public policy considerations at play other than pure economic efficiency, and that the corporation's governance mechanism needs to have some way of taking those considerations into account if it is to achieve the government's goals.

The second observation is that the choice of a Crown corporation as a vehicle for producing goods or delivering services in a commercial context implies a governmental belief that economic efficiency in the government enterprise's operations is an important element of the success of the enterprise. Moreover, the corporate form of governance is being adopted, in part at least, because of a belief that it can assist in achieving this aspect of the government's goals for the enterprise. The qualification is an important one because not all government-owned corporations in Canada operate in a commercial context. For example, at the federal level, the *Financial Administration Act (FAA)*[8] draws an explicit distinction between "departmental corporations," which perform activities of noncommercial nature, and "Crown corporations," which have a broader mandate that can encompass commercial activity. The *Act* further distinguishes between two different types of Crown corporations based on a number of criteria that essentially reflect whether or not there is an expectation that the corporation will be profitable.[9] In a similar vein, Douglas Stevens described the scope of his very useful study of the systems of institutional control employed in selected

Crown corporations in Alberta, Saskatchewan, and Manitoba in the following terms:

> By "crown corporations" we mean corporations at least 50 per cent owned by the government which are incorporated under acts of legislation or companies acts, have boards of directors some, if not all, of whose members are appointed by the government, whose emphasis is on the pursuit of profits as a part of their mandates and are competitive with private sector corporations. Excluded are natural monopolies (public utilities, for example), companies in which the maximization of net revenues is not part of the firm's mandate, and so-called mixed enterprises.[10]

It is not necessary for the purposes of this chapter to defend the merits of any particular line of demarcation for the distinction between commercial and noncommercial Crown corporations. It is sufficient to take a relatively conservative approach and say that the remarks in this paper address corporate entities that are wholly owned by government (or the wholly owned subsidiaries of such corporations), that have boards of directors appointed by government, that are significantly engaged in activities that are competitive with private sector corporations, and that have a significant emphasis on the pursuit of profits. Whether or not the adoption of a corporate form of organization can produce benefits for governmental entities that are not commercial in the sense identified above raises a number of interesting questions. Nevertheless, we want to set them to one side in order to concentrate on those government-owned enterprises whose structure and functions provide the strongest case for comparison with private sector governance models.

The third observation is linked to the second, in that it is useful to draw a distinction between the wholly owned commercial Crown corporations that are the focus of this inquiry and various kinds of mixed-ownership corporations, joint ventures, public investment in private enterprises, and other forms of public/private economic partnership. This is not to say that this form of enterprise is insignificant or to deny that it raises significant corporate governance and public policy questions.[11] Nevertheless, it is worthwhile to begin by concentrating on meeting the governance challenges of the relatively simple cases of wholly owned government enterprises. If the British Columbia Auditor General is to be believed, these challenges have had a way of eluding us, at least in this province, so they seem to deserve attention even at the expense of excluding other issues.

By making these qualifications to the scope of our inquiry into the governance of Crown corporations, we hope to finesse the privatization debate by suggesting that it is the mix of economic efficiency motivations (and pressures) and other public purposes that makes the problems of commercial

Crown corporation governance distinctive. Our governments can solve these problems for us by making one or the other of these purposes overwhelmingly dominant, but it seems reasonable to believe that there will be some circumstances in which governments will want to continue to pursue both within a single enterprise. Thus, it makes sense to consider how governance models can help to address this tension.

This observation also begins to explain the second proposition on which Mr. Morfitt's governance recommendations were premised, namely, the view that some degree of corporate autonomy from government is necessary if the Crown corporation is to achieve these objectives. It is a well-accepted feature of the Canadian literature on Crown corporation governance that the central challenge for those designing governance regimes is to strike an appropriate balance between corporate autonomy and accountability to government.[12] To take just one example, the Economic Council of Canada stated in its 1986 report, *Minding the Public's Business:*

> The fundamental challenge in structuring a control regime is to establish an appropriate balance between the competing requirements for managerial autonomy and public control. Excessive control will undermine the independent status of the corporation and dissipate the benefits that are available from a delegation of decision-making responsibilities. Inadequate direction and control, on the other hand, will jeopardize the role and usefulness of public corporations as instruments of public policy.[13]

Douglas Stevens has expressed skepticism about whether there is a single best or most appropriate model for organizing the relationship between governments and Crown corporations.[14] Whether or not Stevens is correct in this assessment, his research on the actual design and functioning of selected Crown corporations in Alberta, Saskatchewan, and Manitoba strongly suggests that, as a matter of practice, widely differing approaches to the balance between corporate independence and accountability have been employed in this country, along with different institutional arrangements for maintaining that balance.[15] For the purposes of this chapter, the important point is that some degree of institutional autonomy is generally regarded as an essential corollary to the choice made by government to use a commercial Crown corporation as an instrument of public policy. Thus, it is worth addressing how our arrangements for Crown corporation governance reflect that institutional independence within the framework of an overall system of accountability to government.

Why Have More rather than Less Corporate Autonomy?
So far this chapter has identified two propositions that underlie the Auditor General's advice about what we can learn from the fast ferry fiasco, and has

developed a set of qualifications that, in our view, assist in forming a basis for confidence in the soundness of those two propositions. This leads to the third proposition, which is that the failure of corporate governance that the fast ferry project is said to exemplify is the result of insufficient corporate autonomy from government. This third proposition deserves more scrutiny.

The point we are trying to make here is not that the Auditor General's account of the various errors in judgment that resulted in the financial failure of the fast ferry project is somehow erroneous or flawed. This chapter assumes that the Auditor General's report accurately describes the ability of the responsible minister and the Crown Corporations Secretariat to induce the boards of directors of BC Ferries and Catamaran Ferries International Inc. (CFI) to make decisions that turned out to be financially improvident. It is an unfortunate fact of life that the decisions of the boards of directors of private sector corporations as well as those of public corporations occasionally turn out badly. In our view, the interesting question is when we should ascribe these unfortunate results to failures in the system of governance of the enterprise, and when we should attribute them simply to the shortcomings of the decision makers themselves. The fast ferry example is an especially instructive one because some members of the CFI board of directors actually attempted to assert the company's autonomy from governmental direction, but when they did so they were removed and replaced by more compliant directors.[16] Looking back on how events unfolded, it is easy to see that the original CFI board was justified in having concerns about the progress of the fast ferry project. Without the benefit of hindsight, however, how do our institutions of corporate governance allow us to determine when the views of the directors of commercial Crown corporations ought to prevail over those of the minister who is ultimately responsible to the legislature for the performance of the corporation?

In fact, the central concern expressed in some of the early literature and public debate on the governance of Crown corporations relates to the absence of sufficient accountability on the part of Crown corporations to Parliament or provincial legislative assemblies.[17] More recent commentary has tended to place greater emphasis on the need for Crown corporations to have greater autonomy from government, especially in relation to day-to-day operations as distinct from the overall policy direction of the corporation.[18] This trend tends to be associated with an increased emphasis on the pursuit by Crown corporations of economic efficiency goals as distinct from other public policy goals. It is hardly surprising, therefore, that the Auditor General should fasten onto this line of thinking as an antidote to the financial disaster of the fast ferry project. The point we would simply make in passing is that there are advocates of a greater emphasis on the non-economic dimension of the purposes served by Crown corporations and of the importance of ensuring that the corporations are sensitive to these considerations.[19]

Whatever degree of independence from government control the directors of a commercial Crown corporation ought to possess, it seems that two challenges for the directors emerge from the existence of broader governmental objectives for the corporation that have to be reconciled with the more traditional corporate law notion of the obligation of directors to act in the best interests of the corporation, defined in terms of the corporation's long-term economic prosperity. The first is the extent to which it is appropriate for the directors themselves to qualify the pursuit of the corporation's profit-making goals in order to further these other objectives. And the second is the extent to which it is appropriate for the directors to be influenced by governmental preferences for these other objectives over the corporation's purely economic interests. There is no doubt about the virtue of clearer articulation of these non-economic goals. Likewise, there is no reason to doubt the ability of directors to identify situations in which governmental actors are seeking to pressure the corporation to pursue illegitimate goals, and the obligation of directors to resist that type of pressure. The interesting situations are the ones where a director's best business judgment dictates one course of action and the pursuit of the various policy goals the government may have for the corporation dictates another. What this chapter is designed to consider is whether the law, either in the form of traditional public law doctrines or in the form of traditional corporate law concepts, gives the corporate director any guidance in the resolution of this dilemma.

Public Law Principles and the Role of Directors of Commercial Crown Corporations

At a superficial level, it might seem attractive to have recourse to public law concepts in order to resolve what could be characterized as a conflict between spheres of authority. In other words, what the law could try to do is identify clear lines of exclusive authority and confine each of the relevant actors to their own mandate. Some aspects of corporate governance would fall under the exclusive authority of the board and others would fall under the exclusive authority of the responsible minister or some central agency such as a Crown corporations secretariat. On this theory, the courts would use the same judicial review doctrines in policing the boundaries between the authority of directors and the authority of government that they employ to confine administrative decision makers to action that falls within the scope of their authority. In all likelihood, most of the interesting questions would involve control over the exercise of discretion rather than narrower questions of statutory interpretation or fair procedure that tend to preoccupy courts reviewing the decisions of administrative tribunals.

Nevertheless, Canadian public law does have a number of doctrines that are used in a more or less satisfactory manner to shape the exercise of discretion by administrative decision makers. These include doctrines that are designed to protect the independence of administrative decision makers from undue pressure;[20] doctrines that control or limit the extent to which administrative decision makers may delegate the authority they have been given to others;[21] and doctrines that can be used to invalidate the exercise of discretion for improper purposes or based on irrelevant considerations[22] or, in their modern guise, to invalidate discretionary decisions that are either "unreasonable"[23] or "patently unreasonable."[24]

In practice, however, these principles are unlikely to prove to be of significant assistance for a variety of reasons. Some of these reasons are doctrinal. The first is that courts have been reluctant to accept the initial proposition that the commercial decisions of Crown corporations are amenable to judicial supervision using "public law" doctrines as distinct from "private law" principles such as contract or tort. This reluctance has been grounded historically on the view that public law remedies are available (and public law duties are owed) only in situations in which the organization whose conduct is at issue is engaged in activity that can be characterized as governmental rather than private or commercial.[25] The mere fact that commercial Crown corporations are creatures of statute has not been regarded, at least to date, as sufficient to bring their commercial operations within the scope of judicial supervision using public law remedies.[26] Recently courts have begun to be more willing to recognize that some kinds of contractual activity engaged in by public bodies have a governmental character and are thus amenable to supervision using public law remedies.[27] It is not obvious, however, how easy it would be to extend this line of authority to decisions made by commercial Crown corporations. Presumably much would turn on whether the decision in question could be characterized as one that turned on the public, as distinct from the commercial, aspect of the corporation's mandate.

Similar doctrinal hurdles exist with respect to the application of at least some of the other public law concepts to the decisions of commercial Crown corporations. For example, the rationale for guaranteeing the independence of members of administrative bodies who carry out adjudicative functions is expressly tailored to the needs of parties to be confident in the impartiality of the individuals who are deciding their dispute. It seems too great a stretch to attempt to base the decision-making autonomy of directors of commercial Crown corporations on the same principle.[28] Even if a court were willing to stretch the principle of adjudicative independence to encompass the directors of commercial Crown corporations, these principles are subordinate to the decision-making structures set out in legislation.[29] As discussed in more detail below, the legislation governing Crown corporations typically states that directors of Crown corporations serve on an "at pleasure" basis.

Even where public law doctrines, such as the proper purposes and relevant considerations doctrines, could be said to have notional relevance to the oversight of decisions made in the course of governance of commercial Crown corporations, the power of these doctrines is severely undercut if a multiplicity of purposes or considerations can be said to be relevant to the decisions made by corporate decision makers. This is especially true where the relevant purposes or considerations are not articulated clearly in legislation, which is typically the case with respect to commercial Crown corporations. The courts have recognized that their supervisory role, even of more classic administrative tribunals, is bound to be extremely limited in areas where the tribunal is called upon to engage in a polycentric balancing of interests.[30] It would seem likely that most of the commercial decisions made by the directors of Crown corporations would fall into this category.

The main weaknesses of judicial review as a mechanism for reinforcing the ability of directors of commercial Crown corporations to exercise decision-making authority in a manner that is independent from government are, however, practical rather than doctrinal. The first is the difficulty of neatly separating policy direction from operational control. Obviously, one can come up with a number of explanations, not all of which are flattering to government, for the reluctance observed by the Auditor General to embrace recommendations made in the past for the establishment of a clear demarcation of roles and authority.[31] It is, however, possible that government officials have been concerned that narrowing their governance role in relation to commercial Crown corporations, or relinquishing it altogether in certain areas, represents too great a sacrifice in terms of the government's ability to use the Crown corporation as an instrument for pursuing a broad range of public policies, not all of which will be consistent with the pursuit of maximal corporate profitability.

The second weakness is that public law doctrines are structured primarily as vehicles to ensure the lawfulness of administrative action rather than as mechanisms for enhancing the quality of administrative performance.[32] Even those doctrines that have a quality control element, such as the right to a speedy hearing,[33] tend to set minimum standards of acceptable performance rather than serve as effective vehicles for quality control. Yet if the fast ferries example can be treated as typical, the problems that arise from excessive governmental interference in the operation of commercial Crown corporations are likely to be precisely the type of performance problems that judicial review does not address particularly well even in the administrative justice context. To suggest that this mechanism will suddenly become more effective in the commercial Crown corporation context seems inherently implausible.

The final observation is linked to the previous one, which is that the primary focus of our system of judicial review is the validation or invalidation of decisions. For the system to work effectively, somebody who is affected by the decision has to know that it has been taken and be in a position to launch a judicial challenge to it. Once again, if the fast ferries situation can be used as an example, the point at which the consequences of bad decisions become apparent is often well after the decisions themselves have been taken. Even if there is somebody who is in a position to launch a legal challenge to the validity of the underlying decision or chain of decisions, the damage will already have been done. To the extent that these unfortunate consequences flow as a result of directors of commercial Crown corporations doing what they were told to do by governmental officials, it is hard to imagine that the harm done to the corporation itself would be the subject of compensation, even if there were a legal basis for a determination that the decisions in question were invalid.

The point to be made here is not that the actions of directors of commercial Crown corporations are or ought to be immune from judicial oversight using public law doctrines where those doctrines are applicable. Rather, it is that conventional public law doctrines are unlikely to serve as a particularly effective vehicle for bolstering the practical ability of directors of commercial Crown corporations to adopt an independent course of action when they are under pressure to bow to governmental policy objectives that do not correspond to the directors' business sense about what action would be in the best financial interests of the corporation. We now turn to the question of whether the application of traditional corporate law principles to the directors of commercial Crown corporations is likely to serve that goal more effectively.

Corporate Law Principles and the Role of Directors of Commercial Crown Corporations

A simple definition of "corporate governance" frequently referred to in connection with private business corporations is the following one formulated by the Cadbury Committee in the United Kingdom:

> Corporate governance is the system by which companies are directed and controlled. Boards of directors are responsible for the governance of their companies. The shareholders' role in governance is to appoint the directors and the auditors and to satisfy themselves that an appropriate governance structure is in place.[34]

The traditional corporate law principles governing the managerial authority and duties of directors of private corporations do not translate comfortably to their counterparts in commercial Crown corporations. As one writer has astutely observed:

It is tempting to think that theories and models developed to explain organization structures and decision-making in private sector organizations might be applied to public sector corporate organizations. However, members of private and public organizations behave and reach their decisions within different incentives systems and structures.[35]

Below we compare and contrast the functions and obligations of directors in private and Crown corporations, respectively, in order to point out the difficulties in utilizing corporate law principles in both cases. We recognize that this chapter's discussion of these points of comparison is largely descriptive rather than prescriptive, and that the current legal environment could fairly be considered by some to be symptomatic of the problematic state of the law with respect to commercial Crown corporation governance. The point of this discussion is to illustrate how great the gulf is between the assumptions the law makes about the powers and duties of directors of private sector corporations and the corresponding position of directors of commercial Crown corporations, and to suggest that bridging that gap may be more challenging than the Auditor General's recommendations for reform of Crown corporation governance might lead us to believe.

Managerial Authority

Private Corporations

Once elected or appointed, the board of directors becomes the primary organ of management in the private business corporation. (We exclude from our discussion any consideration of the more flexible management structure possible in closely held corporations.) By statute, the directors are required to manage the business and affairs of the corporation.[36] The effect of such a provision is to vest in the board the exclusive authority to exercise every power of the corporation not otherwise allocated to the shareholders by statute. In other words, the directors are able to manage the corporation virtually free of any shareholder interference whatsoever. The shareholders are not entitled to initiate any managerial decisions on their own, nor are they entitled to overrule any exercise of managerial discretion made by the board. Consider, by way of illustration, the matter of dividends. While entitlement to dividends is regarded as one of the fundamental attributes of share ownership, it is for the directors and the directors alone in the exercise of their business judgment to determine whether profits should come out by way of dividends or be kept in the corporation for reinvestment or reserves. This is a classic feature of the modern business corporation – the separation of ownership from control.

One additional point might be made here. While as a matter of theory shareholders unhappy with a director they have chosen may seek to remove him or her before the expiration of his or her term of office,[37] "the practical difficulties in the way of effectively exercising even this measure of supervision are very great owing to the directors' control over the proxy-voting machinery."[38]

Commercial Crown Corporations

While the focus of this chapter is on the Crown corporation wholly owned by government, it is apparent that virtually none of the statutes incorporating the individual Crown corporations at both the provincial and federal levels are identical in every respect. For the sake of convenience, we will concentrate on the federal *Financial Administration Act*,[39] which applies to most federal Crown corporations, and a few selected provincial statutes. These legislative enactments adequately reflect the differences that we wish to emphasize between the managerial authority of directors of private corporations and directors of Crown corporations. There are provisions found in Crown corporation statutes that at first blush appear to vest in the directors of these entities managerial authority similar to that found in private corporations. For example, Section 109 of the *FAA* provides that "the board of directors of a Crown corporation is responsible for the management of the businesses, activities and other affairs of the corporation." Similarly, Section 3(7) of the *Ferry Corporation Act*[40] states that "the directors must manage the affairs of the corporation or supervise the management of those affairs." In addition, it is worth setting out a portion of Section 13(1) of the Manitoba *Crown Corporations Public Review and Accountability Act*[41] enacted in 1988:

Duties of Boards

s. 13(1) Subject to specific requirements or restrictions contained in the Act by or under which a corporation is established and to this Act, a board shall
   (a) exercise the powers of the corporation directly or indirectly through the employees and agents of the corporation;
   (b) direct the management of the business and affairs of the corporation;
   (c) ensure that the corporation complies with the laws of the Province of Manitoba

However, any thought that provisions such as these truly make the board of a Crown corporation the primary organ of managerial authority is totally inaccurate. The separation of ownership from control, which is a hallmark of the governing structure in private corporations, completely breaks down when one analyzes the typical commercial Crown corporation. For one thing, the security of tenure that is a characteristic of a director in a private corporation has no place in the Crown corporation setting. The directors are always appointed by the government, and hold office at its pleasure.[42] Obviously, a director who insists on maintaining a position at odds with that of the government in question runs the risk of being removed at any time. It might also be noted that Cabinet generally also appoints the chair and/or the chief executive officer (CEO) of the Crown corporation, and determines their remuneration.[43]

Of even more importance is the fact that directors of Crown corporations are not entitled to make fundamental policy decisions free from government involvement and, at times, direct interference. For example, Section 89 of the *FAA* authorizes Cabinet to give a directive to the directors of a Crown corporation that they must implement in a prompt and efficient manner. By virtue of Section 89(5), compliance with such a directive is "deemed to be in the best interests of the corporation." While apparently this government prerogative is rarely used,[44] we expect that this is because the government is able to realize its goals through more informal means. The government is not only involved in management of a Crown corporation through the use of an instrument as blunt as a directive. Under the *FAA*, for example, the board must submit an annual corporate plan,[45] an annual operating budget,[46] and an annual capital budget[47] for approval by Cabinet.

A significant role of government in the management decision-making process of commercial Crown corporations is hardly surprising, given that Crown corporations are, after all, instruments of government and fulfill public policy objectives. The difficulties arise when the board of directors of a Crown corporation are not given clear instructions as to the nature of their functions and mandate.[48]

Consider the political decisions made by the British Columbia government during the 1990s to freeze automobile insurance rates. These were policy decisions to be implemented regardless of the views of the directors of the Insurance Corporation of British Columbia. We do not suggest that there was anything wrong with this decision, or that the board of ICBC took issue with the government's decision as a matter of its business judgment: the point is simply that in such a circumstance the directors must comply with government policy.

Perhaps a classic example of a difference between the authority of directors in a private corporation and their counterparts in a Crown corporation relates to the board's discretion regarding the distribution of profits. As noted above, it is exclusively within the jurisdiction of the board of a private corporation whether or not to distribute profits to shareholders, and, if so, in what amount. But in a Crown corporation, the situation is very different. On the instructions of Cabinet, a Crown corporation may be compelled to "dividend" to government such portion of any surplus as is deemed appropriate.[49]

The real challenge for directors of a Crown corporation, as noted by the Secretariat of the Treasury Board of Canada, is to "be sensitive to the need to balance the Crown's broad policy objectives and priorities with the corporation's commercial objectives."[50]

Directors' Duties

Private Corporations

It is clear beyond doubt that directors of a private corporation are fiduciaries, and as a consequence owe various fiduciary obligations to the corporation itself. The precise nature of these obligations is fairly well understood, and is based in part on provisions found in the general incorporation statutes and in part on general equitable principles. For example, Section 122 of the *Canada Business Corporations Act (CBCA)* provides as follows:

> s. 122. (1) **Duty of care of directors and officers** – Every director and officer of a corporation in exercising his powers and discharging his duties shall
> (a) act honestly and in good faith with a view to the best interests of the corporation; and
> (b) exercise the care, diligence and skill that a reasonably prudent person would exercise in comparable circumstances.
> (2) **Duty to comply** – Every director and officer of a corporation shall comply with this Act, the regulations, articles, by-laws and any unanimous shareholder agreement.[51]

In addition, as an illustration of the principle that directors and officers must avoid situations where their personal interests may conflict with their duties to the corporation (the "conflict of interest and duty" principle), Section 120 of the *CBCA* requires that these fiduciaries disclose any material interests in material contracts of the corporation.[52] Equity also demands by virtue of the conflict of interest and duty principle that directors avoid competing with their corporations or taking advantage of business opportunities that their corporations might wish to pursue.

It is appropriate to comment here on what is meant by the phrase "the best interests of the corporation" set out in Section 122(1)(a) above, given that (as will be noted shortly) similar language is frequently employed when describing the duties of directors of Crown corporations. To say that directors of private corporations must act "in the best interests of the corporation" has been judicially determined to mean that their primary purpose at all times must be the interests of the shareholders from a long-term perspective, and in particular that their focus be on the maximization of wealth for shareholders. The following passage from *Dodge* v. *Ford Motor Co.*[53] clearly reflects the prevailing view of Anglo-Canadian and American courts:

A business corporation is organized and carried on primarily for the profit of the stockholders. The powers of the directors are to be employed for that end. The discretion of directors is to be exercised in the choice of means to attain that end, and does not extend to a change in the end itself, to the reduction of profits, or to the nondistribution of profits among stockholders in order to devote them to other purposes.

This view of what is meant by "the best interests of the corporation" does not preclude the directors in decision making from having regard to the interests of other corporate constituents – such as employees, creditors, and customers – or even the community at large, provided that it may be said that the board's actuating motive in arriving at any decision was the long-term profitability of the enterprise.[54]

Crown Corporations

We would not dispute that directors of Crown corporations, like their private corporation counterparts, are fiduciaries. But simply characterizing their status in this manner is not particularly helpful. As noted by Mr. Justice Frankfurter in *Securities and Exchange Commission* v. *Chenery Corp.*:

To say that a man is a fiduciary only begins analysis; it gives discretion to further inquiry. To whom is he a fiduciary? What obligations does he owe as a fiduciary? In what respect has he failed to discharge these obligations?[55]

One writer has suggested that the duties imposed upon directors of private corporations "are appropriate for application to directors of [Crown] corporations"[56] and the BC Auditor General appears to share this view.[57] Indeed, in terms of statutory statements of directors' duties, both Section 115(1) of the *FAA* and Section 16(1) of the Manitoba *Crown Corporations Public Review and Accountability Act* simply reproduce Section 122 of the *CBCA* noted above, thereby regarding these obligations as applicable to and appropriate for directors of Crown corporations. Both statutes also include (in Section 116 of the *FAA* and Section 17 of the Manitoba legislation), the obligation of directors and officers to disclose material interests in material contracts of the Crown corporation.

We have no difficulty in applying the same "conflict of interest and duty" restraints imposed upon directors of private corporations by statute or equity to their counterparts in Crown corporations. At the heart of the conflict of interest and duty principle is the twofold requirement that directors be completely impartial when making corporate decisions and avoid personally benefiting from their positions without the knowledge and consent of the corporation. This underlying policy should apply with equal force to directors and officers of both private and Crown corporations.

From our perspective, the real problem arises in seeking to impose an obligation on directors of commercial Crown corporations to act in "the best interests of the corporation" without redefining that phrase in the context of Crown corporations. Commercial Crown corporations are not intended merely to maximize wealth for its owner (i.e., the government) from a long-term, let alone short-term, perspective: they are also intended to carry out public policy objectives. To employ the same language without clarifying what is meant by "the best interests of the corporation" would appear to serve no useful purpose whatsoever.

In Canada, only Saskatchewan appears to have recognized the problems inherent in simply adopting the corporate law "best interests of the corporation" standard. In Section 46(1)(a) of the *Crown Corporations Act, 1993*,[58] it is stated that every officer and director of a Crown corporation shall:

> act honestly and in good faith with a view to the best interests of the Crown corporation or designated subsidiary Crown corporation while taking into account the public policy and business objectives of the Crown corporation or designated subsidiary Crown corporation.

Here at least is explicit recognition that a Crown corporation is an instrument of government concerned not only with profit maximization but also with public policy objectives.

We have no particular concerns regarding applying the corporate law standard for liability in negligence to directors of Crown corporations, although there appears to be considerable merit in reformulating the duty of care along the lines set out in the Queensland statute discussed immediately below. In any event, the absence of objective criteria such as a market for the shares of a Crown corporation,[59] along with the significant role government plays in the decision-making process, would appear to make it quite difficult as a practical matter ever to find the directors liable for negligence. Special mention should perhaps be made of the Queensland *Government Owned Corporations Act, 1993*,[60] which sets out rather elaborate provisions governing the duties of directors of Crown corporations.

There is clear acknowledgment in the legislation that a Crown corporation director stands on a different footing from his or her private corporation counterpart. Thus, Section 136(2) provides that a director of a Government Owned Corporation (GOC) "must act honestly in the exercise of powers, and discharge of functions, as an officer of the GOC"; the phrase "best interests of the corporation" does not appear at all. In a similar vein, Section 136(3) requires directors of Crown corporations to "exercise the degree of care and diligence that a reasonable person in a like position in a statutory GOC would exercise in the statutory GOC's circumstances." Section 136(9) then elaborates on the duty of care contained in subsection (3):

(9) In determining for the purposes of subsection (3) the degree of care and diligence that a reasonable person in a like position in a statutory GOC would exercise in the circumstances of the statutory GOC concerned, regard must be had to –
  (a) the fact that the person is an officer of a statutory GOC; and
  (b) the application of this Act to the GOC; and
  (c) relevant matters required or permitted to be done under this Act in relation to the GOC;
  including, for example –
  (d) any relevant community service obligations of the GOC; and
  (e) any relevant directions, notifications or approvals given to the GOC by the GOC's shareholding Ministers.

Thus it can be seen that liability for negligence would be found only after a court took into account public policy considerations and the role of government.[61] It should be noted that a violation of any of these statutorily defined duties constitutes an offence, and in such circumstances directors leave themselves open to the possibility of fine and/or imprisonment.[62]

Enforcement of Commercial Crown Corporation Directors' Duties
Finally, a few words should be added about the enforceability of duties imposed upon directors of Crown corporations. There is no doubt that the Crown corporation could bring suit in respect of a breach of any of these obligations, and in all likelihood it would appear that the Crown itself would also have standing. This conclusion is supported by language found in many of the Crown corporation statutes. For example, where directors fail to disclose their interest in Crown corporation contracts, the *FAA*,[63] the Saskatchewan *Crown Corporations Act*,[64] and the Manitoba *Crown Corporations Public Review and Accountability Act*[65] all provide that either the corporation or the Crown is entitled to apply to court for relief.

While the matter is not entirely free from doubt, it seems highly unlikely that individual members of the public could bring suit against the directors of a Crown corporation for any breach of duty. The recent Supreme Court of Canada decisions in *Edwards* v. *Law Society of Upper Canada* [66] and *Cooper* v. *Hobart*[67] support the view that public regulators will not be regarded as owing a duty of care in negligence to individual members of the public. Perhaps the clearest (if not the only) statement that directors of Crown corporations do not owe any duties to individual members of the public is to be found in *Northeast Marine Services* v. *Atlantic Pilotage Authority.*[68] In that case, the defendant authority – a Crown corporation to which the *FAA* applied – did not take the lowest tender offered by the plaintiff in order to prevent the plaintiff from having a monopoly on pilot boat services in the area. The plaintiff brought suit for both breach of contract and liability in tort for negligence. It may be recalled that Section 115(1) of the *FAA* requires a director of a Crown corporation to act in the best interests of the corporation and to exercise the care, diligence, and skill that a reasonably prudent person would employ. In the course of his judgment, Mr. Justice McNair said the following about Section 115:

> In my opinion, the fiduciary duty or obligation imposed on directors and officers of the defendant by virtue of [Section 115] of the Financial Administration Act is one imposed on them in their capacity of agents and trustees for the Crown corporation and is not something which might enure to the benefit of a third party stranger.

Assuming that Mr. Justice McNair is correct in his assessment of Section 115, the effect is simply to reinforce the dominant position of government in relation to the directors of commercial Crown corporations.

Conclusion

The BC Auditor General's report on the fast ferry project makes a number of important recommendations about the governance of commercial Crown corporations. Broadly speaking, these recommendations are that the boards of directors of Crown corporations be composed of individuals who understand the mandate they have been given and have the skills and attributes necessary to carry out that mandate. It is difficult to gainsay the wisdom of these recommendations, either at this general level or in the more detailed form in which they were presented in the report,[69] and we have not attempted to do so in this chapter. The difficulty that we have tried to identify is with respect to translating a generalized mandate to operate in an independent fashion according to sound business principles into the day-to-day reality of running any particular commercial Crown corporation.

No doubt it is the case that if governments are willing to take a hands-off approach to Crown corporations or to establish a clear set of limits in relation to their interactions with Crown corporations, it will be possible for directors who are familiar with the governance of private sector corporations to carry that experience forward into an analogous role in the governance of Crown corporations. The suggestion advanced in this chapter is that if we take the public policy role of Crown corporations seriously, it may not be a simple matter to disentangle this role from the efficient allocation of the corporation's resources, which is the traditional goal of directors of private sector corporations. More importantly, at least for present purposes, it is not obvious that either public law or traditional corporate law principles give the directors of commercial Crown corporations meaningful guidance about how to resolve conflicts between efficiency goals and broader governmental objectives. At the end of the day, it does not appear to us that exhortations to directors of commercial Crown corporations to act in a more independent, businesslike fashion are likely to overcome the fundamental weaknesses in the position of the directors in the current legal environment. Whether or not changes to that environment could be made that would improve the practical ability of the directors to act independently without fundamentally compromising the public policy purposes that justify the existence of the Crown corporation as a public entity is another question, one that we are prepared to leave for another occasion.

Acknowledgments
The authors are grateful for research assistance provided by Ruby Chan, Geeta Gill, Mandy Javahery, and Carmen Tham.

Notes
1 Auditor General of British Columbia, *A Review of the Fast Ferry Project: Governance and Risk Management,* Report 5 (October 1999) c. 1 and 4, <http://www.oag.bc.ca/pubs/1999-00/report-5/sec-1.htm>.
2 *Ibid.* at 9. The Report included, at 43, the following statement concerning recommendations for corporate governance (notes omitted):

> Our 1996 study is only one of a number of reports and studies that have shown a high degree of consensus as to good governance practices. One Canadian authority [CCAF-FCVI Inc., a Canadian research and educational foundation] summarized the main principles succinctly, when it said governing bodies should:
>
> • be composed of people with the necessary knowledge, ability and commitment to fulfill their obligations;
> • understand their purposes and whose interests they represent;
> • understand the objectives and strategies of the organizations they govern;
> • understand what constitutes reasonable information for good governance and obtain it;
> • once informed, be prepared to act to ensure that the organization's objectives are met and that performance is satisfactory; and
> • fulfill their accountability obligations to those whose interests they represent by reporting on their organization's effectiveness.
>
> Two of the guidelines developed by the federal Treasury Board Secretariat (which, in turn, built on guidelines adopted by the Toronto Stock Exchange) are also particularly appropriate:
>
> • the board of directors should ensure that the board can function independently; and
> • in recognition of the importance of the position of CEO (chief executive officer), the board of directors of every Crown corporation should periodically assess the CEO's position and evaluate the CEO's performance.

3 *Ibid.* at 12.
4 For useful discussions of what these justifications might be, see, for example, M. Trebilcock and R. Prichard, "Crown Corporations: The Calculus of Instrument Choice" in R. Prichard, ed., *Crown Corporations in Canada: The Calculus of Instrument Choice* (Toronto: Butterworths, 1983) 1 at 39-74; E. Kirsch, *Crown Corporations as Instruments of Public Policy: A Legal and Institutional Perspective,* Economic Council of Canada Discussion Paper No. 295 (Ottawa: Economic Council of Canada, 1985) at 122-54.
5 See, for example, A. Tupper and G. Doern, eds., *Privatization, Public Policy and Crown Corporations in Canada* (Halifax: Institute for Research on Public Policy, 1988).

6 See, for example, S. Estrin, "State Ownership, Corporate Governance and Privatisation" in Organization for Economic Cooperation and Development Proceedings, *Corporate Governance, State-Owned Enterprises and Privatisation* (Paris: OECD, 1998) 11 at 12-18; J. Brumby and M. Hyndman, "State Owned Enterprise Governance: Focus on Economic Efficiency," *ibid.* 33 at 38-42.

7 See, for example, J.K. Laux and M.A. Molot, *State Capitalism: Public Enterprise in Canada* (Ithaca, NY: Cornell University Press, 1988) at 175-202.

8 R.S.C., c. F-10.

9 S. 83(1) of the *FAA* defines a "Crown corporation" as "a parent Crown corporation or its wholly owned subsidiary." A "parent Crown corporation" means "a corporation that is wholly owned directly by the Crown, but does not include a departmental corporation." S. 2 of the *Act* defines a "departmental corporation" as "a corporation named in Schedule II." S. 3(1)(a.1) empowers the Governor in Council to "add to Schedule II the name of any corporation established by an Act of Parliament that performs administrative, research, supervisory, advisory or regulatory functions of a governmental nature." S. 3(4) prevents the Governor in Council from adding parent Crown corporations to Schedule III of the *Act* if the corporation meets the criteria established for Schedule II corporations. In a roundabout way, then, the *Act* distinguishes between Schedule II corporations that perform functions of an essentially noncommercial nature and Schedule III corporations whose activities can include activity of a more commercial nature. Schedule III corporations are themselves divided into two classifications. Pursuant to s. 3(5), corporations listed in Schedule III, Part II, are restricted to corporations of which the Governor in Council is satisfied that "(a) the corporation (i) operates in a competitive environment, (ii) is not ordinarily dependent on appropriations for operating purposes, and (iii) ordinarily earns a return on equity; and (b) there is a reasonable expectation that the corporation will pay dividends."

10 D. Stevens, "Corporate Autonomy and Institutional Control: The Crown Corporation as a Problem in Organization Design" (1991) 34 Canadian Public Administration 286 at 293-94.

11 See S. Brooks, *Who's in Charge? The Mixed Ownership Corporation in Canada* (Halifax: Institute for Research on Public Policy, 1987).

12 For a very instructive survey of this literature, see D. Stevens, *Corporate Autonomy and Institutional Control: The Crown Corporation as a Problem in Organization Design* (Montreal and Kingston: McGill-Queen's University Press, 1993) at 1-32.

13 Economic Council of Canada, *Minding the Public's Business* (Ottawa: Minister of Supply and Services Canada, 1986).

14 Stevens, *supra* note 12 at 5, 180-86.

15 *Ibid.* at 53-151, 182-85; Stevens, *supra* note 10 at 294-311.

16 See Auditor General of British Columbia, *supra* note 1 at 32-38.

17 See C.A. Ashley and R.G.H. Smails, *Canadian Crown Corporations: Some Aspects of Their Administration and Control* (Toronto: Macmillan of Canada, 1965) at 39-94; A.T. Lambert, *Royal Commission on Financial Management and Accountability Final Report* (Ottawa: Supply and Services Canada, 1979) and the discussion of the Lambert Report in P. Garant, "Crown Corporations: Instruments of Economic Intervention – Legal Aspects" in I. Bernier and A. Lajoie, eds., *Regulations, Crown Corporations and Administrative Tribunals* (Toronto: University of Toronto Press, 1985) at 39-40, 57-63.

18 See, for example, M. Gordon, *Government in Business* (Montreal: C.D. Howe Institute, 1981); Economic Council of Canada, *supra* note 13.

19 For example, see the opinion of the dissenting members of the Economic Council of Canada: Economic Council of Canada, *ibid.* at 147-49; Laux and Molot, *supra* note 7 at 191-202.

20 See, for example, *Ocean Port Hotel Ltd.* v. *British Columbia (General Manager, Liquor Control and Licensing Branch)*, 2001 S.C.C. 52, [2001] 2 S.C.R. 781; *2747-3174 Québec Inc.* v. *Quebec (Régie des permis d'alcool)*, [1996] 3 S.C.R. 919; *Canadian Pacific Ltd.* v. *Matsqui Indian Band*, [1995] 1 S.C.R. 3; *Tremblay* v. *Québec (Commission des affaires sociales)*, [1992] 1 S.C.R. 952.

21 See, for example, *Roncarelli* v. *Duplessis*, [1959] S.C.R. 121; *R.* v. *Sandler* (1971), 21 D.L.R. (3d) 286 (Ont. C.A.); *Lavender and Son Ltd.* v. *Minister of Housing and Local Government*, [1970] 1 W.L.R. 1231 (Eng. Q.B.).

22   *Oakwood Development Ltd.* v. *Rural Municipality of St. François Xavier,* [1985] 2 S.C.R. 164; *Roncarelli* v. *Duplessis, ibid.; Smith and Rhuland Ltd.* v. *The Queen ex rel. Brice Andrews,* [1953] 2 S.C.R. 95; *Padfield* v. *Minister of Agriculture, Fisheries and Food,* [1968] A.C. 997 (Eng. H.L.).

23   *Baker* v. *Canada (Minister of Citizenship and Immigration),* [1999] 2 S.C.R. 817.

24   *Mount Sinai Hospital Centre* v. *Quebec (Minister of Health and Social Services),* 2001 S.C.C. 41, [2001] 2 S.C.R. 281.

25   See, for example, *Vander Zalm* v. *British Columbia (Acting Commissioner of Conflict of Interest)* (1991), 56 B.C.L.R. (2d) 37 (B.C.S.C.).

26   *Canadian Metal Co.* v. *Canadian Broadcasting Corporation (No. 2)* (1975), 11 O.R. (2d) 167 (Ont. C.A.); *Cairns* v. *Farm Credit Corp.* (1991), 7 Admin. L.R. (2d) 203 (F.C.T.D.); *Wilcox* v. *Canadian Broadcasting Corporation,* [1980] 1 F.C. 326 (F.C.T.D.); *Ainsworth Electric Co.* v. *Exhibition Place* (1987), 58 O.R. (2d) 432 (Ont. Div. Ct.); *Midnorthern Appliances Ind. Corp.* v. *Ontario Housing Corp* (1977), 17 O.R. (2d) 290 (Ont. Div. Ct.). In the first three cases, the courts came to the conclusion that the respondent corporations were not federal boards, commissions, or tribunals within the meaning of the *Federal Court Act,* R.S.C. 1985, c. F-7, and thus were not amenable to supervision by the Federal Court of Canada under that *Act.* In the latter two cases, the Ontario Divisional Court reached a similar conclusion with respect to the use of the Ontario *Judicial Review Procedure Act,* R.S.O. 1990, c. J.1, to supervise the commercial activity of the respondent public corporations. It is worth noting, however, that courts have sometimes found that public corporations can have public law duties. For example, in *Webb* v. *Ontario Housing Corp.* (1978), 22 O.R. (2d) 257 (Ont. C.A.), the court ruled that the Ontario Housing Corporation owed a duty of procedural fairness to a tenant who was being evicted from subsidized housing. The distinction between the *Webb* and *Midnorthern Appliances* cases seems to turn on whether the court viewed the corporation as being engaged in carrying out a public program as distinct from a purely or predominantly commercial activity.

27   See, for example, *Shell Canada Products Ltd.* v. *Vancouver (City),* [1994] 1 S.C.R. 231; *Associated Respiratory Services Inc.* v. *British Columbia (Purchasing Commission)* (1994), 87 B.C.L.R. (2d) 70 (B.C.C.A.); *Oil Sands Hotel (1975) Ltd.* v. *Alberta (Gaming and Liquor Commission)* (1998), 19 Admin. L.R. (3d) 121 (Alta. Q.B.).

28   See Garant, *supra* note 17 at 43. For analogous reasons, Garant is of the view that the rules against unauthorized subdelegation do not apply to Crown corporations: *ibid.* at 13.

29   *Ocean Port Hotel, supra* note 20.

30   See *Pushpanathan* v. *Canada (Minister of Citizenship and Immigration),* [1999] 1 S.C.R. 982.

31   Auditor General of British Columbia, *supra* note 1 at 12.

32   See P. Bryden and R. Hatch, "British Columbia Council of Administrative Tribunals Research and Policy Committee Report on Independence, Accountability and Appointment Processes in British Columbia Tribunals" (1999) 12 Can. J. Admin. L. and Prac. 235; M. Priest, "Structure and Accountability of Administrative Agencies" in *Administrative Law, Principles, Practice and Pluralism, Special Lectures of the Law Society of Upper Canada* (Scarborough, ON: Carswell, 1993) at 11.

33   See *Blencoe* v. *British Columbia (Human Rights Commission),* [2000] 2 S.C.R. 307.

34   A. Cadbury, *Report of the Committee on the Financial Aspects of Corporate Governance* (London: Burgess Science Press, 1992) [hereinafter *Cadbury Report*].

35   Stevens, *supra* note 10 at 291.

36   *Canada Business Corporations Act,* R.S.C. 1985, c. C-44, as am. by S.C. 2001, c. 14, s. 102 [hereinafter *CBCA*]; *British Columbia Company Act,* R.S.B.C. 1996, c. 62, s. 117(1) [hereinafter *BCCA*].

37   *CBCA, supra* note 36, s. 109 (1); *BCCA, supra* note 36, s. 130(3).

38   L.C.B. Gower, *Principles of Modern Company Law,* 4th ed. (London: Stevens, 1979) at 152.

39   *Supra* note 8.

40   R.S.B.C. 1996, c. 137.

41   R.S.M. c. C336.

42   *FAA, supra* note 8, s. 105(1); *Ferry Corporation Act, supra* note 40, s. 31.

43   *FAA, ibid.,* s. 108; *Ferry Corporation Act, ibid.,* s. 3(2) and (3).

44 See Canada, Treasury Secretariat, *Directors of Crown Corporations: Introductory Guide to Their Roles and Responsibilities* (July 1993), <http://www.tbs-sct.gc.ca/si-si/ccpi-pise/ig/4.e.htm>.

45 *FAA, supra* note 8, s. 122.

46 *Ibid.,* s. 123.

47 *Ibid.,* s. 124.

48 See Auditor General of British Columbia, *supra* note 1.

49 *FAA, supra* note 8, s. 130; *Insurance Corporation Act,* R.S.B.C. 1996, c. 228, s. 26.

50 Canada, Treasury Secretariat, *supra* note 44.

51 See also *BCCA, supra* note 36, s. 118.

52 *Ibid.,* s. 120.

53 N.W.668 (Mich. S.C. 1919).

54 For interesting discussions of the phrase "best interests of the corporation" and suggestions that its meaning be expanded beyond shareholder wealth maximization, see, for example, the chapters by Janis Sarra (Chapter 2) and Gil Yaron (Chapter 4) in this book.

55 U.S. 80 at 85 (U.S.S.C. 1943).

56 See M.A. Kimuli, "Legal Aspects of Public or Crown Corporations in Canada" (LL.M. Thesis, University of British Columbia, 1980) at 137 [unpublished].

57 See Auditor General of British Columbia, *Crown Corporations Governance Study, Report 2* (1996-97), <http://bcauditor.com/PUBS/1996-97/REPORT-2/TOC.HTM>.

58 R.S.S. c. C-50.101.

59 See Estrin, *supra* note 6.

60 Statutes of Queensland, 1993, No. 28.

61 This statute also provides that a director is not to make improper use of information acquired by virtue of his/her position (s. 136[4]) or to improperly benefit from his/her position (s. 136[5]).

62 For an in-depth discussion of the Queensland legislation, see D. McDonough, "Corporate Governance and Government Owned Corporations in Queensland" (1998) 10 Bond L. Rev. 272.

63 *Supra* note 8, s. 118(1).

64 *Supra* note 58, s. 47(9).

65 *Supra* note 41, s. 17(9).

66 S.C.C. 80, [2001] 3 S.C.R. 562. In this case, the public had paid money into the solicitor's trust fund. The funds had been improperly used and the Law Society had received previous notice of this fact, two years before it took action against the said solicitor. It was held that the Law Society owed no duty of care to individual members of the public for having been tardy in taking action.

67 S.C.C. 79, [2001] 3 S.C.R. 537. In this case, the Registrar of Mortgage Brokers had frozen assets in the account of a mortgage broker for failure to comply with the *BC Mortgage Brokers Act* R.S.B.C. 1996, c. 313. It was held that the Registrar did not owe the investing public a duty of care.

68 (1992) 57 F.T.R. 80 (F.C.T.D.).

69 For the full text of the recommendations, see *supra* note 2.

10
Synchronizing Individual Corporate Self-Interest Goals and Sector Development Responsibilities: The BC Seafood Processing Industry Experience
Kathleen Porter and Joe Weiler

Corporate Decision Making: Introduction to the Problem

In recent years, policy makers and regulators have increasingly focused their attention on reforms that would enhance the legal and institutional framework within which corporations operate. Central to these efforts is the question of corporate governance, that is, the adoption of value-maximizing norms and strategies regulating the decision-making process within a corporation. For example, in 2001 the European Commission issued a Green Paper on *Promoting a European Framework for Corporate Social Responsibility,*[1] and most recently, the Canadian Democracy and Corporate Accountability Commission released its final report, *The New Balance Sheet: Corporate Profits and Responsibility in the 21st Century.*[2] Both reports address the optimal legal framework and the range of relevant factors that corporate decision makers should utilize in their decisions to better reflect the interests of shareholders and other relevant stakeholders who are impacted by corporate decisions and whose views and interests should be considered in these decisions.

These recent contributions to the discussion about the focus of corporate decision making view the current corporate decision-making process as incomplete because it is almost entirely geared towards the interests of shareholders. The prevailing view of a corporation is one of a nexus of contracts between the shareholders and the corporation, with the shareholders' interests playing the pivotal role. The interests of other potential collateral stakeholders in the network of ongoing contractual relations of a typical corporation, such as employees, subcontractors, suppliers, and strategic alliance partners are considered only marginally in the current legal system, at least as it applies to the duties and responsibilities of directors and executives of a corporation. In the case of employees, their interests are usually considered only in the context of the legal liability of directors making a decision about downsizing or insolvency, and solely with reference to issues such as unpaid wages, severance, and pensions.

Consistent with this narrow view of the range of corporate decision-making responsibility, the employee, creditor, or adjacent landowner is considered a potential "victim" of corporate irresponsibility. Corporate governance rules are designed primarily to ameliorate or avoid this situation. We call this perspective the "negative responsibility" approach to the legal regulation of corporate governance. One suggested response to curbing this kind of potentially socially destructive corporate conduct is by government regulation to ensure corporate social responsibility.[3] Yet the advocates of shareholder rights vehemently oppose this corporate social responsibility approach as a violation of shareholder property rights and a failure to understand how the market, if properly allowed to operate, could address these issues without the need to "expropriate" shareholder interests.

There is a third response to the issue of the optimal approach to corporate decision making, which was adopted by the British Columbia seafood processing industry in response to the recommendations of the report of the Fish Processing Strategic Task Force.[4] The seafood processing industry created a sector council, jointly chaired by senior representatives of labour and management. This industry experience provides the focal point for the discussion presented in this chapter about the ways to synchronize corporate self-interest and sectoral governance. This chapter suggests that the implementation of a sector council avoids the need for statutory regulation of corporate decision making, and at the same time provides a concrete structure that will help avoid the negative impact on nonshareholder interests arising from corporate decisions. Rather than rely on the role of the "market" to influence corporate decision making, or on intrusive statutory standards as the basis for corporate social responsibility, we propose a middle ground that affords protection for shareholder and relevant stakeholder interests by providing mechanisms of self-governance both internally (in the company) and externally (in the industry and the community in which the company operates). These mechanisms will provide better outcomes; however, they will not occur on their own, and require vision, leadership, commitment, and a reallocation of resources. There is a growing level of experience in the use of these mechanisms that should help provide managers and directors with clues about how to engage in new forms of decision making without the heavy hand of government forcing this approach on unwilling corporate directors and officers.

Lacking in the discourse about the optimal regulatory approach to corporate decision making is what we call the "positive responsibility" aspect of corporate governance, that is, additional steps in internal corporate decision making that will likely produce more informed and better-implemented decisions. These decisions arise from a broader involvement of more internal company participants. While this may result in a longer decision-making time frame at the outset, it will ultimately involve a shorter implementation period and result in a more mistake-free operation. For example, the corporation would engage in an internal consultation process that includes employees in decisions with respect to major issues such as restructuring, the development of new business strategies, the implementation of new technologies, and decisions on workplace efficiencies or creating ideas for new work that are suited to the company's core business. This would require all company owners and managers (as well as senior union officials where the firm's employees are represented by a union) to support the change from a traditional hierarchical, command-and-control management decision-making system to a more participatory management system that will provide higher levels of corporate social responsibility.

What is involved in this alteration of internal corporate decision making is the acceptance of the need to change, and a more open mind about the kind of change that will work for the particular company and industry involved. This positive responsibility approach rejects the idea that there is a "one size fits all" mode of corporate decision making that will work in any context. There is a significant change in corporate culture inherent in this approach, and a rejection of the view that current legal and market forces are sufficient to avoid the negative impacts that occur when decision makers utilize limited perspectives without the benefit of broader inputs into their decision-making process.

In the positive responsibility approach to corporate decision making, the range of inputs internal to a company's decision making process would likely expand so that the company's decisions would have the benefit of information and experience of fellow companies in the same sector. In the context of a vertical or horizontal connection or alliances to the market for a firm's goods or services, we refer to the experience of value chains and supply chains and how these structures can help individual companies make smart decisions for the benefit of shareholders, employees, and fellow chain members. Finally, in the context of regional production centres in which most companies operate, we discuss the issues involved in regional economic development and the role of individual corporate players in participating in these multi-stakeholder processes. The discussion concludes with suggestions about how these structures and mechanisms can operate without jeopardizing shareholder interests and without the need for government rule making. These systems of decision making are more democratic and usually longer term in their focus, and none are inconsistent with current legal regulation of corporate governance. In each case, they force decision makers to take into account a wider range of interests and provide a mechanism to do so without mandating any particular outcomes or adding any new forms of legal liability to corporate decision makers.

The review of corporate governance structures in this chapter describes four modes of decision making that display the positive responsibility models of corporate decision making. The first model involves internal enterprise decision-making processes designed to more fully engage both labour and management in the overall definition and implementation of best practices and new business opportunities. The second model involves enterprises in joint decision making in the best interest of the sector; often the focus is on the human resource. The third model, the value chain, involves a series of businesses working together in order to respond more strategically to changes in the market. The fourth model is a regional decision-making process where a number of value chains operate in concert based on the global competitive advantage to be gained through inter-sectoral and intra-sectoral collaboration. An enterprise can operate following all four models or engage in any model independently of the others. Our contention is that a company that engages in these types of decision-making processes can meet the goal of corporate social responsibility without jeopardizing the decision-making authority or interests of the shareholder.

Corporate Governance in the Context of Internal Decision-Making Processes

Employee Involvement in Corporate Decision Making

A typical example of employee participation in corporate governance involves placing an employee representative on the board of directors. This may be mere tokenism, however, and is likely the weakest form of employee involvement. Broader and more powerful forms of participation in governance are needed that would provide a platform for the voice and the initiatives of the employees, who, by sharing their experience and ideas as well as by facilitating the implementation of these ideas, could greatly contribute to the quality of corporate governance.

The idea of replacing the prevalent command-and-control feature of corporate governance with a broader participatory structure is not difficult to grasp. It is the implementation of this idea in practice that poses the real challenge because the process is an evolution that takes place over time and involves a shift in a number of aspects in company management. These include the shift from a single-skill employee to a multi-skill employee, from managers who direct to managers who coach, from risk avoidance to risk appraisal practices, and from a hierarchical climate to a collaborative climate.

In this agenda, the questions that need to be addressed include: Which particular processes and/or individuals will enhance decision making? At what time, early in the planning stages to late in the implementation stage, should the constituents be brought into the process of corporate decision making? Who can be trusted with access to confidential corporate decisions or information? What expertise exists or could be developed that would add to the quality of decisions? What decisions or issues should be left to a collective bargaining process aimed at formal collective agreements? What information or range of decisions can be delegated to a process that would be ongoing and whose output would not appear in formal contractual documents? What expertise is needed to make these processes work effectively? Finally, what kind of neutral facilitation, if any, is needed at different stages of this joint consultation process?[5]

While almost all of the experiments in the development of these kinds of joint consultative processes have been done at individual workplaces and were done without the benefit of any public policy or mandate, there is some legislative recognition of the advantages of this approach in the current version of the British Columbia *Labour Relations Code*.[6] This includes Section 53 of the *Code,* which requires every collective agreement to have some sort of joint consultation committee, and Section 54, which requires employers to give adequate notice and then to bargain in good faith with the union about any substantial change in the company's operations occurring during the term of a collective agreement that would significantly impact terms and conditions in the collective agreement. There is no right to strike or lockout over these issues, but public policy is clear that the parties must make every reasonable effort to agree. This provision is particularly important in the context of an impending plant closure, a shutdown of a significant part of an employer's operation, or other examples of restructuring.

There is no implied substantive outcome mandated by these provisions, but rather the expectation that if the parties do seriously attempt to wrestle with the implications of such an operational decision, better outcomes in terms of maximizing a range of interests will probably occur. These may include amendments to the collective agreement itself, such as compensation or work rules, that may be needed to save jobs or investments or to provide a sensible allocation of resources, or out-placement services for workers that are terminated as a result of the downsizing or restructuring.

These statutory provisions assume that there is a range of corporate stakeholders beyond the shareholders. These stakeholders' interests must be considered before any decision of serious impact to these interests can be made and implemented. However, there is no obligation that corporate decision makers must accede to the wishes of workers or must reach agreement that satisfies employees' concerns. What is embedded in this provision is the need to seriously attempt to arrive at a consensus about the way to address the looming potentially negative decision.

Scholarly commentaries by industrial relations experts contain many examples of circumstances where this kind of eleventh-hour bargaining did result in innovative responses and amendments to collective agreements that allowed the company to continue operating pursuant to new work rules and compensation systems. Almost invariably these new provisions have involved continued monitoring of the situation through ongoing joint consultation mechanisms. These latter mechanisms provide the context for further attempts to innovate.

It is important to note that these provisions do not hamstring corporate decision makers in deciding what is in the best interests of shareholders. They do provide, however, a concrete means for these decisions to be informed about broader interests beyond those of the shareholders and the corporate decision makers, of which they might not otherwise be aware. It also avoids the potentially meddlesome and politically charged intrusion of government. What is needed to better understand the pros and cons of joint consultation in the workplace is much better tracking of individual experiences of how these mechanisms are working, when they operate well, when they fail, and why. This research agenda was proposed by the British Columbia Labour Relations Board chair a few years ago, but the fractious labour and employer central organizations in this province refused to cooperate even on participating in a forum on how joint consultation is working in British Columbia companies. In a similar vein, in 1998 the Labour Relations Code Review Committee recommended that these kinds of joint labour-management consultation structures be encouraged by government and that the experience of these firm-level initiatives be researched, analyzed, and publicized so that other parties could learn from this experience. To date, there has been no significant response from government to these recommendations from its Review Committee.[7]

The experience in the British Columbia seafood processing industry shows that the development of joint labour-management initiatives as a part of corporate governance has been a useful tool for the industry to successfully respond to its growing competitiveness challenge. Joint committees in this sector seek joint solutions to a wide range of productivity-related issues in the company's current scope of operations, and attempt to develop new work opportunities such as the processing of new products and exploration of niche-market opportunities. Some committees have a mandate to deal with issues relating to hiring, the development of optimal human resource deployment and compensation systems, and investment in human capital through training initiatives.

The experience with such initiatives in the British Columbia seafood processing industry and in other resource sectors in this province suggests that there are a host of examples of how firms have achieved innovation that has both enhanced the quality of working life and income of workers, while at the same time increasing the profitability and shareholder value of these enterprises. The examples of successful innovation appear to share the following features:

- They recognize the long-standing contractual nature of the relationship of the parties as providing the foundation upon which these innovations could be achieved.
- These innovations were implemented in a step-by-step, incremental fashion.
- The changes made to the contractual relationship involved trade-offs that changed long-standing contractual provisions for the benefit of both parties, rather than consisting only of contract concessions that benefited only the party who sought the innovation.
- Business relations between competitor companies improved as information and training began to extend beyond the confines of individual companies.
- Changes in productivity resulted in similar programs being implemented in non-union facilities as the "best practices" and "lessons learned" were disseminated through the public education programs of the sector council.

The bottom line of this experience is that these joint labour-management consultation structures complement rather than subvert traditional management decision-making systems. When other stakeholders (i.e., the employees) are involved in the decision-making process, the decisions tend to be better informed and easier to implement. Moreover, this broader involvement in decision making creates an atmosphere that is more conducive to achieving necessary trade-offs in pre-existing terms and conditions of employment that need to be adjusted in order to move ahead with the new jointly developed operational initiative. The net result is a win-win situation for both shareholders and employee stakeholders, who in a narrow view of corporate governance would never have participated in these kinds of decisions.

The fact that there are a growing number of firm-level examples of innovation in human resources measures in British Columbia (both within and outside the seafood processing industry) suggests that there is a need for a sectoral-level service that would help to identify and analyze these innovations and educate others about their nature and experience. The sector council mechanism offers an ideal institutional framework in which the industry can develop organizational innovations through the establishment of firm-level measures and initiatives involving both management and employees. Among other things, a sector council offers an ideal platform for accessing and sharing information crucial to such innovation initiatives and providing consulting services through which the participants in innovative organizational changes at the enterprise level can share their experience with one another.

A corporation's responsibilities for its decisions do not end solely with its shareholders and employees. The interests of key suppliers, subcontractors, and other industry participants in some circumstances should be taken into account in the corporate decision-making process in order to maximize the positive impact of these decisions in the larger community in which the company operates. This can be done in a way that enhances rather than dilutes shareholder interests. When decision makers are better informed of the polycentric impact of their firm-level decisions, they can better assess the potential for these individual decisions to contribute to innovation, productivity, product or service quality, and the reputation of the larger industry in which they operate. In our view, in order for this to happen, there needs to be a structure in which this broader impact assessment can be made that allows for these deliberations to be conducted based on accurate information and with the benefit of focused ongoing dialogue with other industry participants. The sector council type of mechanism is proving to be a useful tool in this broader decision-making landscape.

Corporate Governance in the Context of Sectoral Development
There is no single specific model that will fit every industry setting and accomplish the desired level of industry consultation and collaboration for every sector. The important point for the purposes of this chapter is that individual firm-level decisions are likely to better serve the interests of both the individual firm and its sector if they are made with the benefit of the collective intelligence of the industry as a whole, where it can be gathered and shared. If decisions are made in this context, the likelihood of unforeseen negative impacts of individual firm decisions is greatly reduced, and the incentive for government or other external stakeholder intervention is therefore removed.

The important feature of the sector-level mechanism a specific industry will utilize is that it contributes to the level of industrial self-governance that the industry wishes to exercise. This may vary from industry to industry and will depend, for example, on whether the sector has a large union presence (in which case the sector may choose to have a bipartite labour-management structure), or if the sector is made up primarily of large vertically integrated firms (in which case the sector-level organization may choose to create a mechanism geared more towards policy development), or if the sector is made up primarily of smaller, more niche-market producers who rely on inter-firm transactions to get their product or service to market (in which case the industry-level organization will have a larger board structure and a focus on more business-to-business linking programs). Whatever the particular configuration or purpose of the sector-level organization will be, the experience of these types of sectoral entities would seem to contribute to better firm-level decision making because of the potential to pool resources and share information about best and worst practices in the participant firms' individual businesses.

The utility of a sector-level organization reflects the fact that a corporation has a responsibility not only to its shareholders but also to the larger community in which it operates. One only has to think of the health and safety implications of substandard industry practices that soured the public impression about the cattle industry in the United Kingdom as a result of mad cow and hoof and mouth disease, or the salmon aquaculture industry as a result of mass escapes due to defective pen placement or management, or the auto industry as a result of poor tire and sport utility vehicle (SUV) design, to realize that poor operational practices by some companies will have a negative impact on all others in the sector and increase the need for government intervention and regulation. The issue then becomes, at which point do the interests of the individual firm and the sector in which the firm operates intersect, complement, or diverge? How can the individual firm participate in an industry-level mechanism without sacrificing its potential to innovate or contribute to its bottom line? What is the proper balance between the individual firm's immediate self-interest and its sector's longer-term interests? Why would a firm participate in a sector public policy-building exercise that may mean curbing some of its own ability to influence policy development? What level of information sharing will a firm exercise when its own competitive advantage may be served by learning the best practices of others while offering none of its own to other industry members? The following experience of the origins, growing pains, triumphs, and mistakes of the British Columbia Seafood Sector Council offers some useful information for other sectors that wish to tread the path of sectoral self-governance.

Introducing a Sectoral Strategy to the British Columbia Seafood Processing Industry

In an effort to address the challenges facing the British Columbia seafood processing industry, the British Columbia government in 1993 created the Fish Processing Strategic Task Force consisting of prominent industry leaders. In late 1994, the twelve Task Force members unanimously recommended a strategy for their industry that involved better maintenance of fish habitat, more value-added processing, better utilization of underdeveloped species, more investing in human resources, and improving productivity in the plants. In order to ensure some movement to implement these recommendations, the Task Force recommended that a sector council be created by the industry. The council would follow up on the recommendations and to provide ongoing leadership for the sector in guiding it through the period of rapid transformation that was anticipated because of volatile consumer markets and unreliable access to seafood resources. The deliberations of the Task Force about the appropriate forum of a sector-level leadership mechanism provides a useful analysis of the options available to any sector that wishes to create a sector-level organization.

In search of the most effective way to reorganize the British Columbia seafood processing industry, the Task Force considered several models of industry organization: subsectoral associations, advisory bodies, task-focused business-labour initiatives, and service delivery bodies, sector councils, or peak associations. Ultimately, the Task Force recommended a "sector council model" with bipartite labour-management leadership as the appropriate mechanism for this sector, because the longest-existing industry organizations were formed along collective bargaining lines and these two labour-management entities were willing to participate in a nonadversarial entity in order to better serve their constituents.

General Characteristics of a Sector Council

A sector council is an industry-level entity that brings together a number of subsector groups within an industry. Sector councils thus have the advantage of power sharing among groups through their membership in a sector-level entity. An important role of the sector council is to represent the macro-level issues in the industry to government, to subsectors, and to related industries.

The function of the sector council is threefold:

- Address the human resource issues of the sector on an ongoing basis.
- Develop, market, and deliver products and services to implement human resource planning on a cost-recovery basis (i.e., basic costs of development and delivery plus adequate overhead expenses to ensure continuation of the program as long as it is needed).
- Carry out an advocacy role within the sector and with all levels of government to provide advice to stakeholders within the sector.

A sector council is not intended to usurp the specific roles of its members. Thus, collective bargaining in industries where unions exist will still be handled separately by the bargaining parties, in the manner to which they have agreed. A sector council is not designed to resolve disputes. However, where there are problems with the collective bargaining mechanism, a sector council may be used to discuss and build consensus about solutions designed to improve the collective bargaining relationship. Finally, a sector council is not a lobbying organization. However, it is a useful tool for developing consultative partnerships with government in order to ensure policies that serve the common needs of the subsector groups represented by the sector council, and it helps government to introduce appropriate regulatory measures to protect all its constituents.

In terms of structure, the bipartite (or multipartite) nature of the sector council membership is its distinguishing feature. The membership in a sector council must build in the central alliance of businesses and, where relevant, labour organizations and other groups as appropriate in the given industry. In order to consider strategic issues, a sector council must assemble an appropriate selection of senior players from the entire spectrum of the industry instead of relying solely on groups representing labour and management. Members should be selected to serve on the council by their own constituencies in equitable proportion. Normally, in a sector council serving an industry with significant union representation of the workforce, equal numbers of seats are reserved for business and labour representatives, with the balance of seats distributed among other interests groups and, in some cases, government officials. Through this kind of structure, joint decisions are encouraged where possible. The theme of employee participation in sector-level leadership is an important aspect of the sector council model. Since a more productive and harmonious relationship between workers and employers usually increases productivity and contributes to a more competitive industry, various sector-level labour-management initiatives and services could be developed under the auspices of the sector council that incorporate both worker and management direction. A neutral chair, or labour-management co-chair mechanism, may be used to break decision-making deadlocks as necessary.

The sector council is also in a position to work with government and educational institutions on policy developments. This is achieved by ensuring that the sector council staff have strong working relationships with the appropriate government agents (in the bureaucracy), and that the sector council's board of directors (as senior industry leaders) establishes its own relationship with the politicians. In this way, the sector council can become an effective strategic vehicle for education, research, benchmarking, and public policy development.

In order for the sector council to successfully perform its role, it must have solid revenue resources. Without some degree of certainty that the ongoing costs of the council will be supported by committed funding sources, it is impossible for a sector council to contemplate issues in the long-term, strategic manner prescribed. Second, its funding sources should be arranged to shift over time from the public to the private sector, from private sources according to the benefit derived from the sector council's work, with the leading organizations in the industry perhaps playing an additional lead sponsorship role. Where direct service delivery is part of the sector council's mandate, a fee-for-service arrangement further encourages the relationship between the flow of benefits and the burden of costs.

The legal status of a sector council may vary, but a nonprofit society with open, inclusive membership policies is recommended. The constitution and bylaws governing its internal workings must be developed and agreed to by the private parties involved. Government support, even to the extent of legislating the existence of the sector council, should be built in after this initial level of agreement is reached between the lead founding members of the council.

In order for a sector council to be successful, it must develop comprehensive representation from the entire industry over time. A well-functioning sector council also enjoys the benefits of subsector representation, as it can address the needs of a number of subsectors by focusing on the generic issues and providing services or promoting to government a change in policy from which all subsectors will benefit. At the same time, the sector council model does not have to face the challenges of fragmentation and potential conflicts resulting from the coexistence of a large number of pluralistic subsector organizations. While subsectors can be specifically represented as such on the board of directors, this should not limit the board members' responsibilities to the sector as a whole.

A sector council model represents a private value-maximizing type of governance that promotes the interests of the whole industry rather than an immediate benefit to a particular member entity. Sector councils are multipartite and demonstrate the kind of strategic leadership that is possible when subsectors agree to delegate the level of interaction with government to that single coordinated body. The benefits are wide-ranging, and include not only access to government through the association but also identifying joint venture and investment opportunities and potential employees, optimal pooling of public and private resources for sectoral development and identification of synergies among members for firm-level development.

Sectoral organization and mobilization is a complex agenda. A number of key factors must be in place in order for a sectoral organization to succeed to the full extent of its mandate. Several industry members must be strong advocates for the success of the council. It is through their leadership that other, possibly subsector-focused individuals can be brought to the table to explore and experience the opportunity. The industry itself must be sufficiently buoyant that its members have time to contribute to an industry association.

For members to be attracted to the sector council, individual enterprises must believe in the benefits to be derived from working together as an industry and speaking with one voice not only to government but also to the rest of the industry, related industries, and subsector associations. Subsectors must also see the benefit of a sectoral organization and be willing to provide input on their particular needs as a way of addressing the needs of the entire industry.

The Experience of the British Columbia Seafood Sector Council: An Instrument of Sectoral Self-Governance

Over the past five years, the development of the British Columbia Seafood Sector Council (BCSSC) has provided useful lessons for any sector that wishes to engage in this kind of sector-level activity. In order for the BCSSC to attract members, its strategy was to focus in its early years on issues of common industry concerns about which there was little potential disagreement or controversy. Accordingly, the projects undertaken in the initial life of the BCSSC dealt with human resource skills enhancement, productivity and new work joint consultation training to achieve minimum standards in seafood processing required under international trade law. Most of these programs involved training workers in various producing regions along the West Coast in conjunction with local community and technical colleges delivery systems. Many industry participants were assisted by the BCSSC before choosing whether to become dues-paying members. This made the decision to join easier because they had already experienced the benefits of BCSSC services. These BCSSC-sponsored training programs enhanced the skills levels of individual firms and the British Columbia seafood processing sector generally, and brought together management and workers in the common cause of investing in the human capital of the industry.

From the perspective of corporate governance, there were really no conflict-of-interest issues between shareholders and industry interests with respect to these human resource skills enhancement programs. Consequently, it was an easy decision for managers to participate in these programs and to require their workforce to participate in them, because many of the skill sets involved were required by international trade rules from foreign markets for British Columbia seafood products.

The second phase of the BCSSC development involved the delivery of much more firm-specific value-adding consultation services through the efforts of the BCSSC's Director of Business Development. These kinds of consultation services were often delivered in a public/private partnership model in collaboration with British Columbia Ministry of Fisheries personnel. Often, these services were provided to firms facing closure because of the decline of wild salmon stocks. The consultation services helped the target company reassess its current business plan, make necessary adjustments, and find the appropriate tools to develop new products or to process different species in order to survive in the volatile seafood business. In every case, the consultant team was made privy to very confidential firm-specific information that could not be shared with any other members of the BCSSC. In the BCSSC's entire existence, private information has remained private and proprietary, and there has been no breach of confidentiality. Thus, much of this firm-specific business development diversification and value-added product development work involves information that cannot be shared, and member companies rest comfortably knowing that their private information is never divulged.

The growing treasure chest of ideas, information, and analysis about what works and what does not work at the individual firm level has accumulated initially in the person of the BCSSC's Director of Business Development and ultimately in the institutional memory of BCSSC staff generally. This expertise is then delivered to industry clients requiring these services by a variety of BCSSC paid consultants. Because the specific identity of the source of the industry knowledge base is always kept private, there have been no conflicts or tensions in firm-level clients' decision making about whether to divulge private information. The use of this information, however, serves the greater industry goals of enhancing other firms' chances of survival and profitability.

Ultimately, the BCSSC has developed a reservoir of data and analysis that has formed the basis for more generic private advice to clients. In many cases, BCSSC members also receive advice through public educational programs about how to manage change and prosper in the new competitive marketplace. These micro-level experiences become more macro-level tried and true business strategies by being shared among all industry members, with utmost care being taken not to breach client confidentiality.

The kind of firm-level analysis that has been acquired by BCSSC-sponsored consultants providing the full range of services ultimately available through the Council has now grown to include human resource matters such as labour-management relations, workers compensation, health and safety, and more product-focused expertise such as product handling, equipment purchasing, access to financial support through the myriad of government programs, and generic information for potential new markets for client products. The BCSSC has now developed programs in technology transfer and sponsors members and consultants who visit plants and attend conferences in other jurisdictions to acquire knowledge and contacts for human development. The precondition for participation in these missions is that members will share all nonproprietary information with their colleagues in the British Columbia industry. The experience has been that participants have little difficulty distinguishing which information acquired is private and proprietary, and which should be shared through the public education and communication services of the Council. As members have gained more experience with these technology transfer missions, they have become more comfortable with sharing not only information gained in these programs but also their own firms' repository of information that might be relevant to fellow industry participants. Not surprisingly, the one area where members do not divulge much information is in new product development, where "first to market" tends to require such confidentiality.

One valuable by-product of the wide range of group activities sponsored by the BCSSC is the new or deeper relationships that participants develop in these programs. This kind of industry-level contact has spawned a variety of joint ventures and value chains as members experience the benefit of teaming up with other industry participants to pool resources, create economies of scale and share common experiences of how to access financing or government assistance. Consequently, in a host of areas, members can promote the interests of individual firm shareholders by participating in sector-level programs. This has spawned new subgroup activities, where various producers of similar specialty products (for example, smoked salmon) have teamed up to share new market information about nontariff trade barriers and generic labelling. Through this kind of contact at the industry level, synergies can be identified and pursued. Likewise, these industry-level contacts help companies avoid the waste and mistakes that are more likely to occur if a firm operates alone, without the benefit of industry support.

In summary, an industry-level entity such as the BCSSC can be a valuable resource to individual firms, who gain knowledge and contacts that enable them to make informed decisions, taking into account a broad range of stakeholder interests. In this way, the time and experience of participating in sector-level activity pays dividends if a sufficient number of firms actively engage in these activities, thereby generating the critical mass of activity necessary to sustain the sector council itself.

The alternative to the above-noted approaches is to continue to operate as an "island unto oneself." Unfortunately, the tendency in this case is that when things go wrong, and other stakeholders are negatively affected by a firm's decisions, those suffering are likely to call for more intrusive government regulation of all firms in the sector or region, depending on the nature of the harm caused.

The sector council approach provides a useful alternative to more government regulation for an industry that would like to engage in sector self-governance. A defined structure with an effective ongoing public/private working relationship with government bureaucracy, as seen in the BCSSC experience, makes it far easier for government to rely on industry peer pressure to encourage industry participants to adhere to best practices that are regularly discussed at industry-sponsored events. The payback for this level of industry participation may take the form of government's allowing industry to conduct its business pursuant to market demands.

The Emergence of Value Chains

One of the important recent initiatives in the sector council's development has been the value chain program. Value chains involve a minimum of three businesses that form a strategic collaboration for the purpose of meeting specific market objectives over the longer term and for the mutual benefit of all links of the chain. As will be discussed here, a value chain can provide both an effective business response and an effective sectoral strategy to enhance the overall productivity of the industry.

The presence of a sector-level entity such as the sector council can contribute significantly to the success of value chains as a useful new tool in sectoral development. This is not to say, however, that other forms of business-to-business structures should be disregarded. The path to value chains typically begins with the identification of sector-wide issues or issues among traditional business partners. The coexistence of an industry-level structure with other forms of business organization models, such as vertically integrated companies and supply chains, increases industry competitiveness by linking a greater number of structurally different players to market-driven issues.

Value Chains: General Observations

Corporate decision making involves choosing appropriate business-to-business development strategies. Several models are being pursued by businesses; the two most prevalent are the vertical integration model and the supply chain model. As the appetite for implementing collaborative business practices grows, however, the elements of a value chain model are starting to develop through industries to replace these traditional business models.

Value chains are a substantively different approach to business network relations. The key focus in this business strategy is the need to send information through a system to better enable the various links to respond to a client. The value chain model (like the supply chain) is market-driven. However, value chains differ in that they are based on the idea that the competitive advantage is gained through collaboration and negotiation *as partners*. This design enables the "chain" businesses to respond to the demands of the customer more effectively and efficiently while retaining their autonomy from larger corporations. It helps firms increase competitiveness by either reducing operating costs or improving services such as distribution, inventory management, or communication, and by allowing value chain participants to focus on their individual core competencies. The disadvantage of this business strategy is that it is aimed at the long-term benefit of all parties, rather than the maximization of the immediate individual profits of chain members. The success of these systems depends on the degree to which value chain shareholders buy into the strategy that by sharing information and collaborating to solve problems, everyone benefits in the long run. Further, value chain participants must also wrestle with the possibility – as experience has suggested – that the benefits of value chains may not be realized in the pricing structure but are more likely to come from nonprice issues such as efficient consumer response, longer-term contracts, guaranteed supply, and reduced inventory levels, all of which affect the bottom line and therefore the net profit of all value chain members.

Several factors have been identified as being essential to the development of a value chain initiative: a committed individual who identifies an opportunity for his or her business and becomes the proponent and leader of the chain development; knowledge about markets, technology, and organizational innovation; the ability to cooperate with other companies or organizations to create win-win situations; information systems and a sharing attitude for intra-chain communications; the capability to change faster and to continuously adapt to the changing environment; and skilled and objective third-party management assistance, hired from outside the chain. This third-party facilitation gives all the chain players an equal opportunity to air their concerns and search for a mutually beneficial strategy.

British Columbia Seafood Processing Industry Experience

Systems based at the sector level create value by linking business, government, and academia. Business strategies at the simplest level of value chain create firm-to-firm links from harvest to consumption. The British Columbia Seafood Sector Council (BCSSC) has played a value-chain-style role by bringing diverse groups together to engage in a consensus-based dialogue aimed at taking action to respond to seafood processing industry issues. The key to the success of these meetings has been the focus on information sharing and collaboration on projects identified as broadly based and mutually beneficial to the industry as a whole, such as industry training and education, value-added production, and technology transfer. Seafood processing industry stakeholders have consistently expressed their interest in the concept of value chains. This, combined with the lively interest in worldwide value chains, in particular in the agri-food industry, points to tremendous potential opportunities for the British Columbia seafood processing industry if it can successfully deploy value chain strategies.

The seafood sector, however, has a number of characteristics that result in special challenges to value chain formation. Perhaps more than any other industry, access to the resource is tightly regulated, products are highly perishable in nature, and the industry has a distinct commodity orientation. Value chains nevertheless constitute an effective business response mechanism to several emerging market drivers in the seafood processing industry, including quality assurance, food safety, consumer communications, new markets, animal and social welfare, environmental impact, production life cycles, and profit margins. Several important development issues have been identified as a result of activities conducted to introduce the value chain concept and to initiate the development of value chains in the British Columbia seafood processing industry.

The value chain strategy is a process or system for collaboration among existing enterprises, but it does not necessarily follow that the businesses interested in investigating value chains are operating successfully. In fact, the need to form a value chain may often arise out of a crisis in the industry or subsector. The purpose of a value chain, then, is not to enhance the individual links in the chain but rather to create a tool to enhance interaction among a group of existing enterprises in relation to a particular issue or need that has been broadly identified by a sufficient number of businesses in the industry who want to band together in order to meet a particular challenge. The formation of a value chain is based on several readiness factors: the enterprise must already be operational in order to fully participate in a value chain; the links must be actively involved in delivering a specific core product or service; one individual must promote and drive the formation of the chain; and the participants must adjust their view of business relationships to a collaborative business management approach.

The collaborating enterprises or agencies must agree on a clear end product or goal such as market differentiation, logistical efficiencies, or quality control. One of the major challenges that the British Columbia seafood processing industry faces is the fact that a single enterprise may not have the capacity to provide adequate product to a particular market, as this capacity may be dependent upon the availability of the resource. For example, in recent years, several British Columbia companies producing groundfish worked together to supply a particular market, but the project never became a fully operational value chain. Nevertheless, by pooling their resources, they did develop a business network wherein they were able to ensure a level of supply to satisfy the end user. With the implementation of a value chain approach, companies become even more interdependent, and as such, they can provide a level of reassurance to the end user, which when combined with other criteria for quality control, results in an even more successful long-term business relationship.

The first step in initiating value chains is to educate potential stakeholders through public and private information sessions about the process, benefits, and challenges before they begin to invest time and effort in an actual value chain. Some of the common challenges and opportunities that lead enterprises to work together strategically in a chain format have been identified in the agri-food, high tech, automotive, health care, and forestry sectors. These challenges include intense competition for limited resources such as land, water, energy, and naturally occurring plants and animals. The demand is high for specialized services, transportation, and skilled labour. There is also a need for cost-effective production. With the value chain approach, it is possible to develop strategies to optimize the sustainable use of these resources to the mutual benefit of all users.

Future Role of the British Columbia Seafood Sector Council with Respect to Value Chains: Developing Self-Sufficiency

Having benefited from the BCSSC's value chain development services, each value chain that reaches the commercialization stage will be asked to make a financial contribution to the Council to pay for the development of new value chains. This ongoing contribution is a key factor in the sector council's ongoing move towards full self-sufficiency. The value chain development initiatives of the BCSSC were supported initially by government funds but ultimately must become self-financing. On an ongoing basis, value chains will require industry, government, and academia (i.e., research and educational institutions) to work together to form new and more collaborative alliances. A key objective of the BCSSC is to maintain its important role of assisting businesses in the industry to work together through BCSSC initiatives to help businesses develop new strategies, business alliances, and the management expertise to support other initiatives.

In summary, the first requirement for any value chain is that an individual identifies an opportunity for his or her business and becomes a committed proponent and leader of the chain development. Second, it is important that third-party chain management be brought to the potential chain at the earliest opportunity. A skilled facilitator with knowledge of the value chain development process can keep the project on track and often move the stakeholders through difficult stages, including the development of trust and the negotiation of the many business commitments that comprise the chain.

Further work is required to complete the pilot projects now under development in British Columbia. The nature of the seafood processing industry is such that partners in several chain pilot projects that are operating but that are not yet secure in capturing their desired market response are still unwilling to discuss their plans publicly. They have agreed, however, to share their experience with the industry once the pilot projects are completed and the chains are fully operational (and the customers are in the bag!).

Various strategies being contemplated by industry, government, and agencies would provide several viable opportunities to proceed with this new value chain business strategy in a regional context. These are discussed in the following section. What has been demonstrated to date is that the participants in the BCSSC value chain pilot projects are extremely pleased with the results of their newfound business strategy.

Value Chains in the Regional Context

The reason for a regional sectoral development process is to pursue a regional economic development strategy for a certain industry based on the ideas and experience of stakeholders living and working in the particular region. As previously indicated, the third-party facilitation and management services available through a sector council, utilizing a value chain mechanism where appropriate, can be most beneficial.

The Mount Waddington Regional Project[8] tested the idea in practice. It brought together the various stakeholder groups in the Mount Waddington Regional District in north Vancouver Island in order to determine how they could work together for their mutual benefit, rather than (as has traditionally been the case) acting in relative isolation in responding to challenges facing their particular business operation or the seafood processing industry generally in their producing region.

The ensuing report, *Pulling Together: A Regional Seafood Economic Development Strategy for the Mount Waddington Regional District,*[9] is a template for sustainable regional economic development in the seafood processing industry in this region. The theoretical approach and the development process in this region are transferable to other regions as well as other industries where there is the need and desire for businesses in a region to act in a synchronized and collaborative manner.

The lessons learned from this experience about the process of creating a regional sectoral development strategy are as follows:

- The process should be driven from the bottom up rather than from the top down.
- Leadership within the community and within local industry must commit to promoting the process.
- A pilot project should be established as an outcome, whereby aspects of the development strategy can be implemented in an incremental fashion.

At the outset of the project, regional seafood industry participants identified three common obstacles to industry development in the north Island region: poor industry/government relations and industry regulations that are out of step with industry needs and present realities; short-term opportunistic behaviour by industry participants; and inadequate human and financial resources.

The outcome of the process was that the regional participants were able to come to a shared vision of where they wished to go as a regional production centre and what steps businesses individually and as a group needed to take in order to move ahead. What is apparent is that these discrete businesses were able to identify how they would benefit in the longer term if they could find ways to cooperate in building their regional capacity to produce at world-class standards and to get this product to market by forming value and supply chains in order to realize their optimal potential. In the myriad of individual contractual negotiations that are needed to form this integrated web of supply and value chains, these businesses must be conscious of the need to preserve the chain as a whole and not simply to maximize their firm's own advantage to the detriment of other businesses in the regional seafood processing industry. The whole of the regional seafood processing industry is greater than the sum of its parts.

The iterative participatory process of this initiative, which involved scores of meetings between the BCSSC and individuals and groups involved in the North Island seafood processing industry, culminated in a vision, shared by regional processors and suppliers, of the direction in which they wished to lead their regional industry. In addition, participants described what each was prepared to do to implement this shared purpose. In this way, the elements of a regional seafood economic development strategy were identified. The key aspects of the strategy were diversification, integration, collaboration, and sustainability. Towards the culmination of the project, the formation of an aquatic resources processors working group within a regional seafood development facility provided a crucial mechanism for the further pursuit of this emerging regional seafood development strategy.

The processors were able to come to a shared sense of the optimal sectoral strategy for their industry because through the course of this project they came to appreciate that by acting in concert with other firms in the region, they would be much stronger than if they pursued their individual business plans. Each of the processors realized that they could be very good at some discrete aspects of seafood processing and that they need not be a jack of all trades. None had the desire or the resources to go it alone. Rather, these individual firms chose to see themselves as part of a diversified, integrated regional industry that could operate through supply chains or value chain systems that would enable them to maximize returns from their individual contributions to these larger business networks. It is important to note that although the larger firms in the process were already involved in supply chains, they engaged in value chain development. As a result of their investment in this project, they became much more knowledgeable about value chains and consequently much more amenable to participating in these business-to-business relationships if it meant that the region as a whole would benefit.

In order for these business networks to function effectively so that no individual participant took undue advantage of its position in the network to the detriment of the whole, it was crucial that every participant share the same vision of how these business networks should operate within a greater regional seafood development strategy. Maintaining these inter-corporate links required facilitation by skilled supply chain or value chain managers. In this way, individual contractual relationships could be conducted within the overlay of the broader chain dynamic and be consistent with the even larger regional seafood development strategy.

From the perspective of corporate governance, it is apparent that the businesses involved in the development of this regional seafood strategy were able to see beyond their own firm's immediate needs and to collectively grasp the potential advantages that are possible if the various firms in the regional sector work together. Each firm needs to show restraint in optimizing its position in various contractual arrangements that will form the web of this regional seafood production engine. From the perspective of shareholder interests, managers and directors of these firms need to have an accurate grasp of how their firms fit into the larger strategy in order to exercise appropriate judgment on how to advance the fortunes of their firms in the context of the larger agenda. With the assistance of the facilitators who managed the process, the participants were able to see themselves as part of a larger production community and to understand that their shareholders' interests were well served by building on individual strengths in the development of this greater regional production facility. This attitude could be viewed as the embodiment of corporate social responsibility values and principles. These neighbours in the north Island region saw it simply as good business.

Conclusion

The European Commission Green Paper and the Broadbent-Bennett Commission Report illustrate the growing public support for government regulation to promote more corporate social responsibility. This movement reflects the concern that corporate decision making that responds solely to the objective of increasing profits may be problematic for an increasingly integrated global economy.

When the corporate social responsibility worldview is dissected, it advocates that firms take into account nonshareholder interests, including stakeholders such as employees, local communities, and their industry participants. Advocates of corporate social responsibility encourage government to regulate corporate behaviour by such processes as regular social audits so that the goals of corporate social responsibility are advanced in corporate decision making. Opponents of this view argue that this approach amounts to a confiscation of shareholder interests in favour of nonshareholder stakeholders.

Based on the experience of the British Columbia seafood processing sector over the past ten years, many of the goals of corporate social responsibility, such as the need to take into account the interests of employees, fellow sector participants, and communities, have been promoted by the seafood processing industry participants solely for the purpose of enhancing shareholder value in their particular enterprise. In no case was shareholder value (looked at within a reasonable time frame) diluted as a result of the collaborative behaviour both within firms and within industries that is described in this chapter. In every case, firms reacted to market dictates by engaging in consultative and collaborative activities that encompassed a broader range of participants in the decision-making process either as decision makers or at the very least as information providers.

The net effect of this more collaborative decision-making process is that this sector has gone through an extremely difficult restructuring and refocusing period without collapsing, despite the extremely volatile nature of its resources and markets. As a result of new public and private working relationships, the transition has been proceeding without a net loss in the value of production in the sector. This transition experience of the industry has been helped by the fact that new mechanisms of consultation and collaboration have emerged, both internal and external to the seafood processing companies. These collaborative structures, which have enabled more informed decisions by individual firms, have successfully lubricated the restructuring of the sector. These mechanisms have been not foisted on the industry through any government regulation. Rather, they have been piloted and tested (with the help of some initial government subsidy) and then left to survive in the marketplace of ideas and systems. They have survived because they have proved to be valuable to the firms and other organizations that comprise this industry. In this way, the industry has taken important steps towards self-governance rather than succumb to more top-down, government-imposed regulation. In the process, British Columbia seafood sector firms have shown that the goals of corporate social responsibility can be advanced because of their direct economic value to shareholders. Their contribution to the overall social welfare is a bonus, not the raison d'être for these activities. It is their contribution to the bottom line of the balance sheet that has provided the sustaining power for these collaborative decision-making processes.

Acknowledgment
We would like to thank Lenka Radkova of the University of British Columbia Faculty of Law for her extremely helpful research and editing assistance.

Notes
1 European Commission, *Promoting a European Framework for Corporate Social Responsibility*, Green Paper of the European Commission (July 2001), <http://europa.eu.int./comm.off/green/index_en.htm#2001>.
2 Canadian Democracy and Corporate Accountability Commission, *The New Balance Sheet: Corporate Profits and Responsibility in the 21st Century*, Final Report (January 2002), <http://www.corporate-accountability.ca>.
3 See European Commission, *supra* note 1; Canadian Democracy and Accountability Commission, *ibid.*

4 Fish Processing Strategic Task Force, *Building a Sustainable Fishing Industry: A Sectoral Strategy for Prosperity and Resource Health* (October 1994) (Co-chairs: Don Millerd and Jack Nichol) [unpublished, on file with authors].
5 J. Markus and K. Porter, Growing Into Ownership: Employee Ownership and Investment Association (1997) at 7 [unpublished, on file with authors].
6 *British Columbia Labour Relations Code*, R.S.B.C. 1996, c. 224.
7 Labour Relations Code Review Committee, *Managing Change in Labour Relations*, Final Report (Victoria: Minister of Labour, 25 February 1998).
8 British Columbia Seafood Sector Council North Island Project (OP 042) [unpublished, on file with authors].
9 J.P. Weiler, *Pulling Together: A Regional Seafood Economic Development Strategy for the Mount Waddington Regional District* (British Columbia Seafood Sector Council, June 2001) [unpublished].

Part 4
Governance of the Financially Distressed Corporation

11

Under Pressure: Governance of the Financially Distressed Corporation
Geoffrey B. Morawetz

One might think that a director would never be in a more vulnerable position than when he or she is on the board of a corporation in formal restructuring proceedings. In fact, that is not the case. Once a corporation has filed for creditor protection under the *Bankruptcy and Insolvency Act (BIA)*[1] or the *Companies' Creditors Arrangement Act (CCAA),*[2] the pressure on a director is substantially alleviated. Director decision making under the *BIA* or the *CCAA* becomes less relevant because most of the decisions made by the board are subject to scrutiny and review by creditors or their representatives and, in certain circumstances, approval by the court. Directors may also be protected by compromises of claims against them that arose before the commencement of proceedings.[3] It is also common to find a first-ranking director's charge in *CCAA* proceedings to cover certain liabilities that could result in personal liability for directors in the event that the restructuring does not succeed.

It is the pre-filing stage of insolvency that finds directors sitting in the hottest seats. Actions taken by the board of a financially distressed corporation prior to formal insolvency proceedings are made without the safety net of court approval and will receive heightened scrutiny by corporate stakeholders if they prove unsuccessful. In particular, creditors will examine every significant decision made by the board in search of sources of recovery of their consequent losses.

Directors' Fiduciary Duties
It is settled law that the primary duty of directors is to act "in the best interests of the corporation." Courts have held that to act in the best interests of the corporation is to maximize profits for the indirect benefit of shareholders who are the corporation's owners. Directors, who are elected by shareholders, could likewise be replaced by shareholders and are well advised to make shareholder interests paramount when the corporation is solvent.

The standard against which directors' fiduciary duties will be measured is articulated in federal and provincial corporate statutes. Pursuant to Section 122(1) of the *Canada Business Corporations Act*,[4] every director or officer of a corporation must act honestly and in good faith, and exercise the care, diligence, and skill that a reasonably prudent person would exercise in comparable circumstances. The standard, therefore, is a blended objective and subjective one.

Unfortunately, in a context where directors are called on to make decisions that will bear on the very existence of the corporation, there is very little guidance for them. The legal standards against which their actions are measured are unclear, yet the scope of their responsibility arguably widens. Exacerbating the uncertainty is the need for directors to identify the point at which the corporation has entered the "vicinity of insolvency." Traditionally, insolvency has been defined as the point at which a corporation is unable to pay its debts or the corporation's liabilities exceed its assets at a fair valuation. Under this test, a corporation can be insolvent even if it has not commenced proceedings under the *BIA* or the *CCAA*.[5]

Corporate Stakeholders: To Whom Directors' Duties Are Owed

When a corporation is in the vicinity of insolvency, it is a challenge for a board to identify to whom their fiduciary duties are owed. It is clear that when the corporation is solvent, shareholder interests in the going-concern value of the corporation are paramount, but as the equity value in the corporation erodes, shareholder interests become less of a priority and the interests of other stakeholders take the spotlight. The fiduciary standard becomes whether the directors acted in the best interests of the corporation having regard to the interests of those stakeholders who have claims on the residual value of the assets of the corporation, namely the creditors.[6]

For several years, British, Australian, and American courts have held that, at least where a corporation is insolvent or near insolvency, directors must consider the interests of creditors. The recognition of creditor rights is articulated in the Australian case of *Walker* v. *Wimborne*.[7] In that case, Mr. Justice Mason (as he then was) stated that the directors' duty to a corporation as a whole extends in an insolvency context to not prejudicing the interests of creditors. The English court approved the Australian approach in *Winkworth* v. *Edward Baron Development Co. Ltd. et al.*[8]

The cases extending the principle of a fiduciary duty to creditors recognize that creditors are particularly vulnerable at this stage, because they lack the information that directors and officers have with respect to the distressed state of the corporation. Directors who are in the best position to protect the value of the assets available to creditors could use their exclusive knowledge to the disadvantage of creditors.[9] For example, directors could misrepresent the financial situation of the corporation to obtain additional financing or credit, or continue to place orders for supplies knowing that the corporation cannot afford them. Directors could take actions that have the effect of depleting the security held by creditors.

Although to date Canadian courts have stopped short of identifying a direct duty to creditors of financially distressed corporations, they have encouraged directors to have regard to the interests of creditors as residual claimants to the value of assets of the insolvent corporation.[10] In *Peoples Department Stores Inc.* v. *Wise*,[11] Mr. Justice Greenberg of the Quebec Superior Court found that as the corporation approaches insolvency, directors' and officers' fiduciary obligations expand to consider the interests of creditors as claimants to the residual value of the assets of the corporation. In *Peoples*, the Court held that the directors ought to have known that their decisions regarding the domestic inventory procurement policy that benefited the parent company without value to the subsidiary were likely to cause a loss to creditors or threaten the continued existence of the company. The directors have an obligation to ensure that an insolvent corporation is properly administered and that its assets are not dissipated or exploited in a manner that is prejudicial to creditors, because only creditors have a meaningful stake in the assets.[12] Similarly, in *Canbook Distribution Corporation* v. *Borins*,[13] the Ontario Superior Court of Justice held that the law in Canada appears to be moving in the direction of recognizing a fiduciary duty to creditors. This is especially applicable in a situation in which a transaction was entered into, which in itself rendered the corporation insolvent.[14]

Remedies Available to Stakeholders against Directors

Oppression Remedy
Whether or not it is determined that directors owe a fiduciary duty to creditors, directors should be mindful of the fact that the oppression remedy operates as a statutory lifting of the corporate veil for conduct of directors that is oppressive, unfairly prejudicial to the interests of stakeholders, or unfairly disregards the interests of stakeholders.[15]

An oppression action may be brought by those who can be defined as a complainant. "Complainant" has been broadly construed in the case law to include creditors.[16] The court in *Levy-Russell*[17] set out the criteria for granting status to creditors under oppression provisions. The creditor must be in a position that is analogous to that of a minority shareholder in that it has a particular legitimate interest in how the corporation is being managed or has a direct financial interest in the way the directors are conducting the business of the corporation. The court will decline to grant status where the interest is too remote, where the creditor is not proceeding in good faith, where the complainant was not a creditor at the time of the impugned action, or where the acts complained of have nothing to do with debt.[18]

As well, in determining complainant status, the court will have regard to whether there has been unfair prejudice resulting from the protection of the underlying expectation of the creditor in its arrangement with the corporation, whether the acts complained of were foreseeable, whether the creditor could reasonably have protected itself from the directors' acts, and whether the actions resulted in a detriment to the interests of the creditor.[19] When oppressive conduct has occurred, the court has a very broad discretionary power "to make an order to rectify the matters complained of."[20] In *Sidaplex*, the Ontario Court of Appeal held that it is appropriate, where circumstances warrant, to require the corporation's directors and officers to pay a creditor.[21] In that case, a judgment creditor was secured via a letter of credit that was intended to be renewable automatically. Through inadvertence, the letter of credit was for a fixed term, and when it expired, the judgment creditor's debt was left unsecured. Subsequently, the sole director and officer sold the bulk of the corporation's assets. The proceeds of the sale were used to satisfy the corporation's indebtedness to the bank, thereby eliminating the sole director's liability to the bank and satisfying other indebtedness. The judgment creditor's debt was not satisfied and the corporation was left with no assets. The Court ordered the sole director to pay the creditor the amount owing.

It is expected that the use of the oppression remedy will increase over the next few years, whether it is used on its own or in conjunction with other creditor remedies under insolvency statutes such as the *BIA*. Two Ontario decisions in insolvency cases have broadened the opportunities to utilize the oppression remedy.

The first was the 1997 decision of *Re Sammi Atlas Inc.*[22] Sammi Atlas Inc. (Sammi) had filed for protection under the *CCAA*. A Trade Creditors' Committee (TCC) was established pursuant to an order of Mr. Justice Houlden, with a mandate to represent the trade creditors of Sammi. During the course of the *CCAA* proceedings, the TCC became concerned over past conduct that Sammi had been engaged in with its American affiliate, Al Tech. There was concern that over a period of years, Sammi sold products to Al Tech, with which it shared certain elements of management, for significantly more money than it collected. The TCC wished to bring an action against certain directors and officers of Sammi for allowing this situation to develop and not taking corrective action on a timely basis.

After reviewing the order that established the TCC, as well as the evidence in support of the application, Mr. Justice Farley of the Ontario Superior Court concluded that the TCC was a "proper person" to take on the role of "complainant" concerning the Al Tech situation. Having determined that the TCC was to be given the status of complainant, the Court also found it appropriate to lift the *CCAA* stay of proceedings to allow the TCC to give notice of its intention to bring an action if Sammi did not. Although this action did not proceed to the point of being decided on the merits, the decision does sound a warning to directors and officers that they should be mindful of creditor interests in discharging their duties.

The second case arose out of the 1992 *CCAA* proceedings filed by Olympia & York Developments Ltd. (OYDL). OYDL initially filed for protection under the *CCAA,* but by 1996 the proceedings had been transferred from the *CCAA* to the *BIA.* An action was subsequently commenced by the trustee in bankruptcy of OYDL against certain subsidiaries of OYDL and the trustee relied upon the reviewable transaction provisions of the *BIA* and the oppression provisions of the *Business Corporations Act* (Ontario).The facts giving rise to the cause of action are very complicated, and in order to appreciate the decision of Mr. Justice Farley (which is currently under appeal), it is necessary to reproduce the annotation that this author submitted to *Canadian Bankruptcy Reports.*[23] At the opening of business on 16 March 1992:

(i)   Olympia & York Developments Limited (OYDL) owned 100 percent of the common shares of Olympia & York Realty Corp. (OYRC) and OYRC owned 100 percent of the shares of Olympia & York SF Holdings Corporation (OYSF).

(ii)   OYSF owed OYDL approximately $391 million under a promissory note from OYSF to OYDL (OYSF Note).

(iii) OYSF had provided non-recourse guarantees to a number of financial institutions which had made advances to OYDL and had pledged marketable securities to support its guarantees.

(iv)   OYSF had entered into a Custodial and Pledge Agreement with the European Investment Bank (EIB) under which OYSF had deposited with EIB marketable securities to support a guarantee of a loan facility made by EIB to an OYDL entity. The Agreement provided that the securities deposited by OYSF were not to constitute a security interest in favour of EIB until an attachment event or an event of default occurred, including an insolvency of OYDL.

(v)   OYRC owed Citibank approximately US $250 million.

On March 16, 1992 OYSF provided a solvency certificate to HongKong Bank of Canada in support of its guarantee of a $25 million loan facility from HongKong Bank to OYDL.

On March 16, 1992, and prior to giving the solvency certificate to HongKong Bank, a complicated transaction (Transaction) was entered into amongst OYDL, OYRC and OYSF under which new common shares of OYSF were issued to OYRC, new common shares of OYRC were issued to OYDL and the OYSF Note of $391 million to OYDL was retired by OYSF from the subscription price for the new common shares issued that day (a swap of equity for debt).

On May 14, 1992 OYDL, OYRC, OYSF and other companies filed for protection under the *CCAA*, and OYDL was eventually adjudged bankrupt. After the insolvency of OYDL, marketable securities worth approximately $612 million owned by OYSF and pledged to the financial institutions to support OYSF's guarantees of OYDL loan facilities were sold and the proceeds paid to the financial institutions.

The Trustee of OYDL claimed in this action that the Transaction under which the OYSF Note was retired should be reviewed or reversed and that the remaining cash assets of OYSF of approximately US $30 million should be paid to it as Trustee of OYDL. The Trustee claimed (i) under s. 100 of the *Bankruptcy and Insolvency Act* that the value of the OYSF Note was conspicuously greater than the value of the common shares of OYRC received by it in the Transaction (ii) that the Transaction was oppressive under s. 248 of the *OBCA* as disregarding the interests of the creditors of OYDL and (iii) that the Transaction was a fraudulent conveyance in favour of Citibank contrary to s. 95 of the *BIA*. The fraudulent conveyance claim was not advanced at the trial.

The defendant creditor interests of OYRC contended that the Transaction enhanced the equity interests of OYDL in OYRC, that OYRC, which held OYDL's US real estate interests, had value at the time of the Transaction and that OYDL received these enhanced equity interests in the Transaction. They also contended that even if OYSF owed $391 million to OYDL under the OYSF Note, there should be set off against that amount the amount of $612 million representing the value of the marketable securities owned by OYSF and sold to pay off OYDL loans guaranteed by OYSF and that therefore the OYSF Note had no value at the time it was retired in the Transaction. They further contended that any sale of the OYSF Note would have resulted in the bankruptcy of OYDL and that OYDL would therefore have never sold the OYSF Note.

While Citibank and Citibank Canada were not direct participants in this litigation, it was noted that Citibank ended up with a 25 percent interest in OYRC in the ultimate restructuring of OYDL's US real estate interests. Citibank was a significant creditor of OYRC at the relevant time, the size and percentage of such interest being sufficient to support the claim that Citibank was a privy of OYRC/OYDL.

OYDL need not have entered into the Transaction in order to obtain the balance of the $25 million credit from the HongKong Bank of Canada since that process was ostensibly entered into (solely) for the purpose of providing the Bank with the (unnecessary) solvency certificate; rather the money could have been obtained on the basis of the wholly owned subsidiary exception.

In addition, OYRC was a wholly owned "private" subsidiary of OYDL. Before the Transaction, OYDL owned 100 percent of OYRC and after the Transaction, it owned the same 100 percent. There was no value created which OYDL could have utilized (if OYDL had wished to sell (or pledge) the 30 percent of OYRC shares, then it could have done so by utilizing the same percentage out of its existing 100 percent ownership it had of OYRC prior to the transactions).

After reviewing the evidence, the trial judge held that there was a conspicuous difference in fair market value between what OYDL received for the OYSF Note and what the OYSF Note was worth (on a fair market value analysis) – namely OYDL received more shares of OYRC, but it already had 100 percent of this wholly owned subsidiary thus, no further value was put into OYRC and the 30 percent of OYRC shares that it received in addition carried with them no value in the sense that the original 100 percent of the shares were worth exactly the same as the 100 percent original shares plus the 30 percent, but in return for this "nothing," OYDL gave up a OYSF Note which, on the evidence, had a fair market value of some tens of millions of dollars and likely in the neighbourhood of some $30-$50 million.

In accordance with the requirements set out in *Standard Trustco Ltd. (Trustee of)* v. *Standard Trust Co.*,[24] the trial judge then reviewed the equities of the case and noted that the onus of raising equitable considerations and proving that they apply to the particular case must be borne by the party asserting them. The defendants, in this case, offered no reasonable explanation why the wholly owned subsidiary exemption was not put to HongKong Bank as a complete and absolute answer. The defendants also argued that OYDL was at best owed $390 million by OYSF, but that OYDL and its creditors took $611 million of OYSF's assets as security for OYDL's indebtedness, both direct and through its guarantees. However, this was a historical or in place situation and did not impact on the equities which must take what is in place as a given factor, before applying equity.

The trial judge was not persuaded that the defendants had done anything more than raise the issue of applying the equities as envisioned by Weiler J.A. in the *Standard Trustco* case. They did not put forward anything specific subject to some general comments concerning set-off which, in the view of the trial judge, were sufficiently dealt with in *Mitchell, Houghton Ltd.* v. *Mitchell, Houghton (Que.) Ltd.*[25] In this case, OYDL was owed $391 million by OYSF, but OYDL did not owe OYSF anything. The escrow pot only arose after the bankruptcy. Vis-à-vis the question of equitable set-off affecting fair market value of the OYSF Note and hypothetical or notional market, at the time of the assumed sale, OYSF would have no claim against OYDL.

The trial judge also held that a trustee in bankruptcy can be a "proper person" to bring an oppression claim pursuant to ss. 245-248 *OBCA*. While the bankrupt's trustee takes the property of the bankrupt as he finds it and the trustee stands in the shoes of the bankrupt, the trustee has, as its primary obligation, the protection of the creditors of the estate of the bankrupt. Where there is superadded to the equation allegations/facts to support one of the three claims of either (a) "oppression"; (b) "unfairly prejudicial"; or (c) "unfairly disregards," then creditors have been permitted to be complainants pursuant to s. 245(c) as a "proper person." If a creditor could bring such an oppression action, then the characterization of the trustee in bankruptcy as the creditors' representative should be recognized as allowing the trustee in bankruptcy to bring a "representative" oppression action on behalf of the creditors in a proper case.

While OYRC/OYSF did not as affiliates of OYRC oppress the creditors of OYDL, it was reasonable to conclude that they as affiliates participated in at least unfairly disregarding the interest of those creditors. OYRC/OYSF participated in the Transaction with, and at the behest of, OYDL. A better way of looking at the oppression side of this case (as opposed to the s. 100 *BIA* side) would be to visualize the creditors of OYDL suing not only OYRC and OYSF, but also OYDL. As a result of the Transaction, OYDL creditors were inappropriately deprived of the value of some US $22 million to which they would have otherwise been entitled – and which the creditors of OYRC/OYSF would not have been entitled to.

Held: – under either the s. 100 *BIA* claim or the oppression claim, the plaintiff trustee was entitled to the funds held in escrow of some US $22 million, plus interest.

Although this action was not brought against the directors of OYRC or OYSF, the case is nevertheless noteworthy as it specifically states that a trustee in bankruptcy can utilize the oppression provisions of the *OBCA*. A line of cases previously held that a trustee who steps into the shoes of the bankrupt could not challenge the conduct of the bankrupt that gave rise to the oppressive conduct.[26] The OYDL decision extends the role of the trustee to a party that can pursue an oppression remedy where the objective is to ensure *pari passu* treatment for creditors.

Derivative Action
Derivative actions, which involve a remedy for the benefit of the corporation as a whole, may also be instituted by creditors pursuant to Section 239 of the *CBCA*. The party seeking status must have given reasonable notice to the directors of the corporation or its subsidiary of the intention to apply to the court, the complainant must be acting in good faith, and the action

must appear to be in the interests of the corporation. In *Re Daon Development Corporation,* the court held that derivative actions are available only in very limited circumstances.[27] The interest of the creditor must be a direct financial interest or a particular legitimate interest in the manner in which the affairs of the corporation are being managed. The creditor seeking to bring the action must be in a position somewhat analogous to that of a minority shareholder where it has no right to influence management conduct it considers contrary to the corporation's interests.

The Extent of Director Liability
Following the collapse of the corporation, stakeholders, and in particular creditors, will consider taking remedial action against directors to recover their losses. Directors are exposed to liability from a number of provincial and federal statutes, some of which impose strict liability while others depend heavily on the directors' decision making while in the vicinity of insolvency.

Breach of Fiduciary Duty
It is no surprise that directors are at risk of being sued for failing to discharge their basic duties, namely, the duty to act in good faith while exercising due diligence. Directors should be aware that most companies are prohibited from indemnifying directors for a breach of fiduciary duty.[28]

Misrepresenting the Solvency of the Corporation
In the period prior to insolvency, there is considerable scope for wrongful conduct because directors and officers may know that the company is in financial distress but creditors may be left in the dark. Pursuant to Section 198(1)(d) of the *BIA,* directors of bankrupt companies are guilty of an offence, which may include a fine and/or a term of imprisonment, if any books or documents relating to the bankrupt corporation's property or affairs have been concealed, destroyed, mutilated, falsified, omitted, or disposed of, after or within one year preceding the date of an initial bankruptcy event.[29] The same is true where a bankrupt corporation obtains credit or property by false representations made by the bankrupt or by others with the bankrupt's knowledge, pursuant to Section 198(1)(e) of the *BIA.*[30] In order to obtain a conviction, the Crown must prove that at the time of the commission of the alleged offence, the director knew that the corporation would become bankrupt or was willfully blind to that situation.

The Ontario Court of Appeal in *NBD Bank, Canada* v. *Dofasco Inc.* (hereinafter *NBD Bank*) held that officers are liable for their tortious acts in the insolvency context, even if acting in the best interests of the corporation.[31] In *NBD Bank,* the corporate officer made a negligent misrepresentation to the bank in connection with an advance under an existing unsecured credit facility. The officer had advised the bank that the corporation, Algoma Steel – Restructuring #1, was merely having short-term cash problems due to a lengthy strike by employees. The officer also promised that certain US funds that had been previously encumbered were available as security to the bank. Two weeks after the bank loaned the funds, the corporation announced that it was insolvent, and the bank lost $2 million. Because the officer held himself out as capable of making decisions on the corporation's behalf and ought to have foreseen that the bank would rely on the representations made, the officer was held to be personally liable to the creditor.

Directors must also remember that although creditor interests and residual asset value become paramount as the corporation enters insolvency, shareholder interests cannot be forgotten altogether. Misrepresentations made to shareholders will also create liability for directors. In *Triax Resource Limited Partnership* v. *Research Capital Corp.,* the Ontario Superior Court permitted a claim by shareholders against officers and directors to proceed to trial.[32] In this action, the shareholders argued that the directors and officers made misleading and false statements about the corporation's solvency during a purchase of the corporation's shares just before it became insolvent.

Reviewable Transactions *(BIA)*

Where directors enter into a transaction with a person who is not at arm's length within one year before the "date of the initial bankruptcy event,"[33] and conspicuously less than fair market value was received by the corporation, directors or other parties privy to the transaction may be liable for the difference between what the corporation received and fair market value.[34] Persons related to each other are deemed not to be dealing at arm's length.[35] Surprisingly, few cases have been decided under this section, but directors would be wise not to overlook this *BIA* provision. The reviewable transaction provisions were also considered in the discussion of the oppression remedy above.

Wrongful Trading

In the period prior to insolvency, there is a range of conduct, particularly vis-à-vis trade suppliers and lien claimants, that may also attract personal liability if the director or officer knew or ought to have known that the corporation was unable to pay its debts at the time of the transaction. This is particularly so since during those months, the corporation continues to receive goods and services on normal credit terms despite the fact that the corporation may not be able to pay for the goods and services. Directors find themselves in a "Catch-22 situation." If the corporation does not receive any goods and services on credit, the corporation is almost definitely out of business, and if it does, the corporation may very well be unable to pay for them.[36]

The oppression remedy has been used by creditors with respect to allegations of wrongful trading against directors. In *Prime Computer of Canada Ltd. v. Jeffrey*, for example, the oppression remedy was sought by a particular trade creditor whose indebtedness had significantly increased prior to the date of the collapse of the corporation.[37] While the indebtedness increased to the trade creditor, the corporation's sole director's salary also increased by a substantial amount. The court concluded that given the director's position with the corporate respondent, he must have been aware of the financial affairs of the company and the fact that it was unable to meet its payment obligations to the applicant at the time he received his payments. The court ordered the director to compensate the trade creditor directly.

Declaration of Dividends Where Corporation Is Insolvent or Rendered Insolvent

Where a court finds that a bankrupt corporation has paid a dividend,[38] or redeemed or purchased for cancellation any shares of its capital stock,[39] at a time when the corporation was insolvent or where such transaction rendered the corporation insolvent, directors may be personally liable. The same is true under the *BIA* if a dividend is paid or shares redeemed within one year before the date of the initial bankruptcy event when the corporation was insolvent or rendered insolvent.[40] The court may give judgment to a trustee of a subsequently bankrupt corporation against the directors of the corporation jointly and severally in the amount of the dividend, redemption, or purchase price, with interest. The directors' only recourse under the *BIA* is to demonstrate that either the corporation was not insolvent at the time of the dividend or the director was reasonably unaware of the insolvency of the corporation.[41]

In *SCI Systems Inc. v. Gornitzki Thompson & Little Co.*,[42] an Ontario court found that the payment of a dividend and other corporate transactions, which rendered the corporation insolvent, deprived creditors of the realization of their claims and that the directors were therefore liable to the creditors for their losses.

Statutory Deductions and GST

The *Income Tax Act*[43] and the *Excise Tax Act*[44] impose personal liability on corporate directors for failure by a corporation to remit deductions for income taxes from employee wages and for failure to remit amounts collected for Goods and Services Tax (GST). Liability also extends to directors for unpaid deductions relating to the Canada Pension Plan[45] and Employment Insurance.[46] As companies experience difficult financial times, corporations and directors tend to pay key creditors whose goods and services are necessary to the continued operation of the business, rather than amounts owing for taxes.[47]

A director must show that the corporation's inability to pay was not known to the director at the time the tax liability was accruing, in order to potentially escape personal liability. Similarly, where a creditor has placed controls on the activities of the corporation such that the directors are no longer in control of the corporation's ability to meet tax payments, the directors may not be held personally liable.[48] All directors should ensure that a reliable system is in place to meet statutory tax remittance obligations, as failure to do so may result in liability.[49]

Employee Wages and Benefits

Pursuant to Section 119 of the *CBCA*, directors are personally liable for all debts not exceeding six-month wages for services performed by employees for the corporation. This creates an incentive for directors to ensure that these obligations to employees are met, even where the corporation is financially distressed. Directors have a defence against such liability if they relied in good faith on reports prepared by professional advisors that the wage liability would be satisfied.[50] Liability for vacation pay under certain statutes can also be significant, since amounts relating to this obligation are usually accrued and unpaid at the time an employee is terminated or the company becomes insolvent.

Pension legislation is another concern, since it may impose liability on a director who acquiesced or participated in a company's failure to contribute to the plan in contravention of the applicable legislation.[51] The potential liability under pension benefits legislation seems to be the broadest because the applicable legislation does not necessarily cap the maximum amount of director's liability, unlike employment standards and corporation legislation.

Environmental Protection

Directors and officers must be attuned to environmental concerns, since they can face potential personal liability under environmental statutes in addition to the corporation's own liability. This ranges from fines, terms of imprisonment, and liability for cleanup costs. As the corporation approaches insolvency, it is less likely to have assets available to satisfy claims for environmental harm or meet requirements for cleanup or remediation of contaminated sites.[52] Consequently, unremediated environmental damage may deplete the security of creditors. Problems arise with those corporations that have failed to implement effective systems or have failed to maintain them as the corporation approaches insolvency. Absent strong enforcement programs by environmental authorities, remediating environmental harm drops down on the priority list as corporate officers struggle to meet ongoing debt repayment obligations.

Protection for Directors

Resignation from the Board

The possibility of exposure to liability when a corporation is insolvent is daunting for directors. This is particularly so for independent, outside directors who have joined boards in response to corporate governance reforms. Outside directors are not involved on a daily basis in the decision-making process, but remain liable to corporate stakeholders. Directors should be aware that they cannot avoid their responsibilities or liabilities by resigning from the board. Resignation will, however, limit a director's exposure, in that a director will be liable only for actions that occurred while he or she was actually on the board.[53]

The Business Judgment Rule

The business judgment rule, which is less codified in Canada than in the United States, stresses the need not to second-guess the judgment of corporate directors. It affords some protection to the decisions made by directors. The court in *R. v. Bata* held that courts will give deference to the business judgment of corporate boards because honest errors in judgment should not impose liability, provided the requisite standard of care is met by directors.[54] As well, it is the directors, not the courts, that are familiar with the daily operations of the corporation.[55]

The business judgment rule is a presumption that, in making any decision, the directors acted on an informed basis, in good faith, and in the honest belief that the decision was in the best interests of the corporation. If directors follow appropriate procedures and act honestly, in good faith, and in the best interests of the corporations in making decisions, the courts generally will not second-guess the board's judgment, even if, in hindsight, the judgment ultimately turns out to be wrong. Acts that could lead to loss of protection include breach of fiduciary duty, acting in conflict of interest, preferential treatment of certain stakeholders, failure to disclose material aspects of a transaction, or acting without the requisite information or deliberation.

Accordingly, the directors should remain mindful of their fiduciary duties and the interests of creditors and other stakeholders in taking any action. Advice of outside professionals should be sought for any significant board action, including advice regarding the application of fiduciary duties in any alternative to the proposed course of action. In certain cases, directors are entitled to rely in good faith on reports prepared by officers of the corporation or outside experts. Directors should take all appropriate steps to maximize the benefits of these "safe harbour" rules, where appropriate, by obtaining reports of officers and outside experts. Directors should ensure that decisions are made only after appropriate deliberation and due consideration of all relevant material. Any transactions with insiders should be the subject of special scrutiny. Finally, support for directors' decisions, such as reports of officers or outside advisors, should be obtained, reviewed by the board and reflected in the records of the board's deliberations.

At the time that counsel for the debtor actively engages in negotiations with creditors, he or she should have an adequate understanding of the pressing issues facing the debtor and hopefully have an idea as to how to solve them. In addition, counsel should ensure that management and the board have a realistic view of what can be achieved in the negotiations and that they have a clear understanding of the expectations of, and obligations to, all stakeholders involved in the process.

Due Diligence Defence
Establishing a due diligence defence will generally require some positive action on the part of the directors. The nature of the diligence required will depend in part on the statute under which the liability arises. In many situations, directors will be protected from liability if they rely in good faith on the company's audited financial statements, on statements made to them by management, or on the advice of outside advisors.[56] However, directors should always confirm that they are entitled to rely on the documentation or advice on which they are basing their decisions, particularly in view of the overlay of good faith on all types of reliance.

Dissent
Directors have the right to dissent from a particular course of action even though there are comparatively few situations in which a dissent in and of itself relieves a director of liability. However, a record of a director's dissent may prove very helpful in any litigation arising from the action.[57]

Indemnification and Insurance
Indemnification by the corporation may not assist directors if the corporation no longer has assets available to satisfy claims. Corporations may generally purchase insurance only in order to indemnify directors and officers from liability arising out of their good faith but mistaken conduct.[58] It has been suggested that directors should ensure that they obtain indemnities from the company and from its parent and major subsidiaries to create a contractual obligation between the directors and the corporate entity that will have the funds available to indemnify directors.[59] If the company is insolvent, however, the company's indemnity will be of no value and directors' and officers' insurance will be the only protection directors have.

The Shifting Sands: Chief Restructuring Officer

The past decade has also seen a shift in approach to restructuring, as well as the definition of what is a successful restructuring. This has largely been as a result of an increased use of the *CCAA* to compromise the interests of secured creditors. It is also a result of the 1992 amendments to the *BIA*, which enabled a debtor to compromise obligations owing to secured creditors. The decade also saw considerable development in the combined use of the insolvency statutes and corporate statutes, which enable equity to be restructured as well as debt. Gone are the days when an insolvency proposal involved a simple compromise of debts that left the position of the equity holder intact. Creditors have become more sophisticated and more open-minded to solutions that involve not only a compromise of debt owed to them by the insolvent entity but also the conversion of a certain portion of their debt to equity.

Key aspects of current reorganizations focus less on the ability of a debtor to repay outstanding debts and concentrate more on the valuation of the business, taking into account valuations on both a liquidation basis and a going-concern basis, as well as a debt capacity analysis. The valuation and the debt capacity analysis in turn drive the extent of a debt compromise, as well as the formula to govern the conversion from debt to equity. Creditors have become more involved in the decision-making process. They have become less tolerant of the position of equity holders and more involved in assessing the capability of existing management and boards. The independence of a board from management ought to be carefully reviewed. It is acknowledged that there is a role to be played by existing management and boards who have something of value to contribute to the enterprise. However, if either or both of these groups are found to be lacking, creditors will have very little patience with the status quo.

The 1997 reorganization of Sammi, discussed above, illustrates a number of these points. The ultimate parent corporation in the Sammi group was headquartered in South Korea. It was insolvent and had sought protection under South Korean insolvency law. At that time, the applicable law in South Korea provided an infinite amount of time for the debtor to restructure its affairs. This was unacceptable to a number of trade creditors of the Canadian subsidiary. The parent had for a number of years supported the Canadian subsidiary, but when it ran into its own financial difficulties, this support was cut off. The Canadian subsidiary was forced to file under the *CCAA*. It had two main creditor groups, both of which were unsecured. The first group consisted of a number of institutional creditors, which for the most part was composed of a number of South Korean and international banks. The trade creditor group was roughly of equal size. The creditors were organized under a trade creditors' committee. The institutional creditors also combined their efforts so that they had a representative at the bargaining table.

The debtor company pressed on with its reorganization efforts, but did not seem to take into account the fact that there was a new regime. Although the entity was hopelessly insolvent, the debtor continued to give significant deference to its shareholder in attempting to formulate a restructuring proposal. This led to a number of months in which there was a fundamental disconnect between the company, which was taking direction from its management and board, and the creditor groups. The creditor representatives refused to accept that existing equity should have a significant decision-making role in the restructuring. The situation was further exacerbated by the fact that the board seemed to lack a degree of independence. The debtor planned to sell its assets and in fact brought an application for court approval of an asset sale, an application that was opposed by both creditor groups. It was clear that the reorganization plan as proposed by the debtor was doomed to fail. Evidence was brought forward to the court at the time of the hearing that the institutional investors had sold their claims to debt traders primarily based in New York. A significant amount of the trade creditor debt had also been similarly purchased by these debt traders. A dysfunctional reorganization was saved only through the efforts of a chief restructuring officer (CRO), who stepped in and conducted direct negotiations with the debt traders, who stated a clear preference for a restructuring based on a conversion of debt to equity.

The Sammi case also involved other governance issues. The first was the engagement of a CRO. The second was the role the CRO was expected to play. The suggestion of hiring a CRO may not be popular with management, but may be considered advisable by an independent board and by significant creditors. The terms of engagement of a CRO have to be clearly specified. In order to be effective, a CRO should have a position commensurate with that of a chief executive officer (CEO). The compensation package for the CRO is also something that has to be given careful consideration, as is the balancing act that the CRO must play in attempting to reconcile the objectives of a board. Compensation may be based on success, but in today's environment, success is difficult to define. Is the definition of success to be based on preserving a slice of equity for existing shareholders or on maximizing the enterprise value for creditors? Does it also involve the preservation of a business, which will affect the continued employment of the workforce? In all likelihood, it is a combination of the above.

Any CRO who accepts an appointment at an insolvent corporation will be looking for full and complete indemnity from the hazards of being associated with an insolvent corporation. This will involve coverage under the directors' and officers' policy, as well as some form of indemnity from the major lenders. In addition, the compensation package should be reviewed by the major lenders so that no disagreements arise during the mandate of the CRO. The CRO will also want to ensure that the CRO contract itself will not be the subject of a compromise.

The issue of accountability of a CRO is also undergoing development on a case-by-case basis. In one extreme, the board may be of the view that the equity of the company does have value, although it may be currently impaired. In this case, the CRO will be discharging his or her duty only if an attempt is made to preserve a meaningful portion of equity for existing shareholders. At the other end of the spectrum is the entity that is clearly insolvent, and the CRO may recognize that success will be achieved by dividing up the existing equity among the creditors and saving the existing enterprise. In this scenario, the only asset potentially left for existing equity would be the value of assets that can be accessed only with the cooperation of existing equity, such as tax loss carryforwards. There is no doubt that we will continue to see a range of treatment for equity holders in restructured entities, and we will also see CROs continuing to balance the various interests accordingly. One of the advantages that the CRO has over an existing board is that past loyalties and vested interests are less likely to be entrenched in the mind of the CRO.

As we move forward, there is now a clear recognition that the acceptable limits of exposure to liability for directors of insolvent corporations need to be clarified and controlled so as to ensure that the conduct of directors can remain subject to review but without unduly interfering with the ability of current and incoming directors to act in the best interests of corporations. Directors, particularly independent directors, require special protections while a corporation is insolvent. Competent directors are valuable during this time and the stakeholders who have a vested interest in the outcome of the restructuring have to face the reality that, if there is inadequate protection for directors, there will be a strong incentive for directors to resign at the time that the presence of a respected board is essential. It is also clear that regardless of whether or not there will be a successful reorganization, all stakeholders will be best served if a chaotic situation can be avoided. A sudden receivership or forced liquidation will not yield optimum results for any stakeholders.

The Future

The federal government is aware of the need for reform in this area. Consultations are proceeding for the next round of statutory reform. Discussion papers have been submitted on the area of governance and directors' duties and liabilities. A subcommittee of members of the Insolvency Institute of Canada prepared a discussion paper that raised the following points: mechanisms to give directors protection from no-fault liabilities; clarification of the role and duties of directors; mechanisms to encourage directors experiencing financial difficulties to bring in experienced independent professionals to replace or assist existing senior management; and mechanisms to permit creditors to replace directors and/or senior management.[60]

The discussion paper subsequently gave rise to a number of reform proposals from the Institute, the merits of which are currently being discussed. These proposals are as follows:

1 *Alternatives:* (A) the debtor's independent directors have protection from any personal statutory liability otherwise arising from the debtor's failure to pay pre-filing debts (e.g., wages, GST, etc.) so long as the debt is not more than seven (7) days overdue at the time of the commencement of a *CCAA* or *BIA* proposal case; or

(B) the debtor's directors and officers have the protection afforded under option (A) if they meet a due diligence defence.

2 Provide that during the course of *CCAA* or *BIA* proposal cases, the Court has the authority to grant a Court-ordered lien up to a fixed amount in favour of the debtor's directors and officers to indemnify them against third party liability for post-filing conduct to the extent that insurance is not available on reasonable terms for such liability, with exclusions for wilful misconduct and gross negligence.

3 Provide that the same rules concerning registration, priority, appeals, etc. shall apply to charges in favour of directors and officers as apply to debtor-in-possession liens.

4 Provide that when deciding whether or not to grant a charge in favour of the directors and officers, particularly in *CCAA* cases, the Court shall consider whether the debtor's board has established appropriate governance mechanisms, whether by establishing an independent board committee, retaining a CRO or other means, for the proper management of the debtor's affairs during the course of the restructuring proceedings.

5 Provide that during the course of a *CCAA* or *BIA* proposal case, the Court has the authority to replace some or all of the existing directors of the debtor if the governance structure of the debtor is impairing or could impair the process of developing and implementing a going concern solution.

In conclusion, it is interesting to note that the above reform proposals are consistent with global initiatives that have been endorsed by the World Bank. Gordon W. Johnson, Senior Counsel, Legal Department of the World Bank, presented a paper at the INSOL Sixth World Congress in July 2001 in London, England.[61] Section II of his paper discussed the process of developing global consensus on the framework for a set of international insolvency principles. Three principles relate to this topic and are reproduced below:

Principle 7   Director and Officer Liability

Director and officer liability for decisions detrimental to creditors made when an enterprise is insolvent should promote responsible corporate behavior while fostering reasonable risk taking. At a minimum, standards should address conduct based on knowledge of or reckless disregard for the adverse consequences to creditors.

Principle 11   Governance: Management

A. In liquidation proceedings, management should be replaced by a qualified Court-appointed official (administrator) with broad authority to administer the estate in the interest of creditors. Control of the estate should be surrendered immediately to the administrator except where management has been authorized to retain control over the company, in which case the law should impose the same duties on management as on the administrator. In creditor-initiated filings, where circumstances warrant, an interim administrator with reduced duties should be appointed to monitor the business to ensure that creditor interests are protected.

B. There are two preferred approaches in a rehabilitation proceeding: exclusive control of the proceeding by an independent administrator or supervision of management by an impartial and independent administrator or supervisor. Under the second option complete power should be shifted to the administrator if management proves incompetent or negligent or has engaged in fraud or other misbehavior. Similarly, independent administrators or supervisors should be held to the same standard of accountability to creditors and the Court and should be subject to removal for incompetence, negligence, fraud or other wrongful conduct.

Principle 12   Governance: Creditors and the Creditors' Committee

Creditor interests should be safeguarded by establishing a creditors committee that enables creditors to actively participate in the insolvency process and that allows the committee to monitor the process to ensure fairness and integrity. The committee should be consulted on non-routine matters in the case and have the ability to be heard on key decisions in the proceedings (such as matters involving dispositions of assets outside the normal course of business). The committee should serve as a conduit for processing and distributing relevant information to other creditors and for organizing creditors to decide on critical issues. The law should provide for such things as a general creditors assembly for major decisions, to appoint the creditors committee and to determine the committee's membership, quorum and voting rules, powers and the conduct of meetings. In rehabilitation proceedings, the creditors should be entitled to select an independent administrator or supervisor of their choice, provided the person meets the qualifications for serving in this capacity in the specific case.

In the past ten to fifteen years, we have witnessed a dramatic shift in attitude as to how to deal with a financially challenged business enterprise. In the late 1980s and the early 1990s, it was a relatively straightforward world of receivership, wherein once appointed, the receiver would try to sell the assets of the debtor on a going-concern basis. If that failed, liquidation would follow. Since that time, the process and the legal system have been flexible enough to entertain a variety of ways of restructuring business enterprises with an ever-increasing emphasis on the conversion of debt to equity. Concurrent with this shift in attitude has been a recognition that the governance role of director has changed. It has evolved from the protection of shareholder interests to recognition that there is a duty not to disregard the interests of a creditor. More recently, responsible boards have taken a more independent role and have recognized that once there is a formal insolvency proceeding, the role of the director is not only to consider the interests of the creditor but also to examine, review, and facilitate methods by which creditors can, in effect, take control over the restructured entity. The economic realities of the situation dictate that a successful restructuring ought to be measured by the survival rate of businesses, even if restructuring involves a reallocation of ownership between creditors, management, the board, and, to an extent, existing equity. By focusing on the survival of viable enterprises, it is hoped that we can also achieve the benefit of minimizing loss for the economy as a whole.

Acknowledgments
We are grateful for assistance from Maureen Bellmore and Melaney Wagner, Associates at Goodmans LLP, and Cathy Costa and Erin Nicholas, Students-at-Law, Goodmans LLP.

Notes
1 R.S.C. 1985, c. B-3, as am. [hereinafter *BIA*].
2 R.S.C. 1985, c. C-36, as am. [hereinafter *CCAA*].
3 *BIA, supra* note 1, ss. 50(13), (15); *CCAA, ibid.,* s. 5.1.
4 R.S.C. 1985, c. C-44, as am. by S.C. 2001, c. 14 [hereinafter *CBCA*].
5 See also the definition of "insolvent person" in s. 2(1) of the *BIA*.
6 J.P. Sarra and R.B. Davis, *Director and Officer Liability in Corporate Insolvency: A Comprehensive Guide to Rights and Obligations* (Toronto: Butterworths, 2001). See also *Federal Deposit Ins. Corp.* v. *Sea Pines Co.,* 692 F.2d 973 at 977 quoting *Davis* v. *Woolf,* 147 F.2d 629 at 633 (4th Cir. 1945).
7 (1976), 50 A.L.J.R. 446 (H.C.).
8 [1987] 1 All E.R. 114.
9 Sarra and Davis, *supra* note 6.
10 The Canadian approach is different from the approach taken by US courts, where directors have been held to owe a fiduciary duty to creditors directly; see *Geyer* v. *Ingersoll Publications,* 621 A.D. 784 (Del. Ch. 1992). At the point of insolvency, directors may even be deemed trustees for the benefit of corporate creditors; see *Automatic Canteen Co.* v. *Wharton,* 358 F.2d 587 at 590 (2d Cir. 1996).
11 [1998] Q.J. No. 3571 (Q.S.C. Bankruptcy and Insolvency Division) [hereinafter *Peoples*].
12 For an extensive discussion of *Peoples*, see Christopher Nicholls, "Liability of Corporate Officers and Directors to Third Parties" (2001) 35 Can. Bus. L.J. 1 at 31.

13 (1999), 45 O.R. (3d) 565 (Ont. S.C.J.).

14 See also *Sidaplex-Plastic Suppliers Inc.* v. *Elta Group Inc.* (1998), 40 O.R. (3d) 53 (Ont. C.A.) [hereinafter *Sidaplex*], which held that directors and officers acquire fiduciary duties to consider the interests of creditors at the point of insolvency.

15 J.S. Ziegel, "Creditors as Corporate Stakeholders – The Quiet Revolution – An Anglo-Canadian Perspective" (1993) 43 U.T.L.J. 551.

16 See s. 238 of the *CBCA, supra* note 4, for the extended definition of "complainant." See also *Royal Trust Corporation of Canada* v. *Hordo* (1993), 10 B.L.R. (2d) 86 (Ont. Ct. (Gen. Div.)); *Levy-Russell Ltd.* v. *Shieldings Inc.* (1998), 41 O.R. (3d) 54 (Ont. Ct. (Gen. Div.)) [hereinafter *Levy-Russell*].

17 *Levy-Russell, ibid.*

18 See also *Jacobs Farms Ltd.* v. *Jacobs*, [1992] O.J. No. 813 (Ont. Ct. (Gen. Div.)); *Noral Lighting Partners Ltd.* v. *Cornwall Street Railway Light and Power Co.*, [1999] O.J. No. 2749 (Ont. S.C.).

19 *First Edmonton Place Ltd.* v. *315888* (1989), 45 B.L.R. 110 (Alta. C.A.) and *Sidaplex, supra* note 14. See also *369413 Alberta Ltd.* v. *Pocklington*, [2000] A.J. No. 1350 (Alta. C.A.); *Adecco Canada Inc.* v. *J. Ward Broome Ltd.* (2001), 21 C.B.R. (4th) 181 (Ont. S.C.J.); *ADI Ltd. 052987 N.B. Inc.*, [2000] N.B.J. No. 467 (N.B.C.A.), (2000) 22 C.B.R. (4th) 1; *Bull HN Information Systems Ltd.* v. *L.I. Business Solutions Inc.* (1994), 23 Alta. L.R. (3d) 186 (Alta. Q.B.); *American Reserve Energy Corp.* v. *McDorman*, [1999] N.J. No. 198, (Nfld. S.C.), (1999) 48 B.L.R. (2d) 167.

20 *CBCA, supra* note 4, s. 241(3).

21 *Sidaplex, supra* note 14.

22 (1998), 49 C.B.R. (3d) 165 (Ont. Ct. (Gen. Div.) [Commercial List]).

23 *Olympia and York Developments Ltd. (Trustee of)* v. *Olympia and York Realty Corp.* (2002), 28 C.B.R. (4th) 294, additional reasons at (2002), 32 C.B.R. (4th) 83. The author was provided with a copy of the Agreed Statement of Facts introduced in evidence, which was used in preparation of the annotation.

24 (1995), 36 C.B.R. (3d) 1 (Ont. C.A.).

25 (1970), 14 C.B.R. (N.S.) 301 (Ont. S.C.).

26 *Canada (Attorney General)* v. *Standard Trust Co.* (1991), 9 C.B.R. (3d) 41, 5 O.R. (3d) 660 (Gen. Div.)

27 (1984), 54 B.C.L.R. 235 (B.C.S.C.).

28 *CBCA, supra* note 4, s. 124(4).

29 See definition of "date of initial bankruptcy event" in s. 2(1) of the *BIA, supra* note 1.

30 See *R.* v. *Reed* (1992), 13 C.B.R. (3d) 124 (B.C.C.A.).

31 (1999), 46 O.R. (3d) 514 (Ont. C.A.), appeal for leave to S.C.C. dismissed 6 April 2000 [hereinafter *NBD Bank*].

32 (1999), 96 O.T.C. 290 (Ont. S.C.J.).

33 See definition of "date of the initial bankruptcy event" in s. 2 of the *BIA, supra* note 1.

34 *BIA, ibid.*, ss. 100(1), (2).

35 See definition of "related persons" in s. 4 of the *BIA, ibid.*

36 D.R. Dowdall, *Restructuring Insolvent Companies*, Osgoode Hall Law School, York University, Professional Development Programme (Toronto: Edmond Montgomery Publications, 1998).

37 (1991), 6 O.R. (3d) 733 (Gen. Div.).

38 *CBCA, supra* note 4, s. 42.

39 *CBCA, ibid.*, s. 34(2).

40 *BIA, supra* note 1, s. 101(2). In *633746 Ontario Inc. (Trustee of)* v. *Salvati* (1990), 73 O.R. (2d) 774 (Ont. S.C.), the court held that the *BIA* can be read in conjunction with the *CBCA* for this transaction.

41 *BIA, ibid.*, s. 101(5).

42 (1998), 1 C.B.R. (4th) 164 (Gen. Div.), aff'd (1998) 110 O.A.C. 160 (Ont. Div. Ct.).

43 *Income Tax Act*, R.S.C. 1985 (5th Supp.), c. 1, as am.

44 *Excise Tax Act*, R.S.C. 1985, c. E-15, as am.

45 *Canada Pension Plan*, R.S.C. 1985, c. C-8, as am.

46 *Employment Insurance Act,* S.C. 1996, c. 23, as am.

47 *Soper* v. *Canada* (1997), 149 D.L.R. (4th) 297 (F.C.A.); and *Canada A.G.* v. *Consolidated Cdn. Contractors Inc.,* [1999] 1 F.C. 209 (Fed. C.A.).

48 *Bohn* v. *Canada,* [2000] T.C.J. No. 264 (T.C.C.). Directors are personally liable for GST where there is a failure to remit; see *Brown* v. *Canada,* [1998] T.C.J. No. 521 (T.C.C.) and *Ruggles* v. *Canada,* [1999] T.C.J. No. 612, [2000] C.C.S. No. 2501 (T.C.C.).

49 *Lemay* v. *Canada,* [1998] T.C.J. No. 86 (T.C.C.); *Redmond* v. *Canada,* [2000] T.C.J. No. 206 (T.C.C.); and *Ferguson* v. *Canada,* [1999] T.C.J. No. 203 (T.C.C.).

50 *CBCA, supra* note 4, s. 123(4). See *Westar Mining Corporation* (1996), 136 D.L.R. (4th) 564 (B.C.C.A.).

51 C. Hansell and J. Gillies, "Nearing the Brink: Financial Crisis and Issues for the Unrelated Director" in Queen's Annual Business Law Symposium, *Corporate Restructurings and Insolvencies: Issues and Perspectives* (Toronto: Carswell, 1995) 159.

52 For example, in *Legal Oil and Gas Ltd.* v. *Alberta (Minister of Environment),* [2000] A.J. No. 684 (Alta. Q.B.), the court held that directors can be held liable as principals of the corporation for the costs of cleanup of contaminated sites.

53 *Brown* v. *Shearer,* [1995] 6 W.W.R. 68 (Man. C.A.).

54 (1992), 9 O.R. (3d) 329 (Ont. C.J.).

55 See discussion of the business judgment rule in R.M. Cieri *et al.,* "The Fiduciary Duties of Directors of Financially Troubled Companies" (1994) 3(4) J. Bankruptcy Law and Practice 405; H.R. Miller, "Corporate Governance in Chapter 11: The Fiduciary Relationship Between Directors and Stockholders of Solvent and Insolvent Corporations" (1993) 23(4) Seton Hall L. Rev. 1467.

56 See, for example, *CBCA, supra* note 4, s. 123(4).

57 See *CBCA, ibid.,* s. 123; Hansell and Gillies, *supra* note 51.

58 *CBCA, ibid.,* s. 124.

59 Hansell and Gillies, *supra* note 51.

60 D. Dowdall *et al., Governance/Directors' Duties and Liabilities – Discussion Paper* (Insolvency Institute of Canada, St. Andrews, NB, October 2002) [unpublished], and subsequently incorporated into Joint Task Force on Business Insolvency Law Reform, *A Joint Report of the Insolvency Institute of Canada and the Canadian Association of Insolvency and Restructuring Professionals* (15 March 2002) [on file with author].

61 G.W. Johnson, *The World Bank's Consensus Building Role: Developing Principles for Effective Insolvency and Creditor Rights Systems and Related Efforts to Strengthen Capacity* (INSOL Sixth World Congress, July 2001).

12

Governance of the Financially Distressed Corporation in Global Capital Markets: Selected Aspects of the Financing and Governance of Canadian Enterprises in Cross-Border Workouts

Edward A. Sellers, Natasha J. MacParland,
and F. James Hoffner

As Canadian enterprises move further into global capital markets, the issues they face in terms of governance will become increasingly complex.[1] Perhaps at no time are the issues relating to governance and capital markets more acute than when a corporate issuer finds itself in financial distress. The tensions that exist between fairly well understood duties for those involved in the governance of corporations in Canada[2] and the discipline that both global capital markets and other interested parties bring to bear on an enterprise, and those in control of its helm, are heightened when dealing with financial distress. The situation becomes more taut when the financial distress involves the prospect of formal insolvency proceedings in multiple jurisdictions.

Corporate governance is many things, but it is perhaps most simply stated as the stewardship aimed at ensuring the optimal and appropriate use of corporate assets.[3] While corporate governance may be thought of typically in terms of safeguarding shareholders' interests, it also extends to the interests of creditors and others, especially in the "vicinity of insolvency."[4] Indeed, some have categorized insolvency as a litmus test for determining the optimal deployment of financial resources when evaluating governance and insolvency regimes.[5]

It is not possible to canvass all aspects of financing and governance in cross-border workouts. Accordingly, this chapter builds on Geoffrey Morawetz's analysis of governance of the financially distressed corporation (Chapter 11) by examining some specific challenges facing those involved in deploying or adopting financing techniques; some of the financing techniques utilized by financially distressed Canadian enterprises that have accessed global capital markets; and some of the considerations to which directors and officers of financially distressed Canadian enterprises and others should turn their minds as they attempt to meet the challenges of working out corporate financial problems.

For illustrative purposes, the issues discussed in this chapter will be approached in the context of a financially distressed Canadian enterprise having the following: senior syndicated debt facilities administered by a Canadian chartered bank (in which there are participants in both Canada and the United States), with advances made thereunder being fully secured against all of the assets of the enterprise; so-called public debt (whether secured, unsecured, or subordinated) in the form of bonds, debentures, or commercial paper issued in either Canada or the United States; and a form of publicly traded equity listed on one or more of the Toronto Stock Exchange, the New York Stock Exchange, or the NASDAQ Stock Market.[6] This illustrative financially distressed enterprise will be considered as if it were a single legal entity, although most often such enterprises are a consolidated group of companies.

Some of the Challenges

Knowing the Duties Owed
The governance of a Canadian enterprise in financial distress is not for the fainthearted and involves managing duties to and the interests of the corporation, its shareholders, employees, creditors, and others. Although a comprehensive treatment of all of the duties and obligations facing those involved in the governance of financially distressed Canadian enterprises is beyond the scope of this chapter, a brief outline of some of those duties and obligations is necessary.[7]

The Canadian Landscape
A developing body of scholarship is emerging in Canada concerning whether directors (and potentially others) of financially distressed Canadian enterprises are subject to a fiduciary duty in favour of creditors in addition to their fiduciary duty to the corporation and its shareholders, and to their statutory duties of honesty, good faith, care, skill, and diligence, and duty not to oppress creditors,[8] in the context of decisions taken in the direction and management of the affairs of a financially distressed enterprise.[9] The extent to which such duties exist in Canada and in what form is still the subject of debate. Nonetheless, as the interests of shareholders and creditors diverge in proximity to insolvency, a potential dilemma is created for directors who owe a fiduciary obligation to the corporation and its shareholders. They may also owe a fiduciary duty to the corporation's creditors, and, at the very least, have the statutory obligations referred to above.

That period in the financial life of a commercial entity when its solvency may be in doubt has been referred to as being the "twilight"[10] or the "vicinity of insolvency."[11] While in the twilight, it is not unusual for financially distressed Canadian enterprises to carry on business without the certainty of knowing that each and every one of the creditors they induce to extend credit will be repaid in full, in part because it is difficult to know exactly when insolvency arises and also because there is a natural inclination on the part of people within an enterprise to attempt to keep it alive as long as possible. Whether the directors and others involved in the governance of financially distressed corporations ought to direct that those transactions be entered into or to acquiesce in same is another matter.[12]

Detecting Insolvency
There can be many reasons for the financial decline of a business. For example, the enterprise can be involved in a "sunset industry,"[13] it can suffer a catastrophic event,[14] or there could have been a fraud perpetuated on the corporation that contributed significantly to its financial distress.[15] Not every business in financial distress encounters a significant event that automatically raises the spectre of insolvency, and it can be difficult for directors and others involved in the enterprise to know on an operational level exactly when it becomes insolvent. There are also some definitional problems associated with determining when exactly an entity is insolvent.

There are statutory definitions for insolvency contained in the *Bankruptcy and Insolvency Act (BIA)*[16] and the *Canada Business Corporations Act (CBCA)*[17] and its various provincial counterparts, which tend towards a three-part test and which at first blush seem straightforward:

1   A corporation is unable to meet its obligations as they generally come due;
2   A corporation has ceased meeting obligations as they generally come due (together with [1], "liquidity insolvency"); or
3   The property of the corporation at fair value is not sufficient to enable payment of all obligations due and accruing due ("balance sheet insolvency").

However, there seems to be a lack of consistency in the judicial decisions interpreting those provisions that cast doubt on some aspects of a director's ability to know when insolvency arises legally. For example, an appellate decision of the Divisional Court of the Ontario Court of Justice (General Division) in *SCI Systems Inc.* v. *Gornitzki, Thompson & Little*,[18] dealing with an oppression action alleging a wrongful dividend payment under Section 38(3) of the *Business Corporations Act* (Ontario),[19] upheld the determination that deferred taxes were to be included as a liability when considering corporate solvency, notwithstanding that the period for reassessment of the original tax year had expired. The Court indicated that in determining balance sheet insolvency, the reasonable starting point is the financial statements of the corporation. The Court also indicated that if there is clear evidence that an adjustment is appropriate, it should be made and directors are not entitled to be selective about the adjustments that ought to be made – in other words, there is to be no picking and choosing of which liabilities to consider in determining solvency.[20] The Divisional Court in *SCI Systems* also upheld the trial court decision that a court is entitled to consider accounting evidence as well as the actual performance of a corporation in the months following decisions taken by the directors when determining the appropriateness of their conduct in the context of an alleged insolvency.[21]

A somewhat different approach was taken in the *Semi-Tech* proceedings.[22] The Ontario Superior Court of Justice determined that financial statements, on which directors may rely,[23] do not rebut a finding of balance sheet insolvency simply because they show positive equity, as they are historic and based on going-concern assumptions. The Court also held that the concept of accruing obligations for the purpose of determining balance sheet insolvency does not include all long-term debt on the balance sheet and, accordingly, "fair valuation" is to be measured against current payables or amounts properly chargeable for the relevant accounting period.[24] *Semi-Tech* was a case dealing with whether a creditor-sponsored application under the *Companies' Creditors Arrangement Act (CCAA)*[25] – Canada's equivalent to an involuntary petition under Chapter 11 of Title 11 of the US *Bankruptcy Code*[26] – would be allowed to force insolvency proceedings on the debtor over its objections. One could suspect, with respect, that the decision in *Semi-Tech* was somewhat results-oriented, but it has contributed to the uncertainty facing directors in determining when balance sheet insolvency has occurred.

Some of the issues surrounding the state of knowledge of a director regarding a corporation's liquidity insolvency were dealt with by the British Columbia Supreme Court in *Maple Homes*.[27] The case dealt with an application to approve a proposal to creditors of an insolvent private corporation. There was evidence that there had been a decline in sales and a loss of orders that the corporation's sole director clearly knew about prior to the commencement of formal insolvency proceedings. The director admitted in evidence that he knew that the corporation could not make ends meet and could not meet its debts at a time when he determined to allow the corporation to transact on credit prior to taking formal insolvency proceedings. The Court determined that the concentrated efforts of the director as principal in keeping the business in operation, including his continuing efforts to bid for work, was consistent with a good-faith effort rather than trading with knowledge of insolvency. The Court did not deal in its reasons with the state of the corporation's financial reporting in determining the state of the director's knowledge of insolvency.

Whether the decision in *Maple Homes* would be readily applied in the context of an enterprise that has accessed global capital markets is an interesting question. Part of the price of admission to those markets is the ability of issuers to maintain sophisticated information systems concerning their financial health and, for those involved in the governance of issuers, to take decisions based on that information. Whether similar "concentrated efforts" of those involved in the governance of enterprises that have accessed global capital markets would be viewed as good-faith efforts rather than trading with knowledge of insolvency seems doubtful. Although the directors of Canadian enterprises are entitled by statute to rely upon financial statements provided to them,[28] and may not be involved on an executive basis in the day-to-day affairs of the enterprise, it seems likely that if the directors of a financially distressed Canadian enterprise participating in global capital markets knew that the enterprise could not make ends meet while continuing to transact on credit, the directors would be taken to have known of the insolvency of the enterprise.

Sources of Liability
Quite apart from the issue of knowing whether an enterprise is insolvent are the possible sources of liability for directors of corporations trading while insolvent, which include but are not limited to offences under the *Criminal Code*[29] and the *BIA*,[30] the oppression remedy[31] and other corporate statute liabilities,[32] breaches of fiduciary duty,[33] and other tortious liabilities.[34] A brief discussion of some of those sources follows for illustrative purposes, but is much more fully dealt with elsewhere.[35]

Criminal and Quasi-Criminal Offences   Section 361 of the *Criminal Code* concerns obtaining credit by false pretences. There is case law that suggests that a positive or negative exaggeration made to obtain credit is not false pretence in and of itself but is a question of fact in each instance. Also, a mere statement of opinion is not enough to find liability for false pretence with respect to a representation such as a promise or statement of intention. Accordingly, in *R. v. Godfrey,* it was determined that a promise to pay in the future without a representation of a present fact as to solvency was not a criminal offence.[36] Similarly, Section 362 of the *Criminal Code* deals with obtaining credit by fraud. In *R. v. Cohen,*[37] the Quebec Court of Appeal determined that it was not concerned with present or forward-looking statements as to solvency in the context of determining fraud, and indicated in the result that a false statement serving to keep open an existing credit line did not fall within the offences contemplated by Section 362 of the *Criminal Code*. Given the *Godfrey* and *Cohen* decisions, it is unlikely that the necessary *mens rea* or intent can be proved beyond a reasonable doubt in order to obtain a conviction under the *Criminal Code* for obtaining credit either by fraud or under false pretences in the context of financing or restructuring a financially distressed business in Canada.

Sections 198, 199, 200, and 204 of the *BIA* also provide for quasi-criminal offences.[38] These sections do not apply to financially distressed enterprises generally and are applicable only if the enterprise becomes bankrupt; that is, an assignment is made or a receiving order is made or deemed to be made against the enterprise under the *BIA*. However, as the *BIA* offence provisions apply to actions that are taken within one year immediately preceding the date of an initial bankruptcy event, due regard must be had for these offences when involved in the governance of a financially distressed enterprise.

As the *BIA* offences are quasi-criminal offences, intent must be established to find liability. For example, under Section 198(1)(e) of the *BIA*, the false representation sought to be sanctioned must have been intentionally made or there must have been an intent to defraud.[39] This requirement will likely protect those who acted without malfeasance. However, Section 204 of the *BIA* specifically contemplates and sanctions the actions of a director who acquiesces in a corporation committing an offence. As a result, it is possible that a director who does not actively participate in the company's wrongdoing under the *BIA* may still be found guilty of an offence under Section 204.

While not creating an offence per se, the reviewable transaction provisions of the *BIA* should give the directors of financially distressed enterprises some pause.[40] The reviewable transaction provisions give a court the authority to review every transaction entered into "with another person otherwise than at arm's length" within one year before the date of the initial bankruptcy event. If the reviewable transaction occurred for greater than or less than fair market value, then judgment may be rendered against the transferee for the difference in value. Generally the judgment is granted against the other party to the transaction, but Section 100(2) of the *BIA* specifically provides that judgment may be rendered "against any other person being privy to the transaction with the bankrupt."[41]

Oppression   By statute, a remedy may be sought by a complainant against a director or officer of a corporation for any conduct that is oppressive, is unfairly prejudicial to, or unfairly disregards the interests of that complainant and, if appropriate, the court before which the complaint is brought may make any order that it thinks fit in the circumstances.[42] Many cases have determined that creditors are complainants for the purposes of oppression proceedings.[43] Apparently "future" creditors may not be proper complainants, only those who were creditors at the time of the alleged wrongdoing.[44] However, even then not all those creditors qualify.[45]

Of particular note in the context of the governance of financially distressed corporations is the decision of the Alberta Court of Queen's Bench in *First Edmonton Place*.[46] The Court held that it was not mere prejudice or disregard but "unfair" prejudice or disregard that resulted in liability for oppressive conduct.[47] The Court also indicated the criteria that should be looked to when determining whether or not to find liability for oppressive conduct:

- the protection of the underlying expectations of the creditor;
- whether the acts complained of were unforeseeable by the creditor at the time it agreed to advance credit;
- whether the creditor could have reasonably protected itself from the acts complained of; and
- who benefited in the circumstances.[48]

Along similar lines, the Ontario Court of Appeal in *Leon Van Neck & Son* v. *McGorman*[49] affirmed the approach in *First Edmonton Place* and indicated that the principles for finding oppressive conduct were not applicable unless the transactions complained of diverted assets away from the reach of creditors or, in the context of a closely held corporation, directors gained an advantage or reduction in liability. A mere expectation of solvency by a creditor was not enough to find liability, and even if the director misled, guaranteed, or was less than truthful, there was no basis for finding oppression unless there were transactions under which the director personally benefited.[50]

In an earlier decision, *Sidaplex-Plastic*,[51] the Ontario Court of Appeal did not find it necessary for a director to have personally benefited in order to find oppressive conduct, although the director and sole shareholder did in fact personally benefit. In that case, the creditor's security in the debtor's assets had lapsed because the debtor inadvertently provided as security a letter of credit with a fixed term instead of a term renewable automatically. Neither party was aware of the error and both expected the security to continue to be in force. The debtor subsequently sold its assets and the proceeds were used to eliminate the liability of the director and sole shareholder under a personal guarantee to the debtor's bank. The Court upheld the trial court's finding that the "omission" of renewing the letter of credit was unfairly prejudicial when other creditors, including the director, had been paid from the proceeds. In doing so, the Court focused on the ongoing business relationship between the parties and the mutual expectation of the security's continued validity. The Court also upheld the trial court's finding that the director ought to be personally liable for the conduct of the corporation because in a small, closely knit company the director and corporation are functionally the same.[52]

It appears that application of the *Leon Van Neck* and *Sidaplex-Plastic* decisions would hold directors or officers liable for oppressive conduct if it could be established that they authorized transactions that diverted assets away from the reach of the corporation's creditors, but that misleading statements concerning the solvency of the corporation may not be enough to assist in finding liability under the oppression remedy. However, the purposive approach that appears to have been adopted by the Ontario Court of Appeal in *Sidaplex-Plastic,* albeit in the context of a closely held corporation, may well be applicable in the context of a public company complaint where a court is prepared to categorize any such misstatement as being "unfair" so as to grant a remedy for oppressive conduct.

Fiduciary Duty   As recently as 1980, a Canadian Court of Appeal found that the directors of a corporation did not owe the corporation's creditors a fiduciary duty.[53] Subsequent *obiter dicta* comments of the Alberta Court of Queen's Bench in the *Trizec*[54] proceedings led many to believe that a fiduciary duty owed by directors to creditors arising at some point along the continuum between solvency and insolvency had become "intermingled" with the traditional duties owed to a corporation and its shareholders by directors.

Since then, there have been a number of conflicting decisions concerning the existence of a fiduciary duty owed to creditors by directors of insolvent corporations or the absence of same. Perhaps the high-water mark in the camp favouring the finding of a fiduciary duty are the decisions in *Peoples Department Stores Inc. (trustee of)* v. *Wise*[55] *(Peoples)* and *Canbook Distribution Corp.* v. *Borins*[56] *(Edwards Books).*

In *Peoples,* the directors of a solvent, wholly owned subsidiary implemented a new inventory procurement policy under which the subsidiary would purchase inventory and then transfer some to its financially distressed parent company. No financial controls were implemented to ensure payment for the inventory, which caused the subsidiary's receivables to grow unchecked. The Quebec Superior Court found that the directors failed to act in accordance with the duties of loyalty and care required by Section 122 of the *CBCA* in compromising the interests of the subsidiary.[57]

The Court also surveyed Commonwealth decisions holding that directors owe a fiduciary duty to creditors.[58] However, the Court then cited the House of Lords' decision in *Winkworth,* which held that "a company owes a duty to its creditors, present and future."[59] After citing *Winkworth,* the Court held that "the general rationale of that Judgment applies in the present case."[60] In terms of the other Commonwealth decisions, the Court hedged its language by holding: "We agree with the thrust of those judgments and find that Canadian Corporate Law should evolve in that direction."[61] The Court did not specifically identify the extent and scope of the "general rationale" and "thrust" to which it agreed.

In *Peoples,* it was the trustee in bankruptcy that brought suit against the directors, as the trustee had standing to assert a wrong against the company. The Court, by taking into account creditors' interests, found the directors liable for breaching their duties to the company. The best interests of the company were therefore interpreted to include the interests of creditors, but an express finding was not made in *Peoples* that directors of a corporation owe that corporation's creditors a fiduciary duty.

In *Edwards Books,* an unsecured creditor sought relief against the directors and solicitors of the debtor for breach of fiduciary duty in the granting of security by the debtor while on the eve of insolvency to a corporation related to the debtor's directors. The solicitors brought a motion for summary judgment to have the action against them dismissed. The Ontario Superior Court of Justice determined that the creditor did have the necessary status to commence an action in its capacity as a creditor of the debtor to whom the debtor's directors owed a fiduciary duty, but this could not be extended to the debtor's solicitors. The Court did not dismiss the action outright but limited the scope of the action to negligence by finding that there was no basis for an action in fiduciary duty against the solicitors.

Despite the language of the case seemingly establishing a directors' fiduciary duty to creditors, a full reading of the case reveals that the Ontario Superior Court of Justice found that directors *may* owe a fiduciary duty to creditors in circumstances where goods have been ordered on credit by a corporation having granted security over all of its assets in favour of a company related to its directors. In coming to its decision, the Court quoted extensively from *Peoples* and noted that Canadian law "appears to be moving" towards recognition of a fiduciary duty owed by directors to creditors, "particularly" where the corporation is insolvent or where the impugned transaction renders the corporation insolvent.[62]

Judicial enthusiasm for expanding a potential directors' fiduciary duty in this manner seems to have lessened somewhat. For example, the courts in *Lakehead Newsprint*[63] and *USF Red Star Inc.*[64] were less willing to find the existence of such a fiduciary duty. In *Lakehead Newsprint,* the Ontario Superior Court of Justice referred to *Peoples* and *Edwards Books* but noted only that directors "may" have a fiduciary duty to creditors where the corporation is insolvent or rendered insolvent by the directors' action. Where the corporation is not insolvent, the Court found that "there is no authority offered that suggests that there is a fiduciary duty owed at large by directors to creditors of the company."[65]

In *USF Red Star,* the Ontario Superior Court of Justice did not find a director to be personally liable when the corporation continued to order services from a creditor even though the corporation was insolvent. The reported decision is ambiguous in that the Court did not explicitly identify on which grounds (i.e., fiduciary duty or oppression) the plaintiff made its case. The Court nonetheless distinguished the case at bar by narrowly interpreting *Peoples* as a proceeding to recover funds in a "reviewable transaction" and *Edwards Books* as an instance of preference. The Court went on to find that:

directors of a company may, with impunity, cause the company to order goods and services which they have no objective reason to believe the company can pay for in the absence of a preference or fraudulent activities which impair the company's ability to meet its obligations.[66]

Rounding out the field on whether a fiduciary duty exists at large to creditors on the part of directors is an earlier Ontario Divisional Court decision in *SCI Systems*.[67] In that case, the debtor corporation sold its assets and distributed the proceeds as dividends. The plaintiff creditor sought damages from the directors personally for oppressive conduct. The directors argued that the creditor could reasonably have protected itself by negotiating covenants in the credit agreement to prevent the debtor from selling assets.[68] The Court rejected this argument and found that creditors can reasonably expect directors to operate the corporation in accordance with its legal obligations and their common law and statutory obligations, which were summarized as acting honestly and faithfully in the best interests of the corporation and exercising the diligence required of the reasonably prudent person.[69] By stripping the corporation of assets and paying dividends, the directors rendered the company insolvent and unable to pay its creditors, which the Court found unfairly prejudicial to or unfairly disregarded the interests of creditors.[70]

The Court also held that although the "business judgment rule" protects the decisions of directors from judicial second-guessing, the Court is "equally strict" in not exempting directors from their fiduciary duty and duty of care – duties, it noted, which have "evolved in the light of new corporate concerns and societal expectations."[71] Where there is a potential conflict in directors also being shareholders, the Court further held that their actions should be "scrutinized more carefully" and that the test applied to their "fiduciary obligations must necessarily be elevated."[72] The Court did not, however, expressly find liability for breach of fiduciary duty.

To the extent that courts have not been unequivocal or unanimous as to whether and how directors' fiduciary duties should be broadened to include a duty owed to creditors of an insolvent corporation, the Supreme Court of Canada's findings on fiduciary duty in *Cadbury Schweppes* may give reason to rethink this development.[73] The Court referred to earlier Supreme Court of Canada judgments that held that a fiduciary duty does not normally arise in arm's length commercial dealings where parties can protect themselves in the bargain.[74] The Court held that the "overriding deterrence objective applicable to situations of particular vulnerability to the exercise of a discretionary power" did not apply in the case at bar.[75] This statement suggests that a finding of fiduciary duty in commercial settings may be a function of the degree of vulnerability and the potential for deterrence.

In extending directors' fiduciary duties to include a duty owed to creditors of insolvent corporations, the courts seem to be seeking to protect creditors' entitlement to repayment of a debt obligation, not the debt obligation as a medium of a pre-existing fiduciary relationship. There is no great spectre of vulnerability attendant on creditors. They can choose to extend credit or not. To the extent deterrence is required to prevent directors from knowingly inducing extensions of credit at a time when a corporation is insolvent, there are other avenues of redress against directors available in appropriate cases.

With respect, the extension of a judicially developed directors' fiduciary duty to creditors of insolvent corporations is capricious. Directors already have a fiduciary duty to a corporation and its shareholders. Shareholder and creditor interests often conflict in an insolvency, which makes impossible the expectation of pure loyalty to both. Any expectation that such a conflict could be avoided by shifting the duty from shareholders to creditors at a clearly definable moment is unrealistic given the uncertainties involved in knowing when a corporation becomes insolvent. For that matter, Canadian jurisprudence that has contemplated a fiduciary duty to creditors of an insolvent corporation is unclear about when the duty arises. For example, does it arise when an enterprise is insolvent in fact, or when a particular transaction might imperil solvency, or when the directors "know" that the corporation is insolvent or in the vicinity of insolvency? A similar lack of clarity surrounds the issue of to whom the duty is owed. Is it to all creditors, or creditors in existence before insolvency, or creditors in existence after insolvency? Since the interests of creditors are often in conflict when competing for priority over diminished assets, fostering such a general fiduciary duty would place directors in an untenable position when called upon to decide which of any number of creditor interests are paramount. The standards by which to judge duties of loyalty and care in such situations are poorly defined and open-ended. The oppression remedy, in contrast, is legislatively mandated and stipulates that the requirement of unfairness be present to provide some standard of review.[76]

Notwithstanding this critique and the unsettled jurisprudence about whether a directors' fiduciary duty to creditors of insolvent corporations exists in Canada, and what its extent and scope may be, directors of financially distressed enterprises should be aware that they may be open to liability for breach of a potential fiduciary duty to creditors.

Tort Liabilities Two fairly recent cases brought to light the potential for liability founded in tort against directors and others involved in the governance of financially distressed corporations for inducing creditors to advance credit. In *ADGA*,[77] the Ontario Court of Appeal considered whether actions against a director and two employees of a competitor company should be struck out. The alleged torts included inducement of breach of contract and breach of fiduciary duty. After surveying case law, the Court held that there was no principled basis to protect the director and employees from liability in tort even though their actions were taken in pursuit of corporate interests. The Court did, however, suggest that an exception should exist for the protection of directors, officers, and employees in limited circumstances, such as where parties contract voluntarily and accept the risks of dealing with a limited liability company.[78]

In *NBD Bank*,[79] the defendant officer was found to have made a number of misrepresentations, including misstating that receivables in the amount of $2-$3 million were unencumbered, in order to obtain a credit facility on behalf of a corporation. The Ontario Court of Appeal affirmed that while directors and officers will not ordinarily be personally liable for actions carried out under a corporate name, they can be personally liable for acts that are themselves tortious.

The Court did not reconcile the apparent inconsistency of its findings in these two cases, as it seemed clear that the plaintiff in *NBD Bank* had contracted voluntarily and accepted the risk of dealing with a limited liability corporation.

The US Landscape

Similar duties and obligations can be owed by nonresident directors of nonresident corporations if the corporations have a place of business or assets in the United States.[80] For those involved in the governance of financially distressed Canadian enterprises that have participated in global capital markets, the existence of such duties and obligations and the potential liability for breach of such duties and obligations may affect their decision making while attempting to refinance or restructure the enterprise.

Sources of Liability

Criminal and Quasi-Criminal Offences   Title 11 of the US *Bankruptcy Code* provides a comprehensive code of bankruptcy in the United States.[81] It includes Chapter 7, similar in effect to an assignment or receiving order under the *BIA*, and Chapter 11, similar in effect to the *CCAA*.[82] This comprehensive code includes a number of "offence" provisions, including Rule 9011, which provides for sanctions in the event that misrepresentations are made to the court and Section 362, which provides for damages in the event of a willful violation of the stay of proceedings.[83] Both of the example provisions entail an element of intent.

Chapter 8 of Title 18 of the US *Bankruptcy Code*, titled "Crimes and Criminal Procedure – Bankruptcy," contains the legislative provisions dealing with criminal offences concerning bankruptcy. It provides for a number of offences, including concealment of assets,[84] false oaths and claims,[85] bribery,[86] embezzlement against the estate,[87] knowing disregard of bankruptcy law or rule,[88] and bankruptcy fraud.[89] These sections incorporate the relevant provision of Title 11 by reference and specifically refer to an intent requirement.[90]

Oppression   States such as Delaware do not have a statute-based cause of action comparable to the oppression remedy in Canada. Directors can face personal liability pursuant to a variety of statutes, however. A number of jurisdictions, including Delaware, have adopted the *Uniform Fraudulent Transfer Act*. Directors can be held personally liable if they breach their fiduciary duty to creditors if they vote for or permit an insolvent corporation to undertake or commit a fraudulent transfer. As well, directors and officers can be held liable, notwithstanding an absence of a breach of fiduciary duty, if they receive property from the insolvent corporation on a fraudulent basis.[91]

Fiduciary Duty   In the United States, directors of financially distressed enterprises clearly owe fiduciary duties to creditors when the enterprise is insolvent, and possibly even at the point when the enterprise is in the vicinity of insolvency.[92] The origins of this fiduciary duty in the United States arise from the "trust fund doctrine," which posits that the assets of an insolvent company are held in trust for the creditors by the directors as trustees. It is likely that the lack of recourse for creditors under a statutory equivalent to the oppression remedy has led to the unambiguous existence of a judicially developed fiduciary duty in the United States.

Tort Liabilities   The breadth of duties in the United States giving rise to potential director liability for misrepresentation and other tortious conduct is extensive. As in Canada, directors and officers will not be shielded by the enterprise's limited liability against their own tortious acts such as negligent and fraudulent misrepresentation.[93] The comparative ease with which class actions are certified has led to the phenomenon of mass tort actions. Such tort claims have led to a developing trend in the United States to use Chapter 11 reorganization proceedings as a means of dealing with the numerous tort claimants.[94] For enterprises with assets, creditors, or claimants in the United States, the possibility of such mass tort claims can affect the enterprise's solvency, influence its ability to finance its operations, and colour the duties owed by directors to creditors.[95]

Managing Market Relationships

Keeping an Eye on Equity

When financing Canadian companies in financial distress, equity is typically not the form through which additional funds are obtained, although there are instances where a rights offering or other form of equity solicitation has been implemented to assist a challenged enterprise.[96] In most cases involving financially distressed Canadian enterprises participating in global markets, the principal focus relating to those capital markets becomes the debt markets and their participants. Accordingly, the principal focus of directors and officers gravitates away from maintaining relationships with and access to equity markets in dealing with financing and governance issues for financially distressed Canadian enterprises. However, maintaining market confidence and adhering to the regulatory requirements of equity markets is an important aspect of dealing with any issuer's financial distress.

Focusing on Debt

It perhaps goes without saying that, in financially distressed circumstances, the value of an issuer's debt and equity is subject to great speculation. They may end up being worth substantially less than the original value at which they were issued or substantially more than the acquisition price if acquired at a discount to original value. It is generally understood by sophisticated issuers that both senior debt and public debt may be the subject of secondary market activity in that the debt may be traded to parties other than the original holder. In the case of syndicated senior debt, it is not unusual for that debt to trade at a discount in the event of financial distress, either through private sales (by discreet transactions or by auctions) or through the protocols adopted by trading associations, whether at par or at discount.[97] In the case of public debt, such debt frequently trades freely over the counter between sophisticated investors through the auspices of "market makers" or traders, largely situated in New York City. The rules of participation for issuers in those markets (and in the equity markets) vary and are also beyond the scope of this chapter.

Managing relationships with the holders of senior debt and public debt becomes one of the most important aspects of accomplishing any financing or restructuring of a financially distressed enterprise. In situations involving syndicated senior debt, there is typically an agent lender through whom most communication is channelled in dealing with both information requests and negotiations concerning present and future support for the enterprise. So while the holders of the senior debt may change, and although specialized account managers may be introduced into the situation by the agent lender, it is not usual for there to be substantial change in the institutional relationship between the issuer and the agent for holders of the senior debt while the financing and restructuring effort is pursued.

The situation is quite different with respect to the public debt market. Although there are many circumstances in which the initial holders of the debt remain the same, the tendency in financially distressed circumstances is for the debt to trade and for the holders of that debt to have substantially different objectives in conjunction with their investments than the original or intervening holders. It is not always the case that the beneficial owners of public debt are identifiable or well organized at the early stages of an issuer's financial distress. However, as distressed debt trades, ad hoc committees tend to form to represent the interests of public debt holders in dealing with the issuer. Frequently, members of the ad hoc committee subsequently serve as members of a formal committee of bondholders (secured or unsecured) in the context of formal proceedings. The role that the new investors in public debt play in the context of the governance of a financially distressed corporation depends upon many factors, including the amount of the public debt they hold, whether the issuer requires covenant waivers to avoid breaches or enforcement action, the extent to which the public debt is secured against the assets of the issuer, and the extent to which they represent a creditor constituency whose support must be obtained in conjunction with any financing or restructuring.[98]

Information Gathering and Disclosure

Requests for information from market participants and others usually increase when an issuer is in financial distress. Obtaining adequate and reliable information concerning the business and financial affairs of a distressed enterprise can be a challenge but it is critical to a successful financing and restructuring. It is not unusual for financially distressed enterprises to cut corners and restrict or reduce investment in the necessary human or capital resources to support adequate information systems. It is also not unusual that a number of employees involved in the information gathering and disclosure functions, indeed any function, leave for greener pastures. Augmenting the enterprise's existing internal resources with those of external suppliers in developing financial and other information to be disseminated in support of the enterprise's mission may be required.

Typically, information is disseminated on a confidential basis by an issuer to the syndicated debt market and, conversely, on a nonconfidential basis to the public debt market.[99] Managing the dissemination of that information and attempting to ensure an equality of access so as to avoid inadvertent disclosure of information or disclosure to a select number of market participants, while ensuring the accuracy and consistency of the information, represents one of the highest challenges facing financially distressed enterprises. This is not only because of the regulatory requirements that may be applicable but also because enterprises participating in the capital markets typically have many points of contact through which information can be requested and disseminated. Market participants can prove to be very resourceful in obtaining access to information that was not intended to be disclosed at the time of its disclosure or that is incorrect. Adopting and implementing effective communication programs for market participants as well as employees, suppliers, and customers is critical to a successful financing and restructuring of financially distressed enterprises.

Keeping Employees Focused

Keeping the employees of a financially distressed enterprise focused on the issues facing the enterprise and moving towards implementing solutions for its financing or restructuring is also a significant challenge. People working inside financially distressed enterprises are typically subject to substantially increased stress levels because of uncertainty and the increased demands placed on them by the need for enhanced information flow and the disappearance of colleagues, whether through layoffs or voluntary departures. It is also not unusual for headhunters to surface, attempting to lure employees away from a financially distressed enterprise, and for significant management changes to occur during the period of financial distress that alter reporting relationships and the comforts previously associated with job positions.

A large part of keeping employees focused relates to the communication programs referred to above, and also to finding ways in which to instill confidence in the employee group and others so that they continue to believe in the future prospects of the enterprise. Finding a win or two, no matter how small, during the course of the financing and restructuring can go a long way towards convincing both employees and other interested parties that there is a viable and worthwhile enterprise to remain associated with, to finance, and to restructure.

Losing Control

The skill sets required of those involved in governance and in taking executive action in ordinary circumstances are not necessarily sufficient to accomplish a financing or restructuring of a financially distressed enterprise. One of the questions to be asked early in the process by those involved in the governance of a financially distressed enterprise is whether additional skills and resources are required in order to accomplish a financial restructuring (and how they can be paid for). It is not unusual for existing management to underestimate the challenges that will be faced in effecting the financing or restructuring, whether because of the insufficiency of their skill sets or in an attempt to try to postpone events so as to avoid blame. Nonetheless, determining whether senior management or governance changes are required is a necessary aspect of governance and a potential linchpin component of achieving financing for a financially distressed corporation and implementing a successful restructuring.

Board Committees and CROs

It is not unusual for those involved in the most senior positions in a financially distressed enterprise to be asked to relinquish some or all of their control over the enterprise as a component of a financing or restructuring. Canadian corporate history is replete with a number of circumstances where senior management has "fallen on its sword" as a component of a major financial restructuring. Examples in this regard involving enterprises that have accessed global capital markets include the insolvency proceedings of Dome Petroleum Ltd.,[100] Dylex Ltd.,[101] and the Loewen Group Inc.[102]

There is a developing trend in Canada towards the appointment of special committees of boards of directors and/or chief restructuring officers (CRO) in order to steer financially distressed enterprises through their financing and restructuring attempts.[103] Recent examples include cases involving Consumers Packaging Inc.,[104] Laidlaw Inc.,[105] the Loewen Group Inc.,[106] and Algoma Steel Inc.,[107] all Canadian enterprises that have accessed global capital markets. The timing of the appointment of a special committee and/or a CRO can vary. For example, in the recent *Algoma* proceedings, formal insolvency proceedings were commenced prior to the appointment of a CRO, but the usual practice is to retain the services of a CRO prior to commencement of formal proceedings.[108]

The role CROs play is as varied as the circumstances in which they are appointed, but ultimately they can significantly influence the outcome of the financing and restructuring process and will be looked to closely in the governance aspects of the enterprise. The CRO can have reporting relationships with one or more of the senior management, the directors (or a committee of directors), controlling shareholders, or a supervising court.[109]

In circumstances where confidence in the enterprise and senior management is intact, the CRO may work with existing senior management and focus on financing, negotiating with stakeholders, and managing important relationships in order to implement a restructuring. If the enterprise is to continue as a going concern, the CRO can act as a buffer to deal with tough negotiations and issues while preserving the business relationships between the existing directors, senior management, and third parties. In such cases, a successful financing or restructuring is the result of collaboration by the existing senior management and CRO, and is reflected in the day-to-day control of the enterprise. However, in circumstances where lenders, shareholders, or other important stakeholders have lost confidence in management or the business affairs of a financially distressed enterprise, the CRO may replace some or all of the existing senior management and assume full control of the financing and restructuring effort.

Lenders and Public Debt Holders

Senior lenders and public debt holders typically play significant roles in influencing the governance of a financially distressed enterprise.[110] Beyond the covenants contained in the applicable credit agreement or instrument,[111] the ability of senior lenders and public debt holders to influence the direction of a financially distressed enterprise is based on the additional restrictions they may place on the enterprise in return for providing additional financing; waivers of one or more defaults under the applicable credit agreements or instruments, and the potential remedies and rights of enforcement they may pursue; and their consent to or active participation in supporting a financing or restructuring plan in order to achieve a successful outcome.

Difficult Claims

In estimating whether a financing or restructuring attempt will be successful, focus must be placed on whether there are significant claims outstanding against either the enterprise or its directors that would serve as an impediment to the financing or restructuring, such as mass tort claims with respect to securities losses[112] or tort liabilities for personal injury.[113] Those types of liabilities may be too large or owed to too many to make administration and settlement of those liabilities possible on any basis other than within formal insolvency proceedings. Unless those liabilities are dealt with, there is no realistic prospect of being able to finance or restructure the enterprise.

Choosing to File

There are many reasons why financially distressed Canadian enterprises participating in global capital markets may find themselves faced with the choice of whether to seek protection from their creditors. There is usually a period prior to that decision being made where attempts are made at an informal workout of the financial problems facing the enterprise. This is not always possible, whether because of aspects relating to the enterprise's business, the nature and location of its creditor groups, or other factors.

Commencement of formal insolvency proceedings is both a blessing and a bane. It is intended to provide some breathing room during which the debtor can reorganize itself. However, it typically has the collateral effect of heightening the requirement for information flow and disclosure and places great burdens on the individuals involved in governance and management of the enterprise. Nonetheless, a formal insolvency proceeding can be quite beneficial in terms of providing opportunities for financing and effecting a restructuring for a financially distressed enterprise.

Determining whether, when, and where to commence formal insolvency proceedings to best position a financially distressed enterprise to finance or restructure itself is part art and part science. Many, many factors go into making those decisions and are beyond the scope of this chapter. However, certain aspects relating to the financing of financially distressed Canadian businesses discussed below will suggest that a filing can be made either in Canada pursuant to the provisions of the *CCAA*, or in the United States pursuant to the provisions of Chapter 11, or both.

Some Financing Techniques

There are a number of types and sources of financing involving financially distressed Canadian enterprises, although most people automatically think only of what is referred to as debtor-in-possession (DIP) financing, where "new money" is provided by a lender or lenders obtaining the benefit of a court-ordered charge under the *CCAA* or Section 364 of Chapter 11 for the purpose of permitting the debtor to remain in business while it works out its affairs with its creditors.

Accessing Existing Credit

Simply because a company is in financial distress does not mean that all of its "old money" forms of credit financing terminates. Ordinarily, they become subject to negotiation and amendment concerning the basis upon which they may be utilized, but this does not mean they disappear altogether. So-called old money credit financing arrangements are typical in informal workouts but also apply in formal insolvency proceedings in Canada, although on a somewhat different basis.

Current Assets

In the absence of formal insolvency proceedings, financially distressed Canadian enterprises may continue to use their accounts receivable and inventory in the ordinary course of business in order to finance corporate activities. They may also do so within the confines of a *CCAA* proceeding without demonstrating that the interests of any secured parties therein are adequately protected.[114] In addition, within the confines of a *CCAA* proceeding, accounts receivable and inventory may be realized upon and utilized out of the ordinary course of business even though subject to charges in favour of secured parties, without demonstrating "adequate protection," unless restrictions contained in any order issued under the *CCAA* proceedings have limited their use.[115] These two characteristics of current asset financing inside *CCAA* proceedings contrast sharply with the requirement to establish adequate protection in Chapter 11 proceedings.[116]

Asset Dispositions

Disposition of assets in the ordinary course of business (such as owned, obsolete machinery and equipment) is sometimes readily done in order to raise cash, even though those assets are subject to charges in favour of secured parties.[117] In the context of an informal workout, it is not unusual for a financially distressed enterprise to obtain specific permission from relevant secured parties for such asset dispositions to be made in order to provide a ready source of cash to fund corporate activities. It is a very different matter with respect to leased assets and non-obsolete and substantial fixed assets. Typically, lenders involved in informal workouts are not inclined to see significant assets disposed of until such time as they are satisfied that the proceeds of disposition are going to be applied against their loans or otherwise significantly enhance their recoveries.

Within the confines of proceedings under the *CCAA*, however, it is usual for the debtor to receive court permission to dispose of such assets as it thinks is appropriate in order to accomplish a restructuring, subject to prescribed maximums within the court order granting the debtor authority to take such steps. This authority is typically granted to the debtor notwithstanding the existence of charges of secured parties and without any requirement to establish adequate protection.[118] The authority to sell leased assets subject to financing leases containing title-retention language is not yet well developed in Canada. However, such sales have been allowed as part of a going-concern sale, subject to reserves being established on the value to be shared with the affected lessor.[119]

The US approach to asset sales under Chapter 11 is significantly different. A debtor-in-possession may raise cash by using, selling, or leasing assets other than in the ordinary course of business, provided the interest of any creditor in the asset is protected. The debtor can deal with assets with the consent of affected parties or by court order granted after a hearing with appropriate notice given.[120] Any affected party at any time can request the court to restrict or prevent any dealing in the asset to ensure adequate protection of the affected party's interest.[121]

Existing Credit Facilities

Prior to the commencement of proceedings under the *CCAA*, financially distressed enterprises are subject to normal contractual restrictions on the availability of advances. Subsequent to the commencement of *CCAA* proceedings, there is no authority for a Canadian court to compel a lender to make a further advance of credit.[122] It is not clear, however, whether that limitation relates to amounts greater than the amount outstanding at the time of commencement of the *CCAA* proceedings but less than the contractually provided for availability that might otherwise apply.[123] In practice, both in the context of informal workouts and in the context of a *CCAA* proceeding, existing revolving credit facilities can be and are made available by lenders under the terms of either the existing credit arrangements or forbearance arrangements, and in the case of *CCAA* proceedings, under the terms of applicable court orders, insofar as the lenders are satisfied that continuing availability is coincident with maximization of value and an enhanced prospect of recovery of their loans. This situation contrasts sharply with the financing practices in the United States, where so-called pre-petition credit facilities typically terminate and are replaced by so-called DIP financing facilities.[124]

Trade Credit

It is not unusual for trade credit to become more restricted prior to the commencement of formal insolvency proceedings, so that in many instances the debtor finds itself paying on a cash-on-delivery basis prior to commencing proceedings in any event. As is the case with revolving credit facilities established by lenders, there is no authority on the part of a Canadian court to order any supplier to provide additional credit to a debtor subsequent to the commencement of proceedings under the *CCAA*.[125] However, there is no express requirement under the *CCAA* that goods or services that are obtained on credit during the period of court protection (the Administrative Period) be paid for or that the suppliers of those goods and services enjoy any form of priority for payment.[126] This position also contrasts sharply with practice in the United States, where administrative expense priority is extended to the suppliers of goods and services to the debtor during the Administrative Period.[127]

Financing Charges

There is a developed body of case law under the *CCAA* that has determined that during the currency of the Administrative Period a debtor need not make payment with respect to interest or principal amounts for financing arrangements.[128] This has recently been extended to include payments with respect to financing leases.[129] Consequently, one of the significant potential sources of financing for a financially distressed enterprise is the cash flow that becomes available on the commencement of *CCAA* proceedings and the implementation of a moratorium on payment of interest and principal. However, interest and principal moratoriums on secured debt are typically the subject of negotiation in the context of *CCAA* proceedings, and the debtor may be required to provide for payment of senior debt financing charges to secure senior lender cooperation. For example, in the recent *Algoma* proceedings, the syndicate of senior lenders negotiated the inclusion of a provision in the *CCAA* Order permitting the debtor to pay all "interest, fees and reasonable expenses or other amounts pursuant to the Existing Facility" during the Administrative Period.[130]

Accessing New Credit

Changing Lenders

Changing operating lenders is rarely easy, even in the best of times, given the time, effort, and expense required. It may also be restricted by covenants contained in an issuer's public debt instruments. However, there are circumstances where financially distressed enterprises may benefit from a change in lenders because additional credit availability might be provided (such as through asset-based lending arrangements), or existing lending relationships have become overly strained. There has been a substantial increase in asset-based lending in Canada over the course of the past number of years, but such facilities are typically not in place for Canadian companies involved in global capital markets.

Increasing Existing Credit

Most often, financially distressed enterprises in Canada are obliged to approach their exiting senior lenders with a request for increased availability of credit. The nature of the approach and the tone of the discussions that may ensue in conjunction with the request for additional credit vary with each case. However, it is typically the precursor to a wide-ranging discussion on the operational and financial health of the enterprise and what might be done to address the situation. Where additional financing is made available, it is possible to obtain additional advances under amended existing credit facilities. However, where formal insolvency proceedings are to be taken, there is a developing trend towards providing additional credit to financially distressed enterprises in Canada under new facilities. Those facilities are most often arranged and made available by the existing participants in the issuer's senior debt facilities, as opposed to new lenders or holders of public debt.

Canadian DIP Financing

It is possible for financially distressed Canadian enterprises to raise additional senior or public debt to avoid a liquidity crisis and the prospect of a formal insolvency filing usually from their existing lenders as they attempt to preserve value and ward off the deleterious effects to the enterprise of a looming insolvency. Where a formal insolvency filing is selected or becomes necessary, however, there is a developing trend towards "new money" financing of distressed enterprises in Canada to be accomplished as so-called debtor-in-possession (DIP) financing.[131]

What Is It?

DIP financing in the nature of "new money" granted in exchange for the provision of court-ordered charges over some or all of the assets of the debtor is available in Canada only under the auspices of a court exercising jurisdiction over an insolvent debtor pursuant to the provisions of the *CCAA*. The nature of the charges granted to lenders to secure advances made under DIP financing arrangements vary greatly but can be subordinate, *pari passu* or in priority to existing contractual charges. The uses for which DIP financing is sought also vary greatly but are typically to finance and secure:

- professional costs associated with the debtor's reorganization effort[132]
- director and officer liability exposure[133]
- specific maintenance programs[134]
- insurance premium payments (for both director and officer liability policies[135] and for property and casualty coverage)[136]
- bonding requirements[137]
- general working capital purposes.[138]

When Will It Be Available?
The *CCAA* is silent as to whether and upon what terms DIP financing may be obtained. In order to further the objects of the *CCAA*, however, a number of Canadian courts have taken a purposive approach in holding that they have sufficient inherent jurisdiction to permit insolvent debtors to obtain financing supported by court-ordered charges in the course of *CCAA* proceedings, including over the objections of existing secured creditors.[139] The Supreme Court of Canada's views on the limitations on inherent jurisdiction[140] have been alluded to by at least one court of first instance in limiting an application for DIP financing.[141] Accordingly, the scope of availability of DIP financing in Canada is uncertain. Notwithstanding the absence of certainty as to the legal foundation for the availability of DIP financing in Canada and the basis upon which court-ordered charges supporting DIP financing might be varied, DIP financing continues to be sought and granted.[142]

The following principles were referred to by a working group of the Insolvency Institute of Canada's Joint Task Force in Business Insolvency Law Reform (the IIC Joint Task Force) and presented at its annual conference in October 2001 as having emerged from the *CCAA* cases that have considered the issue of when DIP financing may be granted (the IIC 2001 Joint Task Force Guidelines):[143]

- a company with a viable basis for restructuring will be permitted to borrow funds for working capital and grant security for such borrowings that ranks ahead of the claims of unsecured creditors;[144]
- super-priority DIP financing will be approved where all or substantially all the existing secured creditors acquiesce or consent;[145]
- super-priority DIP financing will be granted where existing secured creditors will not be adversely affected thereby because the financing results in the creation of new collateral assisting in repaying the DIP financing, specifically new receivables;[146]

- super-priority DIP financing will be approved where the funds are used to pay essential expenditures that have priority in any event over existing secured lenders, who will therefore suffer little overall prejudice as a result, particularly where the new financing is "not very significant ... relevant to the overall numbers involved";[147]
- the court's inherent jurisdiction to grant super-priority financing does not extend so as to permit it to grant DIP financing super-priority over security interests that, by statute, are afforded priority over all other interests (such as builders liens);[148]
- deciding whether to grant super-priority DIP financing is an exercise of balancing the interests of the debtor and its stakeholders. The court should not permit super-priority DIP financing unless there is cogent evidence that the benefit of DIP financing clearly outweighs the potential prejudice to the lenders whose security is being subordinated;[149]
- the interests of existing secured creditors can be prejudiced by the granting of super-priority financing only if the court is satisfied this is justified in the circumstances of the case. The court will not be satisfied that there is such justification where the secured creditors have "a high level of distrust" and "wide-ranging lack of confidence" in the debtor's managers and directors, and the appointment of an interim receiver under the *BIA* is found to be the more appropriate course of action. An order authorizing super-priority DIP financing "is only rarely made unless the security for such financing can be provided by hitherto unsecured assets."[150]

These principles were discussed and debated by senior insolvency professionals at the conference. As a result, the following reform proposals for legislative and policy reform relating to interim financing were submitted by the IIC Joint Task Force to Industry Canada as part of a report dated 15 March 2002 (hereinafter the IIC 2002 Joint Task Force Report):[151]

(a) provide in CCAA cases for an express statutory power to authorize borrowing ("DIP Loans") and grant security in specified amounts for post-filing advances and supplies of goods and services necessary to fund the debtor during the restructuring proceedings, such power to be authorized according to criteria to be specified in the statute;

(b) provide that in deciding whether or not to authorize a DIP Loan, the court should consider amongst other things, the following factors:

  (i) what arrangements have been made for the governance of the debtor during the proceedings;

  (ii) whether management is trustworthy and competent, and has the confidence of significant creditors;

(iii) how long will it take to determine whether there is a going con-cern solution, either through a reorganization or a sale, that creates more value than a liquidation;

(iv) whether the DIP Loan will enhance the prospects for a going concern solution or rehabilitation;

(v) the nature and value of the assets of the debtor;

(vi) whether any creditors will be materially prejudiced during that period as a result of the continued operations of the debtor; and

(vii) whether the debtor has provided a detailed cash flow for at least the next 120 days;

(c) provide automatic statutory protection for DIP lenders and debtors against tort damages and other claims for entering into court authorized DIP Loans in breach of pre-filing covenants and other obligations;

(d) provide that the court order itself can create the DIP lien on the property of the debtor described therein without the need for security documents;

(e) provide that the DIP lien need not be registered in order to be effective against pre-filing creditors or a trustee in bankruptcy, but notice of the order must be registered under the provincial property security laws applicable in the locality of the debtor, and against title to real estate in order to have priority over subsequent purchasers (with protection for purchasers acting in the ordinary course of business) and secured lenders acting for value and without notice of the court order;

(f) provide that the court has jurisdiction to provide that the DIP lien has priority ("prime") over all or such other existing security interests as may be specified by the court (except source deduction deemed trusts);

(g) provide that the court shall not prime a registered or possessory security interest without at least 48 business hours notice to the affected secured creditor;

(h) provide that in deciding whether to exercise the power to prime other security interests, the court should be required to use the existing balancing of prejudices/limited prejudice test developed by the courts when exercising inherent jurisdiction;

(i) provide that at the time a priming DIP lien is authorized, the court be given the statutory power to authorize and create liens to protect the primed secured creditors to the extent that they are prejudiced by reason that upon enforcement the proceeds of the collateral of such secured creditors are used to repay the DIP Loan (with the same rules concerning registration, priority, appeals, etc. applying to such liens as apply to DIP liens);

(j) provide that in the event that a priming DIP lien is enforced, the court has the authority to allocate on a just and equitable basis how the burden of the DIP lien is ultimately to be borne by the primed secured creditors;

(k) provide that with respect to advances authorized by a court order and made prior to receipt by the DIP lender of written notice of any subsequent order (whether made by way of appeal or otherwise) varying, staying or rescinding the authorizing order, that the rights of DIP lender under the authorizing order with respect to such advances shall not be affected by such subsequent order;

(l) provide (in both *CCAA* and *BIA* proposal cases) that unsecured claims for goods and services (including real property and true personal property leases) provided (in the ordinary course of business and consistent with the statutes and any court orders) post-filing have priority over pre-filing unsecured claims;

(m) provide (in both the *CCAA* and *BIA* proposal cases) that after filing, the debtor should not obtain additional credit from any person, including a supplier or a lender, without first giving the person appropriate notice of the proceeding;

(n) provide that the court shall not permit a *CCAA* or *BIA* proposal case to continue if it is not satisfied that adequate arrangements have been made for payment for post-filing goods and services;

(o) provide (in both *CCAA* and *BIA* proposal cases) that no payments are to be made or security granted with respect to pre-filing unsecured claims without prior court approval (obtained after the initial order), except that with the prior written consent of the monitor/trustee (unless otherwise ordered by the court) the following pre-filing claims can be paid:

    (i)   source deductions;

    (ii) wages (including accrued vacation pay), benefits and sales tax remittances not yet due or not more than seven (7) days overdue at the date of filing; and

    (iii) reasonable professional fees (subject to subsequent assessment) incurred with respect to the filing;

(p) provide (in both *CCAA* and *BIA* proposal cases) that no payments are to be made or additional security granted with respect to pre-filing secured claims (including security leases) that are subject to the stay without the prior approval of the court; and

(q) provide that during a reorganization proceeding if there is no readily available alternative source of reasonably equivalent supply, then in order to prevent hostage payments the court has jurisdiction, on notice to the affected persons, to order any existing critical suppliers of goods and services (even though not under pre-filing contractual obligation to provide goods and services) to supply the debtor during the reorganization proceeding on normal pricing terms so long as effective arrangements are made to assure payment for post-filing supplies.[152]

There are a number of other possible circumstances where a Canadian court may approve DIP financing in *CCAA* cases. As Dr. Sarra suggests, Canadian courts frequently concern themselves with the potential economic consequences to employees, local trade suppliers, communities, and other unsecured creditors when determining to exercise their jurisdiction to grant DIP financing.[153] They may well be prepared to move beyond the IIC 2001 Joint Task Force Guidelines and IIC 2002 Joint Task Force Report in appropriate cases.

The judicial tests that are being applied by Canadian courts in granting DIP financing requests are not yet fully articulated, but, as has been noted by the British Columbia Supreme Court, a mere demonstration that the DIP financing would be "beneficial" is not a sufficient threshold.[154] Rather, what is required is that the DIP financing be "critical for the business to continue to operate in order ... to successfully restructure its affairs."[155]

A somewhat different standard was articulated by the Ontario Court of Justice (General Division) in the *Royal Oak* proceedings, where the Court held that extraordinary relief such as DIP financing with priority status should be granted in an initial *CCAA* Order only in an amount that is reasonably necessary to meet the debtor's urgent needs over the "sorting out period."[156] The Court held that the DIP financing should be enough to "keep the lights on" and enable the debtor to meet appropriate preventative maintenance measures, but that an initial order under the *CCAA* should approach DIP financing in a judicious and cautious manner, ordering DIP financing facilities only where it is reasonably necessary for the continuing operation of the debtor corporation during a brief but realistic period on an urgent basis.[157]

The treatment of a request for a DIP facility in the recent *Algoma* proceedings was not quite so restrictive.[158] The application for an initial order under the *CCAA* was taken on an urgent basis and Algoma's noteholders, who had an existing first charge on the fixed assets, did not receive advance notice of the hearing. Algoma sought and obtained a DIP facility in its initial order.[159] The operating lenders that had an existing first charge on Algoma's current assets were also the lenders under a $50 million DIP facility to be secured by a first charge over the fixed assets and a second charge over the current assets. Professional and directors' charges were also granted with security over Algoma's fixed assets in priority to the noteholders' security for amounts up to Cdn$500,000. An attempt to minimize the effect of the DIP facility on the noteholders' security was to limit draws on the DIP facility to $20 million in the first month.[160] The net effect, however, was to prime the noteholders' security without notice. Upon receiving notice, the noteholders launched an application for leave to appeal and a motion to vary the initial order. The Ontario Court of Appeal dismissed the leave to appeal application, finding that it was premature given the outstanding motion to vary.[161] Ultimately, the DIP facility was not materially altered.

Although the matter was not specifically addressed in *Royal Oak* or *Algoma*, there appears to be a different standard for determining whether to order DIP financing for general working capital purposes as opposed to funding professional fees and certain other debtor-in-possession needs. In the *United Used Auto*[162] proceedings, both the court of first instance and the British Columbia Court of Appeal declined a request for DIP financing generally but determined that it was appropriate to grant a super-priority charge for the legal fees the debtor would incur in connection with the restructuring exercise so long as they were capped. The British Columbia Court of Appeal placed no such limits on the fees and expenses to be incurred by the monitor (a court officer whose appointment is statutorily prescribed under the *CCAA*) and its counsel, which were also granted a court-ordered charge.

US DIP Financing

There is greater legal certainty as to the availability of DIP financing in the United States.[163] Section 364 of Chapter 11 expressly permits a court to authorize DIP financing with, in effect, three distinct levels of priority in relation to existing debt:

1   Unsecured indebtedness with administrative expense status (Sections 364[a] and [b])
2   Credit or indebtedness with priority over all administrative expenses and/or secured by a lien on unencumbered property or a junior lien on encumbered property (Section 364[c])
3   Credit or indebtedness secured by a lien that has priority equal or superior to existing liens or security interests (Section 364[d]).

Unsecured credit obtained in the ordinary course of business receives administrative expense priority without a court order, which is not the case in Canada. The other forms of DIP financing referred to above are available only with express judicial authorization. Such authorization can be given only following notice and an opportunity for objecting parties to have a hearing.[164] In addition, in order to obtain financing that is either secured or that has super-priority administrative expense status (i.e., under Sections 364[c] and [d]), the debtor must demonstrate that credit is unavailable on more favourable terms.

In order to obtain financing that has priority equal or superior to existing liens, the debtor must also establish that existing secured creditors have been or will be given "adequate protection." Section 361 defines adequate protection to include periodic cash payments, additional or replacement liens, and other relief that will preserve the value of the creditor's security.[165] Section 364(e) provides that the priorities and liens granted to lenders under the provisions outlined above are protected from reversal on appeal as long as the order granting the priority was sought in good faith and as long as a stay pending appeal was not obtained by a party opposing the grant of the priority or lien.

In practice, interim financing is typically offered under Sections 364(c) or (d), although DIP financing is rarely provided under Section 364(d) without the existing secured creditors' consent.[166] It is also worth noting that Section 363 permits a Chapter 11 debtor to use the "cash collateral" of a secured creditor, but only after express judicial authorization, which can be given only following notice and an opportunity for objecting parties to be heard. In order to authorize the use of cash collateral, the court must be satisfied that the secured creditor in question has been or will be given adequate protection.[167]

A corporation does not have to be insolvent to file for protection under Chapter 11, so there may be equity remaining in the corporation, a not usual but nonetheless possible situation. This has the potential to encourage existing equity holders in corporations subject to Chapter 11 to participate in interim funding arrangements in appropriate cases because in doing so they are capable of preserving their existing investment to the extent possible.[168]

Some Additional Considerations

Those involved in the governance of financially distressed enterprises are called upon to consider numerous factors in determining whether continuing to access existing financing or obtaining new financing is possible or appropriate. Those considerations should be viewed not only in the context of the statutory and common law duties discussed above but also with regard to whether corporate action to effect a financing or restructuring can be implemented.[169] Some additional considerations are discussed below.

Viability

Is There a Business?

As indicated above, there can be many reasons for an enterprise's financial distress. Those involved in governance have a responsibility to seek to identify and rectify those reasons as soon as possible. During the identification phase, it may become apparent that the entire enterprise is incapable of being financed or restructured, such as has occurred recently in conjunction with a number of technology and telecom enterprises, and liquidation should be pursued. However, more often there is either a "hived down" business that is capable of being refinanced and restructured, as in *Philip Services Corporation*,[170] or a going-concern sale of the enterprise that can be implemented in order to keep it intact but change its ownership and capital structure, such as occurred in the *Red Cross*,[171] *CPI*,[172] and *PSINet*[173] *CCAA* proceedings. Determining which outcome is to be pursued depends, in part, upon the projected financial and operational viability of the restructured business.

Some have suggested that granting the benefit of court-ordered charges to finance the activities of financially distressed enterprises should be done only where there is some firm prospect of a plan.[174] Not every case lends itself to such a conclusion at the commencement of proceedings, however. Indeed, occasionally formal insolvency proceedings need to be commenced to take protective steps,[175] and the plan that emerges is one of any number of possibilities that have been entertained in the twilight period prior to the commencement of proceedings or that arise during the proceedings.

Implementation

In order to achieve the refinancing or restructuring of a financially distressed enterprise, the support of a number of constituents is required. Whether and how those involved in the governance of the financially distressed enterprise go about obtaining the support of those constituents can and frequently does determine the outcome of the financing or restructuring effort.

Lenders' Support

Notwithstanding the availability of super-priority DIP financing under the *CCAA* or Chapter 11, implementing a financing or a restructuring generally requires the support of a class of senior debt holders. In both Canada and the United States, the holders of senior debt will typically be required to vote in favour of a plan implementing a restructuring. Determining the "price" of obtaining senior lender support is important, not only to the prospects of a successful outcome but also because an evaluation should be made of whether the price is justifiable when considered in the context of competing claims and alternative recoveries for the senior lenders.

Creditors' Support Generally

In order to achieve plan implementation, support is also required of each and every class of creditor affected by a *CCAA* plan in Canada.[176] In the United States, that is not necessarily the case, given the "cram down" provisions under Chapter 11.[177] However, it may be necessary to "buy" support of a class of unsecured creditors in order to justify the financing effort and implement a restructuring. In such circumstances, and where it is necessary or desirable to implement a consensual restructuring plan through a sale of the enterprise and distribution of the proceeds of a going-concern sale, consideration should be given to whether the return to claimants generally is sufficient to justify the potential for enhanced recoveries by others. For example, where going-concern sales of businesses under court protection are used to implement a restructuring, all or a substantial number of the trade creditors may be left unaffected by the insolvency as the purchasers may want to assume payment of the trade debt in order to maintain the goodwill of the enterprise, as was the case in *PSINet*.[178]

There are also many other constituents whose support may be crucial to the successful implementation of a financing and restructuring, such as employees, landlords, licensors, customers, and other contractual counterparties. Their interests should be considered in the determination of whether necessary levels of support are available and at what price.

Timing

Implementing a refinancing or restructuring solution for financially distressed Canadian enterprises operating in global capital markets takes time, particularly where formal insolvency proceedings are pursued. Under the *CCAA*, there is an initial 30-day period where a protective stay of proceedings may be granted by court order. Subsequent extensions of the stay may be granted if the debtor demonstrates good faith and due diligence in pursing the restructuring.[179] Typically, such extensions are granted for 60- to 90-day periods, although substantially longer and some shorter periods have been granted.[180] In a Chapter 11 case, the initial 120-day period of exclusivity, along with the notice and disclosure periods applicable to the presentation of a plan, usually indicate an initial six-month period.[181]

It is not unusual for *CCAA* proceedings to take between six and nine months or more before interested parties determine viability, structure a plan, create the necessary level of consensus for implementation, effect the requisite notices, hold the necessary meetings, and achieve implementation. In the context of Chapter 11 proceedings, a substantially longer period appears to be the norm.[182] There are techniques used in preparing for and implementing a restructuring, including prepackaged and prearranged plans, so as to truncate the Administrative Period as far as possible. However, when determining whether or not to pursue DIP financing in order to implement a restructuring, those involved in the governance of a financially distressed enterprise need to approach the matter understanding that the enterprise needs financing for between six months and a year, at a minimum, in order to be able to implement a restructuring.

Reducing Personal Risk

It is not easy to adequately fulfill the role of those involved in the governance of financially distressed enterprises. Significant demands are placed on the individuals involved, both as to their time commitments and in terms of their potential personal exposure. Thankfully, there are mechanisms available under both *CCAA* and Chapter 11 proceedings that make it possible to substantially reduce the potential personal exposure of directors and others.

Releases

The *CCAA* expressly contemplates that certain liabilities of directors may be compromised as part of a plan,[183] and plans of reorganization proposed and adopted under Chapter 11 have had extremely broad release language extending not only to directors but also to officers and others.[184]

Director and Officer Charges

As indicated above, there are also court-ordered charges that may be made available as part of a *CCAA* proceeding that serve to limit the exposure of directors and others by charging the corporation's assets to support payment of any claims made against them. Accordingly, pursuing formal insolvency proceedings may be a preferred option if there is a reasonable likelihood of being able to obtain financing and achieve some measure of protection for those involved in the governance of a financially distressed enterprise.

However, commencing proceedings for the purpose of obtaining reduced personal exposure through court-ordered charges, without due regard for the welfare of the enterprise or in circumstances where its viability is doubtful, is not to be countenanced.[185] Commencing *CCAA* proceedings for the purpose of obtaining reduced personal exposure, either through the implementation of a director's and officer's charge or through the releases contemplated as part of an implemented plan, should not be the primary focus of those involved in the governance of a financially distressed enterprise that have accessed global capital markets. Achieving that protection should be a collateral benefit to be conferred on those who have fulfilled or continue to fulfill their statutory and common law duties to the corporation, its shareholders, and others.

Liability Audits

Conducting an audit of the risk factors associated with personal liability is a helpful exercise for those involved in the governance of financially distressed enterprises. Such an audit should be performed prior to seeking court protection, if possible, particularly if a court-ordered charge is to be sought in favour of directors and officers, as the scope of the potential liability of those benefiting from the charge and its possible priority will impact on the availability of DIP financing and the recovery of many other claimants. The scope of such an audit will vary in each case but should include at least a determination as to the following matters relevant to the financing and governance of the enterprise:

- whether directors and officers knew that the enterprise was insolvent at a time it obtained credit

- whether any creditor's exposure to the enterprise changed materially subsequent to such knowledge arising
- the extent to which directors have acquiesced or actively participated in the management and affairs of the enterprise during the twilight period
- whether any transactions that were into during the twilight period were not at fair market value
- whether any personal benefit was derived by those in positions of governance with respect to any transactions that the enterprise entered into
- whether any unfair statements or misrepresentations have been made by such individuals and in what regard and to whom
- whether any other tortious acts have been committed by or at the direction of such individuals, and in what regard and against whom
- whether such individuals have any potential criminal or quasi-criminal exposure, and in what regard.

A Sober Second Look

At some point, a sober second look needs to be taken by those involved in the governance of a financially distressed enterprise as to whether it makes sense to attempt a financing or restructuring through formal insolvency proceedings. At that time, there should be reflection on whether the proceedings are merely "dashing the ship on the rocks" as an alternative to relinquishing control and abandoning the financing or restructuring attempt.

Consideration should be given to whether the enterprise, existing management, and employees are capable of coming within striking distance of meeting the challenges associated with attempting a financing and restructuring, and, if not, whether they can be augmented by external services. Consideration should then be given to whether pursuing the financing and restructuring opportunity available is in the best interests of the corporation and its various stakeholders.

Choice of Forum

As indicated above, many factors should be looked at in determining the appropriate jurisdiction in which to commence formal insolvency proceedings for Canadian enterprises that have accessed global capital markets. Among those factors are: the scope and certainty associated with the duties of directors and officers of such enterprises and the anticipated treatment in any examination of the exercise of those duties; the availability of DIP financing arrangements; process issues (e.g., the timelines and exclusivity periods that must be adhered to); the situs of assets and creditors and the extent to which: (a) creditor involvement is permitted, mandated, or desired, and (b) creditors' need to be bound by the proceedings; the treatment of contracts, leases, and assets sales under the insolvency regime; and whether insolvency is a prerequisite to qualification for protection.

A Recent Example

The recent *CCAA* proceedings involving Consumers Packaging Inc.[186] (CPI) provide an interesting illustration on the creative use of both "old money" and "new money" DIP financing sources for a financially distressed Canadian enterprise that has participated in global capital markets and commenced formal insolvency proceedings. They also highlight some of the governance issues facing financially distressed enterprises and some of the choices made by those involved in the governance of CPI in financing its activities and accomplishing a going-concern sale of its primary business operations in implementing a restructuring.

Assets

CPI was Canada's principal manufacturer and supplier of glass bottles, representing approximately 82 percent of domestic demand with consolidated net sales of $1.5 billion. It had operations in six plants, all located in Canada, along with extensive warehouse and distribution assets in the United States. CPI was a public company, listed on the Toronto Stock Exchange, although 63.6 percent of its stock was owned directly or indirectly by one individual who also served as chairman of its board of directors and its chief executive officer.

Debts

Before seeking protection from its creditors, CPI had approximately $71 million in revolving operating loans outstanding from a syndicate of three-Canadian based banks, one of which was a subsidiary of a large foreign bank whose loan account was administered out of New York City. The originally committed operating facility was $90 million but had been reduced by agreement with CPI in the months leading to its seeking protection under the *CCAA*. Advances under the operating line were secured against accounts receivable and inventory. A potential pension deficit of approximately $35-$45 million also faced CPI and its creditors upon a complete winding up of its pension plan. As a result of the potential priority position of certain pension deficits under the *Pensions Benefits Act*,[187] as against accounts receivable and inventory,[188] there was some doubt as to the sufficiency of current assets in order to be able to completely retire the operating loans in the event of a liquidation.

CPI also had approximately US$245 million in advances outstanding from bondholders (largely located in the US) secured against its fixed assets, which were aging and had a "heavy" industry profile. CPI had undertaken an aggressive modernization and upgrading program that was funded by public debt issues. Long before CPI commenced formal insolvency proceedings, an ad hoc committee of bondholders formed and they engaged counsel and financial advisors to protect their interests.

CPI's unaudited consolidated balance sheet as at 31 March 2001 indicated "accounts payable and accrued liabilities" of approximately $350 million, a significant portion of which was trade debt. CPI used large amounts of raw materials such as sand, limestone, and corrugated packaging materials in its manufacture and production of glass products. Interruption of service or increase in the cost of these materials to CPI were significant concerns. Accordingly, certain critical suppliers were paid in full for their pre-filing claims, and cash deposits were made on account or prepayment arrangements were made by CPI to ensure future supply.

Operational Challenges

CPI faced many operational challenges including seasonality, aging capital assets, and an enormous increase in its input costs as a result of the spike in natural gas prices in 1999 and 2000. Many of CPI's administrative accounting functions were run out of an indirect subsidiary's systems and premises in the United States, and its CFO function was filled by an individual who also served as CFO of that US subsidiary.[189] The US subsidiary was also subject to certain operational challenges and covenants owed to its own group of public debt holders. CPI had entered into certain long-term fixed price contracts for the supply of glass containers with certain of its customers that did not provide for price adjustments in the event of significant changes in input costs. CPI began losing money and was unable to obtain the necessary adjustments to its contract prices with its customers. It began swapping blocks of business with certain of its subsidiaries so as to attempt to achieve operating efficiencies.

Approaching the Banks

CPI required financing to fund its operating losses and "bridge" it to the completion of its restructuring process. It approached its existing lending syndicate on the matter, but the syndicate was not receptive to providing additional funding. Lengthy negotiations led by the majority shareholder and the CFO ensued without resulting in any additional financing being offered by the operating lenders.

Changes in Governance

After the apparent failure of initial negotiations for additional credit from its existing lenders, in February 2001 CPI's board of directors struck an Independent Restructuring Committee consisting of directors who were independent of the majority shareholder. Apparently CPI's board recognized the need for independence in the circumstances, as the majority shareholder would have been affected by a "change of control" clause in certain public debt instruments and related party guarantees if a substantial dilution of interest or sale of assets occurred at CPI. Such a change in control could have resulted in: acceleration of certain bonds of a related party; certain repurchase obligations of the related party being triggered, which it could not fund; and foreclosure on the common shares held by the majority shareholder. The Committee became active in order to deal with CPI's finances and potential restructuring, including a possible sale as a going concern. The independent committee hired a well-regarded CRO, who in turn hired a well-regarded chief financial officer. Together they assumed the burden of dealing on a day-to-day basis with the parties interested in CPI's financial well-being and the operational issues facing CPI. At or about the same time, CPI engaged financial advisers to assist in dealing, in particular, with its lenders and bondholders, and also to assist in providing administrative support to "backstop" the administrative services supplied by the US subsidiary.

An Active Majority Bondholder

In the spring of 2001, CPI defaulted on interest payments under its bonds. For many months prior, CPI's Independent Restructuring Committee had been dealing with aggressive manoeuvres by a European competitor who wished to acquire CPI's business and become a key international player in the industry. After having had its overtures to purchase CPI rebuffed on numerous occasions, the potential purchaser started to acquire large blocks of the issued bonds, eventually acquiring 50.9 percent, with the stated intention of obtaining a controlling equity interest in CPI. Upon its purchase of a majority of the bonds, the potential purchaser indicated that it would take steps to accelerate the indebtedness due under the bonds unless CPI commenced proceedings under the *CCAA*.[190] Notwithstanding the majority position of this bondholder, CPI continued in dialogue with the professional advisors to the ad hoc committee of bondholders concerning the arrangements being discussed with the operating lenders.

The Bank Deal

At about that time, agreement emerged between CPI and its operating lenders that CPI's restructuring should implement a disposition of its principal operating assets as a going concern under a court-supervised process. A complex arrangement was struck involving utilization of the "old money" operating facilities, which were not retracted by the lenders, and the availability of "new money" under a $20 million DIP facility, to be provided by the same operating lenders pursuant to the terms of a term sheet that was incorporated into the initial order taken out under the *CCAA*[191] and recognized and implemented in the United States pursuant to Section 304 of Chapter 11.[192]

Negotiated Priority of Charges

The funding arrangements with the operating lenders included a negotiated priority of charges under the terms of the initial *CCAA* Order that ranked as follows:

- statutorily created liens and trusts against all of the *CCAA* Applicants that would have priority over contractual claims
- liabilities under the "old money" credit facilities, secured by the accounts receivable and inventories of CPI
- potential liabilities of the directors and officers of all of the *CCAA* Applicants for certain statutory liabilities and the pension plan shortfall amounts, all subject to a $20 million maximum and available only after any and all applicable insurance proceeds had been accessed
- liabilities under the "new money" DIP financing to the extent of $20 million secured against all of the *CCAA* Applicants' assets
- administrative fees and expenses in favour of the monitor under the *CCAA* proceedings and its counsel, as well as counsel for the *CCAA* Applicants
- claims of the bondholders insofar as any of the priority charges granted under the *CCAA* Order diminished the extent of recovery that the bondholders might otherwise have become entitled to in the event of a liquidation (a so-called replacement lien)
- all other potential liabilities of the *CCAA* Applicants' directors and officers for whatever liabilities they may face in serving as directors and officers.

"Old Money" Forbearance

The terms of the forbearance arrangement entered into with the operating lenders with respect to the "old money" were remarkably "vanilla" in that they did not extend to include any number of provisions that ordinarily find their way into such an arrangement. What CPI was required to agree to in the context of the forbearance arrangement was:

- an affirmation of the debt with respect to the principal amount outstanding, the continuing accrual of interest, and the applicable fees and costs being subject to the existing security over accounts receivable and inventory
- an affirmation of the security for the existing debt being validly given and enforceable
- an acknowledgment of existing defaults and that there had been no waiver in respect thereof
- an acknowledgment of the receipt of demand for repayment and a notice of intention to enforce security issued pursuant to Section 244 of the *BIA*
- a series of specified dates by which the asset divestiture program adopted by CPI was to have resulted in: (a) the submission of offers, (b) the negotiation

of terms, (c) court approval of an agreement, and (d) implementation of a sale transaction that would "take out" the operating loans
- a series of intervening events that would terminate the entitlement to availability under the "old money" arrangements
- a reservation of rights in favour of the operating lenders
- stipulations that whatever plan might be filed in the context of the *CCAA* would not affect the "old money" arrangements and the lenders in respect thereof
- mandatory repayment of the "old money" advances through a weekly and permanent reduction in the availability of credit by paying 70 percent of the value any reduction in CPI's working capital assets during the Administrative Period (to compensate the operating lenders for a reduction in collateral value)
- releases and covenants not to sue granted by each of the *CCAA* Applicants in favour of the operating lenders in respect of the manner in which the credit had been operated to date.

Other items that might ordinarily find their way into a forbearance arrangement were not included. For example:

- significant cash controls involving the institution of lock box and blocked account arrangements
- mandatory repayments out of interim asset sales
- "ring fencing," so as to limit the purpose for which monies might be used and to keep advances away from the "challenged" aspects of the business
- the retraction of availability of certain types of advances (for example, bankers' acceptance and LIBOR advances, which are usually based on availability for specified periods)
- inquiries into a complex series of transactions involving related corporations.

"New Money" DIP Financing
The DIP financing facility was the subject of only a term sheet (there was no credit agreement) and the initial *CCAA* Order. In essence, the term sheet specified: (1) how the funds under the DIP facility might be used generally; (2) minimum content of the order of the *CCAA* court implementing same (mostly as to priority of the facility and the absence of any requirement to document or register the change); (3) a series of cash flows that had been prepared by the *CCAA* Applicants in conjunction with their financial advisors; and (4) repayment obligations, including specified dates by which certain milestones had to be reached, which coincided exactly with the divestiture program set out in the forbearance arrangements relating to the

"old money." Otherwise, the ability of CPI to be able to access the DIP financing facilities was largely unrestricted.

Ultimately, the "old money facility" was capped and terminated during the *CCAA* proceedings prior to completion of the prospective sale as a result of certain continuing defaults. Thereafter, all financing for CPI came from its cash flow and the DIP facility. There had been no draw down on the DIP facility until the "old money" facility was terminated.

A Going-Concern Sale

CPI instituted a court-approved and supervised sale process to solicit fully financed offers for its assets. The sale process netted three competing offers. Ultimately, an agreement of purchase and sale of all of CPI's Canadian glass operations, together with all the shares of a US-based subsidiary, was reached that contemplated an aggregate cash purchase price of approximately $235 million, subject to working capital adjustments. This represented approximately $61 million more than CPI's estimated liquidation value. Under the transaction, the purchaser assumed the pension plan shortfall and other employee obligations. While one division was excluded from the sale, the agreement required the purchaser to purchase that division at a minimum price in the event that CPI could not find another buyer by 31 October 2001. The entire transaction was subject to court and regulatory approval.

Initially, the purchaser had requested that the operating lenders consent to the assumption by the purchaser of CPI's syndicated operating debt. However, the operating lenders did not consent to an assumption and ultimately were paid out in full from the proceeds of sale. The major bondholder, which was also an unrequited bidder, unsuccessfully opposed the transaction.

Choices Made

A number of choices were made by those involved in the governance of CPI that affected the interest of its shareholders and creditors, including those who had advanced credit through global capital markets, and that impacted on its ability to successfully implement a financing and restructuring. Of particular note are:

1   change in governance involving the establishment of the Independent Restructuring Committee, the appointment of a CRO and an independent chief financial officer, and the engagement of external financial advisors. This allowed for an assessment to be made by CPI as to the viability of its business, its financing needs, the establishment or shoring up of administrative systems, and the assessment of various financing and restructuring alternatives relatively free from self-interest.

2 The determination to pursue a going-concern sale as the means of achieving a restructuring of CPI's business. That decision was driven by a number of factors, including:

- value maximization for almost all interested parties (notwithstanding the effect on CPI's majority shareholder)
- the demands of the operating lenders that such a sale process be implemented and that they be paid by a specified date
- the agitations of the majority bondholder notwithstanding, the prospect of the failure to accomplish a going-concern sale leaving a liquidation value for aging and "heavy industry" assets to fulfill the liquidation entitlements of the bondholders
- preservation of supply relationships for ordinary trade creditors and over 2,400 direct jobs
- obtaining a successor employer to cure the potential pension deficit, which otherwise had the prospect of eroding the recoveries of the operating lenders and increasing the liabilities of the directors personally
- avoiding the prospect of a major disruption in the Canadian glass container and beverage market.

3 The filing of a full plenary case was made under the *CCAA* alone, rather than also under Chapter 11, and seeking ancillary orders under Section 304 of the US *Bankruptcy Code* enforcing orders issued in the *CCAA* proceedings. This had the effect of making specific charges over CPI's assets available to:

- secure payment of the professional fees and costs necessary to the process
- permit confirmation of availability under the "old money" facility
- support borrowings under a Canadian DIP facility without having to establish adequate protection with respect to the assets charged – which would not have been possible given the nature of the assets and the extent of the indebtedness owed
- allow for payments to critical vendors of pre-filing claims at the discretion of CPI
- give protection to CPI's directors and officers in order to try to implement the financing and restructuring.

In terms of the implementation of the financing arrangements with the existing operating lenders, the net effect of the CPI debt financing arrangements were to set up a potential transfer to the operating lenders of security from the entire asset base of all of the Applicants: (a) by virtue of the broadened security pool made available under the "new money" DIP financing, and (b) the staged reduction in availability under the "old money" facility as a result of the reduction in working capital asset values. It was part of the price of liquidity for CPI and its other stakeholders. In compensation, CPI sought and obtained a replacement lien in favour of its bondholders to cover off any potential diminution in the value of their collateral as a result of the court-ordered charges granted priority over the fixed assets.

The roles the Independent Restructuring Committee, the CRO, and the financial advisors to CPI played in effecting its refinancing and restructuring is completely known only by those involved directly. However, from the perspective of those who represented a member of the operating lender's syndicate, there was a marked change in the manner in which the financial distress of CPI was approached and the solutions implemented subsequent to their involvement.

Conclusion

The issues facing those involved in the governance of financially distressed enterprises can be highly complex and the duties they owe daunting. Successfully financing and restructuring a financially distressed Canadian enterprise that has accessed the global capital markets requires skill, the support and involvement of many, judicial acumen, and a fair amount of luck. Often creditors and others from foreign jurisdictions may not appreciate the subtleties involved in the Canadian insolvency regime, particularly with respect to its DIP financing rules and the effect they may have on interests acquired in global capital markets. As illustrated through the *CCAA* proceedings of CPI, it is possible for such a financing and restructuring to be accomplished when appropriate regard is given to the governance of a financially distressed enterprise and the need to enlist the support of those possessing the skills and resources necessary to implement the process.

Notes

1 For example: Joint Committee on Corporate Governance, *Beyond Compliance: Building a Governance Culture*, Final Report (Toronto: TSX/CNDX/CICA, 2001); Toronto Stock Exchange Committee on Corporate Governance in Canada, *Where Were the Directors? Guidelines for Improved Corporate Governance in Canada* (Toronto: Toronto Stock Exchange, 1994); R.J. Daniels and E.J. Waitzer, "Challenges to the Citadel: A Brief Overview of Recent Trends in Canadian Corporate Governance" (1994) 23 Can. Bus. L.J. 23.

2 See generally the survey of Canadian jurisprudence on directors' fiduciary duty in the judgment of Weiler J.A. in *Pente Investment Management Ltd.* v. *Schneider Corp.* (1998), 44 B.L.R. (2d) 115 at 127 (Ont. C.A.); and the finding of McKinlay J.A. that majority shareholders do not owe a fiduciary duty to minority shareholders in *Brandt Investments Ltd.* v. *KeepRite Inc.* (1991), 3 O.R. (3d) 289 at 301 (Ont. C.A.).

3 See R.J. Daniels and G.G. Triantis, "The Role of Debt in Interactive Corporate Governance" (1995) 83 Calif. L. Rev. 1073 at 1079. In explaining their theory of "Interactive Governance," Daniels and Triantis "adopt a broad definition of 'Governance' that embraces the collective objective of firm value maximization and includes the activities of non-equity stakeholders [creditors]."

4   A term first reported in *Credit Lyonnais Bank Netherland, N.V.* v. *Pathe Communications Corp.,* [1991] WL 277613 at 55 [hereinafter *Credit Lyonnais*].

5   G.G. Triantis, "Debt Financing, Corporate Decision Making, and Security Design" (1995-96) 26 Can. Bus. L.J. 92 at 102 [hereinafter "Debt Financing"].

6   National Association of Securities Dealers Automated Quotation System.

7   For example, the paper does not generally discuss potential liabilities under legislation relating to securities, workplace health and safety, or environmental issues.

8   For example, those under the *Canada Business Corporations Act,* R.S.C. 1985, c. C-44, as am. by S.C. 2001, c. 14, ss. 122, 241 [hereinafter *CBCA*]. Similar provisions are found in the provincial corporation acts. For ease of reference, all further general statutory references relevant to corporate matters will relate to the *CBCA*.

9   See generally the *Fiduciary Duty* section of this chapter, below, and the discussions in J.P. Sarra and R.B. Davis, *Director and Officer Liability in Corporate Insolvency* (Markham, ON: Butterworths, 2002) at 15-21, and C.C. Nicholls, "Liability of Corporate Officers and Directors to Third Parties" (2001) 35 Can. Bus. L.J. 1.

10 G. Morawetz *et al.,* "Canada" in G. Stewart *et al.,* eds., *Directors in the Twilight Zone* (London: INSOL International, 2001) at 47 [hereinafter *Twilight Zone*].

11 *Credit Lyonnais, supra* note 4.

12 See generally *Twilight Zone, supra* note 10 at 82-84. See also *NBD Bank, Canada* v. *Dofasco Inc.* (2000), 46 O.R. (3d) 514 (Ont. C.A.) [hereinafter *NBD Bank*], in which an officer was found personally liable in tort for inducing an extension of credit by a bank to a company in financial distress.

13 See, for example, the insolvency proceedings of Quintette Coal Limited at *Re Quintette Coal Limited* (1990), Vancouver A901 507 (B.C.S.C.).

14 See, for example, the insolvency proceedings of Curragh Inc. as reported at *Canada (Minister of Indian Affairs and Northern Development)* v. *Curragh Inc.* (1994), 27 C.B.R. (3d) 148 (Ont. Ct. (Gen. Div.)) [hereinafter *Curragh*].

15 See, for example, the class action proceedings involving Philip Services Corp. as reported at *Menegon* v. *Philip Services Corp.* (1999), 11 C.B.R. (4th) 262 (Ont. Sup. Ct.). Although not proven at this point, allegations of fraud exist against the vendors and the corporation's directors for misrepresentations that overvalued a metals division.

16 *Bankruptcy and Insolvency Act,* R.S.C. 1985, c. B-3, s. 2(1), as am. [hereinafter *BIA*].

17 *CBCA, supra* note 8 at ss. 42, 44.

18 (1997), 147 D.L.R. (4th) 300 (Ont. Ct. (Gen. Div.)), varied at (1997), 36 B.L.R. (2d) 207, aff'd (1998), 110 O.A.C. 160 (Div. Ct.) [hereinafter *SCI Systems*].

19 *Business Corporations Act* (Ontario), R.S.O. 1990, c. B-16, as am. s. 38(3).

20 *SCI Systems, supra* note 18 at 310 (Ont. Ct. (Gen. Div.)).

21 *Ibid.* at 311-12.

22 *Enterprise Capital Management Inc.* v. *Semi-Tech Corp.* (1999), 10 C.B.R. (4th) 133 (Ont. Sup. Ct.) [hereinafter *Semi-Tech*].

23 *CBCA, supra* note 8, s. 123(4).

24 *Semi-Tech, supra* note 22 at 139.

25 R.S.C. 1985, c. C-36 [hereinafter *CCAA*].

26 U.S.C. Chap. 11 (1978) [hereinafter Chapter 11].

27 *Re Maple Homes Ltd.* (2000), 21 C.B.R. (4th) 87 (B.C.S.C.).

28 *CBCA, supra* note 8, s. 123(4).

29 *Criminal Code,* R.S.C. 1985, c. C-46, ss. 361, 362.

30 *BIA, supra* note 16, Part VIII.

31 *CBCA, supra* note 8.

32 *CBCA, supra* note 8, ss. 118, 119.

33 *Supra* note 9.

34 For example, negligent misrepresentation, fraudulent misrepresentation, fraud and interference with contractual relations. See generally *ADGA Systems International Ltd.* v. *Valcom Ltd.* (1999), 43 O.R. (3d) 101 (Ont. C.A.) [hereinafter *ADGA*].

35 See generally Sarra and Davis, *supra* note 9.

36 (1972), 9 C.C.C. (2d) 386 (Ont. C.A.).

37 (1984), 15 C.C.C. (3d) 231 (Que. C.A.).

38 *BIA, supra* note 16. Liability for an offence under the *BIA* is extended to directors, officers, and agents pursuant to s. 204: "204. Where a corporation commits an offence under this Act, any officer, director or agent of the corporation, or any person who has or has had, directly or indirectly, control in fact of the corporation, who directed, authorized, assented to, acquiesced in or participated in the commission of the offence is a party to and guilty of the offence and is liable on conviction to the punishment provided for the offence, whether or not the corporation has been prosecuted or convicted."

39 *BIA, supra* note 16. See *R.* v. *Reed* (1992), 13 C.B.R. (3d) 124 (B.C.C.A.).

40 *BIA, ibid.*

41 *Ibid.* Courts have interpreted the word "privy" in this section on a number of occasions. Each case supports the conclusion that a director, officer, or principal who had knowledge of the transaction may be privy to the transaction. There does not appear to be a requirement that the director, officer, or principal have personally benefited from, or even have approved, the reviewable transaction. See: *Lagden Equipment Ltd. (Trustee of)* v. *Lagden* (1989), 77 C.B.R. (N.S.) 285 (Que. Sup. Ct.); *Re Westfield Construction Inc.* (1988), 72 C.B.R. (N.S.) 108 (Ont. Sup. Ct.); *H.R. Doane Ltd.* v. *Acadia Auto. and Indust. Supplies Ltd.* (1982), 43 C.B.R. (N.S.) 282 (N.S.T.D.).

42 *CBCA, supra* note 8, s. 241.

43 See generally Sarra and Davis, *supra* note 9 at 35-36.

44 *Lakehead Newsprint (1990) Ltd.* v. *893499 Ontario Ltd.* (2001), 23 C.B.R. (4th) 170 (Ont. Sup. Ct.) [hereinafter *Lakehead Newsprint*], partially rev'd [2001] Carswell Ont. 3388 (O.C.A.), 28 C.B.R. (4th) 53.

45 The right of creditors to bring an action, however, varies across jurisdictions, and courts have limited its use in debt cases. See: *Royal Trust Corp. of Canada* v. *Hordo* (1993), 10 B.L.R. (2d) 86 (Ont. Ct. (Gen. Div.)) [hereinafter *Hordo*]. The Court in *Hordo* held that creditors should not be given standing where the interest of the creditor in how the affairs of the company are managed is too remote or illegitimate, "where the complainants of a creditor have nothing to do with the circumstances giving rise to the debt," or where the proceeding is in bad faith. Creditors should also not be given status as complainants, the Court held, where the position of the creditor is not "analogous" to that of a minority shareholder.

46 *First Edmonton Place Ltd.* v. *315888 Alberta Ltd.* (1988), 60 Alta. L.R. (2d) 122 (Alta. Q.B.).

47 *Ibid.* at 143.

48 *Ibid.* at 145.

49 (2000), 135 O.A.C. 293, aff'd [1998] O.J. No. 4813 (Ont. Ct. (Gen. Div.)) [hereinafter *Leon Van Neck*].

50 *Ibid.*, paras. 101, 110.

51 *Sidaplex-Plastic Suppliers, Inc.* v. *Elta Group Inc. et al.* (1996), 131 D.L.R. (4th) 399 (Ont. Ct. (Gen. Div.)), aff'd (1998), 40 O.R. (3d) 563 at 566-67 (Ont. C.A.) [hereinafter *Sidaplex-Plastic*].

52 *Ibid.* at 404-7.

53 *Western Finance Company Ltd.* v. *Tasker Enterprises Ltd.,* [1980] 1 W.W.R. 323 at 333 (Man. C.A.). Specifically, Huband J.A. held after reviewing texts on Canadian and British company law: "The creditor relationship and the fact of common shareholders are not sufficient, in this case, to create a fiduciary relationship so as to impose liability on Tasker to account to Western Finance for profits earned by Tasker out of a business relationship with Red River [of which Tasker was director and Western Finance was creditor]."

54 *Re Trizec Corp.* (1995), 20 B.L.R. (2d) 202 at 214. Forsyth J. further held: "I acknowledge that a specific duty to shareholders becomes intermingled with a duty to creditors when the ability of a company to pay its debts becomes questionable. However, a wholesale transfer of fiduciary duty to creditors likely does not occur at the stage of proceedings where an arrangement is sought as opposed to a case where liquidation occurs."

55 (1998), 23 C.B.R. (4th) 200 (Que. Sup. Ct.).

56 (1999), 45 O.R. (3d) 565 (Ont. Sup. Ct.) [hereinafter *Edwards Books*].

57 *Peoples, supra* note 55, paras. 69, 80; *CBCA, supra* note 8.

340 *Edward A. Sellers, Natasha J. MacParland, and F. James Hoffner*

58 *Peoples, ibid.,* paras. 190, 191, 195, 199.
59 *Peoples, ibid.,* para. 197; *Winkworth* v. *Edward Baron Development Co. Ltd. et al.,* [1987] 1 All. ER. 114 at 118.
60 *Peoples, supra* note 55, para. 198.
61 *Ibid.,* para. 200.
62 *Edwards Books, supra* note 56 at 572, 574. As this was a motion for summary judgment, the court noted that it was a question of fact to be determined whether the corporation was insolvent at the time of the challenged transactions or whether the transactions threatened the solvency of the corporation.
63 *Lakehead Newsprint, supra* note 44.
64 *USF Red Star Inc.* v. *1220103 Ontario Ltd.* (2001), 13 B.L.R. 295 (Ont. Sup. Ct.) [hereinafter *USF Red Star*].
65 *Lakehead Newsprint, supra* note 44 at 180.
66 *USF Red Star, supra* note 64 at 299-300. The court went on to note: "As Farley J. said in *Royal Trust Corp.* v. *Hordo,* 'It does not seem to me that debt actions should be routinely turned into oppression actions.'"
67 *SCI Systems, supra* note 18.
68 *Ibid.* at 307.
69 *Ibid.* at 308.
70 *Ibid.* at 312-13.
71 *Ibid.* at 314.
72 *Ibid.*
73 *Cadbury Schweppes Inc.* v. *FBI Foods Ltd.,* [1999] 1 S.C.R. 142, para. 164 [hereinafter *Cadbury Schweppes*]. In this case about the obligation of a recipient of confidential information, the party who negotiated for confidential information from the plaintiff later sold that information to the respondent, who breached the pre-existing confidentiality agreement.
74 *Ibid.,* referring to *Frame* v. *Smith,* [1987] 2 S.C.R. 99 at 137-38; *Hodgkinson* v. *Simms,* [1994] 3 S.C.R. 377 at 414. The presence of a commercial relationship will not exclude the presence of a fiduciary relationship, if other indicators of such relationship exists.
75 *Cadbury Schweppes, supra* note 73, para. 164.
76 But see J.S. Ziegel, "Directors' Fiduciary Obligations to Creditors: A Re-examination" in Queen's Annual Business Law Symposium, *Corporate Restructurings and Insolvencies, Issues and Perspectives, 1995* (Toronto: Carswell, 1996) 334 at 337, 338.
77 *ADGA, supra* note 34 at 113.
78 *Ibid.* at 113.
79 *NBD Bank, supra* note 12.
80 *Twilight Zone, supra* note 10 at 421-22. In Delaware, courts can impose personal jurisdiction on any nonresident who in person or through an agent, among other activities, transacts any business in the state: 10 Del. C. s. 3104 (1958).
81 Chapter 11, *supra* note 26.
82 *CCAA, supra* note 25.
83 Bankruptcy Rule 9011; Chapter 11, *supra* note 26 at s. 362(h).
84 U.S.C. s. 152 (1948). Concealment of assets is a continuing offense until the debtor has been discharged, which means that the limitation period does not run until such discharge: 18 U.S.C. s. 3284 (1948).
85 *Ibid.*
86 *Ibid.*
87 *Ibid.,* s. 153.
88 *Ibid.,* s. 156.
89 *Ibid.,* s. 157.
90 Each section cited uses the words "intending," "knowingly," and/or "fraudulently."
91 Del. C. s. 1311 (2001); *Twilight Zone, supra* note 10 at 407.
92 *Geyer* v. *Ingersoll Publications Co.,* 621 A.2d 784 (Del. Ch. 1992) [hereinafter *Geyer*]; *Credit Lyonnais, supra* note 4; D. Thomson, "Directors, Creditors and Insolvency: A Fiduciary Duty or a Duty Not to Oppress?" (2000) 58 U.T. Fac. L. Rev. 31.

93 See generally *Preston-Thomas Constr., Inc.* v. *Central Leasing Corp.*, 518 P.2d 1125, 1127 (Okla. Ct. App. 1973); *Avondale Shipyards, Inc.* v. *Vessel Thomas E. Cuffe*, 434 F. Supp. 920, 930 (E.D. La. 1977).

94 See generally B.J. Houser, "Symposium on Mass Torts: Chapter 11 as a Mass Tort Solution" (1998) 31 Loy. L.A. L. Rev. 451.

95 See generally *Twilight Zone, supra* note 10 at 407-12.

96 Such as Microsoft Corporation's investment in Corel Corporation in 2000 by purchasing 24 million nonvoting convertible preferred shares.

97 Such as through the Loan Syndication and Trading Association.

98 For a discussion of some aspects of the role such investors play in Canadian insolvency proceedings, see J.R. Fogarty and L.A. Goldback, "Vulture Culture: The Changing Dynamics of *CCAA* and *BIA* Restructurings" (2001) 18(5) Nat'l. Insolv. Rev. 61.

99 Due largely to the traditional duty of confidentiality owed by a banker to its customer and customary contractual provisions included in syndicated credit agreements.

100 See the Dome Petroleum Ltd. insolvency proceedings at *Re Dome Petroleum Limited* (1987), Calgary 10361 (Alta Q.B.).

101 See the Dylex Ltd. *CCAA* proceedings at *Re Dylex Limited* (1995), Toronto B4/95 (Ont. Ct. (Gen. Div.)) [hereinafter *Dylex*].

102 See the Loewen Group Inc. *CCAA* proceedings at *Re The Loewen Group Inc. et al.* (1999), Toronto 99-CL-3384 (Ont. Sup. Ct.) [hereinafter *Loewen*].

103 For a useful discussion of the emerging role of CROs in Canada, see M. Forte, "The Recognition and Roles of the Chief Restructuring Officer in Canadian Insolvency Proceedings (Part 1)" (2001) 14 Comm. Insol. R. 4.

104 See the Consumers Packaging Inc. *CCAA* proceedings at *Re Consumers Packaging Inc. et al.* (2001), Toronto 01-CL-4147 (Ont. Sup. Ct.) [hereinafter *CPI*].

105 See the Laidlaw Inc. *CCAA* proceedings at *Re Laidlaw Inc. et al.* (2001), Toronto 01-CL-4178 (Ont. Sup. Ct.) [hereinafter *Laidlaw*].

106 *Loewen, supra* note 102.

107 See the recent Algoma Steel Inc. *CCAA* proceedings at *Re Algoma Steel Inc.* (2001), Toronto 01-CL-4115 (Ont. Sup. Ct.) [hereinafter *Algoma*].

108 As was the case in *CPI, supra* note 104, and *Laidlaw, supra* note 105.

109 See the Starcom International Optics Corp. *CCAA* proceedings at *Re Starcom International Optics Corp.*, (1998) Vancouver A980298 (B.C.S.C.), where the CRO was appointed by and reported to the court, as opposed to the directors.

110 See the discussion in Daniels and Triantis, *supra* note 3.

111 See the discussion in "Debt Financing," *supra* note 5.

112 See the Philip Services Corp. *CCAA* proceedings at *Re Philip Services Corp. et al.* (1999), Toronto 99-CL-3442 (Ont. Sup. Ct.) [hereinafter *Philip*].

113 See the Canadian Red Cross Society *CCAA* proceedings at *Re The Canadian Red Cross Society* (1998), Toronto 98-CL-2970 (Ont. Sup. Ct.) [hereinafter *Red Cross*].

114 See the Silcorp Ltd. *CCAA* proceedings at *Silcorp Limited* v. *Canadian Imperial Bank of Commerce* (1992), Toronto B152/92 (Ont. Ct. (Gen. Div.)).

115 *Ibid.*

116 Chapter 11, *supra* note 26, s. 361.

117 Pursuant to typical exceptions in negative covenants contained in syndicated credit agreements and public debt instruments.

118 For example, in the PSINet Ltd. *CCAA* proceedings, the Initial Order permitted the debtors to "dispose of redundant or non-material assets provided that no sale of assets with net proceeds exceeding $10 million ... shall be agreed upon without leave of this Honourable Court first having been obtained" *Re PSINet Limited et al.* (31 May 2001), Toronto 01-CL-4155 (Ont. Sup. Ct.) [hereinafter *PSINet*].

119 *Ibid.* (26 September 2001). The court required the Monitor to hold back an amount "equal to the full contractual value of the claims of equipment lessors subject to secured financing leases ... with respect to equipment which forms part of the sale assets."

120 Chapter 11, *supra* note 26, ss. 363(a), 363(f).

121   *Ibid.*, s. 363(e).
122   *CCAA, supra* note 25, s. 11.3.
123   An issue discussed at the annual meeting of the Insolvency Institute of Canada (IIC) held at St. Andrews by the Sea in October 2001.
124   For a brief discussion of some of the financing practices in the United States, see G. Triantis, *Law and Economics of Debtor in Possession Financing* (Industry Canada, 1999) [unpublished].
125   *CCAA, supra* note 25, s. 11.3.
126   *Ibid.*
127   Chapter 11, *supra* note 26, s. 364.
128   See, for example, *Re Philips Manufacturing Ltd.* (1992), 12 C.B.R. (3d) 133 (B.C.S.C.) aff'd (1992) 12 C.B.R. (3d) 145 (B.C.C.A.).
129   A financing lease is defined as "a lease which secures the payment or performance of an obligation": *Personal Property Security Act*, R.S.O. 1990, c. P.10, as am., s. 2. As off–balance sheet financings such as financing leases have become more common, there have been numerous cases discussing the characterization of a financing lease. See *Crop and Soil Services Inc.* v. *Oxford Leaseway Ltd.* (2000), 48 O.R. (3d) 291 (Ont. C.A.), and *PSINet, supra* note 118. Chapter 11 also provides for the recharacterization of certain equipment leases by court process. If the leases are recharacterized, the Chapter 11 debtor is not required to make payments during the Administrative Period. Chapter 11, *supra* note 26.
130   *Algoma, supra* note 107. Interestingly, the Initial Order also authorized a $50 million DIP facility with only $20 million of the facility available to Algoma in the first month.
131   For a thorough discussion of the nature and availability of DIP financing in Canada, see J. Sarra, "Debtor in Possession Financing: The Jurisdiction of Canadian Courts to Grant Super-Priority Financing in *CCAA* Applications" (2000) 23(2) Dal. L.J. 337. This type of financing differs from so-called exit financing extended upon the completion of a restructuring.
132   See generally *Re United Used Auto and Truck Parts Ltd.* (2000), 16 C.B.R. (4th) 141 (B.C.C.A.), leave to appeal to the Supreme Court of Canada granted but appeal discontinued, [2000] B.C.C.A. No. 142 (QL) [hereinafter *United Used Auto*].
133   See *CPI, supra* note 104, and see the Canada 3000 Inc. *CCAA* proceedings at *Re Canada 3000 Inc. et al.* (2001), Toronto 01-CL-4314 (Ont. Sup. Ct.) [hereinafter *Canada 3000*].
134   See the Royal Oak Mines Inc. *CCAA* proceedings at *Re Royal Oak Mines* (1999), Toronto 99-CL-3278 (Ont. Sup. Ct.) [hereinafter *Royal Oak*].
135   *Philip, supra* note 112.
136   *Curragh, supra* note 14.
137   *Philip, supra* note 112.
138   *Re Westar Mining Ltd.* (1992), 14 C.B.R. (3d) 88 (B.C.S.C.) [hereinafter *Westar*]; *Re T. Eaton Co Ltd.* (1997), 46 C.B.R. (3d) 293 (Ont. Ct. (Gen. Div.)) [hereinafter *Eaton's*].
139   *United Used Auto, supra* note 132. See also D.B. Light, "Involuntary Subordination of Security Interests to Charges for DIP Financing under the *Companies' Creditors Arrangement Act*" (2002) 30 C.B.R. (4th) 245.
140   *Baxter Student Housing Ltd.* v. *College Housing Co-operative Ltd.* (1975), 57 D.L.R. (3d) 1 (S.C.C.).
141   *Re Royal Oak Mines Inc.* (1999), 7 C.B.R. (4th) 293 at 304 (Ont. Ct. (Gen. Div.)).
142   See Light, *supra* note 139 at 259 for a selective survey of DIP financing caselaw under the *CCAA*.
143   First articulated by M. Rotsztain, "Debtor-in-Possession Financing in Canada: Current Law and a Preferred Approach" (2000) 33 Can. Bus. L.J. 283.
144   *Westar, supra* note 138; *Eaton's, supra* note 138.
145   *Willan Investments Limited et al.* v. *Bank of America Canada et al.* (6 February 1991), Toronto B22/91 (Ont. Ct. (Gen. Div.)).
146   *Dylex, supra* note 101.
147   *Re SkyDome Corporation et al.* (27 November 1988), Toronto 98-CL-3179 (Ont. Sup. Ct.).
148   *Royal Oak, supra* note 134.
149   *United Used Auto, supra* note 132; *Re Sharp-Rite Technologies Ltd.* (21 January 2000), Vancouver A993276 (B.C.S.C.).
150   *General Electric Capital Canada Inc.* v. *Euro United Corp.* (24 December 1999), Toronto 99-CL-3592 (Ont. Sup. Ct.).

151 Joint Task Force on Business Insolvency Law Reform, *A Joint Report of the Insolvency Institute of Canada and the Canadian Association of Insolvency and Restructuring Professionals* (15 March 2002) [hereinafter the *IIC 2002 Joint Task Force Report*] [on file with author].

152 Additionally, the *IIC 2002 Joint Task Force Report* contained recommendations for legislative and policy change relating to corporate governance of businesses' debtors during insolvency and near-insolvency situations.

153 Janis Sarra, *Creditor Rights and the Public Interest: Restructuring Insolvent Corporations* (Toronto: University of Toronto Press, 2003) at 21-25.

154 *United Used Auto, supra* note 132, para. 29.

155 *Ibid.*

156 *Re Royal Oak Mines Inc.* (1999), 6 C.B.R. (4th) 314 at 321.

157 *Ibid.*, para. 24.

158 *Algoma, supra* note 107.

159 *Ibid.*

160 This was varied by the Court to increase draw limits on the DIP facility to $23 million in the first two months of the proceedings. Subsequently, there were additional restrictions on draw downs.

161 (2001), 25 C.B.R. (4th) 194 (Ont. C.A.).

162 *United Used Auto, supra* note 132.

163 See generally Rotsztain, *supra* note 143; Zimmerman, *infra* note 169. The following discussion is excerpted from Joint Task Force on Business Insolvency Law Reform, "Report to the Insolvency Institute of Canada and the Canadian Association of Insolvency and Restructuring Professionals" (Paper presented at the Annual Meeting of the Insolvency Institute of Canada, St. Andrews by the Sea, NB, October 2001) [unpublished] and the affidavit of K. Klee, sworn 9 March 1999, which was submitted in the proceedings reported at *Re Royal Oak Mines Inc.* (1999), 7 C.B.R. (4th) 293 (Ont. Ct. (Gen. Div.)) [hereinafter *Klee*]. At the time of this case, K. Klee was Acting Professor of Law at the Law School of the University of California at Los Angeles and counsel to the law firm of Stutman, Treister and Glatt PC, in Los Angeles. Klee was offered as an expert in the field of US insolvency. See also Light, *supra* note 139 at 248.

164 Bankruptcy Rule 4001(c)(2) and 9006(c)(2) require fifteen days' notice before commencing a final hearing on a motion to obtain credit. A court can hold an interim hearing, a motion for credit during this notice period, provided that affected parties receive reasonable notice. As well, only credit that is necessary to avoid "immediate and irreparable harm" will be given in an interim hearing.

165 "If prospective lenders could not rely on the existence of these provisions in the event of a borrower's insolvency, the ready availability of capital, which is a primary underpinning of our system of commerce, would be undermined severely": *Klee, supra* note 163, para. 22.

166 "A United States Bankruptcy Court would not allow the interest of an undersecured party (i.e., a party with a secured interest in property that may not have sufficient value to insure the full satisfaction of such party's claim), or a party likely to be rendered undersecured by the proposed transaction, to be subordinated to that of a DIP lender without such undersecured party's consent unless: (a) such party had been provided with reasonable notice and an opportunity to be heard in opposition to the request for relief, including the opportunity to contest the debtor's evidence of valuation and present evidence on other matters relevant to the impact of the proposed subordination; (b) the debtor had demonstrated by competent evidence that (i) it was unable, despite appropriate efforts, to obtain credit on an unsecured or non-priming secured basis, (ii) the credit transaction was necessary to preserve the debtor's assets, (iii) the terms of the transaction were fair, reasonable and adequate under the circumstances, and (iv) the debtor has at least a reasonable prospect of successful reorganization; and, of critical importance, (c) if all the debtor's property were encumbered, the debtor had demonstrated by competent evidence that there would be adequate protection of the marginal secured party in the form of (i) periodic cash payments, from an assured source, designed to counteract the diminution of the value of its interest in the relevant collateral or (ii) a demonstrated increase in the value of the collateral, as a direct result of the new capital, equal to or in excess of the value of such

new capital. In my experience, such relief is rarely granted over the objection of an existing lienholder with an interest in the collateral": *Klee, supra* note 163.

167 For a useful discussion of the different positions of a lender whose cash collateral is used and a lender who extends post-petition financing under s. 3764 see D.A. Warfield, "Is It Use of Cash Collateral or Post-Petition Borrowing: How Much Protection Does the Creditor Deserve?" (1989) 94 Com. L.J. 369.

168 *Klee, supra* note 163.

169 For additional discussion, see H.A. Zimmerman, "Financing the Debtor-in-Possession" (Paper presented at the Tenth Annual Meeting and Conference of the Insolvency Institute of Canada, Scottsdale, AZ, 1999) [unpublished], and Sarra, *supra* note 131.

170 *Philip, supra* note 112.

171 *Red Cross, supra* note 113.

172 *CPI, supra* note 104.

173 *PSINet, supra* note 118.

174 *Supra* note 169.

175 For example, in *PSINet, supra* note 118, proceedings were commenced earlier than originally contemplated as a result of broadband access being denied by a creditor. Other examples include: the second Eaton's insolvency proceedings, which were commenced earlier than planned when the sheriff arrived at a store to enforce a writ by taking monies from the cash register; and *Canada 3000, supra* note 133, where proceedings were commenced when an airplane was seized by airport authorities.

176 *CCAA, supra* note 25, s. 6.

177 Chapter 11, *supra* note 26, s. 1129(b); G.G. Triantis, "Mitigating the Collective Action Problem of Debt Enforcement through Bankruptcy Law: Bill C-22 and Its Shadow" (1992) 20 Can. Bus. L.J. 242 at 252 [hereinafter "Mitigating the Collective Action"].

178 *PSINet, supra* note 118.

179 *CCAA, supra* note 25, s. 11.

180 *Loewen, supra* note 102.

181 "Mitigating the Collective Action," *supra* note 177 at 253.

182 *Ibid.*

183 *CCAA, supra* note 25, s. 5.1.

184 See, for example, *Philip, supra* note 112.

185 *Canada 3000, supra* note 133. In this proceeding, the directors and officers were granted a charge in the Initial Order, but once the airline ceased operation, the directors' and officers' charge was retracted and an order was granted removing the charge *nunc pro tunc.*

186 *CPI, supra* note 104. The applicants were CPI, Consumers International Inc., and 164489 Canada Inc.

187 R.S.O. 1990, c. P.8.

188 *Personal Property Security Act,* R.S.O. 1990, c. P.10, s. 30(7).

189 It is common in an undertaking the size of CPI for there to be a number of subsidiaries, affiliates, and complex indirect relationships. CPI was the sole shareholder of 164489 Canada Inc., Consumers Glass s.r.l., CUS II, Inc., and Consumers International Inc. Indirectly, CPI controlled GGC LLC, a wholly owned subsidiary of CUS II, Inc., and Consumers US Inc., a wholly owned subsidiary of Consumers International Inc. CPI also indirectly controlled Anchor Glass Container Corporation through the majority equity interest of Consumers US Inc. In addition, CPI had a majority equity interest in Consumers Sklo-Zorya and a minority equity interest in Phonecia Glass Works.

190 Ultimately, this party participated in the divestiture process but was unsuccessful in its attempts to acquire CPI. In fact, an application for leave to the Court of Appeal was taken by the unsuccessful purchaser after the Ontario Superior Court of Justice approved the sale of CPI to another bidder. This application was also unsuccessful. See *Re Consumers Packaging Inc.* (2001), 27 C.B.R. (4th) 197 (Ont. C.A.).

191 *CPI, supra* note 104.

192 *Re Consumers Packaging Inc., Case No. 01-1865 (U.S. Bkty. Crt. D. Del. 2001) (30 May 2001 and 12 June 2001).*

13

The Role of Court-Appointed Officers in the Governance of Financially Distressed Corporations
John Sandrelli

Whether a corporation is a large multinational publicly traded corporation, a Canadian-controlled private company, or a form that is something in between, governance issues are magnified when the company experiences financial distress. Governance can have an impact on multiple stakeholders in a business, including shareholders, employees, creditors, and perhaps others. In recent times, there appears to be a renewed focus on governance issues across the regulatory spectrum. As companies continue to expand and move into global capital markets, becoming more international in nature, the Canadian landscape with respect to governance issues is likely to change. Most significantly, it is where companies are facing financial difficulty due to poor governance practice or competitive global market pressures that debates about director oversight and manager skills can become more pointed and, in some cases, accusatory.

This chapter examines the financially distressed corporation from the perspective of court-appointed officers, and includes a discussion of the expanding nature of their role. It also explores the benefits to both a business and its stakeholders of introducing a court-appointed officer to the restructuring process in order to aid the financially distressed corporation in meeting its objective of a successful reorganization. Although there are numerous interesting and unique insolvencies where court-appointed officers have taken on an important role in governing the financially distressed company, this chapter highlights a few that are notable in terms of the utilization and expansion of the role of the court-appointed officer.

Governance Issues for the Financially Distressed Corporation

Financially troubled companies differ greatly from healthy ones. They generally suffer on all fronts, including cash flow problems, lack of morale, and, in the case of public companies, shareholder unrest. Of course, it is not uncommon for management to be blamed for these problems. It is well established that the board of directors, in combination with the management that it appoints, is in charge of the governance of a corporation. However, the problems facing the financially distressed company often invite the question of what role the board of directors and management should play. Generally speaking, their credibility is questioned by both creditors and shareholders in terms of whether the directors and managers are the appropriate parties to continue running the company. At the same time, the directors and officers might question their own willingness to attempt to steer the corporate ship through troubled waters. Not only are they frequently accused of being responsible for the current state of affairs, they are also exposed to potential personal liability to creditors or others. The possibility of personal liability is brought to the forefront once it becomes clear that a company is insolvent or on the verge of insolvency. Thus, it is not difficult to envision why the introduction of an independent insolvency practitioner can bring value to what is undoubtedly a difficult situation. A passing on of the governance issues, either in whole or in part, to an experienced practitioner can be the first step in a successful reorganization under which a number of stakeholders can benefit.

Expanding Nature and Role of Court-Appointed Officers

In the last ten to fifteen years, the very nature and description of the court-appointed officer has expanded. Before the late 1980s, the only court-appointed officer of any real significance in terms of assuming governance matters was a Receiver or Receiver/Manager. While there are some differences, this chapter refers to both as Receivers. Generally speaking, a Receiver is appointed at the request of a secured creditor, predominantly a financial institution, to liquidate the financially distressed corporation. While a sale of the business as a going concern is often considered by a Receiver, it is a somewhat rare occurrence for a Receiver to actually run a business for more than a reasonably brief period of time, let alone attempt to restructure it prior to sale. Rather, the focus of the Receiver is to generate a reasonable value for the assets within a reasonable time frame.

In contrast, there are a range of insolvency officers that may be involved in the governance of financially distressed companies, including court-appointed Receivers and Interim Receivers, appointed under the provisions of the *Bankruptcy and Insolvency Act (BIA),* and Monitors,[1] a role that is now mandatory under the *Companies' Creditors Arrangement Act (CCAA).* Most recently, there has also been an emergence of the chief restructuring officer (CRO) as an officer brought in to assist with the workout. The extent to which these different officers become involved in governance varies from situation to situation, but at the very least, all have some role in decision making. Appointments of Receivers, Interim Receivers, and CROs frequently result in the powers of the directors being significantly attenuated or eliminated completely. Even the Monitor appointed in a *CCAA* proceeding can be very influential in terms of decision making. One common thread that runs through all of these roles is that they are court-appointed, and thus the powers of the officers evolve and derive from the court orders appointing them. In most situations, the statutes governing the appointment are flexible. They rely in part on the equitable jurisdiction of the court to do what practicality demands; the role is arguably limited only by the creativity of counsel and the officer involved.

The Role of the Court-Appointed Officer and Its Justifications

There has been a clear recognition by lenders that the reorganization of a business, or at least the running of a financially distressed business for some period of time, can generate a better return for all stakeholders. At the same time, however, it is typical to place blame for the downfall of the financially distressed corporation on the board of directors and management. Moreover, it is often the case that if management had addressed critical issues facing a company long before the introduction of an insolvency professional, the company might not be in such dire straits. Unfortunately, by this point, corporate officers have likely lost credibility in the eyes of their secured lenders, as well as other stakeholders such as suppliers or shareholders. As a result, the use of a court-appointed officer to assist in or take control of the reorganization process and, by definition, the governance of the company, is sometimes imperative to its success. In most cases, a court-appointed officer can introduce instant credibility, as its goal is defined and clear: to maximize the value of the assets for creditors while at the same time balancing the obligations to other stakeholders such as employees, suppliers, and shareholders. There is a recognition by all that the court-appointed officer will not be preferring its own interests to the interests of the stakeholders, which may not always be the case with management when dealing with a financially distressed corporation.

In large measure, what lends the court-appointed officer its credibility is the expertise it brings to the situation. The insolvency practitioner regularly deals with companies in financial difficulty, and most have been involved in a plethora of different industries and situations. The experience that a court-appointed officer brings to an assignment is invaluable, provided that the officer can also recognize his or her limitations by engaging the team necessary to succeed in the objective. So what then does the court-appointed officer bring to the table? What is to be expected of him or her, and why could it be in the interests of the debtor to cooperate with such an appointment?

First, it is imperative to build or strengthen the relationship with existing lenders to allow for the stabilization of the business and the recognition of the need to work together. The court-appointed officer will undoubtedly give comfort to the lender by way of a commitment to the continuous supply of information, reporting, and communication. Additionally, even if the lender does not have an ability to control the governance of the corporation and the decisions that will be made by the court-appointed officer, the lender will be left with the impression of having some influence over the decision-making process.

Second, the introduction of the court-appointed officer will bring some certainty with respect to an assessment of the underlying value of the assets. The officer will also provide an independent opinion as to whether a reorganization is possible or whether a more efficient and cheaper process of liquidation should be pursued. The judgment of the court-appointed officer is more likely to be accepted by a lender than that of management. In my experience, the debtor is the eternal optimist. While such an attitude can be valuable in building a business, a realistic assessment of the situation at hand is required for the financially distressed corporation to succeed in any reorganization.

Third, the court-appointed officer can take on more than just a governing role. As indicated previously, the outside stakeholders will look to the court-appointed officer as a source of information that can be readily available to all that are interested. In addition, creditors and others value the independence of any investigation or review that occurs and are confident of responses to their inquiries. Given that there may be a certain element of mistrust with respect to the previous conduct of those governing the corporation, an independent review that concludes by supporting the prior conduct of those in charge can be a blessing in disguise to corporate officers. Of course, if there are misdeeds or other circumstances to which an independent party would be critical, prior management will not benefit. However, in many cases of financial distress, corporate managers can be blamed for nothing more than being overly optimistic and perhaps working too hard. In these situations, the introduction of the court-appointed officer has the potential to be the best decision that management ever made.

Fourth, the court-appointed officer, making the most of its credibility, can act as a mediator in an effort to keep current management and stakeholders focused on the task of developing a workout strategy. By facilitating a team approach to a difficult situation and by putting aside any personal feelings and emotions that may have created hostility in the past, time and valuable resources can be directed towards accomplishing the goal without distraction. Finally, from the debtor's perspective, a court-appointed officer can be welcome as it will permit current managers to focus on the business issues at hand and on clients and key investors, as opposed to focusing on the more difficult decisions of a financial restructuring such as the termination of employees, termination of leases, downsizing, and change of business focus. The debtor will also benefit from the re-establishment of credibility with the lender and others.

In summary, the employment of a court-appointed officer has frequently proven to be a critical step forward and a turning point in the salvation of the distressed company. A CRO, Interim Receiver, or Monitor can often have a dramatic and positive impact on the restructuring effort. In particular, the CRO enters the situation with none of the baggage from previous bad decisions. The CRO has instant credibility, which previous management will likely never regain, and demonstrates experience that does not otherwise reside in the management team. All of this creates confidence that the company is headed in the right direction. While many companies are reluctant to bring in a CRO, seeing it as an admission that it is in serious trouble, usually the only persons who are having trouble recognizing that the company is in serious trouble are those currently governing the company.

Interim Receivers

There has been an increase in the use of Interim Receivers appointed as a tool in corporate reorganizations or restructurings since Sections 47 and 47.1 were added to the *BIA* in 1992. Section 47 of the *BIA* provides for the court appointment of an Interim Receiver at the request of a secured creditor. The appointment can include very broad powers to take control of the assets of a business as well as operate the business itself. In other words, the Interim Receiver can supplant the board of directors of a company. Section 47.1 permits a similar application to be made where a debtor has filed a Proposal or Notice of Intention to Make a Proposal under the *BIA* and thus has commenced a reorganization proceeding. Upon such filing, creditors are stayed from enforcing any claims against the debtor, and secured creditors are prohibited from enforcing their security.[2] The potential broad powers and duties of an Interim Receiver appointed pursuant to Section 47.1 are identical to that of Section 47.[3]

Prior to the 1992 amendments, the role of the Interim Receiver was to simply preserve the assets for the benefit of the estate during the period between the filing of a Petition in Bankruptcy and the appointment of a Trustee.[4] Given that the focus of the Petition and the proceedings was on bankruptcy, and thus liquidation as opposed to reorganization, it is not surprising that the role of the Interim Receiver was quite limited. The pre-1992 Interim Receiver would play little, if any, role in the governance of the business. While there are a few cases in which an Interim Receiver fulfilled a larger managerial role, such cases were infrequent. The role has historically been, and continues to be, generally more limited to controlling receipts and disbursements, acting as a "watchdog" and sometimes disposing of perishables or assets of deteriorating value. Thus, the powers and duties of an Interim Receiver appointed under Section 46 of the *BIA* typically include taking conservatory and protective measures only.[5] While it is possible for a court to give to the Interim Receiver more control over the business, the language in the section specifically limits the jurisdiction so as not to unduly interfere with the debtor in the carrying on of its business.[6]

Thus, an Interim Receiver appointed under Section 46 will generally not take any steps that would be considered governing the corporation. In *Plaskett & Associates Ltd.* v. *Minister of National Revenue*,[7] the court held that ordinarily in the exercise of its duties, an Interim Receiver could not make business decisions, hire and fire employees, or dispose of the corporation's assets. As a result, the Interim Receiver was held not to be liable for income tax deductions for employees' wages. Mr. Justice Sobier of the Tax Court of Canada contrasted the position of an Interim Receiver appointed under Section 46 of the *BIA* with other types of court-appointed officers who "administer, manage, distribute, wind up, control or otherwise deal with the property of a corporation and who, in such capacity, specifically authorize or cause the payment of salaries and wages."[8]

Following the amendments to the *BIA* and the addition of Sections 47 and 47.1 in 1992, the court may now appoint an Interim Receiver to take possession of all or part of the debtor's property; exercise such control over that property and the debtor's business as the court considers advisable; and take such other action as the court considers advisable.[9] In practice, courts have used their broad discretion and equitable jurisdiction to empower the Interim Receiver to take control of the reorganization itself and, in essence, step into the shoes of and replace the board of directors.[10] Below, I discuss specific case studies illustrating the broad power and jurisdiction of the court to fashion relief given any particular situation. The most significant difference in an Interim Receiver appointed under Sections 47 or 47.1 is that those statutory provisions contain no limitation of unduly interfering with the carrying on of business. Thus significantly greater powers can be granted to an Interim Receiver.

Notable Interim Receiverships
One of the first cases to deal with Section 47 or Section 47.1 of the *BIA* and the powers available to the court for the appointment of an Interim Receiver involved the appointment of an Interim Receiver over the Faro Mine of Curragh Inc. in the Yukon Territory in 1993 *(Curragh)*.[11] As a result of the need to protect against massive potential environmental liability associated with the mine, as well as the need to convey title to a purchaser, the court appointment of an Interim Receiver was viewed as necessary. The Ontario Court (Gen. Div.) ultimately granted a Vesting Order (which was interesting in itself, given that the mine was located in the Yukon) but left the Yukon Court to determine certain priority issues involving lien claimants.

In *Curragh,* the Interim Receivership Order gave the Interim Receiver power to market and sell the mine. While *Curragh* might be described as simply an example of utilizing the appointment of an Interim Receiver for liquidation purposes as opposed to the restructuring of a financially distressed company, the Interim Receiver in *Curragh* maximized value by way of a going-concern sale in a way that no other process would have. Further, the case is noteworthy for endorsing the expanded role of the Interim Receiver under Sections 47 and 47.1 of the *BIA.* Mr. Justice Farley of the Ontario Superior Court noted the vital role of the Interim Receiver in the case at hand:

> It would not be generally said that interim receivers have "sale powers" – beyond of course the aspect of disposing of perishable goods or those items with a predilection to depreciation in value. These aspects are referred to in s. 46(2); it would not seem reasonable to assume that a s. 47(1) interim receiver had less authority in this regard. Although we may observe that one is not dealing with fruit which is subject to rot, one is dealing with mining properties which involve certain potential environmental frailties and the possibility of safety risks if not attended to. It is perhaps unfortunate that certain of those directly involved in the protection of the public (i.e. the governmental organizations) have not taken a more aggressive and positive role in funding the activities of the IR since it is only the IR which stands in between the band-aid environmental solution and the abandonment of the property with ensuing environmental risks. Indeed the environmental legislation regime appears to have frozen the situation with the likelihood that the IR will "continue" until the Faro mine is in fact sold. It appears that the object of the process at the present time is to maintain the property on a shoestring (which has thus far worked) while marketing it with a view towards its sale. With a sale the new owner would then take charge of the property, with the general requirement to maintain it in good condition for environmental purposes and exploiting it in due course when it is determined that conditions are favourable.[12]

Shortly following *Curragh* was *Bruce Agra Foods Inc.* v. *Everfresh Beverages Inc. (Receiver of).*[13] The reorganization of this cross-border business in 1995-96 is notable for a number of reasons, not the least of which is that it is one of the few cases where management itself sought the order appointing the Interim Receiver. The court order gave the Interim Receiver broad powers, including the ability to facilitate the sale of the business on a going-concern basis. Interestingly, from a governance perspective, it was the prior and continuing management that legally controlled the sale process. The powers of the board of directors were not removed, except as varied by an order of the court, and the power to manage the business continued unaltered. It was evident, however, that behind the scenes, the debtor had implicitly agreed to give up the ultimate decision-making power to the Interim Receiver, who had the confidence and support of the major operating lender based in the United States. The case is also noteworthy as one of the first cross-border cases where a Canadian court-appointed officer was in charge of both the Canadian and US operations.

In late 1995, Everfresh Beverages Inc. encountered significant financial difficulties. Everfresh was an integrated multinational manufacturer and distributor of beverages and beverage products, with operations on both sides of the Canada/US border. Its financial distress was accelerated by the loss of confidence of its suppliers and operating lender. Through consultation with the major operating lender, corporate officers approved the concurrent filing under both Chapter 11 of the *Bankruptcy Code*[14] in the United States and the proposal provisions of the *BIA* in Canada. However, given the lender's unease with respect to the management of company operations, the creditors and managers agreed to the appointment of an Interim Receiver to supervise and monitor the financially distressed company but not to manage or administer its affairs. Thus, while existing management, albeit pared down, continued to govern the company, the role of the Interim Receiver was sufficiently broad to give comfort to the various stakeholders and to provide credibility and expertise to the process. In turn, this ensured a successful restructuring and ultimately the sale of the reorganized operations on both sides of the border. Moreover, the approval of both a reorganization plan filed under the United States *Bankruptcy Code* and a proposal under the *BIA* was sought and obtained. In fact, *Everfresh* was one of the first times, if not the first, that an Interim Receiver was given the role of formulating and filing the proposal on behalf of the debtor.

A few years later, *BIA* proposal proceedings were again combined with the appointment of an Interim Receiver in the successful reorganization of J.S. McMillan Fisheries Ltd.[15] J.S. McMillan Fisheries Ltd. was, and continues to be, an integrated fishing and processing company based in British Columbia. In late 1997, the company was in financial distress, as revenues had been seriously eroded and the significant secured debt carried on the balance sheet became almost insurmountable. Upon consultation with its various creditors, the directors and officers authorized the filing of a Notice of Intention to Make a Proposal under the *BIA* and immediately thereafter all resigned. As the company had no management, an order was made appointing an Interim Receiver to essentially supplant the board of directors and management. The Interim Receiver was charged with the task of reorganizing the business and ultimately negotiating and filing a proposal to creditors. The case is interesting as it is one of the few where the appointment of an Interim Receiver was conceded by the board of directors and officers, yet following the successful reorganization of the business, management of the business was returned to the shareholders. To this day, the

McMillan family continues to maintain ownership, the business is profitable, and significant value was preserved and recovered for all concerned.

The utilization of an Interim Receiver has also occurred in the conduct of restructurings under the *CCAA*. *Re Royal Oak Mines Inc. (Royal Oak)* is probably the most notable.[16] Royal Oak was a publicly traded mining company whose crown jewel was its then recently constructed Kemess Mine property located in British Columbia. Due to falling world prices for gold and copper, as well as the cost of construction, Royal Oak applied for and was granted protection under the *CCAA* in early 1999. A Monitor was appointed in the proceedings. There was nothing unusual about the initial appointment of the Monitor from a governance perspective, and the Monitor had the usual powers and duties of supervising the process and reporting to all stakeholders. Later in 1999, however, the Monitor recommended to the court that it be appointed as Interim Receiver under Section 47 of the *BIA* to market Royal Oak's mining assets on a "structured basis" in order to preserve certain tax pools. Apparently, the tax savings associated with such a sale could be achieved only through a restructuring that would convert a portion of the existing debt to equity. The court approved the approach and appointed the Monitor as Interim Receiver.

In its new role as Interim Receiver, the Monitor assumed a much more active role in terms of governance, restructuring, and the ultimate sale of the Kemess Mine. The powers of the Interim Receiver included the sale of non-essential assets, which assisted in the streamlining of Royal Oak's operations, the abandonment of various real properties, and the power to sell in conjunction with the conversion of debt to equity. In essence, the Interim Receiver was able to govern Royal Oak in such a way that it could dispose of the detrimental assets, leaving the most prized ones. Finally, as with *Everfresh*, the Interim Receiver negotiated, formulated, and filed the proposal under the *BIA*, instead of filing a plan under the *CCAA*. In *Royal Oak*, the successful introduction of an Interim Receiver allowed the business to emerge from the process and continue with its viable mining operations. The non-equity stakeholders were able to maximize recovery, jobs were maintained, suppliers retained an important customer, and others undoubtedly benefited.

Monitors and Restructuring Officers

Orders in favour of a company under the *CCAA* must provide for the appointment of a Monitor to supervise the debtor company as it attempts to restructure. As with Interim Receivers, the role and powers of the Monitor have increased correspondingly with the creativity and ingenuity of counsel. While the norm is to limit the Monitor's duties to those of reporting to the court and creditors, advising and assisting the debtor with the preparation of a plan of restructuring, and the administering of the meetings of creditors and claims process, there have been numerous cases in the last several years expanding this role. In this regard, Monitors have been empowered to approve transactions, control payment arrangements, and assist in the negotiations among stakeholders.

The *CCAA* permits compromises or arrangements to be made between an insolvent company and its creditors. The *CCAA* has a broad remedial purpose to permit a financially distressed company the breathing room necessary to allow the company to formulate a plan to meet the demands of creditors. This can be accomplished through refinancing with new lending, equity, or the possible sale of the business as a going concern. The *CCAA* process can maintain the status quo for a period of time while the insolvent company attempts to get approval from its creditors of a proposed arrangement that will enable the company to remain in operation for the future benefit of all stakeholders. Generally speaking, an application under the *CCAA* is initiated by the debtor. Thus, from a governance perspective, the existing board of directors and management remain in place through the period of the stay of proceedings.[17] There can be a benefit to the introduction of an independent officer, and there have been numerous occasions when an Interim Receiver was appointed at the request of influential secured creditors. This most often occurs when a secured creditor most affected by a restructuring proposal is prepared to support the restructuring process but does not have enough faith in management or wishes a more active role in directing the restructuring, such that it insists on an Interim Receiver being appointed. Permitting the secured creditors to assist in or run the restructuring process can sometimes benefit all stakeholders. The alternative, of course, is to attempt to appease the creditors with the Monitor, who is now required to be appointed in all *CCAA* cases.

The Emergence of Chief Restructuring Officers

Finally, the emergence of chief restructuring officers (CROs) in Canada, usually in conjunction with a Monitor appointed under the *CCAA*, adds an entirely new dimension to the governance of a financially distressed corporation. While the "turnaround management" field has been long developed in the United States, it is a relatively new phenomenon in Canada. Creditors and financial institutions have become much more experienced and sophisticated in insolvency matters, with the corresponding recognition that a properly orchestrated restructuring will generally lead to a better return than a receivership or liquidation would. The CRO is becoming the leader of choice to displace the existing management with a view to reorganizing the insolvent corporation. As with Monitors and Interim Receivers, the CRO's powers are typically embodied in the order appointing it, usually under the auspices or within the framework of the *CCAA*.[18]

While the following case studies discuss the specific powers that can be given to a CRO, generally a CRO will assume the role of president and chief executive officer. At the same time, the powers of the board of directors will be given to the CRO by way of court order, and the CRO essentially becomes the sole governing body of the financially distressed corporation, subject to the ongoing direction of the court that is supervising the matter.

One of the first cases in which the court recognized and approved the appointment of a CRO was *Re Starcom International Optics Corporation et al. (Starcom)*.[19] Starcom initially obtained protection under the *CCAA* as well as Chapter 11 of the US *Bankruptcy Code*. Its business was operating a fibreoptic telecommunications system with cable running between Seattle and Vancouver. The major secured creditors were AT&T and Lucent Technologies. The initial filing under the *CCAA* was made *ex parte,* and early in the proceedings the lenders moved, without success, to set aside the *CCAA* Order or alternatively to appoint a Receiver. The lenders continued to be adversarial to the debtor and criticized management, which they perceived as untrustworthy and inexperienced in dealing with a financially distressed business. After much litigation and several months, a CRO was appointed at the request of the lenders and the apparent concession by management. The CRO had the power to supervise and authorize certain actions.

While the CRO was appointed as an agent of the Monitor, the *Starcom* Order gave the CRO the independent ability to seek the approval of certain actions, even when the debtor and/or Monitor did not concur. In essence, the CRO became, and ultimately evolved into, the debtor-in-possession itself. Paragraph 10A of the *Starcom* Order provided:

THIS COURT FURTHER ORDERS THAT the Monitor shall retain William Drake, or such other person as may be appointed by the court and approved by AT&T and the Petitioner to act as Chief Restructuring Officer ("CRO") of the Petitioner and such CRO shall be an agent of the Monitor and an officer of the court having the following powers and duties:

(a) to provide information to the Monitor, to the Petitioner and to AT&T and to fully apprise those parties of events with respect to restructuring of the Petitioner and seek their input on an ongoing basis;

(b) to, as the CRO considers necessary, apprise Lucent and BNR of events with respect to the restructuring;

(c) to oversee the operation of the business of the Petitioner;

(d) to pursue refinancing and restructuring options with a right to instruct an investment banker to negotiate with creditors, investors, potential purchasers and others using, as the CRO considers appropriate and necessary, the internal resources and contacts of the Petitioner and any other persons or parties the CRO deems appropriate;

(e) to review and approve operating budgets and forecasts;

(f) with the approval of the Monitor, and the Petitioner, or in the event such approval is denied, upon approval of the court;

(i) to enter into definitive agreements relating to equity arrangements or other restructuring endeavors and, subject to paragraph 4 of this Order asset sales, financing leases and sales of [indefeasible rights of use];

(ii) to finalize and plan the Plan of Arrangement on behalf of the Petitioner;

(iii) to approve capital expenditures subject to the approval of the court;

(iv) to hire, discharge, or change the remuneration of any of the Petitioner's employees or agents including, for cause, any investment banker;

(v) to initiate or continue any legal action where the CRO considers it appropriate for the operation of the business; and

(vi) to enter into a contract with an investment banker, if such contract terms are consented to by AT&T, the Petitioner and the investment banker providing for remuneration of the investment banker as agreed by those parties with payment to be made to the investment banker from the proceeds of applicable transactions upon closing of those transactions.

Notably, it was ultimately the CRO that negotiated, prepared, filed, and implemented the Plan of Arrangement that provided for the sale of various strands of fibreoptic operations and the remainder of the business to a third-party purchaser. *Starcom* appears to be the first time in Canada that a CRO was appointed by a court, as opposed to being contractually negotiated and implemented. The case is also interesting as it is one of the first cross-border cases in which a CRO was recognized by a US court as a "foreign representative" for purposes of commencing an ancillary case under Section 304 of the United States *Bankruptcy Code*.[20]

From the debtor's perspective, the *CCAA* appears to be flexible enough that the traditional role of the Monitor can be advanced as a solution to creditor distrust. The powers can be formulated in such a way that the board of directors and management can continue to participate in governance of the business while still appeasing any concerns of creditors or others. The more expansive role of a CRO may be satisfactory to current management only in situations where they perceive little hope of preserving equity for shareholders. *Re Agro Pacific Industries Ltd. (Agro)* was such a situation.[21] *Agro* involved a major animal feed and crop product supplier to the farming industry based in British Columbia. In early 2000, on the eve of its annual general meeting, it became clear that Agro's board and management were somewhat dysfunctional, the business was in financial distress, and a reorganization was necessary. At the same time, it was clear to the lenders that significant value could be generated for the business if it could be restructured properly prior to being offered for sale. Given the difficult situation with the board, some form of court-appointed officer was necessary to see the matter through. Accordingly, at the initiation of the major creditors, and with the consent of the board of directors and management, Agro filed for protection under the *CCAA* in April 2000. As part of the Initial Order, which was later confirmed at the comeback hearing, the court appointed a CRO with broad powers to oversee and manage the operation of the business. Paragraph 11(d) of the Initial Order provides a sense of the broad powers given to the CRO:

> 10. THIS COURT FURTHER ORDERS that Colin Rogers be appointed until further order of this court as Chief Restructuring Officer of the Petitioner with the following powers and duties:
>
> ...
>
> (d) To pursue refinancing and restructuring options with a right to instruct an investment banker to negotiate with creditors, investors, potential purchasers and others using, as the Chief Restructuring Officer considers appropriate and necessary, the internal resources and contacts of the Petitioner [Agro] and any other persons or parties the Chief Restructuring Officer deems appropriate;

While the existing members of the board did not resign, their powers were significantly, if not wholly, attenuated. Whether or not the board of directors and the managers appreciated the significance of the role of the CRO and the powers that they were giving up is unclear. However, all stakeholders were of the view that the route pursued and the successful restructuring ultimately completed by the CRO would not have occurred without its involvement.

The court order in *Agro* went somewhat further than *Starcom* in appointing the CRO. The CRO was not appointed as an agent of the Monitor, but rather as an independent officer with separate powers and duties. Additionally, the court extended the protection of the *CCAA* Order normally afforded to the Monitor to this newly created officer. The CRO received security for its remuneration, costs, and disbursements in the form of an administrative charge against the assets of Agro. As the appointment of the CRO was made on consent of the various parties, there are no reasons of the court supporting the Order. Thus it remains to be seen whether other courts will follow the lead of the British Columbia court in giving a CRO all of the protections that would normally be afforded to the Monitor in a *CCAA* proceeding.[22]

Conclusion

Financially troubled companies differ greatly from healthy ones. The financially distressed company requires, at the very least, an adjustment to its governance structure. In some cases a complete overhaul is necessary. The introduction of a court-appointed officer can be critical, whether to act as Monitor of the business and ease the concerns of nervous lenders and suppliers, or to take on a more expansive governing role in terms of reorganizing the business with a view to returning control to the pre-existing shareholders or towards maximizing value by way of a going-concern sale. After all, the financially distressed company requires everything that existing management never had or has likely lost: expertise, credibility, independent judgment, and diplomatic skills, all of which the court-appointed officer can bring to the situation.

Notes

1 Although the appointment of a Monitor was not mandatory under the *Companies' Creditors Arrangement Act (CCAA)* until 1997, the appointment was made as a matter of practice as early as the late 1980s. However, the role of the Monitor has undoubtedly expanded in recent cases.
2 Pursuant to s. 69.1(2) of the *BIA*, secured creditors are exempted from the stay in the event that the secured creditor gave notice of its intention to enforce security under s. 244(1) more than ten days before the filing. The *BIA* also permits an application to lift the stay.
3 For an excellent discussion of Interim Receivers, see the article by Allan Rutman, John Varley, and Jeff Carhart, "Interim Receivers under the *Bankruptcy and Insolvency Act*" (2001) 9 C.B.R. (4th) 89.
4 Under what is now s. 46 of the *BIA*.
5 S. 46 of the *BIA* provides as follows:

> Appointment of interim receiver – The court may, if it is shown to be necessary for the protection of the estate of a debtor, at any time after the filing of a petition for a receiving order and before a receiving order is made, appoint a licensed trustee as interim receiver of the property of the debtor or of any part thereof and direct him to take immediate possession thereof on such undertaking being given by the petitioner as the court may impose with respect to interference with the debtor's legal rights and with respect to damages in the event of the petition being dismissed.

> Powers of interim receiver – The interim receiver appointed under subsection (1) may, under the direction of the court, take conservatory measures and summarily dispose of property that is perishable or likely to depreciate rapidly in value and exercise such control over the business of the debtor as the court deems advisable, *but the interim receiver shall not unduly interfere with the debtor in the carrying on of his business except as may be necessary for the conservatory purposes or to comply with the order of the court.* (emphasis added)

6 In the case of *Re Down*, Vancouver 188266 VA/98 (B.C.S.C.), Arthur Andersen Inc. was appointed as an Interim Receiver under s. 46 of the *BIA* with, some would argue, very broad powers. Notwithstanding these broad powers, the role of the Interim Receiver was to conserve the property of the estate. Moreover, while there were numerous pieces of real estate subject to the Order, there was no active business per se.
7 (1991), 2 C.B.R. (3d) 13 (T.C.C.).
8 *Ibid.*
9 See s. 47(2) of the *BIA*.

10 S. 183(1) confers jurisdiction in equity as will enable the court to exercise original, auxiliary, and ancillary jurisdiction in bankruptcy. Since the bankruptcy court is a court of equity, it is bound to give equitable relief to suitors entitled thereto. Moreover, it is said that the bankruptcy court has "inherent" power or "inherent" jurisdiction given the language of s. 183.

11 *Canada (Minister of Indian Affairs and Northern Development)* v. *Curragh Inc.* (1994), 27 C.B.R. (3d) 148 (Ont. Ct. (Gen. Div.)).

12 *Ibid.* at 152. The decision is also noteworthy for the oft-quoted phrase of Mr. Justice Farley with respect to the inherent jurisdiction of the bankruptcy court to do not only what "justice dictates" but also what "practicality demands" (see also 158-59).

13 *Bruce Agra Foods Inc.* v. *Everfresh Beverages Inc. (Receiver of)* (1996), 45 C.B.R. (3d) 169 (Ont. Ct. (Gen. Div.)).

14 U.S.C., Chap. 11.

15 *Re J.S. McMillan Fisheries* (1998), Vancouver 178071 VA/97 (B.C.S.C.).

16 *Re Royal Oak Mines Inc.* (1999), Toronto 99-CL-3278 (Ont. Sup. Ct).

17 It is fairly common, however, for non-essential directors to resign prior to a filing, given individual liability concerns associated with directing or managing an insolvent business.

18 Undoubtedly, there will also be situations where a CRO is appointed outside of a formal insolvency proceeding. In the restructuring of *Money's Mushrooms* for instance (no formal court proceedings commenced in Canada), the US entity filed under Chapter 11 of the US *Bankruptcy Code* while the Canadian entity was left out of a formal proceeding under the *CCAA* or otherwise. The lender syndicate appointed a CRO to run both the US restructuring as well as the Canadian company by way of contract with the cooperation of management.

19 *Re Starcom International Optics Corp.,* (1998) Vancouver A980298 (B.C.S.C.).

20 S. 304 of the *Bankruptcy Code* permits the commencement of a limited proceeding in aid of a foreign judicial or administrative bankruptcy proceeding. Pursuant thereto, the US bankruptcy court may enjoin any actions against the debtor or the debtor's property located in the United States, usually in aid of the foreign stay of proceedings. In order to qualify for relief, the application must be made by a "foreign representative" as defined in the *Code*.

21 *Re Agro Pacific Industries Ltd.* (2000), Vancouver L001146 (B.C.S.C.).

22 For a discussion of two further recent cases, *Re Algoma Steel Inc.* and *Re Dantel Inc. et al.,* see Mario J. Forte, "The Recognition and Roles of the Chief Restructuring Officer in Canadian Insolvency Proceedings" (2001) 14 Comm. Insol. R. 4.

Contributors

Philip Bryden, B.A. (Dalhousie), B.A. and B.C.L. (Oxford), LL.M. (Harvard), Associate Professor, Faculty of Law, University of British Columbia (UBC)

Lynne L. Dallas, J.D. (Harvard), Professor, University of San Diego School of Law

Ronald B. Davis, LL.B. (Toronto), S.J.D. candidate, Faculty of Law, University of Toronto, Capital Markets Fellowship, Faculty of Law, University of Toronto

F. James Hoffner, student-at-law, Osler, Hoskin & Harcourt LLP, Toronto

Natasha J. MacParland, B.A. (Memorial), LL.B. (Dalhousie), Osler, Hoskin & Harcourt LLP, Toronto

Robert Mansell, B.A. (Toronto), LL.B. (Queen's), Torys, Toronto

Geoffrey B. Morawetz, Goodmans LLP, Toronto

Christopher C. Nicholls, Purdy Crawford Chair in Business Law, Faculty of Law, Dalhousie University

Kathleen Porter, Executive Director, British Columbia Seafood Sector Council, Vancouver

Brian Prill, B.A., M.B.A. (Calgary), LL.B. (Calgary), Torys, Toronto

Stéphane Rousseau, S.J.D. (Toronto), Assistant Professor, Faculty of Law and Centre for Business Law and International Trade, Université de Montréal

John Sandrelli, LL.B. (Toronto) Fraser Milner Casgrain LLP, Vancouver

Janis Sarra, B.A., M.A. (Toronto); LL.B., LL.M., S.J.D. (Toronto), Faculty of Law, University of British Columbia

Edward A. Sellers, B.A. (Winnipeg), LL.B. (Manitoba), Osler, Hoskin & Harcourt LLP, Toronto

Barry Slutsky, B.A. and LL.B. (UBC), PhD (London), Associate Professor, Faculty of Law, University of British Columbia

Cheryl L. Wade, Harold F. McNiece Professor of Law, St. John's University School of Law

Joe Weiler, Professor, Faculty of Law, University of British Columbia

Gil Yaron, B.A. & Sc. (McMaster), L.L.B. (Ottawa), L.L.M. (UBC), Director of Law and Policy, Shareholder Association for Research and Education (SHARE), Vancouver

Index

accountability
  business judgment rule, 161, 183, 287-88, 306
  corporate veil, 131, 141-42
  criminal offences, 301-2, 308-9
  governance standards and, 112, 143-47, 149-50
  multinational enterprises, 133, 142-44, 149-50, 155n96
  oppression remedy, 277-82, 285, 302-4, 306, 307, 309, 339n45
  two-tiered board structures, 50-51
  See also community accountability; directors: liabilities; disclosure of corporate information; disclosure of governance practices; shareholder activism
accounting standards, 56, 61, 62
  See also financial reporting
acquisitions. *See* mergers and acquisitions; takeovers
Adelphia Communications Inc., 156
agency costs, xvii, 5-6, 28, 41, 44, 58, 202-4, 208-9
  market for corporate control, 89-96
  multinational enterprises, 149
Agro Pacific Industries Ltd., 356-57
Al Tech, 278-79
Algoma Steel, 283-84, 313, 323
Alien Tort Claims Act (ATCA) (United States), 142-43
Allen, Tom, 20
analysts, xi, 62-63, 82n105, 83n109, 157
Aon, 156
Arthur Andersen, 57
ASB. *See* Canadian Accounting Standards Board (ASB)
Asia, 46
  governance norms, 49, 53, 54

Japan, 51-52, 81n55
asset dispositions, 315-16, 341n118, 341n119
Association de protection des épargnants et investisseurs du Québec, 129n63
ATCA. *See Alien Tort Claims Act (ATCA)*
audit committees, ix-x, 13, 59, 68, 195, 196
  See also external auditors
Australia
  Government Owned Corporations Act (Queensland), 241-42

balance sheet insolvency, 299, 300
Bankruptcy and Insolvency Act (BIA) (Canada), 275, 283, 284, 299, 302, 339n38, 359n10, 359n20
  court-appointed officers, 346, 349-50, 358n5
Bankruptcy Code (United States), 308-9
banks
  Europe, 47, 49-50, 51
  Japan, 51, 52
Bata Industries Ltd., 176-77, 183, 287
BC Ferries. *See* British Columbia Ferry Corporation
Beyond Compliance: Building a Governance Culture, 13, 43, 44, 59, 92, 102n56, 181-82
BIA. *See Bankruptcy and Insolvency Act (BIA)* (Canada)
blockheld corporate structures, 49, 72, 86, 98n10, 130n92, 155n92
  Europe, 49, 51
  market for corporate control and, xvii-xviii, 86-88
  transition economies, 54-55
  See also banks
Blue Ribbon Committee, 196

boards of directors, ix, xxi-xxii, 8-9, 12, 191
Bryce Commission report, 10-11
co-determination model, 50-51, 73-74
committees, ix, 198, 211, 212; audit
committees, ix-x, 13, 59, 68, 195,
196; compensation committees, x, xi,
195-97; governance committees, 197;
management succession, 198; nominating committees, viii, 196, 197
composition, viii, 11, 57-58, 59-60,
68-69, 204-5, 214-15; diversity, vii-viii,
192, 199-202, 210-11, 214, 219n73;
inside directors, 203; insider/outsider
ratios, 192, 194-95, 205-6, 208-11, 213,
215, 216n17, 223n137; outside
directors, 198, 202, 203, 204, 216n9,
217n19; relationship to corporate
performance, 208-11, 215
Enron Corporation, 56-57
in-camera meetings, viii, 67, 191, 197,
214, 218n46
independent board leaders, vii, 13, 59,
67, 197, 214, 218n50
monitoring role, 40, 41, 48, 191, 192,
194-98, 211-12, 213; transition to,
14-16; workplace discrimination
oversight, 158-60, 170n32
obligations of legal compliance, 175-78
ombudspersons, 193, 213, 215
relational role, 191-92, 193, 198-202,
204-6, 213, 214, 216n7, 222n119
Revlon duty, 95, 105n92, 106n97
role conflicts, 192, 211-13
Saucier Committee report, 13
stewardship role, 12, 42, 59, 102n56,
206, 297
strategic role, viii-ix, 179-87, 192, 206-7,
213, 214
structures, 12; dual board structure,
192-94, 212-13, 214; German two-
tiered structures, 50-51, 212
See also directors; disclosure of governance practices
British Columbia
British Columbia Ferry Corporation,
225-26; views of Auditor General on
fast ferry project, 225-26, 230-31, 243,
244n2
See also seafood processing industry
Broadbent Report. *See* Canadian Democracy and Corporate Accountability
Commission
Bryce Commission, 10-11
business development
sector councils, 254-62; value chains,
263-69

business judgment rule, 161, 183, 287-88,
306
business review boards, 193-94

Cadbury Schweppes Inc. v. *FBI Food Ltd.*,
306, 340n73
California Public Employees' Retirement
System (CalPERS), 22, 117, 128n49
CalPERS. *See* California Public Employees'
Retirement System
Canada 3000 Inc., 344n175, 344n185
Canada Business Corporations Act (CBCA),
4-5, 91, 299
amendments, 65-66, 118-20, 121
fiduciary obligations, 173-74, 178, 179,
182, 239, 276
Canadian Accounting Standards Board
(ASB), 62, 82n104
Canadian Coalition for Good Govern-
ance, 66-67
Canadian Democracy and Corporate
Accountability Commission, xi-xii,
70-71
Canadian Depository System (CDS), 122
Canadian Institute of Chartered Account-
ants (CICA), 13
Canadian Venture Exchange (CDNX), 13
Canbook Distribution v. *Borins*, 277, 304,
305
capital markets, 72-77, 88
See also global capital markets
Caremark International Inc., 160-61, 162
Catamaran Ferries International, 231
See also British Columbia Ferry
Corporation
CBCA. *See Canada Business Corporations
Act (CBCA)*
CCAA. *See Companies' Creditors Arrange-
ment Act (CCAA)* (Canada)
CDNX. *See* Canadian Venture Exchange
CDS. *See* Canadian Depository System
(CDS)
CEOs. *See* chief executive officers
CERES. *See* Coalition of Environmentally
Responsible Economies (CERES)
CFI. *See* Catamaran Ferries International
Chapter 7. *See Bankruptcy Code* (United
States)
Chapter 11. *See Bankruptcy Code* (United
States)
chief executive officers, xi, 193, 203, 212,
214, 222n119
compensation, 218n36
evaluation, 204, 209-10
chief restructuring officers, 289-91, 292,
293, 313, 346, 349, 354-57, 359n18

CICA. *See* Canadian Institute of Chartered Accountants (CICA)

Citibank, 279-2803

City Code on Takeovers and Mergers (UK), 96-97

Civil Rights Act (United States), 163, 171n40

co-determination model, 50-51

Coalition of Environmentally Responsible Economies (CERES), 144

Coca-Cola, 157, 159, 163, 164

communication

financially distressed corporations, 311-12

ombudspersons, 193, 213, 215

See also disclosure of corporate information; disclosure of governance practices; decision-making structures

communitarian theory, 127n37

community accountability, 45-46

See also social responsibilities; stakeholders

Companies' Creditors Arrangement Act (CCAA) (Canada), 275, 289, 300

court-appointed officers, 346-47, 353, 354

compensation

chief executive officers, 218n36

directors, ix, x-xi, 199, 218n61

employee wages and benefits, 286

concessionist theory, xix, 116, 124-25, 127n37

conflicts boards, 192-93

Consumers Packaging Inc., 330-37, 344n189, 344n190

contractual theory, xvi, 5, 44, 45, 116, 248

convergence of corporate regimes, 47-55, 74-75, 86, 99n19

factors in, 88-89, 99n15, 99n19, 100n20

governance norms, xvii, 41, 46-48, 52, 53-55, 74-75, 76

hostile takeover legislation, 94-96

Cooper v. *Hobart,* 242

corporate control regimes, 87

separation of ownership and control, 6, 27, 89, 96, 154n86, 236

See also blockheld corporate structures; convergence of corporate regimes; market for corporate control; ownership patterns

corporate governance

definition, 235, 297

See also boards of directors; decision-making structures

corporate misconduct

identification of, 159

impact of, 156-58

legal compliance and, 159-65

oppression, 277-82, 285, 302-4, 306, 307, 309, 339n45

See also accountability; Enron Corporation; managerial discipline

corporate veil, 131, 141-42

corporations

long-term viability, 103n62, 179, 182-83, 186-87

as nexus of contracts, xvi, 5, 44, 45, 116, 248

See also corporate control regimes; Crown corporations; financially distressed corporations; multinational enterprises (MNEs)

costs

externalization, 45, 64, 76; pension funds and, 134, 136

See also agency costs; litigation

Council of Institutional Investors, 128n50

CPI. *See* Consumers Packaging Inc.

creditors, 51, 63, 81n79

insolvency situations, 63-64, 289-90, 293-94, 326-27; fiduciary obligations of directors, 275-77, 294n10, 304-7, 339n53, 339n54

use of oppression remedy, 277-82, 285, 302-4, 306, 307, 309, 339n45

Criminal Code (Canada), 301

criminal offences

director liabilities, 301-2, 308-9

CROs. *See* chief restructuring officers

Crown corporations, 245n9

corporate autonomy, 226, 227-28, 230-32, 243-44; role of corporate law principles, 235-43; role of public law principles, 232-35

governance structures, 226-32, 244n2

managerial authority, 237-39

roles, 225, 226-27, 228, 241

types, 228-29

See also British Columbia Ferry Corporation

Crown Corporations Act (Saskatchewan), 241, 242

Crown Corporations Public Review and Accountability Act (Manitoba), 237, 240, 242

debt markets, 310-11

debtor-in-possession financing. *See* DIP financing

decision-making structures

participatory models, 249-51; employee involvement, 251-54, 257, 258; sector councils, 256-69

See also boards of directors
Delaware, 200
    corporate laws, 94-96, 106n96, 106n99,
        107n108, 309
    judicial decisions, 162, 340n80
    *In re Caremark International Inc. Derivative
        Legislation,* 160-61, 162
derivative actions, 282-83
Dey, Peter, 11
Dey Committee, 11-12, 26
    Report (*See Where Were the Directors?*)
Dickerson Committee, 4-5, 102n48
DIP financing, 315, 318-25, 343n166
directors, viii-ix, xxii, 197-98
    compensation, ix, x-xi, 199, 218n61
    Crown corporations, 231, 237-38,
        240-43
    evaluation, x-xi, 197, 218
    foreign directors, 201
    independence, 57
    inside directors, 203
    liabilities, 173, 185; business judgment
        rule, 161, 183, 287-88, 306; financially
        distressed companies, 283-88, 291,
        292, 293, 300-309, 327-29; wrongful
        trading, 284-85, 300-301
    minority directors, 200-201, 205,
        219n75
    outside directors, 82n90, 198, 202, 203,
        204, 216n9, 217n19
    recruitment, viii, 68-69, 185
    resignation, 287
    views on governance practices, 67-69
    women directors, 68, 200-201, 220n77,
        220n85, 220n91, 220n92
    See also boards of directors; fiduciary
        obligations
disclosure of corporate information,
        40-41, 61-62, 65, 77, 122
    financial practices, 61-62, 122
    multinational enterprises, 142-47,
        148-49
    views of Canadian public on, 70-71
disclosure of governance practices, 12, 14,
        16-21, 61
    access to information, 24-25
    credibility, 20-21, 26
    enforcement of, 17-18, 19, 26
    TSX guidelines, 17-18, 19, 20-21, 60
discrimination. *See* workplace
        discrimination
dividends, 101n47, 103n60
    Crown corporations, 238
    during insolvency, 285
    policies, 92, 103n59
Dow Chemical California, 180-81

Eaton's, 344n175
Edwards Books. *See Canbook Distribution
    v. Borins*
Edwards v. Law Society of Upper Canada, 242
efficiency, 41, 44-45
    creditors and, 63-64
    definition, xvi, xviii, 22, 44
employees, 69, 71, 260, 286, 312
    board representatives, 194, 213, 215,
        251
    labour shedding, 64-65
    participatory decision making, 251-54,
        257, 258
    as stakeholders, 50, 51, 69, 74, 75-76,
        102n58, 194, 248
    See also human capital investment;
        workplace discrimination
Enron Corporation, xi, 40-41, 56-57, 156,
        158, 159, 198, 212, 215n3
    violations of fiduciary obligations, 58
        162-63, 164-65
*Enterprise Capital Management Inc. v. Semi-
    Tech Corp.,* 300
environmental issues, 184
    disasters, 132, 137-42
    legislative obligations, 176-78, 182, 286
    management systems, xxi, 177-78,
        179-81
    proactive practices, xxi, 183-84
    strategic planning and, xxi, 173, 179-87
Environmental Protection Act (Ontario), 176
equity capital, xviii, 41, 77
Europe
    European Union standards, 47, 145-47
    governance norms, 49-51, 53, 54
    hostile takeover legislation, 96-98
Everfresh Beverages Inc., 351-52
Excise Tax Act (Canada), 285-86
executives, 220n92
    compensation, 197
    financially distressed companies, 312-13
    manager monitoring and, 202-4
    See also chief executive officers; chief
        restructuring officers
external auditors, x, 11, 60, 68
    Enron Corporation, 56-57
externalization of costs, 45, 64, 76
    pension funds and, 134, 136

FAA. See Financial Administration Act (FAA)
    (Canada)
faith-based institutional investors, 119
Faro Mine of Curragh Inc., 350-52
Fastow, Andrew, 162
fiduciary obligations, 70-72, 101n46,
        102n57, 199-200, 239-40, 283

in cases of insolvency, 275-77, 294n10, 298-99, 304-7, 309
to the corporation, 43, 70, 90-92, 101n46, 101n47, 173-75, 178-79, 181
Crown corporations, 240-43
institutional investors, 112, 113-15, 117, 124-25, 135-36
monitoring of legal compliance, 160-65, 170n32
prudent investment, 135, 151n14
shareholder primacy norm and, 90-92, 101n46, 101n47, 102n48, 102n49
Financial Administration Act (FAA) (Canada), 237, 240, 242
financial institutions, 47, 49-50, 51, 52, 77
financial reporting
  accounting standards, 56, 61, 62
  disclosure practices, 61-62, 122
  earnings management, 56, 196, 199
  See also audit committees; external auditors
financially distressed corporations, xxii-xxiii, 297-99, 345-46
  asset dispositions, 315-16, 341n118, 341n119
  communication, 311-12
  Consumers Packaging Inc., 330-37, 344n189, 344n190
  large tort claims, 314
  refinancing, xxiii, 309-11, 313-14, 315-25, 326
  viability, 325-27, 329
  the vicinity of insolvency, xxiii, 276-77, 283-84, 298-99, 309
  See also insolvencies
financing leases, 342n129
First Edmonton Place Ltd. v. *315888 Alberta Ltd.*, 302-3
Fish Processing Strategic Task Force, 249, 256
Five Years to the Dey, 43, 68
France, 54
free-rider problem, 104n78, 123

gender discrimination. *See* workplace discrimination
Germany, 97
  governance norms, 47, 49-51, 193-94, 212
global capital markets, 46-47, 46-55, 99n15
Global Governance Forum, 54
Global Reporting Initiative (GRI), 144-45
governance norms, xvii, 4, 6-10, 42-44, 45, 77

international convergence, xviii, 41, 46-48, 52, 53-55, 74-75, 76
path-dependency, 47-48, 88
  See also convergence of corporate regimes; governance standards; shareholder wealth maximization
governance standards, 112, 143-47, 149-50, 153n66, 155n88
  Global Reporting Initiative (GRI), 144-45
  See also governance norms; legislation
Government Owned Corporations Act (Queensland), 241-42
Graham v. *Allis-Chalmers Mfg. Co.*, 162
GRI. *See* Global Reporting Initiative (GRI)

Hampel Committee, 99n19, 102n56
High Level Group of Company Law Experts, 97
Home Depot, 163, 170n24
hostile takeovers
  defence measures, 94-98, 97-98, 107n108, 203
  effects on firm value, 93-94, 100n32, 104n70
  minority shareholders, 94, 104n78
  percentages of, 85-86
human capital investment, 74, 75-76, 78
Japan, 51-52
  See also employees

ILO. *See* International Labour Organization (ILO)
ImClone Systems Inc., 156
Income Tax Act (Canada), 175-76, 285-86
indemnification, 288, 290
India, 54
industrial sectors
  oil and gas industry, 183-84
  seafood processing industry, 249, 253-54, 256-69
  sector councils, x, 249, 254, 256-63, 257-60
  tulip industry, 180
  value chains, 262-69
insolvencies
  court-appointed officers, xxiii-xxiv, 292, 293, 345, 346-49; chief restructuring officers, 289-91, 292, 293, 313, 346, 349, 354-57, 359n18; interim receivers, 346, 349-53, 354, 358n5, 358n6; monitors, 346, 353-57, 358n1; receivers, 346
  detection, 299-301
  director's liabilities, 275, 283-88, 291, 292, 293

duties to shareholders, 284
duties to stakeholders, xxiii, 276-77
filing, 314; choice of jurisdictions, 315, 329; factors, 315-29
misrepresentation of, 283-84, 307-8, 309, 338n12
proposed legislative and policy reform, xxiii, 291-93, 319-22
reviewable transactions, 279-82, 284, 302
United States, 308-9
the vicinity of insolvency, xxiii, 276-77, 283-84, 298-99, 309
wrongful trading, 284-85, 300-301
See also creditors; financially distressed corporations
Insolvency Institute of Canada, 291-91, 319-22
institutional investors, 58, 113-14, 123, 126n25, 216n10
activism, 15-16, 49, 112-25, 126n14; shareholder proposals, 66, 164-65, 166-67
beneficial shareholders, 120, 121-22, 123
exit choices, 28, 49
intervention in governance, 15-16, 22, 28-29, 30, 31, 49, 194, 199
as universal owners, 112-15, 116
Insurance Corporation of British Columbia, 238
international capital markets. *See* global capital markets
international convergence. *See* convergence of corporate regimes
International Labour Organization (ILO), 146
international law, 131
ISO 14000, 153n66

Japan, 51-52, 81n55
Johnson, Gordon W., 292
Joint Committee Corporate Governance Project. *See* Saucier Committee
Joint Committee on Corporate Governance. *See* Saucier Committee
J.S. McMillan Fisheries Ltd., 352-53

Keiretsus, 51-52, 81n55
Korea, 54

labour-management consultation, 251-54
Labour Relations Code (British Columbia), 252
labour shedding, 64-65
Laird, Alexander (Sandy), 153n56

Lakehead Newsprint (1990) Ltd. v. *893499 Ontario Ltd.,* 305
laws. *See* legislation; regulatory controls
Lay, Kenneth, 162-63
legislation
Alien Tort Claims Act (United States), 142-43
anti-takeover statutes, 94, 105n83, 106n96
Bankruptcy and Insolvency Act (Canada), 275, 283, 284, 299, 302, 339n38, 359n10, 359n20; court-appointed officers, 346, 349-50, 358n5
Canada, 118-19
Canada Business Corporations Act, 4-5, 91, 299; amendments, 65-66, 118-20, 121; fiduciary obligations, 173-74, 178, 179, 182, 239, 276
Civil Rights Act (United States), 163, 171n40
civil vs. common-law countries, 99n15
Companies' Creditors Arrangement Act (Canada), 275, 289, 300; court-appointed officers, 346-47, 353, 354
compliance with, 158-65, 167-68 (*See also* corporate misconduct)
Crown Corporations Act (Saskatchewan), 241, 242
Crown Corporations Public Review and Accountability Act (Manitoba), 237, 240, 242
enabling philosophy, vii, xvii, 4-6, 8, 25-26
environmental issues, 176-78, 182
Environmental Protection Act (Ontario), 176
Europe, 47, 50, 96-98
Excise Tax Act (Canada), 285-86
Financial Administration Act (Canada), 237, 240, 242
Government Owned Corporations Act (Queensland), 241-42
Income Tax Act (Canada), 175-76, 285-86
international law, 131, 155n96
Japan, 52
Sarbanes-Oxley Act of 2002 (United States), 61, 157-58, 196
Securities Exchange Act (United States), 165, 167
United States, 94-96, 101n36, 105n83, 106n96, 106n99, 107n108
See also regulatory controls
lenders
insolvency situations, 347-48
Leon Van Neck & Son v. *McGorman,* 303
Levy-Russell Inc. v. *Shieldings Inc.,* 277

liquidity insolvency, 299, 300
liquidity of markets, xvi, 46
litigation
  discrimination issues, 159-64, 168
  See also shareholder activism; creditors
Loney, John E., 153n56

managerial discipline, 24, 47
  dispersion of shareholders and, 48-49
  market for corporate control and, 86, 88, 93-94
managers. *See* agency costs; executives; officers
Maple Homes Ltd., 300
Marcopper Mining Corporation, 132, 137-42
market for corporate control, 86, 89, 93-96
  agency problems, 89-96
  See also hostile takeovers
market fund portfolios, 151n14
Martin v. *Gibson*, 91
mergers and acquisitions, 85
  See also hostile takeovers
minority directors, 200-201, 205, 219n75
misconduct. *See* corporate misconduct
Mitsubishi, 163
MNEs. *See* multinational enterprises (MNEs)
Money's Mushrooms, 359n18
MR Holdings, 138
multinational enterprises (MNEs), xix-xx, 73, 111-12, 131-32
  disclosure of corporate information, 142-47, 148-49
  home countries, 132, 133, 136-37, 142, 151n17
  host countries, 132, 133, 141-42, 151n17
  investor control of harmful activities, xx, 131-32, 133-37, 143-44, 147-50
  See also Placer Dome Inc.
mutual fund portfolios, 151n14

NBD Bank, Canada v. Dofasco Inc., 283-84, 308, 338n12
New York Stock Exchange (NYSE), 196, 197
NLERS. *See* governance norms
nonlegally enforceable rules and standards. *See* governance norms
norm entrepreneurs, 23
norms. *See* governance norms
Northeast Marine Services v. *Atlantic Pilotage Authority*, 242
NYSE. *See* New York Stock Exchange (NYSE)

OECD. *See* Organization for Economic Cooperation and Development (OECD)
officers
  chief executive officers, xi, 193, 203, 212, 214, 222n119; compensation, 218n36; evaluation, 204, 209-10
  chief restructuring officers, 289-91, 292, 293, 313, 346, 349, 354-57, 359n18
  See also executives; insolvencies: court-appointed officers
oil and gas industry, 183-84
Olympia & York Developments Ltd. (OYDL), 279-82
ombudspersons, 193, 213, 215
Ontario Inc. v. *Harold E. Ballard*, 181
Ontario Teachers' Pension Plan (OTPP), 66
oppressive conduct, 277-82, 285, 302-4, 306, 307, 309, 339n45
Organization for Economic Cooperation and Development (OECD), 54, 103n62, 134
OTPP. *See* Ontario Teachers' Pension Plan (OTPP)
ownership
  separation from control, 6, 27, 89, 96, 154n86, 236
ownership patterns
  Canada, 98n10, 100n20
  concentration, 72, 87-88, 98; agency costs and, 6; Canada, 123, 130n92, 155n92; institutional investors, 49. *See also* blockheld corporate structures
  dispersion, 48-49, 72; corporate control regimes and, 87, 88, 99n17
OYDL. *See* Olympia & York Developments Ltd. (OYDL)

path-dependency, 47-48
pension benefits, 286
pension funds, 67, 71, 123, 124, 134
  Canada, 114-15
  multinational enterprises and, 132, 133, 134-37, 143-44, 147-49
  See also institutional investors
Pente Investment Management Ltd. (Maple Leaf) v. *Schneider*, 174
People's Department Stores v. *Wise*, 277, 304-5
Percival v. *Wright*, 91
Philippines. *See* Marcopper Mining Corporation
Placer Dome Inc., 132, 137-42
pollution, 132, 137-42, 180
  See also environmental issues
pooling, 100n23

Prime Computer of Canada Ltd. v. *Jeffrey,*
   285
proposals. *See* shareholder activism
proxies, 66-67, 118, 123, 125
   shareholder proposals and, 165-67,
   171n58, 171n59
   shareholder rights concerning, 116, 120
PSINet, 341n118, 344n175
public regulation. *See* regulatory controls
Publix Supermarkets, 163
Purdy, Crawford, 62

Qwest Communications International,
   156

R. v. *Bata Industries Ltd.,* 176-77, 183, 287
R. v. *Cohen,* 301
R. v. *Godfrey,* 301
racism, 171n53
   See also workplace discrimination
reform committees, 3, 4-6, 10, 11, 12, 14,
   26, 31
   See also Dey Committee; Saucier
   Committee
regional economic development, 256-69
regulatory controls, vii, 25-26, 41, 76, 77,
   78, 113
   Anglo-American norms, 74-75
   corporate control regimes and, 87-89
   industry sector councils and, 262, 270
   legislation, 3-4, 8-10, 25-32, 43
   multinational entreprises, xx, 132-33
   pressures for deregulation, 75, 77-78,
   111
   See also legislation; Securities and
   Exchange Commission (SEC)
restructuring, 289-91
   See also chief restructuring officers;
   financially distressed corporations
reviewable transactions, 279-82, 284, 302
Revlon duty, 95, 105n92, 106n97
Ringuet v. *Bergeron,* 102n58
risk-taking activities, 209-10
Royal Commission on Corporate Concentration. *See* Bryce Commission
Royal Oak Mines, 323, 353

Sammi Atlas Inc., 278-79, 289-90
Sarbanes-Oxley Act of 2002 (United States),
   61, 157-58, 196
Saucier Committee, 12-14, 20, 21, 26
   *See also Beyond Compliance: Building a
   Governance Culture*
Schafer v. *International Capital Corp.,* 183
SCI Systems Inc. v. *Gornitzki Thompson &
   Little Co.,* 285, 299-300, 306

seafood processing industry
   labour-management consultation,
   253-54
   sector council, 249, 254, 256-57, 260-63
   value chains, 264-69
SEC. *See* Securities and Exchange Commission (SEC)
sector councils, x, 257-60
   seafood processing industry, 249, 254,
   256-57, 260-63
   value chains, 262-69
Securities and Exchange Commission
   (SEC), 156
   regulatory amendments, 157, 196
   shareholder proposals, 66-67, 120,
   165-67
Securities Exchange Act (United States), 165,
   167
Securities Industry Committee on Analyst
   Standards, xi, 62
sexual discrimination. *See* workplace
   discrimination
shaming mechanisms, 22-25
SHARE. *See* Shareholder Association for
   Research and Education (SHARE)
share structures, 122-23
shareholder activism, xviii-xix, 27, 29,
   30-31, 65-67, 118-20, 126n14, 165
   correlated with corporate performance,
   117-18, 128n49, 128n50
   institutional investors, 15-16, 49,
   112-25, 126n14
   Japan, 52
   shaming function, 22-23
   shareholder proposals, 65-66, 120,
   154n87, 155n98; beneficial shareholders, 120, 121-22; corrections of monitoring problems and, 164-68; dispute
   resolution, 120-21, 129n79; institutional investors, 66, 164-65, 166-67;
   rights to present, 171n58, 171n59
   See also litigation
Shareholder Association for Research and
   Education (SHARE), 66, 117, 129n63
shareholder primacy norm. *See* shareholder wealth maximization paradigm
shareholder proposals. *See* shareholder
   activism
shareholder wealth maximization
   paradigm, xvi, xvii, xix, 41, 43,
   101n36, 103n61, 104n67, 106n95
   agency problems, 89-92
   contractarian theory and, 45
   corporate best interests and, 44, 70, 90-
   92, 101n46, 101n47, 102n48, 174-75,
   178-79, 181

market for corporate control, 93-96, 100n32
power relationships within, 59-60
shareholders, 62, 67, 198-99, 276
access to governance information, 16-21, 64-65
apathy, 15, 26-28, 123
co-determination model, 50
communication regulations, 66, 119, 165
conflicts with the company and stakeholder interests, 174-75, 178, 186, 307
exit choices, 44-45, 60, 65
meeting attendance, 27, 118, 129n58
ownership model, 147, 154n84, 236-37
participation in governance principles, xviii, 26-31
power in corporation management, 6, 9, 27
protection of interests, 73, 87-88, 99n15, 99n17
small investors, 58, 60, 72
See also institutional investors; ownership; ownership patterns; shareholder activism; shareholder wealth maximization paradigm
Shoney's, 163, 170n24
Sidaplex-Plastic Suppliers Inc. v. *Elta Group Inc.*, 278, 303-4
Skilling, Jeffrey, 212
social norms, 7-8, 14-16
Asia, 51, 53
effectiveness, 21-25, 30-31
See also governance norms
social responsibilities, xi, xii, 199, 249, 269-70
European Union, 146-47
institutional investors and, 113
views of Canadian public on, 70-71, 115, 127n33, 151n16
views of directors on, 69
See also environmental issues; sector councils; workplace discrimination
Soper v. *Canada (C.A.)*, 176
stakeholders, xii, xxii, 73-74, 101n36, 248, 252
board memberships and, 198-202
Canadian paradigm, 60-61, 70, 71, 75-76, 91-92, 102n58
European governance models, 50
obligations of directors to, 175-87
transition economies, 55
See also creditors; employees; shareholders
Starcom International Optics Corporation, 355-56
State Tax Commission v. *Aldrich et al.*, 175

stock options, ix, xi, 197, 199, 218n61

takeovers, 194
European norms, 47
Revlon duty, 95, 105n92, 106n97
See also hostile takeovers; market for corporate control
Taskforce on the Churches and Corporate Responsibility, 119, 129n63
Teck Corporation Ltd. v *Millar*, 102n58, 174, 181
Texaco, 159, 161-62, 163, 164, 170n32
Thirteenth Directive (European Union), 97
Toronto Stock Exchange (TSX)
Company Manual, 12, 14, 16-17, 20-21, 59-61, 67, 179, 182; corporate compliance, 14, 17-19, 29-31, 43-44
dual-class share structures, 122-23
institutional investors, 114-15
recommended disclosure practices, 16-18, 19, 43-44, 59, 60, 185
Toronto Stock Exchange Committee on Corporate Disclosure, 20
Toronto Stock Exchange Committee on Corporate Governance in Canada. *See* Dey Committee
Toronto Stock Exchange Joint Committee on Corporate Governance. *See* Saucier Committee
tort liabilities, 283-84, 307-8, 309, 338n12
Alien Tort Claims Act (ATCA), 142-43
trade agreements, 71
transactions. *See* reviewable transactions
transition economies, 46-47, 54-55, 81n78
Triax Resource Limited Partnership v. *Research Capital Corp.*, 284
trusteed pension plans. *See* pension funds
TSX. *See* Toronto Stock Exchange (TSX)
tulip industry, 180
twilight period, xxii, 276-77, 283-84, 298-99, 309
Tyco International Ltd., 156

UBC Governance Survey, 67-69, 83n128
UNEP. *See* United Nations Environment Project (UNEP)
unethical conduct. *See* corporate misconduct; workplace discrimination
Uniform Fraudulent Transfer Act, 309
United Kingdom
City Code on Takeovers and Mergers, 96-97
Hampel Committee, 99n19, 102n56
shareholders, 51
United Nations Environment Project (UNEP), 144

United Used Auto and Truck Parks Ltd., 324
University of British Columbia Governance Survey, 67-69, 83n128
USF Red Star Inc. v. *12200103 Ontario Ltd.,* 305-6

value chains, 262-69
the vicinity of insolvency, xxii, 276-77, 283-84, 298-99, 309

wages, 286
Walker v. *Wimborne,* 276
Wall Street Project, 170n23
Walt Disney Company, 164-65
Where Were the Directors? 12, 19, 43, 179, 182, 185

shareholder primacy, 92, 102n55, 103n61
stakeholders, 60, 70, 175, 179
Winkworth v. *Edward Baron Development Co. Ltd. et al.,* 276, 304
Winter, Jaap, 97
women directors, 68, 200-201, 220n77, 220n85, 220n91, 220n92
workers. *See* employees
workplace discrimination, xx
  boards of directors responsibilities, 158-60, 170n32
  litigation concerning, 159, 161-62, 163-64
  shareholder proposals and, xx, 165, 166-67, 168
World Bank, 54, 134, 292-93
WorldCom Inc., 156

Printed and bound in Canada by Friesens

Set in Stone by Artegraphica Design Co. Ltd.

Copy editor: Francis Chow

Proofreader: Jeannie Scarfe

Indexer: Christine Jacobs